CARS, TRAINS, AND PLANES

THE DEFINITIVE VISUAL HISTORY OF LAND AND AIR TRANSPORTATION

CARS, TRAINS, AND PLANES

THE DEFINITIVE VISUAL
HISTORY OF LAND AND
AIR TRANSPORTATION

EDITORIAL TEAM
Suhel Ahmed, Sam Atkinson, Alexandra Beeden,
Sreshtha Bhattacharya, Tanya Desai, Jemima Dunne, Rod Green,
Megha Gupta, Kathryn Hennessy, Nicola Hodgson, Gaurav Joshi, Anita Kakar,
Manisha Majithia, Vibha Malhotra, Scarlett O'Hara, Antara Moitra,
Monica Saigal, Ankush Saikia, Suparna Sengupta, Steve Setford, Chris Stone,
Alison Sturgeon, David Summers, Andrew Szudek, Miezen van Zyl

DESIGN TEAM
Shomik Chakraborty, Tannishtha Chakraborty, Amy Child, Devan Das,
Paul Drislane, Philip Fitzgerald, Arijit Ganguly, Natalie Godwin, Niyati Gosain,
Anna Hall, Richard Horsford, Roshni Kapur, Swati Kayal, Vansh Kohli, Alex Lloyd,
Mark Lloyd, Supriya Mahajan, Payal Rosalind Malik, Nidhi Mehra, Simon Murrell,
Anjana Nair, Namita, Pallavi Narain, Amy Orsborne, Pooja Pipil, Divya PR,
Vaibhav Rastogi, Chhaya Sajwan, Mahua Sharma, Neha Sharma, Riti Sodhi,
Shruti Singh Soharia, Helen Spencer, Sharon Spencer, Steve Woosnam-Savage

Production Manager Pankaj Sharma
Pre-production Manager Balwant Singh
Senior DTP Designers Harish Aggarwal, Dheeraj Arora, Jagtar Singh, Sachin Singh
DTP Designers Nand Kishor Acharya, Neeraj Bhatia, Jaypal Singh Chauhan,
Arjinder Singh, Bimlesh Tiwary, Mohd. Usman, Tanveer Abbas Zaidi
Photographers Deepak Aggarwal, James Mann, Gary Ombler, Paul Self
Picture Researchers Nic Dean, Jenny Faithfull, Julia Harris-Voss,
Ria Jones, Aditya Katyal, Myriam Mégharbi
Picture Research Manager Taiyaba Khatoon
DK Picture Library Claire Bowers, Claire Cordier,
Laura Evans, Emma Shepherd, Romaine Werblow
Jacket Designers Dhirendra Singh, Mark Cavanagh
Managing Jackets Editor Saloni Singh
Jacket Design Development Manager Sophia MTT
Pre-production Ben Marcus, Jamie McNeill, Nikoleta Parasaki
Producer Linda Dare
Managing Editors Camilla Hallinan, Pakshalika Jayaprakash,
Gareth Jones, Esther Ripley, Rohan Sinha
Managing Art Editors Sudakshina Basu, Lee Griffiths,
Karen Self, Arunesh Talapatra
Art Director Phil Ormerod
Publishers Laura Buller, Sarah Larter
Associate Publishing Director Liz Wheeler
Publishing Director Jonathan Metcalf

Special Sales and Custom Publishing Manager Michelle Baxter

General Consultants Tony Streeter (**Trains**), Giles Chapman (**Cars**),
Philip Whiteman (**Planes**)

Contributors Trains: Julian Holland, Keith Fender, Gary Boyd-Hope,
Jonathan Randle Falconer, Peter Herring, Keith Langston, Ashwani Lohani,
Malcolm McKay, David Wilcock; **Cars:** Charles Armstrong-Wilson,
Richard Heseltine, Keith Howard, Phil Hunt, Malcolm McKay, Andrew Noakes,
Jon Presnell; **Planes:** Malcolm McKay, Dave Unwin, Philip Whiteman,
Steve Bridgewater, Joe Coles, Patrick Malone, Peter R March, Mick Oakey,
Elfan ap Rhys, Nick Stroud, Graham White, Richard Beatty

Content previously published in *The Train Book* (2014),
The Car Book (2011), and *The Aircraft Book* (2013)
This edition published in Great Britain in 2016 by
Dorling Kindersley Limited 80 Strand, London WC2R 0RL

Copyright © 2016 Dorling Kindersley Limited
A Penguin Random House Company

2 4 6 8 10 9 7 5 3 1

001–294465–April/2016

A CIP catalogue record for this book
is available from the British Library.
ISBN: 978-0-2412-6277-1
Printed in China

A WORLD OF IDEAS:
SEE ALL THERE IS TO KNOW

www.dk.com

Contents

TRAINS **BEFORE 1894**

TRAINS **1895–1939**

TRAINS **1940-1959**

TRAINS **1960 TO PRESENT**

CARS **BEFORE 1929**

CARS **1930-1949**

CARS **1950-1979**

CARS **1980 TO PRESENT**

AIRCRAFT **BEFORE 1929**

AIRCRAFT **1930-1949**

AIRCRAFT **1950-1979**

AIRCRAFT **1980 TO PRESENT**

Car dates: The date given for each catalogue entry refers to the year that the model was first released. In some cases the accompanying photograph shows a later edition of the model, in these cases the year of the later edition is mentioned in the caption.

Trains

Before 1894

A British Invention

During the 18th century the British inventors Thomas Newcomen and James Watt led the way in the development of the low-pressure, stationary steam engines that played a vital role in the early years of the Industrial Revolution. A major breakthrough took place in the early 19th century when Cornish inventor Richard Trevithick successfully demonstrated the world's first working high-pressure, steam railway locomotive. From then on, British inventiveness, led by the "Father of Railways", George Stephenson, brought a rapid development, which culminated in 1830 with the opening of the world's first inter-city railway, between Liverpool and Manchester.

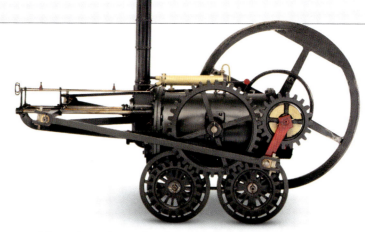

△ **Pen-y-darren locomotive, 1804**

Wheel arrangement	0-4-0
Cylinders	1
Boiler pressure	25 psi (1.75 kg/sq cm)
Driving wheel diameter	48 in (1,220 mm)
Top speed	approx. 5 mph (8 km/h)

Richard Trevithick's high-pressure steam locomotive hauled the world's first train on the Pen-y-darren Ironworks tramway in Merthyr Tydfil, South Wales on 13 February 1804. The train was carrying 10 ton (10.2 tonnes) of coal and 70 men.

◁ **Catch Me Who Can, 1808**

Wheel arrangement	2-2-0
Cylinders	1
Boiler pressure	25 psi (1.75 kg/sq cm)
Driving wheel diameter	48 in (1,220 mm)
Top speed	approx. 12 mph (19 km/h)

Richard Trevithick's *Catch Me Who Can* was demonstrated to the public on a circular track at a steam circus in Bloomsbury, London, in 1808. Unfortunately the train overturned when a rail broke, so the public was not convinced.

◁ **Puffing Billy, 1813**

Wheel arrangement	0-8-0 (final form 0-4-0)
Cylinders	2
Boiler pressure	40 psi (2.8 kg/sq cm)
Driving wheel diameter	48 in (1,220 mm)
Top speed	approx. 5 mph (8 km/h)

Weighing 7.25 tons (7.4 tonnes) and built by William Hedley for the Wylam Colliery in Northumberland, *Puffing Billy* was the world's first commercial adhesion steam engine. Now preserved at London's Science Museum, it is considered the oldest surviving locomotive.

▷ **Locomotion No. 1, 1825**

Wheel arrangement	0-4-0
Cylinders	2
Boiler pressure	50 psi (3.51 kg/sq cm)
Driving wheel diameter	48 in (1,220 mm)
Top speed	approx. 15 mph (24 km/h)

Built by George and Robert Stephenson, *Locomotion No. 1* hauled the first train on the Stockton & Darlington Railway, the world's first public railway, in 1825. This locomotive has been preserved and can be seen at the Darlington Railway Museum, County Durham.

△ *Rocket*, 1829

Wheel arrangement 0-2-2

Cylinders 2

Boiler pressure 50 psi (3.51 kg/sq cm)

Driving wheel diameter 56¾ in (1,435 mm)

Top speed approx. 30 mph (48 km/h)

Robert Stephenson & Co.'s advanced and innovative *Rocket* was the clear winner of the Rainhill Trials held on the Liverpool & Manchester Railway in 1829. The *Rocket* is shown pulling a first-class passenger carriage; luggage was carried on the roof.

▷ *Agenoria*, 1829

Wheel arrangement 0-4-0

Cylinders 2

Boiler pressure 40 psi (2.8 kg/sq cm)

Driving wheel diameter 48 in (1,220 mm)

Top speed approx. 8 mph (13 km/h)

One of only four steam locomotives built by Foster, Rastrick & Co. of Stourbridge, *Agenoria* worked on the Earl of Dudley's Shutt End Colliery Railway, Staffordshire, for 35 years. The same company built the *Stourbridge Lion*, the first locomotive to be exported to the US.

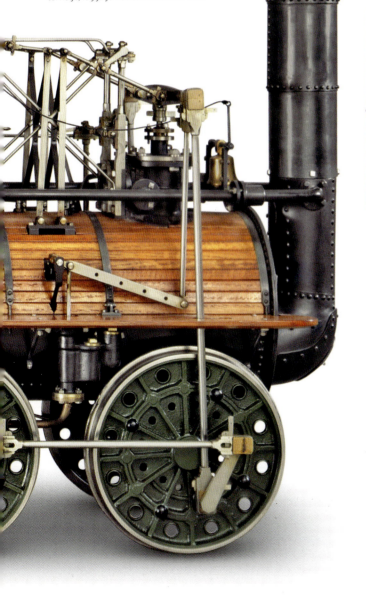

◁ *Sans Pareil*, 1829

Wheel arrangement 0-4-0

Cylinders 2

Boiler pressure 50 psi (3.51 kg/sq cm)

Driving wheel diameter 54 in (1,372 mm)

Top speed approx. 18 mph (29 km/h)

Built by Timothy Hackworth, *Sans Pareil* (meaning "without equal") performed well in the Rainhill Trials on the Liverpool & Manchester Railway in 1829 but exceeded the permitted weight, so was not considered for the prize.

▷ *Novelty*, 1829

Wheel arrangement 0-2-2WT

Cylinders 2

Boiler pressure 50 psi (3.51 kg/sq cm)

Driving wheel diameter 54 in (1,372 mm)

Top speed approx. 28 mph (45 km/h)

Although it was one of the fastest locomotives at the 1829 Rainhill Trials, John Ericsson and John Braithwaite's lightweight *Novelty* proved unreliable and was withdrawn. It was the first locomotive to have its cylinders within the frames.

Steam for Home and Export

The success of Stephenson's *Rocket* and the opening of the world's first public railway in 1825 and the inter-city route in 1830 led to demand for British-built steam railway locomotives at home and abroad. The most successful of the early builders was Robert Stephenson & Company of Newcastle-upon-Tyne, founded by George and his son Robert in 1823. Its early locomotives were built for the Stockton & Darlington Railway but it also supplied locomotives for the first railways in Egypt and Germany as well as the US.

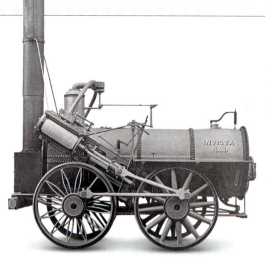

◁ *Invicta*, 1829-30

Wheel arrangement 0-4-0
Cylinders 2
Boiler pressure 40 psi (2.81 kg/sq cm)
Driving wheel diameter 48 in (1,220 mm)
Top speed approx. 20 mph (32 km/h)

Robert Stephenson & Co. built *Invicta* in Newcastle, then shipped it to Kent (UK) by sea. *Invicta* hauled the first train on the Canterbury & Whitstable Railway in 1830. The locomotive was named after the motto "invicta" (undefeated) on the flag of Kent. It is on display at Kent's Canterbury Museum.

▽ *John Bull*, 1831

Wheel arrangement 0-4-0 (as built)
2-4-0 (as modified)
Cylinders 2 (inside)
Boiler pressure 45 psi (3.16 kg/sq cm)
Driving wheel diameter 66 in (1,676 mm)
Top speed approx. 30 mph (48 km/h)

Built by Robert Stephenson & Co., *John Bull* was exported to the US, where it worked on the Camden & Amboy Railroad from 1831 to 1866. US engineer Isaac Dripps added his two-wheel bogie, to which he attached the first cowcatcher, as well as a headlight, spark-arresting chimney, and covered tender and cab.

▷ *Planet*, 1830

Wheel arrangement 2-2-0
Cylinders 2 (inside)
Boiler pressure 45 psi (3.16 kg/sq cm)
Driving wheel diameter 66 in (1,676 mm)
Top speed approx. 35 mph (56 km/h)

Planet was the first type to have inside cylinders and the ninth locomotive built for the Liverpool & Manchester Railway. Designed by Robert Stephenson & Co., *Planet* was the first engine type to be built in large numbers.

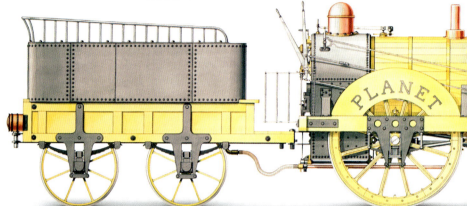

JOHN BULL AS FIRST CONSTRUCTED, 1831

▽ **Adler, 1835**

Wheel arrangement	2-2-2
Cylinders	2 (inside)
Boiler pressure	48 psi (3.37 kg/sq cm)
Driving wheel diameter	54 in (1,372 mm)
Top speed	approx. 17 mph (27 km/h)

The *Adler* (meaning "eagle") was the first successful steam railway locomotive to operate in Germany. It was built for the Bavarian Ludwig Railway by Robert Stephenson & Co. *Adler* remained in service until 1857. In 1935 a replica was built to mark the centenary of the German railways.

▽ **Bury, 1831**

Wheel arrangement	0-4-0
Cylinders	2 (inside)
Boiler pressure	50 psi (3.52 kg/sq cm)
Driving wheel diameter	66 in (1,676 mm)
Top speed	approx. 40 mph (64 km/h)

These locomotives were built with bar frames to reduce weight and were noted for their round-topped fireboxes. Designed by Edward Bury & Co., the Bury was popular in the US where light track was laid quickly to cover vast distances.

△ **Hawthorn *Sunbeam*, 1837**

Wheel arrangement	2-2-0
Cylinders	2 (inside)
Boiler pressure	50 psi (3.52 kg/sq cm)
Driving wheel diameter	60 in (1,524 mm)
Top speed	approx. 40 mph (64 km/h)

Sunbeam was built by R. & W. Hawthorn & Co. of Newcastle for the Stockton & Darlington Railway. Hawthorn built marine and stationary steam engines as well as locomotives for the broad-gauge Great Western Railway.

◁ **North Star, 1838**

Wheel arrangement	2-2-2
Cylinders	2 (inside)
Boiler pressure	50 psi (3.52 kg/sq cm)
Driving wheel diameter	84 in (2,134 mm)
Top speed	approx. 40 mph (64 km/h)

Robert Stephenson & Co.'s *North Star* hauled the inaugural director's train on the broad-gauge Great Western Railway in 1838. The locomotive was rebuilt in 1854 and withdrawn from service in 1871.

▷ **Lion, 1838**

Wheel arrangement	0-4-2
Cylinders	2 (inside)
Boiler pressure	50 psi (3.52 kg/sq cm)
Driving wheel diameter	60 in (1,524 mm)
Top speed	approx. 35 mph (56 km/h)

Lion was one of the first two locomotives built by Todd, Kitson & Laird. The other one was called *Tiger*. *Lion* worked on the Liverpool & Manchester Railway until 1859 before it was retired to Liverpool Docks as a stationary pumping engine.

World Pioneers

By the mid 1820s, pioneering inventors and engineers in continental Europe and the US were experimenting with their own designs. Some of these developments, such as US civil engineer John B. Jervis's swivelling leading bogie or Frenchman Marc Séguin's multitube boiler, would soon be incorporated into locomotives around the world. By the late 1830s rapid technological advances in steam locomotive design led to a massive expansion of railway building. In the US, the Baltimore & Ohio Railroad was the first to operate scheduled freight and passenger services. By 1837 the service had extended from Baltimore over the iconic Thomas Viaduct to Washington DC and across the Potomac River to Harper's Ferry.

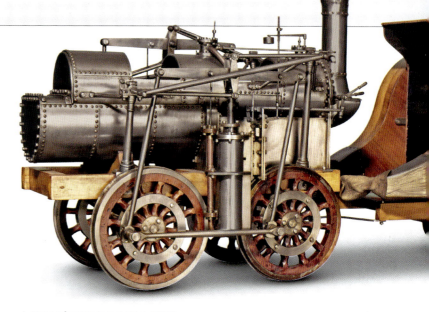

▽ John Stevens's *Steam Waggon*, 1825

Wheel arrangement	early rack-and-pinion
Cylinders	1
Boiler pressure	approx. 100+ psi (7.03 kg/sq cm)
Driving wheel diameter	57 in (1,450 mm)
Top speed	approx. 12 mph (19 km/h)

Colonel John Stevens's *Steam Waggon* demonstrated the practicability of very high-pressure steam railway locomotives. This was the first engine to run on rails in the US. Stevens ran it on a circular track on his estate in Hoboken, New Jersey.

△ Marc Séguin's locomotive, 1829

Wheel arrangement	0-4-0
Cylinders	2
Boiler pressure	approx. 35 psi (2.46 kg/sq cm)
Driving wheel diameter	approx. 54 in (1,372 mm)
Top speed	approx. 15 mph (24 km/h)

Fitted with a multitube boiler, enormous rotary blowers, and a large firebox, Marc Séguin's innovative steam locomotive was the first to be built in France. It was tested on the Saint-Étienne & Lyon Railway in November 1829 and entered regular service in 1830.

The Best Friend, from William H. Brown, *The History of the First Locomotives in America*, New York, 1874

THE CHARLESTON & HAMBURG RAILROAD

△ *Best Friend of Charleston*, 1830

Wheel arrangement	0-4-0
Cylinders	2
Boiler pressure	approx. 35 psi (2.46 kg/sq cm)
Driving wheel diameter	approx. 57 in (1,450 mm)
Top speed	approx. 25 mph (40 km/h)

The first steam locomotive to be constructed entirely in the US, *Best Friend of Charleston* was built by the West Point Foundry in New York. It operated a passenger service on the South Carolina Railroad until it was destroyed by a boiler explosion.

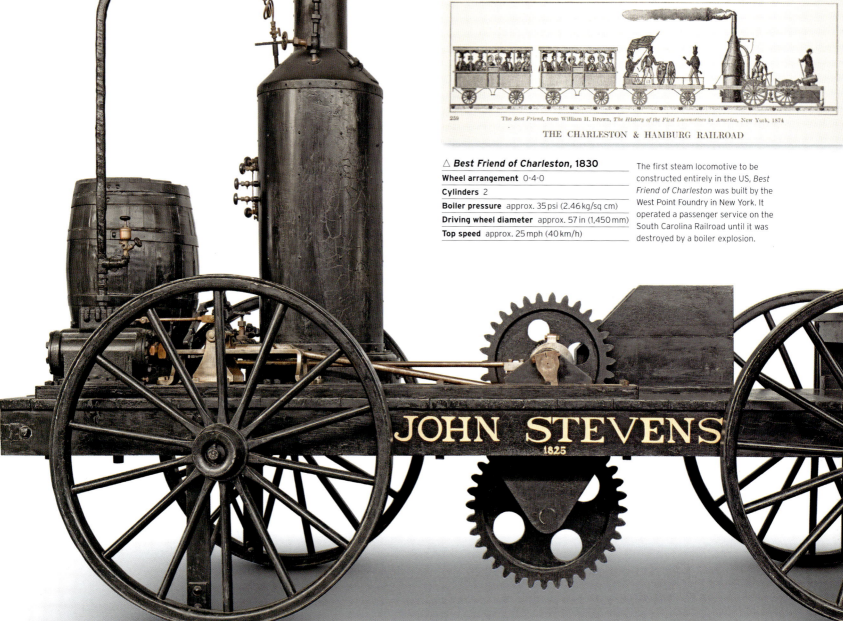

JOHN STEVENS
1825

Marc Séguin, 1786–1875

Born in the Ardèche region of France, engineer, inventor, and entrepreneur Marc Séguin built innovative steam locomotives for the Saint-Étienne & Lyon Railway. His engines were fitted with an ingenious multi-tube boiler, which he patented in 1827, as well as mechanically driven fans to improve draughting for the fire and a firebox enclosed by a water jacket for greater heating capacity. Séguin developed the first suspension bridge in continental Europe and went on to build 186 bridges in France.

Engineering Innovation Marc Séguin was inspired by George Stephenson's *Locomotion No. 1*, which he saw in action on the Stockton & Darlington Railway in 1825.

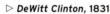

◁ *Tom Thumb*, 1830

Wheel arrangement	2-2-0
Cylinders	1
Boiler pressure	approx. 35 psi (2.46 kg/sq cm)
Driving wheel diameter	approx. 33 in (840 mm)
Top speed	14 mph (23 km/h)

This locomotive was built by US inventor and, later, presidential candidate Peter Cooper. The Baltimore & Ohio Railroad raced *Tom Thumb* against a horse to decide whether they should adopt steam power or horse traction; the train lost, but the railroad saw its potential. Weighing only 1.1 ton (1 tonne), *Tom Thumb* had a vertical boiler with inner tubes fashioned from gun barrels.

▷ *DeWitt Clinton*, 1831

Wheel arrangement	0-4-0
Cylinders	2
Boiler pressure	approx. 35 kg/sq cm)
Driving wheel diameter	approx. 58¾ in (1,520 mm)
Top speed	approx. 20 mph (32 km/h)

The first steam locomotive to operate in New York State, the *DeWitt Clinton* was built for the Mohawk & Hudson Railroad. Passengers travelled in converted stage coaches. It was named after a governor of New York State who was responsible for the construction of the Erie Canal.

◁ *Experiment*, 1832

Wheel arrangement	4-2-0
Cylinders	2
Boiler pressure	approx. 50 psi (3.51 kg/sq cm)
Driving wheel diameter	approx. 72 in (1,830 mm)
Top speed	approx. 60 mph (96 km/h)

This engine was designed by John B. Jervis, chief engineer for the Delaware & Hudson Canal & Railroad. *Experiment*, later named *Brother Jonathan*, was built by the West Point Foundry, New York, for use on the Mohawk & Hudson Railroad. It was the first locomotive with a leading bogie that became the 4-2-0 type.

Railroad Expansion

The earliest US railroads were operated using horse power. In 1830 the Baltimore & Ohio Railroad (B&O) was one of the first to introduce steam. While some railroads bought designs from fledging manufacturers such as Baldwin, the B&O started constructing their own, including the long-lived "Grasshoppers". In 1836 William Norris introduced the four-wheel leading bogie, which became common worldwide until the end of steam in the 20th century. Two years later Johann Schubert's *Saxonia* became the first successful steam engine to be built and operated in Germany.

Old Ironsides

△ Baldwin *Old Ironsides*, 1832

Wheel arrangement	2-2-0
Cylinders	2
Boiler pressure	50 psi (3.51 kg/sq cm)
Driving wheel diameter	54 in (1,372 mm)
Top speed	approx. 28 mph (45 km/h)

Designed by US inventor Matthias Baldwin, *Old Ironsides* was the first commissioned steam locomotive built at the Baldwin Locomotive Works, for the Philadelphia, Germantown & Norristown Railroad.

▷ B&O *Atlantic*, 1832

Wheel arrangement	0-4-0
Cylinders	2
Boiler pressure	50 psi (3.52 kg/sq cm)
Driving wheel diameter	35 in (890 mm)
Top speed	approx. 20 mph (32 km/h)

Built by US inventor and foundry owner Phineas Davis for the Baltimore & Ohio Railroad, *Atlantic* was the prototype for 20 more similar locomotives nicknamed "Grasshoppers".

1832 BALTIMORE & OHIO R. R. ATLANTIC 1832

Early Coaches

The first railway passenger coaches in the US were primitive affairs, often based on existing designs for turnpike stagecoaches and originally intended for low-speed, horse-operated railroads. The rail companies soon learnt that they were impractical: seats were uncomfortable, passengers in open-air carriages not only had to brave the elements but also the smoke, hot ash, and cinders blown out by the equally primitive steam locomotives that hauled the coaches.

◁ Director's Car, 1828

Type	4-wheel
Capacity	12 passengers
Construction	iron and wood
Railway	Baltimore & Ohio Railroad

Originally horsedrawn, in August 1830 the Baltimore & Ohio Director's Car carried the railroad's directors in the first steam-hauled train along the railway to Ellicott's Mills behind *Tom Thumb*. This is a replica built in 1926 for the Fair of the Iron Horse and can be seen at the B&O Railroad Museum, Baltimore.

▷ B&O *Lafayette*, 1837

Wheel arrangement	4-2-0
Cylinders	2
Boiler pressure	60 psi (4.21 kg/sq cm)
Driving wheel diameter	54 in (1,372 mm)
Top speed	approx. 35 mph (56 km/h)

William Norris's *Lafayette* was the first in the world to feature a leading four-wheel bogie on a production model. A replica, built in 1927, can be seen at the Baltimore & Ohio Railroad Museum, Baltimore.

△ B&O "Grasshopper" *John Hancock*, 1836

Wheel arrangement	0-4-0
Cylinders	2
Boiler pressure	50 psi (3.51 kg/sq cm)
Driving wheel diameter	35 in (889 mm)
Top speed	approx. 20 mph (32 km/h)

Fitted with a driver's cab, *John Hancock* was one of 20 "Grasshopper" locomotives built by the Baltimore & Ohio Railroad. It remained in service as a switcher until 1892.

▷ *Saxonia*, 1838

Wheel arrangement	0-4-2
Cylinders	2
Boiler pressure	60 psi (4.21 kg/sq cm)
Driving wheel diameter	59 in (1,500 mm)
Top speed	approx. 37 mph (60 km/h)

Designed by Johann Schubert, *Saxonia* was the first practical working steam locomotive built entirely in Germany. It was used on the Leipzig to Dresden Railway –Germany's first long-distance line. By 1843 *Saxonia* had clocked up more than 5,300 miles (8,500 km).

◁ Maryland Coach, 1830

Type	4-wheel
Capacity	14 passengers
Construction	iron and wood
Railway	Baltimore & Ohio Railroad

Based on a stagecoach, Richard Imlay's double-deck coach was one of six built for the inaugural steam train on the Baltimore & Ohio Railroad. The carriage body was perched on unsprung wheels cradled on leather straps. It was unstable and offered little protection for top deck passengers.

▷ Nova Scotia Coach, 1838

Type	4-wheel
Capacity	6 passengers
Construction	iron and wood
Railway	General Mining Association of Nova Scotia

Built by Timothy Hackworth of London (UK), the Nova Scotia Coach carried the Director of Nova Scotia's General Mining Association on the colliery railway on Cape Breton Island in Canada. Also known as the bride's car, it was said to have originally carried the director's new bride to their home after their marriage ceremony.

The US Forges Ahead

The British locomotives imported into the US were often too heavy for the lighter, quickly laid rail tracks, and not powerful enough to cope with the steeper gradients. So US engineers developed designs tailored to their railways' needs. A leading truck, first with two wheels then four, was fitted to guide the engines through the many sharp curves. Improved traction led to the 4-4-0 becoming the standard type, soon followed by the more powerful 4-6-0. Cowcatchers, headlights, and warning bells were fitted to cope with the unfenced tracks. American designers built locomotives capable of hauling heavy loads over a railroad system that by 1871 linked two oceans.

▷ **B&O L Class No. 57 *Memnon*, 1848**

Wheel arrangement	0-8-0
Cylinders	2
Boiler pressure	75 psi (5 kg/sq cm)
Driving wheel diameter	44 in (1,118 mm)
Top speed	approx. 30 mph (48 km/h)

Bought by the Baltimore & Ohio Railroad in 1848 for freight working, *Memnon* was later used in the Civil War, for hauling troops and supplies. Eight driving wheels gave this locomotive its extra power and traction.

▽ **CVR No. 13 *Pioneer*, 1851**

Wheel arrangement	2-2-2
Cylinders	2
Boiler pressure	100 psi (7 kg/sq cm)
Driving wheel diameter	54 in (1,372 mm)
Top speed	approx. 40 mph (64 km/h)

Pioneer hauled the short passenger trains of the Cumberland Valley Railroad of Pennsylvania and western Maryland until 1890. It survived the destruction of the railway's workshops by the Confederate troops in 1862.

TALKING POINT

Financing the Railroads

Railroad promoters looked to the commercial centres of Philadelphia, Boston, and New York, as well as European money markets to raise capital to develop the railways. Investors preferred bonds to stocks since these offered a guaranteed income. At the same time, the US government offered federal land grants to the rail companies, who then sold the land they did not need to raise more funds.

B&O stocks The value of shares in the US's new Baltimore & Ohio Railroad exceeded $3 million in 1839 when this $100 certificate was issued.

▷ **W&A No. 39 *The General*, 1855**

Wheel arrangement	4-4-0
Cylinders	2
Boiler pressure	140 psi (10 kg/sq cm)
Driving wheel diameter	60 in (1,524 mm)
Top speed	approx. 45 mph (72 km/h)

Built by the Western & Atlantic Railroad, *The General* pulled passenger and freight trains between Atlanta, Georgia, and Chattanooga, Tennessee, from 1856 until 1891.

△ **B&O Class B No. 147**
Thatcher Perkins, **1863**

Wheel arrangement	4-6-0
Cylinders	2
Boiler pressure	175 psi (12.30 kg/sq cm)
Driving wheel diameter	60 in (1,524 mm)
Top speed	approx. 50 mph (80 km/h)

The Baltimore & Ohio's *Thatcher Perkins* (named after the company's Master of Machinery who designed it) is a survivor from among 16,500 "Ten-Wheelers" (4-6-0s) that were built for American railroads up to 1910. Its power was deployed climbing the steeply graded lines of West Virginia.

▽ **UP No. 119, 1868**

Wheel arrangement	4-4-0
Cylinders	2
Boiler pressure	85 psi (6 kg/sq cm)
Driving wheel diameter	60 in (1,524 mm)
Top speed	approx. 45 mph (72 km/h)

This is a replica of the Union Pacific's No. 119 first built by Roger's Locomotive Works of Paterson, New Jersey. The original was stationed at Ogden, Utah, and called upon to mark the completion of the first transcontinental railroad in May 1869. It served the route until 1903.

◁ **CP No. 60 *Jupiter*, 1868**

Wheel arrangement	4-4-0
Cylinders	2
Boiler pressure	110 psi (8 kg/sq cm)
Driving wheel diameter	60 in (1,524 mm) later changed to 61 in (1,600 mm)
Top speed	approx. 45 mph (72 km/h)

Jupiter was built in New York, shipped in kit-form to San Francisco via Cape Horn, then transported by barge to Sacramento, where it was reassembled. The locomotive represented the Central Pacific Railroad at the "golden spike" ceremony on completion of the transcontinental railroad. This replica was built in 1979.

Britain Advances

This period of British railway history features both successes and failures. The Grand Junction Railway's famous Crewe Works opened on a green-field site in 1840 and was soon turning out graceful, single-wheeler express locomotives. While in Liverpool, Edward Bury pursued his bar-frame design, which became popular in North America. On the downside, Brunel's atmospheric railway in Devon was an unmitigated disaster, and the failure of John Fowler's underground steam locomotive caused the designer much embarrassment.

△ FR No.3 "Old Coppernob", 1846

Wheel arrangement	0-4-0
Cylinders	2 (inside)
Boiler pressure	100 psi (7 kg/sq cm)
Driving wheel diameter	57 in (1,448 mm)
Top speed	approx. 30 mph (48 km/h)

Nicknamed "Old Coppernob" because of the copper cladding around its firebox, this locomotive was designed by Edward Bury, and built at Bury, Curtis & Kennedy of Liverpool for the Furness Railway in northwest England. It is normally at the National Railway Museum, York, and is the only survivor of the bar-frame design in the UK.

△ Fireless locomotive "Fowler's Ghost", 1861

Wheel arrangement	2-4-0
Cylinders	2 (inside)
Boiler pressure	160 psi (11.25 kg/sq cm)
Driving wheel diameter	72 in (1,830 mm)
Top speed	approx. 20 mph (32 km/h)

This experimental locomotive, designed by John Fowler and built by Robert Stephenson & Co., was intended for use on London's broad-gauge Metropolitan underground railway. The engine was fitted with condensing apparatus to prevent steam and smoke emissions; it was a complete failure.

▷ GJR *Columbine*, 1845

Wheel arrangement	2-2-2
Cylinders	2
Boiler pressure	120 psi (8.43 kg/sq cm)
Driving wheel diameter	72 in (1,830 mm)
Top speed	approx. 40 mph (64 km/h)

The locomotive *Columbine*, designed by Alexander Allen, was the first to be built at the Grand Junction Railway's Crewe Works. It was subsequently used to haul the London & North Western Railway's Engineering Department Inspection Saloon. It hauled passenger trains until 1877 and was withdrawn in 1902. It is now a static exhibit at London's Science Museum.

◁ **FR *Prince*, 1863**

Wheel arrangement	0-4-0ST
Cylinders	2
Boiler pressure	160 psi (11.25 kg/sq cm)
Driving wheel diameter	24 in (610 mm)
Top speed	approx. 20 mph (32 km/h)

Businessman and engineer George England designed and built *Prince*. It was one of the first three steam locomotives delivered to the slate-carrying 1-ft 11½-in- (0.60-m-) gauge Ffestiniog Railway in North Wales in 1863. It was returned to service in 2013 for the 150th anniversary of steam on the railway, and is the line's oldest working engine.

▷ **LSWR Class 0298, 1863**

Wheel arrangement	2-4-0WT
Cylinders	2
Boiler pressure	160 psi (11.25 kg/sq cm)
Driving wheel diameter	67 in (1,702 mm)
Top speed	approx. 40 mph (64 km/h)

The Class 0298 was designed by Joseph Beattie for the London & South Western Railway to provide suburban passenger services in southwest London. A total of 85 of these well-tank locomotives were built, the majority by Beyer Peacock & Co.

◁ **LNWR *Pet*, 1865**

Wheel arrangement	0-4-0ST
Cylinders	2 (inside)
Boiler pressure	120 psi (8.43 kg/sq cm)
Driving wheel diameter	15 in (380 mm)
Top speed	approx. 5 mph (8 km/h)

John Ramsbottom, the locomotive superintendent of the London & North Western Railway, designed this engine. *Pet* is a small cabless steam locomotive that worked on the 1-ft 6-in- (0.45-m-) narrow-gauge Crewe Works Railway until 1929. It is now a static exhibit at the National Railway Museum, York.

TECHNOLOGY

Brunel's Atmospheric Railway

British engineer Isambard Kingdom Brunel built the broad-gauge South Devon Railway between Exeter and Totnes as an "atmospheric" railway. Dispensing with locomotives, trains were pushed along by a long piston enclosed in a cast-iron tube in the middle of the track. The vacuum to move the piston was created at stationary pumping houses (such as the one above). The railway opened in 1847, but failed within a year. In 1848 it was converted to operate with conventional haulage, because the grease that was applied to the leather flap that sealed the pipe melted during hot weather, or was eaten by rats.

Atmospheric railway track This section of Brunel's broad-gauge track with its cast-iron vacuum pipe is on display at Didcot Railway Centre.

Euro Progress

The 1840s saw rapid railway building across Europe, with many locomotive designs still heavily influenced by British engineering expertise; many had set up workshops in France and Austria. By the 1850s Thomas Crampton's unusual long-boilered, "single-wheeler" engines were hauling trains between Paris and Strasbourg at speeds exceeding 70 mph (113 km/h). The design and craftsmanship of locomotives built by fledgling European builders such as Strauss of Munich stood the test of time with many remaining in service well into the 20th century.

▷ **Oldenburgische Class G1 No. 1 *Landwührden*, 1867**

Wheel arrangement	0-4-0
Cylinders	2
Boiler pressure	142 psi (9.98 kg/sq cm)
Driving wheel diameter	59 in (1,500 mm)
Top speed	37 mph (60 km/h)

The first locomotive to be built by Georg Krauss of Munich, No.1 *Landwührden* won a gold medal for excellence of design and workmanship at the World Exhibition in Paris in 1867. After first working on the Grand Duchy of Oldenburg State Railways' branch lines this lightweight engine was retired in 1900 and is now on display at the Deutsches Museum in Munich.

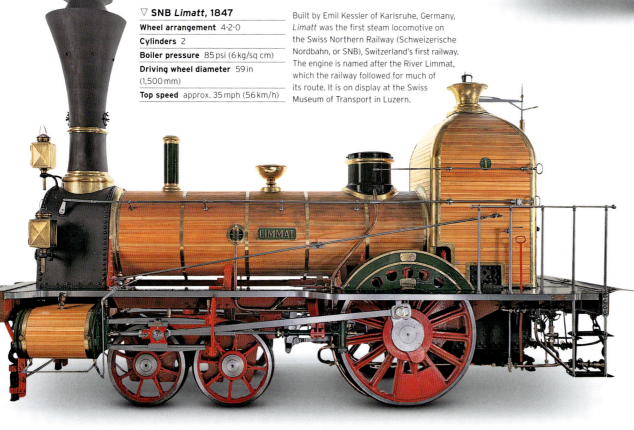

▽ **SNB *Limatt*, 1847**

Wheel arrangement	4-2-0
Cylinders	2
Boiler pressure	85 psi (6 kg/sq cm)
Driving wheel diameter	59 in (1,500 mm)
Top speed	approx. 35 mph (56 km/h)

Built by Emil Kessler of Karlsruhe, Germany, *Limatt* was the first steam locomotive on the Swiss Northern Railway (Schweizerische Nordbahn, or SNB), Switzerland's first railway. The engine is named after the River Limmat, which the railway followed for much of its route. It is on display at the Swiss Museum of Transport in Luzern.

▷ **CF de l'Est Crampton, 1852**

Wheel arrangement	4-2-0
Cylinders	2
Boiler pressure	120 psi (8.43 kg/sq cm)
Driving wheel diameter	84 in (2,134 mm)
Top speed	79 mph (127 km/h)

These fast locomotives, designed by British engineer Thomas Crampton, featured a large driving wheel at the rear and a low mounted boiler. Built by Jean-Francois Cail, No. 80 *Le Continent* hauled express trains between Paris and Strasbourg, retiring only in 1914 after covering 1.5 million miles (2.4 million km).

◁ **Südbahn Class 23 GKB 671, 1860**

Wheel arrangement	0-6-0
Cylinders	2
Boiler pressure	98 psi (6.89 kg/sq cm)
Driving wheel diameter	49 in (1,245 mm)
Top speed	28 mph (45 km/h)

This engine was built by the Lokomotivfabrik der StEG of Vienna to haul freight trains on the Graz-Köflacher Railway in southern Austria. Still used to haul excursion trains, GKB 671 is the oldest steam locomotive in continuous use in the world.

△ **CF de l'Ouest Buddicom Type 111 No. 33 Saint-Pierre, 1844**

Wheel arrangement	2-2-2
Cylinders	2
Boiler pressure	80 psi (5.62 kg/sq cm)
Driving wheel diameter	75 in (1,905 mm)
Top speed	37 mph (60 km/h)

Built in Rouen, France, by British engineer William Buddicom for the new Paris to Rouen railway, No. 33 Saint-Pierre had a long and successful career, retiring only in 1912. It is the oldest original steam locomotive still preserved on the European mainland, and is on display at the Cité du Train Museum in Mulhouse.

◁ **BG Type 1B N2T Muldenthal, 1861**

Wheel arrangement	2-4-0
Cylinders	2
Boiler pressure	110 psi (8 kg/sq cm)
Driving wheel diameter	48 in (1,220 mm)
Top speed	30 mph (48 km/h)

Sächsische Maschinenfabrik of Chemnitz built the Type 1B N2T Muldenthal to haul coal trains on the newly opened Bockwaer Railway in Saxony. When retired in 1952 it was the oldest operational locomotive in Germany. It is now on display at the Dresden Transport Museum.

Class Travel

From the very early days, rail passengers were sorted according to their ability to pay and their position in society. While first-class passengers got sumptuous seating and plenty of space, second class was often very overcrowded and the seats were generally wooden. Those in third class travelled in uncovered wagons open to the elements, and to the smoke, cinders, and ash from the steam engine at the front.

FIRST CLASS

SECOND CLASS

THIRD CLASS

A Day at the Races, **1846** This cartoon from the *London Illustrated News* shows the social distinctions of class travel on the railways in Britain.

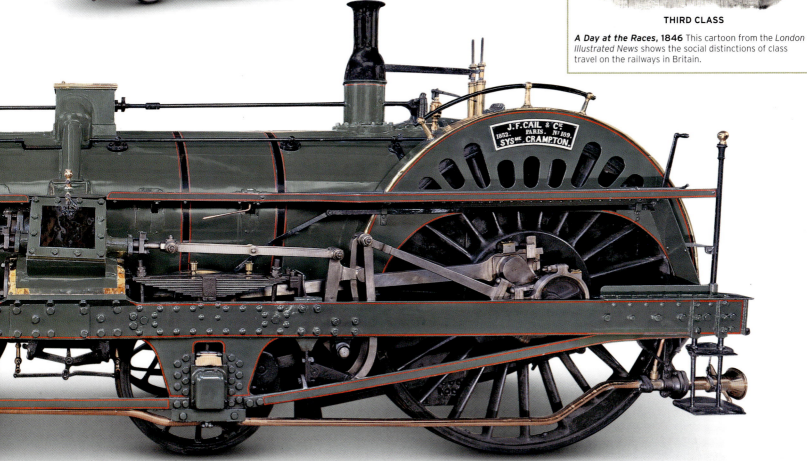

The GWR's Broad Gauge

While other British railways were being built to the standard gauge of 4 ft 8½ in
(1.435 m), engineer Isambard Kingdom Brunel used the broad gauge of 7 ft ¼ in (2.14 m)
when building the Great Western Railway, which opened from London Paddington to
Bristol in 1841. Brunel had argued that his design offered higher speeds, smoother
running, more stability, and increased comfort for passengers when compared to standard-
gauge railways. In many ways he was right, but the spread of the standard gauge not
only in Britain but also in many other parts of the world, including North
America, led to Brunel's broad gauge becoming an anachronism.
The GWR's last broad-gauge train ran on 21 May 1892.

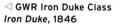

◁ **GWR Firefly Class**
Fire Fly, 1840

Wheel arrangement	4-2-2
Cylinders	2 (inside)
Boiler pressure	100 psi (7 kg/sq cm)
Driving wheel diameter	84 in (2,134 mm)
Top speed	approx. 58 mph (93 km/h)

Designed by Daniel Gooch, Firefly was one of
61 express passenger locomotives built for the
Great Western Railway by various builders
between 1840 and 1842. The class was known
for its speed with the original *Fire Fly* travelling
from Twyford to Paddington in only 37 minutes.
Built in 2005, this working replica is the 63rd *Fire
Fly*. It operates at Didcot Railway Centre.

◁ **GWR Iron Duke Class**
Iron Duke, 1846

Wheel arrangement	4-2-2
Cylinders	2 (inside)
Boiler pressure	100 psi (7 kg/sq cm)
Driving wheel diameter	96 in (2,440 mm)
Top speed	approx. 77 mph (124 km/h)

Twenty-nine Iron Duke Class express
passenger locomotives, designed by
Daniel Gooch, were built at the Swindon
Works of the Great Western Railway
and Rothwell & Co. of Bolton-le-Moors
between 1846 and 1855. The
working replica *Iron Duke*, seen
here, was built in 1985 and is on
display at Didcot Railway Centre.

◁ **GWR Iron Duke Class *Sultan*, 1857**

Wheel arrangement	4-2-2
Cylinders	2 (inside)
Boiler pressure	100 psi (7 kg/sq cm)
Driving wheel diameter	96 in (2,440 mm)
Top speed	approx. 77 mph (124 km/h)

One of the Great Western Railway's Iron Duke Class express locomotives, *Sultan* was originally built in 1847, but was involved in an accident at Shrivenham a year later when it ran into a goods train. The prototype of this class, *Great Western*, was originally fitted with one pair of carrying wheels at the front as a 2-2-2. As with other members of the class, *Sultan*'s driving wheels had no flanges to allow movement on curves.

▷ **GWR Iron Duke Class
Lord of the Isles, 1851**

Wheel arrangement	4-2-2
Cylinders	2 (inside)
Boiler pressure	140 psi (10 kg/sq cm)
Driving wheel diameter	96 in (2,440 mm)
Top speed	approx. 77 mph (124 km/h)

Another express passenger locomotive designed by Daniel Gooch for the Great Western Railway, *Lord of the Isles* was an improved version of the Iron Duke Class with higher boiler pressure, sanding gear, and a better driver's "cab". When new, it was exhibited at the Great Exhibition of 1851, and then in Chicago in 1893. It was withdrawn in 1884.

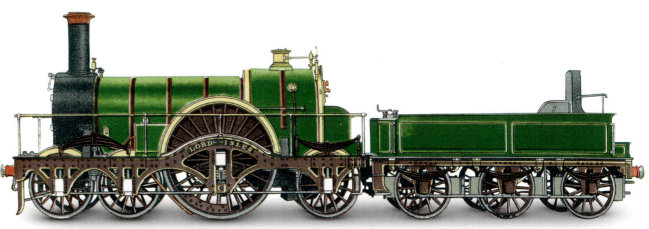

◁ **GWR Rover Class, 1870/1871**

Wheel arrangement	4-2-2
Cylinders	2 (inside)
Boiler pressure	145 psi (10.19 kg/sq cm)
Driving wheel diameter	96 in (2,440 mm)
Top speed	approx. 77 mph (124 km/h)

Built between 1871 and 1888, the Great Western Railway's Rover Class of express locomotives was similar to the Iron Duke Class, but with a small increase in boiler pressure and more protective driver's cabs. They used names previously carried by Iron Dukes and stayed in service until the end of the broad gauge in 1892.

TECHNOLOGY

Battle of the Gauges

There were major problems for passengers who were forced to change trains at stations where the Great Western Railway's broad gauge met standard-gauge tracks. In 1846 the British Government passed the Railway Regulation (Gauge) Act, which mandated the 4-ft 8½-in (1.435-m) gauge for UK and 5 ft 3 in (1.6 m) for Ireland. Brunel was overruled, and by 1892 all the GWR's lines were converted to standard gauge.

***Break of Gauge at Gloucester*, 1846** This political cartoon depicts the confusion caused at Gloucester station where passengers with luggage had to change trains from the broad-gauge Great Western Railway to the standard-gauge Midland Railway and vice versa.

△ **GWR Broad Gauge Coach, 1840**

Type	6-wheel, Second Class
Capacity	48 passengers
Construction	iron chassis, wooden coach body
Railway	Great Western Railway

This replica of a Great Western Railway, broad-gauge, second-class carriage was built by London's Science Museum to run with their replica *Iron Duke* locomotive, to celebrate the anniversary of the railway in 1985. It now operates with *Fire Fly* at Didcot Railway Centre.

Mass Movers

As railways expanded, so did their roles and with that the need for engines designed for specific purposes. Express passenger engines had large driving wheels, which increased the distance travelled in each rotation. For goods trains, haulage power was transmitted through six, eight, or ten smaller wheels that provided the adhesion necessary for trains to move heavy loads. Suburban passenger services kept to timetables by using tank engines that could run equally well smokebox- or bunker-first. For branch line and shunting engines, size and weight were key factors, so the short wheelbase 0-4-0 and the 2-4-0 and 0-6-0 types were preferred.

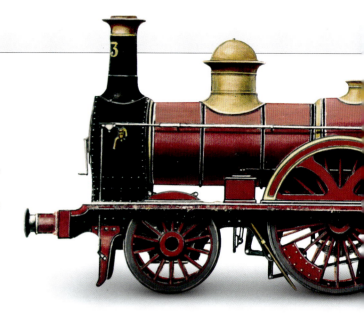

◁ S&DR No. 25 *Derwent*, 1845

Wheel arrangement	0-6-0
Cylinders	2
Boiler pressure	75 psi (3.5 kg/sq cm)
Driving wheel diameter	48 in (1,220 mm)
Top speed	approx. 10-15 mph (16-24 km/h)

From the middle of the 19th century, the six-wheel goods engine became the principal British locomotive. One of the earliest, Timothy Hackworth's *Derwent* of 1845, served the Stockton & Darlington Railway, in northeast England, until 1869.

▷ Met Class A No. 23, 1864

Wheel arrangement	4-4-0T
Cylinders	2
Boiler pressure	120.13 psi (8.46 kg/sq cm); later 150 psi (10.53 kg/sq cm)
Driving wheel diameter	60½ in (1,537 mm)
Top speed	approx. 45 mph (72 km/h)

Tank locomotives built by Beyer Peacock & Co of Manchester were the mainstay of London's Metropolitan Railway from the 1860s until the advent of electrification. To cut pollution, exhaust steam was returned to the water tanks where it was condensed for reuse.

Wagons and Carriages

Unsurprisingly, the designs of the earliest railway vehicles were based on proven ideas. Carriages adopted the design of the road coach; wagons were no more than enlarged versions of the iron and wooden, four-wheel tubs that had been used in mines for centuries. However, increasing loads – both passenger and goods – faster speeds, and the call for greater comfort and facilities brought about rapid advances.

△ SH Chaldron Wagon, 1845-55

Type	Bucket-type coal wagon
Weight	3⅓ tons (3.35 tonnes)
Construction	Iron platework and chassis
Railway	South Hetton Colliery

The design of the chaldron – a medieval measure used for weighing coal – was adopted for the earliest type of wagon. This one was used on George Stephenson's railway at the South Hetton Colliery, County Durham, which opened in 1822.

◁ **LNWR "Large Bloomers", 1851**

Wheel arrangement 2-2-2

Cylinders 2

Boiler pressure 100 psi (7 kg/sq cm); later 150 psi (10.53 kg/sq cm)

Driving wheel diameter 84 in (2,134 mm)

Top speed approx. 50-60 mph (80-96 km/h)

Designed by James McConnell, 74 of these single-wheeler passenger engines were built for the London & North Western Railway up to 1862. They mainly worked between London and Birmingham. The nickname, "Large Bloomers", is attributed to American reformer Amelia Bloomer who scandalized Victorian society by wearing trousers.

▷ **S&PR No. 5 *Shannon*, 1857**

Wheel arrangement 0-4-0WT

Cylinders 2

Boiler pressure 120 psi (8.43 kg/sq cm)

Driving wheel diameter 35 in (889 mm)

Top speed approx. 10-12 mph (16-19 km/h)

London's George England & Co. built this well tank for the Sandy & Potton Railway in Bedfordshire. In 1862 *Shannon* was sold to the London & North Western Railway, spending 16 years as a works shunter before ending its career on the Wantage Tramway in Oxfordshire.

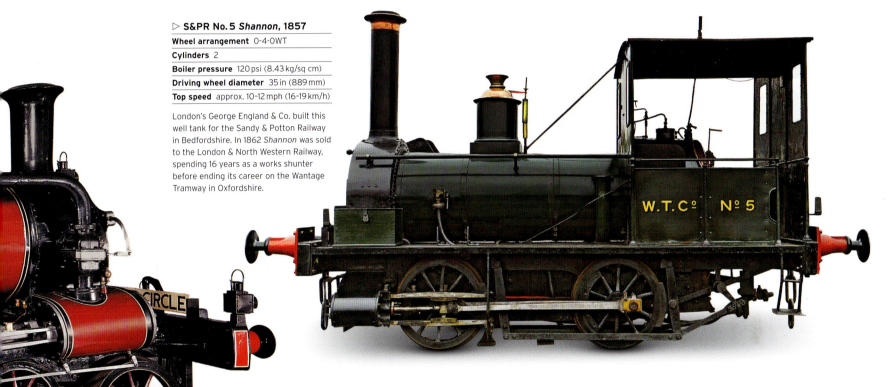

◁ **L&BR Queen Adelaide's Saloon No. 2, 1842**

Type Passenger carriage with fold-down beds

Capacity 10 passengers

Construction Wooden body, iron chassis

Railway London & Birmingham Railway

This "stagecoach on wheels" transported Adelaide, Queen Consort to Britain's William IV. While the chassis was entrusted to the London & Birmingham Railway's Euston Works, the body was the work of a London coach builder. This is the oldest preserved carriage in Europe and is in the National Railway Museum, York.

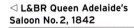

△ **NBR Dandy Car No. 1, 1863**

Type Horse-drawn rail car

Capacity 30 passengers (12 first and second class, 18 third class)

Construction Wooden body and frame

Railway North British Railway

Between 1863 and 1914 passengers on the Port Carlisle Railway in northwest England travelled in this horse-drawn Dandy Car, the horse trotting between the rails. First- and second-class passengers sat inside, while third class sat on benches at either end.

Nations and Colonies

The success of the early British railways and steam engines attracted interest from across Europe and North America. As a result the newly industrialized countries such as US, France, and Germany began to lay the foundations for their own national systems, so became less and less dependent on British expertise.

However, Britain had a wider sphere of influence: its empire – the first railway outside Europe being built in the British colony of Jamaica. There were both economic and political reasons for the British to build railways in Australia, Canada, South Africa, and elsewhere. The vastness of India was controlled through its railway system, while the efficiency, and therefore profitability, of its mining, logging, and agriculture was completely transformed by the new transport.

DIE ERSTE BORSIG-LOKOMOTIVE
AUS DEM JAHRE 1841

△ I-class No. 1, 1855

Wheel arrangement 0-4-2

Cylinders 2

Boiler pressure 120 psi (8.43 kg/sq cm)

Driving wheel diameter 66 in (1,676 mm)

Top speed approx. 20 mph (32 km/h)

One of four I-Class locomotives built by Robert Stephenson & Co of Newcastle-upon-Tyne, England, No.1 was delivered to the Sydney Railway Co. in January 1855. Train services were inaugurated in Australia that May. No.1 was retired in 1877 having run 156,542 miles (250,467 km).

△ Borsig No. 1, 1840

Wheel arrangement 4-2-2

Cylinders 2

Boiler pressure 80 psi (5.62 kg/sq cm)

Driving wheel diameter 54 in (1,372 mm)

Top speed approx. 40 mph (64 km/h)

August Borsig opened a factory in Berlin in 1837 and three years later delivered his first locomotive to the Berlin–Potsdam Railway. In 1840, No.1 outpaced a British-built competitor, ending Germany's reliance on imports and helping make Borsig one of the world's leading engine builders.

▷ EIR No. 22 *Fairy Queen*, 1855

Wheel arrangement 2-2-2

Cylinders ?

Boiler pressure 80–100 psi (5.62–7 kg/sq cm)

Driving wheel diameter 72 in (1,830 mm)

Top speed approx. 25 mph (40 km/h)

One of the first locomotives to haul passenger trains in India, *Fairy Queen* was built by Kitson, Hewitson & Thompson of Leeds, England, for the East Indian Railway. An outside-cylinder, 2-2-2 well tank, it is part of the historic locomotive collection in New Delhi and has a claim to be the world's oldest working engine.

△ *La Porteña*, 1857

Wheel arrangement 0-4-0ST

Cylinders 2

Boiler pressure 140–160 psi (9.84–11.25 kg/sq cm)

Driving wheel diameter about 48 in (1,219 mm)

Top speed approx 16 mph (26 km/h)

Arriving in Argentina from Britain on Christmas Day, 1856, the outside-cylindered, four-wheel saddletank *La Porteña* hauled the first train over the Buenos Aires Western Railway on 29 August 1857. Built by E.B. Wilson of Leeds, it remained in service until 1899 and is now exhibited at the museum in Luján.

◁ **Hawthorn No. 9 *Blackie*, 1859**

Wheel arrangement	0-4-2
Cylinders	2
Boiler pressure	130 psi (9.14 kg/sq cm)
Driving wheel diameter	54 in (1,372 mm)
Top speed	approx. 30 mph (48 km/h)

Hawthorn & Co. assembled this 0-4-0 at its works in Leith, Scotland, for contractor Edward Pickering, who used it in the construction of the 45-mile (72-km) Cape Town to Wellington Railway. South Africa's first locomotive, it was rebuilt as an 0-4-2 in 1873–74 and is now exhibited at Cape Town's main station.

△ **O&RR Class B No. 26, 1870**

Wheel arrangement	0-6-0
Cylinders	2
Boiler pressure	160-180 psi (11.25-12.65 kg/sq cm)
Driving wheel diameter	52 in (1,320 mm)
Top speed	approx. 40 mph (64 km/h)

This locomotive was built by Sharp, Stewart & Co. of Manchester, England, for the 5-ft 6-in- (1.67-m-) gauge Oudh & Rohilkhand Railway of northern India. No. 26 is typical of British engines exported at the time.

TECHNOLOGY

Challenging Railways

With mountain ranges, deserts, and jungles to be overcome, India posed a huge challenge to railway builders. Nevertheless, the first 25-mile (40-km) stretch between Bombay (now Mumbai) and Thane opened in November 1852, and by 1880 around 9,000 miles (14,484 km) of track had been laid. Twenty years on, the network had extended to 40,000 miles (64,374 km). A committee set up by the Governor General, Lord Dalhousie, led to the setting up of the Great Indian Peninsular Railway, the East India Railway, and the Darjeeling Himalayan Railway.

Construction site Workers photographed in 1856 on the wooden staging used in the building of the viaduct at the mouth of tunnel No. 8 (out of 28) on the Bhor Ghat Railway.

19th-century Racers

The development of sleek express steam engines in the late 19th century led to publicity-seeking railways in both the US and UK competing for the fastest journey times on rival intercity routes. In the UK the famous "Races to the North" of 1888 and 1895 saw the railways of the rival East Coast and West Coast Main Lines between London and Scotland engage in a dangerous high-speed struggle for supremacy. In the US there was fierce competition between the Pennsylvania Railroad and the New York Central & Hudson River Railroad on their New York to Buffalo routes during the 1890s. This triggered electrifying performances by the latter company's celebrity locomotive No. 999 while hauling the *Empire State Express*.

◁ **GNR Stirling Single Class, 1870**

Wheel arrangement	4-2-2
Cylinders	2
Boiler pressure	170 psi (11.95 kg/sq cm)
Driving wheel diameter	97 in (2,464 mm)
Top speed	85 mph (137 km/h)

Patrick Stirling designed this locomotive for the Great Northern Railway. A total of 53 of these single-wheeler locomotives were built at Doncaster Works between 1870 and 1895. The locomotives hauled express trains on the East Coast Main Line between London King's Cross and York and were involved in the "Races to the North" of 1888 and 1895. No. 1, shown here, is preserved at the National Railway Museum in York, UK.

Races to the North

Headlined in newspapers as the "Race to the North", railway companies unofficially raced each other on two main lines between London and Edinburgh in 1888. The West Coast Main Line trains were operated by the London & North Western Railway and the Caledonian Railway; and the East Coast Main Line trains, by the Great Northern Railway, the North Eastern Railway, and the North British Railway. Following the completion of the s Forth Bridge in 1890, the companies raced between London and Aberdeen. After a derailment at Preston in 1896, the practice was banned and speed limits were enforced.

Record run A Caledonian Railway postcard shows Engine No. 17 and driver John Souter at Aberdeen after their race-winning run on 23 August 1895.

▷ **LNWR Improved Precedent Class, 1887**

Wheel arrangement	2-4-0
Cylinders	2 (inside)
Boiler pressure	150 psi (10.54 kg/sq cm)
Driving wheel diameter	81 in (2,057 mm)
Top speed	approx. 80 mph (129 km/h)

A total of 166 Improved Precedent Class express locomotives, designed by F.W. Webb, were built at the London & North Western Railway's Crewe Works between 1887 and 1901. No. 790 *Hardwicke* set a new speed record between Crewe and Carlisle during the "Race to the North" on 22 August 1895. It is preserved at the National Railway Museum in York, UK.

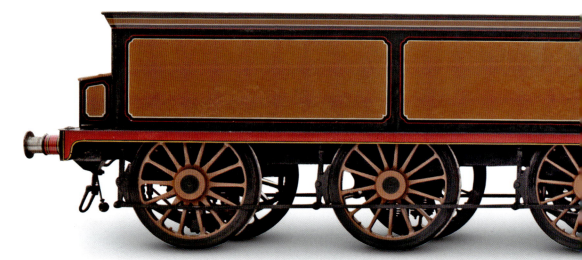

◁ **CR No. 123, 1886**

Wheel arrangement	4-2-2
Cylinders	2 (inside)
Boiler pressure	160 psi (11.25 kg/sq cm)
Driving wheel diameter	84 in (2,134 mm)
Top speed	approx. 80 mph (129 km/h)

Built as an exhibition locomotive by Neilson & Co. of Glasgow for the Caledonian Railway in 1886, this unique single-wheeler hauled expresses between Carlisle and Glasgow. Following retirement in 1935 it was preserved and is now on display at the Riverside Museum in Glasgow.

TECHNOLOGY

Standard Rail Time

Confusion reigned on the early railways as clocks at stations were set at local time, causing difficulty for railway staff and passengers alike. In the UK the Great Western Railway introduced a standardized "London Time" for their station schedules in 1840. This synchronization used Greenwich Mean Time (GMT) set by the Royal Observatory at Greenwich, which later became accepted as the global standard time. In 1883 railways in the US and Canada split both countries longitudinally into geographic time zones and introduced Railroad Standard Time.

Time regulation Made by American jeweller Webb C. Ball in 1889, this precision regulator clock helped maintain the accuracy of other timepieces on the Baltimore & Ohio Railroad.

▷ **NYC&HR No. 999, 1893**

Wheel arrangement	4-4-0
Cylinders	2
Boiler pressure	180 psi (12.65 kg/sq cm)
Driving wheel diameter	86¹/₂ in (2,197 mm)
Top speed	approx. 86 mph (138 km/h)

Alleged to have travelled at over 100 mph (161 km/h), No. 999 was built in 1893 to haul the New York Central & Hudson River Railroad's flagship train, the *Empire State Express*, between New York and Buffalo. This celebrity locomotive was exhibited at the Chicago World's Fair before being retired in 1952. Nicknamed the "Queen of Speed", No. 999 is on display at the Chicago Museum of Science & Industry.

▽ **LB&SCR B1 Class, 1882**

Wheel arrangement	0-4-2
Cylinders	2 (inside)
Boiler pressure	150 psi (10.53 kg/sq cm)
Driving wheel diameter	78 in (1,980 mm)
Top speed	approx. 70 mph (113 km/h)

The B1 Class locomotives were designed by William Stroudley for the London, Brighton & South Coast Railway. A total of 36 were built at Brighton Works between 1882 and 1891. Hauling heavy expresses between London and Brighton, they were named after politicians, railway officials, or places served by the railway. The last survivor was retired in 1933, and No. 214 *Gladstone* is preserved at the National Railway Museum in York.

London Locals

Growing prosperity and personal mobility enabled people to move away from the centre of London. Railroads supplied transportation links from the new suburbs to the city, giving birth to the commuter train. While the Great Eastern Railway among others provided a peak-time, steam-hauled service, electric traction – overground and underground – was the future. The first deep-level "tube" line, the City & South London Railway, which opened in 1890 was the nucleus of London's underground system. Other cities soon followed London's example: Liverpool in northwest England and Budapest and Paris in Continental Europe. In the US, the Boston subway opened in 1897 and, by 1904, had been joined by New York's.

△ GWR 633 Class, 1871

Wheel arrangement	0-6-0T
Cylinders	2
Boiler pressure	165 psi (11.6 kg/sq cm)
Driving wheel diameter	54½ in (1,384 mm)
Top speed	approx. 40 mph (64 km/h)

Designed by George Armstrong and built at Wolverhampton Works, several of the 12-strong 633 Class were fitted with condensing apparatus to take Great Western Railway trains through the tunnels, so gaining the nickname "Tunnel Motors". Much modified, some lasted until 1934.

△ LB&SCR A1 Class, 1872

Wheel arrangement	0-6-0T
Cylinders	2
Boiler pressure	150 psi (10.53 kg/sq cm)
Driving wheel diameter	48 in (1,220 mm)
Top speed	approx. 60 mph (96 km/h)

The London, Brighton & South Coast Railway's suburban network was the domain of William Stroudley's small, six-coupled tanks. Fifty were built between 1872 and 1880, and the bark of their exhaust earned them the nickname of "Terriers". They were named after places they served, in the case of No. 54 *Waddon* (1875), a district near Croydon.

◁ NLR 75 Class, 1879

Wheel arrangement	0-6-0T
Cylinders	2
Boiler pressure	160 psi (11.24 kg/sq cm)
Driving wheel diameter	52 in (1,321 mm)
Top speed	approx. 30 mph (48 km/h)

John C. Park supplied the North London Railway with this shunting engine to serve the dock system around Poplar. Thirty were built up to 1905 and, as they rarely left the docks, no coal bunker was fitted; fuel was stored on the footplate.

◁ LSWR 415 Class, 1882

Wheel arrangement	4-4-2T
Cylinders	2
Boiler pressure	160 psi (11.25 kg/sq cm)
Driving wheel diameter	67 in (1,702 mm)
Top speed	approx. 45 mph (72 km/h)

Designed by William Adams of the London & South Western Railway, 71 of the 415 Class were built from 1882 to 1885. Put to work on suburban services out of London's Waterloo, three ended their days on the southwest Lyme Regis branch, where their short wheelbase and leading bogie were ideal to negotiate the severe curves.

London's Carriages

Both the Metropolitan and District railways began by using locomotive-hauled carriages. However, few offered the upholstered luxury of the Metropolitan's "Jubilee" coach. Most followed the pattern of the District's No. 100, with 10 passengers to each compartment. The distinction between the classes even extended to lighting: first class travellers enjoyed two gas jets, while second and third class passengers made do with one. Conditions improved little with the coming of the City & South London Railway, which became known as the "sardine tin railway".

◁ C&SLR "Padded Cell", 1890

Type	underground passenger carriage
Capacity	32 passengers
Construction	wooden body on two 4-wheel bogies
Railway	City & South London Railway

Tunnel diameter restricted carriage size on this first "tube" line. Coaches were fitted with high-backed seating, running along the length, and gates at either end to allow passengers on and off. With the only windows being slits above seats, and air entering through roof ventilators, the nickname "padded cells" was appropriate.

△ **C&SLR electric locomotive, 1889**

Wheel arrangement	0-4-0 (Bo)
Power supply	0.5 kV DC third rail
Power rating	100 hp (74.60 kW)
Top speed	25 mph (40 km/h)

The first important railway to use electric traction was the City & South London Railway. When opened in 1890 the line had six stations and ran from City to Stockwell. Operated by 14 locomotives, one of which – with a train of later steel-bodied carriages with full-length windows – is passing Borough Junction in this 1922 photograph.

▽ **GER S56 Class, 1886**

Wheel arrangement	0-6-0T
Cylinders	2
Boiler pressure	180 psi (12.65 kg/sq cm)
Driving wheel diameter	48 in (1,220 mm)
Top speed	approx. 60 mph (96 km/h)

James Holden designed a small but powerful, six-coupled tank for the Great Eastern Railway's inner-suburban services in 1886. It was equipped with Westinghouse compressed air brakes, ideal where stations were close together. The sole survivor, No. 87 of 1904, is part of Britain's National Collection.

△ **Met C Class, 1891**

Wheel arrangement	0-4-4T
Cylinders	2
Boiler pressure	140 psi (9.84 kg/sq cm)
Driving wheel diameter	66 in (1,676 mm)
Top speed	approx. 60 mph (96 km/h)

The Metropolitan Railway's C Class consisted of just four engines built by Neilson & Co. of Glasgow. After the Met's expansion into Hertfordshire and Buckinghamshire, they hauled trains from the city out to Watford, Amersham, and Aylesbury.

▷ **Met Jubilee Coach No. 353, 1892**

Type	four-compartment, first-class passenger coach
Capacity	32
Construction	original wooden body on later 4-wheel steel chassis
Railway	Metropolitan Railway

This carriage served the Metropolitan Railway from 1892 until 1907 when it was sold to the Weston, Clevedon & Portishead Light Railway. Restored to mark the railway's 150th anniversary in 2013, it is now at the London Transport Museum.

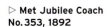

△ **DR Coach No. 100, 1884**

Type	four-compartment, third-class passenger carriage
Capacity	40
Construction	original wooden body on later 4-wheel steel chassis
Railway	District Railway

The origins of coach No. 100 of the District Railway are uncertain. What is definite is that the body finished up as a storage shed in Kent. It was rescued, placed on a new chassis, and now runs on the Kent & East Sussex Railway, where a District Railway brown livery was applied.

Specialist Steam

Initially used for hauling coal, railways were soon adapted to play similar roles in the fast-growing industrial landscape. Narrow-gauge lines and engines were ideal for quarries, foundries, shipyards, brickworks, and some military sites. Dock railways required small but powerful engines that could weave their way along quaysides, while in chemical plants and munitions factories the danger posed by stray sparks was overcome by developing fireless locomotives. Ingenious engines and track were used to scale mountains. There were few places where the steam locomotive could not serve.

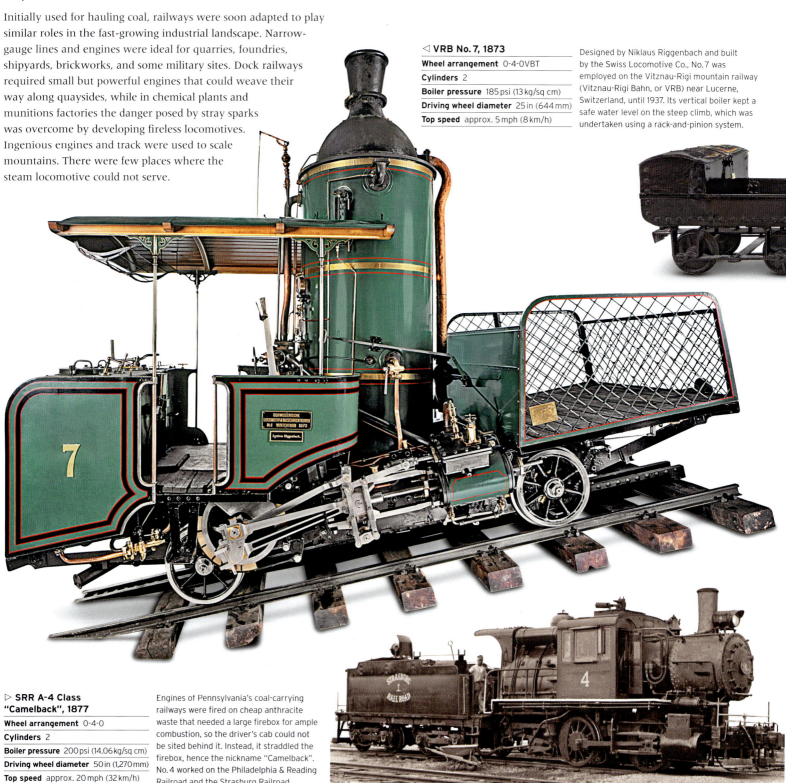

◁ **VRB No. 7, 1873**

Wheel arrangement	0-4-0VBT
Cylinders	2
Boiler pressure	185 psi (13 kg/sq cm)
Driving wheel diameter	25 in (644 mm)
Top speed	approx. 5 mph (8 km/h)

Designed by Niklaus Riggenbach and built by the Swiss Locomotive Co., No.7 was employed on the Vitznau-Rigi mountain railway (Vitznau-Rigi Bahn, or VRB) near Lucerne, Switzerland, until 1937. Its vertical boiler kept a safe water level on the steep climb, which was undertaken using a rack-and-pinion system.

▷ **SRR A-4 Class "Camelback", 1877**

Wheel arrangement	0-4-0
Cylinders	2
Boiler pressure	200 psi (14.06 kg/sq cm)
Driving wheel diameter	50 in (1,270 mm)
Top speed	approx. 20 mph (32 km/h)

Engines of Pennsylvania's coal-carrying railways were fired on cheap anthracite waste that needed a large firebox for ample combustion, so the driver's cab could not be sited behind it. Instead, it straddled the firebox, hence the nickname "Camelback". No.4 worked on the Philadelphia & Reading Railroad and the Strasburg Railroad.

◁ **FR Double Fairlie No.10** *Merddin Emrys*, **1879**

Wheel arrangement	0-4-4-0T
Cylinders	4
Boiler pressure	160 psi (11.25 kg/sq cm)
Driving wheel diameter	32 in (813 mm)
Top speed	approx. 35 mph (56 km/h)

Following a design by British engineer Robert Fairlie, *Merddin Emrys* was the first locomotive built by the Ffestiniog Railway's workshops. A double-ended, articulated tank engine riding on powered bogies, today's No.10 is much rebuilt.

TECHNOLOGY

Crane Tanks

Used in industrial locations from docks and factories to shipyards and ironworks, crane tanks combined shunting with the ability to distribute loads. The Pallion shipyard in Sunderland, in northeast England, employed a fleet of five, while the nearby Shildon Ironworks in County Durham saw the last use of the type in Britain. Crane tanks were chiefly a product of the 19th century, although one – built for the North London Railway – remained in service until 1951.

Southern Railway No. 234S, 1881 This crane tank was used at Ashford Locomotive Works and Folkestone Harbour, both in Kent, and at Lancing Carriage Works in Sussex. It was retired in 1949.

△ LYR *Wren*, 1887

Wheel arrangement	0-4-0ST
Cylinders	2
Boiler pressure	170 psi (11.95 kg/sq cm)
Driving wheel diameter	16¹/₂ in (418 mm)
Top speed	approx. 5 mph (8 km/h)

Wren was one of eight small saddletanks employed on the 7¹/₂-mile- (12-km-), 1-ft 6-in- (0.46-m-) gauge track serving the Lancashire & Yorkshire Railway's works at Horwich, Lancashire. The engine was built by Beyer Peacock & Co. of Manchester, and remained in use until 1962.

◁ Hunslet *Lilla*, 1891

Wheel arrangement	0-4-0ST
Cylinders	2
Boiler pressure	120 psi (8.43 kg/sq cm)
Driving wheel diameter	26 in (660 mm)
Top speed	approx. 10-12 mph (16-19 km/h)

Lilla is a survivor from 50 saddletanks built by the Hunslet Engine Co. of Leeds, England, between 1870 and 1932 for Welsh slate quarries. It was retired from Penrhyn Quarry in 1957 and is now preserved on the Ffestiniog Railway in North Wales.

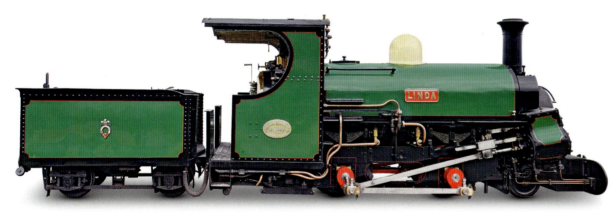

◁ Hunslet *Linda*, 1893

Wheel arrangement	0-4-0STT
Cylinders	2
Boiler pressure	140 psi (9.9 kg/sq cm)
Driving wheel diameter	26 in (660 mm)
Top speed	approx. 12-18 mph (19-29 km/h)

From the same stable as *Lilla* but more powerful, *Linda* was used on the Penrhyn Quarry's "mainline", which ran from Bethesda to Port Penrhyn, near Bangor, Wales. Another Ffestiniog veteran, *Linda* has been rebuilt there as a 2-4-0 saddletank tender engine.

▷ Saxon IV K Class, 1892

Wheel arrangement	0-4-4-0T
Cylinders	4 (compound)
Boiler pressure	174 psi/203 psi/217 psi (12.23 kg/sq cm/14.27 kg/sq cm/ 15.25 kg/sq cm) (variations within class)
Driving wheel diameter	30 in (760 mm)
Top speed	approx. 19 mph (30 km/h)

Germany's most numerous narrow-gauge class, 96 of these were built for the Royal Saxon State Railways from 1892 to 1921. They were articulated, and used the Günther-Meyer system of powered bogies; only 22 survive.

Shrinking the World

The introduction of steam engines on the narrow-gauge, slate-carrying railway at Ffestiniog in Wales in 1863 had led to the adoption of other narrower-gauge railways around the world. These lines were suited to mountainous regions as they were cheaper to construct and could cope with sharper curves and steeper gradients. In the 1870s India built its first locomotive using parts imported from Britain, and in 1872 Japan opened its first railway. Elsewhere, larger engines were being introduced and the mass production of freight locomotives had begun.

◁ **Japan's No. 1, 1871/2**

Wheel arrangement	2-4-0T
Cylinders	2
Boiler pressure	140 psi (10 kg/sq cm)
Driving wheel diameter	52 in (1,320 mm)
Top speed	approx. 30 mph (48 km/h)

Built in the UK by the Vulcan Foundry in 1871, No. 1 was the first steam locomotive to operate on Japan's inaugural public railway, from Tokyo to Yokohama, which opened in 1872. From 1880 it went to work on other Japanese railways before retiring in 1930. It is now on display at the Saitama Railway Museum.

▷ **V&TRR No. 20 *Tahoe*, 1875**

Wheel arrangement	2-6-0
Cylinders	2
Boiler pressure	130 psi (9.14 kg/sq cm)
Driving wheel diameter	48 in (1,220 mm)
Top speed	approx. 30 mph (48 km/h)

Built by the Baldwin Locomotive Works, Philadelphia, in 1875, No. 20 *Tahoe* worked on the Virginia & Truckee Railroad in Nevada, US, until 1926. The 41.88-ton (38-tonne) locomotive was temporarily brought out of retirement during WWII. It has since been restored and is now on display at the Railroad Museum of Pennsylvania in Strasburg.

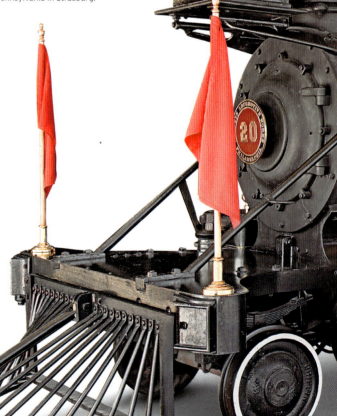

TALKING POINT

Prince of Wales's Coach

Constructed at the Agra Workshops of the 3-ft 3-in- (1-m-) gauge Rajputana Malwa Railway in 1875, this elegant coach was specially built for the then Prince of Wales (later King Edward VII) for his visit to India in 1877. The prince travelled to India for the Royal Durbar, which celebrated the coronation of his mother Queen Victoria as Empress of India. With all of its original fittings intact, this coach is now on display at the National Rail Museum, New Delhi.

Royal transport This unique, four-wheel coach features balconies at each end with seating for four armed guards. The carriage has sunshades on both sides and is decorated with emblems of the British Crown.

△ **Indian F Class, 1874**

Wheel arrangement	0-6-0
Cylinders	2
Boiler pressure	approx. 140 psi (10 kg/sq cm)
Driving wheel diameter	approx. 57 in (1,448 mm)
Top speed	approx. 30 mph (48 km/h)

Derived from the British-built 3ft 3-in- (1-m-) gauge F Class mixed traffic locomotives introduced in 1874, F1 Class No. 734 was the first locomotive to be assembled in India, using imported parts. It worked on the Rajputana Malwa Railway from 1895, and is now an exhibit at the National Rail Museum, New Delhi.

▷ FR Single Fairlie *Taliesin*, 1876

Wheel arrangement 0-4-4T
Cylinders 2
Boiler pressure 150 psi (10.53 kg/sq cm)
Driving wheel diameter 32 in (810 mm)
Top speed approx. 20 mph (32 km/h)

Built for the 1-ft 11½-in- (0.60-m-) gauge
Ffestiniog Railway in North Wales by
the Vulcan Foundry, Single Fairlie
Taliesin worked slate and passenger
trains between Blaenau Ffestiniog and
Porthmadog until withdrawn and
scrapped in 1935. A working replica,
using a few parts from the original
engine, was built at the railway's Boston
Lodge Workshops in 1999.

△ DHR Class B, 1889

Wheel arrangement 0-4-0ST
Cylinders 2
Boiler pressure 140 psi (10 kg/sq cm)
Driving wheel diameter 26 in (660 mm)
Top speed approx. 20 mph (32 km/h)

A total of 34 of these locomotives were built
by Sharp Stewart & Co. and others for the
2-ft- (0.60-m-) gauge Darjeeling Himalayan
Railway in India from 1889 to 1927. Some of
them still run on this steeply graded line,
which was declared a World Heritage Site
by UNESCO in 1999.

△ Russian O Class, 1890

Wheel arrangement 0-8-0
Cylinders 2
Boiler pressure 156-213 psi (11-15 kg/sq cm)
Driving wheel diameter 47¼ in (1,200 mm)
Top speed approx. 35 mph (56 km/h)

Over 9,000 of the Russian O Class freight
engines were built between 1890 and
1928, making it the second most numerous
class of steam locomotives in the world.
Armoured versions of this class were
widely used to haul trains during WWI,
the Russian Civil War, and WWII.

▷ CGR Class 7, 1892

Wheel arrangement 4-8-0
Cylinders 2
Boiler pressure 160-180 psi (11.25-12.65 kg/sq cm)
Driving wheel diameter 42½ in (1,080 mm)
Top speed approx. 35 mph (56 km/h)

Thirty-eight of these powerful freight
locomotives were built in Scotland in 1892 for
the 3-ft 6-in- (1.06-m-) gauge Cape Government
Railway in South Africa. They worked on the
newly formed South African Railways from 1912,
until their withdrawal in 1972. Some saw service
on the Zambesi Sawmills Railway in Zambia.

Trains
1895-1939

Express Steam for the UK

This period of British railway history saw major advances in the design and construction of British express passenger steam locomotives. Innovations – often developed in other countries – such as compounding using high- and low-pressure cylinders, larger and higher pressure boilers, superheating, and longer wheel arrangements all contributed to more efficient locomotives. These graceful machines were able to haul longer and heavier trains at greater speeds on Britain's busy main lines.

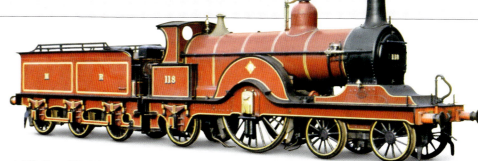

△ MR Class 115, 1896

Wheel arrangement	4-2-2
Cylinders	2 (inside)
Boiler pressure	170 psi (11.95 kg/sq cm)
Driving wheel diameter	93 in (2,370 mm)
Top speed	approx. 90 mph (145 km/h)

These express locomotives, designed by Samuel W. Johnson, were built at the Midland Railway's Derby Works till 1899. Class 115s were nicknamed "Spinners" for the spinning motion of their pair of huge driving wheels.

△ GNR Class C2 Small Atlantic, 1898

Wheel arrangement	4-4-2
Cylinders	2
Boiler pressure	170 psi (11.95 kg/sq cm)
Driving wheel diameter	93 in (2,370 mm)
Top speed	approx. 90 mph (145 km/h)

Named *Henry Oakley*, No. 990 was the first of 22 C1 Class express locomotives designed by Henry Ivatt and built at the Great Northern Railway's Doncaster Works. Nicknamed "Klondyke", it was passed to the London & North Eastern Railway, which went on to classify this small boiler version as C2.

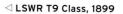

◁ LSWR T9 Class, 1899

Wheel arrangement	4-4-0
Cylinders	2 (inside)
Boiler pressure	175 psi (12.30 kg/sq cm)
Driving wheel diameter	79 in (2,000 mm)
Top speed	approx. 85 mph (137 km/h)

Nicknamed "Greyhounds", 66 T9 Class passenger locomotives were built between 1899 and 1901. The class was designed by Dugald Drummond for the London & South Western Railway.

◁ **MR Compound 1000 Class, 1902**

Wheel arrangement	4-4-0
Cylinders	3 (2 outside low-pressure; 1 inside high-pressure)
Boiler pressure	220 psi (15.46 kg/sq cm)
Driving wheel diameter	84 in (2,134 mm)
Top speed	approx. 85 mph (137 km/h)

Designed by Samuel W. Johnson, these express compound locomotives were built at the Midland Railway's Derby Works from 1902. Some 45 were constructed.

▷ **LNER Class C1 Large Atlantic, 1902**

Wheel arrangement	4-4-2
Cylinders	2
Boiler pressure	170 psi (11.95 kg/sq cm)
Driving wheel diameter	80 in (2,030 mm)
Top speed	approx. 90 mph (145 km/h)

Developed from the Great Northern Railway's Class C2 Small Atlantic, 94 of these large boiler express locomotives were built at Doncaster Works between 1902 and 1910. Under London & North Eastern Railway's ownership, it retained its C1 classification to distinguish it from its small boiler relatives.

▽ **GWR, 3700 Class or City Class, 1902**

Wheel arrangement	4-4-0
Cylinders	2 (inside)
Boiler pressure	200 psi (14.06 kg/sq cm)
Driving wheel diameter	80 in (2,030 mm)
Top speed	approx. 100 mph (161 km/h)

Designed by George Churchward, 20 of these express locomotives were built at the Great Western Railway's Swindon Works between 1902 and 1909. In 1904, No. 3440 *City of Truro* was claimed to be the first steam locomotive to reach 100 mph (161 km/h).

◁ **GWR 4000 Class or Star Class, 1907**

Wheel arrangement	4-6-0
Cylinders	4 (2 outside, 2 inside)
Boiler pressure	225 psi (15.82 kg/sq cm)
Driving wheel diameter	80 in (2,030 mm)
Top speed	approx. 90 mph (145 km/h)

Another of George Churchward's designs, 73 Star Class express passenger locomotives were built at the Great Western Railway's Swindon Works between 1907 and 1923. The prototype, No. 4, was given the name *North Star*, then renumbered 4000. This is No. 4005 *Polar Star*, which remained in service until 1934.

British Evolution

By the end of the 19th century Britain's railway network had expanded to serve nearly every part of the country. Coal mines, quarries, ironworks, factories, ports, and harbours were all connected to the railway system, and the rapid growth of freight traffic led to the development of more powerful steam locomotives capable of handling heavier and longer trains. These freight workhorses were so successful that many remained in service for more than 50 years. At the same time, passenger traffic connecting cities with their suburbs also saw a rapid expansion, with new types of tank locomotives capable of fast acceleration hauling commuter trains to tight schedules.

△ **Met E Class No. 1, 1898**

Wheel arrangement	0-4-4T
Cylinders	2 (inside)
Boiler pressure	150 psi (10.53 kg/sq cm)
Driving wheel diameter	65³/₄ in (1,670 mm)
Top speed	approx. 60 mph (96 km/h)

No. 1 was the last locomotive built at the Metropolitan Railway's Neasden Works and spent its early years hauling commuter trains between Baker Street and Aylesbury. As London Transport No. L44, it remained in service until 1965 and is now preserved.

△ **CR 812 Class, 1899**

Wheel arrangement	0-6-0
Cylinders	2 (inside)
Boiler pressure	160 psi (11.25 kg/sq cm)
Driving wheel diameter	59³/₄ in (1,520 mm)
Top speed	approx. 55 mph (88 km/h)

John F. McIntosh designed this tender locomotive for the Caledonian Railway. A total of 79 of the 812 Class were built between 1899 and 1909. Most remained in service for more than 50 years.

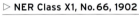

▷ **NER Class X1, No. 66, 1902**

Wheel arrangement	2-2-4T
Cylinders	2 (compound, inside)
Boiler pressure	175 psi (12.30 kg/sq cm)
Driving wheel diameter	67³/₄ in (1,720 mm)
Top speed	approx. 55 mph (88 km/h)

Built for the North Eastern Railway in 1869 to haul its Mechanical Engineer's saloon, No. 66 *Aerolite* was rebuilt as a 4-2-2T in 1886 and as a 2-2-4T in 1902.

Shifting Freight

The railway companies built thousands of four-wheel covered and open freight wagons to carry raw materials, finished goods, and food perishables around Britain. Individual companies also owned large fleets of private-owner wagons and displayed their names on the sides. At docks and harbours, small tank locomotives with short wheelbases carried out shunting operations on the tightly curved railways.

◁ **Alexandra Docks (Newport and South Wales) & Railway Co. No. 1340, 1897**

Wheel arrangement	0-4-0ST
Cylinders	2
Boiler pressure	160 psi (11.25 kg/sq cm)
Driving wheel diameter	35³/₄ in (910 mm)
Top speed	approx. 30 mph (48 km/h)

Built by the Avonside Engine Company of Bristol, this engine spent much of its life shunting around Newport Docks before being sold to a Staffordshire colliery in 1932. Now named *Trojan*, it is preserved at Didcot Railway Centre.

▷ GWR 2800 Class, 1903/1905

Wheel arrangement 2-8-0

Cylinders 2

Boiler pressure 225 psi (15.82 kg/sq cm)

Driving wheel diameter 55½in (1,410 mm)

Top speed approx. 50 mph (80 km/h)

Eighty-four of these heavy freight locomotives, designed by George Churchward, were built at the Great Western Railway's Swindon Works between 1903 and 1919. Most were in service until the early 1960s.

◁ GWR Steam Railmotor, 1903

Wheel arrangement 0-4-0 + 4-wheel unpowered bogie

Cylinders 2

Boiler pressure 160 psi (11.25 kg/sq cm)

Driving wheel diameter 48 in (1,220 mm)

Top speed approx. 30 mph (48 km/h)

Built by the Great Western Railway, these self-propelled carriages were fitted with a steam-powered bogie and a vertical boiler at one end, and a driver's compartment at both ends. The railmotors operated suburban passenger services in London, and on country branch lines in England and Wales. A re-creation was completed by the Great Western Society in 2011 using an original body and a new power bogie.

△ LTSR Class 79, 1909

Wheel arrangement 4-4-2T

Cylinders 2

Boiler pressure 170 psi (11.95 kg/sq cm)

Driving wheel diameter 78 in (1,980 mm)

Top speed approx. 65 mph (105 km/h)

Four of these suburban tank engines, designed by Thomas Whitelegg, were built for the London, Tilbury & Southend Railway's commuter services from Fenchurch Street station in 1909. Retired in 1956, *Thundersley* is now part of the UK's national collection.

◁ GWR Iron Mink Covered Wagon, 1900

Type 4-wheel

Weight 10 tons (10.16 tonnes)

Construction iron

Railway Great Western Railway

More than 4,000 of these covered wagons were built by the Great Western Railway from 1886 to 1902. Ventilated and refrigerated versions carried meat, fish, and fruit. Bogie versions weighing 30 tons (30.5 tonnes) were built between 1902 and 1911.

△ The Royal Daylight Tank Wagon, 1912

Type 4-wheel

Weight 14 tons (14.2 tonnes)

Construction iron

Railway private owner

Built for the Anglo-American Oil Co. by Hurst Nelson of Motherwell, UK, this private-owner tank wagon carried imported American lamp oil branded as Royal Daylight. It is now displayed at Didcot Railway Centre.

Continental Glamour

Railways had conquered most parts of Europe, and trains were now carrying vast quantities of raw materials and finished goods as well as large numbers of passengers. Travelling times between European cities had been cut significantly thanks to improvements in track and signalling, and also to modern coaches and powerful locomotives capable of sustaining higher speeds for greater lengths of time. New technology led the way as superheated and compound engines rolled off the production lines in ever greater numbers, while the US-influenced 4-6-2 "Pacific" type also started to make an appearance.

◁ Nord Compound, 1907

Wheel arrangement	4-6-0
Cylinders	4 (compound)
Boiler pressure	232 psi (16.3 kg/sq cm)
Driving wheel diameter	69 in (1,750 mm)
Top speed	approx. 70 mph (113 km/h)

French engineer Alfred de Glehn designed these compound express locomotives. Built for railways in France and abroad, some remained in service until the 1960s.

△ Bavarian Class S3/6, 1908

Wheel arrangement	4-6-0
Cylinders	4 (compound)
Boiler pressure	213 psi (15 kg/sq cm)
Driving wheel diameter	73½ in (1,870 mm)
Top speed	approx. 75 mph (120 km/h)

Designed by the German company Maffei, a total of 159 of these express locomotives were built over a period of nearly 25 years – 89 for the Royal Bavarian State Railways and 70 (known as Class 18.4-5) for the Deutsche Reichsbahn – between 1908 and 1931. This example was modernized in the 1950s.

1895 Paris Crash

On the afternoon of 22 October 1895 an express train from Granville hauling three baggage cars, a post van, and six passenger carriages approached the Montparnasse terminus, Paris. The train was travelling too fast, the air brake failed, and it crashed through the buffer stop at 30 mph (48 km/h), then travelled across the station concourse, through the station wall, and down to the street. A woman pedestrian was killed, but amazingly there were no fatalities on the train.

The infamous accident Locomotive No. 721 lies upended on its nose after crashing through the 2-ft- (60-cm-) thick wall of the terminus and falling 33 ft (10 m) onto the street below.

▽ Prussian Class P8, 1908

Wheel arrangement	4-6-0
Cylinders	2
Boiler pressure	170 psi (11.95 kg/sq cm)
Driving wheel diameter	69 in (1,750 mm)
Top speed	approx. 68 mph (110 km/h)

One of the most successful European steam locomotive designs, around 3,700 of the Prussian state railways superheated Class P8s were built between 1908 and 1926. Designed by Robert Garbe, they were built in several different German factories.

△ SJ B Class, 1909

Wheel arrangement	4-6-0
Cylinders	2
Boiler pressure	171 psi (12 kg/sq cm)
Driving wheel diameter	69 in (1,750 mm)
Top speed	approx. 65 mph (105 km/h)

Swedish state railways (Statens Järnvägar, or SJ) built 96 of these powerful superheated locomotives between 1909 and 1920. Three more were made in 1944. The engines were used to haul express passenger and freight trains.

◁ PO Pacific, 1910

Wheel arrangement	4-6-2
Cylinders	2
Boiler pressure	approx. 200 psi (14.06 kg/sq cm)
Driving wheel diameter	67 in (1,702 mm)
Top speed	56 mph (90 km/h)

Built for the Paris à Orléans Railway, these express locomotives were the first "Pacific" type in mainland Europe. Fifty were built in the US by the American Locomotive Co. (ALCO).

△ FS Class 740, 1911

Wheel arrangement	2-8-0
Cylinders	2
Boiler pressure	171 psi (12 kg/sq cm)
Driving wheel diameter	55 in (1,400 mm)
Top speed	approx. 56 mph (90 km/h)

A total of 470 of these mixed-traffic engines were built for the Italian state railways (Ferrovie dello Stato, or FS) between 1911 and 1923, some remaining in service until the 1970s. No. 740.423 has been restored to operational condition in Sardinia, and is occasionally used on charter trains.

△ Prussian Class T18, 1912

Wheel arrangement	4-6-4T
Cylinders	2
Boiler pressure	170 psi (11.95 kg/sq cm)
Driving wheel diameter	65 in (1,650 mm)
Top speed	approx. 62 mph (100 km/h)

The last tank locomotive designed for the Prussian state railways, 534 Class T18s were built between 1912 and 1927. Some were still in service in the 1970s with Deutsche Bundesbahn in West Germany and Deutsche Reichsbahn in East Germany.

Rapid Development

With railways now well established, this period saw rapid developments in the design of both passenger and freight locomotives around the world. Mass production of heavy freight engines reached new heights with more than 1,000 of the Prussian state railways Class G8 along with another 5,000 of the later Class G8.1 being built over the following years. However, the world record for the most numerous class of locomotive goes to the Russian E Class, of which around 11,000 were built.

▷ **Austrian Gölsdorf Class 170, 1897**

Wheel arrangement	2-8-0
Cylinders	2 (compound)
Boiler pressure	185 psi (13 kg/sq cm)
Driving wheel diameter	51 in (1,298 mm)
Top speed	approx. 37 mph (60 km/h)

Designed by Karl Gölsdorf for the Imperial Royal Austrian State Railways, the Class 170 freight locomotives were the first to be fitted with radially sliding coupled axles, known as Gölsdorf axles.

△ **Prussian Class G8, 1902**

Wheel arrangement	0-8-0
Cylinders	2
Boiler pressure	170 psi (11.95 kg/sq cm)
Driving wheel diameter	53 in (1,350 mm)
Top speed	approx. 35 mph (56 km/h)

More than 1,000 of these superheated freight locomotives were built in Germany for the Prussian state railways. After WWI hundreds were given to Germany's enemies as reparations. Some saw service during the building of the Baghdad Railway in Turkey in 1916.

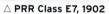

△ **PRR Class E7, 1902**

Wheel arrangement	4-4-2
Cylinders	2
Boiler pressure	205 psi (14.4 kg/sq cm)
Driving wheel diameter	78½ in (2,000 mm)
Top speed	approx. 80 mph (129 km/h)

The original Class E7 No. 7002 was built at the Pennsylvania Railroad's Altoona Works, Pennsylvania, US. It was once claimed to be the world's fastest steam engine, supposedly reaching 127 mph (204 km/h), but this is disputed. First numbered 8063, this locomotive was renumbered after the first 7002 was scrapped and is now in the Pennsylvania Railroad Museum.

◁ **Indian Class EM, 1907**

Wheel arrangement	4-4-2
Cylinders	2
Boiler pressure	190 psi (13.4 kg/sq cm)
Driving wheel diameter	78 in (1,980 mm)
Top speed	approx. 60 mph (96 km/h)

Originally built as a 4-4-0 by the North British Locomotive Co. for the Great Indian Peninsula Railway, the Class EM remained in service until the late 1970s. EM No. 922 was rebuilt in 1941 by the Mughalpura workshops.

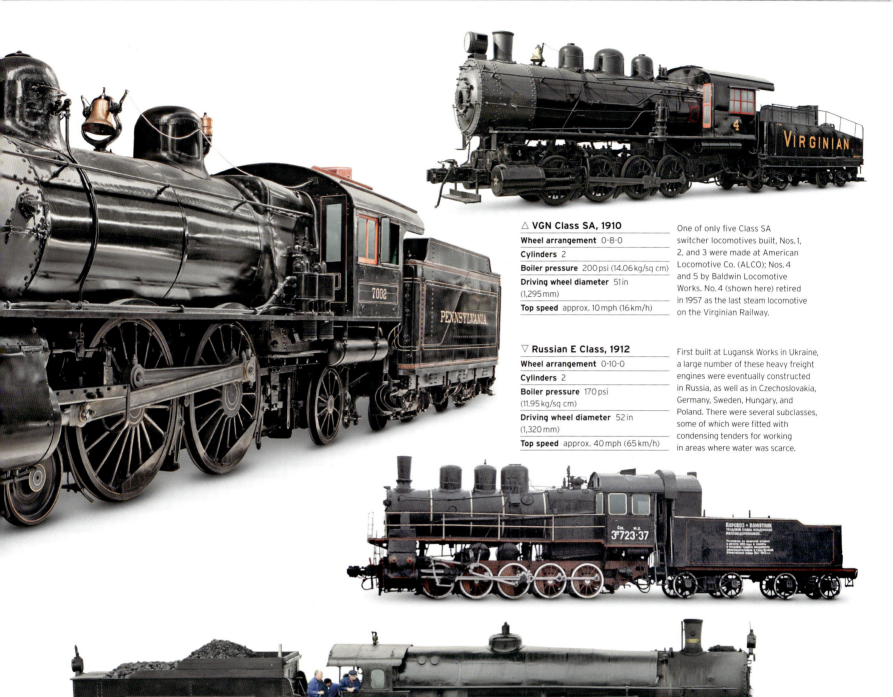

△ VGN Class SA, 1910

Wheel arrangement	0-8-0
Cylinders	2
Boiler pressure	200 psi (14.06 kg/sq cm)
Driving wheel diameter	51 in (1,295 mm)
Top speed	approx. 10 mph (16 km/h)

One of only five Class SA switcher locomotives built, Nos. 1, 2, and 3 were made at American Locomotive Co. (ALCO); Nos. 4 and 5 by Baldwin Locomotive Works. No. 4 (shown here) retired in 1957 as the last steam locomotive on the Virginian Railway.

▽ Russian E Class, 1912

Wheel arrangement	0-10-0
Cylinders	2
Boiler pressure	170 psi (11.95 kg/sq cm)
Driving wheel diameter	52 in (1,320 mm)
Top speed	approx. 40 mph (65 km/h)

First built at Lugansk Works in Ukraine, a large number of these heavy freight engines were eventually constructed in Russia, as well as in Czechoslovakia, Germany, Sweden, Hungary, and Poland. There were several subclasses, some of which were fitted with condensing tenders for working in areas where water was scarce.

△ Austrian Gölsdorf Class 310, 1911

Wheel arrangement	2-6-4
Cylinders	4 (compound)
Boiler pressure	220 psi (15.5 kg/sq cm)
Driving wheel diameter	84 1/4 in (2,140 mm)
Top speed	approx. 62 mph (100 km/h)

Designed by Karl Gölsdorf, 90 of the Class 310 four-cylinder compound express locomotives were built for the Imperial Royal Austrian State Railways from 1911 to 1916. This was one of the most elegant locomotives of the period.

TECHNOLOGY

Geared Locomotives

US-built, lighter-weight geared steam locomotives such as the Shay, Heisler, and Climax types had wheels driven by reduction gearing. These locomotives were designed for the quick and cheap-to-lay industrial railways used by logging, sugar-cane, mining, and quarrying industry operations where speed was not needed and gradients were often steep.

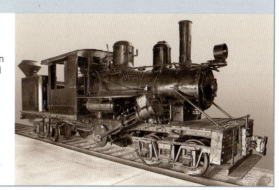

Climax Moore-Keppel No. 4 Built in 1913, this logging locomotive was designed to be powerful, agile, and cheap and its light weight made it a popular export model. It is now on display at the Railroad Museum of Pennsylvania.

On Other Gauges

George Stephenson introduced the 4-ft 8½-in- (1.435-m-) gauge for British railways in 1830 and before long it became the standard gauge for many railways around the world. However, there were, and still are, many exceptions. In India a broader gauge of 5 ft 6 in (1.67 m) was used for many mainline railways, but more lightly laid lines had narrower gauges of 3 ft 3 in (1 m) or, for mountain railways, only 2 ft (0.61 m). While the standard gauge was usually the norm in mainland Europe and the US, there was also widespread use of narrow gauges in mountainous regions. The most extensive narrow-gauge network in the US was the Denver & Rio Grande Railroad's 3-ft- (0.91-m-) gauge system in Arizona, Utah, and New Mexico.

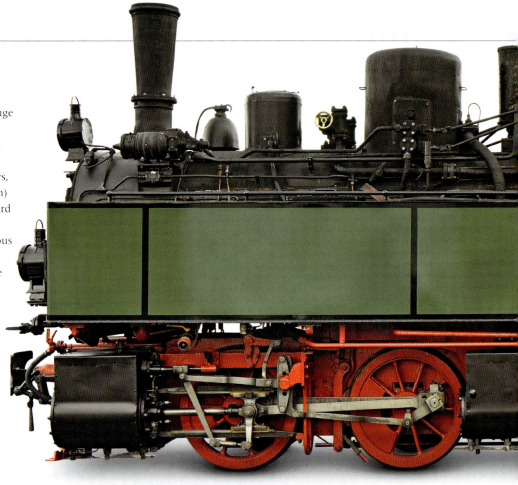

▷ NWE Mallet, 1897

Wheel arrangement	0-4-4-0
Cylinders	4
Boiler pressure	200 psi (14 kg/sq cm)
Driving wheel diameter	39½ in (1,000 mm)
Top speed	approx. 18 mph (30 km/h)

This engine was one of 12 powerful articulated steam locomotives built for the 3-ft 3-in- (1-m-) gauge Nordhausen-Wernigerode Railway in Germany. Several were lost in WWI but three are now with the NWE's successor the Harzer Schmalspurbahnen on the Harz Mountains in central Germany.

△ NWR ST, 1904

Wheel arrangement	0-6-2T
Cylinders	2 (inside)
Boiler pressure	150 psi (10.53 kg/sq cm)
Driving wheel diameter	51 in (1,295 mm)
Top speed	approx. 30 mph (48 km/h)

One of the first locomotives built at India's North Western Railway's Mughalpura Workshops, ST No. 707 was made from parts supplied by North British Locomotive Co. of Glasgow. Weighing 55 tons (55 tonnes), this 5-ft 6-in- (1.67-m-) gauge locomotive was employed for shunting duties. It is now on display at the National Rail Museum, New Delhi.

△ KS Wren Class, 1905

Wheel arrangement	0-4-0
Cylinders	2
Boiler pressure	140 psi (9.84 kg/sq cm)
Driving wheel diameter	20 in (500 mm)
Top speed	approx. 15 mph (24 km/h)

A total of 163 of these narrow-gauge locomotives were built by the British company Kerr Stuart for use on industrial railways around the world between 1905 and 1930. However, *Jennie* was made in 2008 for the 2-ft- (0.60-m-) gauge Amerton Railway, Staffordshire, by the Hunslet Engine Co.

▷ Indian SPS, 1903

Wheel arrangement	4-4-0
Cylinders	2 (inside)
Boiler pressure	160 psi (11.25 kg/sq cm)
Driving wheel diameter	78 in (1,980 mm)
Top speed	approx. 50 mph (80 km/h)

A range of standard designs was introduced for India, including the Standard Passenger (SP); when superheating was added it became the SPS. British designed, some of these engines had extremely long working lives. After partition in 1947, this one ran on the new Pakistan Railways until the 1980s.

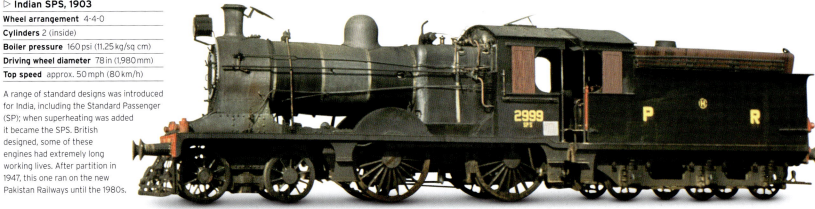

△ Mh 399, 1906

Wheel arrangement	0-8+4
Cylinders	2
Boiler pressure	180 psi (12.65 kg/sq cm)
Driving wheel diameter	36 in (910 mm)
Top speed	approx. 25 mph (40 km/h)

Built by Krauss of Linz, this locomotive was made for the Austrian Railways' 2-ft 6-in- (0.76-m-) narrow-gauge Mariazell Railway. It had rear wheels that are also driven by coupling rods. Seen here is No. 399.06 preserved on the Mariazellerbahn, Austria.

△ TGR K Class Garratt, 1909

Wheel arrangement	0-4-0+0-4-0
Cylinders	4
Boiler pressure	195 psi (13.70 kg/sq cm)
Driving wheel diameter	31½ in (800 mm)
Top speed	approx. 25 mph (40 km/h)

The world's first Garratt-type articulated steam locomotive, No. K1 was built by Beyer Peacock & Co. of Manchester, England, for the Tasmanian Government Railway, Australia. It ran on the 2-ft- (0.60-m-) gauge North East Dundas Tramway. This historic locomotive was returned to Britain in 1947 and now hauls trains on the Welsh Highland Railway.

△ EIR No. 1354 *Phoenix*, 1907

Wheel arrangement	0-4-0WT
Cylinders	2 (inside)
Boiler pressure	120 psi (8.44 kg/sq cm)
Driving wheel diameter	36 in (910 mm)
Top speed	approx. 20 mph (32 km/h)

One of five railmotors built in England by Nasmyth Wilson & Company, *Phoenix* was made for the 5-ft 6-in- (1.67-m-) East Indian Railway in 1907. Later, in 1925, the coaches were removed and *Phoenix* was rebuilt in India as a small shunting engine. It is now on display at the National Rail Museum, New Delhi.

▷ Lima Class C Shay, 1906

Wheel arrangement	B-B-B
Cylinders	3
Boiler pressure	200 psi (14.06 kg/sq cm)
Driving wheel diameter	36 in (910 mm)
Top speed	approx. 15 mph (24 km/h)

Designed by US inventor Ephraim Shay, the Class C geared three-truck steam locomotive was first introduced in 1885. This Shay No. 1 was built by the Lima Locomotive & Machine Co. for a standard-gauge logging railroad in Pennsylvania in 1906. It can be seen at the Railroad Museum of Pennsylvania, Strasburg.

Competition From the New Electrics

While steam traction was enjoying its heyday in the late 19th and early 20th centuries other forms of faster and cleaner rail transport were being developed. Electric trams, or streetcars, first started appearing in Europe and the US during the 1880s, and the technology began to appear on railways by the early 20th century. Using a mixture of either third-rail or overhead catenary power supplies, electric traction had been introduced on many city commuter lines in the UK and the US by the outbreak of World War I. With their fast acceleration these trains were ideal for lines with high-density traffic; they also eliminated the problem of pollution in built-up areas and in tunnels. In the US the electrification of the 2³/₄-mile (4.23-km) Cascade Tunnel in Washington State in 1909 was an early example of clean electric locomotives replacing the asphyxiating fumes of steam engines in confined spaces.

△ Budapest Metro car, 1896

Wheel arrangement 2 x 4-wheel powered bogies with 28 PS motors

Power supply 300 V DC, overhead supply

Power rating 28 hp (20.59 kW) per engine

Top speed approx. 30 mph (48 km/h)

Fitted with two Siemens & Halske traction motors, 20 of these double-ended, electric subway cars were built for Continental Europe's first electric underground railway, which opened in Budapest, Hungary in 1896. Plans for extending the metro with two extra routes were made in 1895, but the lines only opened more than 70 years later in 1970 and 1976. Following retirement in the early 1970s, car No.18 was preserved and is on display at the Seashore Trolley Museum in Kennebunkport, US.

◁ NER petrol-electric autocar, 1903

Wheel arrangement 2 x 4-wheel bogies (1 powered)

Transmission 2 traction motors

Engine petrol

Total power output 80 hp (59.6 kW)

Top speed approx. 36 mph (58 km/h)

Two of these petrol-electric railcars were built in 1903 in the UK at the North Eastern Railway's York Works. The original Wolseley four-cylinder engine that drove generators to power the two electric traction motors was replaced by a six-cylinder 225 hp (168 kW) engine in 1923. The railcars had been withdrawn by 1931. One is being restored at the Embsay & Bolton Abbey Steam Railway in Yorkshire.

▷ Drehstrom-Triebwagen, 1903

Wheel arrangement 2 x 6-wheel bogies, outer axles motorized

Power supply 6-14 kV (25-50 Hz) AC

Power rating 1,475 hp (1,100 kW)

Top speed 130 mph (210 km/h)

Built by Siemens & Halske and AEG of Germany and fitted with three-phase induction motors, two prototype high-speed Drehstrom-Triebwagen railcars were tested on the Prussian military railway south of Berlin in 1903. Taking overhead power from a triple catenary, the AEG-built railcar reached 130 mph (210 km/h) between Zossen and Marienfelde on 28 October 1903, a world rail-speed record not broken until 1931.

▷ NER electric locomotive, 1905

Wheel arrangement Bo-Bo

Power supply 600-630 V DC, third-rail or catenary

Power rating 640 hp (477 kW)

Top speed approx. 27 mph (43 km/h)

Drawing power from either a third-rail or an overhead catenary, two of these locomotives were built by British Thomson-Houston for the North Eastern Railway in 1903-04 but was not operational until 1905 when the line was electrified. They worked on a steeply graded freight line to a quayside in Newcastle-upon-Tyne until 1964. One is preserved at the Locomotion Museum in Shildon, County Durham.

NORTH

Ticketing on the Railways

Early railway companies issued tickets to passengers on handwritten pieces of paper. This was time-consuming and open to fraud by unscrupulous ticket clerks. Invented by Thomas Edmondson, an English station master, the Edmondson railway ticket system was introduced in 1842. Using preprinted, durable cards was not only a faster means of issuing tickets but they were also given unique serial numbers that had to be accounted for by booking clerks each day. Ticket inspectors at stations and on trains punched holes in the tickets to prevent reuse.

Ticket punch Featuring a decorative, three-pointed spike, this silver ticket punch was made by the Bonney-Vehslage Tool Co. for the Baltimore & Ohio Railroad in 1906.

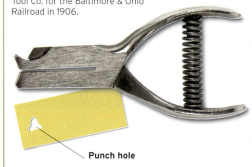

Punch hole

△ B&O Bo Switcher, 1895

Wheel arrangement	Bo (0-4-0)
Power supply	approx. 450 V, catenary
Power rating	approx. 15 hp (11.2 kW)
Top speed	approx. 10 mph (16 km/h)

Opened in 1860, the Baltimore & Ohio Railroad's network of railways serving waterfront warehouses at Fells Point in Baltimore was originally horsedrawn. Overhead streetcar power lines were introduced in 1896 with small electric switchers, like this No.10 built by General Electric in 1909, taking over from horsepower.

▷ Schynige Platte Class He2/2, 1910

Wheel arrangement	0-4-0
Power supply	1,500 V DC, overhead catenary
Power rating	295 hp (220 kW)
Top speed	approx. 5 mph (8 km/h)

The 2-ft 7½-in- (0.8-m-) gauge Schynige Platte Railway in the Swiss Bernese Oberland opened using steam power in 1893. This steeply graded mountain rack railway was electrified in 1914. Four of the original electric engines built by the Swiss Locomotive & Machine Works and Brown Boveri still operate on the railway.

EASTERN

Locomotives for World War I

Following the outbreak of World War I, the Railway Operating Division (ROD) of the British Royal Engineers was formed in 1915 to operate railways in the European and Middle East theatres of war. The British network of narrow-gauge trench railways was operated by the War Department Light Railways, while the French had already standardized portable, 1-ft 11¾-in (0.60-m) gauge, military Decauville equipment to supply ammunition and stores to the Western Front. The Germans used a similar system for their trench railways – the Heeresfeldbahn. The entry of the US into the war in 1917 saw many US-built locomotives shipped across the Atlantic for service in France.

△ GWR Dean Goods, 1883
Wheel arrangement	0-6-0
Cylinders	2 (inside)
Boiler pressure	180 psi (12.65 kg/sq cm)
Driving wheel diameter	61¾in (1,570 mm)
Top speed	approx. 45 mph (72 km/h)

Designed by William Dean, 260 of these standard-gauge freight locomotives were built at the Great Western Railway's Swindon Works between 1883 and 1899. In 1917 the Railway Operating Division commandeered 62 of them to operate supply trains in northern France. Some also served in France during WWII.

△ Baldwin Switcher, 1917
Wheel arrangement	0-6-0T
Cylinders	2
Boiler pressure	190 psi (13.4 kg/sq cm)
Driving wheel diameter	48 in (1,220 mm)
Top speed	approx. 30 mph (48 km/h)

Built in the US by the Baldwin Locomotive Works, the 651–700 Series of Railway Operating Division shunting (or switching) locomotives was introduced in 1917 for use by the British Military Railways in France. After the war they became Class 58 of the Belgian National Railways.

▽ Henschel metre-gauge, 1914
Wheel arrangement	0-6-0T
Cylinders	2
Boiler pressure	200 psi (14 kg/sq cm)
Driving wheel diameter	31½in (800 mm)
Top speed	approx. 18 mph (29 km/h)

Built by the German company Henschel in 1914, two of these 3-ft 3-in- (1-m-) gauge locomotives were originally supplied to the Army Technical Research Institute. They were later transferred to the Nordhausen-Wernigerode Railway in the Harz Mountains in central Germany, where they hauled trains carrying standard-gauge freight wagons.

▷ O&K Feldbahn, 1903
Wheel arrangement	0-8-0T
Cylinders	2
Boiler pressure	approx. 180 psi (12.65 kg/sq cm)
Driving wheel diameter	approx. 22¾in (580 mm)
Top speed	approx. 15 mph (24 km/h)

Introduced in 1903, around 2,500 of these 1-ft 11¾-in- (0.60-m-) gauge "Brigadelok" locomotives were built by several German companies, and widely used on the military light railways constructed to supply forward positions of the German army. The locomotive shown here is No. 7999, an Orenstein & Koppel engine built in 1915 with Klein–Linder articulation of the front and rear axles.

△ GCR Class 8K, 1911
Wheel arrangement	2-8-0
Cylinders	2
Boiler pressure	180 psi (12.65 kg/sq cm)
Driving wheel diameter	56 in (1,420 mm)
Top speed	approx. 45 mph (72 km/h)

The Great Central Railway's Class 8K freight locomotive introduced in 1911 was chosen as the standard British Railway Operating Division 2-8-0 locomotive during WWI. A total of 521 were built, with many seeing service hauling troop and freight trains in France. During WWII many of these locomotives were sent on active service to the Middle East.

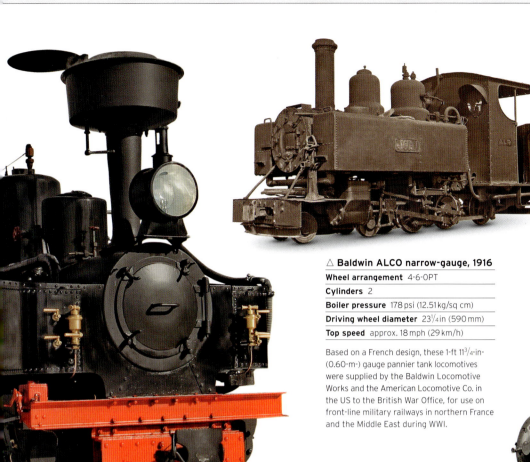

△ **Baldwin ALCO narrow-gauge, 1916**

Wheel arrangement 4-6-0PT

Cylinders 2

Boiler pressure 178 psi (12.51 kg/sq cm)

Driving wheel diameter 23$\frac{1}{4}$in (590 mm)

Top speed approx. 18 mph (29 km/h)

Based on a French design, these 1-ft 11$\frac{3}{4}$-in-(0.60-m-) gauge pannier tank locomotives were supplied by the Baldwin Locomotive Works and the American Locomotive Co. in the US to the British War Office, for use on front-line military railways in northern France and the Middle East during WWI.

TECHNOLOGY

Armoured Engines

The British pioneered the use of small, armoured, narrow-gauge petrol locomotives to operate on the temporary railways that served the front line during World War I. Unlike steam locomotives, which could easily be spotted by the enemy, these locomotives could haul ammunition trains to forward positions during daylight hours without being detected.

Simplex locomotive Built for the British War Office by Motor Rail Ltd in 1917, this 1-ft 11$\frac{3}{4}$-in (0.60-m), four-wheel, engine hauled 15-ton (15.2-tonne) ammunition trains at 5 mph (8 km/h) to the trenches in northern France.

△ **Pershing Nord, 1917**

Wheel arrangement 2-8-0

Cylinders 2

Boiler pressure 189 psi (13.28 kg/sq cm)

Driving wheel diameter 56 in (1,420 mm)

Top speed 56 mph (90 km/h)

The North British Locomotive Co. in Glasgow supplied 113 Consolidation Pershings for the Compagnie des Chemins de fer du Nord in France. While the railway was happy to run these large locomotives at up to 56 mph (90 km/h), other French railways preferred lower operating speeds.

△ **Baldwin "Spider", 1917**

Wheel arrangement 4-6-0

Cylinders 2

Boiler pressure 190 psi (13.4 kg/sq cm)

Driving wheel diameter 61$\frac{3}{4}$in (1,570 mm)

Top speed approx. 65 mph (105 km/h)

Nicknamed "Spiders" by British soldiers, 70 of these mixed-traffic locomotives were built with bar frames by the US Baldwin Locomotive Works between 1917 and 1918 for service on the Western Front during WWI. Later they became Class 40 of the Belgian National Railways.

Fast and Powerful

The introduction of longer and heavier express passenger trains in Europe and the US during the 1920s and 1930s led to the building of more powerful and faster types of locomotives to standard designs. In Britain, Sir Nigel Gresley led the way with his three-cylinder A1 and A3 Pacific 4-6-2s of which *Flying Scotsman* is justifiably world famous. Other British locomotive engineers such as the Great Western Railway's Charles Collett and the London, Midland & Scottish Railway's Henry Fowler favoured a 4-6-0 wheel arrangement. In the US, Germany, and France, the Pacific type became the favoured express passenger locomotive type.

△ **PRR Class K4s, 1914**

Wheel arrangement	4-6-2
Cylinders	2
Boiler pressure	205 psi (14.4 kg/sq cm)
Driving wheel diameter	80 in (2,030 mm)
Top speed	approx. 70 mph (113 km/h)

The Class K4s Pacific locomotives, of which 425 were built in the US between 1914 and 1928, were the Pennsylvania Railroad's premier express steam locomotive. They were often used in double or triple headers to haul heavy trains.

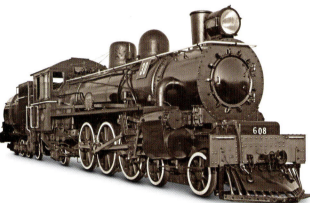

◁ **NZR Class Ab, 1915**

Wheel arrangement	4-6-2
Cylinders	2
Boiler pressure	180 psi (12.65 kg/sq cm)
Driving wheel diameter	54 in (1,372 mm)
Top speed	approx. 60 mph (96 km/h)

One of a class of 141 locomotives, New Zealand Railways Class Ab Pacific locomotive No. 608 is named *Passchendaele* in memory of NZR staff killed in WWI. Ab engines were replaced by diesels in the 1960s but five have been preserved.

◁ **SOU Class Ps-4, 1923**

Wheel arrangement	4-6-2
Cylinders	2
Boiler pressure	200 psi (14.06 kg/sq cm)
Driving wheel diameter	73 in (1,854 mm)
Top speed	approx. 80 mph (129 km/h)

Finished in a striking green livery, the 64 Class Ps-4 Pacific-type express passenger locomotives were built for the Southern Railway of the US by the American Locomotive Company (ALCO) and the Baldwin Locomotive Works between 1923 and 1928. Designed to haul the railroad's heavy expresses, they had been replaced by diesels by the early 1950s. No. 1401 is on display in the Smithsonian Institution in Washington, DC.

△ **PRR Class G5s, 1924**

Wheel arrangement	4-6-0
Cylinders	2
Boiler pressure	205 psi (14.4 kg/sq cm)
Driving wheel diameter	68 in (1,730 mm)
Top speed	approx. 70 mph (113 km/h)

This engine was designed by William Kiesel to work commuter trains on the Pennsylvania Railroad. The Class G5s was one of the largest and most powerful 4-6-0s in the world. No. 5741 is on display in the Railroad Museum of Pennsylvania.

▷ **LMS Royal Scot Class, 1927**

Wheel arrangement	4-6-0
Cylinders	3
Boiler pressure	250 psi (17.57 kg/sq cm)
Driving wheel diameter	81 in (2,057 mm)
Top speed	approx. 80 mph (129 km/h)

Designed by Sir Henry Fowler, 70 Royal Scot Class locomotives were built to haul long-distance express trains on the London, Midland & Scottish Railway. They were later rebuilt by William Stanier with Type 2A tapered boilers, and remained in service until the early 1960s.

BUILDING THE 'ROYAL SCOT' ENGINE

◁ DR Class 01, 1926

Wheel arrangement 4-6-2

Cylinders 2

Boiler pressure 232 psi (16.3 kg/sq cm)

Driving wheel diameter 78 3/4in (2,000 mm)

Top speed approx. 81 mph (130 km/h)

A total of 241 (including 10 rebuilt Class 02s) of these standardized Class 01 express locomotives were built for the Deutsche Reichsbahn between 1926 and 1938. Some engines remained in service in East Germany until the early 1980s.

△ LNER Class A3, 1928

Wheel arrangement 4-6-2

Cylinders 3

Boiler pressure 220 psi (15.46 kg/sq cm)

Driving wheel diameter 80 in (2,030 mm)

Top speed 108 mph (174 km/h)

Britain's Sir Nigel Gresley designed the A3 for the London & North Eastern Railway. These locomotives hauled express trains between London's King's Cross and Scotland. No. 4472 *Flying Scotsman* is the only example preserved.

△ GWR Castle Class, 1936

Wheel arrangement 4-6-0

Cylinders 4

Boiler pressure 225 psi (15.82 kg/sq cm)

Driving wheel diameter 80 1/2 in (2,045 mm)

Top speed approx. 100 mph (161 km/h)

These express locomotives were designed by Charles Collett for the Great Western Railway. Its Swindon Works built 171 Castle Class engines between 1923 and 1950. Shown here is No. 5051. They had all been retired by 1965, but eight have now been preserved. No. 5051 *Drysllyn Castle* is at Didcot Railway Centre.

△ GWR King Class, 1930

Wheel arrangement 4-6-0

Cylinders 4

Boiler pressure 250 psi (17.57 kg/sq cm)

Driving wheel diameter 78 in (1,980 mm)

Top speed approx. 90 mph (145 km/h)

The King Class was designed by Charles Collett for the Great Western Railway. Thirty of these express locomotives were built at Swindon Works in England between 1927 and 1936. They were replaced by diesels in the early 1960s; three including this one, No. 6023 *King Edward II*, have been preserved.

▷ Nord Pacific, 1936

Wheel arrangement 4-6-2

Cylinders 4 (compound)

Boiler pressure 240 psi (16.87 kg/sq cm)

Driving wheel diameter 75 1/2 in (1,918 mm)

Top speed approx. 81 mph (130 km/h)

French engineer André Chapelon designed these powerful locomotives for the Compagnie du Nord. They hauled express trains such as the *Flèche d'Or* in northern France. Shown here is No. 3.1192, which is exhibited at the Cité du Train, Mulhouse, France.

Mixed-traffic Movers

By the 1930s the standardization of machine parts by European and US locomotive builders had reduced construction and maintenance costs significantly. Powerful engines designed to haul express freight and passenger trains were soon coming off the production lines in great numbers. In Britain both Charles Collett of the Great Western Railway (GWR) and William Stanier of the London, Midland & Scottish Railway (LMS) made standardization a common theme when designing their new 4-6-0 locomotives, while in Germany the Class 41 2-8-2s built for the Deutsche Reichsbahn incorporated parts simultaneously developed for three other classes.

△ **LMS Class 5MT, 1934**

Wheel arrangement 4-6-0
Cylinders 2
Boiler pressure 225 psi (15.82 kg/sq cm)
Driving wheel diameter 72 in (1,830 mm)
Top speed approx. 80 mph (129 km/h)

Designed by William Stanier for the London, Midland & Scottish Railway, many of these powerful mixed-traffic locomotives, "Black Fives", saw service in Britain until the end of steam in 1968. A total of 842 were built.

◁ **SR S15 Class, 1927**

Wheel arrangement 4-6-0
Cylinders 2
Boiler pressure 175-200 psi (12.30-14 kg/sq cm)
Driving wheel diameter 67 in (1,700 mm)
Top speed approx. 65 mph (105 km/h)

These powerful British locomotives were a modified version of an earlier Robert Urie design, introduced by Richard Maunsell. They were built by the Southern Railway at its Eastleigh Works in Southern England.

◁ **NZR Class K, 1932**

Wheel arrangement 4-8-4
Cylinders 2
Boiler pressure 200 psi (14.06 kg/sq cm)
Driving wheel diameter 54 in (1,372 mm)
Top speed approx. 65 mph (105 km/h)

Built to haul heavy freight and passenger trains on New Zealand's mountainous North Island, 30 of the Class Ks were built at Hutt Workshops for New Zealand Railways between 1932 and 1936. They were gradually withdrawn from service between 1964 and 1967.

GREAT WESTERN   5900

△ LNER Class V2, 1936

Wheel arrangement 2-6-2

Cylinders 3

Boiler pressure 220 psi (15.46 kg/sq cm)

Driving wheel diameter 74 in (1,880 mm)

Top speed approx. 100 mph (161 km/h)

These engines were designed by Sir Nigel Gresley for the London & North Eastern Railway and hauled both express passenger and express freight trains. No. 4771 *Green Arrow* is the only preserved example.

TALKING POINT

Fresh Milk

Transporting perishable goods such as milk, fish, and meat by rail called for specialized freight wagons. In Britain, milk was first conveyed in milk churns loaded into ventilated wagons at country stations, but from the 1930s it was carried in six-wheeled milk tank wagons loaded at a creamery. The wagons were marshalled into trains and hauled by powerful express steam locomotives to depots in and around London. The last milk trains to operate in Britain ran in 1981.

London's dairy supplier With a capacity of 3,000 gallons (13,638 litres), the Express Dairy six-wheel milk tank wagon weighed as much as a loaded passenger coach when full. This wagon was built by the Southern Railway in 1931 and rebuilt in 1937.

△ DR Class 41, 1937

Wheel arrangement 2-8-2

Cylinders 2

Boiler pressure 290 psi/228 psi (20.39 kg/sq cm/16 kg/sq cm)

Driving wheel diameter 63 in (1,600 mm)

Top speed approx. 56 mph (90 km/h)

Built with parts that were designed for several different locomotive types, these powerful, fast freight engines were constructed for the Deutsche Reichsbahn between 1937 and 1941.

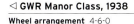

◁ GWR Manor Class, 1938

Wheel arrangement 4-6-0

Cylinders 2

Boiler pressure 225 psi (15.82 kg/sq cm)

Driving wheel diameter 68 in (1,730 mm)

Top speed approx. 65 mph (105 km/h)

With their light axle loading, these Great Western Railway mixed-traffic locomotives could operate on secondary and branch lines as well as main lines in England and Wales. This engine is No. 7808 *Cookham Manor*.

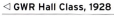

◁ GWR Hall Class, 1928

Wheel arrangement 4-6-0

Cylinders 2

Boiler pressure 225 psi (15.82 kg/sq cm)

Driving wheel diameter 72 in (1,830 mm)

Top speed approx. 70 mph (113 km/h)

A total of 259 of these versatile engines, designed by Charles Collett, were built at the Great Western Railway's Swindon Works between 1928 and 1943. This is No. 5900 *Hinderton Hall*.

Versatile Engines

While the development of more powerful and faster express steam locomotives gathered pace during the 1920s and 1930s there was also the parallel development of smaller engines designed for shunting (or switching) at freight yards, railway workshops, and stations, or to carry out passenger and freight duties on country branch lines. Many of these versatile locomotives remained in active service until the end of the steam era, while some have since been restored to service on heritage railways.

▷ **P&R Switcher No.1251, 1918**

Wheel arrangement	0-6-0T
Cylinders	2
Boiler pressure	150 psi (10.53 kg/sq cm)
Driving wheel diameter	50 in (1,270 mm)
Top speed	approx. 25 mph (40 km/h)

Rebuilt in 1918 from a Class 1-2a Consolidation locomotive, No.1251 spent its life as a switcher at the Philadelphia & Reading Railroad Shops in Reading, Pennsylvania. It was retired in 1964 as the last steam engine on a US Class 1 railroad, and is now on display at the Railroad Museum of Pennsylvania.

△ **LMS Class 3F "Jinty", 1924**

Wheel arrangement	0-6-0T
Cylinders	2 (inside)
Boiler pressure	160 psi (11.25 kg/sq cm)
Driving wheel diameter	55 in (1,400 mm)
Top speed	approx. 40 mph (64 km/h)

These tank locomotives, nicknamed "Jintys", were designed by Henry Fowler for the London, Midland & Scottish Railway. Widely used for shunting and local freight work in the Midlands and northwest England, 422 were built with the last examples remaining in service until 1967.

△ **GWR 5600 Class, 1924**

Wheel arrangement	0-6-2T
Cylinders	2 (inside)
Boiler pressure	200 psi (14.06 kg/sq cm)
Driving wheel diameter	55½ in (1,410 mm)
Top speed	approx. 45 mph (72 km/h)

Designed for the Great Western Railway by Charles Collett, 150 of these powerful tank engines were built at the company's Swindon Works and 50 by Armstrong Whitworth in Newcastle-upon-Tyne. They mainly saw service in the South Wales valleys hauling coal trains, but were also used on local passenger services.

▽ **L&B *Lew*, 1925**

Wheel arrangement	2-6-2T
Cylinders	2
Boiler pressure	160 psi (11.25 kg/sq cm)
Driving wheel diameter	33 in (840 mm)
Top speed	approx. 25 mph (40 km/h)

Completed at the Ffestiniog Railway's Boston Lodge Works in 2010, *Lyd* (shown) is a replica of *Lew*, which was built by Manning Wardle in 1925 for the Southern Railway's 1-ft 11¾-in (0.60-m) gauge Lynton to Barnstaple line. The line, closed in 1935, is now in the process of being reopened by enthusiasts.

Battery Power

Battery locomotives are powered by huge onboard batteries that are recharged in between duties. These engines were once used on railways serving industrial complexes, such as explosives and chemical factories, mines, or anywhere else where normal steam or diesel locomotives could present hazards, such as fire risk, explosion, or fumes. In England, the London Underground uses battery-electric locomotives when the normal electric power is turned off during periods of night-time maintenance.

English Electric EE788 0-4-0 Battery Locomotive This four-wheel, 70-hp (52-kW), battery-electric locomotive was built by English Electric at their Preston factory in England in 1930 and worked for many years at their Stafford Works. It is currently on display at the Ribble Steam Railway Museum in Preston.

△ GWR 4575 Class Prairie Tank, 1927

Wheel arrangement	2-6-2T
Cylinders	2
Boiler pressure	200 psi (14.06 kg/sq cm)
Driving wheel diameter	55½ in (1,410 mm)
Top speed	approx. 50 mph (80 km/h)

Designed by Charles Collett, the 4575 Class of Prairie tank was built at the Great Western Railway's Swindon Works between 1927 and 1929. Of the 100 built, many saw service on branch line passenger and freight duties in England's West Country. No. 5572 shown here was one of the six fitted for push-pull operations. It is preserved at Didcot Railway Centre.

△ GWR 5700 Class Pannier Tank, 1929

Wheel arrangement	0-6-0PT
Cylinders	2 (inside)
Boiler pressure	200 psi (14.06 kg/sq cm)
Driving wheel diameter	55½ in (1,410 mm)
Top speed	approx. 40 mph (64 km/h)

One of the most numerous classes of British steam engine, 863 of these Pannier Tanks were built for the Great Western Railway and British Railways between 1929 and 1950. They were usually seen at work on shunting duties or hauling passenger and freight trains on branch lines. Of the 16 preserved, No. 3738, seen here, is on display at Didcot Railway Centre.

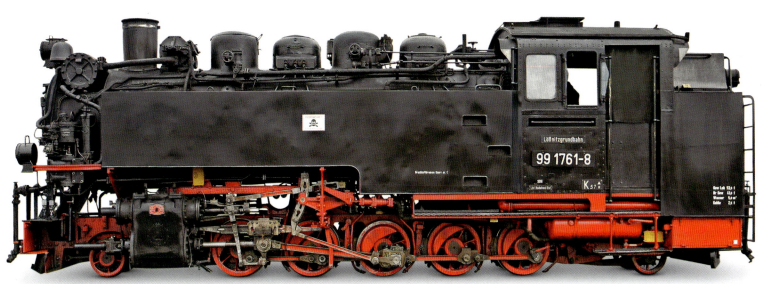

△ DR Class 99.73-76, 1928

Wheel arrangement	2-10-2T
Cylinders	2
Boiler pressure	200 psi (14.06 kg/sq cm)
Driving wheel diameter	31½ in (800 mm)
Top speed	approx. 19 mph (31 km/h)

The Deutsche Reichsbahn had these tank engines built as a new standard design for 2-ft 5½-in- (0.75-m-) gauge lines in Saxony, eastern Germany. A number of these and a modified version introduced in 1950s are still in service today.

△ EIR Class XT/1, 1935

Wheel arrangement	0-4-2T
Cylinders	2
Boiler pressure	160 psi (11.25 kg/sq cm)
Driving wheel diameter	57 in (1,448 mm)
Top speed	approx. 40 mph (64 km/h)

Built by Freidrich Krupp AG of Berlin, Germany, for the 5-ft 6-in- (1.67-m-) gauge East Indian Railway, these locomotives were first introduced in 1929 and were used for light passenger work. No. 36863 (shown) was built in 1935 and is on static display at the National Rail Museum, New Delhi.

Freight Shifters

As train speeds rose, they increasingly carried a variety of goods, including perishable food items. Freight locomotives evolved accordingly. Mainland Europe and North America discarded the six-wheeler for front-rank duties, but the UK continued to build them. The 2-8-0, and variants on the eight-coupled wheelbase, became the main types. Canada, China, Germany, and the USSR built 10-coupled designs, but, especially in the US, the loads and terrain demanded nothing short of the giants.

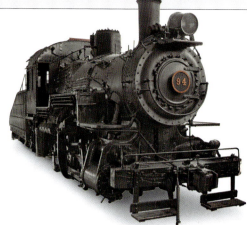

◁ PRR Class A5s, 1917

Wheel arrangement	0-4-0
Cylinders	2
Boiler pressure	185 psi (13 kg/sq cm)
Driving wheel diameter	50 in (1,270 mm)
Top speed	approx. 25 mph (40 km/h)

The Pennsylvania Railroad served many industrial sites around Baltimore, Philadelphia, and New York, where a short-wheelbase switcher, or shunter, was essential to negotiate the tight clearances. One of the most powerful 0-4-0s ever, 47 of the Class A5s were built at the railroad's workshops in Altoona, Pennsylvania, up to 1924.

△ XE Class, 1928/30

Wheel arrangement	2-8-2
Cylinders	2
Boiler pressure	210 psi (14.8 kg/sq cm)
Driving wheel diameter	61¹/₂ in (1,562 mm)
Top speed	approx. 30 mph (48 km/h)

Aside from articulated types, the XE (X Eagle) Class of British-built Mikados (2-8-2s) were the largest steam locomotives on the subcontinent. A total of 93 of these broad-gauge (5-ft 6-in/1.67-m) designs were built, of which 35 were based in Pakistan after partition. No. 3634 *Angadh* is shown here.

▷ CP T1-C Class Selkirk, 1929

Wheel arrangement	2-10-4
Cylinders	2
Boiler pressure	285 psi (20.03 kg/sq cm)
Driving wheel diameter	63 in (1,600 mm)
Top speed	approx. 65 mph (105 km/h)

This semi-streamlined class of engines was built by Canadian Pacific Railway to master the Selkirk Mountains. Thirty of these oil-burners were built up to 1949, and were the largest and most powerful, non-articulated locomotives in the British Commonwealth. They hauled trains 262 miles (422 km) over the mountains from Calgary, Alberta, to Revelstoke, British Columbia.

▷ DR Class 44, 1930

Wheel arrangement	2-10-0
Cylinders	3
Boiler pressure	228 psi (16 kg/sq cm)
Driving wheel diameter	55 in (1,400 mm)
Top speed	approx. 50 mph (80 km/h)

The Deutsche Reichsbahn acquired the first 10 in 1926, but delayed further orders until 1937, after which no fewer than 1,979 were built up to 1949. Unusually for a freight design they had three cylinders, helping them to haul trains of up to 1,181 tons (1,200 tonnes).

Goods Wagons

By the 20th century, railways hauled loads ranging from salt to sugar, petrol to milk, and cattle to coal. Wagons evolved to cater for specific roles: hoppers transported coal, ores, and stone; tankers carried liquids and gases; and refrigerated cars carried perishable goods. Whatever the load, before the introduction of continuous braking, every train had a brake van. From here the guard kept watch over the train, using his brake to keep control of the loose-coupled wagons on down gradients and when stopping.

△ GWR "Toad" brake van, 1924

Type	Brake van
Weight	20 tons (20.32 tonnes)
Construction	wooden body on 4-wheel steel chassis
Railway	Great Western Railway

At a time when most UK goods trains lacked any form of through braking, the role of the guard was critical in controlling the train. From 1894 the Great Western Railway's guards manned "Toads", the name deriving from the electric telegraph code for brake vans.

FRUIT GROWERS EXPRES

F.G.E.X.

57708

CAPY 75000
LD.LMT. 77000
LT.WT.55400 AX.6 47

◁ **UP Challenger CSA-1 Class/ CSA-2 Class, 1936**

Wheel arrangement	4-6-6-4
Cylinders	4
Boiler pressure	280 psi (19.68 kg/sq cm)
Driving wheel diameter	69 in (1,753 mm)
Top speed	approx. 70 mph (113 km/h)

Union Pacific Railroad's Challenger proved that a simple articulated engine could haul huge loads at high speed. Each set of driving wheels was powered by two cylinders, with four trailing wheels to support the huge firebox. The American Locomotive Co. (ALCO) built 105 from 1936 to 1944. Two have been preserved, No. 3977 and No. 3985.

▷ **SAR Class 15F, 1938**

Wheel arrangement	4-8-2
Cylinders	2
Boiler pressure	210 psi (14.8 kg/sq cm)
Driving wheel diameter	60 in (1,524 mm)
Top speed	approx. 60 mph (96 km/h)

Most numerous of South African Railway's classes, the 15F was used predominantly in the Orange Free State and Western Transvaal. Construction spanned WWII; 205 were built by UK companies and a further 50 by German. Several have survived. The 1945-built No. 3007 is in the city of its birth at Glasgow's Riverside Museum.

◁ **GWR 2884 Class, 1938**

Wheel arrangement	2-8-0
Cylinders	2
Boiler pressure	225 psi (15.81 kg/sq cm)
Driving wheel diameter	55½ in (1,410 mm)
Top speed	approx. 45 mph (72 km/h)

The Great Western Railway's 2800 Class of 1903 – the first British 2-8-0 – was a success, persuading the GWR to add to the original total of 83. Modifications, though minor, merited a new designation – the 2884 Class, 81 of which were built from 1938 to 1942. No. 3822 is one of nine preserved.

◁ **FGEX fruit boxcar, 1928**

Type	Express refrigerated boxcar
Weight	24.73 tons (25.13 tonnes)
Construction	wooden body with integral cooling system mounted on steel underframe with two 4-wheel bogies
Railway	Fruit Growers' Express

A leasing company jointly owned by 11 railroads in the eastern and southeastern US, the Fruit Growers' Express built and operated several thousand refrigerated vehicles. Retired in the late 1970s, No. 57708 was preserved by the Cooperstown & Marne Railroad.

△ **ACF 3-dome tank wagon, 1939**

Type	Three-dome bogie oil tank wagon
Weight	18.08 tons (18.37 tonnes)
Construction	steel superstructure mounted on a double bogie steel chassis
Railway	Shippers' Car Line Corporation

The American Car & Foundry Co. remains one of the major rolling stock manufacturers in the US. It built three-dome tank wagon No. 4556 in 1939 for the Shippers' Car Line Corporation. Riding on two four-wheel bogies, and used for transporting propane and liquid petroleum gas, the tank wagon has a capacity of 3,790 gallons (17,230 litres).

Streamlined Steam Around Europe

The 1930s was the Golden Age of high-speed, steam-hauled trains in Europe. With national pride at stake, railways competed for the coveted title of the world's fastest train. In Britain the Great Western Railway's *Cheltenham Flyer* was first off the mark in 1932. Hauled by Sir Nigel Gresley's new streamlined A4 Pacifics, the London & North Eastern Railway's *Silver Jubilee* (1935) and *Coronation* (1937) services set new standards in speed, luxury, and reliability. Steam speed records continued to be broken, first by the German Class 05 in 1936 and then by Gresley's *Mallard* in 1938. World War II ended this high-speed excitement, although *Mallard*'s record has never been broken.

△ LNER Class P2, 1934

Wheel arrangement	2-8-2
Cylinders	3
Boiler pressure	220 psi (15.46 kg/sq cm)
Driving wheel diameter	74 in (1,880 mm)
Top speed	approx. 75 mph (121 km/h)

Sir Nigel Gresley's Class P2 locomotives hauled heavy express passenger trains between London and Aberdeen. Six of the powerful engines were built at the London & North Eastern Railway's Doncaster Works between 1934 and 1936. The class was rebuilt as Class A2/2 Pacifics during WWII.

△ LMS Coronation Class, 1938

Wheel arrangement	4-6-2
Cylinders	4
Boiler pressure	250 psi (17.57 kg/sq cm)
Driving wheel diameter	81 in (2,057 mm)
Top speed	approx. 114 mph (183 km/h)

Designed by William Stanier, a total of 38 of these powerful express locomotives were built at the London, Midland & Scottish Railway's Crewe Works between 1937 and 1948. Ten were built with a streamlined casing that was removed after WWII. No. 6229 *Duchess of Hamilton*, refitted with its streamlined casing, has been preserved.

△ DR Class 05, 1935

Wheel arrangement	4-6-4
Cylinders	3
Boiler pressure	290 psi (20.39 kg/sq cm)
Driving wheel diameter	90½ in (2,299 mm)
Top speed	125 mph (201 km/h)

Three of the streamlined Class 05 passenger expresses were built for the Deutsche Reichsbahn in Germany between 1935 and 1937. During 1936 No. 05.002 set a world speed record for steam locomotives of 125 mph (201 km/h) between Berlin and Hamburg. No. 05.001 is preserved in Nürnburg.

▷ LNER Class A4, 1935

Wheel arrangement	4-6-2
Cylinders	3
Boiler pressure	250 psi (17.57 kg/sq cm)
Driving wheel diameter	80 in (2,030 mm)
Top speed	126 mph (203 km/h)

British engineer Sir Nigel Gresley designed the Class A4 streamlined locomotive. Thirty-five of them were built at the London & North Eastern Railway's Doncaster Works between 1935 and 1938. No. 4468 *Mallard* set an unbeaten world speed record for steam engines of 126 mph (203 km/h) on the East Coast Main Line in 1938.

△ **SNCB Class 12, 1938**

Wheel arrangement	4-4-2
Cylinders	2 (inside)
Boiler pressure	256 psi (18 kg/sq cm)
Driving wheel diameter	82½ in (2,096 mm)
Top speed	103 mph (166 km/h)

The Class 12 was designed by Raoul Notesse for the Belgian state railways. Six of these Atlantic-type locomotives were built between 1938 and 1939 to haul the Brussels to Ostend boat trains. They were retired in 1962 and No. 12.004 has since been preserved.

TALKING POINT

Travelling Exhibit

The London, Midland & Scottish Railway's streamlined *Coronation Scot* train was shipped across the Atlantic to appear in Baltimore, US. It travelled over 3,000 miles (4,828 km) around the US before being exhibited at the New York World's Fair in 1939. It was unable to return to Britain because of the onset of World War II. The locomotive, No. 6229 *Duchess of Hamilton*, masquerading as No. 6220 *Coronation*, was eventually shipped back to the UK in 1942 but the coaches remained in the US where they were used by the US Army as an officer's mess until after the war, when they too were returned.

***Duchess of Hamilton*'s headlamp** One of the two headlamps fitted to *Duchess of Hamilton*, this one remained in the US and is now on display at the Baltimore & Ohio Railroad Museum in Baltimore.

◁ **DR Class 03.10, 1939**

Wheel arrangement	4-6-2
Cylinders	3
Boiler pressure	290 psi (20.38 kg/sq cm)
Driving wheel diameter	78¾ in (2,000 mm)
Top speed	87 mph (140 km/h)

A total of 60 of these streamlined express passenger locomotives were built for the Deutsche Reichsbahn between 1939 and 1941. After WWII the class was split between East and West Germany and Poland. The German locomotives were rebuilt without their streamline casing, retiring in the late 1970s.

TECHNOLOGY

The Silver Jubilee Service

Named to honour the 25-year reign of King George V, the *Silver Jubilee* high-speed express train was introduced by the London & North Eastern Railway between London King's Cross and Newcastle-upon-Tyne in 1935. Painted in two-tone silver and grey, the articulated train was hauled by one of four of Sir Nigel Gresley's new Class A4 streamlined Pacific locomotives named *Silver Link*, *Quicksilver*, *Silver King*, and *Silver Fox*. The service ceased on the onset of World War II.

Inaugural run LNER Class A4 No. 2509 *Silver Link* departs King's Cross station with the inaugural *Silver Jubilee* express to Newcastle on 30 September 1935.

The Age of Speed and Style

Symbolized by the futuristic designs of the trains, planes, and automobiles of that period, the decade before World War II could rightly be called "The Age of Speed". Across the world railway companies were introducing modern high-speed expresses designed to entice the travelling public on board with their luxurious interiors, slick service, and dependable fast schedules. Apart from a few diesel-powered streamliners in Germany and the US, these iconic trains were hauled by the latest Art Deco-style steam locomotives, many designed by some of the world's leading industrial designers.

▷ Japan/China Class SL7, 1935

Wheel arrangement	4-6-2
Cylinders	2
Boiler pressure	220 psi (15.5 kg/sq cm)
Driving wheel diameter	78³/₄ in (2,000 mm)
Top speed	87 mph (140 km/h)

Built by Kawasaki Heavy Industries in Japan and the Shahekou Plant in the Kwantung Leased Territory in China, the 12 Pashina-type locomotives hauled the *Asia Express* during Japanese control of the South Manchuria Railway between 1934 and 1943. Designated Class Shengli 7 after the war, they remained in service in China until the 1970s.

△ VR S Class, 1937

Wheel arrangement	4-6-2
Cylinders	3
Boiler pressure	200 psi (14.06 kg/sq cm)
Driving wheel diameter	73 in (1,854 mm)
Top speed	86 mph (138 km/h)

First introduced in 1928, the four Australian Victoria Railways' S Class Pacific-type locomotives were given a streamlined casing in 1937 to haul the new non-stop, Art Deco-style, *Spirit of Progress* express between Melbourne and Albury. They had all been scrapped by 1954 after the introduction of diesels.

▽ MILW Class A, 1935

Wheel arrangement	4-4-2
Cylinders	2
Boiler pressure	300 psi (21.09 kg/sq cm)
Driving wheel diameter	84 in (2,134 mm)
Top speed	112¹/₂ mph (181 km/h)

Designed to haul the US *Hiawatha* expresses, four of these high-speed Atlantic-type Class A locomotives were built for the Milwaukee Road (MILW) from 1935 to 1937. Locomotive "A" No. 2 achieved 112¹/₂ mph (181 km/h) between Milwaukee and New Lisbon in May 1935.

△ **CN Class U-4-a, 1936**

Wheel arrangement	4-8-4
Cylinders	2
Boiler pressure	275 psi (19.33 kg/sq cm)
Driving wheel diameter	77 in (1,956 mm)
Top speed	90 mph (145 km/h)

Five of these streamlined Confederation-type express passenger locomotives were built for Canadian National Railways by the Montreal Locomotive Works in 1936. They remained the premier express locomotives between Toronto and Montreal until replaced by diesels in the 1950s.

Rail and Road

By the mid-1930s, American Art Deco-style cars and streamlined steam trains were capable of achieving speeds of 120 mph (193 km/h). Industrial designers such as the American Gordon Buehrig, the Franco-American Raymond Loewy, the Englishman John Gurney Nutting, and Italian-born Frenchman Ettore Bugatti all left their mark on the brief but exciting period of technological progress that ended with the onset of World War II.

Speed rivalry Now highly sought after, Jack Juratovic's iconic "Road and Track" prints of 1935 feature a Duesenberg Torpedo Phaeton car racing a streamlined steam train.

△ **NSWGR Class C38, 1943**

Wheel arrangement	4-6-2
Cylinders	2
Boiler pressure	245 psi (17.22 kg/sq cm)
Driving wheel diameter	69 in (1,750 mm)
Top speed	80 mph (129 km/h)

Designed in 1939, five of the standard-gauge Australian Class C38 express passenger locomotives were actually delivered to the New South Wales Government Railways by Clyde Engineering of Sydney between 1943 and 1945. After hauling expresses they were retired between 1961 and 1976.

△ **PP&L "D" Fireless locomotive, 1939**

Wheel arrangement	0-8-0
Cylinders	2
Boiler pressure	130 psi (9.14 kg/sq cm)
Driving wheel diameter	42 in (1,067 mm)
Top speed	20 mph (32 km/h)

Streamlined, but not fast, this Pennsylvania Power & Light Co. fireless shunter was built by Heisler for the Hammermill Paper Co. in Erie. Used in industrial plants where inflammable fuel would be a hazard, fireless locomotives stored steam in their boilers. The largest of this type built, No. 4094-D is on display in the Railroad Museum of Pennsylvania in Strasburg, US.

Raymond Loewy

Nicknamed "The father of Streamlining", French-born Raymond Loewy (1893–1986) was an American industrial designer known for his wide-ranging work for US industry. In addition to designing world-famous logos for oil companies, such as Shell, and railways, he also left his mark on Studebaker cars and iconic railway locomotives such as the Pennsylvania Railroad's Class K4s, T1 and S1 streamlined steam engines. After opening an office in London in 1930, Loewy went on to restyle the Baldwin Locomotive Co.'s early diesel locomotives. Loewy returned to live in his native France in 1980 and died a few years later.

Standing tall Raymond Loewy stands on one of his iconic designs, Pennsylvania Railroad's unique Class S1 6-4-4-6 experimental streamliner locomotive, the US's largest and fastest high-speed locomotive.

Diesel and Electric Streamliners

The 1930s saw the introduction of high-speed diesel and electric trains in Europe and North America. Designed by leading engineers such as Ettore Bugatti and tested in wind tunnels, these streamliners caught the public's imagination, broke world speed records, and ushered in the new age of high-speed rail travel. In Europe the Germans led the way with their *Flying Hamburger*, the forerunner of today's intercity expresses, and in the US the *Pioneer Zephyr* reached new heights of futuristic modern design. Sadly the onset of World War II brought an abrupt end to this exciting progress.

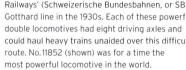

△ DR Class SVT 137
Fliegender Hamburger, 1935

Wheel arrangement	two-car articulated set – front and rear bogies 2' Bo' 2'
Transmission	each car electric (1 traction motor)
Engine	each car Maybach 12-cylinder diesel 8,850 cc
Total power output	810 hp (604 kW)
Top speed	99 mph (160 km/h)

With a prototype built in 1932, the Deutsche Reichsbahn train entered service in 1935 between Berlin and Hamburg; it had a buffet and seated 98. The diesel-electric *Fliegender* (flying) *Hamburger* established the world's fastest regular train service with an average speed of 77 mph (124 km/h). Inactive during WWII, it saw service in France in 1945–49, then returned to operate in Germany until 1983.

△ SBB Class Ae8/14, 1931

Wheel arrangement	(1'A)A1A(A1') + (1A')A1A(A1')
Power supply	15 kV 17 Hz AC, catenary
Power rating	7,394–10,956 hp (5,514–8,173 kW)
Top speed	62 mph (100 km/h)

Three prototype Class Ae8/14 electric locomotives were built for the Swiss Federal Railways' (Schweizerische Bundesbahnen, or SBB) Gotthard line in the 1930s. Each of these powerful double locomotives had eight driving axles and could haul heavy trains unaided over this difficult route. No. 11852 (shown) was for a time the most powerful locomotive in the world.

▷ Bugatti railcar (autorail), 1932/33

Wheel arrangement	each car 2 x 8-wheel bogies, 2 or 4 axles powered
Transmission	mechanical
Engine	each car 2 or 4 Bugatti 12,700 cc
Total power output	4 engines 800 hp (596 kW)
Top speed	122 mph (196 km/h)

Designed by Ettore Bugatti and built in the Bugatti factory in Alsace, France, these petrol-engined railcars were supplied as single-, double-, or triple-car units. The most comfortable and fastest was the 48-seat, two-car, four-engined "Presidentiel", which set a world rail-speed record of 122 mph (196 km/h) in 1934.

▷ GWR streamlined railcar, 1934

Wheel arrangement	2 x 4-wheel bogies, 1 powered
Transmission	mechanical
Engine	8,850 cc AEC diesel
Total power output	130 hp (97 kW)
Top speed	approx. 63 mph (100 km/h)

First introduced by the Great Western Railway in 1934, these streamlined diesel railcars were nicknamed "Flying Bananas" and remained in service on British Railways until the early 1960s. Production versions, including parcels cars and articulated buffet sets, were fitted with two AEC diesel engines allowing a top speed of 80 mph (129 km/h).

TECHNOLOGY

German Experiment

The *Schienenzeppelin*, or "rail zeppelin", was an experimental railcar with an aluminium body, which looked like a Zeppelin airship. The front-end design of this prototype bore an uncanny resemblance to the Japanese *Bullet Train* of the 1960s.

Weighing only 20 tons (20.32 tonnes), this 85-ft (26-m) long propeller-driven car was powered by a BMW 12-cylinder petrol aircraft engine producing a power of 600 hp (447 kW). In June 1931 it set a world land-speed record for rail vehicles using air propulsion when it reached 143 mph (230 km/h) on the Berlin to Hamburg line. The railcar was scrapped in 1939 to provide material for the German war effort in World War II.

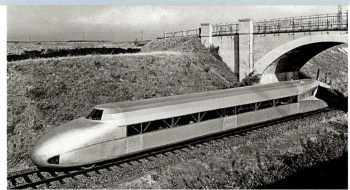

Zeppelin train Built by Franz Kruckenberg of Hannover the *Schienenzeppelin* only had two axles and was designed to carry 40 passengers.

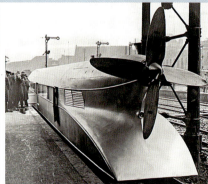

Rear fairing The wind-tunnel-designed fairing had a four-bladed propeller made of ash wood.

◁ **PRR Class GG1, 1934**

Wheel arrangement 2-C+C-2

Power supply 11 kV 25 Hz AC, catenary

Power rating 4,620 hp (3,446 kW)

Top speed approx. 100 mph (161 km/h)

A total of 139 of these powerful electric locomotives, nicknamed "Blackjacks", were built for the Pennsylvania Railroad between 1934 and 1943. They entered service in 1935 hauling express passenger trains on the newly electrified New York to Washington DC main line. Relegated to freight service in the 1950s they had all been withdrawn by 1983. No. 4935 is preserved at the Railroad Museum of Pennsylvania.

◁ **CB&Q _Pioneer Zephyr_, 1934**

Wheel arrangement 3 x articulated cars on 4 bogies

Transmission mechanical

Engine 8-cylinder Winton diesel

Total power output 600 hp (447 kW)

Top speed 112¹/₂ mph (181 km/h)

Built by the Budd Co. for the Chicago, Burlington & Quincy Railroad, the _Pioneer Zephyr_ was a streamlined train of three stainless-steel cars articulated with Jacobs bogies and powered by a submarine engine. On its inaugural run between Denver and Chicago it averaged 77 mph (124 km/h) for the 1,015-mile (1,633-km) journey, reaching a top speed of 112¹/₂ mph (181 km/h).

▷ **SBB Doppelpfeil, 1939**

Wheel arrangement 2 x 4-wheel powered bogies (single unit)

Power supply 15 kV 17 Hz AC, catenary

Power rating single units 528 hp (394 kW); twin units 1,126 hp (840 kW)

Top speed 77 mph (125 km/h)

Seven of the Schweizerische Bundesbahnen's "Rote Pfeil" (or Red Arrow), streamlined electric single-unit railcars were introduced in 1935 for service on the Swiss Gotthard Railway, a major international railway link between Germany and Italy via the 49,222-ft (15,003-m) Gotthard Rail Tunnel. Three twin units known as "Doppelpfeil", (or Double Arrows), were introduced in 1939.

Practical Diesels and Electrics

World War I had left Europe's railways in tatters; coal was scant and expensive, and, while steam was still popular, other forms of traction would soon emerge to herald the end of an era. In mountainous countries such as Italy and Switzerland, an abundance of clean and cheap hydroelectric power made possible the electrification of main lines. Powerful electric locomotives, such as the Swiss "Krocodils", were soon hauling heavy trains over demanding routes, while in Italy speed records were being broken on Mussolini's new high-speed railway. At the other end of the scale, small diesel and electric shunters (or switchers) were being introduced in Europe and North America as a more efficient way of marshalling trains.

▷ SBB Class Ce 6/8 II and Ce 6/8 III, 1919-20

Wheel arrangement	1-C+C-1
Power supply	15 kV 17 Hz AC, catenary
Power rating	3,647 hp (2,721 kW)
Top speed	47 mph (76 km/h)

Serving until 1980, 51 of these electric engines were built to haul heavy freight on the Swiss Federal Railways' (Schweizerische Bundesbahnen, or SBB) Gotthard line from 1919 to 1927. Their long noses, for which they were nicknamed "Krokodils" (crocodiles), contain the motors.

△ GIPR Class WCP 1, 1930

Wheel arrangement	1'Co2'
Power supply	1.5 kV DC, catenary
Power rating	2,158 hp (1,610 kW)
Top speed	75 mph (121 km/h)

The first electric locomotives to be used in India, 22 of these powerful passenger engines were built from 1930 by Metropolitan-Vickers in the UK for the Great Indian Peninsula Railway. The first of these, No. 4006 *Sir Roger Lumley*, is on display at the National Rail Museum, New Delhi.

▷ DR E04, 1933

Wheel arrangement	1'Co1'
Power supply	15 kV 17 Hz AC, catenary
Power rating	2,694 hp (2,010 kW)
Top speed	75 mph (121 km/h)

A total of 23 Class E04 electric locomotives were built for Deutsche Reichsbahn for service on the newly electrified Stuttgart to Munich main line. Members of the class stayed in service in West Germany until 1976 and in East Germany until 1982. Several of these have been preserved.

▷ GHE T1, 1933

Wheel arrangement	A1 (0-2-2)
Transmission	mechanical
Engine	4-cylinder diesel
Total power output	123 hp (92 kW)
Top speed	25 mph (40 km/h)

This unique four-wheel 3-ft 3-in- (1-m-) gauge diesel railcar (or *Triebwagen*) was built by Waggonfabrik Dessau in 1933 for the Gernrode-Harzgeroder Railway in Germany. After WWII it became No. 187.001 of the East German Deutsche Reichsbahn and was used as a workman's tool wagon. Seating 34 passengers, this restored railcar runs on the Harz narrow-gauge railways.

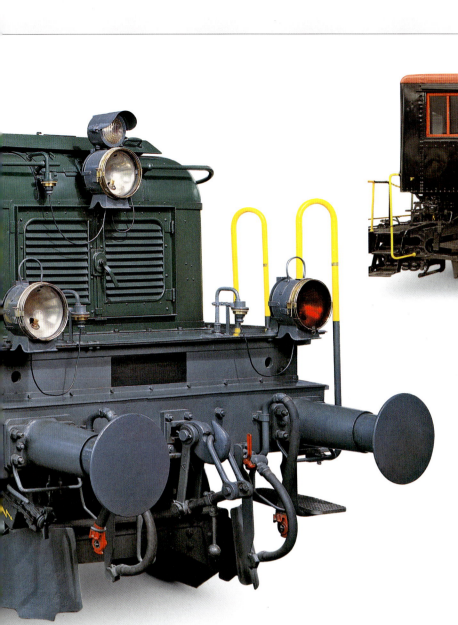

△ **PRR Class B1, 1934**

Wheel arrangement	C (0-6-0)
Power supply	11 kV 25 Hz AC, catenary
Power rating	697 hp (520 kW)
Top speed	25 mph (40 km/h)

Fourteen of these single-unit electric switchers were built at Altoona Works by the Pennsylvania Railroad in 1934. They spent most of their life performing empty carriage movements in and out of Penn Station in New York, US, before retiring in the early 1970s.

△ **DR Class Kö, 1934**

Wheel arrangement	B (0-4-0)
Transmission	mechanical
Engine	79 hp (59 kW) diesel as modified
Total power output	18–22 kW (24–29 hp)
Top speed	11 mph (18 km/h)

These small diesel mechanical shunters, known as *Einheitskleinlokomotiven*, served at small stations on the Deutsche Reichsbahn. Fitted with only a foot brake, some were converted to run on LPG during WWII. Three of these, including No. 199.011 shown, have been converted to operate as Class Kö II on the 3-ft 3-in- (1-m-) gauge Harz railways.

▷ **LMS Diesel Shunter No. 1831, 1931**

Wheel arrangement	C (0-6-0)
Transmission	hydraulic
Engine	Davey Paxman 6-cylinder diesel
Total power output	400 hp (298 kW)
Top speed	25 mph (40 km/h)

This was the first experimental diesel-hydraulic shunter in the UK. It was built by the London, Midland & Scottish Railway at its Derby Works in 1931 using the frame and running gear of a Midland Railway 1377 Class 0-6-0 steam locomotive of the same number. It was not successful and was officially withdrawn in 1939.

◁ **FS Class ETR 200, 1937**

Wheel arrangement	3-car articulated on 4-wheel bogies
Power supply	3 kV DC, catenary
Power rating	1,408 hp (1,050 kW)
Top speed	126 mph (203 km/h)

Entering service between Milan and Naples in 1937, a total of 18 of these three-car electric multiple units were built by Breda for the Italian state railways. The streamlined shape was designed after wind tunnel tests, and in July 1939 unit ETR 212 set a world record for electric rail traction of 126 mph (203 km/h). The class was in regular service until the 1990s, and ETR 212 has since been preserved.

TECHNOLOGY

Track Inspection

During the 19th century the maintenance of thousands of miles of railway track, often in places inaccessible by road, was only made possible by teams of gangers walking the lines or travelling on unpowered handcars (also known as pump cars or jiggers). These were propelled by pushing a wooden arm up and down. By the 20th century more ingenious methods had been introduced, such as motorized road vehicles fitted with flanged wheels. Road-rail inspection vehicles are still used today on remote railways around the world. In the US these are known as hi-rail vehicles; in Scotland, Land Rovers are adapted for use on the West Highland Line.

Buick Ma&Pa Car No. 101, 1937 Originally used as a funeral car, this vehicle was converted to run on the Maryland & Pennsylvania Railroad to test a radio communication system between locomotives and the railway's offices.

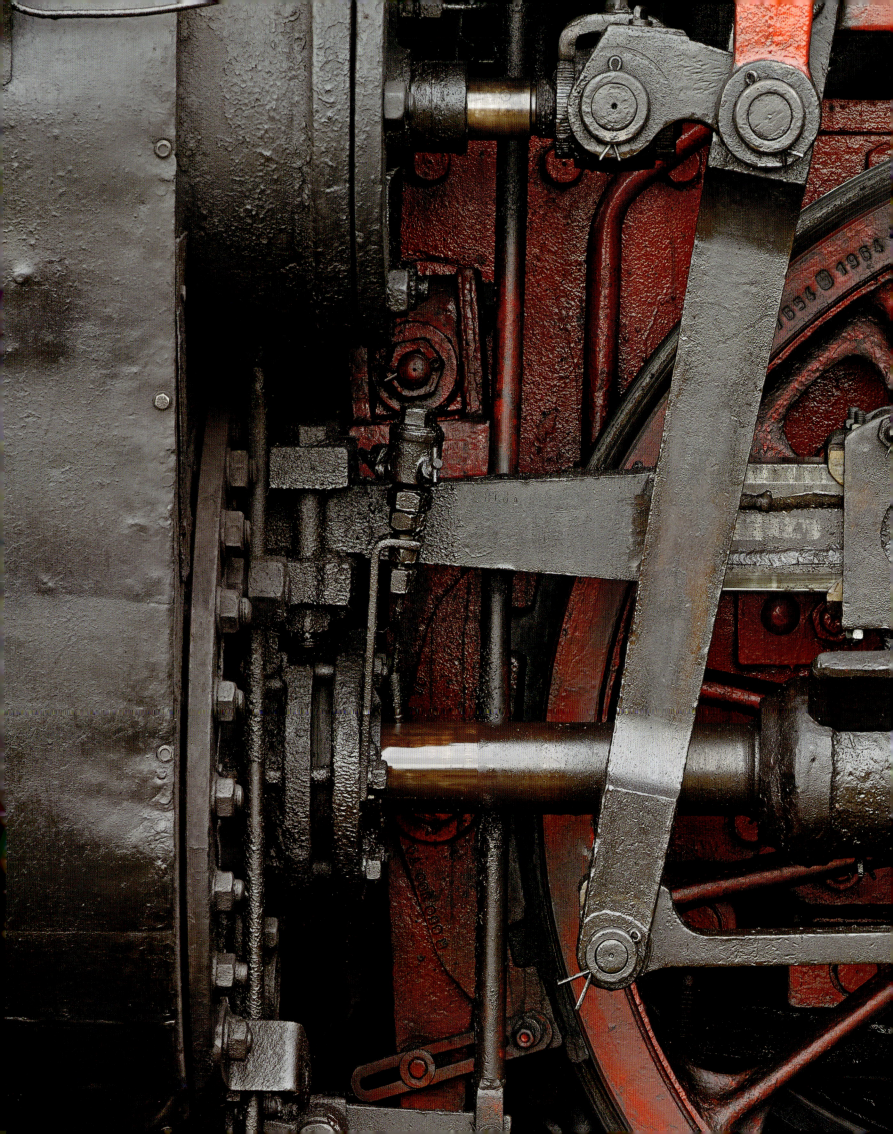

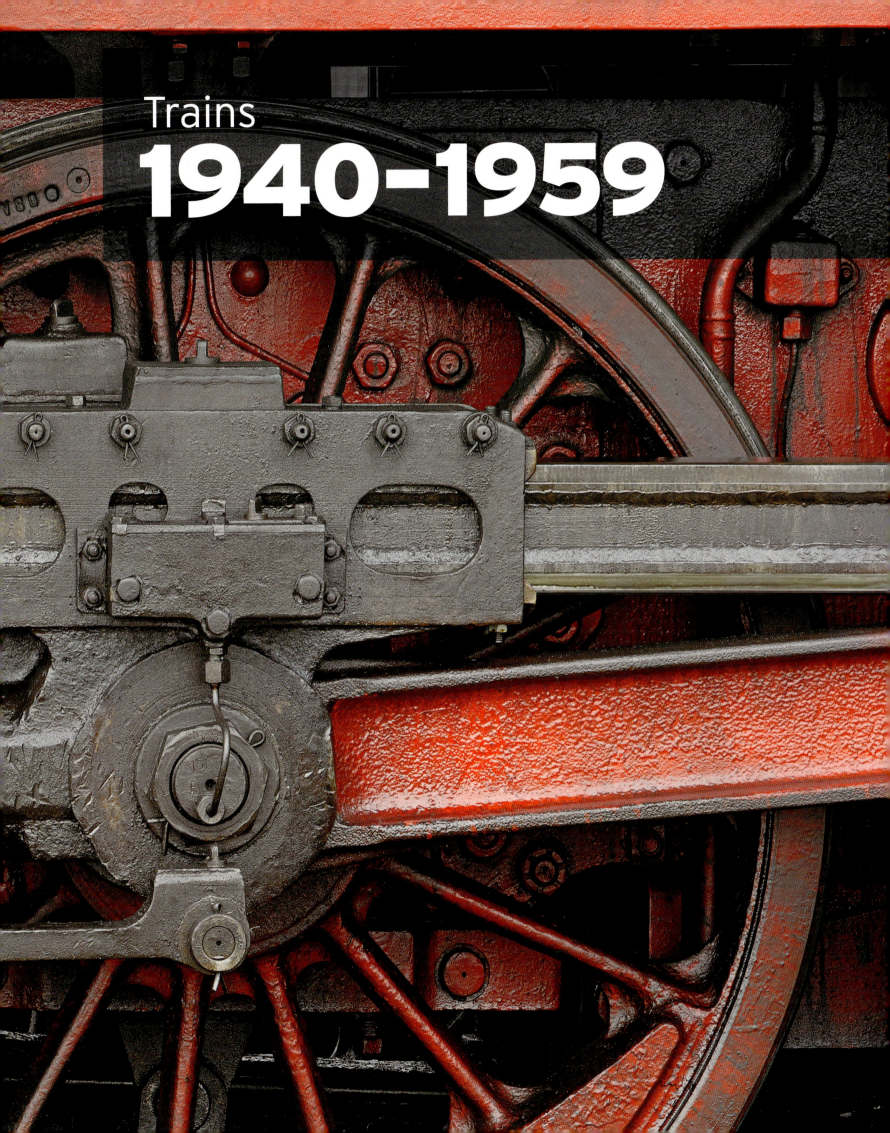

Trains
1940–1959

World War II Logistics

The transportation of raw materials, troops, military equipment, and ammunition by rail was of strategic importance to the warring powers in World War II. As a result, cheaply constructed powerful freight locomotives – mass-produced in Germany, Britain, and the US – saw active service in war zones. After the war many ran on European national railways – as replacements or as war reparations. A large number of engines, built for the United States Army Transportation Corps (USATC), were sent to Asia under lease-lend agreements and, after the war, by the UN Relief & Rehabilitation Administration.

◁ LMS 8F, 1935

Wheel arrangement	2-8-0
Cylinders	2
Boiler pressure	225 psi (15.82 kg/sq cm)
Driving wheel diameter	56 1/4 in (1,430 mm)
Top speed	approx. 50 mph (80 km/h)

Designed by William Stanier for the London, Midland & Scottish Railway, these were the standard British freight locomotives for part of WWII. They saw service for Britain's War Department in Egypt, Palestine, Iran, and Italy - 25 were sold to Turkey in 1941. Of the 852 built, some remained in British service until 1968, while Turkish examples ran into the 1980s.

△ DR Class 52 "Kriegslok", 1942

Wheel arrangement	2-10-0
Cylinders	2
Boiler pressure	232 psi (16.3 kg/sq cm)
Driving wheel diameter	55 in (1,400 mm)
Top Speed	50 mph (80 km/h)

Around 7,000 of these Deutsche Reichsbahn heavy freight locomotives were built mainly for service on the Eastern Front. A small number remain in service in Bosnia even today, while many, like this Class 52 No. 52.8184-5 rebuild, have been preserved.

◁ USATC S160, 1942

Wheel arrangement	2-8-0
Cylinders	2
Boiler pressure	225 psi (15.82 kg/sq cm)
Driving wheel diameter	56³/₄ in (1,440 mm)
Top speed	approx. 45 mph (72 km/h)

Of the 2,120 austerity Consolidation-type heavy freight locomotives built for the USATC, 800 were shipped to Britain for use in Europe after D-Day. After the war they saw service on many European railways as well as in North Africa, China, India, and North and South Korea.

▷ USATC S100, 1942

Wheel arrangement	0-6-0T
Cylinders	2
Boiler pressure	210 psi (14.8 kg/sq cm)
Driving wheel diameter	54 in (1,370 mm)
Top speed	approx. 35 mph (56 km/h)

Built for the USATC, 382 of these locomotives were shipped to Britain and used in Europe after the D-day landings of June 1944. Britain's Southern Railway later bought 15 as shunters.

△ Class V36 Shunter, 1937

Wheel arrangement	0-6-0
Transmission	hydraulic
Engine	Deutsche Werke/MAK diesel
Total power output	360 hp (268 kW)
Top speed	approx. 37 mph (60 km/h)

Fitted with four axles but only three pairs of driving wheels, these diesel locomotives were built for the German armed forces (Wehrmacht) and were used for shunting duties. They saw widespread use in Europe and North Africa after the war.

▷ Armoured Car, 1942

Type	4-wheel
Capacity	130 (whole train)
Constuction	armour-plated steel
Railway	German Wehrmacht

This camouflaged car formed part of a German Wehrmacht BP42 armoured train that protected supply and transport trains in the Balkans and Russia. An armoured Class 57 0-10-0 steam locomotive was positioned in the centre of the train, which consisted of a combination of infantry, navigating, anti-aircraft, and artillery wagons, with converted tank turrets.

▷ **SR Class Q1, 1942**

Wheel arrangement	0-6-0
Cylinders	2 (inside)
Boiler pressure	230 psi (16.17 kg/sq cm)
Driving wheel diameter	61 in (1,550 mm)
Top Speed	50 mph (80 km/h)

Designed by Oliver Bulleid for the Southern Railway, these freight locomotives were lightweight, which enabled them to operate over most of the company's network. A total of 40 were built, and they all remained in service on the Southern Region of British Railways until the 1960s. This is No. C1, the first of the series.

The Maryland Car

In 1947, US journalist Drew Pearson set out to help the people of war-stricken France and Italy. A Friendship Train travelled around the US gathering $40 million of relief supplies. In response, the French sent a Merci (thank you) Train filled with gifts back to the US. Arriving in New York in 1949, the train consisted of a series of European boxcars used to transport soldiers and horses during the war. There were 49 cars – one for each US state (although the District of Columbia and Hawaii had to share). The Maryland Car, shown here, was originally built for the Paris, Lyon & Mediterranean Railway in 1915. It is now on display at the Baltimore & Ohio Railroad Museum, Baltimore.

△ **WD Austerity, 1943**

Wheel arrangement	2-8-0
Cylinders	2
Boiler pressure	225 psi (15.82 kg/sq cm)
Driving wheel diameter	56¼in (1,430 mm)
Top speed	approx. 45 mph (72 km/h)

Designed by R.A. Riddles for the British War Department, these freight trains were "austerity", or cheaper, versions of the LMS 8F. Of the 935 built, many saw service in mainland Europe after D-day in June 1944. After the war, 733 were in operation for British Railways, while others worked in the Netherlands, Hong Kong, and Sweden.

▽ **Indian Class AWE, 1943**

Wheel arrangement	2-8-2
Cylinders	2
Boiler pressure	210 psi (14.76 kg/sq cm)
Driving wheel diameter	61½in (1,562 mm)
Top speed	approx. 62 mph (100 km/h)

These huge locomotives were built by Baldwin Locomotive Works for the USATC for hauling heavy freight trains in India during WWII. They were fitted with 7-ft- (2,134-mm-) diameter boilers and 40 became Indian Railways Class AWE. One of these, No. 22907 *Virat*, has been restored to working order at the Rewari Steam Loco Shed.

US Moves into Diesel

The diesel locomotive represented the greatest advance in US railways during the 20th century. Although diesel engines had been around since the 1890s, the challenge was to make them small and light enough to fit within the confines of a locomotive, yet powerful enough to haul a train. The breakthrough had come in 1935 when General Motors unveiled their 12-cylinder, 2-cycle engine that was 23 per cent smaller and, thanks to lightweight alloys, 20 per cent lighter than its predecessors. Accelerating into the 1940s the diesel began to conquer the US.

◁ **Boxley Whitcomb 30-DM-31, 1941**

Wheel arrangement	0-4-0
Transmission	mechanical
Engine	8-cylinder Cummins
Total power output	150 hp (120 kW)
Top speed	approx. 20 mph (32 km/h)

Built by the Whitcomb company of Rochelle, Illinois, "30" referred to the locomotive weight range in tons and "DM" to its transmission (diesel-mechanical). The Boxley Materials Co. of Roanoke, Virginia bought No. 31 from the Houston Shipbuilding Corporation of Texas in 1953.

◁ **VC Porter No. 3, 1944**

Wheel arrangement	A1-A1
Transmission	electric
Engine	not known
Total power output	300 hp (224 kW)
Top speed	approx. 20 mph (32 km/h)

H.K. Porter Inc. was one of the largest manufacturers of industrial locomotives in the US – by 1950, it had built 8,000. This rod-driven switcher Porter No. 3, built for the Virginia Central Railroad, is the last of the 28 of its type built. It is now preserved at the Virginia Museum of Transportation.

▷ **PMR GM EMD SW-1 No. 11, 1942**

Wheel arrangement Bo-Bo

Transmission electric

Engine EMD Model 567 V-6 engine

Total power output 600 hp (448 kW)

Top speed 45 mph (72 km/h)

The Pere Marquette Railway, which took its name from a 17th-century French Jesuit priest, served the Great Lakes region of the US and Canada. The EMD SW-1 Class was introduced in 1936, but No. 11 was delivered to the railway in April 1942 to begin shunting hoppers at Eireau, Ontario. It was retired in 1984.

△ **GM Class E7a, 1945**

Wheel arrangement A1A-A1A

Transmission electric

Engine 2 x EMD Model 567A, 12-cylinder

Total power output 2,000 hp (1491 kW)

Top speed 85 mph (137 km/h)

Supplied to over 20 railways, General Motors's E7 was one of the first standard American diesels. Between 1945 and 1949, 428 of the E7a cab units were produced along with 82 E7b boosters. The Gulf, Mobile, & Ohio Railroad's No. 103, shown here, was notable for appearing in the film *The Heat of the Night*.

△ **Baldwin Class DS-4-4-660, 1946**

Wheel arrangement Bo-Bo

Transmission electric

Engine 4-cycle engine

Total power output 660 hp (492 kW)

Top speed 60 mph (96 km/h)

The Chesapeake & Western (C&W, known locally as the "Crooked and Weedy") operated over 53½ miles (86 km) of the Shenandoah Valley (US). In 1946 it took delivery of three diesel units. With running costs at 25 cents per mile (as opposed to the 96 cents for steam), it marked a turning point for the CHW. No. 662 was retired in 1964 and languished in a scrapyard before being donated to the Virginia Museum of Transportation.

◁ **Ma&Pa GM EMD Type NW2, 1946**

Wheel arrangement Bo-Bo

Transmission electric

Engine 12-cylinder engine

Total power output 1,000 hp (750 kW)

Top speed 60 mph (97 km/h)

This type was first introduced in 1939. The Maryland & Pennsylvania Railroad (a short line linking Baltimore with York and Hanover, Pennsylvania) took delivery of Nos. 80 and 81, two Type NW2 switchers built by the Electro-Motive Division of General Motors, in December 1946. In total, 1,145 NW2s were shipped between 1939 and 1949 to over 50 railways (in contrast to the Ma&Pa's modest pair, Union Pacific bought 95). No. 81 has been part of the Railroad Museum of Pennsylvania's collection since 1997.

Post-war US

Some railways needed persuading that diesel could match the haulage power of steam, but, once General Motors's freight demonstrator and prototypes had convinced them, the economic argument was irresistible. Mainline locomotives fell into two categories: cab units and hood units. The former, with their sleek bodywork and colourful liveries, handled the expresses and were augmented by boosters for extra power. In the hood unit, the workhorse, the engine (or engines), radiators, and ancillary equipment were mounted on a platform above the chassis with the cab placed at one end or in the centre. The transition from steam to diesel was accomplished within 20 years; by 1960 around 34,000 diesel locomotives operated in the US.

▷ **B&A GE 70-ton switcher, 1946**

Wheel arrangement Bo-Bo

Transmission electric

Engine 2 x Cooper-Bessemer FDL-6T 6-cylinder 4-cycle engines

Total power output 660 hp (492 kW)

Top speed 60 mph (96 km/h)

The Baltimore & Annapolis Railroad was mainly a commuter line that in 1950 succumbed to road competition and replaced passenger trains with buses. That year it bought a solitary diesel, a General Electric 70-ton switcher – No. 50 – for freight operations. The type was introduced in 1946 as a lighter, low-cost option for secondary routes, and 238 were built up to 1955. Retired in 1986, No. 50 is preserved at the Baltimore & Ohio Museum.

△ **Baldwin S12 switcher, 1950**

Wheel arrangement Bo-Bo

Transmission electric

Engine De Lavergne Model 606A SC 4-cycle engine

Total power output 1,200 hp (895 kW)

Top speed 60 mph (96 km/h)

Employing a turbocharged version of the powerful Model 606A engine, the S12 switcher was famous for its hauling prowess, as demonstrated by Baldwin's original No. 1200. Here, masquerading as No. 1200, is Earle No. 7 or, in the records of its operators, the United States Navy, No. 65-000369. The USN took 18 of the 451 S12s shipped between 1951 and 1956 and stationed this unit at its ordnance depot in Earle, New Jersey.

▷ **B&O F7 Class, 1949**

Wheel arrangement Bo-Bo

Transmission electric

Engine EMD 567B 16-cylinder engine

Total power output 1,500 hp (1,119 kW)

Top speed 50-120 mph (80-193 km/h)

The F7 was the most numerous of the General Motors's F Series; 2,341 A units and 1,467 B (booster) units were built by 1953. The speed variation was a product of eight different gear ratios. Though tailored for freight, many US railways used F7s for front-line passenger services until the 1970s. No. 7100, shown, was bought by the Baltimore & Ohio Railroad in 1951 and enjoyed a second career on the Maryland Area Regional Commuter (MARC) system from 1987 to the late 1990s.

◁ **N&W EMD GP9 Class, 1955**

Wheel arrangement Bo-Bo

Transmission electric

Engine EMD 567C 16-cylinder engine

Total power output 1,750 hp (1,305 kW)

Top speed 75 mph (125 km/h)

General Motors's "Geep Nine" remains one of the most successful and long-lasting of diesels, although not the most attractive. Looks did not count for US and Canadian railways, which between them bought 4,087 A units and 165 type B boosters from 1954 to 1963. No. 521 was one of 306 GP9s on the books of the Norfolk & Western, and many remain in service on secondary lines and with industrial users; some Class 1 railways still use them as shunters.

△ Budd RDC railcar, 1949

Wheel arrangement	Bo-2
Transmission	mechanical
Engine	2 x General Motors Type 6-110 6-cylinder engines
Total power output	275 hp (205 kW)
Top speed	85 mph (137 km/h)

After WWII the Budd Co. used its expertise in building lightweight stainless-steel carriages to assemble diesel railcars (or multiple units) for secondary and local passenger services. A prototype Rail Diesel Car (RDC) was unveiled in 1949 and impressed with its economy. By 1962, 398 were in operation. Out west, RDCs provided a stopping service over the 924 miles (1,487 km) between Salt Lake City, Utah, and Oakland, California. The RDC was also exported to Australia, Brazil, Canada, and France.

◁ N&W ALCO T6 (DL440) Class, 1958

Wheel arrangement	Bo-Bo
Transmission	electric
Engine	ALCO 251B 6-cylinder 4-cycle engine
Total power output	1,000 hp (746 kW)
Top speed	60 mph (96 km/h)

The American Locomotive Co. (ALCO) introduced the T6 (the "T" stood for "Transfer") in 1958 believing there was a demand for a switcher capable of shuttling trains between yards and terminals at higher speeds. This was not the case and up to 1969 just 57 had been delivered, of which the Norfolk & Western Railway took 38. Retired in 1985, No. 41 is kept at the Virginia Museum of Transportation, US.

Britain Makes the Change

By the 1940s the rail system in Britain consisted of four major companies and many smaller light railways. In 1948 the "Big Four" and the majority of the smaller railways were nationalized under one umbrella company – British Railways. The new company commissioned a report to look at ways of stemming the losses they were incurring as a result of competition from air and road traffic. Known as the Modernisation Plan and published on 1 December 1954, the report made a number of recommendations, including the replacement of all steam engines. Tests in the late 1950s with "pilot-scheme" diesels were intended to demonstrate which locomotives to order in quantity. Orders for thousands of new diesels would follow in the next decade.

△ **BR (W) Gas Turbine No.18000, 1949**

Wheel arrangement	A1A-A1A
Transmission	electric
Engine	Brown Boveri Gas Turbine
Total power output	2,500 hp (1,865 kW)
Top speed	90 mph (145 km/h)

This revolutionary locomotive was delivered to British Railways in 1949 from Switzerland and was used for 10 years on the BR Western Region. In 1965 it left the UK and was used for research in Switzerland and Austria, returning in 1994 to the UK where it is now preserved.

△ **BR Class 08, 1953**

Wheel arrangement	0-6-0
Transmission	electric
Engine	English Electric 6KT
Total power output	350 hp (261 kW)
Top speed	20 mph (32 km/h)

Based on a wartime design of diesel shunter ordered by the London, Midland & Scottish Railway, over 950 Class 08 locomotives were built by five British Railways workshops between 1953 and 1959. Smaller batches of similar locomotives using different engines were also built. Sixty years on some remain in service. No. 08 604 *Phantom* is preserved at Didcot, UK.

△ **BR Class 05, 1954**

Wheel arrangement	0-6-0
Transmission	mechanical
Engine	Gardner 8L3
Total power output	201 hp (150 kW)
Top speed	17 mph (27 km/h)

This engine was one of several designs of smaller shunting locomotives delivered to British Railways in the 1950s. Later classified as Class 05, 69 were built between 1954 and 1961. Few remained in service for more than a decade as the freight traffic they were built for disappeared after the BR network was reduced following the Beeching Report.

◁ **English Electric prototype *Deltic*, 1955**

Wheel arrangement	Co-Co
Transmission	electric
Engine	2 x Napier Deltic D18-25 engines
Total power output	3,300 hp (2,460 kW)
Top speed	106 mph (171 km/h)

Built speculatively by English Electric, *Deltic* was the prototype for the 22 Type 5 *Deltic* D9000 Class 55 diesel locomotives bought for services on the East Coast route from London to York and Edinburgh. They were to replace the famous London & North Eastern Railway design A4 Pacific steam engines.

▷ BR Type 1 Class 20, 1957

Wheel arrangement Bo-Bo

Transmission electric

Engine English Electric 8SVT MkII

Total power output 986 hp (735 kW)

Top speed 75 mph (121 km/h)

This class was one of the most successful of all the Modernisation Plan locomotives. A total of 227 were built for British Railways between 1957 and 1968. The class saw limited passenger services but could work in multiples and, coupled together, could handle heavy traffic. Some remain in use with UK freight operators nearly 60 years later.

◁ BR Class 42, 1958

Wheel arrangement B-B

Transmission hydraulic

Engine 2 x Maybach MD650 engines

Total power output 2,100 hp (1,566 kW)

Top speed 90 mph (145 km/h)

These locomotives were based upon successful V200 engines that ran in West Germany and used the same engines as their German cousins. Known as *Warships*, they were used by British Railways principally on the Western Region from London Paddington to Devon, Cornwall, and South Wales until withdrawn from service in 1972. This is No. 801 *Vanguard*.

△ BR Class 108, 1958

Wheel arrangement 2-coach multiple unit

Transmission mechanical

Engine 2 x BUT/Leyland 6 cylinder

Total power output 300 hp (224 kW)

Top speed 70 mph (113 km/h)

British Railways's Modernisation Plan led to the replacement of steam locomotives, and more than 4,000 diesel multiple units were ordered. These new self-propelled "Derby Lightweight" trains were much cheaper to operate than the steam trains they replaced.

▷ BR Type 4 Class 40, 1958

Wheel arrangement 1Co-Co1

Transmission electric

Engine English Electric 16SVT MkII

Total power output 1,972 hp (1,471 kW)

Top speed 90 mph (145 km/h))

This class was designed to replace the fastest steam locomotives working express trains initially between London and Norwich and later all over the UK. The initial pilot batch of 10 was expanded to a final class of 200 by 1962.

Europe Follows the US

As Europe emerged from the chaos and damage inflicted by World War II, many railway companies based their future planning on the US where diesels had been replacing steam for nearly a decade. A wide variety of manufacturers using an equally wide choice of diesel engines built locomotives for state railways across Europe. Labour-intensive steam was replaced with diesels, which were cheaper to run although more expensive to buy. The process was gradual in most countries; some steam engines survived until 1977 in West Germany, and they never entirely disappeared in East Germany.

▽ **DB V200 (Class 220), 1954**

Wheel arrangement	B-B
Transmission	hydraulic
Engine	2 x Maybach MD 650 engines
Total power output	2,170 hp (1,618 kW)
Top speed	87 mph (140 km/h)

Designed to replace steam locomotives on heavy express passenger trains in the mid-1950s, the Class 220s were displaced to less important routes by electrification in the 1960s and 70s. All were withdrawn by the Deutsche Bundesbahn by 1984, but many went on to work for other operators in Greece, Switzerland, and Italy.

△ **NSB Class Di.3, 1955**

Wheel arrangement	Co-Co
Transmission	electric
Engine	EMD 16-567-C
Total power output	1,750 hp (1,305 kW)
Top speed	65 mph (105 km/h)

The Swedish firm Nydqvist & Holm AB (NoHAB) built diesel locomotives under license for the major US diesel locomotive builder EMD, then owned by General Motors. As well as the Di.3 locomotives, delivered in two types to Norwegian State Railways (Norges Statsbaner AS, or NSB), similar locomotives were supplied to Denmark and Hungary. The locomotives remain in service with freight operators in several European countries.

Diesel Shunters

While the big mainline diesel engines attracted attention, using diesel locomotives in shunting yards was just as transformational. While labour-intensive steam machines needed a team of operatives and had to be kept "in steam" even when at rest, diesel shunters could be operated by one person, and simply switched off when not in use. Crew conditions were better too and, in many cases, so was the visibility from the cab. The advantages of the diesels were recognized even before World War II, and after the conflict their use became more and more widespread. Many of the 1950s designs had long working lives.

△ **SNCF Class C 61000, 1950**

Wheel arrangement	0-6-0
Transmission	electric
Engine	Sulzer 6 LDA 22
Total power output	382 hp (285 kW)
Top speed	37 mph (60 km/h)

Ordered immediately after WWII in 1945, but not delivered until 1950-1953, the 48 C 61000 locomotives were used for shunting in freight yards and for short-distance freight. Twelve of the locomotives were used with coupled powered "slave" units to double the power available for shunting.

△ **DB VT11.5 (Class 601/602), 1957**

Wheel arrangement	B'2+2'2'+2'2'+2'2'+ 2'2'+2'2'+2'B
Transmission	hydraulic
Engine	2 x MTU engines
Total power output	2,060 hp (1,536 kW)
Top speed	100 mph (160 km/h)

The Class 601s were First Class only diesel-powered train sets used for Trans-Europ Express services from 1957 to 1972, reaching Paris, Milan, Amsterdam, and Ostende. Some were rebuilt as Class 602 from 1970 with 2,1450 hp (1,600 kW) gas turbines in place of the two diesel engines. The train sets were withdrawn from service in 1990.

△ **SNCF Class CC 65000, 1957**

Wheel arrangement	Bo-Bo
Transmission	electric
Engine	2 x SACM MGO VSHR V12
Total power output	1,824 hp (1,360 kW)
Top speed	81 mph (130 km/h)

Because of their shape these locomotives were nicknamed "Sous-marin" (submarines). Twenty were delivered to SNCF to replace steam locomotives in the west of France where they worked until the 1980s; all were withdrawn by 1988. Tested widely when new, their builder Alsthom also exported the design – 37 to Algeria and 25 to Argentina.

◁ **DB VT98 (Class 798), 1955**

Wheel arrangement	single-car rail bus
Transmission	mechanical
Engine	2 x Büssing AG U10 engines
Total power output	295 hp (220 kW)
Top speed	56 mph (90 km/h)

These rail bus vehicles were introduced in West Germany from 1953 to 1962 – initially the single-engined VT95 version, and then this more powerful two-engined VT98 version. In total 913 powered and 1,217 unpowered trailer cars (of both types) replaced steam locomotives on many rural lines across West Germany.

◁ **PKP Class SM30, 1957**

Wheel arrangement	Bo-Bo
Transmission	electric
Engine	Wola V-300
Total power output	295 hp (220 kW)
Top speed	37 mph (60 km/h)

This was the first diesel-electric locomotive designed and built in Poland – its initial models used an engine originally designed for army tanks. Ultimately 909 of the locomotives were built by Fablok in Chrzanów in southern Poland between 1956 and 1970, many for industrial users. Polish State Railways (or PKP) received 302. Some were still in use in 2014.

△ **DR V15 (Class 101), 1959**

Wheel arrangement	0-4-0
Transmission	hydraulic
Engine	6 KVD 18 SRW
Total power output	148 hp (110 kW)
Top speed	22 mph (35 km/h)

The East German V15 (and later V18) diesel shunters were built in large numbers for both the Deutsche Reichsbahn and industrial rail operators such as mines and steelworks. Built in Potsdam by VEB Lokomotivbau Karl Marx Babelsberg, many were also exported to other Eastern Bloc countries.

Electric Charge

In the early part of the 20th century several European railways had already started to use electric rather than steam locomotives on main lines in the Swiss and Austrian Alps – they were among the first to use this powerful new technology. Plans to expand electrified railways were delayed almost everywhere in Europe by World War II, which led to the destruction of much railway infrastructure. As post-war rebuilding got underway, most European countries turned to electrified railways, and the 1950s saw new electric trains being widely introduced.

△ **BR Class 70 No. 20003, 1948**

Wheel arrangement Co-Co

Power supply 750 V DC third rail, overhead lines

Power rating 2,200 hp (1,641 kW)

Top speed 75 mph (120 km/h)

Following two similar locomotives (CC1/CC2) delivered to Southern Railway in 1941, No. 20003 was built at the Ashford Locomotive Works, Kent, in 1948 for British Railways. Like the earlier two it was used until the late 1960s, mainly on the London to Brighton main line and other Sussex routes.

◁ **BLS Ae 4/4, 1944**

Wheel arrangement Bo-Bo

Power supply 15 kV AC, 16²/₃ Hz, overhead lines

Power rating 3,950 hp (2,946 kW)

Top speed 78 mph (126 km/h)

Designed and built in Switzerland during WWII, the Ae 4/4 design was revolutionary, using a light steel body mounted on two-axle bogies. It produced nearly 4,000 hp (2,984 kW), which was the equivalent of two or three steam engines. These design principles have been used for electric locomotives ever since.

▽ **SNCF Class BB 9000, 1954**

Wheel arrangement Bo-Bo

Power supply 1,500 V DC, overhead lines

Power rating 4,000 hp (2,983 kW)

Top speed 206 mph (331 km/h)

This was one of two pairs of experimental express passenger engines using two-axle bogies that were delivered to the French state railways in 1952–54: BB 9003 and 9004 were built in France by Jeumont Schneider. On 29 March 1955 BB 9004 matched the world record of 206 mph (331 km/h) set the previous day by CC 7107, which was not beaten until 2006.

▷ BR Class EM1/ Class 76, 1954

Wheel arrangement Bo-Bo

Power supply 1,500 V DC, overhead lines

Power rating 1,868 hp (1,393 kW)

Top speed 65 mph (105 km/h)

Built for the electrification of the Manchester to Sheffield route via Woodhead, the first prototype was made for British Railways in 1940 but remained unused owing to WWII. It was tested in the Netherlands from 1947 to 1952, and was returned when the Woodhead line's electrification was completed.

◁ FS Class ETR, 1952

Wheel arrangement 7-car EMU

Power supply 3,000 kV DC, overhead lines

Power rating 3,487 hp (2,600 kW)

Top speed 124 mph (200 km/h)

Featuring a driving cab on the roof, and a panoramic lounge at the front with just 11 First Class seats, the "Settebello" (Seven of Diamonds – named after an Italian card game) was the epitome of both high-speed and luxury travel. They were introduced by the Italian state railways in the early 1950s. One "Settebello" still exists.

▷ BR Class AL1/ Class 81, 1959

Wheel arrangement Bo-Bo

Power supply 25 kV AC, overhead lines

Power rating 3,200 hp (2,387 kW)

Top speed 100 mph (161 km/h)

This was the first production AC electric locomotive class built in the UK for the first British 25 kV AC main line electrification of the London to Birmingham/Manchester/Liverpool line. As BR Class 81 the locomotives remained in service until 1991.

▽ DB Class E41/141, 1956

Wheel arrangement Bo-Bo

Power supply 15 kV AC, 16²⁄₃ Hz, overhead lines

Power rating 3,218 hp (2,401 kW)

Top speed 75 mph (120 km/h)

Large-scale plans for electrification of West Germany's railways during the 1950s led to large orders for several "Universal" locomotive types built by consortiums comprising all the major German locomotive-building firms. The E41 was the "universal" design for light passenger and freight trains. In total 451 were built between 1956 and 1971; all have now been withdrawn.

Post-war Steam

While railways played a vital strategic role in Europe during World War II, the ravages of war, destruction of industry, and shortages of raw materials and fuel painted a bleak picture for the Continent's future. Britain's railways and workshops escaped the worst excesses of destruction, and with innovative locomotive designers, such as Oliver Bulleid and Robert Riddles, were introducing new types of successful austerity locomotives towards the end of the war. In contrast, on mainland Europe the national railways were assisted in rebuilding their war-torn networks and rolling stock by deliveries of large numbers of powerful locomotives from US and Canadian manufacturers who were geared up to production through the Lend-Lease programme and the 1948 Marshall Plan.

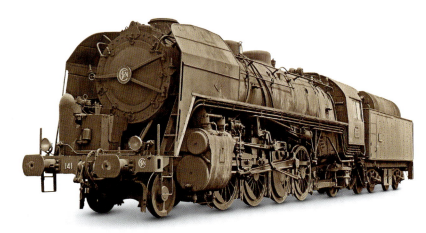

△ **SNCF 141R, 1945**

Wheel arrangement	2-8-2
Cylinders	2
Boiler pressure	225 psi (15.82 kg/sq cm)
Driving wheel diameter	65 in (1,650 mm)
Top speed	approx. 62 mph (100 km/h)

Powerful and economical to maintain, 1,323 Class 141R locomotives were built between 1945 and 1947 for the French state railway (Société Nationale des Chemins de fer Français, or SNCF) by various builders in the US and Canada. Supplied under the Lend-Lease programme to replace engines lost during WWII, around half were oil-burners. Many remained in service until the 1970s.

△ **Hunslet Austerity, 1944**

Wheel arrangement	0-6-0ST
Cylinders	2 (inside)
Boiler pressure	170 psi (11.95 kg/sq cm)
Driving wheel diameter	51 in (1,295 mm)
Top speed	approx. 35 mph (56 km/h)

Designed by the Hunslet Engine Co. of Leeds, these locomotives were chosen by the British War Department for use as its standard shunting engine during WWII. Introduced in 1944, the earlier batches saw action in Europe and North Africa, as well as on military bases and ports across Britain.

▷ **SNCB 29, 1945**

Wheel arrangement	2-8-0
Cylinders	2
Boiler pressure	231 psi (16.24 kg/sq cm)
Driving wheel diameter	59 in (1,500 mm)
Top speed	approx. 60 mph (96 km/h)

After WWII these powerful mixed-traffic engines were built in Canada under the Lend-Lease programme to help in the reopening of Belgium's ruined state railways – Société Nationale des Chemins de fer Belges. Of the 180 built, one example, No. 29.013, has been preserved and is on display at the Belgian national railway museum at Schaarbeek.

◁ **SR Bulleid Light Pacific, 1945**

Wheel arrangement	4-6-2
Cylinders	3 (1 inside)
Boiler pressure	280 psi (19.68 kg/sq cm)
Driving wheel diameter	74 in (1,880 mm)
Top speed	approx. 80 mph (129 km/h)

Built under wartime conditions, Oliver Bulleid's "Battle of Britain" and "West Country" Class Light Pacific locomotives incorporated many cost-saving and innovative features. The 110 locomotives built for the Southern Railway and British Railways between 1945 and 1951 were renowned for their performance but suffered from high coal consumption. Sixty were subsequently rebuilt.

◁ **GWR Modified Hall, 1944**

Wheel arrangement	4-6-0
Cylinders	2
Boiler pressure	225 psi (15.82 kg sq cm)
Driving wheel diameter	70 in (1,778 mm)
Top speed	approx. 75 mph (121 km/h)

Fitted with a large, three-row superheater to make up for the low-quality coal then available, these engines were a development by Frederick Hawksworth of Charles Collett's Hall Class. Between 1944 and 1950, a total of 71 were built at the Great Western Railway's Swindon Works.

◁ **PKP Class Pt47, 1948**

Wheel arrangement	2-8-2
Cylinders	2
Boiler pressure	213 psi (15 kg/sq cm)
Driving wheel diameter	72³/₄in (1,850 mm)
Top speed	approx. 68 mph (109 km/h)

Built by Fablok and Cegielski for the Polish state railways (Polskie Koleje Panstwowe, or PKP from 1948 to 1951, these engines achieved outstanding performances hauling heavy passenger trains over long distances.

△ **SNCF 241P, 1948**

Wheel arrangement	4-8-2
Cylinders	4 (2 high-pressure, 2 low-pressure)
Boiler pressure	284 psi (19.96 kg/sq cm)
Driving wheel diameter	78³/₄in (2,000 mm)
Top speed	75 mph (121 km/h)

These powerful "Mountain"-type express passenger compound locomotives were built by Schneider for the French state railway (SNCF) between 1948 and 1952. Designed to haul trains weighing 800 tons (813 tonnes) on the Paris to Marseilles main line, they were soon made redundant by electrification.

◁ **Andrew Barclay Industrial, 1949**

Wheel arrangement	0-4-0ST
Cylinders	2
Boiler pressure	160 psi (11.25 kg/sq cm)
Driving wheel diameter	35¹/₂in (900 mm)
Top speed	approx. 20 mph (32 km/h)

Scottish locomotive company Andrew Barclay built 100s of these diminutive saddle tanks for use on privately owned industrial railways in Britain and abroad. Their short wheelbase enabled them to operate on the sharply curved lines at collieries, steel and gas works, and docks.

World Steam's Last Stand

With seemingly unlimited supplies of cheap foreign oil, by the 1960s many European and North American railways had replaced their steam engines with modern diesel-electric and electric engines, which were not only more efficient, powerful, and cleaner, but also required less maintenance between journeys. However, in other parts of the world where coal supplies were abundant and labour was cheap, steam continued to reign for a few more decades. In South Africa the development of steam locomotive design reached its pinnacle in the 1980s with the "Red Devil". Ending in 2005, the awesome spectacle of QJ 2-10-2 double-headed freight trains running through the frozen wastes of Inner Mongolia marked the final chapter of steam's 200-year reign.

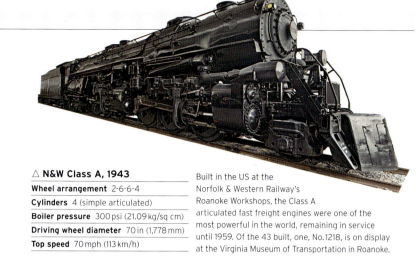

△ N&W Class A, 1943

Wheel arrangement	2-6-6-4
Cylinders	4 (simple articulated)
Boiler pressure	300 psi (21.09 kg/sq cm)
Driving wheel diameter	70 in (1,778 mm)
Top speed	70 mph (113 km/h)

Built in the US at the Norfolk & Western Railway's Roanoke Workshops, the Class A articulated fast freight engines were one of the most powerful in the world, remaining in service until 1959. Of the 43 built, one, No.1218, is on display at the Virginia Museum of Transportation in Roanoke.

△ IR Class WP, 1947

Wheel arrangement	4-6-2
Cylinders	2
Boiler pressure	210 psi (14.78 kg/sq cm)
Driving wheel diameter	67 in (1,700 mm)
Top speed	68 mph (109 km/h)

Featuring a distinctive cone-shaped nose decorated with a silver star, 755 of the Class WP express passenger engines were built for the Indian broad-gauge railways between 1947 and 1967. No.7161 *Akbar* is preserved at the Rewari Steam Loco Shed, India.

◁ Soviet Class P36, 1949

Wheel arrangement	4-8-4
Cylinders	2
Boiler pressure	213 psi (15 kg/sq cm)
Driving wheel diameter	73 in (1,854 mm)
Top speed	78 mph (126 km/h)

Built between 1949 and 1956, the 251 Class P36 were the last Soviet standard class, first working on the Moscow to Leningrad line until replaced by diesels. They later saw service in Eastern Siberia until being put into strategic storage from 1974 to the late 1980s.

▷ N&W J Class, 1950

Wheel arrangement	4-8-4
Cylinders	2
Boiler pressure	300 psi (21.09 kg/sq cm)
Driving wheel diameter	70 in (1,778 mm)
Top speed	70 mph (113 km/h)

A total of 14 J Class express passenger locomotives were built at the Norfolk & Western Railway's Roanoke Workshops between 1941 and 1950. Fitted with futuristic streamlined casings, they were soon replaced by diesels and had all retired by 1959.

▷ UP Class 4000 "Big Boy", 1941

Wheel arrangement	4-8-8-4
Cylinders	4
Boiler pressure	300 psi (21.09 kg/sq cm)
Driving wheel diameter	68 in (1,730 mm)
Top speed	80 mph (129 km/h)

Twenty-five of these monster articulated locomotives were built by the American Locomotive Co. (ALCO) for the Union Pacific Railroad between 1941 and 1944. Nicknamed "Big Boys", they were designed to haul heavy freight trains unaided over the Wasatch Range between Wyoming and Utah before being replaced by diesels in 1959. Eight have been preserved of which No.4014 is being restored to working order.

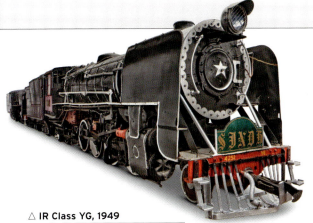

△ IR Class YG, 1949

Wheel arrangement 2-8-2

Cylinders 2

Boiler pressure 210 psi (14.8 kg/sq cm)

Driving wheel diameter 48 in (1,220 mm)

Top speed 50 mph (80 km/h)

The Class YG was the standard freight locomotive on the Indian Railways 3-ft 3-in- (1-m-) gauge system. Around 1,000 were built by various manufacturers in India and overseas between 1949 and 1972. Three, including *Sindh* seen here, are preserved in working order at Rewari Steam Loco Shed southwest of Delhi.

TALKING POINT

Cutting-edge Steam

Apart from the Class 25 condensing engines, South African Railways also took delivery of 50 Class 25NC (non-condensing). Of these, No. 3450 was modified in 1981 at the SAR's Salt River Workshops in Cape Town as the prototype Class 26. Nicknamed the "Red Devil" because of its livery, tests demonstrated vastly increased power and savings; diesel and electric traction had virtually replaced steam by the early 1980s.

The Red Devil This unique engine is seen here leaving Krankuil with a South African rail tour in 1990. It last ran in 2003 and is now preserved in Cape Town.

▷ SAR Class 25C, 1953

Wheel arrangement 4-8-4

Cylinders 2

Boiler pressure 225 psi (15.81 kg/sq cm)

Driving wheel diameter 60 in (1,524 mm)

Top speed 70 mph (113 km/h)

A total of 90 Class 25C locomotives were built for the 3-ft-6-in- (1.06-m-) gauge South African Railways. The engines were originally fitted with an enormous condensing tender so that they could operate across the arid Karoo Desert. Most were later converted to a non-condensing Class 25NC between 1973 and 1980.

△ IR Class WL, 1955

Wheel arrangement 4-6-2

Cylinders 2

Boiler pressure 210 psi (14.8 kg/sq cm)

Driving wheel diameter 67 in (1,702 mm)

Top speed 60 mph (96 km/h)

Featuring a light axle load for work on branch lines, these broad-gauge steam engines were built for the Indian Railways in two batches: the first 10 by Vulcan Foundry (UK) and 94 at the Chittaranjan Locomotive Works (India). No. 15005 *Sher-e-Punjab* is preserved at Rewari.

▷ China Railways Class QJ, 1956

Wheel arrangement 2-10-2

Cylinders 2

Boiler pressure 213 psi (15 kg/sq cm)

Driving wheel diameter 59 in (1,500 mm)

Top speed 50 mph (80 km/h)

One of the most prolific classes constructed in China was the Class QJ heavy freight engine of which at least 4,700 were built between 1956 and 1988. Their service on the Jitong Railway in Inner Mongolia (China) ended in 2005, though some ran on industrial railways until 2010.

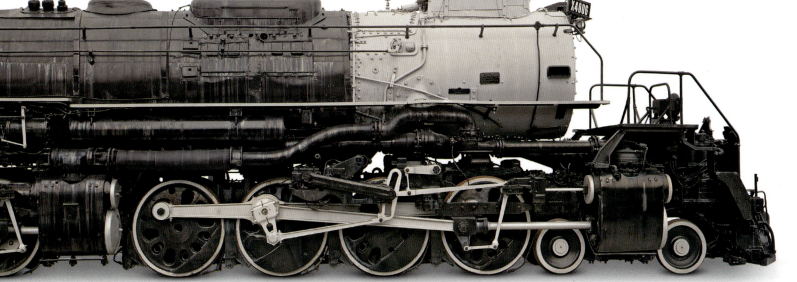

Europe's Last Gasp

With diesel and electric traction rapidly gaining favour, the 1950s saw the last steam locomotives built for Europe's national railways. In West Germany the last one to be built for Deutsche Bundesbahn, No. 23.105, rolled off the production line in 1959. Across the English Channel, Robert Riddles had designed 12 new classes of standard locomotives for the nationalized British Railways. Sadly, many of these fine engines had extremely short working lives owing to the hurried implementation of the ill-conceived Modernisation Plan. Despite this, privately owned British locomotive manufacturers such as Beyer Peacock & Co. of Manchester and Hunslet of Leeds continued to export steam locomotives; the last engine was built by Hunslet in 1971.

◁ DB Class 23, 1950

Wheel arrangement	2-6-2
Cylinders	2
Boiler pressure	232 psi (16.3 kg/sq cm)
Driving wheel diameter	69 in (1,750 mm)
Top speed	68 mph (110 km/h)

This engine was designed to replace the Prussian Class P8 passenger locomotives on the West German Deutsche Bundesbahn. The 105 Class 23s were built between 1950 and 1959. No. 23.105 was the last steam locomotive built for DB. The final examples were retired in 1976 and eight have been preserved.

△ *Bonnie Prince Charlie*, 1951

Wheel arrangement	0-4-0ST
Cylinders	2
Boiler pressure	160 psi (11.25 kg/sq cm)
Driving wheel diameter	24 in (610 mm)
Top speed	20 mph (32 km/h)

Built by Robert Stephenson & Hawthorns in 1951, *Bonnie Prince Charlie* originally worked as a gas works shunter at Hamworthy Quay in Dorset (UK). It was bought by the Salisbury Steam Trust in 1969 and has since been restored at Didcot Railway Centre.

▷ BR Class 4MT, 1951

Wheel arrangement	2-6-4T
Cylinders	2
Boiler pressure	225 psi (15.82 kg/sq cm)
Driving wheel diameter	68 in (1,730 mm)
Top speed	70 mph (113 km/h)

Robert Riddles's Class 4MT tank locomotive was the largest of four standard tank designs built by British Railways. Used primarily on suburban commuter services, a total of 155 were built between 1951 and 1956 but were soon displaced by electrification.

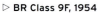

▷ BR Class 9F, 1954

Wheel arrangement	2-10-0
Cylinders	2
Boiler pressure	250 psi (17.57 kg/sq cm)
Driving wheel diameter	60 in (1,524 mm)
Top speed	90 mph (145 km/h)

The Class 9F was the standard heavy freight locomotive built by British Railways between 1954 and 1960. A total of 251 were built with No. 92220 *Evening Star* being the last steam engine built for BR. Although designed for freight haulage, they were occasionally used on express passenger duties. All were retired by 1968, and nine have been preserved.

▷ BR Class 7 Britannia, 1951

Wheel arrangement	4-6-2
Cylinders	2
Boiler pressure	250 psi (17.57 kg/sq cm)
Driving wheel diameter	74 in (1,880 mm)
Top speed	90 mph (145 km/h)

A total of 55 Class 7 Britannia engines, designed by Robert Riddles, were built at British Railway's Crewe Works between 1951 and 1954. After hauling expresses across the BR network, they were relegated to more humble duties. One lasted until the end of BR mainline steam in 1968.

△ DR Class 65.10, 1954

Wheel arrangement	2-8-4T
Cylinders	2
Boiler pressure	232 psi (16.3 kg/sq cm)
Driving wheel diameter	63 in (1,600 mm)
Top speed	56 mph (90 km/h)

The powerful Class 65.10 tank locomotives were built to haul double-deck and push-pull commuter trains on the Deutsche Reichsbahn in East Germany. All 88 built had retired by 1977, but three have been preserved.

◁ DR Class 99.23-24, 1954

Wheel arrangement	2-10-2T
Cylinders	2
Boiler pressure	203 psi (14.27 kg/sq cm)
Driving wheel diameter	39½ in (1,003 mm)
Top speed	25 mph (40 km/h)

Seventeen of these massive 3-ft 3-in- (1-m-) gauge tank locomotives were built for the Deutsche Reichsbahn in East Germany from 1954 to 1956. They still survive on the highly scenic railways in the Harz Mountains with nine currently in working order.

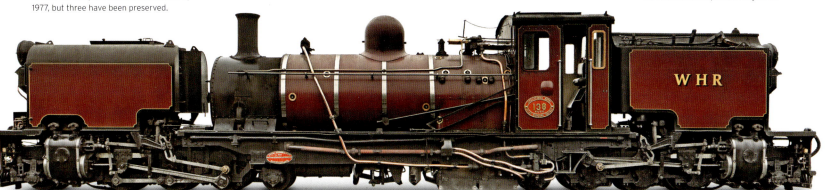

△ Beyer-Garratt Class NG G16, 1958

Wheel arrangement	2-6-2+2-6-2
Cylinders	4
Boiler pressure	180 psi (12.65 kg/sq cm)
Driving wheel diameter	33 in (840 mm)
Top speed	40 mph (64 km/h)

Several European manufacturers built 34 of these engines from 1937 to 1968 for the 2-ft- (0.61-m-) gauge lines of South African Railways. No.138, built by Beyer Peacock & Co., now hauls trains on the Welsh Highland Railway.

Moving People and Goods

Although the very first railways were built to carry freight, some were designed from the start primarily to transport passengers. During the world wars, the railways carried huge quantities of raw materials, military supplies, and troops. However, by the 1950s they struggled against more flexible and cheaper road transport. Meeting this challenge with some success, the railways carved out the vital roles of transporting commuters. They competed with air travel by introducing faster and more luxurious passenger trains and focussed on the long-haul, heavy-freight traffic that remains a core business today.

△ GWR Corridor Composite carriage No. 7313, 1940

Type 2 x 4-wheel bogies

Capacity 24 first-class passengers plus 24 third-class passengers

Construction steel

Railway Great Western Railway

Built by the Great Western Railway at their Swindon Works in 1940, the 60-ft- (18.2-m-) long express passenger coach No. 7313 has four first-Class compartments, four third-Class compartments, and two lavatory cubicles. It is wearing its "wartime economy" brown livery and is preserved at Didcot Railway Centre.

△ N&W Budd S1 sleeper, 1949

Type 2 x 4-wheel bogies

Capacity 22-32 sleeping berths

Construction stainless steel

Railway Norfolk & Western Railway

Twenty of these sleeping cars were built by Budd in 1949 for the Norfolk & Western Railway. They were used on the *Powhatan Arrow*, *The Pochohontas*, and other sleeping car routes on the railway's network. *The Pochohontas*, the N&W's last passenger train, ceased running in 1971. This car is now preserved at the Virginia Museum of Transport in Roanoke.

▷ N&W Pullman Class P2 No. 512, 1949

Type 2 x 4-wheel bogies

Capacity 66 passengers

Construction steel

Railway Norfolk & Western Railway

Seating 66 passengers, this coach was built for the Norfolk & Western Railway's *Powhatan Arrow* by Pullman-Standard in 1949. Introduced between Norfolk, Virginia, and Cincinnati, Ohio, in 1946, the train last ran in 1969. This coach is now on display at the Virginia Museum of Transport in Roanoke.

Freight Cars

Road transport began siphoning off much of the peacetime short-distance, single-load freight traffic, but the railways' trump card was their ability to transport heavy loads more efficiently over long distances. To meet this demand a wide variety of purpose-built freight cars were constructed to carry raw materials such as coal, oil, and iron ore; perishable goods such as fish, meat, fruit and vegetables; and hazardous cargoes such as chemicals and petroleum.

△ Penn Central Wagon No. 32367, 1955

Type Class H34A covered hopper

Weight 62½ tons (63.5 tonnes)

Construction steel

Railway Penn Central

The Wagon No. 32367 was built at the Penn Central Corporation's Altoona Workshops in 1955. The cargo (often grain) was discharged through chutes underneath the wagon. It is now on display at the Railroad Museum of Pennsylvania in Strasburg.

▷ VEB double-deck coach, 1951

Type 2- to 5-car articulated coach sets

Capacity approx. 135 passengers per coach

Construction steel

Railway Deutsche Reichsbahn

Known as Doppelstockwagen in Germany, these double-deck coaches are descended from those introduced on the Lübeck–Büchen Railway in 1935. Built by Waggonbau Görlitz, they were capable of carrying 50 per cent more passengers than single-deck coaches. Seen here are the first of around 4,000 double-deck, articulated coaches built in East Germany on a test run in 1951.

Travelling in Comfort

While the Railway Regulations Act of 1847 made it compulsory for Britain's railways to provide poorer people with travelling accommodation at an affordable price, the well-heeled traveller was charged much more for comfort. Up until 1956 there were three classes of travel – first, second, and third. Second class was then abolished. First-class compartments offered plenty of legroom, and luxury seating, carpets, and curtains. Third-class passengers were squashed into more basic compartments with horse-hair seats.

Class distinction The first-class compartment (below, left) features curtains, carpets, and individual wingbacks and armrests for its six passengers. Third class (below, right) has a less comfortable bench-seat arrangement.

◁ BR(W) Brake Third carriage No. 2202, 1950

Type 2 x 4-wheel bogies

Capacity 24 Third Class passengers plus guard's and luggage compartments

Construction steel

Railway British Railways (Western Region)

Featuring distinctive domed roof ends and designed by the Great Western Railway's last chief mechanical engineer, F. W. Hawksworth, this Brake Third carriage was built in 1950 for British Railways (Western Region) by Metropolitan-Cammell of Birmingham. It is now preserved at Didcot Railway Centre.

◁ DR Acid Cannister Wagon, 1956

Type cannister wagon

Weight 14.6 tons (14.83 tonnes)

Construction steel

Railway Deutsche Reichsbahn

Built in 1956 for the East German state railways, this freight wagon carried 12 clay pots, each containing 220 gallons (1,000 litres) of acid. It is on display at the Stassfurt Museum Shed.

△ MDT/IC No. 13715, 1958

Type refrigerated boxcar

Weight 37½ tons (38 tonnes)

Construction steel

Railway Illinois Central Railroad

This 33-ft- (10-m-) long, insulated, refrigerated boxcar was built by the Pacific Car & Foundry Co. of Renton in Washington State for the Illinois Central Railroad in 1958. Fitted with air circulation fans, this type of car usually carried perishable fruit and vegetables, which were kept chilled by dry ice loaded into roof-mounted bunkers.

Trains
1960 to present

Freight and Passenger Accelerates

During the 1960s and 1970s railways around the world followed the early lead of North America and replaced steam with either diesel or electric locomotives. The growth in car ownership in many Western countries meant that railways had to offer faster and more comfortable trains to persuade passengers to use the train instead. Freight services – historically very slow – gathered speed through the introduction of new locomotives that were twice as fast and twice as powerful as the steam locomotives they replaced.

△ **BR Type 4 Class 47, 1962**

Wheel arrangement	Co-Co
Transmission	electric
Engine	Sulzer 12LDA28-C
Total power output	2,750 hp (2,051 kW)
Top speed	95 mph (153 km/h)

The most numerous main-line diesel locomotives ever used in the UK, the first 20 Class 47s were delivered in 1962/63 and tested on British Railway's Eastern Region. Orders for more soon followed, and a total of 512 were built by both Brush Traction's Falcon Works and BR's Crewe Works. Some remain in use with British operators.

▷ **Soviet Class M62, 1964**

Wheel arrangement	Co-Co
Transmission	electric
Engine	Kolomna V12 14D40
Total power output	1,973 hp (1,472 kW)
Top speed	62 mph (100 km/h)

The Soviet M62 design was exported to Warsaw Pact countries in the 1960s and 1970s, as well as being delivered to Soviet Railways. Between 1966 and 1979 Czechoslovakia received 599 of them from Voroshilovgrad Locomotive works (in present-day Ukraine). Production only ended in 1994 and one is shown here.

△ **DR V180, 1960**

Wheel arrangement	B-B
Transmission	hydraulic
Engine	2 x 12KVD21 A-2
Total power output	1,800 hp (1,342 kW)
Top speed	75 mph (120 km/h)

The V180 was designed to replace steam engines on main-line passenger and freight trains in two versions – as well as the initial 87 four-axle versions, a further 206 more powerful six-axle locomotives, were delivered by 1970 and subsequently renumbered as DR Class 118.

◁ **DR V100, 1966**

Wheel arrangement	B-B
Transmission	hydraulic
Engine	MWJ 12 KVD 18-21 A-3
Total power output	987 hp (736 kW)
Top speed	50 mph (80 km/h)

The East German V100 centre-cab design was first tested in 1964, and in total 1,146 production locomotives of several types were built for the Deutsche Reichsbahn from 1966 to 1985. The V100s were also exported to several other communist countries such as Czechoslovakia and China.

▽ **GM EMD Class SD45, 1965**

Wheel arrangement	Co-Co
Transmission	electric
Engine	20-cylinder EMD 645E3
Total power output	3,600 hp (2,685 kW)
Top speed	65 mph (105 km/h)

General Motors Electro-Motive Division (EMD) built 1,260 SD45 locomotives from 1965 to 1971 for several US railways, using a 20-cylinder version of EMD's then new 645 engine. Some SD45s remain in use in the US freight railroads. Shown here is Erie Lackawanna Railway's No. 3607, which has been preserved.

△ **GM EMD GP40, 1965**

Wheel arrangement	Bo-Bo
Transmission	electric
Engine	16-645E3
Total power output	3,000 hp (2,237 kW)
Top speed	65 mph (105 km/h)

Baltimore & Ohio Railroad bought 380 General Motors Electro-Motive Division (EMD) model GP40 locomotives so had the largest fleet in the US of these successful locomotives. In total 1,221 were built for various operators in North America between 1965 and 1971. They were used for freight trains by B&O but other operators used them for passenger services.

◁ **DB Class 218 (V160), 1971**

Wheel arrangement	B-B
Transmission	hydraulic
Engine	MTU MA 12 V 956 TB 10
Total power output	2,467 hp (1,840 kW)
Top speed	87 mph (140 km/h)

The Deutsche Bundesbahn first ordered the final version of the V160 fleet – Class 218 – in the late 1950s. The prototypes were delivered in 1968 and 1969; series production began in 1971. Fitted with electric train heating, the Class 218 could work with the latest air-conditioned passenger coaches. Of the 418 delivered, around half remain in use.

△ **Chinese DF4, 1969**

Wheel arrangement	Co-Co
Transmission	electric
Engine	16V240ZJA
Total power output	3,251 hp (2,425 kW)
Top speed	62 mph (100 km/h)

The DF4, known as "Dong Feng" (East Wind), is one of a series of locomotives built for the Chinese national railways. Updated versions remain in production over 40 years after the first one was built at China's Dalian Locomotive Works. DF4s replaced steam locomotives throughout China and several thousand remain in use.

TECHNOLOGY

Container Transport

The use of containers to transport freight by ship began in the 1950s. In 1952 Canadian Pacific introduced the "piggyback" transport of containers on wheeled road trailers, although the Chicago North Western Railroad had pioneered this before World War II. During the 1960s rail operators started to offer services to transport the maritime containers (called "intermodal" as they can be transferred from one form of transport to another) to and from ports on specially designed flat wagons. Intermodal freight transport grew substantially in the 1970s and 1980s. In 1957 it accounted for less than one per cent of US rail freight, but by the mid 1980s more than 15 per cent of freight was transported in this way.

B&O Class P-34 No. 9523 This is a 40-ton (40.64-tonne) flat car for carrying road semitrailers. It was built by B&O in 1960 at its workshops in Dubois, Pennsylvania.

High-speed Pioneers

High-speed rail travel began in 1960 when French Railways introduced the world's first 124-mph (200-km/h) passenger train – the "Le Capitole" Paris to Toulouse service. In 1964 the first Japanese Shinkansen line from Tokyo to Shin-Osaka was opened; this was the start of fast passenger train services on a dedicated high-speed rail line. Higher-speed operations began in the UK with the 100-mph (161-km/h) "Deltic" diesels in 1961, and in North America with gas-turbine–powered trains in 1968. In the 1970s the German Class E03/103 began a 124-mph (200-km/h) operation on existing lines in West Germany, while in the UK the new diesel-powered High Speed Train (HST) brought 125-mph (201-km/h) services to several major routes from 1976.

△ JNR Shinkansen Series 0, 1964

Wheel arrangement	12-car EMU, all 48 axles powered
Power supply	25 kV 60 Hz AC catenary
Power rating	11,903 hp (8,880 kW)
Top speed	137 mph (220 km/h)

Japan built brand-new, standard-gauge (4-ft 8½-in/1.4-m) high-speed lines to dramatically improve journey times. The first section of Japan National Railways' Tōkaidō Shinkansen line operated at 130 mph (209 km/h) – at the time the fastest trains in the world.

△ DR Class VT18.16 (Class 175), 1964

Wheel arrangement	4-car DMU
Transmission	hydraulic
Engine	2 x 12 KVD 18/21 engines
Total power output	1,973 hp (1,472 kW)
Top speed	100 mph (160 km/h)

Built by East German industry to operate the Deutsche Reichsbahn's important international express trains, eight four-car VT18.16 trains were delivered from 1964 to 1968. These worked abroad reaching Copenhagen, Denmark; Vienna, Austria; and Malmö, Sweden; plus Prague and Karlovy Vary in Czechoslovakia. The trains were progressively withdrawn in the 1980s, although more than one survives.

▽ BR Type 5 *Deltic* D9000 Class 55, 1961

Wheel arrangement	CoCo
Transmission	electric
Engine	2 x Napier Deltic 18-25 engines
Total power output	3,299 hp (2,461 kW)
Top speed	100 mph (161 km/h)

Based on the *Deltic* prototype of 1955, a total of 22 of these engines were ordered for express passenger trains on British Railways' East Coast main line between London, York, Newcastle, and Edinburgh to replace 55 steam locomotives. Capable of sustained 100 mph (161 km/h) running, the class enabled faster trains to be operated on the route from 1963. Withdrawn in 1981, several have been preserved in working order.

TECHNOLOGY

Amtrak Begins Service

The US National Railroad Passenger Corporation (Amtrak) took over long-distance passenger rail services in May 1971, following a US Congress decision to maintain some level of rail service after many companies had moved to freight only. Amtrak started life with old equipment, but quickly started looking for new diesel and electric trains including new French-built Turboliner trains.

THE TRAIN OF THE FUTURE IS YEARS AHEAD OF SCHEDULE

Amtrak

Amtrak's new turboliner-the train of the future-is here today. Turboliners now serve New York State, Montreal, Chicago, Detroit, Milwaukee, and Port Huron.

The turbo train Amtrak introduced six 125-mph (201-km/h) Turboliner trains from 1973 on services from Chicago. Powered by Turbomeca gas turbines originally designed for helicopters, the trains never got to exploit their high-speed capability.

△ DB Class E03/103, 1970

Wheel arrangement CoCo

Power supply 15 kV AC, 16²/₃ Hz overhead lines

Power rating 10,429 hp (7,780 kW)

Top speed 124 mph (200 km/h)

Five E03 prototypes were delivered from 1965, and after test, another 145 slightly more powerful production engines were ordered. From 1970 until the 1980s the Deutsche Bundesbahn Class 103 worked on all the major express trains in Germany. A small number remain in use; one was used for high-speed test trains until 2013 and allowed to run at 174 mph (280 km/h).

▽ SNCF Class CC6500, 1969

Wheel arrangement CoCo

Power supply 1.5 kV DC overhead lines (21 locos also equipped for 1.5 kV DC third rail)

Power rating 7,909 hp (5,900 kW)

Top speed 124 mph (200 km/h)

Seventy-four powerful CC6500 engines were delivered between 1969 and 1975 to run on the Société Nationale des Chemins de fer Français' "Le Capitole" Paris to Toulouse service. Twenty-one were fitted with third-rail pick-up and pantographs, for use on the Chambéry-Modane "Maurienne" line.

△ UAC Turbo Train, 1968

Wheel arrangement 7-car articulated train set

Transmission torque coupler

Engine 4 x Pratt & Whitney Canada ST6B gas turbines

Total power output 1,600 hp (1,193 kW)

Top speed 120 mph (193 km/h)

United Aircraft Corporation (UAC) entered the market with patents bought from the Chesapeake & Ohio Railway for articulated high-speed train sets using lightweight materials. However, UAC used gas turbines instead of diesel engines. Canadian National Rail bought five sets and the US bought three.

▽ BR HST Class 253/254, 1976

Wheel arrangement BoBo

Transmission electric

Engine (power car) Paxman Valenta 12R200L

Total power output (power car) 2,249 hp (1,678 kW)

Top speed 125 mph (201 km/h)

In 1973 British Rail started trials of the High Speed Train prototype with two power cars. Production trains followed in 1976, with deliveries lasting until 1982. The HST holds the world diesel rail speed record of 148 mph (238 km/h) set in 1987. The trains remain in service as do similar ones in Australia.

Technology in Transition

This was a period of large-scale changes for railways around the world. Car ownership and the impact of new motorways led to the closure of less-used railway routes, particularly in Western Europe, although branch lines still thrived in Eastern Europe. Commodities such as coal and iron ore continued to be carried by the railways. Much of the local goods transport switched to trucks, but the use of intermodal containers to carry long-distance freight by rail continued to grow. In addition, many European cities were expanding existing metro systems or building new ones.

△ BR D9500 Class 14, 1964

Wheel arrangement	0-6-0
Transmission	hydraulic
Engine	Paxman 6YJXL
Total power output	650 hp (485 kW)
Top speed	40 mph (64 km/h)

The 56 locomotives in this class, all built at the British Railways Works in Swindon during 1964, were delivered just as the local freight traffic they were designed for was rapidly disappearing from the UK rail network. As a result many were withdrawn within three years. Most went on to have longer careers with industrial rail operators in the UK and Europe.

◁ Soviet Class VL10, 1963

Wheel arrangement	Bo-Bo+Bo-Bo
Power supply	3,000 V DC, overhead lines
Power rating	6,166 hp (4,600 kW)
Top speed	62 mph (100 km/h)

Built in Tbilisi (now Georgia) the VL10 eight-axle, twin-unit electric was the first modern DC electric locomotive built for Soviet Railways. It shared both external design and many components with the VL80 25 kV AC electric design, also introduced in 1963. Thousands of both classes were built until production ended in the 1980s.

△ DR VT2.09 (Class 171/172), 1962

Wheel arrangement	2 axle rail bus
Transmission	mechanical/hydro-mechanical
Engine	6 KVD 18 HRW
Total power output	180 hp (134 kW)
Top speed	56 mph (90 km/h)

Designed for East Germany's rural branch lines, this train was nicknamed "Ferkeltaxi" (piglet taxi) because farmers sometimes brought piglets along as luggage. An early prototype built in 1957 was followed by orders for production trains, delivered from 1962 to 1969. In 2004 they were withdrawn from regular use in Germany.

TALKING POINT

Track Maintenance

Motorized draisines replaced or supplemented daily track inspections carried out on foot from the 1960s, enabling tools and equipment to be carried to work sites quickly. During the 1960s ultrasonic testing of rails by test vehicles fitted with special equipment became more common in both US and Europe, and regular test trains operated, often at night, to monitor track condition.

Room for two In East Germany the two-axle draisine could carry two people and their tools to repair minor faults.

▷ DR V60 D (Class 105), 1961

Wheel arrangement	0-8-0
Transmission	hydraulic
Engine	12 KVD 18/21
Total power output	650 hp (485 kW)
Top speed	37 mph (60 km/h)

The powerful V60 was designed to replace the Deutsche Reichsbahn steam locomotives for shunting and short freight trains. The engines, enhanced by advances made on the WWII V36 diesels used by the German military, unusually had four axles with the wheels connected by external coupling rods. They were built for the DR and other state railways plus heavy industry in Eastern Bloc countries.

TECHNOLOGY

Battery Locomotives

In many European countries battery-powered engines were used to move locomotives around maintenance depots. Using the battery engines enabled electric locomotives to be transferred to maintenance areas without (hazardous) overhead power lines for traction current and was quicker and cheaper than starting a diesel to move it a few hundred yards. Battery engines continue to be used in this way today.

Akkuschleppfahrzeuge (ASF) Over 500 ASFs (meaning battery-shunting vehicle) were built in East Germany from 1966 to 1990. Used by DR and industrial operators, some are still working.

△ Preston Docks Sentinel, 1968

Wheel arrangement	A-A
Transmission	hydraulic
Engine	Rolls-Royce C8SFL
Total power output	325 hp (242 kW)
Top speed	18 mph (29 km/h)

The Sentinel locomotives were designed to replace steam engines at major industrial sites that operated their own railways. Innovative and easy to use, they had a central driving position in a full-width cab and safe places for shunting staff to travel on the outside of the engines. Several are preserved at UK heritage railways.

△ LT Victoria Line, 1969

Wheel arrangement	4-car units, always operated as pairs
Power supply	630 V DC third and fourth rail system
Power rating	1,137 hp (848 kW)
Top speed	25 mph (40 km/h)

The Victoria Line was the first completely new Tube line in London for 60 years when it opened in 1969. The new trains bought by London Transport were fitted with Automatic Train Operation (ATO) equipment – the train drove itself and the "driver" would normally only open and close doors at stations.

▽ DR V300 (Class 132), 1973

Wheel arrangement	Co-Co
Transmission	electric
Engine	Kolomna 5D49
Total power output	3,000 hp (2,237 kW)
Top speed	74 mph (120 km/h)

Based on the Soviet TE109 design and built at Voroshilovgrad (now Luhansk, Ukraine), the most numerous of the DR V300 locomotives was Class 132, with 709 locomotives. While most have been withdrawn, some remain in service with several German freight operators today.

Deutsche Reichsbahn

105 992-2

Travelling in Style

In the 1960s and 70s railways around the world invested in large numbers of new passenger carriages. The investment was partly driven by the need to offer higher speed and more comfort on intercity routes, and in other cases simply to replace older equipment. Steel became the dominant material for coach bodies, replacing wooden-framed, steam-age vehicles in many cases. Increasing numbers of new multiple-unit trains, both diesel and electric, were built in many countries to replace conventional trains using locomotives and coaches.

◁ Cravens Stock, 1963

Type second-class, open coach	
Capacity 64 passengers	
Construction steel	
Railway CIÉ (Irish railways)	

Fifty-eight of these coaches were assembled in Irish Railways's Inchicore Works in Dublin between 1963 and 1967, using kits provided by Cravens in Sheffield, UK. The coaches were fitted with steam heating and vacuum brakes, and were used for express trains in the 1960s. Several coaches have been preserved.

△ Talgo III, 1964

Type articulated express passenger car	
Capacity 21 passengers	
Construction stainless steel	
Railway RENFE (Spanish state railways)	

In the 1950s the Spanish Talgo company pioneered articulated trains of semi-permanently coupled short cars utilizing single-axle wheel sets. The Talgo III was the third version of the train and the first to be used internationally. Some had variable-gauge axles, which permitted operation from Spain into France.

△ Penn Central/Amtrak Metroliner, 1969

Type snack bar car (powered)	
Wheel arrangement 2-car EMU	
Power supply 11 kV AC 25 Hz, 11 kV AC 60 Hz, and 25 kV AC 60 Hz, overhead lines	
Power rating 1,020 hp (761 kW)	
Top speed 125 mph (200 km/h)	

Budd built 61 Metroliner EMU cars for Penn Central Transportation in 1969 in collaboration with other manufacturers and the US government. The cars were inherited by Amtrak in 1971. Designed for use at 150 mph (241 km/h), the Metroliners never operated that fast and most were withdrawn by Amtrak in the 1980s.

△ Reko-Wagen, 1967

Type second-class, open coach	
Capacity 64 passengers	
Construction steel	
Railway Deutsche Reichsbahn	

The Deutsche Reichsbahn introduced *Reko-Wagen* (reconstructed coaches) in the 1950s and 60s - the reconstruction referred to their rebuild from older designs. Initially, short three-axle coaches were built but in 1967 61-ft- (18.7-m-) long bogie coaches appeared.

△ Eurofima, 1973

Type first- and second-class open	
Capacity 54 (first); 66 (second)	
Construction steel	
Railway SBB (Swiss Railways; and others)	

In the mid-1970s several Western European railways jointly ordered 500 new daytime coaches to a standard design following tests with 10 prototypes. They were funded via Eurofima, a not-for-profit rail financing organization based in Switzerland. In total 500 coaches were built for six different operators.

▽ Mark IIIB First Open, 1975

Type	first class Pullman coach
Capacity	48 passengers
Construction	steel
Railway	British Rail

The first 125 mph (201 km/h) Mark III coaches appeared in 1975 and incorporated steel integral monocoque construction, giving them great body strength. The British Rail High Speed Train (HST) used Mark III coaches and others were built for use with electric locomotives at up to 110 mph (177 km/h).

△ Mark III sleeper, 1979

Type	sleeping coach
Capacity	26 berths in 13 compartments
Construction	steel
Railway	British Rail

In 1976 British Rail ordered a new prototype sleeper with a view to replacing its older cars, but this was cancelled after a fatal fire on Mark I sleepers on an overnight train in Taunton in 1978. BR decided to build a new version that incorporated safety systems onto all sleepers; 236 were ordered in 1979.

▷ Amtrak Superliner, 1978

Type	double-deck long distance
Capacity	up to 74, fewer for sleepers
Construction	stainless steel
Railway	Amtrak

Based upon cars originally built in 1956 for the Atchison, Topeka & Santa Fe Railway and inherited by Amtrak in 1971, the Superliner long-distance cars were built from 1978. Nearly 500 were made over the next 20 years in multiple configurations (sleepers, seating cars, diners, and observation cars).

High Speed Goes Global

Operating at speeds that were impossible on historic railway tracks, high-speed lines had burst upon the world scene in 1964 with the introduction of the Shinkansen in Japan. In Europe the French led the way, building a network of dedicated high-speed lines known as a Train à Grandes Vitesse (TGV), with the first route between Paris and Lyon opening in 1981. Spain's first high-speed line, the Alta Velocidad Española (AVE), opened between Madrid and Seville in 1992. The UK, with its Victorian rail network, lagged behind; despite the opening of the Channel Tunnel in 1994, it would not be until 2007 before the country's first dedicated high-speed railway HS1 was complete, ushering in high-speed rail travel between London and Paris.

▷ Soviet ER200, 1984

Wheel arrangement each car
2 x 4-wheel bogies

Power supply 3 kV DC overhead lines

Power rating 6-car set: 5,150 hp (3,840 kW)/14-car set: 15,448 hp (11,520 kW)

Top speed 124 mph (200 km/h)

Built of aluminium alloy in Riga, the ER200 is a Soviet high-speed train that was first introduced in 1984. At the time it was the first Direct Current (DC) intercity electric multiple-unit train with rheostatic braking. Later versions operate on the Moscow to St Petersburg main line. Unit ER200-15 is on display at the Moscow Railway Museum.

△ AVE S-100, 1992

Wheel arrangement each car
2 x 4-wheel bogies

Power supply 3 kV DC overhead supply/25 kV 50 Hz AC overhead supply

Power rating 11,796 hp (8,800 kW)

Top speed 186 mph (300 km/h)

The Alta Velocidad Española (AVE) is a network of high-speed railways operated in Spain by Renfe Operadora. It was Europe's longest high-speed network and, after China, the world's second longest. The first line between Madrid and Seville opened in 1992 using S-100 dual-voltage, electric multiple units built by Alstom.

▷ Thalys PBKA, 1996

Wheel arrangement 2 power cars
+ 8 passenger cars

Power supply 3 kV DC overhead supply/25 kV 50 Hz AC overhead supply/15 kV $16^2/_3$ Hz AC overhead supply/1,500 V DC overhead supply

Power rating 4,933 hp (3,680 kW) - 11,796 hp (8,800 kW)

Top speed 186 mph (300 km/h)

Built by GEC-Alstom in France, the Thalys PBKA is a high-speed international train service, introduced in 1996, that can operate on four different electrical systems in France, Germany, Switzerland, Belgium, and the Netherlands. The 17 train sets built operate services between Paris, Brussels, Cologne (Köln), and Amsterdam, hence PBKA.

TECHNOLOGY

Transrapid Prototype

Developed in Germany, this high-speed monorail train with no wheels, gear transmissions, or axles, and has no rails or overhead power supply. Instead it levitates, or hovers, above a track guideway using attractive magnetic force between two linear arrays of electromagnetic coils, hence its name "Maglev". Based on a patent from 1934, planning for it began in 1969 and the test facility was completed in 1987. The latest version Maglev 09 can cruise at over 300 mph (482 km/h). The only commercial application to date opened in China in 2002 and operates between Shanghai and its Pudong International Airport.

Revolutionary technology The two-car Maglev Transrapid prototype is seen in action at the test facility at the Emsland test track in Germany in 1980.

▷ Eurostar Class 373/1, 1993

Wheel arrangement each car
2 x 4-wheel bogies

Power supply 25 kV 50 Hz AC overhead supply/3,000 V DC overhead supply/1,500 V DC overhead supply/750 V DC third-rail (not used)

Power rating 4,600 hp (3,432 kW) - 16,360 hp (12,200 kW)

Top speed 186 mph (300 km/h)

Introduced in 1993, the Class 373/1 multi-voltage electric multiple units are operated by Eurostar on the high-speed line between London, Paris, and Brussels via the Channel Tunnel. In the UK these trains operated on the third-rail network to London's Waterloo Station until the completion of the HS1 line in 2007.

▷ SNCF LGV Sud-Est TGV, 1981

Wheel arrangement each car 2 x 4-wheel bogies
Power supply 1,500 V DC overhead supply/
25 kV 50 Hz AC overhead lines
Power rating 4,157 hp (3,100 kW) - 9,115 hp (6,800 kW)
Top speed 186 mph (300 km/h)

The French Train à Grande Vitesse (TGV) was
originally designed to be powered by gas turbines,
but the oil crisis of 1973 led to the first prototypes
being electrically powered. Built by GEC-Alstom,
the first of these dual-voltage high-speed trains
entered service on the LGV (Ligne à Grande Vitesse)
Sud-Est line between Paris and Lyon in 1981.

▷ SJ X2, 1989

Wheel arrangement each car 2 x 4-wheel bogies
Power supply 15 kV 16⅔ Hz AC overhead lines
Power rating 4,370 hp (3,260 kW)
Top speed 124 mph (200 km/h)

Built of corrugated stainless steel, the Swedish railways'
(Statens Järnvägar, or SJ) X2 high-speed tilting train is
designed to operate at speed on the country's existing
rail network. In tests it has reached 171 mph (276 km/h).
One train set was exported to China and others loaned
to Amtrak in the US and to Countrylink in Australia.

▷ DB ICE 1, 1991

Wheel arrangement each car
2 x 4-wheel bogies
Power supply 15 kV 16¾ Hz AC,
overhead supply
Power rating 5,094 hp (3,800 kW)-
6,437 hp (4,800 kW)
Top speed 174 mph (280 km/h)

Introduced in 1991, InterCityExpress
(ICE) 1 was Germany's first truly high-
speed public train. Sixty train sets
were built, each one consisting of
a power car at either end and either
12 or 14 passenger cars; a 12-car set
can accommodate 743 passengers.

Diesel's Next Generation

By the early 1980s the first home-grown generation of diesel–electric locomotives in Europe and North America had reached the end of their working lives. The US engine builders General Electric and the General Motors's EMD brand then began to dominate the scene on both continents with their highly successful, more powerful and efficient heavy-freight machines, which remain in operation today. In the UK, on the other hand, diesel locomotive building ended completely in 1987 when the last engine, BR Class 58 diesel–electric No. 58 050, rolled off the production line at the famous Doncaster Works.

△ **BR Class 58, 1984**

Wheel arrangement	Co-Co
Transmission	electric
Engine	Ruston Paxman 12-cylinder diesel
Total power output	3,300 hp (2,460 kW)
Top speed	80 mph (129 km/h)

Designed with an optimistic eye on export potential, 50 of the Class 58 heavy-freight, diesel-electric locomotives were built by British Rail Engineering Ltd at Doncaster between 1983 and 1987. They had a short working life in Britain with the last retired in 2002. Since then 30 have been hired for railways in the Netherlands, France, and Spain.

△ **Amtrak GE Genesis, 1992**

Wheel arrangement	B-B
Transmission	electric
Engine	General Electric V12 or V16 4-stroke supercharged diesel
Total power output	4,250 hp (3,170 kW)
Top speed	110 mph (177 km/h)

General Electric Transportation Systems built 321 of these low-profile, lightweight, diesel-electric locomotives between 1992 and 2001. They operate most of Amtrak's long-haul and high-speed rail services in the US and Canada. A dual-mode version can also collect 750 v DC current from third-rail in built-up areas such as New York.

△ **IÉ Class 201, 1994**

Wheel arrangement	Co-Co
Transmission	electric
Engine	EMD V12 2-stroke diesel
Total power output	3,200 hp (2,386 kW)
Top speed	102 mph (164 km/h)

Thirty-two of these powerful diesel-electric locomotives were built by General Motors in Ontario, Canada, for Iarnród Éireann in Ireland between 1994 and 1995. Two were also built for Northern Ireland Railways. They are all named after Irish rivers and operate on the Dublin to Cork express trains and on the *Enterprise* between Dublin and Belfast.

▷ **UP GM EMD Class SD60, 1984**

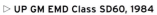

Wheel arrangement	C-C
Transmission	electric
Engine	EMD 16-cylinder diesel
Total power output	3,800 hp (2,834 kW)
Top speed	65 mph (105 km/h)

Built by General Motors, the heavy freight EMD Class SD60 diesel-electric locomotive was introduced in 1984. Production ceased in 1995 by which time 1,140 had been delivered to nine US railways, Canadian National Railways, and Brazil. Union Pacific Railroad bought 85 of the SD60, seen here, and 281 of the SD60M variant.

◁ **BR GM EMD Class 66, 1998**

Wheel arrangement Co-Co

Transmission electric

Engine EMD V12 two-stroke diesel

Total power output 3,000 hp (2,238 kW)

Top speed 75 mph (121 km/h)

A total of 446 of these diesel-electric freight locomotives were built by Electro-Motive Diesel in the US for Britain's railways between 1998 and 2008. Over 650 of this highly successful design have also been sold to several European freight operators as well as the Egyptian State Railways.

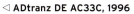

▷ **DWA Class 670 railcar, 1996**

Wheel arrangement 2-axle

Transmission mechanical

Engine MTU 6V 183 TD 13 diesel

Total power output 335 hp (250 kW)

Top speed 62 mph (100 km/h)

Incorporating parts used in buses, six of these double-deck diesel railcars were built by German Wagon AG (DWA) for German state railways in 1996 after a prototype was unveiled in 1994. A number remain in service.

◁ **ADtranz DE AC33C, 1996**

Wheel arrangement Co-Co

Transmission electric

Engine General Electric V12 diesel

Total power output 3,300 hp (2,462 kW)

Top speed 75 mph (121 km/h)

Fitted with General Electric diesel engines these powerful locomotives, nicknamed "Blue Tigers", were built by German manufacturer ADtranz between 1996 and 2004. Eleven units, including No. 250 001-5 seen here, were made for leasing in Germany, while Pakistan Railways ordered 30 and Keretapi Tanah Melayu in Malaysia bought 20.

▷ **HSB Halberstadt railcar, 1998**

Wheel arrangement 2 x 4-wheel bogies (1 powered)

Transmission mechanical

Engine Cummins 6-cylinder 1,080 cc diesel

Total power output approx 375 hp (280 kW)

Top speed 31 mph (50 km/h)

Four of these were built in 1999 by the Halberstadt Works, then part of Deutsche Bahn, for the Harzer Schmalspurbahnen (Harz Narrow-gauge Railway). They still work services at times, running on lines that are lightly used.

A New Wave of Electrics

The demise of steam power in Western Europe during the 1950s and 1960s saw the spread of electrification across much of the continent. The soaring price of oil in the 1970s added further impetus for national railways to switch from hurriedly introduced diesel locomotives to electric haulage. However, the power supplies varied greatly from country to country, and with the growth of transnational railway freight services, a new generation of multivoltage electric locomotives had started to appear by the 1990s.

▷ **CSD Class 363, 1980**

Wheel arrangement	B-B
Power supply	25 kV 50 Hz AC/3,000 V DC, overhead supplies
Power rating	4,102–4,666 hp (3,060–3,480 kW)
Top speed	75 mph (121 km/h)

The prototype Class 363 dual-voltage locomotive was built by Skoda Works for the Czechoslovakian state railways. It was the first multisystem electric engine in the world fitted with power thyristor pulse regulation and has a distinct sound in three frequencies when accelerating.

◁ **DR Class 243, 1982**

Wheel arrangement	Bo-Bo
Power supply	15 kV 16.7 Hz AC, overhead supply
Power rating	4,958 hp (3,721 kW)
Top speed	75 mph (120 km/h)

Over 600 of these mixed-traffic electric locomotives were built by L.E.W. Hennigsdorf for the Deutsche Reichsbahn between 1982 and 1991. Originally classified as DR Class 243, they became Class 143 under the renumbering scheme that followed Germany's reunification.

△ **SNCF Class BB 26000, 1988**

Wheel arrangement	B-B
Power supply	25 kV AC/1,500 V DC, overhead supplies
Power rating	7,500 hp (5,595 kW)
Top speed	124 mph (200 km/h)

These multipurpose, dual-voltage electric engines were constructed for the French state railways between 1988 and 1998; a total of 234 were built. A further 60 triple-voltage locomotives, which were made between 1996 and 2001, are classified as SNCF Class BB 36000.

△ **PKP Class EP09, 1986**

Wheel arrangement	Bo-Bo
Power supply	3,000 V DC, overhead supply
Power rating	3,914 hp (2,920 kW)
Top speed	99 mph (160 km/h)

A total of 47 of the Class EP09 express passenger electric engines were built by Pafawag of Wroclaw for the Polish state railways between 1986 and 1997. First entering service in 1988, they operate trains on main lines from Warsaw and Kraków.

TECHNOLOGY

Glacier Express

Named in honour of the Rhone Glacier, which it passed at the Furka Pass, the Glacier Express was introduced between St Moritz and Zermatt in Switzerland on 25 June 1930. It was originally operated by three 3-ft 3-in- (1-m-) gauge railway companies, the Brig-Visp-Zermatt Bahn (BVZ), the Furka Oberalp Bahn (FO), and the Rhaetian Railway (RhB). While two of the lines were electrified, steam locomotives were used on the FO section until 1942 when that line was also electrified. It runs daily all-year-round but is not exactly an "express" as it takes 7½ hours to cover 181 miles (291 km), much of it on a rack-and-pinion system. Since 2008 much of its route on the Albula and Bernina railways has been declared a UNESCO World Heritage Site.

Scenic ride The train passes through stunning Alpine scenery, crossing 291 bridges, burrowing through 91 tunnels, and gaining height on numerous spirals.

△ BR Class 91, 1988

Wheel arrangement Bo-Bo

Power supply 25 kV AC, overhead supply

Power rating 6,480 hp (4,832 kW)

Top speed 125 mph (204 km/h)

Delivered between 1988 and 1991, 31 of the Class 91 express locomotives were built at Crewe Works for British Rail. Designed to reach 140 mph (225 km/h) but now only used at 125 mph (204 km/h), they operate express trains in a push-pull mode on the East Coast Main Line between London King's Cross and Edinburgh.

△ FS Class ETR 500, 1992

Wheel arrangement power cars: 2 x 4-wheel motorized bogies

Power supply 3 kV DC, overhead supply

Power rating complete train: 11,796 hp (8,800 kW)

Top speed 155 mph (250 km/h)

Following four years of testing, 30 Class ETR 500 high-speed, single-voltage electric trains were introduced on the Italian state railway, between 1992 and 1996. Before the production models were constructed, a prototype motor car was built and tested. Coupled to an E444 locomotive on the Diretissima Line between Florence and Rome, it attained a speed of 198 mph (319 km/h) in 1988.

◁ SBB Cargo Bombardier Traxx, 1996

Wheel arrangement Bo-Bo

Power supply 15 kV 16.7 Hz AC/25 kV 50 Hz AC, overhead supply

Power rating 7,500 hp (5,595 kW)

Top speed 87 mph (140 km/h)

From 1996 the Bombardier Traxx, dual-voltage electric locomotives were introduced on many European railways. Since then around 1,000 have been built at the company's assembly plant in Kassel, Germany, of which 35 of the F140 AC variant, seen here, are operated by SBB Cargo in Switzerland.

▽ BR Class 92, 1993

Wheel arrangement Co-Co

Power supply 25 kV AC, overhead supply/750 V DC third-rail

Power rating 5,360–6,760 hp (3,998–5,041 kW)

Top speed 87 mph (140 km/h)

Designed to haul freight trains through the Channel Tunnel between Britain and France, the 46 Class 92, dual-voltage electric locomotives were built by Brush Traction and ABB Traction and assembled at the former company's erecting shops in Loughborough (UK) between 1993 and 1996. They are operated by GB Railfreight/Europorte 2 and DB Schenker.

▷ Amtrak Class HHP-8, 1999

Wheel arrangement B-B

Power supply 12.5 kV 25 Hz AC/12.5 kV 60 Hz AC/25 kV 60 Hz AC, overhead supplies

Power rating 8,000 hp (5,968 kW)

Top speed 125 mph (201 km/h)

Fifteen of these express passenger electric locomotives were built for Amtrak by Bombardier and Alstom in 1999. The Amtrak locomotives hauled trains on the Northeast Corridor between Washington DC and Boston until they were retired in 2012.

Urban Rail Solutions

While pioneering urban railways such as London's Metropolitan Railway and Chicago's South Side Elevated Railroad originally ran on steam, by the late 1930s electrified railways such as the Budapest Metro, the Moscow Metro and London Underground were carrying huge numbers of commuters between their suburban homes and city-centre offices. With the world's cities still expanding during the late 20th century, modern electrically powered rapid-transit systems (RTS) such as street tramways and surface and underground railways, many using driverless automatic trains, were built to transport millions of passengers each day, very quickly and over short distances.

▷ Vancouver SkyTrain RTS ICTS Mark I, 1985

Wheel arrangement	2-car sets
Power supply	750 V DC, third rail
Power rating	888 hp (640 kW) per 2-car set
Top speed	50 mph (80 km/h)

The 43-mile (69-km) Vancouver SkyTrain is an RTS serving Vancouver and its suburbs. Trains on the Expo Line and Millennium Line are automated and are driven by linear induction motors. The cars run in two- to six-car configurations. This is a four-car Mark I train of the Intermediate Capacity Transit System (ICTS) built by the Urban Transportation Development Corporation of Ontario.

△ SDTI Duewag U2 cars, 1980/81

Wheel arrangement	double-ended, 6-axle, articulated
Power supply	600 V DC, overhead supply
Power rating	408 hp (300 kW)
Top speed	50 mph (80 km/h)

The San Diego Trolley is a 53-station, three-route light rail system in the city of San Diego, California, which opened in 1981. The articulated cars initially used were U2 vehicles built in Germany by Duewag. These cars also worked in Edmonton and Calgary, Canada, and in Frankfurt, Germany.

△ Berlin *U-Bahn* F-type train, 1992/1993

Wheel arrangement	2-car sets
Power supply	750 V DC, third rail
Power rating	734 hp (540 kW) per 2-car set
Top speed	45 mph (72 km/h)

The 152-mile (245-km) Berlin *U-Bahn* (or underground railway), first opened in 1902 and, despite problems caused by the division of Berlin during the Cold War, today serves 170 stations across 10 lines. The system uses both *Kleinprofil* (small profile) trains and *Grossprofil* (large profile) trains, such as the F-type. The trains are worked in four-, six-, or eight-car combinations.

△ T&W Metro, 1980

Wheel arrangement 2-car articulated
(6-axle articulated sets)

Power supply 1,500 V DC,
overhead supply

Power rating 410 hp (301.5 kW)

Top speed 50 mph (80 km/h)

The 46-mile (74-km) Tyne & Wear Metro in Newcastle-upon-Tyne in northeast England is a hybrid light railway system with suburban, interurban, and underground sections. A total of 90 two-car articulated sets, usually coupled together in pairs, were built between 1978 and 1981 by Metro Cammell in Birmingham.

▽ Vienna ULF tram, 1998

Wheel arrangement 2- or 3-car articulated

Power supply 216–480 kW (289–643 hp)

Power rating 653 hp (480 kW)

Top speed 50 mph (80 km/h)

The Ultra Low Floor (ULF) cars, built by the consortium of Siemens of Germany and Elin of Austria, were introduced on Vienna's tram network in 1998 and in 2008 in Oradea, Romania. With a floor only 7 in (18 cm) above the pavement they provide easy access for wheelchairs or children's buggies.

▽ Luas Alstom Citadis tram, 1997

Wheel arrangement 3-, 5-, and 7-car articulated (8-, 12-, and 16-axle articulated sets)

Power supply 750 V DC, overhead lines

Power rating 979 hp (720 kW)

Top speed 44 mph (70 km/h)

The Citadis is a family of low-floor trams built by Alstom in France and Spain and popular in many cities around the world. The 23-mile (37-km) Luas tram system in Dublin, Ireland, uses the three-car 301 and five-car 401 variants on the city's Red Line, while the seven-car 402 variant works on the Green Line.

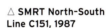

△ SMRT North–South Line C151, 1987

Wheel arrangement 6-car sets

Power supply 750 V DC, third rail/ 1,500 V DC, overhead supply

Power rating 2,937 hp (2,160 kW)

Top speed 50 mph (80 km/h)

Singapore's Mass Rapid Transit system started life when the North–South Line opened in 1987. Since then it has been extended to 93 miles (150 km), serving 106 stations on five routes. Six-car C151 (shown), C151A, and C751B trains collect current from a third rail and have an automatic train operation system. C751A trains, which are fully automatic and driverless, use an overhead supply.

▽ Gatwick Adtranz C-100, 1987

Wheel arrangement 2-car sets with rubber tyres

Power supply 600 V AC

Power rating 110.5 hp (75 kW) per car

Top speed 28 mph (46 km/h)

This elevated, fully automatic, driverless, guided people-mover system began operation in 1987. The train connects the North and South Terminals at London's Gatwick Airport, a distance of ¾ mile (1.2 km). Similar systems have proved popular in airports and cities around the world.

Universal Applications

The beginning of the 21st century saw changes in the way manufacturers dealt with their customers – instead of railway companies telling the equipment manufacturer exactly what they wanted built, the manufacturers started offering railway operators product ranges based on universal "platforms" much like the auto or aviation industries. As a result some commuters in California now travel in similar trains to those in Berlin or Athens, and interoperable locomotives, able to run from multiple traction voltages and using several different signalling systems, are now common in Europe.

△ **Siemens Eurosprinter ES64 U2/U4, 2000**

Wheel arrangement	Bo-Bo
Power supply	1,500 V DC/3,000 V DC and 15 kV AC/25 kV AC, overhead lines
Power rating	8,579 hp (6,400 kW)
Top speed	143 mph (230 km/h)

Siemens introduced the Eurosprinter family of locomotives following big orders from DB in Germany and ÖBB in Austria. The Eurosprinter range has four basic bodyshells and multiple versions. The ES64 U4 (EuroSprinter 6400 kW Universal 4 system) is the most flexible and able to operate in multiple countries.

△ **Siemens Desiro Classic, 2000**

Wheel arrangement	2-car DMU
Transmission	mechanical
Engine	2 x MTU 1800 6R
Total power output	845 hp (630 kW)
Top speed	74 mph (120 km/h)

Siemens has now sold over 600 of its first "Desiro" model, the two-car articulated diesel-powered Desiro Classic. The trains are used for regional passenger services in Europe, and the design has been exported to southern California. Electric versions have also been built for Bulgaria, Greece, and Slovenia.

▽ **Voith Gravita, 2008**

Wheel arrangement	B-B
Transmission	hydraulic
Engine	8 V 4000 R43
Total power output	1,341 hp (1,000 kW)
Top speed	62 mph (100 km/h)

The Gravita family of locomotives, developed by Voith, is designed for freight traffic on lightly used lines. Germany's Deutsche Bahn purchased 130 locomotives of two types – 99 of the Gravita 10BB and 31 of the more powerful 15BB model.

▷ Siemens Desiro-RUS, 2013

Wheel arrangement 2-car EMU

Power supply 3,000 V DC and 25 kV AC, overhead lines

Power rating 3,418 hp (2,550 kW)

Top speed 99 mph (160 km/h)

Desiro EMUs have been built for several countries from the UK to Slovenia, Greece, and Thailand. Russian railways (RZD) ordered 38 Desiro-RUS to operate services at the 2014 Sochi Winter Olympics. The trains, branded "Lastochka" (swallow), were built by Siemens at their Krefeld factory in Germany.

◁ Bombardier ALP45 DP, 2012

Wheel arrangement Bo-Bo

Transmission electric

Engine 2 x Caterpillar 3512C

Power supply 25 kV and 12.5 kV AC, overhead wires

Total power output diesel: 4,200 hp (3,135 kW)/ electric: 5,362 hp (4,000 kW)

Top speed diesel: 100 mph (161 km/h)/ electric: 124 mph (200 km/h)

These engines were designed for through operation from busy electric lines to non-electrified regional routes in North America to facilitate "one-seat rides" – travelling without changing trains. The locomotive can switch from electric to diesel (and vice versa) while moving. Bombardier has sold 46 to New Jersey Transit and Agence Métropolitaine de Transport in Montreal, Canada.

▷ Voith Maxima, 2008

Wheel arrangement C-C

Transmission hydraulic

Engine ABC 16 V DZC

Total power output 4,826 hp (3,600 kW)

Top speed 75 mph (120 km/h)

Voith introduced its most powerful single-engine, diesel-hydraulic locomotive ever built for freight operators in Europe in 2008. Two versions are available – the Maxima 40CC and lower-powered Maxima 30CC. Around 20 have been sold, mostly to Germany-based operators.

△ Vossloh Eurolight, 2010

Wheel arrangement Bo-Bo

Transmission electric

Engine Caterpillar C175-16

Total power output 3,753 hp (2,800 kW)

Top speed 124 mph (200 km/h)

The Eurolight design from Vossloh aims to maximize available power while minimizing axle weight, which enables the locomotive to operate even on rural routes often not built for heavy trains. By using a lighter weight engine and lightweight body, the locomotive weighs under 78 tons (79 tonnes).

△ Vossloh G6, 2010

Wheel arrangement C

Transmission hydraulic

Engine Cummins QSK-23-L

Total power output 900 hp (671 kW)

Top speed 50 mph (80 km/h)

Vossloh builds the G6 diesel-hydraulic locomotive in Kiel in Germany at the former Maschinenbau Kiel (MaK) factory. So far it has been sold mostly to industrial operators in Germany. Verkehrsbetriebe Peine-Salzgitter (VPS) runs a large railway network serving the steel industry at Salzgitter (central Germany) and has bought 40 G6s to replace 43 older diesel shunters.

△ Alstom Prima II, 2010

Wheel arrangement Bo-Bo

Power supply 3,000 V DC and 25 kV AC, overhead lines

Power rating 5,630 hp (4,200 kW)

Top speed 124 mph (200 km/h)

Alstom developed the Prima II prototype in 2008 and has sold 20 to Moroccan railways (ONCF). The locomotives are used for passenger trains on all electrified routes. Able to work from all traction voltages, the Prima II model can be built as four-axle locomotives or six-axle freight versions.

High Speed – The New Generation

By 2000, train speeds had increased significantly since the first high-speed Shinkansen and TGV trains of the 1960s to 1980s. New lines were being designed specifically for trains that could operate at 205 mph (330 km/h), and a new generation of trains was being introduced in several countries. Plans for intercity Maglev (*Mag*netic *Lev*itation) routes were developed in both Germany and Japan although, as yet, none has been built as the construction costs are too high. In the US 150-mph (241-km/h) operation on sections of existing lines was introduced.

△ **Trenitalia ETR 500, 2000**

Wheel arrangement 13-car trains including two power cars

Power supply 3,000 V DC, 25 kV AC, overhead lines

Power rating 11,796 hp (8,800 kW)

Top speed 211 mph (340 km/h)

These trains were based upon an earlier batch of ETR 500 trains built in the mid 1990s for operation on 3,000 V DC electrified lines of the Italian railways (Trenitalia). The new high-speed lines connecting Naples and Rome, and Florence and Milan that opened after 2000 needed trains able to work on 25 kV AC power, which the latest ETR 500 can do. The trains are limited to 186 mph (300 km/h) for current operation in Italy.

△ **DB ICE 3, 2000**

Wheel arrangement 8-coach, high-speed EMU

Power supply 15 kV AC, $16^2/_3$ Hz, 25 kV AC, 3,000 V DC, 1,500 kV DC, overhead lines

Power rating 10,724 hp (8,000 kW)

Top speed 205 mph (330 km/h)

Sixty-seven ICE 3 trains entered service from 2000, just before the new 205-mph (330-km/h) high-speed line connecting Cologne with Frankfurt airport opened in 2002. All had eight cars and featured "panorama lounges" at either end, where passengers could see the driver and the line ahead through a glass screen. Seventeen of the trains were four-voltage international sets, four of which were bought by Dutch Railways.

▷ **SMT/Transrapid, 2004**

Wheel arrangement Maglev (no wheels)

Power supply electromagnetic suspension

Power rating unknown

Top speed 268 mph (431 km/h)

The world's first commercial Maglev system was built at Birmingham Airport, UK in 1984. Work to develop high-speed Maglev systems was led by Japanese and German companies in the 1990s, and the world's only high-speed system opened in China in 2004 with a 19-mile (31-km) route connecting Shanghai city with its Pudong International Airport using German-built trains.

◁ **Chinese Railways CRH$_2$A, 2007**

Wheel arrangement 8-coach, high-speed EMU

Power supply 25 kV AC, overhead lines

Power rating 6,434 hp (4,800 kW)

Top speed 155 mph (250 km/h)

The Chinese Government ordered 60 CRH$_2$A trains from Kawasaki of Japan working with China Southern Rolling Stock Corp. (CSR) in 2004. The train is based on the E2 Shinkansen operated by Japan Railways (JR) East. The first three were built in Japan; the remainder were assembled at CSR Sifang. CSR has built several more versions since 2008 including 16-car sleepers.

△ Amtrak Acela, 2000

Wheel arrangement two Bo-Bo power cars plus 6 passenger cars

Power supply 11 kV AC 25 Hz, 11 kV AC 60 Hz, and 25 kV AC 60 Hz, overhead lines

Power rating 12,337 hp (9,200 kW)

Top speed 165 mph (266 km/h)

Amtrak ordered the new Acela design following trials of several European high-speed trains in the US in the 1990s. Built to unique US standards for crashworthiness, the trains can tilt, enabling higher speed on curves. Current maximum speed is 150 mph (241 km/h) in service, but plans exist for 160-mph (257-km/h) operation on some sections of the Washington, DC–Boston route in the future.

▽ RZD *Sapsan*, 2009

Wheel arrangement 10-coach, high-speed EMU

Power supply 25 kV AC, 3,000 V DC, overhead lines

Power rating 10,728 hp (8,000 kW)

Top speed 155 mph (250 km/h)

German train manufacturer Siemens built eight 10-car broad-gauge (5-ft/1.52-m) versions of its Velaro high-speed train for Russia in 2009–11. Russian Railways (RZD) operate the trains branded *Sapsan* (peregrine falcon) – the fastest bird – between Moscow and St Petersburg/Nizhny Novgorod. Eight more trains are due to enter service in 2014–15.

△ JR N700 Shinkansen, 2007

Wheel arrangement 16-coach, high-speed EMU

Power supply 25 KV AC, overhead lines

Power rating 22,905 hp (17,080 kW)

Top speed 186 mph (300 km/h)

The N700 Shinkansen can accelerate faster than any of the trains it replaced on the Tôkaidô Shinkansen line between Tokyo and Hakata. Built in either 8- or 16-car train sets, most N700s were in service by 2012, and 149 trains will have been delivered by the time production ends in 2016.

TALKING POINT

Meals on the Move

"Bento" is the Japanese name for a carefully crafted takeaway meal in a single, often disposable, container. Bento boxes were historically made from wood or metal, but are now found in a variety of materials and novelty shapes. A wide range of bento box train meals, known as ekiben, are sold at kiosks in railway stations all over Japan to take on board the train.

Novelty boxes
Ekiben packed in boxes shaped like Japanese trains have become collector's items. This one is modelled on the N700 Shinkansen.

Faster and Faster

Many existing high-speed train fleets have been expanded and, as new lines have opened, increasing numbers of fast international services have become possible, connecting France, Germany, Spain, and Switzerland in particular. In France, a specially modified test train built by Alstom, the TGV V150, achieved a new world speed record of 357¼ mph (574.8 km/h) in 2007. In Japan the main railways had been privatized by 2006, and in 2012 the world's first "start-up" private high-speed operator was NTV in Italy, which also began its services with a brand-new train design. However, state-owned operators continue to dominate.

△ NTV AGV ETR 575, 2012

Wheel arrangement 11-coach, articulated, high-speed EMU

Power supply 3,000 V DC, 25 kV AC, overhead lines

Power rating 10,054 hp (7,500 kW)

Top speed 186 mph (300 km/h)

Italian private rail operator Nuovo Trasporto Viaggiatori (New Passenger Transport), started high-speed services from Naples to Rome and Turin in 2012 with a fleet of 25 Alstom-built Automotrice à Grande Vitesse (AGV) high-speed trains. The trains are equipped with three different classes of passenger accommodation.

△ VT Class 390 Pendolino, 2002

Wheel arrangement 9- or 11-coach, high-speed, tilting EMU

Power supply 25 kV AC, overhead lines

Power rating 7,979 hp (5,950 kW)

Top speed 124 mph (200 km/h)

The Virgin Trains's tilting, high-speed Pendolino trains have speeded up journeys on the UK's West Coast Main Line from London to Birmingham, Manchester, and Glasgow since 2002. By leaning on curves the trains can go faster than conventional ones, reducing journey times and increasing track capacity.

▽ LSER Class 395 Javelin, 2009

Wheel arrangement 6-car EMU

Power supply 25 kV AC overhead lines and 750 V DC third rail

Power rating 4,506 hp (3,360 kW)

Top speed 140 mph (225 km/h)

Built by Hitachi in Kasado, Japan, using Shinkansen technology, the Javelin trains have been in service since 2009 serving the London & South Eastern Railway on the UK's domestic high-speed line HS1. They have reduced journey times significantly (in some cases by as much as than 50 per cent) between cities in Kent and London.

TALKING POINT

Steam Train Revival

The UK has led the world in preserving mainline steam locomotives, with many restored to working order since the 1950s. The success in preserving different types has led to groups of volunteers trying to recreate engine classes that never survived. All 49 Peppercorn Class A1 locomotives were scrapped in the 1960s, so in 1990 a group decided to build another – from scratch. Nineteen years later the new engine, based on the original design but with some modern features, started operations. It now works charter trains all over the country. Several other similar projects are now underway in the UK.

Peppercorn Class A1 No. 60163 *Tornado*, 2008
This is the first main-line steam engine built in the UK since 1960.

△ **PKP IC Class ED250, 2014**

Wheel arrangement 7-coach, high-speed EMU

Power supply 15 kV AC, 16²/₃Hz, 25 kV AC, 3,000 V DC, 1,500 kV DC, overhead lines

Power rating 7,373 hp (5,500 kW)

Top speed 154 mph (249 km/h)

Poland's long-distance railway company Polskie Koleje Panstwowe Intercity (PKP IC) ordered 20 Class ED250 trains from Alstom. Based on the "New Pendolino" design, first built for China and Italy, but without the tilt equipment, the trains began to replace older locomotive-operated trains on the Gdynia/Gdansk–Warsaw–Krakow/Katowice route from late 2014.

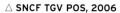

△ **SNCF TGV POS, 2006**

Wheel arrangement 10-car train including 2 power cars

Power supply 15 kV AC, 16²/₃Hz, 25 kV AC, 1,500 kV DC, overhead lines

Power rating 12,440 hp (9,280 kW)

Top speed 199 mph (320 km/h)

Using the new LGV Est high-speed line that connects the Alsace region with Paris, the French national railways' (SCNF) TGV POS (Paris-Ostfrankreich-Süddeutschland, or Paris-Eastern France–Southern Germany) trains started operating from 2006. The TGV POS trains also work through services to Munich and Frankfurt in Germany plus Geneva and Zurich in Switzerland.

◁ **SNCF TGV Euroduplex, 2012**

Wheel arrangement 10-car train including 2 power cars

Power supply 15 kV AC, 16²/₃Hz, 25 kV AC, 1,500 kV DC, overhead lines

Power rating 12,440 hp (9,280 kW)

Top speed 199 mph (320 km/h)

The third-generation "Duplex" (double-deck) TGV train was built for the French national railway SNCF; 95 have been ordered, with deliveries planned until 2017. This is the only double-deck high-speed train capable of operating across several different European rail networks and is used for services between France and Germany and France and Spain.

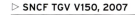

▷ **SNCF TGV V150, 2007**

Wheel arrangement 5-car, TGV train

Power supply 31 kV AC, overhead lines

Power rating 26,284 hp (19,600 kW)

Top speed 357¹/₄ mph (574.8 km/h)

This test train used two new TGV POS power cars and three special cars with powered bogies, all vehicles having specially made, bigger wheels. For the test run on the LGV Est Européenne line, the overhead line voltage was increased for more power. The record of 357¹/₄ mph (574.8 km/h) – 6 miles (9.65 km) per minute – more than achieved the target set.

Into the Future

Investment in the railways around the world is growing, driven by rising passenger numbers as large cities continue to expand, combined with increasing road congestion, and the need to reduce CO_2 emissions. Older-style trains that use locomotives and separate coaches are being replaced by modern, self-powered multiple units. Rail operators, both passenger and freight, are also seeking to reduce maintenance and energy costs; some modern trains are designed to recycle electricity while braking.

◁ Bombardier Omneo Régio2N, 2010

Wheel arrangement 6- to 10-car, articulated EMU

Power supply 25 kV AC, 1,500 kV DC, overhead lines

Power rating 4,291hp (3,200 kW)

Top speed 99 mph (160 km/h)

The Omneo is the world's first articulated, double-deck EMU with a single-deck driving coach at each end, and double-deck, articulated intermediate coaches sandwiched between short, single-deck door sections. The trains can be supplied in lengths ranging from 6 to 10 cars (266-443 ft/81-135 m). The French national railway (SNCF) has agreed a €7-billion-framework contract for up to 860 trains for delivery until 2025.

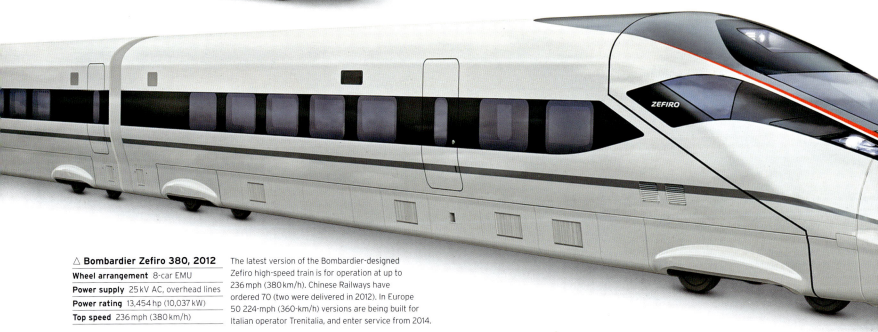

△ Bombardier Zefiro 380, 2012

Wheel arrangement 8-car EMU

Power supply 25 kV AC, overhead lines

Power rating 13,454 hp (10,037 kW)

Top speed 236 mph (380 km/h)

The latest version of the Bombardier-designed Zefiro high-speed train is for operation at up to 236 mph (380 km/h). Chinese Railways have ordered 70 (two were delivered in 2012). In Europe 50 224-mph (360-km/h) versions are being built for Italian operator Trenitalia, and enter service from 2014.

Local Transport Developments

The demand for urban transport has grown significantly in the last 30 years – whether metros under city streets or light-rail systems that run on roads alongside other vehicles. The strongest growth is in Asia and the Middle East where new systems have been built since 1990. For established networks the challenge is to create more capacity through better performance and smart control systems on networks that are more than 100 years old, for example, in London and Paris.

▷ Vossloh Wuppertal Schwebebahn train, 2015

Wheel arrangement 3-section, articulated vehicle

Power supply 750 V DC, third rail adjacent to single running rail

Power rating 322 hp (240 kW)

Top speed approx. 37 mph (60 km/h)

Germany's Wuppertal Schwebebahn is a suspended railway built largely above the River Wupper on massive iron supports. First opened in 1901, it is now a protected national monument, but is still used daily by thousands of commuters. Vossloh will supply 31 new trains from 2015 – part of a comprehensive modernization plan.

◁ **Amtrak Siemens American Cities Sprinter ACS-64, 2014**

Wheel arrangement Bo-Bo

Power supply 25 kV, 12.5 kV, and 12 kV AC, overhead lines

Power rating 8,579 hp (6,400 kW)

Top speed 125 mph (201 km/h)

Siemens is building 70 ACS-64s at its factory in Sacramento, California. Amtrak, which introduced the first ACS-64 in 2014, will use them to replace all its existing electrics on the Washington DC–New York–Boston Northeast Corridor route.

△ **VMS Chemnitz tram-train, 2015**

Wheel arrangement 3-section articulated LRV

Power supply 600 V and 750 V DC, overhead lines plus diesel engines

Power rating electric: 777 hp (580 kW); diesel: 1,046 hp (780 kW)

Top speed 62 mph (100 km/h)

Tram-trains that enable travel to city centres from regional railway lines are now in use in many EU countries. In Germany some use diesel engines on non-electrified rail lines. Chemnitz tram-trains will use this technology from 2015.

TECHNOLOGY

Cargo Efficiency

The major Class 1 Railways in North America have increased operational efficiency and productivity significantly since the 1980s. By operating longer, heavier trains using powerful modern locomotives, operating costs per cargo container have reduced, making rail much cheaper than road. Double-stacked containers are used in North America, Australia, and India. The Brazilian mining company Vale runs the 554-mile (892-km) Carajás Railroad with the world's heaviest trains – 330-wagon, 41,632-ton (42,300-tonne) iron-ore trains run up to 24 times a day to the port at Ponta da Madeira.

BNSF freight train, Cajon Pass, California With two modern GE Evolution Series ES44DC engines at each end, this train can be up to 2^2/$_3$-mile (4.3-km) long. On steep gradients, the engines slow down descending trains, as well as pull them up the inclines.

△ **Siemens Vectron, 2013**

Wheel arrangement Bo-Bo

Power supply 3 kV DC, overhead lines

Power rating 6,974 hp (5,200 kW)

Top speed 99 mph (160 km/h)

Siemens developed the Vectron family of locomotives to replace its previous Eurosprinter model. The first major order received was for 23 Vectron DC electric locomotives from Polish rail freight operator DB Schenker Rail Polska – the first of these entered service in 2013. Subsequent orders for locomotives for use in several countries have been obtained, including a broad-gauge version for Finland.

△ **Siemens ICx, 2017**

Wheel arrangement 7- or 12-coach, high-speed EMU

Power supply 15 kV AC, 16^2/$_3$ Hz

Power rating 13,271 hp (9,900 kW)

Top speed 155 mph (250 km/h)

ICx trains will replace Germany's existing long-distance, locomotive-operated trains, and later the first two types of ICE train. Due for delivery from 2017 are 85 12- and 45 slower 7-coach trains using 92-ft (28-m) long coaches configured as distributed-power EMUs with more seats and space than those they replace.

△ **Calgary Transit C-train System Siemens S200, 2015**

Wheel arrangement 2-car, articulated LRV

Power supply 600 V DC, overhead lines

Power rating 777 hp (580 kW)

Top speed 65 mph (105 km/h)

The Canadian city of Calgary opened its first light-rail line in 1981. Since then the network has expanded and carries 290,000 people daily. To increase capacity and to retire some of the original light-rail vehicles (LRVs), 60 new S200 LRVs are on order for delivery in 2015-16. Calgary Transit expects to increase its fleet from under 200 to 390 over the next 30 years.

△ **London Underground Siemens Inspiro metro concept**

Wheel arrangement 6-car, metro EMU

Power supply 630 V DC, third and fourth rail

Power rating 1,340 hp (1,000 kW)

Top speed 56 mph (90 km/h)

London Underground has seen significant growth in passengers. The "New Tube for London" programme is planning 250 new underground trains, possibly automatic and driverless, to enter service between 2020 and 2035. Three companies are designing trains; shown here is Siemens's proposal.

Cars
Before 1929

Pioneer Vehicles

The 19th century saw tremendous advances in engineering, as mechanisation transformed production in factories. Inventors turned their attention to replacing the horse with something that could go faster and further. Steam, electricity, gas, and petrol were all tried, and in this early period it was hard to say which would win; speed records went first to electric, then to steam.

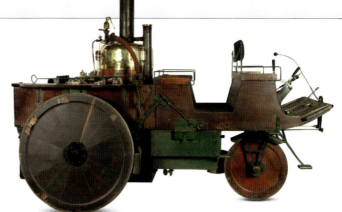

◁ **Grenville Steam Carriage c.1880**

Origin UK

Engine vertical steam boiler

Top speed 20 mph (32 km/h)

Railway engineer Robert Neville Grenville from Glastonbury, UK, was one of dozens of Victorian inventors to build a steam-powered road carriage. Grenville's vehicle has survived.

▷ **Daimler 1886**

Origin Germany

Engine 462 cc, one-cylinder

Top speed 10 mph (16 km/h)

Gottlieb Daimler and Wilhelm Maybach fitted their engine into a stagecoach in 1886, creating the first four-wheeled, petrol-engined vehicle to reach 10 mph.

▷ **Stanley Runabout 1898**

Origin USA

Engine 1,692 cc, straight-two steam

Top speed 35 mph (56 km/h)

Twins Francis and Freelan Stanley built over 200 of these inexpensive and reliable steam cars in 1898-99. In 1906 a more powerful model reached 127 mph (204 km/h).

▽ **Daimler Cannstatt 4HP 1898**

Origin Germany

Engine 1,525 cc, V2

Top speed 16 mph (26 km/h)

In June 1887 Daimler equipped a workshop for 23 employees in Cannstatt, Stuttgart, to build his engines. The engines were still fitted to modified stagecoaches.

◁ Franklin Model A 1902

Origin USA

Engine 1,760 cc, straight-four

Top speed 25 mph (40 km/h)

John Wilkinson designed the first four-cylinder car in the US for Herbert Franklin. The air-cooled engine had overhead valves and was mounted across the wooden chassis.

△ Benz (replica) 1885

Origin Germany

Engine 954 cc, single-cylinder

Top speed 6 mph (10 km/h)

Built in 1885 and patented in 1886, Karl Benz's Motorwagen had many clever features: it was lightweight and had a four-stroke petrol engine, rack steering, and steel spoke wheels.

△ Lanchester 1897

Origin UK

Engine 3,459 cc, straight-two

Top speed 20 mph (32 km/h)

Brothers Frederick, George, and Frank Lanchester ran their first car in 1896 with a single-cylinder engine. The following year they built this car with a two-cylinder engine.

◁ Columbia Electric 1899

Origin USA

Engine single electric motor

Top speed 15 mph (24 km/h)

At the start of the 20th century, when most petrol-car makers were producing a handful of models a year, Columbia was building hundreds of smooth, silent electric cars.

△ Sunbeam-Mabley 1901

Origin UK

Engine 230 cc, one-cylinder

Top speed 20 mph (32 km/h)

John Marston's Sunbeam bicycle factory, along with Maxwell Maberley-Smith, developed this unusual vehicle with a seat either side of a central belt drive.

▷ Clément-Gladiator Voiturette 1899

Origin France

Engine 402 cc, one-cylinder

Top speed 20 mph (32 km/h)

Bicycle magnate Adolphe Clément saw the potential of the motor industry and promoted several marques. This simple voiturette had a 2.5 hp De Dion-type engine under the seat.

◁ Goddu Tandem 1897

Origin USA

Engine cc unknown, two-cylinder

Top speed 30 mph (48 km/h)

Inventor Louis Goddu made only a handful of cars, but pioneered features such as the overhead camshaft in a car that was exceptionally rapid for its time.

◁ Duryea Motor Wagon 1893

Origin USA

Engine 1,302 cc, one-cylinder

Top speed 12 mph (19 km/h)

Bicycle makers Frank and Charles Duryea made the first successful gasoline-powered automobile in the US in 1893. They also won the US's first motor race in 1895.

▷ Panhard et Levassor Phaeton 1891

Origin France

Engine 1,060 cc, straight-two

Top speed 12 mph (19 km/h)

René Panhard and Émile Levassor offered their first car in 1890, building a Daimler engine under licence. They pioneered sliding gear transmission and front engine with rear drive among other modern features.

◁ Arnold Benz 1897

Origin UK

Engine 1,190 cc, single-cylinder

Top speed 16 mph (26 km/h)

William Arnold & Sons built Benz-like cars with their own 1.5 hp engines. One was fitted with the first electric self-start dynamotor, which also assisted the engine on hills.

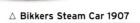

△ Bikkers Steam Car 1907

Origin Netherlands

Engine steam boiler

Top speed 10 mph (16 km/h)

Better known for its steam-driven fire engines, Bikkers also made steam vehicles, such as this one, for cleaning cesspits. This is the oldest commercial vehicle in the Netherlands.

First Cars for Customers

It was one amazing feat to build the first practical motor cars – it was another to start making more and selling them. Just convincing people of their benefits was often difficult. Entrepreneurs, engineers, and aristocrats all played their parts in the earliest faltering steps towards car manufacture. Germany was at the forefront of this development, followed by France, the UK, and the US.

◁ **Adler 3.5HP Voiturette 1901**

Origin Germany

Engine 510 cc, single-cylinder

Top speed 20 mph (32 km/h)

The typewriter and bicycle manufacturer Adler made components for Benz and De Dion cars before starting to make its own De Dion-engined vehicles in 1900.

△ **Arrol-Johnston 10HP Dogcart 1897**

Origin UK

Engine 3,230 cc, flat-two

Top speed 25 mph (40 km/h)

George Johnston conceived his rugged, simple Dogcart – the first British-built car – in Glasgow, Scotland. Powered by an underfloor opposed-piston engine, it remained in production for 10 years.

◁ **US Long Distance 7HP 1901**

Origin USA

Engine 2,245 cc, single-cylinder

Top speed 25 mph (40 km/h)

Ambitiously named for a runabout, this car had its horizontally mounted engine and two-speed epicyclic gearbox under the seat. It was renamed the Standard in 1903.

▷ **Clément 7HP 1901**

Origin France

Engine 7 hp, one-cylinder

Top speed 25 mph (40 km/h)

Adolphe Clément made a fortune from bicycles and pneumatic tyres, and then invested it in car manufacture. His cars were among the first models to feature front-mounted engines and drive shafts.

△ **Rover 8HP 1904**

Origin UK

Engine 1,327 cc, single-cylinder

Top speed 30 mph (48 km/h)

This was Rover Cycle Company's first four-wheeled car. The 8HP featured a tubular "backbone" chassis, column gearchange, and a camshaft brake. One 8HP successfully drove from London to Constantinople in 1906.

◁ **Mercedes 60HP 1903**

Origin Germany

Engine 9,293 cc, straight-four

Top speed 73 mph (117 km/h)

While other makes were building crude machines that were barely faster than a running man, Mercedes was manufacturing magnificent high-speed vehicles like the 60HP.

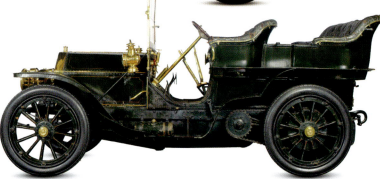

▷ **De Dion-Bouton 3.5HP Voiturette 1899**

Origin France

Engine 510 cc, single-cylinder

Top speed 25 mph (40 km/h)

Count Albert de Dion was one of France's motoring pioneers. His single-cylinder, water-cooled engines were used by dozens of early car makers around the world.

▷ **De Dion-Bouton 8HP Type O 1902**

Origin France

Engine 943 cc, single-cylinder

Top speed 28 mph (45 km/h)

In 1902 De Dion-Bouton adopted wheel steering and front, rather than underfloor, engine position for popular, light cars such as the Type O, which had a long production run.

◁ Renault Voiturette 1898

Origin France

Engine 400 cc, single-cylinder

Top speed 20 mph (32 km/h)

Louis Renault and his brothers started building cars in 1897, and their Voiturette quickly became popular in France thanks to its impressive performances in trials.

◁ Ford Model A 1903

Origin USA

Engine 1,668 cc, flat-two

Top speed 28 mph (45 km/h)

Henry Ford built his first car in 1896, but did not start production until 1903 with the underfloor-engined Model A. This was developed into the Model C of 1904.

▷ FN 3.5HP Victoria 1900

Origin Belgium

Engine 796 cc, straight-two

Top speed 23 mph (37 km/h)

The Belgian armaments manufacturer FN diversified into motorcycle and car making around the turn of the century. About 280 Victorias were made up until 1902.

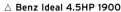

△ Fiat 16/24HP 1903

Origin Italy

Engine 4,180 cc, straight-four

Top speed 44 mph (71 km/h)

With a front-mounted, water-cooled, four-cylinder engine driving the rear wheels via a four-speed gearbox, the 16/24HP was a thoroughly modern car.

△ Maxwell Model A Junior Runabout 1904

Origin USA

Engine 1,647 cc, flat-two

Top speed 35 mph (56 km/h)

Jonathan Maxwell and Benjamin Briscoe of New Jersey developed this simple and effective shaft-driven runabout, which sold for $750. It performed well in trials.

△ Benz Ideal 4.5HP 1900

Origin Germany

Engine 1,140 cc, single-cylinder

Top speed 22 mph (35 km/h)

The maker of the first successful car in 1885. Benz's Ideal had tiller steering. In 1900, 603 cars were made – most car makers of the time produced only a handful each year.

△ Holsman Model 3 Runabout 1903

Origin USA

Engine 1,000 cc, flat-two

Top speed 20 mph (32 km/h)

Harry K. Holsman built significant numbers of rope-drive "highwheelers" in Chicago for sale to mid-west pioneers: large wheels allowed them to drive over virgin prairie.

△ Rexette 1905

Origin UK

Engine 900 cc, one-cylinder

Top speed 28 mph (45 km/h)

One of many marques established in Coventry, Britain's "motor city", Rexette derived its 1904 three-wheeler from one if its motorcycles, adding wheel steering in 1905.

Early Production-line Cars

By the end of the first decade of the 20th century, it was clear that the motor car was here to stay, and carmakers started looking at ways to increase production. De Dion-Bouton in France and Oldsmobile in the US both claimed sales of over 2,000 in 1902, but Henry Ford would eclipse them all, as he introduced the moving production line to motor car manufacture.

◁ **Vulcan 10HP 1904**

Origin UK

Engine 1,500 cc, straight-two

Top speed 35 mph (56 km/h)

Vulcan cars were exceptional value for money. The 1903 single-cylinder cost just £105 and the 1904 twin £200: consequently, sales rocketed during 1904–06.

△ **Wolseley 6HP 1901**

Origin UK

Engine 714 cc, single-cylinder

Top speed 25 mph (40 km/h)

Herbert Austin designed and oversaw manufacture of this Voiturette before setting up his own company. Its efficient design ensured successful production.

△ **Oldsmobile Curved Dash 1901**

Origin USA

Engine 1,564 cc, single-cylinder

Top speed 20 mph (32 km/h)

Ransom Eli Olds conceived the world's first mass-production car. It was light, simple, affordable, and reliable: 2,100 were sold in 1902 and 5,000 more in 1904.

◁ **Speedwell 6HP Dogcart 1904**

Origin UK

Engine 700 cc, single-cylinder

Top speed 25 mph (40 km/h)

Speedwell made a wide range of cars from 6 hp to 50 hp, though it only lasted from 1900 to 1907. The Dogcart used a De Dion-type engine.

▷ **L'Elegante 6HP 1903**

Origin France

Engine 942 cc, single-cylinder

Top speed 28 mph (45 km/h)

Like De Dion-Bouton, L'Elegante cars were built in Paris. They closely resembled De Dion-Boutons and used their engines; the L'Elegante only lasted four years.

▽ **Knox 8HP 1904**

Origin USA

Engine 2,253 cc, single-cylinder

Top speed 28 mph (45 km/h)

Knox sold hundreds of these simple cars, which were notable for full-length springs and an air-cooled, single-cylinder engine covered in screwed-in pins to increase cooling.

△ **Cadillac Model A 1903**

Origin USA

Engine 1,606 cc, single-cylinder

Top speed 35 mph (56 km/h)

Henry Leland set up Cadillac in 1902 after parting with Henry Ford; in 1903 he sold some 2,400 of these simple, well-engineered small cars for $750 each.

△ **De Dion-Bouton 10HP Type W 1904**

Origin France

Engine 1,728 cc, straight-two

Top speed 40 mph (64 km/h)

De Dion-Bouton claimed to be the world's largest car producer, selling 2,000 cars in 1902 alone, and offering a wide choice of popular, easy-to-drive vehicles.

◁ Spyker 12/16HP Double Phaeton 1905
Origin Netherlands
Engine 2,544 cc, square-four
Top speed 45 mph (72 km/h)

The Spijker brothers started selling other marques before producing their own from 1900. From 1904 they made a range of large, advanced cars, including a 4x4.

◁ Ford Model T Tourer 1908
Origin USA
Engine 2,896 cc, straight-four
Top speed 42 mph (68 km/h)

Henry Ford dreamt of bringing motoring to the wider public, and by using a moving assembly line he achieved it with the rugged, reliable, low-cost Model T.

△ CID Baby 1910
Origin France
Engine single-cylinder
Top speed 40 mph (64 km/h)

Cottereau of Dijon was renamed CID in 1910; its best-known product was the Baby, a light car with a Buchet engine driving through a four-speed friction transmission.

▷ Renault AX 1908
Origin France
Engine 1,060 cc, straight-two
Top speed 35 mph (56 km/h)

French manufacturers excelled at making lightweight, practical vehicles and the AX was a perfect example. It was in production for six years, and was popular with taxi drivers.

△ Humber Humberette 1913
Origin UK
Engine 998 cc, V2-cylinder
Top speed 25 mph (40 km/h)

This well-made economy model featured an air-cooled engine. It was classed as a "cyclecar" for tax purposes as it weighed under 320 kg (700 lb).

△ Peugeot Bébé 1913
Origin France
Engine 855 cc, straight-four
Top speed 37 mph (60 km/h)

Ettore Bugatti designed this car for Wanderer, but it was best known as a Peugeot; 3,095 were sold during 1913-16.

◁ Twombly Model B 1914
Origin USA
Engine 1,290 cc, straight-four
Top speed 50 mph (80 km/h)

Mounting the axles above the chassis gave the Twombly unusually low lines. It was very narrow, and its tandem seating was an uncommon feature that proved unpopular.

△ Dodge Model 30 Touring Car 1914
Origin USA
Engine 3,480 cc, four-cylinder
Top speed Unknown

The Dodge brothers were formerly subcontractors to Ford. Their own first car was twice as powerful as the Model T, and was supplied with an all-steel welded body.

◁ Standard 9½ HP Model S 1913
Origin UK
Engine 1,087 cc, straight-four
Top speed 45 mph (72 km/h)

Set up by Reginald Maudsley in 1903, Standard gained a reputation for making good engines, which were also used by other marques; its own cars sold well.

▷ Stellite 9HP 1913
Origin UK
Engine 1,098 cc, straight-four
Top speed 45 mph (72 km/h)

A subsidiary company of Wolseley, which later absorbed it, Stellite's advanced features included rack-and-pinion steering and overhead inlet valves.

Birth of the Competition Car

The idea of proving the speed and durability of new cars by pitting them against each other in long-distance trials, hill climbs, or circuit races came early in the history of the motor car. By the end of the first decade of the 20th century motor sport was thriving throughout Europe and the US, with German, French, Italian, British, and American cars leading the field. In the absence of restrictions on engine capacity, many cars of this era had mammoth engines.

△ Napier Gordon Bennett 1902

Origin UK

Engine 6,435 cc, straight-four

Top speed 70 mph (113 km/h)

The sole British entrant in the 1902 Gordon Bennett Trial, this Napier driven by S.F. and Cecil Edge won. Its colour became known as British Racing Green.

△ Spyker 60HP 1903

Origin Netherlands

Engine 8,821 cc, straight-six

Top speed 80 mph (129 km/h)

The Spijker brothers, Jacobus and Hendrik-Jan, pioneered magnificent cars, most notably this first production six-cylinder with permanent four-wheel drive and four-wheel brakes.

△ Auburn Model 30L Roadster 1910

Origin USA

Engine 3,300 cc, straight-four

Top speed 65 mph (105 km/h)

Auburn built 1,623 cars in 1912. The 30L was sold as a saloon, tourer, and roadster using a Rutenber engine with individually cast cylinders. The Roadster was the cheapest at $1,100.

△ Darracq 12HP "Genevieve" 1904

Origin France

Engine 1,886 cc, straight-two

Top speed 45 mph (72 km/h)

Darracqs were capable cars with light, pressed-steel chassis, but this one is most famous for its starring role in the 1953 comedy film Genevieve, which popularized veteran cars.

△ Darracq 200HP 1905

Origin France

Engine 25,400 cc, V8

Top speed 120 mph (193 km/h)

The world's oldest surviving V8, this car took the world land speed record in 1905 at 110 mph (177 km/h). In 1906 it exceeded 120 mph, and continued setting records up to 1909.

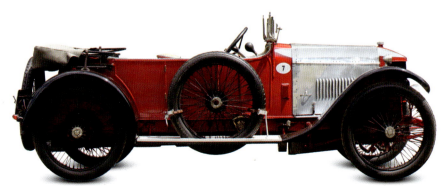

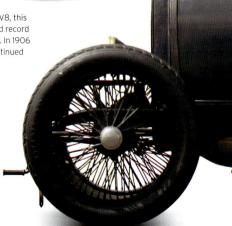

◁ Vauxhall Prince Henry 1910

Origin UK

Engine 3,054 cc, straight-four

Top speed 100 mph (161 km/h)

Vauxhall built three cars for the 1910 Prince Henry Trial in Germany. They went on to win many events, including the Russian Nine-day Trial and the Swedish Winter Cup.

△ Austro-Daimler Prince Henry 1910

Origin Austria

Engine 5,714 cc, straight-four

Top speed 85 mph (137 km/h)

Ferdinand Porsche led Austro-Daimler's split from its German parent. This car's overhead-camshaft engine helped it finish 1-2-3 in the 1910 Prince Henry Trial.

▷ Stutz Bearcat 1912

Origin USA

Engine 6,391 cc, straight-four

Top speed 75 mph (121 km/h)

A roadgoing racer with low build, no doors, and a monocle windscreen, the rakish Bearcat quickly became an icon of its era, winning 25 of the 30 races it entered.

△ Marquette-Buick 1909

Origin USA

Engine 4,800 cc, straight-four

Top speed 90 mph (145 km/h)

Louis Chevrolet drove one of these to victory in the first 5-mile (8-km) race on Indianapolis's "Brickyard" circuit in 1910. It was later disqualified for not meeting the criteria of a stock car.

△ Lancia Tipo 55 Corsa 1910

Origin Italy

Engine 4,700 cc, straight-four

Top speed 85 mph (137 km/h)

Lancia founder Vincenzo was passionate about motor sport and won the 1904 Coppa Florio in Italy. This car also won several races in the US, for the Vanderbilt family.

▷ Panhard et Levassor X-19 Labourdette Torpédo Skiff 1912

Origin France

Engine 2,100 cc, straight-four

Top speed 60 mph (97 km/h)

Coachbuilder Henri Labourdette built this skiff (rowing-boat) body without doors for driver Chevalier René de Knyff. Light and strong, its style appealed to French sportsmen. This is a replica of the 1912 original.

▷ Mercer Type 35R Raceabout 1910

Origin USA

Engine 4,929 cc, straight-four

Top speed 80 mph (129 km/h)

Unusually low-slung with great handling for its time, the Raceabout won five of its first six races in 1911. A four-speed gearbox introduced in 1913 made it even faster.

△ Bugatti Type 15 1910

Origin France

Engine 1,327 cc, straight-four

Top speed 55 mph (89 km/h)

Ettore Bugatti's first production car was the Type 13, also offered as the longer-wheelbase Type 15. Numerous giant-killing race performances boosted its sales.

◁ Fiat S61 Corsa 1908

Origin Italy

Engine 10,087 cc, straight-four

Top speed 97 mph (156 km/h)

A very successful race car derived from a Grand Touring model, the S61 Corsa won races in Europe and the US, including the 1912 American Grand Prix.

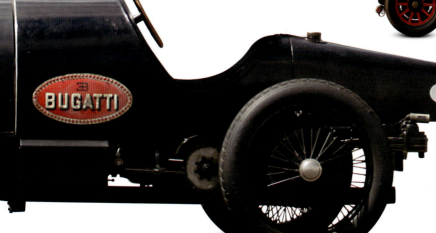

◁ Bugatti Type 18 "Garros" 1912

Origin France

Engine 5,027 cc, straight-four

Top speed 105 mph (169 km/h)

Ettore Bugatti himself won in this 100 bhp chain-drive, Grand Prix car with overhead camshaft and double inlet valves. Others were driven in the Indianapolis 500.

△ Fiat S74 1911

Origin Italy

Engine 14,137 cc, straight-four

Top speed 102 mph (164 km/h)

With a GP limit on engine bore, strokes grew: this OHC engine is so tall the driver has to look around it. David Bruce-Brown won the 1911 American Grand Prix in one.

Luxury and Power

Car makers saved their finest work for their richest customers. Such customers would not tolerate unreliability, and demanded cars that gave far greater performance than traditional horse-drawn carriages. They also demanded comfort – an important factor on the rough roads of the early 20th century – and luxuries such as preselect gearboxes and power steering.

◁ **Nagant Type D 14/16HP Town Car 1909**

Origin Belgium

Engine 2,600 cc, straight-four

Top speed 50 mph (80 km/h)

This Liège marque built its own high quality cars from 1907. The smaller 14/16 hp was remarkable for its efficient sidevalve engine, which was capable of revving to 3,000 rpm.

▷ **HEDAG Electric Brougham 1905**

Origin Germany

Engine Two electric motors

Top speed 15 mph (24 km/h)

A modified horse-taxi with an electric motor in each front wheel, the Brougham had power steering, four-wheel brakes, and electric indicators. It was built under licence from Kriéger of France.

▷ **Panhard & Levassor 15HP Type X21 1905**

Origin France

Engine 2,614cc, straight-six

Top speed 50 mph (80 km/h)

In 1891 Panhard and Levassor laid the foundations of the modern motor car. By 1905 they were producing remarkably quiet and smooth-running cars, such as the X21.

◁ **Regal Model NC Colonial Coupé 1912**

Origin USA

Engine 3,200 cc, straight-four

Top speed 50 mph (80 km/h)

Notable for its low, "underslung" build, which placed its axles above the chassis, the Regal was a light sporting car, though hardly aerodynamic with this body style.

▷ **Rolls-Royce Silver Ghost 1906**

Origin UK

Engine 7,036 cc, straight-six

Top speed 63 mph (101 km/h)

Charles Rolls and Henry Royce focused on making the finest car in the world, and succeeded with this 40/50 hp model. It was quiet, powerful, and superbly built.

△ **Cadillac Model 51 1914**

Origin USA

Engine 5,157 cc, V8

Top speed 55 mph (89 km/h)

Henry Leland stole a march on the opposition with the US's first mass-produced V8. With 70 bhp, it was powerful and reliable. Sales in the first year were over 13,000.

◁ **Brooke 25/30HP Swan 1910**

Origin UK

Engine 4,788 cc, straight-six

Top speed 37 mph (60 km/h)

The work of British engineer Robert Matthewson, of Calcutta, India, the Swan had a beak that sprayed water to clear a path through the crowded streets of Calcutta.

▷ **Lanchester 28HP Landaulette 1906**

Origin UK

Engine 3,654 cc, straight-six

Top speed 55 mph (89 km/h)

Frederick Lanchester was a brilliant engineer whose cars were innovative and original. This car has its original convertible bodywork, mid-mounted engine, and preselect gearbox.

▷ **Peugeot Type 126 12/15HP Touring 1910**

Origin	France
Engine	2,200 cc, straight-four
Top speed	45 mph (72 km/h)

A family company founded in ironmongery, Peugeot was hugely successful in the early 20th century with a wide range of motor cars. Just 350 of this model were sold.

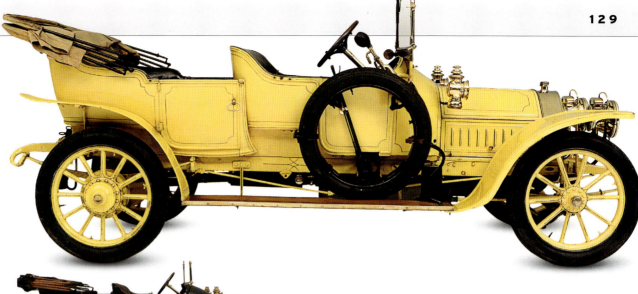

▽ **Mors 14/19HP Landaulette Town Car 1904**

Origin	France
Engine	3,200 cc, straight-four
Top speed	40 mph (64 km/h)

Emile Mors was building 200 cars a year in 1898, so by 1904 his chassis were well developed. This luxury model carries a coachbuilt city-car body by Rothschild of Paris.

◁ **Georges Roy 12HP 1909**

Origin	France
Engine	2,900 cc, straight-four
Top speed	45 mph (72 km/h)

Georges Roy, unusually, built its own car bodies. This model could be either a two- or a four-seater, the rear compartment ingeniously folding back when not required.

▷ **Thomas Flyer Model 6/40M Touring 1910**

Origin	USA
Engine	7,679 cc, straight-six
Top speed	67 mph (108 km/h)

Thomas made increasingly rapid and large-engined cars, and won the New York to Paris race in 1908. From 1910 to 1919 it made more luxurious models, such as this Flyer.

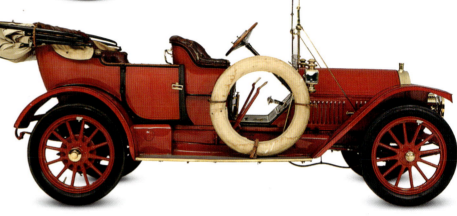

▷ **Argyll 15/30 1913**

Origin	UK
Engine	2,614 cc, straight-four
Top speed	47 mph (76 km/h)

Scotland's biggest car maker in the Edwardian era built splendid cars, such as this sleeve-valve-engined model. It was made in a magnificent, palace-like factory in Alexandria, on the banks of Loch Lomond, Scotland.

△ **Fiat 24/40HP 1906**

Origin	Italy
Engine	7,363 cc, straight-four
Top speed	53 mph (85 km/h)

Fiat produced a broad range of large-engined cars for Italy's elite. These received weighty and luxurious bodies – though a light racer was also made for this chassis.

◁ **Daimler 28/36 1905**

Origin	UK
Engine	5703 cc, straight-four
Top speed	50 mph (80 km/h)

The British Daimler company began by making replicas of German cars. By 1905, however, it had taken a strong lead in the market for quality cars with large engines and four gears, such as the 28/36.

▷ **Lancia Alpha 1907**

Origin	Italy
Engine	2,543 cc, straight-four
Top speed	50 mph (80 km/h)

Vincenzo Lancia founded his company in 1906, after six years racing for the Fiat factory. With a four-speed gearbox, the Alpha was a modern, well-made car in its day.

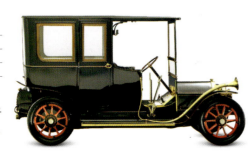

▷ **Pierce-Arrow Model 38 Park Phaeton 1913**

Origin	USA
Engine	6,796 cc, straight-six
Top speed	65 mph (105 km/h)

Pierce-Arrow made some of the US's finest cars. This model, which has an exclusive body by Studebaker, was started by pumping compressed air into its engine.

Competition Cars

The 1920s saw rapid technological progress in the world of competition cars, as the emphasis moved from proving road cars by racing them, to developing and testing advanced engineering in race cars, and then adapting it to road models. This decade saw innovations such as multiple valves and spark plugs per cylinder, double overhead camshafts, and front-wheel drive all proven in motor sport.

△ **Duesenberg 183 1921**
Origin USA
Engine 2,977 cc, straight-eight
Top speed 112 mph (180 km/h)

This was the only all-American car with a US driver – Jimmy Murphy – to win a European Grand Prix, at Le Mans in 1921. Murphy also won the Indianapolis 500 in it in 1921.

▽ **AC Racing Special 1921**
Origin UK
Engine 1,991 cc, straight-six
Top speed 90 mph (145 km/h)

AC made only road cars until co-owner John Weller designed the Light Six engine. With a chain-driven overhead camshaft, it resulted in a series of fast sports cars, including the Special.

△ **OM 665 "Superba" 1925**
Origin Italy
Engine 1,990 cc, straight-six
Top speed 70 mph (113 km/h)

Founded in 1899, OM still exists, making forklifts within the Fiat Group. The 665 won its class at Le Mans in 1925 and 1926, and finished 1-2-3 in the first Mille Miglia in 1927.

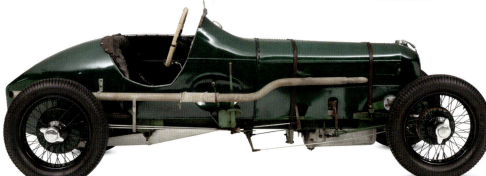

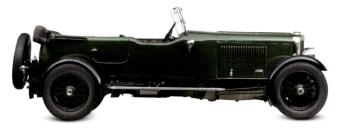

▷ **Mercedes-Benz Type S 36/220 1926**
Origin Germany
Engine 6,789 cc, straight-six
Top speed 106 mph (171 km/h)

Designed by Ferdinand Porsche, this was one of the best and most expensive vintage-era sports cars. It had a supercharger, which boosted power when the throttle was pushed right down.

◁ **Sunbeam 3-litre 1924**
Origin UK
Engine 2,916 cc, straight-six
Top speed 90 mph (145 km/h)

This big car was long and narrow for a racer, but a powerful, dry-sump, double-overhead-camshaft engine kept it competitive. A Sunbeam 3-litre came second at Le Mans in 1925.

▽ **Mercedes-Benz 710 SSK 1929**
Origin Germany
Engine 7,065 cc, straight-six
Top speed 117 mph (188 km/h)

With 170 bhp, boosted to 235 bhp by engaging the supercharger, the Ferdinand Porsche-designed SSK was an effective competition car, impressing in hillclimbs, Grands Prix, and road races.

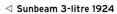

△ **Alfa Romeo P2 1924**

Origin Italy

Engine 1,987 cc, straight-eight

Top speed 123 mph (198 km/h)

Alfa Romeo poached the designer Vittorio Jano from Fiat to create the supercharged P2. Driven by Ascari and Campari, it won the first World Grand Prix Championship in 1925.

△ **Delage V12 1923**

Origin France

Engine 10,600 cc, V12

Top speed 143 mph (230 km/h)

In this car René Thomas set a World Land Speed Record of 143.31 mph (230.6 km/h) in 1924. At Brooklands John Cobb, Oliver Bertram, and Kay Petre all used it to set track records.

◁ **Riley 9 Brooklands 1929**

Origin UK

Engine 1,087 cc, straight-four

Top speed 80 mph (129 km/h)

Percy Riley's 9HP engine with hemispherical combustion chambers gave this sports car great performance for its size. The car's low build gave equally good road-handling.

◁ **Bugatti Type 39 1925**

Origin France

Engine 1,493 cc, straight eight

Top speed 100 mph (161 km/h)

Bugatti reduced the size of its Type 35 engine and used it to develop the Type 39, which was victorious in the 1,500 cc French Touring Grand Prix of 1925.

▷ **Bugatti Type 35C 1926**

Origin France

Engine 1,991 cc, straight-eight

Top speed 125 mph (201 km/h)

Bugatti's most successful racer, the Type 35 won more than 1,000 races in its career. The supercharged 35C triumphed in its debut race, the 1926 Gran Premio di Milano in Italy.

△ **Bugatti Type 35B 1927**

Origin France

Engine 2,262 cc, straight-eight

Top speed 127 mph (204 km/h)

The 35B was built to win Formula Libre races. Its supercharged engine employed a ball-bearing camshaft to help it rev to 6,000 rpm and produce up to 140 bhp.

▷ **Bentley 4½-litre 1927**

Origin UK

Engine 4,398 cc, straight-four

Top speed 92 mph (148 km/h)

One of the most famous British racing cars, the Bentley's advanced engine overcame the car's substantial weight to make it a successful long-distance racer.

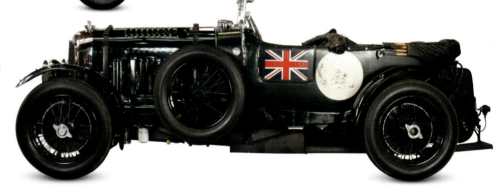

◁ **Fiat Mephistopheles 1923**

Origin Italy/UK

Engine 21,706 cc, straight-six

Top speed 146 mph (235 km/h)

English racing driver Ernest Eldridge fitted a World War I Fiat aero engine into a 1908 Fiat SB4 chassis to create this one-off car. In 1924 he used it to set a new World Land Speed Record of 146.01 mph (234.98 km/h).

▷ **Miller Boyle Valve Special 1930**

Origin USA

Engine 4,425 cc, straight-four

Top speed 140 mph (225 km/h)

Harry Miller was a brilliant engineer, and the race cars and engines he built were by far the most successful in US oval-track racing during the 1920s and 30s.

Luxury and Prestige

Despite the recession that hit much of the world in the aftermath of World War I, there were still plenty of wealthy customers in the 1920s looking for the latest and most opulent carriages to transport them across Europe or the US. Expensive cars were built as chassis complete with running gear, and were clad in the finest examples of the traditional coachbuilders' art.

▷ Hispano-Suiza H6 1919
Origin France
Engine 6,597 cc, straight-six
Top speed 85 mph (137 km/h)

Hispano-Suiza, a Spanish company based in France, made some of the finest cars of the 1920s. Designed by Swiss engineer Marc Birkigt, they featured the first servo brakes.

◁ Spyker C4 All-weather Coupé 1921
Origin Netherlands
Engine 5,741 cc, straight-six
Top speed 80 mph (129 km/h)

Despite royal patronage, and engines shared with Zeppelins, the expensive Spykers sold in very small numbers. The company stopped building cars in 1925.

△ Pierce-Arrow 38HP Model 51 1919
Origin USA
Engine 8,587 cc, straight-six
Top speed 75 mph (121 km/h)

This huge and powerful car had a four-valves-per-cylinder engine. US President Woodrow Wilson liked his official Model 51 so much that he kept it when he left the White House.

▷ Lincoln L Sedan 1922
Origin USA
Engine 6,306 cc, V8
Top speed 82 mph (132 km/h)

Ford rescued Lincoln from receivership in 1922 and produced this magnificent machine. Its luxuries include an electric clock, thermostatic radiator shutters, and a cigar lighter.

◁ Hotchkiss AM 80 Veth Coupé 1929
Origin France
Engine 3,015 cc, straight-six
Top speed 80 mph (129 km/h)

Hotchkiss built high-quality sporting cars. This example was bodied in Arnhem, the Netherlands, by Veth. It features a 29 mph (40 km/h) impact-absorbing front bumper by Overman.

▷ Isotta-Fraschini Tipo 8A Van Rijswijk Dual-cowl Phaeton 1924
Origin Italy
Engine 7,372 cc, straight-eight
Top speed 90 mph (145 km/h)

Italy's top car of the 1920s attracted some magnificent coachbuilt bodies, including this model from the Netherlands. Its 120 bhp engine was designed by Giustino Cattaneo.

△ Lagonda 3-litre 1929
Origin UK
Engine 2,931 cc, straight-six
Top speed 83 mph (134 km/h)

Lagonda produced sporting cars with seven-bearing engines that made them smooth-running and long-lasting. Some had sporting coachwork, other were saloons or limousines.

△ Rolls-Royce 20HP 1922
Origin UK
Engine 3,128 cc, straight-six
Top speed 65 mph (105 km/h)

Underpowered compared with the effortlessly potent larger Rolls-Royces, the 20 hp was a response to post-war austerity. It sold well, despite its limitations.

△ **Stutz Model K 1921**

Origin USA

Engine 5,899 cc, straight-four

Top speed 75 mph (120 km/h)

Alongside its highly successful Bearcat sports cars, Stutz built attractive touring cars with the same engines. From 1921 these had a detachable cylinder head.

△ **Renault 40CV 1921**

Origin France

Engine 9,123 cc, straight-six

Top speed 90 mph (145 km/h)

Renault's biggest luxury car of the 1920s had six cylinders, wooden wheels, and wheelbases of just over 3.6 m (12 ft) or 3.9 m (13 ft). A 40CV won the Monte Carlo Rally in 1925.

△ **Horch Type 350 1928**

Origin Germany

Engine 3,950 cc, straight-eight

Top speed 62 mph (100 km/h)

Horch was Germany's main rival to Mercedes-Benz in the luxury car market. Paul Daimler, son of Gottlieb Daimler, was employed to design this car's double-overhead-camshaft engine.

△ **Minerva 32HP AK Landaulette 1927**

Origin Belgium

Engine 5,954 cc, straight-six

Top speed 70 mph (113 km/h)

Belgium's premier car manufacturer made highly refined cars in the 1920s with Knight sleeve-valve engines. They attracted formal coachwork and multiple royal patronage.

◁ **Packard 443 Custom Eight 1928**

Origin USA

Engine 6,318 cc, straight-eight

Top speed 85 mph (137 km/h)

One of the US's leading luxury marques of the 1920s, Packard built lavish cars on impressively long chassis – in this case with a wheelbase almost 3.6 m (12 ft) long.

△ **Bugatti Type 41 Royale 1927**

Origin France

Engine 12,760 cc, straight-eight

Top speed 120 mph (193 km/h)

With 24 valves and 300 bhp, the Royale was imposing in the extreme, and aimed at royalty worldwide. However, it was prohibitively expensive; just six were built.

▽ **Rolls-Royce Phantom I 1925**

Origin UK

Engine 7,668 cc, straight-six

Top speed 90 mph (145 km/h)

The refined Phantom I, here shown as a sports model, lived up to its reputation of being the "best car in the world". It was often clad in luxurious limousine bodywork.

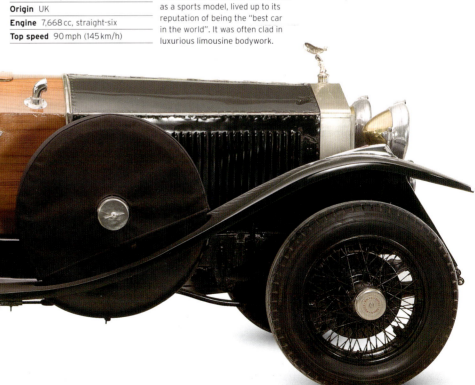

Cars
1930-1949

Economy Models of the Post-Depression Era

The Great Depression that struck the US in 1929 and spread around the world hit car sales hard. Some people still wanted cars, though their aspirations were lower. Upmarket car makers introduced smaller, more affordable versions for the new decade, and manufacturers of small cars made improvements to their models. The new low-price cars were mostly very usable four-seat saloons, much better equipped than earlier economy vehicles.

△ **Singer Junior 8HP 1927**

Origin UK

Engine 848 cc, straight-four

Top speed 55 mph (89 km/h)

Cars such as this one with its lively but economical overhead-camshaft engine made Singer one of the best-selling UK manufacturers in the 1920s. In the 1930s sales declined due to lack of development.

△ **DKW FA 1931**

Origin Germany

Engine 490 cc, straight-two

Top speed 47 mph (76 km/h)

DKW turned its little two-stroke engine sideways and mounted it behind a transverse gearbox to drive the front wheels. This achieved a much lighter and more compact powertrain.

▷ **Goliath Pionier 1931**

Origin Germany

Engine 198 cc, one-cylinder

Top speed 28 mph (45 km/h)

From 1924 Carl Borgward made small commercial vehicles. During the economic crisis he adapted the designs to make this small fabric-bodied car, 4,000 of which were sold.

▷ **Ford Model Y 1932**

Origin UK

Engine 933 cc, straight-four

Top speed 57 mph (92 km/h)

Built in the UK, France, and Germany, the Model Y was perfect for the European market, and cheap enough to give Ford market leadership, a position it held for decades.

△ **Adler Trumpf Junior 1934**

Origin Germany

Engine 995 cc, straight-four

Top speed 57 mph (92 km/h)

This front-wheel-drive "people's car" sold over 100,000 before the war. In two-seat sports form it achieved many successes, including second in class at the Le Mans race in 1937.

△ **Austin Seven Ruby 1934**

Origin UK

Engine 747 cc, straight-four

Top speed 50 mph (80 km/h)

Austin kept the Seven modern with synchromesh on the top three gears, effective four-wheel brakes, shock absorbers, and a sturdy body. However, the extra weight slowed it down.

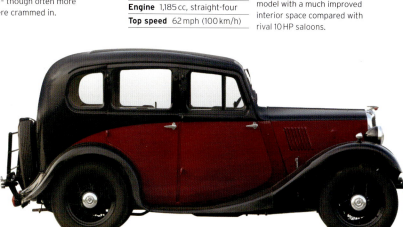

△ Hansa 500 1934
Origin Germany
Engine 465 cc, straight-two
Top speed 40 mph (64 km/h)

Carl Borgward liked small cars; after the Goliath he designed the four-seat Hansa 400 and 500. However, as the economic crisis receded, larger cars were back in demand.

△ Fiat Topolino 500 1936
Origin Italy
Engine 569 cc, straight-four
Top speed 53 mph (85 km/h)

Dante Giacosa designed this "Fiat for the people", with a proper water-cooled engine up front, and two seats – though often more people were crammed in.

△ Hillman Minx Magnificent 1936
Origin UK
Engine 1,185 cc, straight-four
Top speed 62 mph (100 km/h)

Hillman's affordable Minx saloon series began in 1932. In 1936 Hillman offered a better-equipped model with a much improved interior space compared with rival 10 HP saloons.

△ Opel P4 1936
Origin Germany
Engine 1,074 cc, straight-four
Top speed 55 mph (89 km/h)

The P4 was developed from Opel's earlier "Laubfrosch". Conventional in both styling and engineering, it was well constructed and reliable, and popular for those reasons.

△ Morris Eight 1936
Origin UK
Engine 918 cc, straight-four
Top speed 58 mph (93 km/h)

The Eight saved Morris when Austin and Ford had knocked it into third place in the UK. In terms of layout, size, and mechanical specification, it copied the Ford Eight, but it sold well.

△ American Bantam 60 1937
Origin USA
Engine 747 cc, straight-four
Top speed 55 mph (89 km/h)

Production of Austin Sevens under licence in the US had a chequered history from 1929. This restyle by Alexis de Sakhnoffsky did look American, but was too tiny to sell well.

△ Škoda Popular 1938
Origin Czechoslovakia
Engine 995 cc, straight-four
Top speed 62 mph (100 km/h)

Škoda produced innovative small cars in the 1930s. This model featured a wet-liner engine, single-tube backbone chassis, and swing-axle, independent rear suspension.

△ Vauxhall H-type Ten-Four 1937
Origin UK
Engine 1,203 cc, straight-four
Top speed 60 mph (97 km/h)

Vauxhall's entry-level car was a little bigger than its rivals' and boasted monocoque construction, independent front suspension, and hydraulic brakes. Sales reached 42,245.

▷ Lancia Aprilia 1937
Origin Italy
Engine 1,352 cc, V4
Top speed 80 mph (129 km/h)

Probably the most advanced pre-war saloon, the monocoque Aprilia had all-independent suspension, a narrow-angle V4 engine with overhead cam, hydraulic brakes, and pillarless doors.

Racing Cars and Single-seaters

The 1930s saw Italian marques take the lead in European motor racing as French and British opposition waned. However, it wasn't long before German government investment created immensely fast and dominant racing machines. These German cars left other manufacturers looking at lesser formulae where they could compete on an equal footing; only the Italian manufacturers battled on to collect an occasional Grand Prix win.

◁ **Riley Brooklands 1929**
Origin UK
Engine 1,087 cc, straight-four
Top speed 88 mph (142 km/h)

The light, sporting build of Riley cars made them ideal for creating a sports-racing version. The Brooklands raced with great success, winning the 1932 Tourist Trophy.

△ **Hudson Eight Indianapolis 1933**
Origin USA
Engine 3,851 cc, straight-eight
Top speed 130 mph (209 km/h)

To combat reduced race entries during the Great Depression, Indianapolis started the "Junk Formula", welcoming Specials built on production chassis, like this Hudson.

△ **Bugatti Type 51 1931**
Origin France
Engine 2,262 cc, straight-eight
Top speed 140 mph (225 km/h)

Jean Bugatti developed the Type 51 from the Type 35 and added a new twin-cam engine. The car won the 1931 French GP, but later struggled to match German and Italian racers.

△ **Auto Union Type D 1938**
Origin Germany
Engine 2,990 cc, V12
Top speed 205 mph (330 km/h)

Auto Union designer Eberan von Eberhorst produced this complex machine for the new 3-litre Grand Prix category in 1938. Its mid-mounted, three-camshaft V12 produced 420 bhp.

▷ **Auto Union Type A 1934**
Origin Germany
Engine 4,360 cc, V16
Top speed 171 mph (275 km/h)

Ferdinand Porsche designed this revolutionary Grand Prix car, more like modern racers than anything in its day, with a hugely sophisticated engine in front of the rear wheels.

Alfa Romeo

The only racing marque that successfully challenged the all-conquering Germans through the 1930s was Italy's Alfa Romeo, owned and partly financed by the government of dictator Benito Mussolini. With Vittorio Jano as designer, Enzo Ferrari as team manager, and drivers like Tazio Nuvolari, Achille Varzi, and Rudolf Caracciola, Alfa Romeo was able to keep a toehold, but in the end it was an impossible challenge.

▷ **Alfa Romeo 8C 2300 1931**
Origin Italy
Engine 2,336 cc, straight-eight
Top speed 135 mph (217 km/h)

At the start of the decade racing cars still had mechanics on board and, in the case of this Alfa Romeo, even four seats. Built to win Le Mans, this model won it four years in a row.

◁ **Alfa Romeo Tipo B 1932**
Origin Italy
Engine 2,650 cc, straight-eight
Top speed 140 mph (225 km/h)

This was the first successful centre-line single-seater after riding mechanics were dropped. It won the Italian Grand Prix on its debut, challenging German supremacy.

◁ Maserati 8C 3000 1932

Origin Italy

Engine 2,991 cc, straight-eight

Top speed 149 mph (240 km/h)

Maserati's new Grand Prix car for the 1933 season had an ultra-light alloy engine. It beat the Alfa Romeos to win the 1933 French Grand Prix.

△ Maserati 8CTF 1938

Origin Italy

Engine 2,991 cc, straight-eight

Top speed 180 mph (290 km/h)

The double-overhead-camshaft, twin-supercharged 8CTF was built to challenge German domination in European Grands Prix. However, it proved more successful in the US.

▷ Morgan 4/4 Le Mans 1935

Origin UK

Engine 1,098 cc, straight-four

Top speed 80 mph (129 km/h)

Morgan's first four-wheel car was a lively performer with a Coventry Climax engine. Several were raced, and Prudence Fawcett finished 13th in hers at Le Mans (France) in 1938.

◁ Mercedes-Benz W25 1934

Origin Germany

Engine 3,360 cc, straight-eight

Top speed 180 mph (290 km/h)

Encouraged by German government incentives, Mercedes-Benz invested heavily to produce this clean and competitive racer for the new 750 kg (1,654 lb) maximum weight formula.

△ Mercedes-Benz W125 1937

Origin Germany

Engine 5,660 cc, straight-eight

Top speed 205 mph (330 km/h)

The only restriction for the 1937 Grand Prix season was a maximum weight of 750 kg (1,654 lb). Rudolf Uhlenhaut took full advantage to build one of the most powerful GP cars ever.

△ Issigonis Lightweight Special 1938

Origin UK

Engine 750 cc, straight-four

Top speed 90 mph (145 km/h)

Built by Alec Issigonis, who designed the Morris Minor and the Mini, this car has an ultra-light semi-monocoque with all-independent suspension incorporating rubber belts at the rear.

△ Mercedes-Benz W154 1938

Origin Germany

Engine 2,962 cc, V12

Top speed 192 mph (309 km/h)

For 1938 engines were limited to 3.0-litre supercharged or 4.5-litre unsupercharged; Mercedes still managed to achieve 430 bhp with this twin-supercharged, four-cam, V12 racer.

▽ Alfa Romeo 12C-37 1937

Origin Italy

Engine 4,475 cc, V12

Top speed 193 mph (311 km/h)

Alfa Romeo battled bravely to match the dominant German marques in the late 1930s. Vittorio Jano's answer was this 430 bhp V12, but it did not handle well.

△ Alfa Romeo 8C 2300 Monza 1933

Origin Italy

Engine 2,556 cc, straight-eight

Top speed 135 mph (217 km/h)

Scuderia Ferrari (Ferrari's racing division) ran Alfa Romeo's racing team with great success in the 1930s. This may look like a roadgoing sports car, but it won numerous Grands Prix.

Luxury Cars

The 1930s may have been the decade of worldwide depression, but there were still enough wealthy customers to support a fine selection of luxury car manufacturers in the US and Europe. Elegant, comfortable, and often speedy, these cars were usually the first to receive new developments like power brakes, synchromesh gears, and hydraulic brakes.

▷ **Rolls-Royce 20/25 1930**

Origin UK

Engine 3,699 cc, straight-six

Top speed 75 mph (121 km/h)

As the increasing weight of formal luxury coachwork made cars slower, Rolls-Royce upgraded its 20 hp model into the 20/25 with more power.

△ **Rolls-Royce Phantom II 1930**

Origin UK

Engine 7,668 cc, straight-six

Top speed 90 mph (145 km/h)

Magnificent engineering, effortless power, and the ultimate in elegance defined the Rolls-Royce Phantom, even if it could hardly be called advanced mechanically.

◁ **Rolls-Royce 20/25 1930**

Origin UK

Engine 3,699 cc, straight-six

Top speed 75 mph (121 km/h)

The 20/25 was steadily improved through its seven-year production, with synchromesh gears from 1932, but it struggled to maintain the "Best Car in the World" claim.

△ **Cadillac 60 Special 1938**

Origin USA

Engine 5,676 cc, V8

Top speed 92 mph (148 km/h)

Cadillac built some of the most prestigious cars of the 1930s, using not just a large V8, but V12 and V16 engines too. The 60 Special heralded post-war styling in 1938.

Packard

At the top of the luxury car tree in the US stood Packard: it launched the world's first production V12 engine in 1915 and maintained its position through the 1920s. The Great Depression meant a shift of emphasis was vital, broadening its range and appeal, but Packard failed to spot the market turning in the late 1930s, allowing Cadillac to steal its crown.

△ **Packard Super 8 1930**

Origin USA

Engine 6,318 cc, V8

Top speed 100 mph (161 km/h)

Opulent and beautifully built, the Packard Super 8 was one of the top luxury cars at the start of the decade. Buyers were not concerned by its huge fuel consumption.

▽ **Packard Super 8 1932**

Origin USA

Engine 6,318 cc, straight-eight

Top speed 100 mph (161 km/h)

A new chassis design allowed Packard to build lower body styles with a better ride afforded by hydraulic dampers. Power-assisted brakes were fitted from 1933.

◁ **Buick NA 8/90 1934**

Origin USA

Engine 5,644 cc, straight-eight

Top speed 85 mph (137 km/h)

The Buick was spacious and surprisingly good to drive, with a synchromesh gearbox attached to an overhead valve engine – both advanced features at the time.

◁ **Buick Master Series 60 1930**

Origin USA

Engine 5,420 cc, straight-six

Top speed 75 mph (121 km/h)

Buick entered the 1930s with an ancient and thirsty six-cylinder engine, but the cars were still impressive touring machines that found a ready market.

△ **Buick Century Series 60 1936**

Origin USA

Engine 5,247 cc, straight-eight

Top speed 95 mph (153 km/h)

A luxurious family car with a surprising turn of speed, thanks to its 120 bhp engine, the Series 60 Buick proved popular worldwide, offering great value for money.

△ **Talbot 65 1932**

Origin UK

Engine 1,665 cc, straight-six

Top speed 65 mph (105 km/h)

In 1926 chief engineer Georges Roesch gave Talbot one of the smoothest-running six-cylinder engines ever, making this British saloon refined and desirable.

△ **Lincoln K V12 1934**

Origin USA

Engine 6,735 cc, V12

Top speed 100 mph (161 km/h)

Lincoln's luxurious V12 model offered the best of everything, and had pioneering styling updates such as integral, sloping headlights and aerodynamic lines.

◁ **La Salle V8 1931**

Origin USA

Engine 5,840 cc, V8

Top speed 80 mph (129 km/h)

General Motors launched La Salle as a slightly cheaper alternative to its Cadillac brand. Offering similar running gear at a lower price, these elegant and impressive cars sold well.

△ **Packard Super 8 1936**

Origin USA

Engine 5,342 cc, straight-eight

Top speed 90 mph (145 km/h)

Another new chassis design kept Packard at the head of the field, with refinements such as hydraulic brakes. However, competition affected sales.

△ **Packard Super 8 1938**

Origin USA

Engine 5,342 cc, straight-eight

Top speed 95 mph (153 km/h)

The last of Packard's top-of-the-range Super 8s to have their own distinctive coachwork were built in 1938, with a V-screen and more curvaceous lines.

Sports Cars (30s)

New events such as the Mille Miglia in Italy and the Le Mans 24-hour race in France in the 1920s meant that by the following decade competitive automobile racing was thriving. It led to many manufacturers developing models that could be used on both road and track, with marques such as Alfa Romeo and Aston Martin producing fast cars designed to appeal to customers with a competitive edge.

△ **Salmson S4 1929**

Origin France	
Engine 1,296 cc, straight-four	
Top speed 56 mph (90 km/h)	

French carmaker Salmson offered the S4 in a range of body styles, and fitted it with a modern double-overhead-cam powerplant.

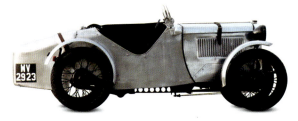

△ **Austin Seven Ulster 1930**

Origin UK	
Engine 747 cc, straight-four	
Top speed 80 mph (129 km/h)	

This aluminium-bodied race version of the Austin Seven, first launched in 1922, added competition success to the model's mainstream popularity.

▷ **Alfa Romeo 8C 2600 1933**

Origin Italy	
Engine 2,556 cc, straight-eight	
Top speed 105 mph (169 km/h)	

This later version of the famed 8C featured a bigger powerplant and was used with further success by Alfa's official racing team.

◁ **Aston Martin MkII 1932**

Origin UK	
Engine 1,495 cc, four-cylinder	
Top speed 80 mph (129 km/h)	

The epitome of the small British sports car of the period, the MkII was lower than its predecessor, thanks to a redesigned chassis.

△ **Aston Martin Le Mans 1932**

Origin UK	
Engine 1,495 cc, straight-four	
Top speed 85 mph (137 km/h)	

Aston's two-seater Le Mans sports model was named in recognition of the marque's participation in the celebrated French endurance event since 1928.

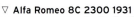

△ **Alfa Romeo 8C 1934**

Origin Italy	
Engine 2,336 cc, straight-eight	
Top speed 105 mph (169 km/h)	

Among the many Italian coachbuilders to clothe Vittorio Jano's iconic 8C model was the legendary Pinin Farina with a typically beautiful interpretation.

▽ **Alfa Romeo 8C 2300 1931**

Origin Italy	
Engine 2,336 cc, straight-eight	
Top speed 105 mph (169 km/h)	

Designed by the automotive genius Vittorio Jano in 1931, the celebrated 8C dominated Blue Riband races such as the Mille Miglia in Italy during the early 1930s.

▷ MG PB 1935

Origin UK

Engine 939 cc, straight-four

Top speed 76 mph (122 km/h)

Revising the 1934 MG PA led to the larger-engined PB a year later, which was available in coupé and convertible body styles.

◁ MG TA Midget 1936

Origin UK

Engine 1,292 cc, straight-four

Top speed 79 mph (127 km/h)

Introduced as a replacement for the PB, the sportier TA Midget featured MG's first hydraulic brakes and, on later models, a synchromesh gearbox.

▷ Fiat Balilla 508S 1933

Origin Italy

Engine 995 cc, straight-four

Top speed 70 mph (113 km/h)

A year after Fiat's new Balilla was launched in 1932, a Sports (S) version of the family model was made available with extra horsepower.

△ Jaguar SS100 1936

Origin UK

Engine 2,663 cc, straight-six

Top speed 95 mph (153 km/h)

Less than 200 examples were made of the SS100 sports model, one of the last before the "SS" was dropped from the company's name.

▷ Morgan Super Sport 3-wheeler 1936

Origin UK

Engine 1,096 cc, V-twin

Top speed 70 mph (113 km/h)

In the 1930s Morgan expanded the technology on its three-wheelers so that buyers could now choose models with three speeds rather than just two.

▽ Morgan 4/4 1936

Origin UK

Engine 1,122 cc, straight-four

Top speed 80 mph (129 km/h)

After 27 years of building three-wheeled vehicles, in 1936 Morgan launched its first four-wheeler in the form of the evergreen 4/4 model.

△ AC 16/80 1936

Origin UK

Engine 1,991 cc, straight-six

Top speed 80 mph (129 km/h)

The six-cylinder engine in the elegant 16/80 was first introduced in 1919, and would go on to power ACs until the early 1960s.

▽ BSA Scout 1935

Origin UK

Engine 1,075 cc, straight-four

Top speed 60 mph (97 km/h)

Known as a manufacturer of cars, motorcycles, and three-wheelers, BSA launched its first modern-looking sports tourer, the Scout, in 1935.

△ BMW 328 1936

Origin Germany

Engine 1,971 cc, straight-six

Top speed 93 mph (150 km/h)

A Le Mans and Mille Miglia winner, the streamlined 328 was one of the finest sports models of the late 1930s.

▷ Wanderer W25K 1936

Origin Germany

Engine 1,963 cc, straight-six

Top speed 90 mph (145 km/h)

The svelte and stylish W25K came from German carmaker Wanderer, which was part of the Auto Union car manufacturing group that included Audi.

Mass-market Models

In the 1930s motoring became popular for the middle classes of Europe and the US, with discerning buyers choosing cars for reliability and power, spaciousness and price. In the US new marques such as Pontiac were created to cater to the mass market and innovations were comfort related, such as automatic transmission to smooth the ride. In Europe Citroën popularized front-wheel drive and monocoque construction.

△ **Citroën 11 Large 1935**

Origin France

Engine 1,911 cc, straight-four

Top speed 76 mph (122 km/h)

André Citroën flouted convention with the monocoque construction, front-wheel-drive Traction Avant series. They functioned well, and were produced until 1957.

◁ **Singer Nine Le Mans 1933**

Origin UK

Engine 972 cc, straight-four

Top speed 70 mph (113 km/h)

Singer's powerful overhead-camshaft engine was its strongest selling point. This was an excellent small sports car to rival MG in the UK.

▷ **Austin 10/4 1935**

Origin UK

Engine 1,125 cc, straight-four

Top speed 55 mph (89 km/h)

The 10/4 was Austin's best-selling model from 1932 to 1940, as customers traded up from the tiny Austin Seven of the 1920s to get a little more space and speed.

△ **Pontiac Six 1935**

Origin USA

Engine 3,408 cc, straight-six

Top speed 75 mph (121 km/h)

Pontiac provided six-cylinder power and stylish bodywork featuring a fencer's mask grille and turret-top lines. The Six saw the company fifth in the US sales league by 1939.

◁ **Ford V8-81 1938**

Origin USA

Engine 3,622 cc, V8

Top speed 85 mph (137 km/h)

Ford's V8 engine gave more performance for the price than any rivals could offer. This helped it to become a worldwide best-seller to follow Models A and T.

△ **Rover 14 1934**

Origin UK

Engine 1,577 cc, straight-six

Top speed 69 mph (111 km/h)

Stylish and solidly middle class with the additional appeal of a six-cylinder engine, Rover's 14HP sold steadily in the UK throughout the 1930s.

▷ **Renault Juvaquatre 1938**

Origin France

Engine 1,003 cc, straight-four

Top speed 60 mph (97 km/h)

An estate version of Renault's first unitary construction model was produced until 1960. It had conventional running gear with mechanical brakes and three gears.

△ **Chevrolet EA Master 1935**

Origin USA

Engine 3,358 cc, straight-six

Top speed 85 mph (137 km/h)

Chevrolet sold over half a million E-series cars in 1935 as car ownership increased massively in the US. Responsive, stylish, and modern, they had a clear appeal.

◁ Hudson Eight 1936

Origin USA

Engine 4,168 cc, straight-eight

Top speed 90 mph (145 km/h)

Hudson moved gradually upmarket in the 1930s, and lost some market share, but this rugged and powerful straight-eight sold well for its size.

△ Hanomag Garant 1936

Origin Germany

Engine 1,097 cc, straight-four

Top speed 52 mph (84 km/h)

A more conventional car than the 1920s Kommisbrot, the Garant proved very popular. Hanomag built no more cars after World War II, despite creating a promising prototype in 1951.

▷ Plymouth P3 1937

Origin USA

Engine 3,300 cc, straight-six

Top speed 75 mph (121 km/h)

Chrysler's bargain basement marque was a sales phenomenon in the US, with its simple, rugged cars at an excellent price. In 1937 566,128 Plymouths were sold.

▷ Dodge D5 1937

Origin USA

Engine 3,570 cc, straight-six

Top speed 85 mph (137 km/h)

Though its body styling was very similar to other cars in the Chrysler group, this didn't stop Dodge selling 295,000 of the D5 in 1937, thanks to strong US demand for mid-range cars.

△ Oldsmobile Six 1935

Origin USA

Engine 3,530 cc, straight-six

Top speed 80 mph (129 km/h)

Oldsmobile was General Motors' mainstream marque, selling on its pioneering features such as hydraulic brakes and synchromesh gears or an optional automatic gearbox.

◁ Dodge D11 1939

Origin USA

Engine 3,570 cc, straight six

Top speed 85 mph (137 km/h)

Absorbed by Chrysler in 1928, Dodge celebrated its 25th anniversary with this modern vee-screen, faired-headlight model that anticipated post-war styling.

◁ Mercedes-Benz 260D 1936

Origin Germany

Engine 2,545 cc, straight-four

Top speed 60 mph (97 km/h)

Claimed to be the first production car with a diesel engine, the 260D was durable but rather slow and noisy. However, the diesel engine was a sign of things to come.

▽ Mercedes-Benz 170H 1936

Origin Germany

Engine 1,697 cc, straight-four

Top speed 68 mph (109 km/h)

When Adolf Hitler demanded a "people's car" to mobilize Germany, Mercedes-Benz came up with the unsuccessful, rear-engined 130H and 170H, which offered open-top motoring with side protection.

Streamlined Cars

The vast majority of drivers in the 1930s were perfectly happy with their spacious, easily-accessed, upright, slab-fronted cars. But now that cars were capable of comfortably exceeding 80 mph (129 km/h) a small number of stylists and engineers, in Europe and the US, were turning their attention to aerodynamics and exploring its potential to increase maximum speeds dramatically and boost stability.

△ Pierce Silver Arrow 1933
Origin USA
Engine 7,566 cc, V12
Top speed 115 mph (185 km/h)

A concept car designed by James R. Hughes, only five Silver Arrows were built in this form. It caused a sensation at the 1933 New York Show, but was too expensive.

▽ Bugatti Type 50 1931
Origin France
Engine 4,972 cc, straight-eight
Top speed 110 mph (177 km/h)

Jean Bugatti styled this Profilée coupé that had the most extreme raked windscreen yet seen on a road car. It combined a luxury road chassis with a double-overhead-camshaft engine.

▷ Cord 810 1936
Origin USA
Engine 4,730 cc, V8
Top speed 93 mph (150 km/h)

The brilliant Cord didn't just boast aerodynamic styling with pop-up headlights: it was front-wheel drive with trailing arm suspension and electric gearchange.

△ Peugeot 402 1935
Origin France
Engine 1,991 cc, straight-four
Top speed 75 mph (121 km/h)

Far more successful than most streamlined cars of the 1930s, mainly due to its low price, 75,000 of the 402 were sold. Retaining a separate chassis allowed Peugeot to offer 16 body styles.

△ Renault Viva Gran Sport 1936
Origin France
Engine 4,085 cc, straight-six
Top speed 89 mph (143 km/h)

With its swept-back, V-shaped grille forming part of the body rather than standing vertically, plus laid-back headlights faired into the front wings, this was an advanced car for its time.

▽ Cord Phantom Corsair 1938
Origin USA
Engine 4,730 cc, V8
Top speed 115 mph (185 km/h)

Designed by millionaire Rust Heinz and built by California coachbuilders Bohmann & Schwartz, based on a Cord 810, this one-off dream car featured in the 1938 film *The Young in Heart*.

▷ Alfa Romeo 6C 2300 Aerodinamica 1935
Origin Italy
Engine 2,309 cc, straight-six
Top speed 120 mph (193 km/h)

Developed secretly on Benito Mussolini's request by Vittorio Jano and Gino and Oscar Jankovits, this car was to have been a V12, but was fitted with a six-cylinder engine.

▷ Alfa Romeo 8C 2900B Le Mans Coupé 1938
Origin Italy
Engine 2,905 cc, straight-eight
Top speed 140 mph (225 km/h)

This sensational aerodynamic coupé, driven by Raymond Sommer and Clemente Biondetti, set the fastest lap at 97 mph (156 km/h), and led for 219 laps at the 1938 Le Mans race – until a tyre blew.

△ **Steyr 50 1936**

Origin Austria

Engine 978 cc, straight-four

Top speed 53 mph (85 km/h)

This teardrop-shaped Austrian people's car was more powerful than some, so it could climb steep Alpine passes. Some 12,000 Steyr 50s were sold up to 1940.

△ **Mercedes-Benz 150H Sport Roadster 1934**

Origin Germany

Engine 1,498 cc, straight-four

Top speed 78 mph (125 km/h)

Designers Hans Nibel and Max Wagner at Mercedes created this mid-engined sports racing prototype, of which just 20 were made. It had great handling, and innovative features such as a coil-sprung, swing-axle rear suspension, and disc wheels.

▷ **Tatra T87 1936**

Origin Czechoslovakia

Engine 2,968 cc, V8

Top speed 99 mph (159 km/h)

With exceptionally aerodynamic bodywork by Paul Jaray and Hans Ledwinka, the rear-engined Tatra was as effective as it was unconventional.

◁ **Chrysler CU Airflow Eight 1934**

Origin USA

Engine 5,301 cc, straight-eight

Top speed 90 mph (145 km/h)

With its wind-tunnel-developed monocoque body, low build, and great handling, the Airflow was way ahead of its time. But the car suffered quality problems, and its sales were poor.

◁ **Lincoln-Zephyr 1936**

Origin USA

Engine 4,378 cc, V12

Top speed 90 mph (145 km/h)

Faired-in headlights and aerodynamic styling made the monocoque-construction Zephyr look very modern, but it still had a side-valve engine and mechanical brakes.

△ **Lagonda V12 Lancefield Le Mans Coupé 1939**

Origin UK

Engine 4,479 cc, V12

Top speed 128 mph (206 km/h)

Lagonda improved its fortunes in the 1930s with a superb V12 engine, which powered two roadsters to 3-4 at Le Mans in 1939. This coupé was finished too late to join them.

▷ **Panhard et Levassor X77 Dynamic 1936**

Origin France

Engine 2,863 cc, straight-six

Top speed 90 mph (145 km/h)

Despite advanced monocoque construction, torsion-bar independent front suspension, and a near-central driving position, the "Art Deco" Dynamic was, however, not popular.

Magnificent and Exotic Body Styles

The 1930s saw the ultimate flowering of the coachbuilder's art. The most exotic chassis, often adapted from state-of-the-art racing cars into roadgoing performance machines, were dressed in the most stylish, streamlined, luxurious, and even decadent bodywork the world had yet seen. It is no surprise that style-conscious France contributed much to this period; even medium-sized French cars were given stunning bodywork.

△ **Cadillac V16 two-seater roadster 1930**

Origin	USA
Engine	7,413 cc, V16
Top speed	95 mph (153 km/h)

The ultimate US status symbol, the Cadillac V16 was a vast car with effortless performance. This rare two-seater belonged to Otis Chandler, publisher of the *Los Angeles Times*.

▷ **Alfa Romeo 8C 2900B Coupé 1938**

Origin	Italy
Engine	2,905 cc, straight-eight
Top speed	100 mph (161 km/h)

Based on the 8C 35 Grand Prix chassis, the 2900B was the finest roadgoing supercar from Alfa Romeo. A handful were sold with this elegant body by Touring.

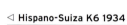

◁ **Hispano-Suiza K6 1934**

Origin	France
Engine	5,184 cc, straight-six
Top speed	90 mph (145 km/h)

The final model from this illustrious Paris car maker was given some fine bodies. This close-coupled saloon had distinctive overlapping doors – a style that saw a revival 70 years later.

▷ **Lancia Astura 1931**

Origin	Italy
Engine	2,973 cc, V8
Top speed	79 mph (127 km/h)

With its narrow-angle overhead-cam V8 engine, the Astura was one of Italy's finest pre-war chassis. This 4th Series Cabriolet was bodied by Pinin Farina.

▷ **Auburn Speedster 1935**

Origin	USA
Engine	4,596 cc, straight-eight
Top speed	104 mph (167 km/h)

Just 500 Speedsters were built in 1935-36, making them highly sought after. Each was tested at 100 mph (160 km/h), which was achievable thanks to 148 bhp from the supercharged engine.

◁ **Bugatti Type 57SC Atalante 1935**

Origin	France
Engine	3,257 cc, straight-eight
Top speed	120 mph (193 km/h)

A mere 17 of these supremely elegant vehicles with low suspension were built. Designed by Jean Bugatti, they had twin-cam engines and independent front suspension.

◁ **Mercedes-Benz 500K Special Roadster 1934**

Origin	Germany
Engine	5,018 cc, straight-eight
Top speed	102 mph (164 km/h)

Using the world's first all-independent suspension, with coil springs and shock absorbers, the 500K offered unparalleled comfort and matching performance.

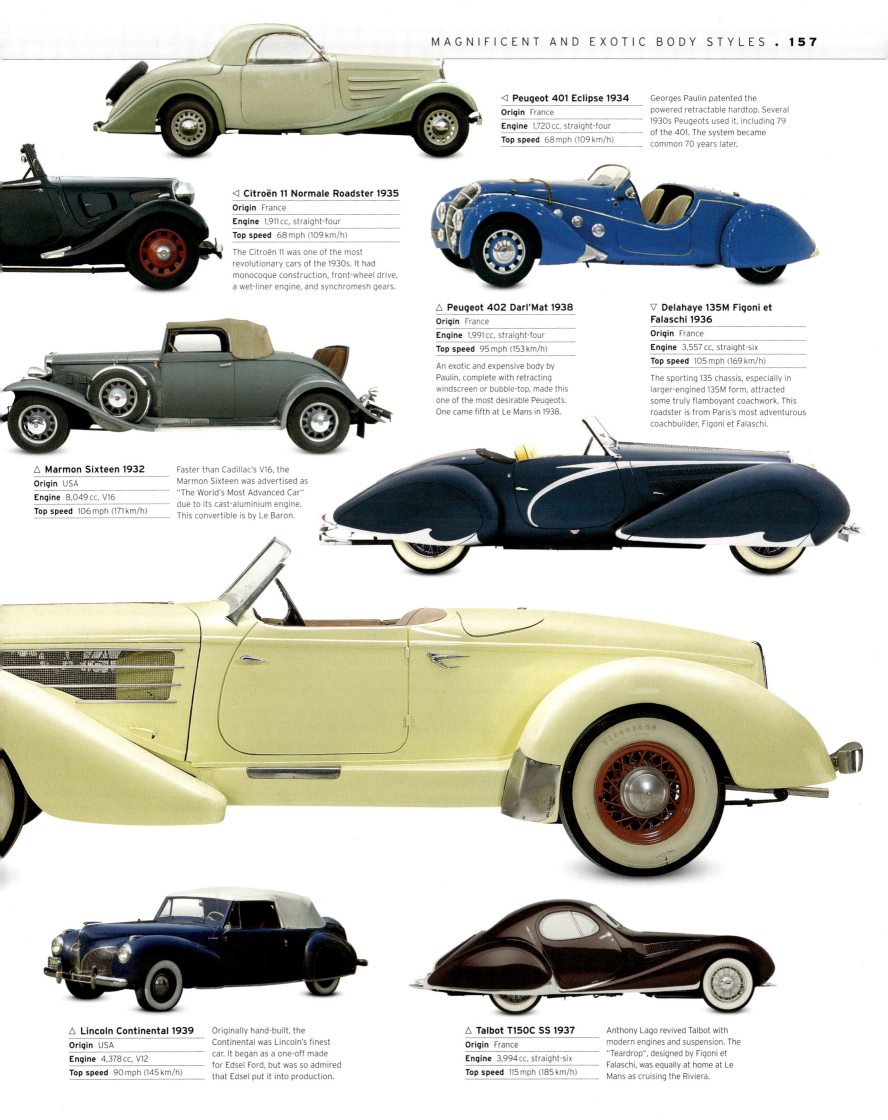

◁ **Peugeot 401 Eclipse 1934**

Origin France

Engine 1,720 cc, straight-four

Top speed 68 mph (109 km/h)

Georges Paulin patented the powered retractable hardtop. Several 1930s Peugeots used it, including 79 of the 401. The system became common 70 years later.

◁ **Citroën 11 Normale Roadster 1935**

Origin France

Engine 1,911 cc, straight-four

Top speed 68 mph (109 km/h)

The Citroën 11 was one of the most revolutionary cars of the 1930s. It had monocoque construction, front-wheel drive, a wet-liner engine, and synchromesh gears.

△ **Peugeot 402 Darl'Mat 1938**

Origin France

Engine 1,991 cc, straight-four

Top speed 95 mph (153 km/h)

An exotic and expensive body by Paulin, complete with retracting windscreen or bubble-top, made this one of the most desirable Peugeots. One came fifth at Le Mans in 1938.

▽ **Delahaye 135M Figoni et Falaschi 1936**

Origin France

Engine 3,557 cc, straight-six

Top speed 105 mph (169 km/h)

The sporting 135 chassis, especially in larger-engined 135M form, attracted some truly flamboyant coachwork. This roadster is from Paris's most adventurous coachbuilder, Figoni et Falaschi.

△ **Marmon Sixteen 1932**

Origin USA

Engine 8,049 cc, V16

Top speed 106 mph (171 km/h)

Faster than Cadillac's V16, the Marmon Sixteen was advertised as "The World's Most Advanced Car" due to its cast-aluminium engine. This convertible is by Le Baron.

△ **Lincoln Continental 1939**

Origin USA

Engine 4,378 cc, V12

Top speed 90 mph (145 km/h)

Originally hand-built, the Continental was Lincoln's finest car. It began as a one-off made for Edsel Ford, but was so admired that Edsel put it into production.

△ **Talbot T150C SS 1937**

Origin France

Engine 3,994 cc, straight-six

Top speed 115 mph (185 km/h)

Anthony Lago revived Talbot with modern engines and suspension. The "Teardrop", designed by Figoni et Falaschi, was equally at home at Le Mans as cruising the Riviera.

Powerful Sports Tourers

Despite the 1929 Wall Street Crash that precipitated a worldwide recession, the 1930s saw small manufacturers continue to make large-engined sports tourers, with ever-increasing refinement as the global economy recovered. The widespread building of high-quality surfaced roads allowed wealthy drivers to cruise at hitherto unimagined speeds and travel hundreds of miles in a few hours, making journeys such as Paris to Monte Carlo or London to Edinburgh a comfortable reality.

△ Bentley 4-litre 1931

Origin UK

Engine 3,915 cc, straight-six

Top speed 80 mph (129 km/h)

The magnificent 8-litre and less-impressive 4-litre models were the swansongs of the independent Bentley company, which would shortly be taken over by Rolls-Royce.

△ Railton Eight 1933

Origin UK

Engine 4,010 cc, straight-eight

Top speed 90 mph (145 km/h)

Reid Railton had the idea of mounting English sporting coachwork on the powerful US Terraplane chassis. The result was the Eight – a fast sporting car available at a competitive price.

▷ Delahaye T135 1935

Origin France

Engine 3,227 cc, straight-six

Top speed 100 mph (161 km/h)

Named "Coupe des Alpes" after success in the challenging Alpine Rally, the T135 had a truck-derived engine, but it performed well on road and track – and looked fabulous.

△ SS I 1933

Origin UK

Engine 2,552 cc, straight-six

Top speed 75 mph (121 km/h)

William Lyons initially built motorcycle sidecars, and then bodies for Austin Sevens. His first complete car was the SS 1 coupé of 1931. It was also available as a tourer from 1933.

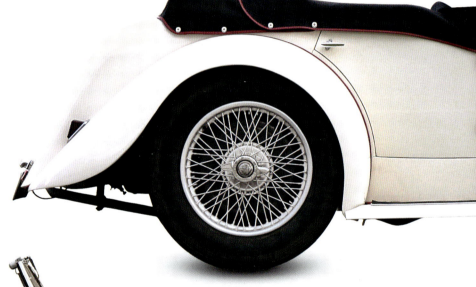

◁ Daimler LQ20 Special 1934

Origin UK

Engine 2,700 cc, straight-six

Top speed 75 mph (121 km/h)

Daimler's owner-driver range had Lanchester-derived engines, fluid flywheel transmission, and servo brakes. Unlike the light Special tourer shown here, the cars were usually heavy-bodied saloons.

◁ Lagonda 3-litre 1933

Origin UK

Engine 3,181 cc, straight-six

Top speed 82 mph (132 km/h)

Lagonda found its luxury tourers hard to sell in the recession, but its 3-litre model was still a fine sporting car that performed well. It offered pre-selector transmission as an option.

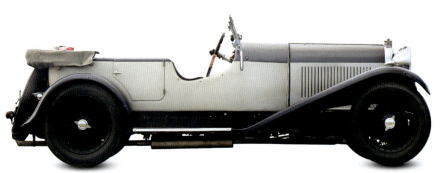

△ Mercedes-Benz 540K 1936

Origin Germany

Engine 5,401 cc, straight-eight

Top speed 106 mph (171 km/h)

Twice the price of a V16 Cadillac, the Mercedes-Benz 540K was a magnificent grand tourer with all-independent suspension, power brakes, and a supercharged engine that gave 180 bhp.

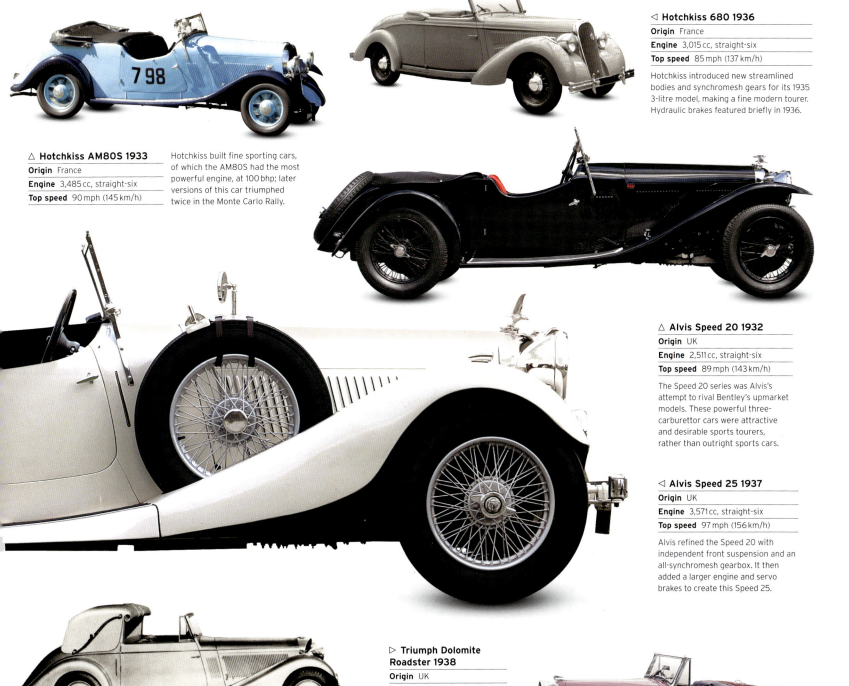

◁ Hotchkiss 680 1936

Origin France

Engine 3,015 cc, straight-six

Top speed 85 mph (137 km/h)

Hotchkiss introduced new streamlined bodies and synchromesh gears for its 1935 3-litre model, making a fine modern tourer. Hydraulic brakes featured briefly in 1936.

△ Hotchkiss AM80S 1933

Origin France

Engine 3,485 cc, straight-six

Top speed 90 mph (145 km/h)

Hotchkiss built fine sporting cars, of which the AM80S had the most powerful engine, at 100 bhp; later versions of this car triumphed twice in the Monte Carlo Rally.

△ Alvis Speed 20 1932

Origin UK

Engine 2,511 cc, straight-six

Top speed 89 mph (143 km/h)

The Speed 20 series was Alvis's attempt to rival Bentley's upmarket models. These powerful three-carburettor cars were attractive and desirable sports tourers, rather than outright sports cars.

◁ Alvis Speed 25 1937

Origin UK

Engine 3,571 cc, straight-six

Top speed 97 mph (156 km/h)

Alvis refined the Speed 20 with independent front suspension and an all-synchromesh gearbox. It then added a larger engine and servo brakes to create this Speed 25.

△ Jensen S-type 1937

Origin UK

Engine 3,622 cc, V8

Top speed 81 mph (130 km/h)

The S-type was the first car made by brothers Alan and Richard Jensen, who began as coachbuilders. They offered it as a drophead coupé, saloon, or tourer, and with a 2.2-litre engine option.

▷ Triumph Dolomite Roadster 1938

Origin UK

Engine 1,991 cc, straight-six

Top speed 80 mph (129 km/h)

With its three-carburettor engine and waterfall grille, the Walter Belgrove-designed Dolomite was a striking car. Accommodation was three seats abreast in the front, and a two-seat dickey behind.

▷ Delage D6-75 1938

Origin France

Engine 2,998 cc, straight-six

Top speed 95 mph (153 km/h)

Despite near bankruptcy and a takeover by Delahaye in 1935, Delage continued making superb sporting cars throughout the 1930s. This replica TT version is more sporty than most D6-75s.

Large Cars

After World War II few people in Europe could afford large, luxurious saloons. Instead, designs were conservative and only figures such as government ministers, ambassadors, or doctors could justify a large, powerful car for their work. Cars were mostly updated pre-war creations with heavy and ponderous engines, many still with side valves and three-speed gearboxes.

▷ **Isotta-Fraschini 8C Monterosa 1947**

Origin Italy

Engine 3,400 cc, V8

Top speed 100 mph (161 km/h)

Inspired by Tatra, engineer Fabio Rapi planned an advanced luxury car, with a rear-mounted V8 engine, rubber springs, and aerodynamic monocoque body. Only five of these were ever built.

▷ **Daimler DE36 1946**

Origin UK

Engine 5,460 cc, straight-eight

Top speed 83 mph (134 km/h)

This huge post-war Daimler was supplied to seven royal families around the world, including the Windsors. It had the UK's last production straight-eight engine.

◁ **Bentley MkVI 1946**

Origin UK

Engine 4,257 cc, straight-six

Top speed 100 mph (161 km/h)

Post-war Bentleys were priced just below the equivalent Rolls-Royce; 80% were sold with factory-built "Standard Steel" bodies, which was cheaper than coachbuilding.

▷ **Opel Kapitän 1948**

Origin Germany

Engine 2,473 cc, straight-six

Top speed 78 mph (126 km/h)

Re-introduced in 1948, the monocoque Kapitän helped Opel get back on its feet after the war. It was a practical and popular car: 30,431 were sold up to 1951.

△ **Wolseley 6/80 1948**

Origin UK

Engine 2,215 cc, straight-six

Top speed 79 mph (127 km/h)

This reliable saloon became the standard police car in the UK in the 1940s, used for both patrol and pursuit duties. It had a factory-supplied, heavy-duty specification.

▷ **Humber Pullman II 1948**

Origin UK

Engine 4,086 cc, straight-six

Top speed 78 mph (126 km/h)

This imposing limousine was a favourite of British government officials. The chassis was an extended Super Snipe, requiring a two-part propeller shaft.

◁ **Humber Super Snipe II 1948**

Origin UK

Engine 4,086 cc, straight-six

Top speed 82 mph (132 km/h)

Preferred by bank managers and government officials, the Super Snipe was the epitome of conservative taste. It inherited its engine from the wartime British army staff car.

▽ **Rolls-Royce Silver Wraith 1946**

Origin UK

Engine 4,257 cc, straight-six

Top speed 85 mph (137 km/h)

The top UK post-war luxury car had its body custom-made, generally panelled in aluminium. It gradually grew in length and engine size until 1959.

△ **Ford V8 Pilot 1947**

Origin UK

Engine 3,622 cc, V8

Top speed 79 mph (127 km/h)

An extremely tough car, the Pilot's flathead V8 engine dated back to the 1930s. Its pulling power was legendary, but it was out of step with the UK's post-war austerity.

▷ **Lagonda 2.6-litre 1948**

Origin UK

Engine 2,580 cc, straight-six

Top speed 90 mph (145 km/h)

A luxury convertible and saloon designed by the great WO Bentley, the Lagonda had all-independent suspension and a double-camshaft 2.6-litre engine that subsequently powered Aston Martins.

△ **Delahaye 235 1951**

Origin France

Engine 3,557 cc, straight-six

Top speed 110 mph (177 km/h)

An updated version of the pre-war 135, Delahaye built 85 of the 235 between 1951 and 1954. Coachbuilt bodywork proved too expensive and was replaced by a factory body.

▷ **Austin A135 Princess 1947**

Origin UK

Engine 3,995 cc, straight-six

Top speed 88 mph (142 km/h)

Triple carburettors and more modern-looking, aluminium bodywork from coachbuilder Vanden Plas helped improve performance. This is the later, long-wheelbase limousine.

◁ **Austin A125 Sheerline 1947**

Origin UK

Engine 3,995 cc, straight-six

Top speed 81 mph (130 km/h)

Razor-edged styling and huge headlamps helped this large Austin resemble a contemporary Bentley, but performance from its truck-derived engine was limited.

US Style-setters

There was a huge appetite for new cars in post-war America, so manufacturers rushed into production, working with essentially pre-war body styles. These styles, however, had seen three seasons' more development than European makes, since the US had joined the war that much later. By 1949 pent-up demand was satisfied, and manufacturers were competing head-on with aerodynamic new styles and with the first signs of fins and chrome.

△ **Lincoln 1946**

Origin USA

Engine 4,998 cc, V12

Top speed 92 mph (148 km/h)

Lincoln, Ford's upmarket brand, was still making pre-war-styled cars in 1946. These were fine cars, but the public was looking for something more modern than this.

△ **Kaiser Frazer F47 1946**

Origin USA

Engine 3,707 cc, straight-six

Top speed 82 mph (132 km/h)

The first US car with true post-war styling – a full-width bodyshell with no front or rear wing mouldings – the Frazer was styled by Howard "Dutch" Darrin.

◁ **Buick Roadmaster Sedanette 1949**

Origin USA

Engine 5,247 cc, straight-eight

Top speed 87 mph (140 km/h)

Buick's 1949 Sedanette was superbly proportioned, its fastback style enhanced by tapering chrome sidebars, spats over the rear wheels, and fighter-aircraft-style "ventiports".

△ **Chrysler Windsor Club Coupé 1946**

Origin USA

Engine 4,107 cc, six-cylinder

Top speed 82 mph (132 km/h)

The Chrysler Windsor was a Chrysler Royal with better trim, including two-tone wool broadcloth seats. This coupé has distinctively post-war rear-end styling, despite still-protruding wings.

▷ **Buick Super 1946**

Origin USA

Engine 4,064 cc, straight-eight

Top speed 82 mph (140 km/h)

Buick's post-war style was a light update of its 1942 models, but it was still more modern than most of its rivals. Elegant and attractive, the convertibles were particularly desirable.

△ **Chevrolet Stylemaster 1946**

Origin USA

Engine 3,548 cc, straight-six

Top speed 80 mph (132 km/h)

The US's best-selling car was a competitively priced, pre-war-styled machine whose Stovebolt Six engine dated back to 1937.

◁ Tucker 48 1948
Origin USA
Engine 5,475 cc, flat-six
Top speed 131 mph (211 km/h)

Even without the personality of its mercurial sponsor, Preston Tucker, this car would have made headlines with its rear-mounted helicopter engine and storming performance.

▽ Pontiac Chieftain Convertible 1949
Origin USA
Engine 4,079 cc, straight-eight
Top speed 85 mph (137 km/h)

Low, sleek, full-width bodies were the hit of 1949 at Pontiac. This was some compensation for the rather unexciting pre-war L-head six- and eight-cylinder engines.

◁ Ford Custom V8 1949
Origin USA
Engine 3,917 cc, V8
Top speed 85 mph (137 km/h)

Ford's new styling came in 1949. It was clean, low, modern, and boxy – all of which was soon to be seen on European Fords too. The public flocked to buy the new models.

▽ Dodge Coronet 1949
Origin USA
Engine 3,769 cc, straight-six
Top speed 80 mph (129 km/h)

Dodge's boxy new look arrived in 1949. Apart from the chrome, US cars were not too different in profile from European cars at this time, but this was soon to change.

△ Cadillac Fleetwood 60 Special 1947
Origin USA
Engine 5,670 cc, V8
Top speed 90 mph (145 km/h)

In 1947 Cadillac was still building a pre-war-styled car, dressing it up with ever more chrome. Slightly wider doors were fitted to the luxury Fleetwood model.

◁ Hudson Super Six 1948
Origin USA
Engine 4,293 cc, straight-six
Top speed 90 mph (145 km/h)

One of the few small firms in post-war US car production, Hudson excelled with its low-built "step down" 1948 models and new, powerful, Super Six engine.

△ Cadillac Series 62 Club Coupé 1949
Origin USA
Engine 5,424 cc, V8
Top speed 92 mph (148 km/h)

General Motors' 1948 body design featured tailfins inspired by the P38 Lockheed fighter plane. 1949 brought a new OHV engine.

▽ Chevrolet Fleetline Deluxe 1949
Origin USA
Engine 3,548 cc, straight-six
Top speed 80 mph (129 km/h)

Chevrolet adopted fully blended front wings in 1949. The wings were still a conservative style, but the marque remained the market leader.

△ Oldsmobile 88 Club Sedan 1949
Origin USA
Engine 4,977 cc, V8
Top speed 100 mph (161 km/h)

Futuramic styling, plus the new high-performance Rocket V8 engine and effective Hydramatic automatic transmission, made the 1949 Oldsmobiles hugely desirable.

▽ Packard Super Eight convertible 1948
Origin USA
Engine 5,359 cc, straight-eight
Top speed 98 mph (158 km/h)

1948 was Packard's finest post-war year, as its clean, modern, "bathtub" styling was a hit with buyers. However, the small company could not afford annual restyles like its rivals.

◁ Studebaker Champion 1950
Origin USA
Engine 2,779 cc, straight-six
Top speed 82 mph (132 km/h)

In 1947 Studebaker was the first big name to introduce post-war styling. By 1950 the Champion was onto its first major revision, with longer nose and aerodynamic lines.

Practical Everyday Transport

The demands and shortages of World War II meant that transport in the 1940s had to concentrate on practicality without frills or luxuries – vans and pick-ups were vital to move food and supplies to where they were needed, and off-road vehicles were required to carry troops over rough terrain. After the war simple, sturdy vehicles were in demand as the world's economies began to recover.

△ **Citroën 11 Large 1935**

Origin France

Engine 1,911 cc, straight-four

Top speed 65 mph (105 km/h)

The longest of the innovative front-wheel-drive Citroëns was over 4.5 m (15 ft) long with a huge turning circle. Ideal for the larger family, or as a taxi, it had three rows of seats.

▽ **Humber Super Snipe staff car 1938**

Origin UK

Engine 4,086 cc, straight-six

Top speed 78 mph (126 km/h)

This Humber was the perfect vehicle for transporting British officers during World War II. Despite being large and lumbering, it was rapid and very strong.

△ **Ford F1 1948**

Origin USA

Engine 3,703 cc, V8

Top speed 70 mph (112 km/h)

Attractive, well proportioned, and adequately powerful in V8 form, the 1948 truck was styled by Bob Gregorie along the lines of the 1939 Ford range and has always been popular.

▽ **International Harvester K-series pick-up 1941**

Origin USA

Engine 3,507 cc, straight-six

Top speed 65 mph (105 km/h)

The pick-up truck became standard transport in rural America by the 1940s. Agricultural machinery maker International Harvester started building light trucks in 1909.

△ **Volkswagen Kübelwagen 1940**

Origin Germany

Engine 985 cc, flat-four

Top speed 50 mph (80 km/h)

Ferdinand Porsche's Beetle-based military transport served in all fields of war, despite being only two-wheel drive. A remarkable 50,435 of these were built from 1940 to 1945.

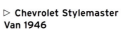

△ **Volkswagen Schwimmwagen Type 166 1941**

Origin Germany

Engine 1,131 cc, flat-four

Top speed 47 mph (76 km/h)

A highly effective amphibian of which 15,584 were built, the Schwimmwagen had a propeller for water propulsion. It was four-wheel drive in first gear only, with two limited-slip differentials.

▷ **Chevrolet Stylemaster Van 1946**

Origin USA

Engine 3,548 cc, straight-six

Top speed 87 mph (140 km/h)

This capacious van was ideal for transporting loads in rural areas. Great value, the durable "Stovebolt Six" engine introduced in 1937 made it a best-seller.

◁ **Standard Vanguard 1948**

Origin UK

Engine 2,088 cc, straight-four

Top speed 77 mph (124 km/h)

Standard's MD Sir John Black's post-war dream was to build a car for worldwide export. In the event, however, sales were confined to British Commonwealth countries.

▽ **Land-Rover Series I 1948**

Origin UK

Engine 1,595 cc, straight-four

Top speed 55 mph (89 km/h)

Rover director Maurice Wilks brilliantly conceived a 4x4 utility for farming families that could go anywhere on the fields, take children to school, and produce to market.

▷ **Land-Rover Series I Station Wagon 1948**

Origin UK

Engine 1,595 cc, straight-four

Top speed 55 mph (89 km/h)

Far more versatile than the Jeep that inspired it, the Land-Rover's wider appeal led to demand for a more civilized vehicle – the 7-seater Station Wagon fulfilled that brief.

◁ **Willys MB "Jeep" 1941**

Origin USA

Engine 2,199 cc, straight-four

Top speed 60 mph (97 km/h)

Willys, Ford, and Bantam competed for the US Army contract to build a light, four-wheel-drive reconnaissance vehicle. Willys won with the MB, and Ford built it as the Ford GPW.

▽ **Willys Jeep Jeepster 1948**

Origin USA

Engine 2,199 cc, straight-four

Top speed 60 mph (97 km/h)

Designed by Brooks Stevens, the Jeepster was an attempt to create a fun sports car from the basic wartime Jeep. It was rear-wheel drive only, and was heavily decorated with chrome.

△ **Jowett Bradford 1946**

Origin UK

Engine 1,005 cc, flat-two

Top speed 53 mph (85 km/h)

Jowett's horizontally opposed flat-twin engine dated back to 1910, but it readily pulled this spacious family estate car. It was typical functional transport built in Yorkshire.

◁ **Hillman Minx Phase III estate 1949**

Origin UK

Engine 1,185 cc, straight-four

Top speed 59 mph (95 km/h)

Estate cars were practical workhorses and Hillman was one of the first British marques to produce an estate car body that was adapted from a monocoque Commer van.

Roadsters and Sports Cars

Instructed to help restore the UK's devastated balance of payments after World War II, British car manufacturers hurried to build sports cars to sell on the lucrative US market, where home-grown products were too bulky to match nimble European cars on twisty roads. Few of these British products would last long into the next decade (the Jaguar XK120 being an exception), and mainland Europe saw only a handful of expensive sports cars produced.

△ Bristol 400 1947

Origin UK

Engine 1,971cc, straight-six

Top speed 94 mph (151 km/h)

Bristol Aeroplanes entered the car market with a repackaged pre-war BMW design, brought back to the UK as "war reparations". It was a good sporting car and sold well.

△ Riley RMC Roadster 1948

Origin UK

Engine 2,443cc, straight-four

Top speed 100 mph (161 km/h)

A somewhat half-hearted attempt to make a sports car out of a four-door sports saloon, the Roadster had a single row of three seats and a very long tail. In all, 507 were made.

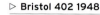

▷ Bristol 402 1948

Origin UK

Engine 1,971cc, straight-six

Top speed 98 mph (158 km/h)

Touring of Italy gave Bristol an attractive post-war style for the 401 saloon and this rare, four-seat convertible, which has a concealed hood and wind-up windows.

△ Ferrari 166 MM Barchetta 1949

Origin Italy

Engine 1,995cc, V12

Top speed 125 mph (201 km/h)

The first true production Ferrari sports car, usually fitted with this fabulous Touring Barchetta body, won the Mille Miglia, Spa, and Le Mans races in 1949.

◁ Jaguar XK120 1948

Origin UK

Engine 3,442cc, straight six

Top speed 125 mph (201 km/h)

William Lyons designed his 120 as simply a test bed for the new twin-cam XK engine. Huge demand, however, persuaded him to put it into production.

Grand Prix Cars

When Grand Prix racing resumed in 1946, in the wake of World War II, the German "Silver Arrows", almost unbeatable in the late 1930s, were nowhere to be seen. The new rules allowed 1.5-litre supercharged or 4.5-litre unsupercharged engines, and saw the small supercharged Italian racers from Alfa Romeo and Maserati dominate. The only car to beat them in the 1940s was the lumbering French Talbot-Lago.

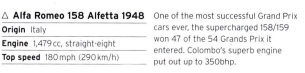

△ Alfa Romeo 158 Alfetta 1948

Origin Italy

Engine 1,479cc, straight-eight

Top speed 180 mph (290 km/h)

One of the most successful Grand Prix cars ever, the supercharged 158/159 won 47 of the 54 Grands Prix it entered. Colombo's superb engine put out up to 350bhp.

▷ **Talbot-Lago T26 Grand Sport 1947**

Origin France

Engine 4,482 cc, straight-six

Top speed 120 mph (193 km/h)

The ultimate Grand Tourer of the 1940s enjoyed a wide range of fabulous coachbuilt bodies, with none finer than this model by Saoutchik. A lighter version won Le Mans in 1950.

◁ **MG TC 1945**

Origin UK

Engine 1,250 cc, straight-four

Top speed 75 mph (121 km/h)

Attractive, light, and fun – if very old-fashioned in its design – the TC sold as fast as MG could build it in the early post-war years.

▽ **MG YT 1948**

Origin UK

Engine 1,250 cc, straight-four

Top speed 71 mph (114 km/h)

An MG sports car tailored for family use, the versatile YT was built only for export. Just 877 were sold between 1948 and 1950.

△ **MG TD 1949**

Origin UK

Engine 1,250 cc, straight-four

Top speed 80 mph (129 km/h)

It still looked like a pre-war car, but the TD was beautifully rounded, readily tunable, and had a left-hand drive version too. Worldwide, 29,664 were sold between 1950 and 1953.

◁ **Austin A90 Atlantic 1949**

Origin UK

Engine 2,660 cc, straight-four

Top speed 91 mph (146 km/h)

Leonard Lord's attempt at making a car that would appeal to US buyers was too small and costly to catch on, despite great PR generated by the records it set at the Indianapolis Speedway.

△ **Healey Silverstone 1949**

Origin UK

Engine 2,443 cc, straight-four

Top speed 107 mph (172 km/h)

Donald Healey added the powerful twin-camshaft Riley engine to his own chassis, which had excellent handling qualities. The result was this ideal club-racing road car.

◁ **Allard P1 1949**

Origin UK

Engine 3,622 cc, V8

Top speed 85 mph (137 km/h)

Sydney Allard put the readily available "flathead" Ford V8 engine in a sporting chassis with light bodywork to produce the P1. In it, he won the Monte Carlo Rally in 1952.

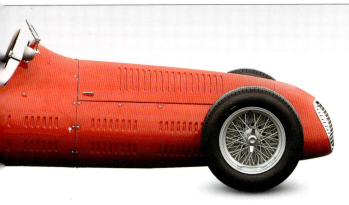

◁ **Maserati 4CLT/48 1948**

Origin Italy

Engine 1,491 cc, straight-four

Top speed 168 mph (270 km/h)

With a new tubular chassis and twin superchargers for 1948, the 16-valve 4CLT became more competitive, and won numerous Grands Prix in 1948 and 1949.

△ **Talbot-Lago T26C 1948**

Origin France

Engine 4,482 cc, straight-six

Top speed 168 mph (270 km/h)

Despite being heavy (it was even burdened with a pre-selector gearbox) and lacking a supercharger, the T26C scored two Grand Prix victories in 1949, thanks to its endurance and reliability.

Small Cars

After World War II there was a new motoring revolution. Most soldiers posted overseas had experienced long-distance travel for the first time. On their return home they wanted to be mobile and take their families much further afield than their fathers had been able to. To meet this demand, manufacturers around the world strove to develop cars for the masses, many of which went on to sell by the million.

◁ Morris Eight Series E 1938
Origin UK
Engine 918 cc, straight-four
Top speed 58 mph (93 km/h)

A pre-war model just modern enough in looks to continue in production post-war, the Series E Morris sold well until the new Morris Minor was ready to take over.

▷ Morris Minor 1948
Origin UK
Engine 918 cc, straight-four
Top speed 62 mph (100 km/h)

Alec Issigonis's brilliant people's car had a monocoque construction, torsion-bar front suspension, four gears, and modern lines – but not the flat-four engine he had wanted.

△ Volkswagen 1945
Origin Germany
Engine 1,131 cc, flat-four
Top speed 63 mph (101 km/h)

Designed by Ferdinand Porsche before the war, the "Beetle" would eventually become the best-selling car of all time thanks to its reliable engine, good space, and low price.

△ Toyota Model SA 1947
Origin Japan
Engine 995 cc, straight-four
Top speed 58 mph (93 km/h)

Japan's first new post-war model, the SA mimicked many features of Volkswagen's Beetle, although its Ford-like engine was mounted at the front rather than the rear.

▷ Ford Taunus G93A 1948
Origin Germany
Engine 1,172 cc, straight-four
Top speed 60 mph (97 km/h)

This German version of Britain's E93A Ford Prefect had much more modern styling than its counterpart, but it was exactly the same beneath the bonnet.

◁ Standard 8HP 1945
Origin UK
Engine 1,009 cc, straight-four
Top speed 60 mph (97 km/h)

Standard rushed its pre-war Eight back into production in 1945, having improved it with a four-speed gearbox. A competent if unexciting car, it sold 53,099 in three years.

◁ **Datsun DB 1948**

Origin Japan

Engine 722 cc, straight-four

Top speed 50 mph (80 km/h)

With styling copied from the US-built Crosley, this was Japan's first modern-looking car. The DB used a pre-war Datsun truck chassis and a side-valve car engine.

▷ **Crosley 1948**

Origin USA

Engine 721 cc, straight-four

Top speed 70 mph (113 km/h)

The slab-sided Crosley showed great promise with its unique sheet-steel, overhead-camshaft engine, but it failed to win over the US car-buying public.

▽ **Fiat 500C 1949**

Origin Italy

Engine 569 cc, straight-four

Top speed 60 mph (97 km/h)

This was the final version of Dante Giacosa's brilliant 1937 "Topolino" (Little Mouse), which mobilized the population of Italy with its well-packaged conventional layout.

△ **Citroën 2CV 1948**

Origin France

Engine 375 cc, flat-two

Top speed 39 mph (63 km/h)

Derived from a 1930s plan to develop a car to replace the horse and cart in rural France, the 2CV became a favourite in both town and country. The 2CV's crude looks belied its high-quality, innovative engineering.

◁ **Renault 4CV 1946**

Origin France

Engine 760 cc, straight-four

Top speed 57 mph (92 km/h)

The 4CV looked similar to its British rival, the Morris Minor, but it had all-independent suspension and a rear-mounted engine; it was also quicker to reach a million sales.

◁ **MG Y-type 1947**

Origin UK

Engine 1,250 cc, straight-four

Top speed 71 mph (114 km/h)

MG lengthened its little TC sports car chassis and added pre-war Morris Eight body panels to create this antiquated but charming saloon, which sold 6,158 from 1947 to 1951.

▷ **Panhard Dyna 110 1948**

Origin France

Engine 610 cc, flat-two

Top speed 68 mph (109 km/h)

Designed by Jean Albert Grégoire, the Dyna 110 had an aluminium structure, an air-cooled aluminium engine, front-wheel drive, and independent suspension.

△ **Austin A40 Devon 1947**

Origin UK

Engine 1,200 cc, straight-four

Top speed 67 mph (108 km/h)

Modelled on a pre-war Chevrolet, Austin's first post-war design was slightly awkward and bulbous-looking, but it sold well thanks to its new overhead-valve engine.

◁ **Bond Minicar 1948**

Origin UK

Engine 122 cc, one-cylinder

Top speed 38 mph (61 km/h)

Petrol rationing and cheap tax for three-wheelers made this two-seater ideal for the austerity of post-war Britain. The two-stroke engine pivoted with the car's front wheel.

▷ **Saab 92 1949**

Origin Sweden

Engine 764 cc, straight-two

Top speed 65 mph (105 km/h)

Aircraft maker Saab gave its 92 the most aerodynamic styling of the time, along with front-wheel drive and a two-stroke engine. The 92 proved a very successful rally car.

Mid-range Family Saloons

Once hostilities were over, factory owners flush with money from war contracts hurried to fill their factories' capacities with car manufacture again. However, shortages of raw materials – especially steel – meant that many stayed initially with old-fashioned construction techniques like wood body frames, aluminium body panels, and fabric-covered roofs. Some rushed pre-war models back into production, while others took the time to develop all-new models.

△ Rover 10 1945

Origin UK

Engine 1,389 cc, straight-four

Top speed 65 mph (105 km/h)

The 10HP was a luxuriously trimmed but underpowered 1930s saloon. It stayed in production post-war and looked identical to the more powerful 1948-49 P3 model that followed.

▷ Riley RMB 1946

Origin UK

Engine 2,443 cc, straight-four

Top speed 95 mph (153 km/h)

Pre-war in appearance only, the RM was among Britain's first new post-war models and, in 2.5-litre form, was a dynamic sports saloon, built to high standards.

▷ Daimler DB18 1945

Origin UK

Engine 2,522 cc, straight-six

Top speed 72 mph (116 km/h)

Daimler's smallest car from directly before the war was the obvious choice to re-introduce post-war. Well engineered and sensible, it exuded quality, but not opulence.

▷ Alvis TA14 1946

Origin UK

Engine 1,892 cc, straight-four

Top speed 74 mph (119 km/h)

Alvis re-entered the market post-war with a quality coachbuilt saloon. Its styling and chassis were firmly rooted in the 1930s, with beam axles and mechanical brakes.

◁ Mercedes-Benz 170V 1946

Origin Germany

Engine 1,697 cc, straight-four

Top speed 67 mph (108 km/h)

Launched in 1936 and very successful due to its quality construction, smooth running, and all-independent suspension, the 170V was re-introduced post-war.

▽ Peugeot 203 1948

Origin France

Engine 1,290 cc, straight-four

Top speed 71 mph (114 km/h)

Post-war Peugeots were built to be resilient. The 203, in particular, had a spacious modern body, a powerful engine for its size, and hard-wearing running gear. It was made until 1960.

△ AC 2-litre 1947

Origin UK

Engine 1,991 cc, straight-six

Top speed 80 mph (129 km/h)

AC quickly launched a quality car with attractive, post-war styling, although it had a pre-war chassis with beam axles. Its powerful engine was designed in 1919.

◁ Triumph 1800 1946

Origin UK

Engine 1,776 cc, straight-four

Top speed 75 mph (121 km/h)

Standard bought Triumph in 1945, and relaunched it as an upmarket marque with razor-edge styling. The 1800's engine was enlarged in 1949, and it lasted until 1954.

△ **Jowett Javelin 1947**
Origin UK
Engine 1,486 cc, flat-four
Top speed 78 mph (126 km/h)

The Javelin was the result of a brave attempt by a small Yorkshire company to build an all-new post-war car. It had a modern engine and was aerodynamic, with good handling.

△ **Volvo PV444 1947**
Origin Sweden
Engine 1,414 cc, straight-four
Top speed 76 mph (122 km/h)

With monocoque construction and a new overhead-valve engine – later tuned to give double the power and a top speed of 95 mph (153 km/h) – the new Volvo was ahead of its time.

▽ **Sunbeam-Talbot 90 1948**
Origin UK
Engine 1,944 cc, straight-four
Top speed 77 mph (124 km/h)

Produced as a quality four-door saloon or two-door drophead, the 90 had an attractive post-war look but still had a beam front axle.

△ **Vauxhall Velox 1948**
Origin UK
Engine 2,275 cc, straight-six
Top speed 74 mph (119 km/h)

A pre-war design with minimal enhancements, the Velox had a strong six-cylinder engine and sold on value for money and reliability. Full post-war styling came in 1951.

△ **Tatra T600 Tatraplan 1948**
Origin Czechoslovakia
Engine 1,952 cc, flat-four
Top speed 80 mph (129 km/h)

With a drag coefficient of just 0.32, the brilliant T600 was extremely aerodynamic. The air-cooled engine was mounted at the rear, giving a spacious interior for six people.

△ **Humber Hawk III 1948**
Origin UK
Engine 1,944 cc, straight-four
Top speed 71 mph (114 km/h)

One of the first British cars to have curved windscreen in a modern body, the Mk III had a pre-war side-valve engine and chassis, but now with independent front suspension.

△ **Holden 48-215 "FX" 1948**
Origin Australia
Engine 2,171 cc, straight-six
Top speed 80 mph (129 km/h)

General Motors acquired Australia's Holden in 1931, but Holden forged its own identity post-war with this monocoque car – intended first as a Chevrolet but too small for the US.

△ **Morris Oxford MO 1948**
Origin UK
Engine 1,476 cc, straight-four
Top speed 71 mph (114 km/h)

The Oxford MO was a large Morris Minor, with the same torsion-bar front suspension, rack-and-pinion steering, and hydraulic brakes. It sold 159,960 in six years despite its slow performance.

△ **Fiat 1500 1949**
Origin Italy
Engine 1,493 cc, straight-six
Top speed 75 mph (121 km/h)

This was the final version of a car introduced in 1935. Very advanced with aerodynamic styling, it had a backbone chassis, independent front suspension, and overhead valves.

△ **Hansa 1500 1949**
Origin Germany
Engine 1,498 cc, straight-four
Top speed 75 mph (121 km/h)

Strikingly modern for its time, the Hansa had a backbone chassis and all-independent suspension, and even pioneered flashing indicators. It could seat six people.

Economical Cars

Europe specialized in the small, economical family car in the 1950s, producing a wide range of practical and often surprisingly civilized vehicles with much more space, pace, and comfort than their pre-war equivalents. However, some marques, such as Ford, bucked the modernizing trend by continuing throughout the decade to sell pre-war cars at rock bottom prices, undercutting the more advanced models.

◁ **Wolseley 1500 1957**

Origin UK

Engine 1,489 cc, straight-four

Top speed 78 mph (126 km/h)

Morris recycled the Minor's floorpan and fitted it with a bigger engine to make this upmarket Wolseley (also available under the Riley name); a popular car, it sold over 140,000.

△ **Ford Prefect E493A 1949**

Origin UK

Engine 1,172 cc, straight-four

Top speed 60 mph (97 km/h)

Ford added faired-in headlamps and quality fittings inside to distract buyers from the car's pre-war origins. The Prefect sold well in the car-starved UK of the post-war era.

△ **Ford Popular 103E 1953**

Origin UK

Engine 1,172 cc, straight-four

Top speed 60 mph (97 km/h)

A hangover from the 1930s, the 103E had rod brakes, a side-valve engine, three gears, and pre-war styling. It was basic and very cheap, and remained in production until 1959.

▷ **Ford Anglia 100E 1953**

Origin UK

Engine 1,172 cc, straight-four

Top speed 70 mph (113 km/h)

Ford built pre-war cars through the 1950s, but this modern-looking saloon brought their small cars up to date. It sold well, despite having a side-valve engine and three gears.

△ **Ford Anglia 105E 1959**

Origin UK

Engine 997 cc, straight-four

Top speed 76 mph (122 km/h)

The 105E, the final model in the Anglia series, was right up to date with its ultra-modern, US-influenced styling, oversquare, free-revving new engine, and slick, four-speed gearbox; the 1,197 cc Super is shown.

◁ **Renault Dauphine 1956**

Origin France

Engine 845 cc, straight-four

Top speed 66 mph (106 km/h)

The Dauphine was an update of the rear-engined, post-war 4CV. With a slightly larger engine, more space inside, and an appealing new body, it sold over 2 million in 12 years.

△ **DKW Sonderklasse 1953**

Origin Germany

Engine 896 cc, straight-three

Top speed 75 mph (121 km/h)

With its light, air-cooled, two-stroke engine and aerodynamic styling, the DKW Sonderklasse was faster than its small engine size suggested; later models could reach 88 mph (142 km/h).

▷ **Morris Minor Traveller 1953**

Origin UK

Engine 1,098 cc, straight-four

Top speed 62 mph (100 km/h)

The attractive, practical, timber-clad Traveller was a popular addition to the hugely successful Morris Minor range. It had side-hinged rear doors and a rear seat that folded away to increase space.

◁ **Simca Aronde Plein Ciel 1957**

Origin France

Engine 1,290 cc, straight-four

Top speed 82 mph (132 km/h)

Simca started by making Fiats under licence, and the Aronde was its first new design. The body of this good-looking but expensive Plein Ciel coupé was built by Facel.

◁ **Nash Metropolitan 1954**

Origin UK/USA

Engine 1,489 cc, straight-four

Top speed 75 mph (121 km/h)

Built in Britain primarily for the North American market, this little coupé was marketed at female drivers, as an about-town car for wealthy housewives.

△ **Fiat 600 1955**

Origin Italy

Engine 633 cc, straight-four

Top speed 62 mph (100 km/h)

The first rear-engined Fiat, with all-independent suspension and monocoque construction, the 600 was a brilliant small car with adequate space for four people.

△ **Fiat 600 Multipla 1956**

Origin Italy

Engine 633 cc, straight-four

Top speed 55 mph (89 km/h)

The well-packaged Multipla could seat six adults yet was only about 3.5 m (11 ft 6 in) long. It pioneered the "MPV" (Multi-Purpose Vehicle) concept, which became especially popular in the 1990s.

△ **Austin A40 1958**

Origin UK

Engine 948 cc, straight-four

Top speed 72 mph (116 km/h)

After Prince Philip remarked on the dumpy look of Austin cars, the company called in Pinin Farina, who turned the staid A40 into this stylish saloon.

△ **Škoda Octavia 1959**

Origin Czechoslovakia

Engine 1,089 cc, straight-four

Top speed 75 mph (121 km/h)

Launched in 1954 as the 440, this Czech people's car was good value for money, but the swing-axle rear suspension could cause problems when cornering for unwary drivers.

Detroit Fins and Chrome

Post-war prosperity in the US brought the most indulgent and flamboyant period ever in car design, as carmakers at all levels of the market dressed up their cars with ever increasing amounts of chrome plating and wild styling excesses: fins, bullets, and aircraft-inspired detail. Cars and engines grew to enormous proportions, peaking in 1959 before blander styling arrived in 1960.

▷ Chevrolet Bel Air 1953

Origin USA
Engine 3,859 cc, straight-six
Top speed 87 mph (140 km/h)

A quarter of a million Bel Air sedans, Chevrolet's luxury model, were made in 1953, helped by competitive pricing and attractive styling with increasing amounts of chrome.

△ Plymouth Fury 1959

Origin USA
Engine 5,205 cc, V8
Top speed 105 mph (167 km/h)

Plymouth was on the way up from 1955, with dramatic new Virgil Exner styling and a lively V8 engine. The Fury two-door coupé was one of its most stylish models.

◁ Chevrolet Bel Air 1957

Origin USA
Engine 4,343 cc, V8
Top speed 106 mph (171 km/h)

Seen as a "baby Cadillac" with its iconic finned styling and hot V8 options, the 1957 Chevrolets are among the marque's most popular classics today.

△ Chrysler New Yorker 1957

Origin USA
Engine 6,424 cc, V8
Top speed 116 mph (187 km/h)

Designer Virgil Exner's new "forward look", plus new torsion-bar front suspension, helped Chrysler win *Motor Trend*'s Car of the Year in 1957 and turn its falling fortunes around.

▷ Lincoln Continental Mark II 1956

Origin USA
Engine 6,030 cc, V8
Top speed 108 mph (174 km/h)

Lincoln reintroduced its top-of-the-line Continental in 1956 with an exceptionally well-proportioned, if large, two-door coupé body style. The price tag was almost $10,000.

◁ Lincoln Capri 1958

Origin USA
Engine 7,046 cc, V8
Top speed 110 mph (177 km/h)

Believing biggest had to be best, Ford's top brand built the largest car of the post-war era. The Capri was over 5.8 m (20 ft) long, with a 375 bhp V8 to lug it along.

▷ Pontiac Bonneville Custom 1959

Origin USA
Engine 6,375 cc, V8
Top speed 114 mph (183 km/h)

The late 1950s saw Pontiac reinvent itself as a sporty marque with low-slung styling and hot V8 engine options, resulting in many stock-car race wins in 1959.

▽ Edsel Corsair 1959

Origin USA
Engine 5,440 cc, V8
Top speed 119 mph (192 km/h)

Ford introduced the Edsel in 1957 to target the mid-range market in the US, but it did not succeed and closed in 1959. Only 1,343 of this attractive and powerful Corsair were built.

▷ **Ford Fairlane 500 Club Victoria 1959**

Origin USA

Engine 4,785 cc, V8

Top speed 98 mph (158 km/h)

The 1959 Fords won the Gold Medal for Exceptional Styling at the Brussels World Fair, and sold well. This two-door Club Victoria was a relative rarity; with just 23,892 sold.

△ **Studebaker Silver Hawk 1957**

Origin USA

Engine 4,736 cc, V8

Top speed 115 mph (185 km/h)

One of the world's oldest road vehicle producers, Studebaker introduced distinctive styling after the war; this two-door body style began in 1953, with fins growing steadily to this 1957 peak.

▷ **Buick Roadmaster Riviera 1957**

Origin USA

Engine 5,965 cc, V8

Top speed 117 mph (188 km/h)

Buick's hardtop Riviera appeared in 1954. By 1957 it had ladles of chrome and big fins, but Buick's popularity was in decline despite 250/300 bhp engines.

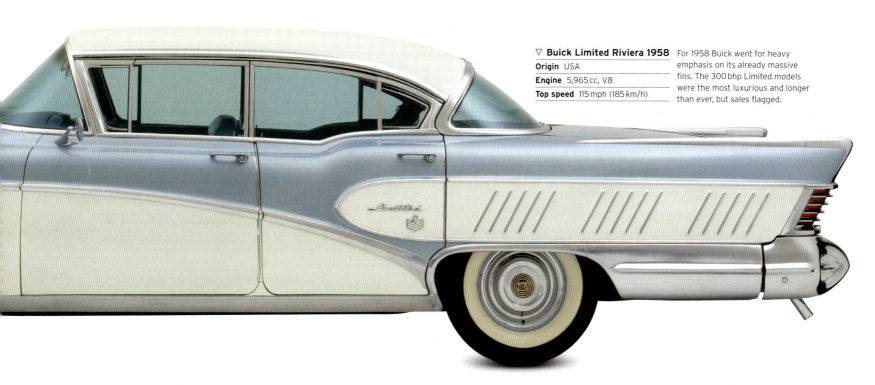

▽ **Buick Limited Riviera 1958**

Origin USA

Engine 5,965 cc, V8

Top speed 115 mph (185 km/h)

For 1958 Buick went for heavy emphasis on its already massive fins. The 300 bhp Limited models were the most luxurious and longer than ever, but sales flagged.

▽ **Cadillac Series 62 Club Coupe 1952**

Origin USA

Engine 5,424 cc, V8

Top speed 98 mph (158 km/h)

Cadillac was the style innovator at the top end of the US market and was a pioneer of big fins, as seen on the back of this luxurious 190 bhp coupé.

▷ **Cadillac Series 62 Convertible Coupe 1958**

Origin USA

Engine 5,981 cc, V8

Top speed 116 mph (187 km/h)

All-new styling brought Cadillac up to the minute in 1957 and the fins grew even bigger in 1958; the engine had grown too, now boasting 310 bhp in standard form.

▷ **Cadillac Series 62 Sedan 1959**

Origin USA

Engine 6,391 cc, V8

Top speed 114 mph (183 km/h)

The massive fins of the 1959 Cadillac were divided by twin-bullet tail lamps and the engine now had 325 bhp. It was surely the most flamboyant of 1950s American car designs.

Opulence and High Performance

The 1950s saw prosperity slowly return after World War II, and with it increasing demand for cars of the highest luxury. But now, as roads improved and people's horizons broadened, ultimate performance was a goal too. The best post-war cars were expected to cruise all day at 100 mph (161 km/h) – more if they claimed to be serious sports cars – and before long, that's what they did.

△ Rolls-Royce Silver Dawn 1949
Origin UK
Engine 4,566 cc, straight-six
Top speed 87 mph (140 km/h)

Rolls-Royce claimed to make the best cars in the world and on engineering integrity, it did. This was its "smallest" car: still the ultimate opulence for four.

◁ Rolls-Royce Silver Cloud I 1955
Origin UK
Engine 4,887 cc, straight-six
Top speed 106 mph (171 km/h)

Still being built on a separate chassis meant that Rolls-Royces could easily be fitted with coachbuilt luxury bodies: this one by Hooper & Co. exudes grace.

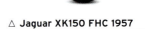

▽ Bristol 403 1953
Origin UK
Engine 1,971 cc, straight-six
Top speed 104 mph (167 km/h)

Still clearly derived from the outstanding pre-war BMWs, the Bristol 403 had 100 bhp, which was put to great effect in this aerodynamic, high-quality four-seater.

▷ Jaguar MkVII 1951
Origin UK
Engine 3,442 cc, straight-six
Top speed 102 mph (164 km/h)

The Mark VII was the car William Lyons was preparing for when he produced the stunning XK120. Fast, stylish, and luxurious, the MkVII was a great saloon.

◁ Jaguar XK140 FHC 1955
Origin UK
Engine 3,442 cc, straight-six
Top speed 124 mph (200 km/h)

Seeing the insatiable demand for its XK sports cars, Jaguar produced variants including this fixed-head coupé with a wood and leather interior.

△ Jaguar XK150 FHC 1957
Origin UK
Engine 3,781 cc, straight-six
Top speed 132 mph (212 km/h)

Sold first in slightly less potent 3.4-litre form, the XK150 FHC was a very civilized sports 2+2, capable of cruising happily all day at 100 mph (161 km/h) in relative silence.

▽ Jaguar MkIX 1959
Origin UK
Engine 3,781 cc, straight-six
Top speed 114 mph (183 km/h)

Jaguar's last separate-chassis saloon boasted 220 bhp, power steering, and all-disc brakes, making it a highly civilized, if heavyweight, gentleman's express.

△ Facel Vega FVS 1954

Origin	France
Engine	5,801 cc, V8
Top speed	134 mph (216 km/h)

One of the first European marques to use US V8 power (in this case, from Chrysler), Facel Vega offered an outstanding "Grand Routier" in the extremely stylish FVS.

△ Mercedes-Benz 300 1951

Origin	Germany
Engine	2,996 cc, straight-six
Top speed	103 mph (166 km/h)

Germany's first prestige car after World War II was built with quality and durability as priorities: around 1,000 a year were built over 10 years.

◁ Lancia Aurelia B20 GT 1953

Origin	Italy
Engine	2,451 cc, V6
Top speed	115 mph (185 km/h)

Brilliantly engineered with the world's first production V6 engine and semi-trailing arm rear suspension, the Aurelia was built to perfection, regardless of cost.

▷ Tatra 603 1956

Origin	Czechoslovakia
Engine	2,474–2,545 cc, V8
Top speed	100 mph (161 km/h)

This top-quality, streamlined saloon was built mainly for Czech diplomats. The 603 has a compact, air-cooled V8 engine, which is mounted at its back.

△ Mercedes-Benz 300SL 1954

Origin	Germany
Engine	2,996 cc, straight-six
Top speed	129 mph (208 km/h)

One of the most iconic cars of the 1950s, the 300SL with its gullwing doors and 250 bhp fuel-injected, dry-sump engine was an outstanding sports coupé.

△ Ferrari 250GT 1956

Origin	Italy
Engine	2,953 cc, V12
Top speed	145 mph (233 km/h)

Ferrari's first volume production GT, the 250 boasted tremendous performance from the triple-Weber carburettor V12, within a luxurious 2+2 coupé styled by Pinin Farina.

△ Kaiser Darrin 1954

Origin	USA
Engine	2,641 cc, straight-six
Top speed	96 mph (154 km/h)

Shipbuilder Henry Kaiser turned to cars after World War II. The glassfibre-bodied Darrin with doors that slid into the front wings was the brainchild of designer Howard "Dutch" Darrin.

◁ Bentley S2 1959

Origin	UK
Engine	6,230 cc, V8
Top speed	113 mph (182 km/h)

Rolls-Royce and Bentley were at a disadvantage in the US, as their six-cylinder engines were considered downmarket. But this changed when this silken V8 was launched.

△ Bentley R-type Continental 1952

Origin	UK
Engine	4,566 cc, straight-six
Top speed	120 mph (193 km/h)

Rolls-Royce finally cashed in on subsidiary Bentley's sporting heritage with this magnificent coachbuilt Grand Touring saloon, the epitome of luxury and speed.

△ Aston Martin DB2/4 1953

Origin	UK
Engine	2,580 cc, straight-six
Top speed	116 mph (187 km/h)

Expensive and exclusive, with W.O. Bentley's twin-overhead-camshaft engine in a tubular chassis, the Aston Martin epitomized racing pedigree and class.

△ Aston Martin DB4 1958

Origin	UK
Engine	3,670 cc, straight-six
Top speed	141 mph (227 km/h)

By the end of the decade the Aston Martin had grown into a true luxury supercar, with exotic Italian styling by Touring and 240 bhp from its new twin-cam engine.

Racing Cars

The 1950s was the decade of successful front-engined racing cars, especially in sports-car racing. European marques derived from roadgoing sports cars dominated, gradually becoming more and more different from their street origins. Disc brakes proved a huge advantage and would be rapidly adopted, along with other improvements such as fuel injection that would filter through to improve road cars in time.

▷ **Talbot-Lago T26 Grand Sport 1951**

Origin France

Engine 4,483 cc, straight-six

Top speed 125 mph (201 km/h)

Based on the chassis and engine from a successful Grand Prix racer, the Grand Sport was an early post-war sports racing car that won at Le Mans in 1950.

△ **Ferrari 375 MM 1953**

Origin Italy

Engine 4,522 cc, V12

Top speed 150 mph (241 km/h)

Built primarily as a competition car, the 375 Mille Miglia won the Spa 24-hour race, Pescara 12-hour race, and Buenos Aires 1,000 km at the start of its glittering racing career.

△ **Kurtis-Chrysler 500S 1953**

Origin USA

Engine 6,424 cc, V8

Top speed 145 mph (233 km/h)

Typical of the effective US-built racers that contested the Carrera Panamericana and US endurance races, this car has the Chrysler Hemi V8 in a light, aluminium body.

◁ **Ferrari 250GT SWB 1959**

Origin Italy

Engine 2,953 cc, V12

Top speed 160 mph (257 km/h)

The gorgeous Pinin Farina-designed SWB dominated the Group III (2-3 litre) racing class, winning many races outright. It was equally at home on the road.

△ **Abarth 205 1950**

Origin Italy

Engine 1,089 cc, straight-four

Top speed 108 mph (174 km/h)

The first complete car from legendary engine tuner Carlo Abarth, the 205 used a tuned Fiat engine in a body styled by Giovanni Michelotti. It was a successful endurance racer.

▽ **Lotus Eleven 1956**

Origin UK

Engine 1,098 cc, straight-four

Top speed 112 mph (180 km/h)

The elegant Lotus Eleven marked a step forward in professionalism from Lotus and proved hugely successful. It came 7th overall at Le Mans in 1956, racing against many larger-engined cars.

△ **Pupulidy-Porsche Special 1954**

Origin USA

Engine 1,582 cc, flat-four

Top speed 130 mph (209 km/h)

American racer Emil Pupulidy built a body inspired by Mercedes' Silver Arrows, fitted it to a VW floorpan, and went racing. He won the car's first race at the Nassau Speed Week in the Bahamas.

▷ **Porsche 550/1500RS 1953**

Origin Germany

Engine 1,498 cc, flat-four

Top speed 136 mph (219 km/h)

When Porsche designed a new engine with double overhead camshafts on each side for its mid-engined 550 racer, it became a race winner. The actor James Dean had a fatal crash in his.

◁ **Porsche 550 Coupé 1953**

Origin Germany

Engine 1,488 cc, flat-four

Top speed 124 mph (200 km/h)

This was Porsche's first purpose-built works racing car. Mid-engined 550s won their class in 1953 events from Le Mans to the Carrera Panamericana.

△ **Aston Martin DBR1 1956**

Origin	UK
Engine	2,922 cc, straight-six
Top speed	155 mph (249 km/h)

The most successful Aston Martin racing car until 2010, the DBR1 had six major international race wins, including Le Mans, Nürburgring, Goodwood, and Spa.

△ **Aston Martin DBR2 1957**

Origin	UK
Engine	3,670 cc, straight-six
Top speed	160 mph (257 km/h)

Aston built two cars to race its new 3.7-litre engine, with semi-backbone chassis and styling like the DBR1; they later raced with 4.2-litre engines in the US.

◁ **Panhard 750 Spider 1954**

Origin	France/Italy
Engine	745 cc, flat-two
Top speed	90 mph (145 km/h)

Built by Tino Bianchi on a 1950 Panhard Dyna rolling chassis, with frame by GILCO and body by Colli, this one-off Special competed in the 1955 Mille Miglia in Italy.

▷ **Mercedes-Benz W196 1954**

Origin	Germany
Engine	2,496 cc, straight-six
Top speed	186 mph (299 km/h)

Mercedes-Benz returned to Formula 1 with a complex spaceframe chassis, desmodromic valves, and fuel injection. The W196 gave race driver Juan Manuel Fangio two world titles.

◁ **Jaguar C-type 1951**

Origin	UK
Engine	3,442 cc, straight-six
Top speed	144 mph (232 km/h)

This roadgoing race car was built to win Le Mans, which it did in 1951 and 1953 (pioneering disc brakes in 1953). It was derived from the XK120, with a lightweight tubular chassis.

△ **OSCA MT4 1953**

Origin	Italy
Engine	1,490 cc, straight-four
Top speed	120 mph (193 km/h)

Superb design by the Maserati brothers and a twin-camshaft, twin-spark engine made the MT4 more competitive than it looked. In 1954 it won the Sebring 12-hour race in the US.

△ **Maserati 250F 1954**

Origin	Italy
Engine	2,494 cc, straight-six
Top speed	180 mph (290 km/h)

The elegant 250F raced throughout the seven years of the 2.5-litre limit in Formula 1, winning eight Grand Prix and giving Juan Manuel Fangio the 1957 World Championship.

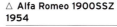

△ **Alfa Romeo 1900SSZ 1954**

Origin	Italy
Engine	1,975 cc, straight-four
Top speed	117 mph (188 km/h)

The Alfa Romeo 1900, marketed as "the family car that wins races", spawned this lightweight special-bodied car by Zagato that was successful in long-distance races.

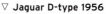

▽ **Jaguar D-type 1956**

Origin	UK
Engine	3,781 cc, straight-six
Top speed	167 mph (269 km/h)

After the XK-derived C-type, Jaguar developed this lightweight racer with monocoque centre section to win Le Mans in France. It won in 1955, 1956, and 1957.

Sports Cars (50s)

Massive demand for sports cars in prosperous post-war America prompted rapid progress in design there and in Europe. This was a golden era for sports cars, as profiles became lower and stylists emphasized this with gorgeous, flowing lines, in the process coming up with some of the most attractive cars ever built.

△ **Chevrolet Corvette 1953**
Origin USA
Engine 3,859 cc, straight-six
Top speed 107 mph (172 km/h)

A Motorama dream car that made it to production, this was the first plastic-bodied car and represented a well-judged leap of faith by Chevrolet.

△ **Sunbeam Alpine 1953**
Origin UK
Engine 2,267 cc, straight-four
Top speed 95 mph (153 km/h)

Based on the four-seat Sunbeam-Talbot 90 chassis, the Alpine was overweight. Good PR from Alpine Rally wins in Europe and a 120 mph (193 km/h) record run were not enough to win sales.

△ **Alfa Romeo Giulietta Spider 1955**
Origin Italy
Engine 1,290 cc, straight-four
Top speed 112 mph (180 km/h)

This beautiful little sports car was built to a very high specification with performance far higher than its 1.3 litres would suggest, thanks to its brilliant twin-cam engine.

△ **Jowett Jupiter 1950**
Origin UK
Engine 1,486 cc, flat-four
Top speed 84 mph (135 km/h)

Innovative but heavy, Jupiters enjoyed good handling thanks to a low, horizontally opposed engine. Jowett was too small to make it in quantity: 899 of these were sold.

▷ **Alfa Romeo 2000 Spider 1958**
Origin Italy
Engine 1,975 cc, straight-four
Top speed 111 mph (179 km/h)

Ahead of contemporary British and US standards, except for its drum brakes, this handsome 2+2 Alfa boasted unitary construction, a five-speed gearbox, and a double-overhead-camshaft engine.

◁ **Triumph TR2 1953**
Origin UK
Engine 1,991 cc, straight-four
Top speed 107 mph (172 km/h)

This fast and entertaining sports car was developed on a shoe-string budget. It was an immediate success in the market, and probably won more rallies than any other car.

△ **Arnolt Bristol 1953**
Origin USA/Italy/UK
Engine 1,971 cc, straight-six
Top speed 109 mph (175 km/h)

S.H. "Wacky" Arnolt of Indiana, USA, commissioned Bristol to build a rolling chassis in England, to be clothed by coachbuilders Bertone of Italy. Just 142 were built.

▷ **Jaguar XK140 1955**
Origin UK
Engine 3,442 cc, straight-six
Top speed 124 mph (200 km/h)

The XK120 grew up into the XK140, with rack-and-pinion steering, more power, and more space inside. Customers could have a roadster, drophead, or fixed-head coupé.

▽ **BMW 507 1956**
Origin Germany
Engine 3,168 cc, V8
Top speed 135 mph (217 km/h)

Just 250 of these gorgeous super sports cars from BMW were built. It was so good, motorcycle World Champion John Surtees has owned one from new.

△ **MGA 1955**

Origin UK

Engine 1,489 cc, straight-four

Top speed 100 mph (161 km/h)

Beautiful lines, a top speed of 100 mph (just), and a fixed-head coupé option made up for the separate chassis in the MGA. It sold well, especially in the US.

◁ **Mercedes-Benz 190SL 1955**

Origin Germany

Engine 1,897 cc, straight-four

Top speed 107 mph (172 km/h)

Launched just after the similarly shaped but much faster 300SL Gullwing, the 190 was a luxurious touring car for two, built to traditional Mercedes-Benz quality standards.

△ **Daimler SP250 1959**

Origin UK

Engine 2,548 cc, V8

Top speed 120 mph (193 km/h)

The maker of staid luxury saloons had a new aluminium V8, and it was used in a glassfibre-bodied sports car with a chassis copied from Triumph.

△ **Austin-Healey 100/4 1952**

Origin UK

Engine 2,660 cc, straight-four

Top speed 103 mph (166 km/h)

Donald Healey conceived an inexpensive sports car using Austin Atlantic parts, Gerry Coker styled a stunning body, and Austin bought the rights to produce it.

△ **Austin-Healey Sprite 1958**

Origin UK

Engine 948 cc, straight-four

Top speed 86 mph (138 km/h)

Targeting the bottom-of-the-market preserve of kit cars, the "Frogeye" ("Bugeye" in the US) Sprite showed that sports cars didn't have to be fast to be fun.

△ **Porsche 356A 1955**

Origin Germany

Engine 1,582 cc, flat-four

Top speed 100 mph (161 km/h)

The lively 356, launched in 1950, grew from its VW roots until, by the end of the decade, it was a 110 mph (177 km/h) flyer, hitting 125 mph (201 km/h) in its twin-cam Carrera form.

◁ **AC Ace 1956**

Origin UK

Engine 1,971 cc, straight-six

Top speed 117 mph (188 km/h)

Launched in 1954 with AC's own engine, the Ferrari-inspired Ace with all-independently sprung chassis came alive with a 120 bhp Bristol engine, and later spawned the Cobra.

△ **Lotus Elite 1957**

Origin UK

Engine 1,216 cc, straight-four

Top speed 118 mph (190 km/h)

This was the world's first glassfibre monocoque: complex with excellent aerodynamics, a powerful Coventry Climax engine, and supple suspension. It was highly sophisticated.

△ **Lotus 7 1957**

Origin UK

Engine 1,172 cc, straight-four

Top speed 85 mph (137 km/h)

Brilliantly simple, Sevens were sold mostly as kits with a choice of engines. Low weight and well-designed suspension made them quick and effective in club racing.

Bubble Cars and Microcars

Inventors had always made tiny, economical motor cars, but consumers rarely bought them. The Suez crisis of 1956 and the subsequent petrol rationing changed that – suddenly fuel economy became a priority. Existing microcars were thrust into the limelight and new models joined the market in droves. But soon these were superseded by small conventional cars like the Fiat 500 and the Mini.

△ **Inter 175 Berline 1953**

Origin France

Engine 175 cc, one-cylinder

Top speed 50 mph (80 km/h)

Built by a French aircraft company, the tandem-seat Inter's front wheels could be folded in to allow it to pass through a doorway or narrow passage for storage.

△ **Heinkel Cabin Cruiser 1957**

Origin Germany

Engine 204 cc, one-cylinder

Top speed 50 mph (80 km/h)

Lightweight construction, typical of an aircraft company, plus brilliant packaging enabled the Heinkel to seat two adults and two children and go as fast as a BMW Isetta.

△ **Vespa 400 1957**

Origin Italy/France

Engine 393 cc, straight-two

Top speed 52 mph (84 km/h)

Designed by Piaggio but built in France, this two-seater was sophisticated for its time, with a fan-cooled engine in the rear, and all-independent suspension.

△ **Austin Mini Seven 1959**

Origin UK

Engine 848 cc, straight-four

Top speed 72 mph (116 km/h)

The Mini had Issigonis's brilliant packaging, its transverse engine and gearbox-in-sump allowing four seats. Priced competitively, it wiped out the bubble cars.

△ **Frisky Family Three 1958**

Origin UK

Engine 197 cc, one-cylinder

Top speed 44 mph (71 km/h)

Engine maker Henry Meadows Ltd began building 4-wheel Frisky cars in 1957, based on prototype styling by Michelotti. A 3-wheel model was cheaper to tax in Britain.

△ **Fiat Nuova 500 1957**

Origin Italy

Engine 479 cc, straight-two

Top speed 51 mph (82 km/h)

Dante Giacosa's brilliant new 500 was only a slow two-seater at first, but repackaged interior space and more power transformed it into a 3.4-million seller.

▷ **Berkeley SE492 1958**

Origin UK

Engine 492 cc, straight-three

Top speed 80 mph (129 km/h)

This brilliant glassfibre and aluminium monocoque sports car had a transverse engine, front-wheel drive, and all-independent suspension, but was let down by unreliable motorcycle engines.

▷ **Goggomobil Dart 1959**

Origin Germany/Australia

Engine 392 cc, straight-two

Top speed 65 mph (105 km/h)

Australian Bill Buckle designed this stylish sports body to fit the chassis and running gear of the German Goggomobil. This model sold 700 with 300 cc or 400 cc engines.

◁ **Subaru 360 1958**

Origin Japan

Engine 356 cc, straight-two

Top speed 60 mph (97 km/h)

Though little-known outside Japan, this clever monocoque four-seater with air-cooled rear engine sold 392,000. It was the people's car of Japan in the 1960s.

△ **Zündapp Janus 1957**

Origin Germany

Engine 250 cc, one-cylinder

Top speed 50 mph (80 km/h)

A mid-mounted engine, back-to-back seating for four adults, and great build quality made this microcar one of the cleverest. However, it was too unconventional to sell well.

△ **BMW Isetta 300 1955**

Origin Germany

Engine 298 cc, one-cylinder

Top speed 50 mph (80 km/h)

Built by BMW under licence from Iso, the 300 was the archetypal bubble car. It developed into a dependable car with two seats and single or close-double rear wheels.

▷ **BMW 600 1957**

Origin Germany

Engine 582 cc, flat-two

Top speed 62 mph (100 km/h)

Isetta customers wanted a four-seater, so BMW obliged with the 600 – one side door served the rear seats. Michelotti transformed the 600 into the larger 700 for 1959.

△ **Messerschmitt KR200 1956**

Origin Germany

Engine 191 cc, one-cylinder

Top speed 60 mph (97 km/h)

Fritz Fend's concept for disabled ex-servicemen was transformed into a practical tandem-seat bubble car with aircraft-like canopy and handlebar steering.

△ **Scootacar 1958**

Origin UK

Engine 197 cc, one-cylinder

Top speed 45 mph (72 km/h)

Although it arrived late on the market, around 1,500 of three different models were built in total of this British tandem-seat microcar. Driver and passenger sat scooter-style astride the engine.

△ **Messerschmitt TG500 1958**

Origin Germany

Engine 490 cc, straight-two

Top speed 80 mph (129 km/h)

With over double the power of a KR200, the four-wheel "Tiger" excelled in small-capacity racing and autotests due to its low centre of gravity and tiny dimensions.

△ **Bambino 200 1955**

Origin Netherlands

Engine 191 cc, one-cylinder

Top speed 53 mph (85 km/h)

This rear-engined German Fuldamobil was built under licence in the Netherlands. Versions were also built in South America, Britain, Sweden, Greece, India, and South Africa.

▷ **Peel P50 1963**

Origin UK

Engine 49 cc, one-cylinder

Top speed 38 mph (61 km/h)

The culmination of the 1950s drive towards miniaturization, the world's smallest production car was a city runabout for one person and a shopping bag or suitcase.

Large Saloons

In 1950s America all saloons were large and sales figures were huge, justifying annual improvements and restyling. In Europe the economic climate was less favourable, with limited demand in the austerity years after World War II. As a result, updated pre-war cars were produced well into the decade in Europe, especially by smaller manufacturers that could not afford the cost of monocoque construction technology or major engineering changes.

▷ **Daimler Conquest Century 1954**

Origin UK

Engine 2,433 cc, straight-six

Top speed 90 mph (145 km/h)

Daimler made good cars, but struggled to update in the 1950s. However, performance modifications on the Century made it much livelier than the basic Conquest.

▽ **Mercury Monterey 1954**

Origin USA

Engine 4,195 cc, V8

Top speed 100 mph (161 km/h)

Mercury's first all-new engine since 1939 powered a clean, modern-styled car that was even available with a green-tinted, plexiglass roof panel, 50 years ahead of its time.

△ **Oldsmobile Super 88 1955**

Origin USA

Engine 5,309 cc, V8

Top speed 101 mph (163 km/h)

With its Futuramic styling and Rocket V8 engine, Oldsmobile was king of NASCAR (the National Association for Stock Car Auto Racing) in the early 1950s.

△ **Hudson Hornet 1954**

Origin USA

Engine 5,047 cc, straight-six

Top speed 106 mph (171 km/h)

This was the last year for Hudson's low-floored "step-down" series, introduced in 1948 with the Super Six engine. It was developed into the NASCAR-winning Hornet in 1951.

△ **De Soto Firedome 1953**

Origin USA

Engine 4,524 cc, V8

Top speed 92 mph (148 km/h)

De Soto introduced the Firedome as its top model in 1952. Its name alludes to the efficient hemispherical combustion chambers in its new V8 engine, which gave 160 bhp.

△ **Alvis TC21/100 Grey Lady 1954**

Origin UK

Engine 2,993 cc, straight-six

Top speed 100 mph (161 km/h)

Alvis kept its post-war big saloon saleable by boosting the engine to 100 bhp, and adding wire wheels and bonnet scoops. Graber saved it with modern styling in 1956.

◁ **Austin A99 Westminster 1959**

Origin UK

Engine 2,912 cc, straight-six

Top speed 98 mph (158 km/h)

Austin's Westminster grew into a distinguished large saloon with Pininfarina styling for the 1960s. It was competitively priced with servo brakes and either overdrive or automatic gearbox.

◁ **Renault Frégate 1951**

Origin France

Engine 1,997 cc, straight-four

Top speed 78 mph (126 km/h)

Nationalized after the war, Renault needed an upmarket saloon. But the Frégate was slow to enter production and was soon outclassed by the Citroën DS.

▷ **Vauxhall Cresta 1955**

Origin UK

Engine 2,262 cc, straight-six

Top speed 80 mph (129 km/h)

Vauxhall's General Motors parentage was conspicuous in the chrome-laden Cresta; the styling was pure 1949 Chevrolet. Despite that, it sold quite well in Britain.

▷ **Rambler Ambassador 1958**

Origin USA

Engine 5,359 cc, V8

Top speed 95 mph (153 km/h)

AMC was formed by the 1954 merger of Nash and Hudson. It was the only major US car maker to increase sales in the recession of 1958, thanks to new Rambler models.

◁ **Chevrolet Bel Air Nomad 1956**

Origin USA

Engine 4,343 cc, V8

Top speed 108 mph (174 km/h)

Mid-1950s Chevrolets had low, sporty styling and a potent V8 engine that made even this estate car model hugely exciting. Of 1.6 million 1956 Chevrolets, a mere 7,886 were Nomads.

△ **Lancia Flaminia 1957**

Origin Italy

Engine 2,458 cc, V6

Top speed 102 mph (164 km/h)

Styling by Pinin Farina gave the Lancia Flaminia a resemblance to the Austin Westminster, but under the skin this was a much more sophisticated car with De Dion transaxle and great handling.

▽ **Armstrong Siddeley Sapphire 1953**

Origin UK

Engine 3,435 cc, straight-six

Top speed 100 mph (161 km/h)

A luxurious car that continued to sell to traditional customers for whom Jaguar appeared too modern, the Sapphire came with pre-selector or Hydramatic gearboxes.

◁ **Rover 90 1957**

Origin UK

Engine 2,639 cc, straight-six

Top speed 91 mph (146 km/h)

Rover's P4 range had radical styling when it was launched in 1950, and stayed fresh into the 1960s. Separate chassis construction and high quality fittings made it a solid car.

△ **Peugeot 403 1955**

Origin France

Engine 1,468 cc, straight-four

Top speed 76 mph (122 km/h)

The 403 is a rugged and well-engineered car whose later 404 version can still be seen in Africa and South America. Over a million were sold. Fictional US detective Columbo drove a convertible 403.

▷ **BMW 502 1955**

Origin Germany

Engine 3,168 cc, V8

Top speed 105 mph (169 km/h)

BMW's aluminium V8 engine appeared in 1954 at 2580cc, but grew the following year to give this big saloon the performance to match its imposing looks and quality fittings.

◁ **Humber Hawk VI 1954**

Origin UK

Engine 2,267 cc, straight-four

Top speed 83 mph (134 km/h)

The last of the separate-chassis Hawks was a solid, well-built, and comfortable saloon. It had good cruising ability thanks to overdrive transmission, but sluggish acceleration.

△ **Humber Super Snipe 1959**

Origin UK

Engine 2,651 cc, straight-six

Top speed 92 mph (148 km/h)

Humber finally adopted monocoque construction but went for slightly too small a six-cylinder engine in this Super Snipe. Later models had 3-litre engines and better performance.

Family Cars

For space, comfort, and fuel economy, family cars of the 1950s were similar to those of today; the big differences were in style, safety, performance, and noise at higher speeds. Any of these family cars would comfortably take you from London to Edinburgh, or from Calais to Nice, in a day – a big improvement on the much slower family cars of the 1930s.

△ **Alfa Romeo 1900 1950**

Origin Italy

Engine 1,884 cc, straight-four

Top speed 103 mph (166 km/h)

Dr Orazio Satta set Alfa Romeo on the road to post-war success with this strikingly modern saloon – a monocoque with a twin-cam engine and aerodynamic full-width styling.

△ **Volvo Amazon 1956**

Origin Sweden

Engine 1,583 cc, straight-four

Top speed 90 mph (145 km/h)

Starting as the 121 in 1956 with four doors and 60 bhp, the strong but light Amazon was steadily improved. In its two-door form it sold until 1970.

◁ **Volvo PV444 1957**

Origin Sweden

Engine 1,583 cc, straight-four

Top speed 95 mph (153 km/h)

Volvo's PV444 was rugged, lively, and popular in the 1950s – a four-speed, all synchromesh gearbox was a boon. The similar PV544 replaced it from 1958.

△ **Riley RME 1952**

Origin UK

Engine 1,496 cc, straight-four

Top speed 78 mph (126 km/h)

Also made in a more responsive 2.5-litre form, the Riley was outdated in its construction but remained a quality, sporting saloon car for a select clientèle.

△ **Borgward Isabella TS 1954**

Origin Germany

Engine 1,493 cc, straight-four

Top speed 93 mph (150 km/h)

A sporty and well-built two-door saloon, the Isabella sold over 200,000 in seven years, but could not save this family company from collapse in 1961.

△ **Ford Consul MkII 1956**

Origin UK

Engine 1,703 cc, straight-four

Top speed 81 mph (130 km/h)

In Britain Ford's small cars retained pre-war characteristics, but its mid-range family cars had modern US styling. The Consul shared a basic bodyshell with the Zephyr.

△ **Ford Zephyr MkII 1956**

Origin UK

Engine 2,553 cc, straight-six

Top speed 90 mph (145 km/h)

A six-cylinder engine plus a light weight gave the Zephyr effortless performance. Overdrive models had six gears to choose from.

▷ **Fiat 1200 Granluce 1957**

Origin Italy

Engine 1,221 cc, straight-four

Top speed 85 mph (137 km/h)

A small but lively saloon with good road-handling, this car sold over 400,000 in three years. There was also an attractive two-seater convertible version.

◁ **MG Magnette ZA 1954**

Origin UK

Engine 1,489 cc, straight-four

Top speed 80 mph (129 km/h)

With an engine from Austin and a body from Wolseley, the MG saloon also boasted twin carburettors, rack-and-pinion steering, and leather and wood trim.

△ Austin A40 Somerset 1952
Origin UK
Engine 1,200 cc, straight-four
Top speed 70 mph (113 km/h)

Comfortable, surprisingly spacious, and agile considering the small engine dimensions, the sturdily built Somerset was a strong seller for Austin - 173,306 in two years.

▷ Henry J 1951
Origin USA
Engine 2,641 cc, straight-six
Top speed 82 mph (132 km/h)

Kaiser-Frazer tried to boost its flagging sales with this cut-price economy saloon with a Willys four- or six-cylinder engine. Production lasted until 1954.

△ Austin A50/A55 Cambridge 1955
Origin UK
Engine 1,489 cc, straight-four
Top speed 75 mph (121 km/h)

Monocoque construction for the Somerset's successor provided lower lines and a lighter weight. The addition of a bigger engine created a serviceable family car for the 1950s.

△ Mercedes-Benz 220 1954
Origin Germany
Engine 2,195 cc, straight-six
Top speed 101 mph (163 km/h)

Mercedes' first monocoque construction saloon arrived in four-cylinder form in 1953; the more powerful six-cylinder version joined it in 1954. Sturdy and well built, they sold well.

▷ Hindustan Ambassador 1958
Origin India
Engine 1,489 cc, straight-four
Top speed 73 mph (117 km/h)

India's best-known car, still in production today, is a locally built Morris Oxford Series II. Slowly updated over the years, since 1992 it has used an Isuzu engine.

△ Vauxhall PA Velox 1957
Origin UK
Engine 2,262 cc, straight-six
Top speed 87 mph (140 km/h)

Vauxhall's US-ownership was apparent in the styling of this Velox with its wraparound windscreen. The look put off the more conservative British buyer.

◁ Volkswagen Kombi 1950
Origin Germany
Engine 1,131 cc, flat-four
Top speed 58 mph (93 km/h)

Volkswagen made the most of the Beetle's platform construction and low-mounted, flat engine to produce the Kombi van, pick-up, camper, and minibus range.

△ Simca Aronde 1958
Origin France
Engine 1,290 cc, straight-four
Top speed 82 mph (132 km/h)

The steadily updated Aronde saloon, estate, convertible, and coupé sold over a million in the 1950s. This was a reliable, spacious saloon with modest performance.

△ Wolseley 15/60 1959
Origin UK
Engine 1,489 cc, straight-four
Top speed 77 mph (124 km/h)

Pinin Farina gave the big Wolseley - and soon Austin, Morris, MG, and Riley too - a new look with a strong hint of US design. The Wolseley was a comfortable, durable car.

Convertible Style

Before World War II open cars were usually the cheap option. In the 1950s, however, they moved upmarket and became more desirable. As manufacturers turned to monocoque construction, convertibles became more costly to build than they had been on separate chassis. With higher prices, open cars had to become more luxurious and sophisticated, and their role turned to leisure transport.

△ Buick Roadmaster 1951

Origin	USA
Engine	5,247 cc, straight-eight
Top speed	85 mph (137 km/h)

Having a Roadmaster parked on your driveway was a status symbol in post-war America. This was Buick's top model, and had automatic transmission; a year later the finned era began.

◁ Healey G-type 1951

Origin	UK
Engine	2,993 cc, straight-six
Top speed	100 mph (161 km/h)

Derived from the far more plentiful Nash-Healey that was built for the US market, just 25 of the Alvis-engined G-type were made by Healey for sale mainly in the UK.

△ Austin-Healey 3000 MkI 1959

Origin	UK
Engine	2,912 cc, straight-six
Top speed	114 mph (183 km/h)

Smooth, stylish, and powerful, the 3000 with its Austin Westminster-derived engine was available either as a two-seater or 2+2 convertible, and sold especially well in the US.

△ Ford Thunderbird 1954

Origin	USA
Engine	4,785 cc, V8
Top speed	115 mph (185 km/h)

Ford's answer to the Chevrolet Corvette and European sports cars, the "T-bird" boasted a 198 bhp V8 engine and a glassfibre hardtop: a soft-top was optional.

◁ Ford Fairlane 500 Skyliner 1958

Origin	USA
Engine	5,440 cc, V8
Top speed	120 mph (193 km/h)

The 1959-model Fords are considered their most elegant ever. This was the last year for the remarkable folding-hardtop Skyliner, a feature that was 50 years ahead of its time.

△ Chevrolet Bel Air 1955

Origin	USA
Engine	4,343 cc, V8
Top speed	100 mph (161 km/h)

1955 was Chevrolet's renaissance year, helped by a smart new body style but especially by the hot new V8 engine, it launched in the Bel Air with 162/180 bhp on tap.

▷ Morris Minor 1000 Tourer 1956

Origin	UK
Engine	948 cc, straight-four
Top speed	73 mph (117 km/h)

The brilliant Morris Minor, originally launched in 1948, offered practical, spacious, economical, everyday transport to millions; the 4–5 seat Tourer is still very popular today.

▷ Chevrolet Bel Air Convertible 1957

Origin	USA
Engine	4,638 cc, V8
Top speed	120 mph (193 km/h)

With 283 bhp (one bhp per cubic inch), the Ramjet fuel-injected top-performance option Bel Air is one of the most sought-after Chevrolets, with styling to match.

◁ Nash Metropolitan 1500 1954

Origin	UK
Engine	1,489 cc, straight-four
Top speed	75 mph (121 km/h)

Austin of England built a remarkable 95,000 of these fun little cars for the North American market, badged as Nash or Hudson, plus nearly 10,000 for other markets.

◁ **Mercedes-Benz 300SL Roadster 1957**

Origin Germany

Engine 2,996 cc, straight-six

Top speed 129 mph (208 km/h)

Fast, exotic, and derived from the legendary Gullwing, the 300SL boasted fuel injection, luxury, and impeccable build quality. Expensive, just 1,858 were built.

▷ **Volkswagen Karmann Ghia 1957**

Origin Germany

Engine 1,192 cc, flat-four

Top speed 77 mph (124 km/h)

Karmann found a market niche by fitting pretty, Ghia-designed coupé and cabriolet bodies on the VW Beetle floorpan. These were steadily improved as 1,300 and 1,500 cc engines were used.

△ **Morgan Plus Four TR 1954**

Origin UK

Engine 1,991 cc, straight-four

Top speed 96 mph (154 km/h)

One of the most long-lived car shapes ever had its genesis in the roadster version. This model is the drophead coupé, a lusty, fun, and pure sports car.

△ **Renault Floride/Caravelle 1958**

Origin France

Engine 845 cc, straight-four

Top speed 76 mph (122 km/h)

Rather underpowered initially with the Renault 4CV engine, the Floride grew into the Caravelle with 956/1108 cc engines and livelier performance – up to 89 mph (143 km/h).

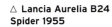

△ **Lancia Aurelia B24 Spider 1955**

Origin Italy

Engine 2,451 cc, V6

Top speed 115 mph (185 km/h)

Lancia's Aurelia saloon of 1950 had the world's first production V6 and semi-trailing arm, independent rear suspension: the B24 Spider put these into a gorgeous but expensive open two-seater.

◁ **Škoda Felicia Super 1959**

Origin Czechoslovakia

Engine 1,221 cc, straight-four

Top speed 87 mph (140 km/h)

Ruggedly built on a tubular backbone chassis, the Škoda was an interesting vehicle to drive, with somewhat unpredictable swing-axle rear suspension.

△ **Citroën DS 1961**

Origin France

Engine 1,911 cc, straight-four

Top speed 86 mph (138 km/h)

The DS was introduced in 1955, wowing the public with its high-pressure hydraulic brakes, steering, and suspension. This version, a luxurious cabriolet, followed five years later.

▽ **Cadillac Eldorado 1959**

Origin USA

Engine 6,390 cc, V8

Top speed 120 mph (193 km/h)

The biggest fins came in 1959 and none more dramatic than those on the 345 bhp Eldorado, which also boasted air suspension and powered everything.

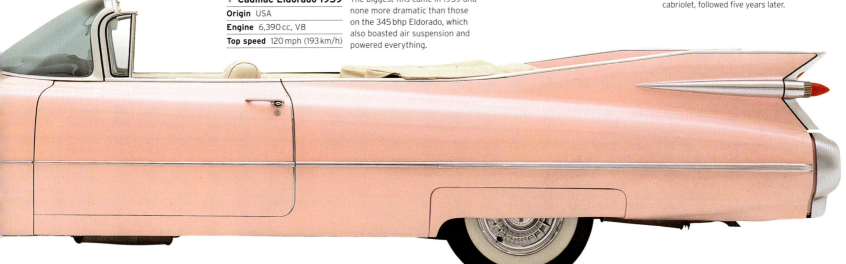

Family Cars

In the 1960s engineers in Europe and Japan had considerable freedom with their designs for compact family transport. Manufacturers chose either a front engine with front-wheel drive, a front engine with rear drive, or a rear engine with rear drive. Styling was also flexible, leading to the production of a variety of cars, each with a clear identity.

△ Peugeot 404 1960

Origin	France
Engine	1,618 cc, straight-four
Top speed	84 mph (135 km/h)

Nearly three million of these outstanding family cars were built. Well engineered and durable, they were driven around the world and in some places are still in use.

◁ Wolseley Hornet 1961

Origin	UK
Engine	848 cc, straight-four
Top speed	71 mph (114 km/h)

BMC expanded the Mini's market by giving it a Wolseley grille, larger boot, and better quality trim. From 1963 it had 998cc and from 1964 Hydrolastic suspension.

△ Mini Moke 1964

Origin	UK
Engine	848 cc, straight-four
Top speed	84 mph (135 km/h)

A fun derivative of the Mini, the Moke was originally designed as an off-road, light reconnaissance vehicle for the British Army, but it was more successful as a beach car.

△ Triumph Herald 1200 1961

Origin	UK
Engine	1,147 cc, straight-four
Top speed	77 mph (124 km/h)

Triumph made the most of limited financial resources manufacturing this separate-chassis small car with all-independent suspension, a great turning circle, and luxury trim.

◁ Lancia Flavia 1961

Origin	Italy
Engine	1,488 cc, flat-four
Top speed	93 mph (150 km/h)

The Flavia had an aluminium boxer engine and dual-circuit servo disc brakes. In 1963 the engine became 1.8 litres, and fuel injection was added in 1965.

△ Ford Cortina Mk I GT 1963

Origin	UK
Engine	1,498 cc, straight-four
Top speed	94 mph (151 km/h)

Hardly innovative – except for the fresh-air ventilation from 1965 – this car was popular for its low-friction oversquare engine, synchromesh gearbox, and spacious body.

△ MG 1100 1962

Origin	UK
Engine	1,098 cc, straight-four
Top speed	85 mph (137 km/h)

The BMC 1100/1300 range sold well. The increased interior space was the result of a transverse engine and front-wheel drive, while the Hydrolastic suspension gave a comfortable ride.

◁ **Hillman Minx/Hunter 1966**

Origin UK

Engine 1,725 cc, straight-four

Top speed 92 mph (148 km/h)

Chrysler's Rootes Group produced this no-nonsense family saloon that performed well. It was built for ten years in the UK, then for several decades more in Iran.

△ **Sunbeam Rapier IV 1963**

Origin UK

Engine 1,592 cc, straight-four

Top speed 92 mph (148 km/h)

Launched in 1955 with 1,390 cc, this two-door saloon based on the Hillman Minx kept Sunbeam's sporting name alive with some rally successes.

▷ **Hillman Imp 1963**

Origin UK

Engine 875 cc, straight-four

Top speed 78 mph (126 km/h)

The Rootes Group's small car had a superb aluminium engine in the back. The Imp sold around half a million units over 13 years, but it was hugely outsold by the Mini.

△ **Renault 8 Gordini 1964**

Origin France

Engine 1,108 cc, straight-four

Top speed 106 mph (171 km/h)

All-disc brakes (standard even on basic model R8s) and a five-speed gearbox helped make the rear-engined 8 Gordini remarkably rapid for its small engine size.

◁ **Citroën Ami 6 1961**

Origin France

Engine 602 cc, flat-two

Top speed 68 mph (109 km/h)

Giving the 2CV this unusual body helped Citroën sell another 1.8 million small cars between 1961 and 1978. It lost the notchback rear window in 1969.

◁ **Amphicar 1961**

Origin Germany

Engine 1,147 cc, straight-four

Top speed 70 mph (113 km/h)

Hans Trippel designed this amphibious car after huge investment in research. It used a Triumph Herald engine in the back and steered with the front wheels.

◁ **Fiat 124 1966**

Origin Italy

Engine 1,197 cc, straight-four

Top speed 85 mph (137 km/h)

Key to Fiat's 1960s success were cars like the 124, which offered excellent carrying capacity and performance with good handling; it lived on for decades more as the Russian Lada.

◁ **Volkswagen 1600 Fastback 1966**

Origin Germany

Engine 1,584 cc, flat-four

Top speed 83 mph (134 km/h)

Faster than a Beetle and with front disc brakes, the 1600 was improved in 1968 with 12-volt electrics, fuel injection, and MacPherson strut front suspension.

▷ **Honda N360 1967**

Origin Japan

Engine 354 cc, straight-two

Top speed 72 mph (116 km/h)

Honda extracted 27 bhp from the overhead-cam 360 engine, improving the performance enough for this Japanese-market *kei* car to sell in other markets.

◁ **Toyota Corolla 1966**

Origin Japan

Engine 1,077 cc, straight-four

Top speed 85 mph (137 km/h)

The first of an incredibly successful line, the Corolla was not exceptional in any way but was well put together and dependable, making it an ideal family car.

Rear/Mid-engined Racers

In the 1960s many racing-car constructors realized the benefits of moving the engine from its traditional position at the front of the car to the middle or rear. Improved weight distribution was just one of the advantages of this configuration. Marques that adopted the new set-up for their racing models soon reaped the rewards in the form of superior handling and performance on the racetrack.

△ Huffaker-Offenhauser Special 1964

Origin USA

Engine 4,179 cc, straight-four

Top speed 180 mph (290 km/h)

Just three Huffaker-Offenhauser Specials were built for Indy Car racing, with the model featuring a liquid suspension system and rear-engine set-up.

△ Simca Abarth GT 1962

Origin France/Italy

Engine 1,288 cc, straight-four

Top speed 143 mph (230 km/h)

Italian tuning company Abarth fitted a new 1,300 cc engine into the French Simca 1000 and transformed it into a winning racer in 1962 and 1963.

△ Maserati Tipo 61 "Birdcage" 1959

Origin Italy

Engine 2,890 cc, straight-four

Top speed 177 mph (285 km/h)

Known as the "Birdcage" because of its intricate tubular chassis, the 61 competed at Le Mans and other endurance events from 1959 to 1961.

▷ Lola T70 1965

Origin UK

Engine 4,736-5,735 cc, V8

Top speed 200 mph (322 km/h)

Raced successfully on home soil in Britain as well as across the Atlantic, the T70 was powered by either a Ford or a Chevrolet V8 engine.

◁ Ford GT40 MkII 1966

Origin USA

Engine 6,997 cc, V8

Top speed 200 mph (322 km/h)

Two years after its 1964 launch, the legendary GT40 was upgraded and the MKII secured a clean sweep at the 1966 Le Mans 24-hour race in France.

▷ Jaguar XJ13 1966

Origin UK

Engine 4,994 cc, V12

Top speed 175 mph (282 km/h)

Jaguar built just one stunning XJ13 model, which despite its new 502 bhp V12 engine was deemed not competitive enough to race at Le Mans.

▷ Eisert Indy racer 1964

Origin USA

Engine 4,949 cc, V8

Top speed 180 mph (290 km/h)

Influenced by Lotus Formula 1 racers of the period, the Eisert was specially built to compete in Indy Car racing in the mid-1960s.

△ Alfa Romeo Tipo 33.2 1967

Origin Italy

Engine 1,995 cc, V8

Top speed 162 mph (261 km/h)

Alfa's decision to develop a new sports prototype model in the 1960s bore fruit with the Tipo 33.2, which won its debut race in 1967.

△ Howmet TX 1968

Origin USA

Engine 2,958 cc, gas turbine

Top speed 180 mph (290 km/h)

Competing in high-profile endurance events during the 1968 season, the Howmet featured a novel gas-turbine powerplant.

△ **Lotus 49 1967**
Origin UK
Engine 2,993 cc, V8
Top speed 180 mph (290 km/h)

The fruits of a collaboration between Lotus, Ford, and Cosworth, the legendary 49 was piloted by the finest Grand Prix drivers of the late 1960s.

△ **Matra Cosworth MS10 1968**
Origin France
Engine 2,993 cc, V8
Top speed 180 mph (290 km/h)

Matra started out in Formula 1 in 1967 with the MS10, which shared the same impressive Cosworth engine as the Lotus 49.

△ **Ferrari 312/68 1968**
Origin Italy
Engine 2,989 cc, V12
Top speed 193 mph (310 km/h)

The 1968 version of Ferrari's 312 F1 racer first unveiled two years previously was the best yet, with Jacques "Jacky" Ickx winning that year's French Grand Prix.

▽ **Ferrari 312P 1969**
Origin Italy
Engine 2,990 cc, V12
Top speed 199 mph (320 km/h)

First raced in 1969, Ferrari's 312P prototype competed in high-profile endurance events such as the Spa 1,000 km and the Le Mans 24-hour race.

△ **March 707 1970**
Origin UK
Engine 8,226 cc, V8
Top speed 200 mph (322 km/h)

Designed in the late 1960s, March competed in the North American CanAm racing series with the 707 model, which was powered by a mighty Chevrolet V8 engine.

△ **Porsche 718 RS 1957**
Origin Germany
Engine 1,587 cc, flat-four
Top speed 140 mph (225 km/h)

Porsche's 718 open-topped endurance racer recorded a number of podium finishes, including third place at the 1958 Le Mans 24-hour race. It continued winning races into the early 1960s.

△ **Porsche 906 1966**
Origin Germany
Engine 1,991 cc, flat-six
Top speed 174 mph (280 km/h)

The first Porsche to incorporate gullwing doors, the 906 from 1966 hit the ground running with class and overall victories in its debut year.

◁ **Porsche 917K 1970**
Origin Germany
Engine 4,494 cc, flat-twelve
Top speed 199 mph (320 km/h)

Conceived in the 1960s with the aim of winning the 1970 Le Mans 24-hour race, the fabled 917 did just that and also won in 1971.

Sports and Executive Saloons

A new breed of saloon, these cars were aimed at hard-driving businessmen. The cars were well able to sustain foot-to-the-floor overtaking and relaxed high-speed cruising, in contrast to earlier counterparts that would shake themselves to pieces, or overheat their engines. Much of the know-how behind these cars was directly derived from the racing track, where saloon cars had fired the minds of engineers.

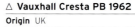

△ **Vauxhall Cresta PB 1962**
Origin UK
Engine 3,294 cc, six-cylinder
Top speed 93 mph (150 km/h)

The Cresta was a large, comfortable car from the British branch of General Motors. From 1965 automatic transmission was introduced.

▷ **Austin/Morris Mini Cooper 1961**
Origin UK
Engine 1275 cc, four-cylinder
Top speed 100 mph (161 km/h)

The Mini was never meant to be a performance saloon, but Formula 1 boss John Cooper spotted its potential. Tuned engines and disc brakes exploited its fantastic roadholding.

△ **Ford Zephyr MkIII 1962**
Origin UK
Engine 2,553 cc, six-cylinder
Top speed 95 mph (153 km/h)

Ford offered four- or six-cylinder engines in its biggest British saloon. This car came with front disc brakes, an all-synchromesh gearbox, and an optional automatic transmission.

△ **Volvo 122S 1961**
Origin Sweden
Engine 1,778 cc, four-cylinder
Top speed 100 mph (161 km/h)

The ultimate engine in this rugged yet capable sports saloon car was a 100 bhp unit. It was a spirited performer, especially with optional overdrive, and was called the Amazon in Sweden.

△ **Ford Falcon 1966**
Origin Australia
Engine 3,277 cc, six-cylinder
Top speed 105 mph (169 km/h)

This was the third generation of Ford's popular "compact". It was designed to thwart the VW Beetle in the US, but was also specifically adapted for the demanding Australian market.

▷ **Wolseley 6/110 1961**
Origin UK
Engine 2,912 cc, six-cylinder
Top speed 101 mph (163 km/h)

The 6/110 was a heavy car, so it had no real spark despite a 120 bhp engine. An already luxurious specification could be enhanced with optional air conditioning and power steering.

▽ **Rover P6 2000 TC 1963**
Origin UK
Engine 1,978 cc, four-cylinder
Top speed 108 mph (174 km/h)

In 1963 the P6 broke new ground for safety and sportiness in saloon cars. The TC (twin carburettor) added extra zest. A later version, the P6 3500, had a V8 engine.

△ **Jaguar XJ6 1968**

Origin	UK
Engine	4,235 cc, six-cylinder
Top speed	124 mph (200 km/h)

Widely hailed as the finest saloon car in the world, the beautiful XJ6 offered a superb compromise between high performance, ride comfort, and roadholding.

◁ **Daimler 2.5-litre V8-250 1962**

Origin	UK
Engine	2,548 cc, V8
Top speed	112 mph (180 km/h)

After Jaguar had taken over Daimler in 1960, it created this compact luxury model by uniting the SP250's refined V8 engine with the Jaguar MkII body. Almost all were automatic.

△ **Jaguar Mk2 1959**

Origin	UK
Engine	3,781 cc, six-cylinder
Top speed	125 mph (201 km/h)

For many, this lithe Jaguar is the epitome of the 1960s sports saloon. The 3.8-litre version was a great saloon racer, although the 3.4 litre was more popular on the road.

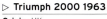

▷ **Triumph 2000 1963**

Origin	UK
Engine	1,998 cc, six-cylinder
Top speed	93 mph (150 km/h)

A stylish and well-liked car among business executives of the 1960s, the 2000 featured all-round independent suspension, front disc brakes, and Italian styling by Giovanni Michelotti.

▷ **Humber Hawk MkIV 1964**

Origin	UK
Engine	2,267 cc, four-cylinder
Top speed	83 mph (134 km/h)

Humber's largest executive cars received a styling revision around the rear window for their final three years, like this MkIV. They still featured a column gearchange.

◁ **Isuzu Bellett 1963**

Origin	Japan
Engine	1,991 cc, four-cylinder
Top speed	118 mph (190 km/h)

Little known in the West, the neat Bellett was one of Japan's first sports saloons and, in GT-R form, a star of Japanese production car racing. Over 170,000 were built.

▷ **Holden Monaro 1968**

Origin	Australia
Engine	5,736 cc, V8
Top speed	115 mph (185 km/h)

The Monaro was a sporty, four-seater coupé derived directly from the HK series Kingswood/Brougham saloon. The ultimate edition of the Monaro was the 5.7-litre GTS 327 Bathurst.

△ **Nissan Skyline GT-R 1969**

Origin	Japan
Engine	1,998 cc, six-cylinder
Top speed	124 mph (200 km/h)

The twin-camshaft engine in the GT-R turned the humdrum Skyline saloon into a serious race winner that notched up 50 race wins in its first three years.

Sedans and Sporty Coupés

Clean, smooth lines and hot-rod performance options were the big trends in 1960s America, as car stylists reacted against the excessive fins and chrome of the previous decade. American carmakers finally found their sports-car niche with the Ford-inspired, compact, and affordable "pony cars". "Coke bottle" styling was to be seen right across the marketplace and, before long, around the world.

△ Buick Skylark 1961

Origin USA

Engine 3,528 cc, V8

Top speed 105 mph (169 km/h)

Buick introduced the Skylark sport coupé to wide acclaim. With its clean, low lines Buick finally abandoned the fins of the 1950s for a popular new look.

△ Buick Riviera 1963

Origin USA

Engine 6,571 cc, V8

Top speed 120 mph (193 km/h)

One of the cleanest examples of the "Coke bottle" styling that swept across the industry in the 1960s was on the long, low, lithe, luxury 1963 Buick Riviera.

△ Plymouth Barracuda 1964

Origin USA

Engine 4,473 cc, V8

Top speed 106 mph (171 km/h)

Plymouth struggled in the 1960s until the Barracuda heralded a remarkable recovery – yet it never came close to the sales success of Ford's Mustang rival.

△ Chrysler 300F 1960

Origin USA

Engine 6,768 cc, V8

Top speed 120 mph (193 km/h)

The 300 Series "Letter cars" were Chrysler's most powerful machines: the 1960's F went to monocoque construction and ram-tuned induction, but forgot to chop the fins.

△ Studebaker Gran Turismo Hawk 1962

Origin USA

Engine 4,736 cc, V8

Top speed 110 mph (177 km/h)

Packard's takeover in 1954 did not help Studebaker for long; it struggled, closing in 1966. The Hawk boosted sales briefly in 1962.

◁ Ford Thunderbird Landau 1964

Origin USA

Engine 6,392 cc, V8

Top speed 118 mph (190 km/h)

The year Ford launched the Mustang, the Thunderbird also received a total new look, with a longer bonnet, shorter roof, and power bulge. Sales went up by 50 per cent.

Ford Mustang

After the record-breaking success of the compact Falcon saloon, Ford saw a niche for a mini-Thunderbird based on the Falcon platform – and created a whole new market with the hugely popular Mustang. It set a new world record, selling 418,000 in its first year: it would have sold more if Ford could have built them faster.

▷ Ford Mustang hardtop coupe 1964

Origin USA

Engine 4,727 cc, V8

Top speed 116 mph (187 km/h)

The Mustang sold in coupé, convertible, and, later, fastback coupé forms, with engines ranging from 3.3-litre straight-six to 4.7-litre V8. This V8 hardtop coupé was by far the most popular.

△ **Chevrolet Corvair Monza 1965**

Origin USA

Engine 2,687 cc, flat-six

Top speed 90 mph (145 km/h)

The compact Corvair with its rear-mounted aluminium engine was too revolutionary for most Americans and criticized by US attorney Ralph Nader; but enthusiasts loved it.

◁ **Chevrolet Camaro 327 1967**

Origin USA

Engine 5,359 cc, V8

Top speed 122 mph (196 km/h)

It took Chevrolet three years to respond to Ford's Mustang, but when it came, the Camaro offered a great range of performance packages in a smooth, attractive body.

△ **Pontiac Tempest GTO 1966**

Origin USA

Engine 6,375 cc, V8

Top speed 122 mph (196 km/h)

The Tempest compact helped make Pontiac the third best-selling US marque of the 1960s and the GTO confirmed its performance credentials: it was a real hot rod.

◁ **Oldsmobile Starfire 1964**

Origin USA

Engine 6,456 cc, V8

Top speed 108 mph (174 km/h)

Oldsmobile moved into the personal luxury market with the Starfire, using its most powerful engine option in an imposing, squared-off, two-door bodyshell.

△ **Mercury Cougar 1967**

Origin USA

Engine 4,727 cc, V8

Top speed 112 mph (180 km/h)

Mercury entered the "pony car" market in 1967, pitting parent Ford against the Chevrolet Camaro. Handsome styling ensured it caught on, selling 150,000 in its first year.

◁ **Dodge Charger R/T 1968**

Origin USA

Engine 5,211 cc, V8

Top speed 113 mph (182 km/h)

"Dodge Fever" arrived with the restyle for 1968 as the marque saw record sales, helped by the new, super-smooth "Coke bottle" styled Charger V8.

△ **Mercury Cyclone 1968**

Origin USA

Engine 4949 cc, V8

Top speed 115 mph (185 km/h)

The Cyclone was Mercury's macho Grand Tourer model from 1964, given "Coke bottle" styling from 1966 that looked best on the most popular Fastback Coupe body.

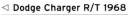

△ **Ford Mustang 1965**

Origin USA

Engine 4,727 cc, V8

Top speed 116 mph (187 km/h)

More than a million Mustangs were sold in the first two years of production. The styling was so universally loved that it won the Tiffany Award for Excellence in American Design.

△ **Ford Mustang Fastback 1965**

Origin USA

Engine 4,727 cc, V8

Top speed 116 mph (187 km/h)

The stylish Fastback bodystyle, sold as the 2+2, joined the range in 1965 and immediately outsold the convertible; in 1966 Mustang took 7.1 per cent of all US car sales.

◁ **Ford Mustang Boss 302 1969**

Origin USA

Engine 4,942 cc, V8

Top speed 121 mph (195 km/h)

Faced with competition from the Camaro, Mustang grew for 1969, both in size and performance, up to the ultimate Boss 302 and Boss 429 monsters.

Ultimate Luxury Limousines

The 1960s saw the final flowering of the separate chassis luxury car. These huge, heavy, traditional, and opulent cars were gradually replaced by lighter, more efficient, modern, monocoque luxury models, with significantly higher performance and sleeker, lower lines. The decade also saw the appearance of much smaller luxury cars based on mainstream models, ideal for city-centre driving.

◁ **GAZ Chaika 1959**

Origin USSR

Engine 5522 cc, V8

Top speed 99 mph (159 km/h)

A close copy of a 1955 Packard, the Chaika was built until 1981. It was strictly for party officials, academics, scientists, and other VIPs who were approved by the Soviet government.

▷ **Cadillac Calais 1965**

Origin USA

Engine 7030 cc, V8

Top speed 120 mph (193 km/h)

Every Cadillac was a luxury car; this model featured curved side windows, remote-controlled exterior mirrors, variable ratio steering, and heated seats.

△ **Nissan Cedric 1962**

Origin Japan

Engine 1,883 cc, straight-four

Top speed 90 mph (145 km/h)

Rarely seen outside Japan at the time, Nissan's large saloon was inspired by US styling but fitted with a 1.5-2.8-litre engine. It was Nissan's first monocoque design.

△ **Nissan President 1965**

Origin Japan

Engine 3,988 cc, V8

Top speed 115 mph (185 km/h)

Nissan's ultimate car for 1965 was a better model than the Cedric, with a 3.0-litre V6 or 4.0-litre V8 and, from 1971, ABS. One was used by Japan's prime minister.

▷ **Mercedes-Benz 300SEC 1962**

Origin Germany

Engine 2996 cc, straight-six

Top speed 124 mph (200 km/h)

One of Germany's finest cars of the early 1960s, the 300SEC had a race-proven, fuel-injected six-cylinder engine in a sophisticated coupé or convertible shell.

△ **Mitsubishi Debonair 1964**

Origin Japan

Engine 1991 cc, straight-six

Top speed 96 mph (154 km/h)

This luxury car for the Japanese market was styled like an early 1960s US car, and stayed almost unchanged until 1986. A bigger engine was added in the 1970s.

△ **Mercedes-Benz 600 1963**

Origin Germany

Engine 6332 cc, V8

Top speed 130 mph (209 km/h)

From 1963 until as recently as 1981, Mercedes offered this large saloon for VIPs to travel in an insulated cabin at speeds of up to 120 mph (193 km/h). Only 2,677 of them were built.

▷ **Rolls-Royce Silver Cloud III 1962**

Origin UK

Engine 6230 cc, V8

Top speed 110 mph (177 km/h)

The last of the separate-chassis mainstream Rolls-Royces was traditional and indulgent, but with a wonderful wood and leather interior; it also had V8 power and modern twin headlamps.

◁ **Checker Marathon Limousine 1963**

Origin USA

Engine 4637 cc, V8

Top speed 90 mph (145 km/h)

Checker built taxis from 1923 to 1959, and then produced a few taxi-derived cars, estates, and limos. This eight-door limo offered a roomy interior.

▷ **Bentley S3 Continental 1962**

Origin UK

Engine 6,230 cc, V8

Top speed 113 mph (185 km/h)

The stately Bentley S3 also came in a coachbuilt "Continental" version. This was a faster and lighter model with an aluminium body and sportier lines.

◁ **Lincoln Continental Convertible 1961**

Origin USA

Engine 7,043 cc, V8

Top speed 115 mph (185 km/h)

The 1961 Continental was one of the most influential auto designs of the decade. It had power-assisted seats, windows, brakes, steering, and gearbox.

▽ **Chrysler New Yorker 1960**

Origin USA

Engine 6,767 cc, V8

Top speed 122 mph (196 km/h)

In 1960 Chrysler began producing its first monocoque construction bodyshells. The New Yorker was the longest and most luxurious, with 350 bhp to speed it along the freeways.

△ **Humber Imperial 1964**

Origin UK

Engine 2,965 cc, straight-six

Top speed 100 mph (161 km/h)

The ultimate Imperial model was discontinued for 10 years by Chrysler's Rootes Group, but they brought it back in 1964-67 as this comfortably equipped, big saloon.

△ **Rolls-Royce Phantom VI 1968**

Origin UK

Engine 6230 cc, V8

Top speed 101 mph (163 km/h)

Huge, heavy, and entirely custom-made, this was the ultimate status symbol for rock stars or royalty. Based on a 1950s design with twin headlamps added, 409 were built up to 1992.

◁ **Radford Mini De Ville 1963**

Origin UK

Engine 1,275 cc, straight-four

Top speed 95 mph (153 km/h)

Harold Radford coachbuilders offered Minis completely reworked with luxury interiors, tuned engines, and special exterior finishes. Customers included British actor Peter Sellers.

△ **Jaguar MkX 1962**

Origin UK

Engine 3,781 cc, straight-six

Top speed 120 mph (193 km/h)

A wide 1960s luxury model with monocoque construction, independent rear suspension, and wood and leather interior, this car was ideal for the US market.

△ **Daimler DS420 1968**

Origin UK

Engine 4,235 cc, straight-six

Top speed 110 mph (177 km/h)

Jaguar based this classy limousine on its MkX/420G platform but extended it at the back. This model was built by Vanden Plas, then by Jaguar from 1979 to 1992.

Compact Coupés

Small, specialist manufacturers created many GT cars in Europe in the 1960s, which, owing to their ingenuity and inventiveness, rivalled those of the big car makers. Hardtop coupés became increasingly popular, and trends towards front-wheel drive or even mid-engine layouts were appearing. Aerodynamic testing produced some very efficient shapes.

◁ TVR Grantura 1958
Origin UK
Engine 1,798 cc, straight-four
Top speed 108 mph (174 km/h)

The TVR wasn't styled, it grew. Its cheeky, chunky looks and lively performance due to its light weight brought small yet steady volume sales and competition success into the 1960s.

△ Porsche 356B 1959
Origin Germany
Engine 1,582 cc, flat-four
Top speed 111 mph (179 km/h)

By 1960 Porsche's brilliant VW-based sports car of 1950 had moved a long way from its roots. This sophisticated 2+2 coupé was well built and reassuringly expensive.

△ Gilbern GT 1959
Origin UK
Engine 1,622 cc, straight-four
Top speed 100 mph (161 km/h)

Wales' only successful carmaker used a spaceframe chassis, attractive glassfibre body, and high quality interiors to sell this handsome MGA/B/Midget-powered coupé.

△ Volvo P1800 1961
Origin Sweden
Engine 1,778 cc, straight-four
Top speed 106 mph (171 km/h)

Initially assembled in Britain by Jensen, but soon transferred to Sweden to improve quality, the P1800 was a stylish and incredibly durable two-seat Grand Tourer.

△ NSU Sport Prinz 1959
Origin Germany
Engine 598 cc, straight-two
Top speed 76 mph (122 km/h)

Italian styling house Bertone worked wonders to create this winsome little coupé for the bravely independent NSU. Over 20,000 were sold in the 1960s.

△ Matra Djet 1962
Origin France
Engine 1,108 cc, straight-four
Top speed 118 mph (190 km/h)

Designed by René Bonnet and built by Matra, the aerodynamic Djet pioneered the mid-engine layout for roadgoing sports cars, and was fast with Renault Gordini power.

△ Ogle SX1000 1962
Origin UK
Engine 1,275 cc, straight-four
Top speed 110 mph (177 km/h)

Industrial designer David Ogle designed this bubble-like coupé, which successfully hid the Mini-Cooper running gear below. Sadly, few were made.

◁ Marcos 1800 1964
Origin UK
Engine 1,778 cc, straight-four
Top speed 115 mph (185 km/h)

Dennis Adams styled this ultra-low two-seater, with fixed lay-back seats and adjustable pedals. A wide range of engines found their way under the long, low bonnet.

△ Broadspeed GT 1965
Origin UK
Engine 1,275 cc, straight-four
Top speed 113 mph (182 km/h)

Broadspeed founder Ralph Broad took the Mini Cooper 1275S and added a glassfibre fastback rear body that, with some engine tuning, made it a real flyer.

◁ **Ford Consul Capri 1961**
Origin UK
Engine 1,498 cc, straight-four
Top speed 83 mph (134 km/h)

Ford's first attempt to make a sporty coupé for Europe just didn't catch on – it was far too American in its styling. Only 18,000 were sold in three years.

△ **Ford Capri 1969**
Origin UK
Engine 1,599 cc, straight-four
Top speed 100 mph (161 km/h)

Five years after the Mustang took the US market by storm, Ford managed the same in Europe with the brilliant Capri, helped by engine options from 1,300 cc to 3,000 cc.

◁ **Lancia Fulvia Coupé 1965**
Origin Italy
Engine 1,216 cc, V4
Top speed 100 mph (161 km/h)

Lancia flouted convention with beautifully built, compact, twin-cam V4 engines and front-wheel drive in designer Pietro Castagnero's 2+2 coupé – the last true Lancia.

◁ **Lotus Elan +2 1967**
Origin UK
Engine 1,558 cc, straight-four
Top speed 123 mph (198 km/h)

Not wanting to lose its keen two-seater buyers when they started families, Lotus developed this upmarket 2+2 Elan, still on the superb-handling, backbone chassis.

△ **Saab Sonett 1966**
Origin Sweden
Engine 1,498 cc, V4
Top speed 100 mph (161 km/h)

Front-wheel drive, a freewheel, and a column gearchange were unusual features derived from the Sonett's saloon parent, but the neat glassfibre body looked good.

△ **Triumph GT6 1966**
Origin UK
Engine 1,998 cc, straight-six
Top speed 112 mph (180 km/h)

Triumph neatly combined the Spitfire chassis and 2000 engine in a pretty, Michelotti-styled body to make the GT6, soon dubbed a "mini E-type". This is the 1970 restyle.

△ **Unipower GT 1966**
Origin UK
Engine 1,275 cc, straight-four
Top speed 119 mph (192 km/h)

The best-looking Mini-based sports car of all, the Unipower had its Mini engine over the rear wheels in a lightweight spaceframe chassis bonded to its glassfibre body.

◁ **Alfa Romeo 1750 GTV 1967**
Origin Italy
Engine 1,779 cc, straight-four
Top speed 116 mph (187 km/h)

Alfa Romeo's Giulia series, launched in 1962-63, was hugely successful. This car was the perfect compact four-seater sporting coupé, with twin-cam power and great handling.

△ **Sunbeam Rapier H120 1969**
Origin UK
Engine 1,725 cc, straight-four
Top speed 106 mph (171 km/h)

Sunbeam's US ownership was clear in the Plymouth Barracuda-derived styling, but the Rapier became an effective sports coupé with Holbay tuning.

Powerful GT Cars

In terms of performance, the most powerful GT cars of the 1960s were on a par with their equivalents today, so efficient were their aerodynamics and engineering. Modern supercar drivers might notice differences in electronic gadgetry, soundproofing, and driver aids – but not in performance. The 1960s also produced some of the finest styling ever seen in this genre.

△ Bristol 407 1962

Origin UK

Engine 5,130 cc, V8

Top speed 122 mph (196 km/h)

The British Bristol marque used a Chrysler V8 engine in the 407, giving this upmarket four-seater the power it needed to merit its pretensions as a status symbol.

△ Aston Martin DB5 1964

Origin UK

Engine 3,995 cc, straight-six

Top speed 148 mph (238 km/h)

Adding the cowled headlamps from the DB4 GT created a much sportier look for the DB5, which was justified by an upgrade to a 314 bhp Vantage engine and a five-speed ZF gearbox.

◁ Aston Martin DB6 1965

Origin UK

Engine 3,995 cc, straight-six

Top speed 140 mph (225 km/h)

The body of this luxurious, heavy model was slightly more spacious than that of the DB5. The flick-up tail balanced the cowled-light front and improved aerodynamic stability.

△ Ferrari 400 GT Superamerica 1961

Origin Italy

Engine 3,967 cc, V12

Top speed 160 mph (257 km/h)

Each 400 Superamerica was built to order and customized for individual owners. With an aerodynamic body styled by Pininfarina, the GT gave shattering levels of performance.

△ Ferrari 275GTB 1965

Origin Italy

Engine 3,286 cc, V12

Top speed 153 mph (246 km/h)

Perfectly proportioned styling by Pininfarina, a five-speed gearbox, and all-independent suspension showed that Ferrari was moving with the times; six-carburettor versions did 165 mph (265 km/h).

△ Chevrolet Corvette Sting Ray 1963

Origin USA

Engine 5,360 cc, V8

Top speed 147 mph (237 km/h)

A dramatic 1963 restyling gave the Corvette a new, aerodynamic profile, with the headlamps hidden behind electrically operated panels. For the first time it was offered as a hardtop coupé as well as a convertible.

△ Dino 246GT 1969

Origin Italy

Engine 2,418 cc, V6

Top speed 148 mph (238 km/h)

Enzo Ferrari named this mid-engined two-seater after his son Dino, who died in 1956; later versions went out under simply the Ferrari name. The stunning styling is by Pininfarina.

▷ Jaguar E-type 1961

Origin UK

Engine 3,781 cc, straight-six

Top speed 140 mph (225 km/h)

With the E-type, Jaguar's Malcolm Sayer and William Lyons created one of the most beautiful and effective sports cars of all time. The E-type was just as at home on the road as it was on the racetrack.

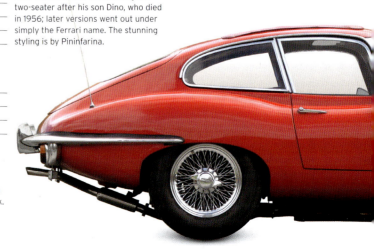

△ Facel Vega Facel II 1962

Origin France

Engine 6,286 cc, V8

Top speed 133 mph (214 km/h)

Big, bold, unquestionably French, and powered by a Chrysler V8, the Facel II was firmly in the Grand Routier tradition. Only 180 of this expensive, exclusive car were made.

△ Ford Mustang GT500 1967

Origin USA

Engine 7,010 cc, V8

Top speed 134 mph (216 km/h)

Carroll Shelby shoe-horned the big-block Ford V8 engine into the Mustang to create the 355 bhp GT500, which offered serious hot-rod performance in a luxury package.

△ Gordon-Keeble 1964

Origin UK

Engine 5,395 cc, V8

Top speed 136 mph (219 km/h)

British engineering, a powerful American V8 engine, and delicately beautiful Italian styling by Bertone created this excellent GT, which some see as offering the perfect combination of speed and style.

△ Iso Grifo A3C 1965

Origin Italy

Engine 5359 cc, V8

Top speed 170 mph (274 km/h)

Giotto Bizzarrini designed the Grifo A3C for racing, and it triumphed in its category at Le Mans in 1965. It was based on Bizzarrini's stunning V8-powered Grifo two-seat coupé.

△ Lamborghini 400GT Monza 1966

Origin Italy

Engine 3,929 cc, V12

Top speed 156 mph (251 km/h)

Lamborghini and Ferrari fought a constant battle to be the top Italian supercar brand. The 400GT's four-cam V12 engine was far more advanced than anything Ferari could offer. The Monza was a one-off edition of the car.

△ Lamborghini Miura 1966

Origin Italy

Engine 3,929 cc, V12

Top speed 177 mph (285 km/h)

Lamborghini eclipsed Ferrari when it introduced the outstanding Miura, the first practical, mid-engined supercar. The breathtaking styling was by Marcello Gandini for Bertone.

◁ Lamborghini Islero 1968

Origin Italy

Engine 3,929 cc, V12

Top speed 160 mph (257 km/h)

This simple and elegant restyling of the 2+2 Lamborghini 400GT was by Carrozzeria Marazzi. Unfortunately, it lacked the commercial appeal that the top stylists could create.

△ Jensen Interceptor 1967

Origin UK

Engine 6,276 cc, V8

Top speed 133 mph (214 km/h)

Jensen commissioned the Italian styling company Vignale to design a new body for this Chrysler V8-engined coupé. The result was a truly elegant, practical 2+2.

▷ Studebaker Avanti 1962

Origin USA

Engine 4,736 cc, V8

Top speed 120 mph (193 km/h)

The fibreglass-bodied Avanti was a bold move for a small manufacturer such as Studebaker, but it failed to save the company. Small numbers were made privately until 1991.

◁ Maserati Ghibli 1967

Origin Italy

Engine 4,719 cc, V8

Top speed 154 mph (248 km/h)

Maserati's magnificent four-cam V8 engine enabled this luxurious coupé to perform like a supercar. The car's perfectly proportioned fastback body was styled by Ghia of Italy.

Sports Cars (60s)

Despite a wide choice of attractive, often extremely potent models, the open sports car was in decline in the 1960s as the popularity of civilized, closed-top Grand Touring cars grew: the vast majority of these sports cars were launched in the first half of the decade and many were conceived in the 1950s. Japan now joined the US and Europe on the world market.

△ **MG Midget 1961**

Origin UK

Engine 948 cc, straight-four

Top speed 86 mph (138 km/h)

Tiny, cute, and enormous fun to drive at speeds much lower than it feels, the Midget was a true fun car and was built – with engines up to 1,500 cc – into the 1980s.

△ **Ferrari 250 California Spider 1959**

Origin Italy

Engine 2,953 cc, V12

Top speed 145 mph (233 km/h)

One of the most beautiful and desirable Ferraris ever made, now worth millions, the California Spider was a car of film stars, and became something of a film star itself.

△ **Jaguar E-type 1961**

Origin UK

Engine 3,781 cc, straight-six

Top speed 149 mph (240 km/h)

With double-overhead-camshaft engine, all-disc brakes, and all-independent suspension, the E-type was a bargain compared with other 1960s supercars.

△ **Maserati Mistral Spider 1963**

Origin Italy

Engine 3,692 cc, straight-six

Top speed 145 mph (233 km/h)

Maserati fuel-injected its twin-cam six to get Jaguar-level performance and commissioned Frua to design this understated and sophisticated two-seat body.

△ **Lotus Super Seven 1961**

Origin UK

Engine 1,498 cc, straight-four

Top speed 103 mph (166 km/h)

The Seven was a 1950s design that refused to die, thanks to uncompromising, timeless styling and fabulous, seat-of-the-pants handling. Versions are still made today.

▷ **Lotus Elan 1962**

Origin UK

Engine 1,558 cc, straight-four

Top speed 122 mph (196 km/h)

Lotus cars were engineered for lightness, giving terrific performance. The glassfibre Elan sat on a steel backbone chassis and it went – and handled – superbly.

◁ **Austin-Healey 3000 MkIII 1963**

Origin UK

Engine 2,912 cc, straight-six

Top speed 121 mph (195 km/h)

Introduced in 1953 with a four-cylinder engine, the "Big Healey" grew up into a comfortable 2+2 touring sports car. Its low build and swooping curves had huge appeal.

◁ **Innocenti Spider 1961**

Origin Italy

Engine 948 cc, straight-four

Top speed 86 mph (138 km/h)

Innocenti of Milan commissioned Ghia to style a more upmarket body for British Austin-Healey Sprite running gear, with a bootlid, wind-up windows, and a heater.

▷ **Mercedes-Benz 230SL 1963**

Origin Germany

Engine 2,306 cc, straight-six

Top speed 120 mph (193 km/h)

The 230SL may look a sophisticated touring car with its pagoda roof and automatic option, but it won the gruelling Liège-Sofia-Liège rally in 1963: they don't come tougher.

△ MGB 1962

Origin	UK
Engine	1,798 cc, straight-four
Top speed	103 mph (166 km/h)

Britain's best-selling sports car sold over half a million in 1962–80. Rugged, reliable, and long-legged, it was a perfectly proportioned, truly practical enthusiast's car.

△ Triumph TR4A 1964

Origin	UK
Engine	2,138 cc, straight-four
Top speed	109 mph (175 km/h)

Designer Giovanni Michelotti restyled the separate-chassis TR sports car for 1961 and Triumph added independent rear suspension in 1964.

△ Sunbeam Tiger 1964

Origin	UK
Engine	4,261 cc, V8
Top speed	117 mph (188 km/h)

Carroll Shelby helped Rootes develop the Tiger from the excellent Sunbeam Alpine. The new engine gave it all the power it needed to fly, winning races and rallies.

△ Chevrolet Corvette Sting Ray 1965

Origin	USA
Engine	5,360 cc, V8
Top speed	147 mph (237 km/h)

A stunning restyle in 1963 turned Corvette into Sting Ray, with ultra-modern lines oozing macho potential, fulfilled in the ultimate 375 bhp fuel-injected "L84" model.

▽ Datsun Fairlady 1965

Origin	Japan
Engine	1,595 cc, straight-four
Top speed	100 mph (161 km/h)

Derived from the 1,500 cc predecessor of 1961, this MGB-beater from Japan was superbly built and tempted US drivers to consider buying Japanese cars.

△ AC Cobra 427 1965

Origin	USA/UK
Engine	6,997 cc, V8
Top speed	164 mph (264 km/h)

Designer Carroll Shelby had the idea to put the Ford V8 in the pretty British AC Ace – and topped it with this big block version, a road-legal race car with monstrous acceleration.

◁ Alfa Romeo Duetto Spider 1966

Origin	Italy
Engine	1,570 cc, straight-four
Top speed	111 mph (179 km/h)

Battista Pininfarina styled this exceptionally lovely roadster, which is also a joy to drive with a lively double overhead camshaft engine and all-disc brakes. It continued into the 1990s.

▽ Fiat Dino Spider 1967

Origin	Italy
Engine	1,987 cc, V6
Top speed	127 mph (204 km/h)

Pininfarina styled this gorgeous Spider, which boasted a Ferrari V6 engine and five-speed gearbox; had it been badged Ferrari, not Fiat, sales would have doubled.

△ Vignale Gamine 1967

Origin	Italy
Engine	499 cc, straight-two
Top speed	60 mph (97 km/h)

Recognizable to millions of children as Noddy's car, Vignale's Gamine fun car was based on Fiat 500 running gear. But it was too expensive to sell well.

Supercars

The 1970s saw a dramatic shift in car styling away from the flowing curves of the 1960s. Now stark, sharp-edged lines were epitomized by the dramatic wedge profiles that swept the motor show circuit. As television boosted the influence of motor racing, supercars were created by manufacturers who had never made them before, to homologate cars that would grab race-winning headlines.

△ Monteverdi 375C 1967
Origin Switzerland/Italy
Engine 7,206 cc, V8
Top speed 155 mph (249 km/h)

Switzerland's only carmaker commissioned Fissore to style his cars and Frua to build them, with Chrysler "hemi" engines. Only a handful were custom-built annually until 1973.

▷ De Tomaso Pantera 1969
Origin Italy
Engine 5,763 cc, V8
Top speed 160 mph (257 km/h)

A big block Ford V8 in an Italian suit, was styled by Ghia and built by De Tomaso in Italy, initially in partnership with Ford USA. It was so stunning, it was built into the 1990s.

◁ Ferrari 365GTB/4 Daytona 1968
Origin Italy
Engine 4,390 cc, V12
Top speed 174 mph (280 km/h)

The last and fastest of Ferrari's front-engine, rear-drive two-seaters had its heyday in the early 1970s: the 365GTB/4 is simple, brutal, and stunningly effective.

▽ Citroën SM 1970
Origin France
Engine 2,670 cc, V6
Top speed 142 mph (229 km/h)

When Citroën bought Maserati, this was the result: an aerodynamic and hydropneumatic French supercar with a powerful Italian V6 engine.

▷ Ferrari 400GT 1976
Origin Italy
Engine 4,823 cc, V12
Top speed 156 mph (251 km/h)

This executive four-seater is a civilized car with an automatic gearbox, and capable of exceeding 150 mph (241 km/h). A fine Ferrari, even if not as exotic as most.

◁ Ferrari 308 GTS 1978
Origin Italy
Engine 2,926 cc, V8
Top speed 155 mph (249 km/h)

Ferrari dropped the Dino name for its 1970s small sports car and gave it a new four-cam V8, mid-mounted as in the 246GT, with a Pininfarina-styled hardtop or targa body.

▷ Lancia Stratos 1973
Origin Italy
Engine 2,418 cc, V6
Top speed 143 mph (230 km/h)

Lancia's first pure sports car, built to homologate the model for rallying, this Bertone-styled supercar with Dino Ferrari power unit was a winner from the start.

◁ BMW 3.0CSL 1972

Origin Germany

Engine 3,003 cc, straight-six

Top speed 133 mph (214 km/h)

One of the first "homologation specials", built primarily to make high performance parts eligible for touring-car racing, the CSL also made a fabulous road car.

△ BMW M1 1979

Origin Germany

Engine 3,453 cc, straight-six

Top speed 162 mph (261 km/h)

BMW turned a race-car project into a roadgoing supercar, with mid-mounted 24-valve six in a sharp suit by Giorgetto Giugiaro, around Lamborghini-designed chassis.

△ Jaguar E-type Series III 1971

Origin UK

Engine 5,343 cc, V12

Top speed 150 mph (241 km/h)

To replace the XK engine, Jaguar needed something special, with more than six cylinders: what better than this aluminium V12 in an enlarged E-type shell?

◁ Porsche 911 1973

Origin Germany

Engine 2,994 cc, flat-six

Top speed 141 mph (227 km/h)

For 1975, Porsche's 911 gained impact-absorbing bumpers to keep it legal in the US; this example has been customized to resemble the earlier 2.7 Carrera RS, which is now a highly-coveted model.

▷ Porsche 934-5 1976

Origin Germany

Engine 2,994 cc, flat-six

Top speed 190 mph (306 km/h)

Derived from the 911 Turbo road car, the 934 was a highly successful sports racer, winning championships in Europe, the US, and Australia into the early 1980s.

△ Mercedes-Benz C111-II 1970

Origin Germany

Engine 4,800 cc (four-rotor Wankel)

Top speed 186 mph (300 km/h)

Mercedes' C111s were experimental cars, starting with a three-rotor Wankel-engined car in 1969. This Phase II version had 350 bhp, but fuel consumption was huge.

◁ Lamborghini Countach LP400 1974

Origin Italy

Engine 3,929 cc, V12

Top speed 170 mph (274 km/h)

When Bertone styled this ultimate wedge-shaped supercar, it could hardly have expected it to enter production and continue being made well into the 1990s.

▽ Alfa Romeo Navajo 1976

Origin Italy

Engine 1,995 cc, V8

Top speed 155 mph (249 km/h)

Bertone used the Alfa Romeo Tipo 33 racing car chassis for this dramatic wedge concept car. Its front and rear spoilers change angle as speed rises.

▷ Vauxhall SRV concept 1970

Origin UK

Engine 2,279 cc, straight-four

Top speed 140 mph (225 km/h)

General Motors sent Wayne Cherry to the UK to shake up Vauxhall's styling department. This concept heralded a "droop-snoot" look across the production range.

▷ Aston Martin V8 1972

Origin UK

Engine 5,340 cc, V8

Top speed 162 mph (261 km/h)

The big, macho Aston Martin V8 with 282–438 bhp was sharply styled by William Towns and proved a huge success, continuing in production for two decades.

◁ Lotus Esprit Turbo 1980

Origin UK

Engine 2,174 cc, straight-four

Top speed 148 mph (238 km/h)

Lotus road cars reached supercar status when the exotic Giugiaro-styled Esprit, introduced in 1976, gained a turbocharger, making this light car fly.

Small Cars

The Mini revolutionized small cars in the 1960s, so in the 1970s manufacturers battled for a slice of its market with their own interpretations of what a small car should include. Almost all kept the Mini's front-engine layout and added a hatchback, but not all were transverse and some still had rear-wheel drive. Some offered more space than the Mini, but none matched its brilliant packaging.

△ **Datsun Cherry 100A 1970**

Origin Japan

Engine 988 cc, straight-four

Top speed 86 mph (138 km/h)

The first front-wheel-drive Datsun was inspired by the Mini and sold 390,000 in five years, a period that saw Nissan's worldwide market share grow enormously.

△ **Fiat 127 1971**

Origin Italy

Engine 903 cc, straight-four

Top speed 83 mph (134 km/h)

Fiat had always been brilliant at well-packaged, quick, small cars; the 127 was another success, with sales of 3.7 million. The 1300 Sport option had a 1,300 cc engine and could reach 95 mph (153km/h).

△ **Mini Clubman 1969**

Origin UK

Engine 998 cc, straight-four

Top speed 75 mph (121 km/h)

By adding a longer, modern-looking front to the Mini, improved trim, and 1- or 1.1-litre engines, British Leyland maintained a presence in the market until the Metro was ready in 1981.

△ **Renault 5 1972**

Origin France

Engine 956 cc, straight-four

Top speed 86 mph (138 km/h)

The class-defining and perhaps most popular supermini, the 5 sold 5.5 million in 12 years. It was reasonably priced, with six engine choices from 782 to 1,397 cc and all-independent suspension.

◁ **Volkswagen Polo 1975**

Origin Germany

Engine 895 cc, straight-four

Top speed 80 mph (129 km/h)

VW completed its modern revolution with the Polo. It had a new overhead-cam front engine, all-independent suspension, and front-wheel drive, with engines from 0.9 to 1.3 litres.

◁ **Mazda Familia/323 1977**

Origin Japan

Engine 985 cc, straight-four

Top speed 80 mph (129 km/h)

First of a long and successful line of small Mazdas, the Familia was old-fashioned, with a front engine and rear-wheel drive, but reliable. Mazda introduced front-wheel drive in 1980.

△ **Mitsubishi/Colt Mirage 1978**

Origin Japan

Engine 1,244 cc, straight-four

Top speed 90 mph (145 km/h)

Sold in some markets as Colt, Mitsubishi's first front-drive car had a two-speed final drive, giving eight forward gears in total, for economy or performance.

△ Opel Kadett 1973

Origin Germany

Engine 993 cc, straight-four

Top speed 74 mph (119 km/h)

The German version of the General Motors T-car was sold with engines from 1.0 to 2.0 litres. The car was rear-wheel drive, betraying its US design ethos.

◁ Citroën 2CV6 1970

Origin France

Engine 602 cc, flat-two

Top speed 68 mph (109 km/h)

Due to its combination of spacious interior, large sunroof, stylish appearance, and economy, the 2CV stayed in production until 1990, selling almost 3.9 million.

△ Toyota Starlet 1978

Origin Japan

Engine 993 cc, straight-four

Top speed 84 mph (135 km/h)

Restricted by its outdated live rear axle, most Starlets were loaded with equipment such as five gears to win sales over the front-wheel-drive, all-independent opposition.

△ Citroën Visa 1978

Origin France

Engine 1,124 cc, straight-four

Top speed 89 mph (143 km/h)

Conceived as an economy saloon to replace the Ami, the lightweight Visa became Citroën's choice for rallying in the early 1980s. It was fitted with engines from 653 cc upwards.

◁ Peugeot 104 1973

Origin France

Engine 954 cc, straight-four

Top speed 84 mph (135 km/h)

Unusually, Peugeot's first supermini was launched as a 5-door model only; a shorter 3-door followed later. The all-new engine and independent suspension added to its appeal.

△ Ford Fiesta 1976

Origin Spain

Engine 957 cc, straight-four

Top speed 79 mph (127 km/h)

Ford's first supermini for Europe was basic, with only four gears, but it had engines up to 1,600 cc and was competitively priced. Sales were 1.75 million by 1983.

△ Vauxhall Chevette HS 1978

Origin UK

Engine 2,279 cc, straight-four

Top speed 115 mph (185 km/h)

Vauxhall made a virtue of a live rear axle by adding a big, tuned dual-cam engine. The Chevette went on to win rallies. Most were 1.3-litre hatchbacks.

◁ Talbot Sunbeam Lotus 1979

Origin UK

Engine 2,174 cc, straight-four

Top speed 121 mph (195 km/h)

The Talbot Sunbeam had a shortened rear-wheel-drive Avenger platform, so was quite outdated. But adding a big, powerful Lotus engine made it ideal for rallying.

4x4 and Off-roaders

In the 1970s Jeep and Land Rover finally saw serious opposition in the off-road market. As a trend towards leisure off-roading and even beach cars developed, thousands of home-build dune buggies were sold in the US, UK, and elsewhere. Alongside capable four-wheel-drive off-roaders, there were early examples of the less serious two-wheel-drive soft-roaders that would become popular 30 years later.

▷ **Toyota Land Cruiser FJ40 1960**
Origin Japan
Engine 3,878 cc, straight-six
Top speed 84 mph (135 km/h)

Japan's answer to the Land Rover was this robust off-roader that saw few changes from 1960 to 1984. Front disc brakes and 3.0- and 4.2-litre engines were added between 1974 and 1976.

◁ **Chevrolet Blazer K5 1969**
Origin USA
Engine 5,735 cc, V8
Top speed 98 mph (158 km/h)

Chevrolet shortened its pick-up truck and added a full cab with two- or four-wheel drive and 6-cylinder or 8-cylinder engines to compete against the Jeep, Ford Bronco, and Scout – it sold well.

△ **Ford Bronco 1966**
Origin USA
Engine 2,781 cc, straight-six
Top speed 76 mph (122 km/h)

Conceived by the same team who gave Ford the Mustang, the Bronco was a brave early take on the SUV concept but was too small to capture the US market; models from 1978 onwards were larger.

△ **Subaru Leone Estate 1972**
Origin Japan
Engine 1,595 cc, flat-four
Top speed 87 mph (140 km/h)

The first of the four-wheel-drive, everyday road cars, the Leone (1600 in the UK and US) Estate was a pioneer, and Subarus were still modelled on it 40 years later.

▷ **Suzuki Jimny LJ10 1970**
Origin Japan
Engine 359 cc, straight-two
Top speed 47 mph (76 km/h)

In 1967 Japan's Hope Motor Co. developed a design for a 4x4 with a Mitsubishi engine; Suzuki bought it and fitted its own engine, creating a successful line of tiny 4x4s.

Fun Cars

As the roads became increasingly clogged with traffic and restricted by legislation, adventurous drivers sought excitement off the tarmac. In the US they ripped bodies off old VW Beetles, bolted on light, open shells, and roared off over the sand in their dune buggies. Meanwhile, in France Matra tried to emulate the Range Rover with a two-wheel-drive leisure vehicle, and in the UK even three-wheelers briefly became trendy and fun.

▷ **Meyers Manx 1964**
Origin USA
Engine 1,493 cc, flat-four
Top speed 90 mph (145 km/h)

Californian Bruce Meyers began the dune buggy craze with his Manx, which won the Baja 1000 race. With a glassfibre roadster body and a VW Beetle floorpan, it sold about 6,000 to 1971.

◁ International Harvester Scout II 1971
Origin USA
Engine 4,981 cc, V8
Top speed 90 mph (145 km/h)

The Scout was launched in 1960 as the world's first SUV. The Scout II, which had a wheelbase of up to 254 cm (100 in) and a choice of 4-, 6-, or V8-cylinder engines, was in production until 1980.

▷ Land Rover Series III 1971
Origin UK
Engine 2,286 cc, straight-four
Top speed 68 mph (109 km/h)

Evolved from the original 1948 Land Rover, the Series III was still the benchmark capable off-roader. With an all-synchromesh gearbox and updated dashboard, it enjoyed a 14-year life.

△ Jeep Commando 1972
Origin USA
Engine 4,980 cc, V8
Top speed 90 mph (145 km/h)

The Commando was the ultimate evolution of the 1940s Jeepster, with short or full cab and a range of AMC 6-cylinder or 8-cylinder engines; 20,223 were sold in two years.

▽ Range Rover 1970
Origin UK
Engine 3,528 cc, V8
Top speed 99 mph (159 km/h)

This step up from the Land Rover offered superb off-road ability and comfort. With vinyl seats and a plastic dashboard, its interior could be hosed clean. Luxury came later, in the 1980s.

△ Jeep Wagoneer 1972
Origin USA
Engine 5,896 cc, V8
Top speed 95 mph (153 km/h)

AMC took over Jeep in 1970 and improved its cars with new engines. The Wagoneer was the original luxury 4x4, with refined Quadra-Trak four-wheel drive added in 1973.

△ Mercedes-Benz G-Wagen 1979
Origin Austria
Engine 2,299 cc, straight-four
Top speed 89 mph (143 km/h)

Expensive but tough, this reliable off-roader came with either two- or four-wheel drive. The G-Wagen had low-ratio gears like the Land Rover, but with the benefit of coil springs for its live axles.

△ Matra-Simca Rancho 1977
Origin France
Engine 1,442 cc, straight-four
Top speed 89 mph (143 km/h)

While not as rugged as a full-blown 4x4, this front-wheel-drive soft-roader was ideal for rural tracks too challenging for normal road cars. It was rebranded as a Talbot in 1979.

△ Leyland Mini Moke 1968
Origin Australia
Engine 998 cc, straight-four
Top speed 75 mph (120 km/h)

Impractical in rainy Britain, Mokes made much more sense in warm, dry climates. Production was in Australia from 1968 to 1981, later transferring to Portugal.

△ Bond Bug 1970
Origin UK
Engine 700 cc, straight-four
Top speed 76 mph (121 km/h)

The three-wheeled Bug embodied the spirit of youth, freedom, humour, and optimism with which Britain entered the 1970s. But fewer than 3,000 people were inspired to buy one.

Saloons

The 1970s saw the production of numerous innovative cars, such as the fuel-injected BMWs, the turbocharged Saabs, and the 16-valve Triumphs, but for mainstream saloon cars it was a decade in which time stood still. An extraordinary number of saloons that were already in production in 1970 were still in production in almost unchanged form in 1980.

◁ Morris Marina 1971
Origin UK

Engine 1,798 cc, straight-four

Top speed 86 mph (138 km/h)

Mechanically little different from the 1948 Morris Minor, the Marina sold surprisingly well for Britain's struggling car maker. It lasted, as the Ital, until 1984.

▷ Wartburg Knight 1966
Origin East Germany

Engine 991 cc, straight-three

Top speed 74 mph (119 km/h)

An East German car with a two-stroke engine, the Knight sold well in Eastern Europe throughout the 1970s. It fared less well in Western Europe, despite incredibly low prices.

△ Triumph Dolomite Sprint 1973
Origin UK

Engine 1,998 cc, straight-four

Top speed 115 mph (185 km/h)

Triumph built innovative cars with attractive styling on a tight budget. The Sprint, which challenged the BMW 2002 series, was one of the first 16-valve family saloons.

△ Citroën CX2400 1974
Origin France

Engine 2,347 cc, straight-four

Top speed 113 mph (182 km/h)

The Citroën DS's successor combined all its predecessor's innovation with a transverse engine for increased space. It had 2.0–2.5-litre engines, and was made until 1989.

▽ Saab 99 Turbo 1977
Origin Sweden

Engine 1,985 cc, straight-four

Top speed 122 mph (196 km/h)

Saab showed the world that turbocharging could be used in a mainstream saloon, not just for racing homologation. It sold well and lifted the company's whole image.

△ De Tomaso Deauville 1970
Origin Italy

Engine 5,763 cc, V8

Top speed 143 mph (230 km/h)

Though styled by Ghia, the Deauville suffered from looking like the Jaguar XJ12 – which offered similar performance – while trying to sell for double its price.

△ Škoda 120S 1970
Origin Czechoslovakia

Engine 1,174 cc, straight-four

Top speed 86 mph (138 km/h)

The "people's car" for communist Czechoslovakia sold on price alone in Europe, being noisy and difficult to drive. This one did remarkably well in its class in rallying.

◁ Hillman Avenger 1970
Origin UK

Engine 1,498 cc, straight-four

Top speed 91 mph (146 km/h)

An all-new design for the 1970s from Chrysler's Rootes Group, the Avenger was thoroughly conventional and lasted until 1981 in various guises.

▷ **BMW 2002Tii Alpina A4S 1972**

Origin Germany

Engine 1,990 cc, straight-four

Top speed 130 mph (209 km/h)

The 02 series from 1966 established BMW as a serious car maker, selling 750,000 in 10 years. Its finest model (apart from the Turbo) was Alpina's tuned, fuel-injected A4S.

◁ **BMW 520 1972**

Origin Germany

Engine 1,990 cc, straight-four

Top speed 106 mph (171 km/h)

Key to BMW's success in the 1970s, the 5-Series combined handsome looks with modern running gear. It offered four- and six-cylinder engines from 1.8 to 3.0 litres.

▷ **Rover 3500 SD1 1976**

Origin UK

Engine 3,528 cc, V8

Top speed 125 mph (201 km/h)

Despite its advanced looks, high specification, and excellent dynamics, the SD1 rapidly gained a reputation for poor quality in the 1970s. Later models fared little better with buyers.

△ **Ford Escort Mk2 RS1800 1973**

Origin UK

Engine 1,835 cc, straight-four

Top speed 112 mph (180 km/h)

Ford boosted sales through motor sport success, and the RS1800, with its BDA engine, was a formidable rally car. It won the 1979 World Rally Championship.

△ **Ford Cortina MkV 1979**

Origin UK

Engine 1,993 cc, straight-four

Top speed 103 mph (166 km/h)

The best-selling Cortina changed little from 1970's MkIII to the last MkV in 1982, and sold over two million, mostly in the UK. It was spacious, efficient, and cheap.

△ **Cadillac Seville 1975**

Origin USA

Engine 5,737 cc, V8

Top speed 115 mph (185 km/h)

General Motors added a more mainstream line to its upper-crust Cadillac marque in 1975. Stylist Bill Mitchell targeted the Mercedes/Rolls-Royce market; it sold well.

△ **Maserati Quattroporte II 1975**

Origin Italy

Engine 2,965 cc, V6

Top speed 125 mph (201 km/h)

Conceived when Maserati was owned by Citroën, the Quattroporte II had a Merak/SM engine and plenty of SM hydraulic equipment. Just five of these four-door models were built.

Sports Cars (70s)

North American safety laws impacted heavily on sports-car design in this decade, often spoiling pretty shapes with big bumpers, and peppy performance with detuned but low-emission engines. The sports car was declining, as "hot hatchbacks" typified by the Volkswagen Golf GTI grabbed the attention of thrill-seeking drivers.

△ **Morgan 4/4 four-seater 1969**

Origin UK

Engine 1,798 cc, straight-four

Top speed 105 mph (169 km/h)

After almost two decades, Morgan suddenly realized some of its devotees also had families, leading to the reintroduction of a four-seater model for the 1970s.

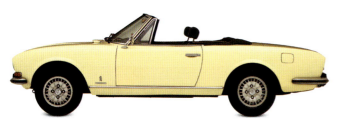

△ **Peugeot 504 Cabriolet 1969**

Origin France/Italy

Engine 2,664 cc, V6

Top speed 110 mph (177 km/h)

This handsome four-seater was designed and built for Peugeot by Pininfarina. There was a coupé version too; both used mechanical parts from the 504 and 604 saloons.

◁ **MG Midget MkIII 1969**

Origin UK

Engine 1,275 cc, straight-four

Top speed 95 mph (153 km/h)

The beloved Sprite/Midget was updated for the 1970s. New features included round rear wheelarches, a Mini Cooper S-type engine, trendy matt-black trim, and a better hood.

◁ **Triumph TR6 1969**

Origin UK

Engine 2,498 cc, straight-six

Top speed 120 mph (193 km/h)

The zenith of the British sports car boasted 150 bhp from the fuel-injected straight-six, rear-wheel drive, fresh air, a loud exhaust, and crisply cool styling.

△ **Triumph Stag 1970**

Origin UK

Engine 2,997 cc, V8

Top speed 118 mph (190 km/h)

Britain's rival to the Mercedes-Benz SL had a distinctive T-shaped rollover bar. The unique V8 engine suffered teething problems, but the Italian styling was a hit.

△ **Triumph TR7 1975**

Origin UK

Engine 1,998 cc, straight-four

Top speed 110 mph (177 km/h)

The TR7 was built to meet anticipated safety laws, which meant a hardtop only; a convertible followed five years later. It was a civilized cruiser and a big seller.

△ **Triumph TR8 1980**

Origin UK

Engine 3,528 cc, V8

Top speed 135 mph (217 km/h)

Fitting Rover's V8 engine gave the TR8 punchy performance as a roadster or coupé. The TR line was axed in 1981, after just 2,500 TR8s had been sold, mostly in the US.

△ **Lotus Elan Sprint 1971**

Origin UK

Engine 1,558 cc, straight-four

Top speed 120 mph (193 km/h)

The fifth, final, and finest incarnation of Colin Chapman's benchmark sports car, this car had superb road manners matched by 126 bhp of power, a five-speed gearbox, and natty livery.

△ **Mercedes-Benz 350SL 1971**

Origin Germany

Engine 3,499 cc, straight-six

Top speed 126 mph (203 km/h)

An all-new SL for the 1970s, this car shared suspension hardware with the S-Class limousine. Powerful, fast, and stylish, it had a standard hardtop for winter.

◁ **Jensen-Healey 1972**

Origin UK

Engine 1,973 cc, straight-four

Top speed 120 mph (193 km/h)

Created by legendary sports-car designer Donald Healey and built by Jensen, this roadster used a Lotus twin-cam engine. It was great to drive and light on fuel, but could be temperamental.

▽ **Matra-Simca Bagheera 1973**

Origin France

Engine 1,442 cc, straight-four

Top speed 110 mph (177 km/h)

This mid-engined coupé was built by an aerospace company, using engines and transmissions from Simca family cars. Three-abreast seating and a plastic body were among its interesting facets.

△ **MGB 1974**

Origin UK

Engine 1,798 cc, straight-four

Top speed 90 mph (145 km/h)

The "rubber bumper" MGB era began in 1974. Together with a raised suspension height and a cleaned-up engine, this made the car legal for US sale, but blunted its feisty character.

△ **MGB GT 1974**

Origin UK

Engine 1,798 cc, straight-four

Top speed 105 mph (169 km/h)

Being more aerodynamic than MG's B Roadster, the GT had a much higher top speed. It was also far more practical, with its rear tailgate and extra luggage space.

△ **Lancia Beta Montecarlo/Scorpion 1975**

Origin Italy

Engine 1,756 cc, straight-four

Top speed 120 mph (193 km/h)

This exhilarating mid-engined two-seater came with a steel or canvas roof. It suffered from poor brakes and was withdrawn from 1978-80 to fix them, returning in 2-litre form.

△ **Fiat X1/9 1972**

Origin Italy

Engine 1,290-1,498 cc, straight-four

Top speed 110 mph (177 km/h)

The X1/9 brought mid-engined sports cars to the masses, and remained popular in Europe and the US until 1989. It was designed and built by Bertone.

▽ **TVR 3000S 1978**

Origin UK

Engine 2,994 cc, V6

Top speed 125 mph (201 km/h)

TVR produced this convertible after three decades of being in business. An open version of the Ford-powered 3000M, abundant power and low weight made it very fast.

△ **Panther Lima 1976**

Origin UK

Engine 2,279 cc, straight-four

Top speed 115 mph (185 km/h)

A Morgan alternative, this car had a 1930s roadster look but offered a modern driving experience owing to the powerful Vauxhall engine underneath its glassfibre body.

Stylish Coupés

The flamboyance of the 1950s and curvaceousness of the 1960s had gone: with the 1970s came wedge profiles, straight lines, and angular shapes. Some cars looked better than others; as so often, it was the Italian stylists who seemed to have the best eye for producing a stunning car – though for the first time, Japanese stylists showed they could do it just as well.

△ **Ford Capri RS 3100 1973**

Origin UK

Engine 3,093 cc, V6

Top speed 123 mph (198 km/h)

With its image kept exciting by wild racing cars like this one, the roadgoing Ford Capris continued to notch up healthy sales – around 750,000 in the 1970s.

△ **Opel Manta GT/E 1970**

Origin Germany

Engine 1,897 cc, straight-four

Top speed 116 mph (187 km/h)

Despite attractive styling and almost half-a-million made, most Mantas have rusted away: a shame, as it was a civilized touring car with engines from 1.2 to 1.9 litres.

▷ **Ford Mustang III 1978**

Origin USA

Engine 4,942 cc, V8

Top speed 140 mph (225 km/h)

The third-generation Mustang was a full four-seater for the first time, as it was a larger car based on Ford's "Fox" platform; it continued, with revisions, until 1994.

△ **Jaguar XJ12C 1975**

Origin UK

Engine 5,343 cc, V12

Top speed 148 mph (238 km/h)

To draw sporting kudos for its XJ6/12-derived coupé, British Leyland campaigned this car – the first factory-backed racing activity since 1956. Prepared by Broadspeed, it took pole at Silverstone in 1975.

▽ **Chevrolet Monte Carlo 1970**

Origin USA

Engine 5,735 cc, V8

Top speed 115 mph (185 km/h)

Chevrolet launched a new coupé for the 1970s, bigger than a Chevelle and more luxurious, but still with a useful turn of speed for stock-car racing.

▷ **Datsun 260Z 1973**

Origin Japan

Engine 2,565 cc, straight-six

Top speed 125 mph (201 km/h)

The 240–280Z series was the world's best-selling sports car in the 1970s, from what, at the time, seemed a most unlikely source. Japanese cars were about to conquer the globe.

△ **Rolls-Royce Corniche 1971**

Origin UK

Engine 6,750 cc, V8

Top speed 120 mph (193 km/h)

The Silver Shadow was a monocoque but this did not stop Rolls-Royce from adapting the structure into this two-door coupé. The Corniche looked very elegant, too.

◁ **Volkswagen Scirocco GTI 1974**

Origin Germany

Engine 1,588 cc, straight-four

Top speed 115 mph (185 km/h)

This car was styled by Giorgetto Giugiaro and built by Karmann on the VW Golf floorpan. The Scirocco was a hit, selling 504,200 in seven years, with three engine specs: from 1.4- to 1.6-litre GTI.

◁ **Buick Riviera 1971**

Origin USA

Engine 7,458 cc, V8

Top speed 125 mph (201 km/h)

Buick's status symbol coupé had a stunning new look for the 1970s, with a centrally divided wraparound rear window and accentuated rear "hips".

△ **Alfa Romeo Junior Zagato 1970**

Origin Italy

Engine 1,290 cc, straight-four

Top speed 105 mph (169 km/h)

Ercole Spada at Zagato achieved the impossible: he took an Alfa Romeo GT Junior and turned it into something even more arresting to look at. Only the cost held back sales.

△ **Maserati Kyalami 4.9 1976**

Origin Italy

Engine 4,930 cc, V8

Top speed 160 mph (257 km/h)

When Alejandro De Tomaso took over Maserati, he developed his 1972 Ghia-designed Longchamp model into the Kyalami, with a choice of potent Maserati V8 engines.

◁ **Lancia Gamma Coupé 1976**

Origin Italy

Engine 2,484 cc, flat-four

Top speed 125 mph (201 km/h)

A striking two-door body by Pininfarina transformed Lancia's big Gamma saloon. Mechanically sophisticated too, it soon became a desirable machine.

▷ **Mazda RX-7 1978**

Origin Japan

Engine 2,292 cc, two-rotor Wankel

Top speed 117 mph (188 km/h)

Mazda succeeded, where German manufacturer NSU had failed, in persuading the world to accept the rotary engine as a serious option: 570,500 were sold in seven years.

△ **Porsche 911S 2.2 1970**

Origin Germany

Engine 2,195 cc, flat-six

Top speed 144 mph (232 km/h)

The 911 gained improved handling for the 1970s by moving the rear wheels back by 5.5 cm (2.2 in) and the fuel-injected S took full advantage, becoming a junior supercar.

◁ **Porsche 924 1976**

Origin Germany

Engine 1,984 cc, straight-four

Top speed 125 mph (201 km/h)

Purists disapprove of the VW van engine, but the front-engined 924 was a best-seller for Porsche and expanded its market beyond the dedicated sporting driver.

△ **Porsche 911T 2.4 Targa 1972**

Origin Germany

Engine 2,341 cc, flat-six

Top speed 128 mph (206 km/h)

Porsche introduced the Targa to offer fresh-air motoring with rollover protection; it was heavier and less sporting than the 911 Coupé, but found a ready market.

△ **Suzuki SC100 Coupé 1978**

Origin Japan

Engine 970 cc, straight-four

Top speed 76 mph (122 km/h)

Suzuki sold 894,000 rear-engined "Whizzkids", mainly on cute looks as they were cramped for four and had poor performance. The Mini was roomier and more nimble.

Muscle Cars

In the late 1960s US manufacturers were bitten by the high-performance bug. Sacrificing efficiency for brute force, they installed powerful V8 engines in otherwise humdrum coupés, hardtops, and convertibles. Fearsome competition cars, they were also thrilling to drive on the road. The "muscle cars" reached their pinnacle in 1970, after which power outputs were drastically reduced in the face of the unfolding oil crisis.

△ **Plymouth Road-Runner Superbird 1970**

Origin	USA
Engine	7,213 cc, V8
Top speed	130 mph (209 km/h)

The Superbird, endorsed by the TV cartoon character Road-Runner, was a NASCAR racer made legal for the road. Just 1,900 of these winged wonders were built.

△ **Oldsmobile 442 1970**

Origin	USA
Engine	7,456 cc, V8
Top speed	120 mph (193 km/h)

The 442 was launched in 1964; the figures signified a four-barrel carburettor, four-speed gearbox, and dual exhausts. It was a standalone model from 1968 to 1972.

▷ **Plymouth Hemi 'Cuda 1970**

Origin	USA
Engine	7,210 cc, V8
Top speed	130 mph (209 km/h)

The 'Cuda crowned the large Plymouth Barracuda series, and with its hemispherical-head Chrysler V8 pumping out up to 425 bhp, it was the series powerhouse.

▽ **Pontiac Firebird Trans Am 1973**

Origin	USA
Engine	7,459 cc, V8
Top speed	132 mph (212 km/h)

Often distinguished by a huge bonnet decal sticker depicting a phoenix, the Trans Am was named after the race series in which Firebirds excelled in the late 1960s.

△ **Pontiac Trans Am 1975**

Origin	USA
Engine	6,556 cc, V8
Top speed	118 mph (190 km/h)

The Firebird was restyled with a longer nose and a bigger rear window to become the Pontiac Trans Am. It was still a race contender, despite a cut in power to 185 bhp forced by tighter emissions rules.

◁ **Dodge Challenger R/T 440 1970**

Origin	USA
Engine	6,276 cc, V8
Top speed	114 mph (183 km/h)

This practical hardtop coupé was enlivened by electric acceleration to rival the hottest Mustangs. A 7.2-litre engine option boosted its bhp from 300 to 385.

▷ **Mercury Cougar 1973**

Origin	USA
Engine	7,030 cc, V8
Top speed	125 mph (201 km/h)

For a time in the 1970s, the Mercury Cougar – especially in 390 bhp XR-7 guise – headed Ford's high-power offerings; it was based closely on the Mustang.

▷ Ford Mustang Mach 1 1972

Origin USA

Engine 5,753 cc, V8

Top speed 130 mph (209 km/h)

The ultimate performance Mustang of the 1970s was also the largest, and starred in a famous two-wheeled stunt in the James Bond film *Diamonds Are Forever*.

◁ Ford Falcon XA hardtop 1972

Origin Australia

Engine 5,673 cc, V8

Top speed 160 mph (257 km/h)

This GT-HO version tore up Australia's race tracks, leading to a public outcry – known as the "Supercar Superscare" – at the prospect of 160 mph (257 km/h) cars speeding on the country's roads.

▽ MGB GT V8 1973

Origin UK

Engine 3,528 cc, V8

Top speed 125 mph (201 km/h)

A short-lived British entry into the muscle car canon, the GT's light alloy Rover V8 engine weighed 18 kg (40 lb) less than the regular four-cylinder MGB motor, boosting agility.

△ Chevrolet Camaro 1966

Origin USA

Engine 6,489 cc, V8

Top speed 136 mph (219 km/h)

The Camaro was Chevrolet's answer to Ford's Mustang, and joined the expanding "pony car" club with its reliable drive train and electric acceleration available for the biggest V8 engine.

▷ Chevrolet Camaro SS 396 1972

Origin USA

Engine 6,588 cc, V8

Top speed 120 mph (193 km/h)

A 240 bhp V8 engine was a hot option on the SS. This Camaro, visually updated like the entire range in 1970, was too polluting to be sold in California.

△ Chevrolet Nova SS 1971

Origin USA

Engine 5,736 cc, V8

Top speed 107 mph (172 km/h)

The fastest of the compact Nova SSs could reach 60 mph (97 km/h) from standstill in under 6 seconds. Abundant wheelspin and heavy steering only boosted the car's macho appeal.

▽ Chevrolet Corvette 1980

Origin USA

Engine 5,733 cc, V8

Top speed 125 mph (201 km/h)

Corvettes of the 1970s, like other sporty US cars, gradually surrendered outright performance to tighter emissions laws. This 1980 model offered a relatively tame 190 bhp.

Racing Cars

In the 1970s it became clear that every category of motor racing needed restrictions to power outputs, to prevent cars from taking off at the speeds of over 200 mph (322 km/h) which many were now capable of. Advances in turbocharging then kept legislators on their toes, as speeds continued to rise.

▽ **Tyrrell-Cosworth 001 1970**

Origin UK

Engine 2,993 cc, V8

Top speed 190 mph (306 km/h)

When Ken Tyrrell was stood up by Matra, he had Derek Gardner design an all-new car to bear the Tyrrell name. This car showed great potential in late 1970.

△ **Ford Escort RS1600 1970**

Origin UK

Engine 1,599 cc, straight-four

Top speed 113 mph (182 km/h)

Fitted with a Cosworth BDA 16-valve double overhead camshaft, which was a development of the basic Ford engine, the RS1600 was a successful rally/race car; around 1,000 were built.

▷ **Mirage-Cosworth GR7 1972**

Origin UK

Engine 2,993 cc, V8

Top speed 200 mph (322 km/h)

The 1972 Mirage M6 was the first Cosworth DFV-powered car to win a Sports Car Championship. It was developed into the GR7 for 1974, and finished fourth at Le Mans.

△ **Tyrrell-Cosworth 002 1971**

Origin UK

Engine 2,993 cc, V8

Top speed 195 mph (314 km/h)

In its first full year as a Formula 1 constructor, Ken Tyrrell's team achieved a fabulous double, World Champion team and driver, the latter for Jackie Stewart.

◁ **Lola-Cosworth T500 1978**

Origin UK

Engine 2,650 cc, V8

Top speed 210 mph (338 km/h)

Indianapolis racers were faster than contemporary Formula 1 cars, due to the high-speed capacity of the oval track. The T500 turbo won the Indy 500 in 1978 at 161.4 mph (260 km/h).

◁ **Brabham-Cosworth BT44 1974**

Origin UK

Engine 2,993 cc, V8

Top speed 200 mph (322 km/h)

The BT44 was designed by Gordon Murray with very clean lines incorporating early thoughts on ground-effect aerodynamics. It took several Grand Prix wins in 1974.

▽ **Lotus 72 1970**

Origin UK

Engine 2,993 cc, V8

Top speed 198 mph (319 km/h)

Colin Chapman and Maurice Philippe achieved a revolutionary design with the 72, using wedge aerodynamics, radiators in side pods, and an overhead air intake.

△ **Lotus 79 1977**

Origin UK

Engine 2,993 cc, V8

Top speed 205 mph (330 km/h)

The first Formula 1 car to take full advantage of ground-effect aerodynamics, which caused it to suck itself to the road for maximum grip on corners, the 79 was a great success.

△ **Matra-Simca MS670B 1972**

Origin France

Engine 2,993 cc, V12

Top speed 210 mph (338 km/h)

Matra wanted to be the first French marque since 1950 to win Le Mans: it succeeded when Henri Pescarolo achieved a hat-trick with the MS670B in 1972, 1973, and 1974.

△ **Porsche 917/10 1971**

Origin Germany

Engine 4,998 cc, flat-twelve

Top speed 213 mph (343 km/h)

The 917 gave Porsche its first Le Mans wins in 1970 and 1971. The 917/10 was turbocharged for the CanAm Challenge; its 850 bhp gave Penske Racing the win in 1972.

▽ **Porsche 936/77 1977**

Origin Germany

Engine 2,142 cc, flat-six

Top speed 217 mph (349 km/h)

Jacky Ickx almost single-handedly took a superb win at the 1977 Le Mans in the 936; he had won with a 936 in 1976 (also winning the WSC), and would win again in 1981.

△ **Alfa Romeo Tipo 33 TT12 1975**

Origin Italy

Engine 2,995 cc, flat-twelve

Top speed 200 mph (322 km/h)

Alfa Romeo fitted the ageing T33 with a new 48-valve engine, slab-sided bodywork, and a huge rear spoiler. It won the World Sportscar Championship with ease.

△ **Surtees-Hart TS10 1972**

Origin UK

Engine 1,975 cc, straight-four

Top speed 150 mph (241 km/h)

World Champion John Surtees turned race-car constructor to win the European Formula 2 title, with Mike Hailwood driving the TS10.

△ **McLaren-Offenhauser M16C 1974**

Origin UK

Engine 2,650 cc, straight-four

Top speed 205 mph (330 km/h)

McLaren won the Indianapolis 500 three times – the second with Johnny Rutherford driving this M16C in 1974. Almost every car taking part had the 770 bhp "Offy" engine.

◁ **Renault RS10 1979**

Origin France

Engine 1,496 cc, V6

Top speed 215 mph (346 km/h)

Thanks to gritty determination by Jean-Pierre Jabouille, this was the first turbocharged car to win a Grand Prix, heralding an era of power outputs up to 1,500 bhp.

▷ **Chevrolet Nova NASCAR 1979**

Origin USA

Engine 5,817 cc, V8

Top speed 200 mph (322 km/h)

North American Stock Car racing used a strict formula of racing chassis clad with silhouette bodies. Dale Earnhardt raced this car in 1979 as a Pontiac and in 1985 as a Chevrolet.

Hatchbacks

Italian designers were the first to introduce rear hatches to compact family saloons, realizing the huge benefits they had in terms of cargo capacity. Previously the style had only been seen on some exotic fastback coupés, but cars such as the Austin A40 Farina showed the way forwards in the 1960s, and as the 1970s progressed, the world's manufacturers increasingly turned to hatchbacks.

▷ **Austin Maxi 1750 1969**

Origin UK

Engine 1,748 cc, straight-four

Top speed 97 mph (156 km/h)

Alec Issigonis's packaging skills were at their best in the transverse-engined, hydrolastic-suspended Maxi. An extremely spacious saloon, it sold well into the 1970s.

▷ **Ford Pinto 1971**

Origin USA

Engine 1,993 cc, straight-four

Top speed 105 mph (169 km/h)

Ford's sub-compact, two-door Pinto of 1970 was joined in six months by the three-door hatchback. It had British 1,600 or German 2,000 cc engines, and four-speed gearboxes.

△ **Chevrolet Vega 1970**

Origin USA

Engine 2286 cc, straight-four

Top speed 95 mph (153 km/h)

Chevrolet's all-new sub-compact for the 1970s was conventional, with an aluminium overhead-cam engine and three-speed manual gearbox. It sold 274,699 in its first year.

◁ **Honda Accord 1976**

Origin Japan

Engine 1,599 cc, straight-four

Top speed 94 mph (151 km/h)

Introduced as hatchback only, and joined by saloon versions in 1978, the Accord was a sophisticated car with five-speed manual or optional Hondamatic transmission.

△ **AMC Pacer 1975**

Origin USA

Engine 3,802 cc, straight-six

Top speed 92 mph (148 km/h)

Short and wide, the Pacer was a development of AMC's pioneering Gremlin hatchback of 1970. Its rounded form contrasted with the boxy shape of its contemporaries.

▷ **Reliant Robin 1973**

Origin UK

Engine 848 cc, four-cylinder

Top speed 80 mph (129 km/h)

This plastic-bodied three-wheeler was popular in the UK during the 1970s fuel crisis. It was thrifty, due to its low weight, and could be driven on a motorbike licence.

▷ **AMC Gremlin 1970**

Origin USA

Engine 3,258 cc, straight-six

Top speed 95 mph (153 km/h)

This first US sub-compact car was cramped in the back and had a column-change three-speed gearbox. It posed little threat to European imports, though the V8 model was popular.

◁ **Volkswagen Passat 1973**

Origin Germany

Engine 1,470 cc, straight-four

Top speed 98 mph (158 km/h)

First of the modern front-wheel-drive VWs, the Passat was based on the Audi 80 and styled by Giugiaro. Fast, modern, and stylish, it sold 1.8 million by 1980.

◁ **Volkswagen Golf GTI 1975**

Origin Germany

Engine 1,588 cc, straight-four

Top speed 112 mph (180 km/h)

The original "hot hatchback" that started a whole new sporting trend was famous for its black trim. It had 110 bhp from its fuel-injected engine and handled beautifully.

△ **Volvo 340 1976**

Origin Netherlands

Engine 1,397 cc, straight-four

Top speed 94 mph (151 km/h)

Volvo's DAF plant in Holland needed a modern small car. Volvo's answer was this long-lived, rear-drive hatch fitted with Renault engines and De Dion rear suspension.

△ **Chrysler Horizon 1977**

Origin France/UK/USA

Engine 1,118 cc, straight-four

Top speed 95 mph (153 km/h)

Chrysler's compact hatchback, intended for sale in Europe and the US, was derived from the Simca 1100, and so had a European style. It had front-wheel drive and all-independent suspension.

△ **Renault 20TS 1975**

Origin France

Engine 1,995 cc, straight-four

Top speed 104 mph (167 km/h)

Renault adopted the hatchback style right across its range, up to the big luxury 20 and 30 saloons, which had 1.6–2.7-litre engines, central locking, and power steering.

▷ **Renault 14 1976**

Origin France

Engine 1,218 cc, straight-four

Top speed 89 mph (143 km/h)

Renault sold almost a million of this bulbous 5-door hatch. It featured a transverse, canted-over Peugeot 104/Citroën Visa-type engine with its transmission in the sump.

▽ **Fiat Strada/Ritmo 1978**

Origin Italy

Engine 1,585 cc, straight-four

Top speed 111 mph (179 km/h)

Fiat were keen to stress that this car was built by robots. Some suggested it had been styled by them too, but the tuned Abarth versions were great fun to drive.

△ **Opel Kadett 1979**

Origin Germany

Engine 1,297 cc, straight-four

Top speed 93 mph (150 km/h)

General Motors' compact hatchback finally adopted front-wheel drive in this version, sold as the Vauxhall Astra in British markets from 1980. It had 1.0–1.8-litre engines.

Cars
1980 to present

Boosted Performance

The 1980s was the decade of the turbocharger, transforming the top echelons of motor sport both in racing and rallying: reliability was heavily affected at first by the increased power output, but soon it became impossible to win without one (or more). As technology sent power and speed soaring, legislators struggled to keep up. In the end, turbos became so heavily penalized that normally aspirated engines returned.

△ Lancia Beta Monte Carlo 1979

Origin Italy

Engine 1,425 cc, straight-four

Top speed 168 mph (270 km/h)

Lancia developed this car to contest the Sports Car Racing World Championship. It dominated the 2-litre class in 1980-81, even beating the Porsche 935s three times.

△ Porsche 956 1982

Origin Germany

Engine 2,650 cc, flat-six

Top speed 221 mph (356 km/h)

Built for the World Sportscar Championship, the aluminium monocoque 956 was a winner from the start. Jacky Ickx and Derek Bell led the 1982 Le Mans (France) to the finish.

▷ Porsche 953 4WD 1984

Origin Germany

Engine 3,164 cc, flat-six

Top speed 150 mph (241 km/h)

Four 953s (effectively four-wheel-drive 911s) were built for the 1984 Paris-Dakar Rally, and two of them finished 1-2. René Metge and Dominic Lemoyne drove the winning car.

△ Ferrari 126C4/M2 1984

Origin Italy

Engine 1,496 cc, V6

Top speed 200 mph (322 km/h)

Despite an 850 bhp power output, the 126C4/M2 struggled against the dominant McLaren MP4/2 in 1984, and finished second in the Formula 1 Constructors' Championship.

△ Lancia Rallye 037 Evo 2 1984

Origin Italy

Engine 2,111 cc, straight-four

Top speed 150 mph (241 km/h)

Through consistency and great handling on tarmac, the 037 beat Audi's quattro to win the 1983 World Rally Championship. Abarth built lighter Evo 2s with 350 bhp for 1984.

▷ Porsche 911 SCRS 1984

Origin Germany

Engine 2,994 cc, flat-six

Top speed 160 mph (257 km/h)

This Group B Porsche lacked four-wheel drive but handled superbly on tarmac, taking Henri Toivonen to second place in the 1984 European Championship.

◁ Opel Manta 400 1985

Origin Germany

Engine 2,410 cc, straight-four

Top speed 130 mph (209 km/h)

Without four-wheel drive, the Mantas couldn't really compete at World Rally Championship (WRC) level, but both Jimmy McRae and Russell Brookes won British Rally Championships in them.

Audi quattros

Audi revolutionized the world of rallying with its four-wheel drive, four-seat quattro coupé. In its first event, the 1981 Monte Carlo Rally, it failed to finish but Hannu Mikkola was a minute faster than the opposition on almost every stage, demonstrating the car's sensational potential. The competition were forced to go 4x4 too, kicking off the super-fast Group B rally phenomenon.

▷ Audi quattro 1980

Origin Germany

Engine 2,144 cc, straight-five

Top speed 138 mph (222 km/h)

Hannu Mikkola and Michèle Mouton were the first quattro works drivers, overcoming teething troubles and showing tremendous pace in 1981.

▷ Lotus-Renault 97T 1985

Origin UK

Engine 1,492 cc, V6

Top speed 200 mph (322 km/h)

With Ayrton Senna at the wheel, the 900 bhp Lotus 97T could have won the 1985 Formula 1 World Championship had it been reliable: it took eight pole positions in the season.

◁ Toyota Celica Twin Cam Turbo 1985

Origin Japan

Engine 2,090 cc, straight-four

Top speed 135 mph (217 km/h)

It was far from the ultimate in Group B technology, but this Toyota did well in Africa, with Björn Waldegård winning two Safari and two Ivory Coast rallies.

△ Peugeot 205 T16 Evo 2 1985

Origin France

Engine 1,775 cc, straight-four

Top speed 155 mph (249 km/h)

With huge turbo, mid-engine, and 4x4, Timo Salonen took the 1985 WRC Drivers' title in the big-wing 500 bhp Evo 2 and won the last Group B event in Europe.

▷ Peugeot 405 T16 GR 1986

Origin France

Engine 1,905 cc, straight-four

Top speed 155 mph (249 km/h)

After Group B rallying was cancelled, Peugeot turned to the Paris–Dakar desert endurance rally: Ari Vatanen won in 1989 and 1990 in the mid-engined 405 T16.

△ McLaren-Honda MP4/4 1988

Origin UK

Engine 1,496 cc, V6

Top speed 210 mph (338 km/h)

McLaren secured the best engine for 1988 and Gordon Murray designed the best chassis to run it, Ayrton Senna and Alain Prost winning all but one race of the 1988 Formula 1 season.

▷ MG Metro 6R4 1984

Origin UK

Engine 2,991 cc, V6

Top speed 155 mph (249 km/h)

Designed by Williams' designer Patrick Head, with a mid-mounted engine later used in the Jaguar XJ220 and four-wheel drive, this was an ultimate Group B rally car.

◁ Benetton-Ford B188 1988

Origin UK

Engine 3,493 cc, V8

Top speed 200 mph (322 km/h)

The Italian-sponsored Benetton Formula 1 team turned to Ford Cosworth DFV non-turbo power for 1988. With Alessandro Nannini and Thierry Boutsen driving, they achieved a couple of third places.

△ Audi Sport quattro 1983

Origin Germany

Engine 2,133 cc, straight-five

Top speed 154 mph (248 km/h)

Audi chopped 32 cm (12.6 in) out of the centre of the quattro to keep it competitive against purpose-built Group B opposition. It had 306 bhp in road form, and double that for rallying.

△ Audi Sport quattro S1 E2 1985

Origin Germany

Engine 2,133 cc, straight-five

Top speed 154 mph (248 km/h)

In a last-ditch fight with the purpose-built Group B cars, Audi added wings and spoilers to make the Evo 2, with 550 bhp. Walter Röhrl won the Sanremo Rally in 1985 with it.

US Compacts

It took a long time for US manufacturers to take much notice of the world trend towards small, fuel-efficient cars. Plentiful inexpensive fuel, wide open roads, and for the most part low traffic densities, encouraged the use of large cruising cars. But the 1980s saw Japanese and European cars make increasing headway into the market, forcing US manufacturers to reconsider.

△ **Dodge Aries 1981**
Origin USA
Engine 2,213 cc, straight-four
Top speed 98 mph (158 km/h)

This spacious front-wheel-drive saloon was *Motor Trend's* Car of the Year in 1981. It sold a million in seven years, helping to improve Chrysler's fortunes in the 1980s.

△ **Pontiac Phoenix 1980**
Origin USA
Engine 2,838 cc, V6
Top speed 109 mph (175 km/h)

Sold as a two-door coupé or a five-door hatchback, Pontiac's first front-wheel-drive compact was more efficient than its rear-wheel-drive predecessor. It was made until 1984.

◁ **Dodge Lancer 1985**
Origin USA
Engine 2,213 cc, straight-four
Top speed 111 mph (179 km/h)

Also available as a 125 mph (201 km/h) turbo, the five-door Lancer was a lively performer. It had a five-speed manual or a three-speed automatic gearbox.

▽ **Buick Reatta 1988**
Origin USA
Engine 3,800 cc, V6
Top speed 125 mph (201 km/h)

Buick's first two-seater for 50 years had touch-screen climate control, a radio, and electronic diagnostics. Unfortunately, its gadgets deterred rather than attracted buyers.

◁ **Pontiac Grand Am 1985**
Origin USA
Engine 3,000 cc, straight-four
Top speed 100 mph (161 km/h)

Pontiac brought back an old name for its mid-80s compact saloon. It had front-wheel drive, 2.5-litre 4-cylinder or 3.0-litre V6 engines, and coupé or sedan body styles.

△ **Pontiac Fiero GT 1985**
Origin USA
Engine 2,838 cc, V6
Top speed 124 mph (200 km/h)

General Motors astonished the world with the mid-engined, part-plastic-bodied Fiero two-seater sports car, which sold 370,158 in five years. Base models had a 4-cylinder engine.

△ **Chrysler LeBaron Coupé 1987**
Origin USA
Engine 2,501 cc, straight-four
Top speed 103 mph (166 km/h)

Turbocharged engine options and a radical new look – including sliding covers over the headlights – gave the LeBaron Coupé, and its convertible counterpart, real 80s appeal.

◁ **Ford Escort 1981**

Origin USA

Engine 1,597 cc, straight-four

Top speed 96 mph (154 km/h)

Not until 1981 was the US market ready for as small a car as the European Ford Escort. This US version became the US's best-selling car for some of the decade.

△ **Chevrolet Spectrum 1985**

Origin Japan

Engine 1,471 cc, straight-four

Top speed 100 mph (161 km/h)

GM's Japanese affiliate built this compact hatchback and saloon as the Isuzu Gemini; it was renamed the Chevrolet Spectrum for the US and Canadian markets.

▷ **Ford Probe 1988**

Origin USA

Engine 2,184 cc, straight-four

Top speed 118 mph (190 km/h)

Originally planned to replace the Mustang, but launched as a new model alongside it, the front-wheel-drive Probe was designed by Mazda and built in its new US factory.

△ **AMC Eagle 1979**

Origin USA

Engine 4,228 cc, straight-six

Top speed 88 mph (142 km/h)

In the late 1970s AMC combined its Jeep-derived four-wheel-drive expertise with its saloon car range. The result was this pioneering US four-wheel-drive crossover vehicle.

△ **Cadillac Cimarron 1981**

Origin USA

Engine 1,835 cc, straight-four

Top speed 100 mph (161 km/h)

In a rush to enter the compact car market – and to compete with European imports – General Motors failed to turn its J-car platform into a convincing Cadillac, despite its high-tech equipment.

◁ **Eagle Premier 1987**

Origin USA

Engine 2,464 cc, straight-four

Top speed 117 mph (188 km/h)

Styled by Giugiaro and developed by AMC and Renault, the Premier boasted electronically controlled four-speed automatic transmission, fuel injection, and air conditioning.

▽ **Volkswagen Jetta 16V 1987**

Origin USA/Germany

Engine 1,781 cc, straight-four

Top speed 126 mph (203 km/h)

Adapting to the US market's resistance to hatchbacks, Volkswagen added a boot to its Golf hatchback in 1979. It sold millions, a third going to the US.

Superminis

Once the British-made Mini had shown how large the market was for compact four-seater cars with small engines, manufacturers worldwide stepped in to satisfy demand. With safety legislation becoming increasingly influential, the minis grew into superminis, which were larger, but still triumphs of packaging. Virtually all manufacturers followed the Mini's example of having a transverse four-cylinder engine and front-wheel drive.

◁ **Austin Mini-Metro 1980**

Origin UK

Engine 998 cc, straight-four

Top speed 84 mph (135 km/h)

Only 21 years after the Mini, in 1980 a new British supermini arrived. The car's engine dated back to 1953, but it was well packaged and had comfortable Hydragas suspension.

▷ **Talbot Samba 1982**

Origin France

Engine 1,360 cc, straight-four

Top speed 87 mph (140 km/h)

Peugeot took over Chrysler's European arm in 1978, so the Samba was no more than a dressed-up Peugeot 104. This meant it was a good car, with 954–1,360 cc options.

△ **Ford Festiva 1986**

Origin Japan/South Korea

Engine 1,138 cc, straight-four

Top speed 93 mph (150 km/h)

The Ford Festiva was designed by Mazda on a Mazda platform for the US, Australasia, and Japan. It was also produced as the Kia Pride by Kia Motors of Korea.

▷ **Peugeot 205 GTi 1984**

Origin France

Engine 1,905 cc, straight-four

Top speed 121 mph (195 km/h)

The sparkling GTi was an impressive derivative of Peugeot's 2.7-million-selling hatchback – even more so when it grew to 1905 cc, 130 bhp, and 121 mph in 1986.

▷ **Nissan Cherry Turbo 1983**

Origin Japan

Engine 1,488 cc, straight-four

Top speed 114 mph (183 km/h)

Nissan's Cherry hatchbacks sold an impressive 1,450,300 between 1983 and 1986. Top of the range was this 114 bhp Turbo, but it suffered from poor handling and turbo lag.

△ **Volkswagen Polo 1981**

Origin Germany

Engine 1,043 cc, straight-four

Top speed 94 mph (151 km/h)

The second-generation Polo sold 4.5 million from 1981 to 1994, the extra space and more powerful engines making it much more competitive. It was restyled in 1990.

◁ **Nissan March/Micra 1983**

Origin Japan

Engine 988 cc, straight-four

Top speed 88 mph (142 km/h)

Nissan's starter car had durable mechanics and 1.0- or 1.2-litre engines. It was not the most elegant supermini, but it was easy to drive and sold two million in nine years.

▷ Opel Corsa/Vauxhall Nova GTE/GSi 1983

Origin Spain

Engine 1,598 cc, straight-four

Top speed 117 mph (188 km/h)

The "hot hatch" GTE joined the Corsa family a bit later than the other 1.0/1.2/1.3/ 1.4-litre models and was by far the best looking. Like Ford's Fiesta, it was built in Spain.

△ Sinclair C5 1985

Origin UK

Engine Electric motor

Top speed 15 mph (24 km/h)

The C5 was a brave attempt to convert the world, starting in the UK, to light electric personal transportation. The converts were few, however, with just 12,000 made.

◁ SEAT Ibiza 1985

Origin Spain

Engine 1,461 cc, straight-four

Top speed 107 mph (172 km/h)

There was some Fiat influence in SEAT's new hatch, although all of its engines were designed by Porsche. Engines ranged from 950 to 1,714 cc.

◁ Fiat Uno 1983

Origin Italy

Engine 1,301 cc, straight-four

Top speed 104 mph (167 km/h)

The 127's successor was a great all-rounder, and sold 6.5 million by 1994. This was thanks to its good packaging, crisp styling by Giugiaro, and nimble handling.

△ Autobianchi Y10 1985

Origin Italy

Engine 999 cc, straight-four

Top speed 88 mph (142 km/h)

Built by Autobianchi and sold in some markets as a Lancia, this compact city car had dramatic styling and good interior space for its size. However, it was a little cramped for long journeys.

△ Renault 5 1984

Origin France

Engine 1,108 cc, straight-four

Top speed 90 mph (145 km/h)

This second-generation Renault 5 had 956–1,721 cc engines turned transverse for more interior space. It was one of the best-selling European cars of the 1980s.

◁ Citroën AX 1987

Origin France

Engine 954 cc, straight-four

Top speed 83 mph (134 km/h)

Available at first as a three-door, then as a five-door model in 1988, the AX shared its running gear with small Peugeots, but had its own chic styling.

△ Honda Civic CRX V-TEC 1987

Origin Japan

Engine 1,590 cc, straight-four

Top speed 129 mph (208 km/h)

Honda's Civic supermini was easily adapted to produce this coupé. With the 150 bhp, V-TEC, variable valve timing, twin-cam engine, it was astonishingly quick.

△ Geo Metro/Suzuki Swift 1989

Origin Japan/USA

Engine 993 cc, straight-three

Top speed 88 mph (142 km/h)

Built by Suzuki as the Cultus, or Swift, and still produced 20 years later in Pakistan, this "world car" was sold by GM in the US and built in seven different countries worldwide.

Ultimate Sports Saloons

By the 1980s saloons were so refined that open sports cars became the preserve of hardy enthusiasts; speed-seeking drivers bought sports saloons instead. The surge in popularity of touring-car racing led manufacturers to build homologation specials – road models adapted to meet racing regulations – that would put their marque's cars at the front of the race grid. These limited-edition performance cars are highly collectable now.

△ **Aston Martin Lagonda 1976**

Origin	UK
Engine	5,340 cc, V8
Top speed	143 mph (230 km/h)

A computerized digital dashboard and harsh wedge styling made the Lagonda seem futuristic in the 1970s. It took until 1979 for the first car to be delivered, the model truly coming of age in the 1980s.

△ **Holden VH Commodore 1981**

Origin	Australia
Engine	5,044 cc, V8
Top speed	125 mph (201 km/h)

Holden of Australia built tough saloons with engines from 1.9 litres upwards; its VH Commodores were successful locally in motor sport. The road version was known as the SS.

△ **Rover 3500 Vitesse 1982**

Origin	UK
Engine	3,528 cc, V8
Top speed	133 mph (214 km/h)

Simple mechanics, modern lines, and a light V8 engine helped the Rover SD1 become European Car of the Year in 1977; the Vitesse was the ultimate performance version in the 1980s.

▷ **Bentley Turbo R 1985**

Origin	UK
Engine	6,750 cc, V8
Top speed	143 mph (230 km/h)

Rolls-Royce transformed Bentley's flagging sales by introducing turbochargers, giving the marque back its sporting credentials: ultimate luxury with a big kick.

△ **Maserati Biturbo 1981**

Origin	Italy
Engine	1,996 cc, V6
Top speed	132 mph (212 km/h)

To expand the market for his Maserati marque, Alejandro de Tomaso launched this two- or four-door, turbocharged saloon; it drove well, but its staid looks and poor build let it down.

△ **BMW M3 1988**

Origin	Germany
Engine	2,302 cc, straight-four
Top speed	143 mph (230 km/h)

In making its E30 3-series fit for racing, BMW produced one of the iconic cars of the 1980s. Terrific performance and handling were matched by luxurious trim.

◁ **Vauxhall Lotus Carlton 1989**

Origin	Germany/UK
Engine	3,615 cc, straight-six
Top speed	177 mph (285 km/h)

Sold in mainland Europe as the Opel-Lotus Omega, this was a modified version of the standard Carlton saloon, with an enlarged engine and twin turbochargers to give phenomenal performance.

▽ **Audi V8 DTM 1988**

Origin Germany

Engine 4,172 cc, V8

Top speed 153 mph (246 km/h)

The four-wheel-drive, 4.2-litre V8 brought Audi credibility as a maker of top-league saloon cars. This smaller 3.6-litre won Germany's DTM race series in 1990 and 1991.

△ **Ford Sierra XR4i 1983**

Origin UK/Germany

Engine 2,792 cc, V6

Top speed 129 mph (208 km/h)

This last rear-wheel-drive muscle car from Ford Europe could be exciting in the wet, but refined high-speed cruising was its forte, the bi-plane spoiler keeping it stable.

◁ **Ford Sierra Cosworth RS500 1987**

Origin UK/Germany

Engine 1,993 cc, straight-four

Top speed 149 mph (240 km/h)

With 224–300 bhp, powerful brakes, and huge spoilers, this turbocharged homologation special kept the Sierra at the forefront of touring-car racing; just 500 cars were made.

△ **Ford Taurus SHO 1989**

Origin USA

Engine 2,986 cc, V6

Top speed 143 mph (230 km/h)

Ford ordered Yamaha engines for a planned sports car: when the car was cancelled, the engines were put in the limited-edition SHO. The SHO was so popular it went into full production.

△ **Lancia Thema 8.32 1987**

Origin Italy

Engine 2,927 cc, V8

Top speed 149 mph (240 km/h)

Trimmed to the highest standard and hugely expensive, the Lancia Thema 8.32 was fitted with an engine from the Ferrari 308 sports car, modified to suit the heavier saloon body.

◁ **Volkswagen Golf Rallye G60 1989**

Origin Germany

Engine 1,763 cc, straight-four

Top speed 134 mph (216 km/h)

For those who thought the Golf GTI wasn't quite fast enough, Volkswagen produced the supercharged, four-wheel-drive G60 for just one year, selling 9,780. Rather surprisingly, it was not built for rallying.

Pace-setting Style from Italian Designers

Producers of ground-breaking car designs since the 1920s, the Italian styling houses were the single most influential styling force in the motoring world by the 1980s. Italian stylists led not just fashion – wedge shapes or rounded – but whole concepts such as the hatchback body style, adding glamour to everything from cheap runabouts to mid-engined supercars.

△ **DeLorean DMC-12 1981**

Origin UK

Engine 2,849 cc, V6

Top speed 121 mph (195 km/h)

Lotus drew up the chassis, Giugiaro styled the body, and it starred in the film *Back to the Future*, but the DeLorean had quality problems that saw it out of production in 1982.

△ **Hyundai Excel/Pony 1985**

Origin South Korea

Engine 1,468 cc, straight-four

Top speed 96 mph (154 km/h)

Hyundai brought in Italdesign to style its first Pony in 1975, replacing it 10 years later with this similar but front-wheel-drive model. It was built up to 1994.

△ **Škoda Favorit 1987**

Origin Czechoslovakia

Engine 1,289 cc, straight-four

Top speed 92 mph (148 km/h)

Škoda's first front-engined, front-wheel-drive model was styled by Bertone and became one of Central Europe's most popular cars. It was simple, with just one engine option.

△ **Lancia Delta Integrale 1987**

Origin Italy

Engine 1,995 cc, straight-four

Top speed 134 mph (216 km/h)

Giugiaro's Delta was very modern for its time, and was European Car of the Year in 1980. This is the 4x4 rally development of what started as a shopping car.

◁ **Chrysler TC by Maserati 1989**

Origin Italy

Engine 2,213 cc, straight-four

Top speed 130 mph (209 km/h)

Though it was built in Italy by Maserati, the TC had a turbocharged Chrysler engine and was styled in the US. Three years in gestation, it took too long to reach the high street and sold poorly.

△ **Citroën BX 1982**

Origin France

Engine 1,905 cc, straight-four

Top speed 106 mph (171 km/h)

Styled by Marcello Gandini of Bertone, 2.3 million BXs were sold in 12 years. They shared the Peugeot 405's floorpan, but with hydropneumatic suspension and 1.1–1.9-litre engines.

▷ **Peugeot 405 1987**

Origin France

Engine 1,905 cc, straight-four

Top speed 116 mph (187 km/h)

Built until 1997 in Europe and still made in Iran, the Pininfarina-styled 405 won European Car of the Year in 1988 and sold 2.5 million worldwide. It has 1.4–2.0-litre engines.

◁ **Volvo 780 1986**

Origin Sweden/Italy

Engine 2,849 cc, V6

Top speed 114 mph (183 km/h)

Built by Bertone, the 780 began life with a live rear axle and an underpowered engine. By 1988 these had been replaced by independent rear suspension and a turbo.

△ **Citroën XM 1989**

Origin France

Engine 2,975 cc, V6

Top speed 143 mph (230 km/h)

Styled by Bertone, and derived from Gandini's Citroën BX, the big, sleek XM had 2.0–3.0-litre engines and electronically controlled hydropneumatic suspension.

△ Fiat Panda 1980
Origin Italy
Engine 1,100 cc, straight-four
Top speed 86 mph (138 km/h)

A Giorgetto Giugiaro-styled classic, this simple, no-frills car set the style for 1980s Fiats. Steadily improved with 650–1,100cc and even a 4x4, it was on sale until 2003.

◁ Fiat Strada/Ritmo Cabriolet 1983
Origin Italy
Engine 1,498 cc, straight-four
Top speed 103 mph (166 km/h)

Bertone gave Fiat the most distinctively styled family hatchback of the 1970s. It was too radical to be popular at first, but by the 1983 Cabriolet launch it had come of age.

◁ Fiat Croma 1985
Origin Italy
Engine 2,500 cc, straight-four
Top speed 121 mph (195 km/h)

Giorgetto Giugiaro styled this big "notchback hatchback" family car with 1.6–2.5-litre engines. It was the world's first passenger car with a direct injection diesel engine.

△ Isuzu Piazza Turbo 1980
Origin Japan
Engine 1,996 cc, straight-four
Top speed 127 mph (204 km/h)

General Motors' Japanese brand had Giugiaro style its new coupé. Sold in the US from 1983 and in Europe from 1985, it was fast, but handled poorly at first.

◁ Ferrari Mondial Cabriolet 1984
Origin Italy
Engine 2,926 cc, V8
Top speed 146 mph (235 km/h)

Pininfarina styled the striking wedge-shaped, mid-engined Mondial, which looked even better with its roof down as it had no rollover bar. Its performance was exhilarating.

△ Lotus Etna 1984
Origin UK/Italy
Engine 3,946 cc, V8
Top speed 180 mph (290 km/h)

Styled by Giugiaro for Italdesign, the Etna was a non-running prototype until 2008 when it finally ran with the intended V8 engine, derived from the Esprit slant-four.

△ Cadillac Allanté 1987
Origin USA/Italy
Engine 4,087 cc, V8
Top speed 119 mph (192 km/h)

Designed and built in Italy, and flown to the US as fully trimmed bodies to be united with the Cadillac chassis, this upmarket roadster was criticized for having front-wheel drive.

▷ Aston Martin V8 Vantage Zagato 1986
Origin UK/Italy
Engine 5,340 cc, V8
Top speed 185 mph (298 km/h)

Echoing the DB4 GT Zagato of the 1960s, just 50 coupés and 25 convertibles of the 1986 V8 Vantage Zagato were built. Though not as elegant, it was brutally fast – and expensive.

Two-seater Excitement

The 1980s was the decade of young, upwardly mobile professionals, or "yuppies", whose fun cars gave rise to a rich heritage of roadsters and coupés. Each had its own flavour at a time when, in retrospect, their manufacturers were generally untroubled by the demands of safety legislation. Evergreen classics mixed it with newcomers boasting front- and four-wheel drive; the brute horsepower of the old guard vied with the cutting-edge technology of the new. There was rarely room for the kids.

△ **Aston Martin Bulldog 1980**

Origin UK

Engine 5,340 cc, V8

Top speed 191 mph (307 km/h)

Here was a fantasy Aston Martin: a mid-engined, twin-turbo, gullwing-door concept car that shocked the car world in 1980. The only car built achieved 191 mph in tests.

△ **Alfa Romeo Spider 1982**

Origin Italy

Engine 1,567–1,962 cc, four-cylinder

Top speed 118 mph (190 km/h)

Launched in 1966, the Spider gained a major facelift in 1982. Purists decried the rubber bumpers and tail spoiler, but these crash precautions kept this living classic legally compliant in the US.

△ **Pontiac Firebird Trans Am 1982**

Origin USA

Engine 5,001–5,733 cc, V8

Top speed 140 mph (225 km/h)

The most aerodynamic GM car ever, this third-generation Firebird was a 2+2 coupé. The Trans Ams were all V8s – one starred as KITT in the popular US TV series *Knight Rider*.

▽ **Chevrolet Corvette Convertible 1986**

Origin USA

Engine 5,733 cc, V8

Top speed 142 mph (229 km/h)

The Corvette was fully redesigned in 1983, and three years later a proper convertible option made a return after a gap of 10 years away. A digital dashboard was a notable feature.

△ **TVR 350i 1984**

Origin UK

Engine 3,528 cc, V8

Top speed 143 mph (230 km/h)

TVR's traditional backbone chassis and glassfibre body blended with Rover's superb aluminium V8 engine made for lightning acceleration and entertaining handling.

▷ **Toyota MR2 1984**

Origin Japan

Engine 1,587 cc, four-cylinder

Top speed 120 mph (193 km/h)

The MR2 (Mid-engined Recreational Two-seater) wasn't the first affordable centrally powered sports car, but it was certainly the best yet; responsive and reliable.

△ **Marcos Mantula 1984**

Origin UK

Engine 3,528–3,947 cc, V8

Top speed 150 mph (241 km/h)

The classic Marcos of the 1960s sprang back to life in the 1980s as the Mantula. Features now included a soft-top, a more aerodynamic nose, and a gutsy Rover V8 engine.

▽ **Caterham Seven 1980**

Origin UK

Engine 1,588–1,715 cc, four-cylinder

Top speed 115 mph (185 km/h)

Based on the 1968 version of the 1957 Lotus Seven, the Caterham grew in popularity during the 1980s. It still used Ford engines, and its handling and acceleration excited a new generation.

△ **Porsche 911 Cabriolet 1982**

Origin Germany

Engine 2,687–3,299 cc, flat-six

Top speed 168 mph (270 km/h)

Fans of the 911 who craved fresh air waited until 1982 before Porsche launched a fully convertible bodystyle. It was eventually offered with standard Carrera and Turbo engines.

◁ **Porsche 959 1986**

Origin Germany

Engine 2,994 cc, flat-six

Top speed 190 mph (306 km/h)

Two hundred of these awesome cars were built to qualify the 959 for Group B rallying. It had four-wheel drive, 405 bhp from its twin-turbo engine, and electronic ride height.

△ **BMW Z1 1986**

Origin Germany

Engine 2,494 cc, six-cylinder

Top speed 140 mph (225 km/h)

Originally a prototype to test suspension parts, BMW decided to market the Z1 and sold 8,000. The doors slid down inside the plastic body for access to the cockpit.

△ **Jaguar XJS 1988**

Origin UK

Engine 5,343 cc, V12

Top speed 150 mph (241 km/h)

This fully convertible XJS (previously, there had been a Targa-top cabriolet) came with an electric hood, anti-lock brakes, Jaguar's silken V12 engine, and abundant style.

◁ **Ferrari Testarossa 1984**

Origin Italy

Engine 4,942 cc, flat-twelve

Top speed 181 mph (291 km/h)

Featuring in the *Miami Vice* TV series, the Testarossa symbolized 1980s glamour. The all-alloy, 390 bhp engine roared from the back of the widest car on sale at the time.

△ **Lotus Esprit 1987**

Origin UK

Engine 2,174 cc, four-cylinder

Top speed 163 mph (262 km/h)

Amazing performance from the 2.2-litre Esprit Turbo engine made it a genuine Ferrari-baiter; 1987 saw a Lotus restyle of the Giugiaro original as part of a big revamp.

▷ **Ferrari F40 1987**

Origin Italy

Engine 2,936 cc, V8

Top speed 201 mph (323 km/h)

From 1987 to 1989 this was the world's fastest production car, thanks to twin turbos, 478 bhp, and lightweight composite bodywork. It marked Ferrari's 40th birthday.

△ **Lotus Elan 1989**

Origin UK

Engine 1,588 cc, four-cylinder

Top speed 136 mph (219 km/h)

Lotus's only front-wheel-drive sports car, this shortlived Elan was exciting to drive, partly due to clever wishbone front suspension. The Isuzu engine was usually turbocharged.

△ **Lamborghini Countach 1988**

Origin Italy

Engine 5,167 cc, V12

Top speed 180 mph (290 km/h)

The wild-child Countach was cleverly restyled for its final two years, to commemorate the supercar-maker's silver jubilee. It gained the widest tyres then fitted to any car.

Multi-purpose Vehicles

The 1980s saw the Sport-Utility Vehicle (SUV) market continue to grow, spawning some powerful 4x4s with exceptional mud-plugging ability, and some comfort-oriented cars with only limited ability on rough terrain. At the same time, a new niche was discovered, for capacious seven-seat Multi-Purpose Vehicles (MPVs), based on car or van platforms and aimed at larger families with a lot to carry.

△ Land Rover 88 SIII 1971

Origin UK

Engine 2,286 cc, straight-four

Top speed 68 mph (109 km/h)

The basic Land Rover continued to be among the best off-road vehicles throughout the 1980s. Creature comforts were limited, especially on this ex-army lightweight model.

◁ Nissan Prairie 1983

Origin Japan

Engine 1,809 cc, straight-four

Top speed 99 mph (159 km/h)

Boxy and spacious, and with sliding rear doors, the Prairie revealed a new market for van-like road cars and sold over a million in six years. It had 1.5- or 1.8-litre engines.

▷ Nissan Patrol 1982

Origin Japan

Engine 3,246 cc, straight-six

Top speed 80 mph (129 km/h)

Rugged and basic compared with more upmarket rivals, the Patrol was an unashamed workhorse with live axles, semi-elliptic springs, and four- and six-cylinder engines.

◁ Land Rover Discovery 1989

Origin UK

Engine 2,495 cc, straight-four

Top speed 107 mph (172 km/h)

Bridging the gap between the luxury Range Rover and the basic Land Rover, the Discovery was superb off-road and had a plush Conran-designed interior. It won a British Design Council award.

△ Mitsubishi Space Wagon 1984

Origin Japan

Engine 1,725 cc, straight-four

Top speed 97 mph (156 km/h)

Also sold as the Chariot, the Nimbus, and the Expo, this compact five- or seven-seater was one of the first ever MPVs. It had two- and four-wheel-drive models.

△ Plymouth Voyager 1984

Origin USA

Engine 2,213 cc, straight-four

Top speed 96 mph (154 km/h)

Plymouth's version of Chrysler's all-new Minivan responded to the new MPV craze previously only served by van adaptations like the Volkswagen Microbus.

▷ Suzuki Vitara 1988

Origin Japan

Engine 1,590 cc, straight-four

Top speed 87 mph (140 km/h)

Suzuki cleverly mixed its off-road expertise with normal road car comforts in this compact soft-roader, and established a niche market for the comfortable mini 4x4.

▽ Mercedes-Benz G-Wagen 1979

Origin Germany/Austria

Engine 2,746 cc, straight-six

Top speed 92 mph (148 km/h)

Coil-sprung live axles gave the G-Wagen a smoother ride than its rival Land Rover, but high price and basic looks limited sales until Mercedes-Benz improved these in 1991.

△ Lamborghini LM002 1986

Origin Italy

Engine 5,167 cc, V12

Top speed 125 mph (201 km/h)

Italian supercar maker Lamborghini gave the LM002 a huge V12 engine feeding from six Weber carburettors. Super-fast on sand, it became a favourite among Arab oil sheikhs.

△ Renault Espace 1984

Origin France

Engine 1,995 cc, straight-four

Top speed 105 mph (169 km/h)

Matra's MPV took years to reach production; scheduled to be a Simca, it ended up a Renault. Features included a galvanised inner shell, glassfibre skin, and seven movable seats.

△ Daihatsu Sportrak 1987

Origin Japan

Engine 1,589 cc, straight-four

Top speed 89 mph (143 km/h)

Sold as the Rocky or Feroza in some markets, the Sportrak was a compact leisure 4x4. Two- and four-wheel-drive options gave fair on- and off-road performance.

△ Rayton Fissore Magnum 1985

Origin Italy

Engine 2,492 cc, V6

Top speed 104 mph (168 km/h)

The Magnum was built by Fissore, using a shortened military Iveco four-wheel-drive chassis. It had Fiat/VM/Alfa 4- or 6-cylinder engines – or a V8 in the US, where it sold as the Laforza.

△ Pontiac Trans Sport 1989

Origin USA

Engine 3,135 cc, V6

Top speed 107 mph (172 km/h)

General Motors responded to the Chrysler Minivans with this rakishly styled, long-nosed MPV. It had a galvanized shell and plastic panels like Matra's Espace.

△ Jeep Cherokee 1984

Origin USA

Engine 2,838 cc, V6

Top speed 96 mph (154 km/h)

The first Jeep to have its chassis combined into a monocoque welded-steel bodyshell was a much more civilized car than its predecessors. It enjoyed greater sales as a result.

△ Jeep Wrangler 1987

Origin USA

Engine 3,956 cc, straight-six

Top speed 105 mph (169 km/h)

Conceived by AMC to rejuvenate the basic Jeep model with overtones of its wartime ancestor, the Wrangler used 2.5-litre 4-cylinder or 4.0-litre 6-cylinder engines.

Premium Luxury

In the 1980s car manufacturers remained convinced that the best way to build a luxury car was with a front engine and rear-wheel drive, plus a good deal of weight. Lightweight construction and materials had yet to influence this sector of the market, and fuel economy was not a priority. The Saab 900 was an exception – a light, front-drive vehicle that opened a new niche in the market for luxury cars.

△ **Aston Martin V8 Vantage 1977**

Origin	UK
Engine	5,340 cc, V8
Top speed	168 mph (270 km/h)

The ultimate 1970s Aston Martin became even more potent in 1986 with 432 bhp. The style remained the same, complete with sumptuous leather and walnut veneers.

△ **Shanghai SH760 1964**

Origin	China
Engine	2,200 cc, straight-six
Top speed	85 mph (137 km/h)

The Shanghai Automotive Industry Corporation built 79,526 of this imposing car almost unaltered from 1964 to 1991. It was inspired by Soviet and Mercedes models.

◁ **Bristol Beaufighter 1980**

Origin	UK
Engine	5,900 cc, V8
Top speed	150 mph (241 km/h)

Based on the 412, rather bluntly styled by Zagato, the niche market Beaufighter had the extra appeal of turbocharging for its Chrysler V8 engine and a lift-off roof panel.

▷ **Lincoln Mark VII 1984**

Origin	USA
Engine	4,949 cc, V8
Top speed	118 mph (190 km/h)

The Mark VII was a two-door coupé with optional designer interiors. Based on the four-door Continental platform, it had BMW turbodiesel or Ford V8 engine choices.

◁ **BMW 3-series Convertible 1986**

Origin	Germany
Engine	2,495 cc, straight-six
Top speed	135 mph (217 km/h)

By engineering rollover protection into the windscreen frame, BMW produced the cleanest-looking convertible of its day. The power hood all but disappeared when it was retracted.

▽ **Rolls-Royce Silver Spirit 1980**

Origin	UK
Engine	6,750 cc, V8
Top speed	119 mph (192 km/h)

The Silver Spirit was the ultimate in luxury and quality of build, but its sheer weight, its ageing engine, and its stately styling lost it sales to more modern luxury cars.

△ Cadillac Fleetwood Brougham 1980

Origin USA

Engine 6,037 cc, V8

Top speed 104 mph (167 km/h)

The top of Cadillac's prestige line remained conventional with large dimensions, a large V8 engine and live rear axle. Luxury trim and power steering came as standard.

△ Jaguar XJ12 1979

Origin UK

Engine 5,343 cc, V12

Top speed 150 mph (241 km/h)

Jaguar's 350 bhp flagship saloon looked more elegant than ever with its makeover by Pininfarina for the 1980s. It continued to make other luxury cars seem overpriced.

△ Cadillac Sedan De Ville 1985

Origin USA

Engine 4,087 cc, V8

Top speed 119 mph (191 km/h)

Cadillac gave the world a front-wheel-drive V8. It had the same interior space as before, but in a smaller bodyshell. US buyers still wanted big cars, however, and sales suffered.

◁ Saab 900 Convertible 1986

Origin Sweden

Engine 1,985 cc, straight-four

Top speed 126 mph (203 km/h)

Despite being no more than a progressively developed 1960s front-drive model, the Saab 900 Convertible sold well into the 1990s, and was spoiled only by its turbo lag.

▷ Lexus LS400 1989

Origin Japan

Engine 3,969 cc, V8

Top speed 147 mph (237 km/h)

The Lexus was Toyota's flagship car of 1989. It successfully challenged existing US and European high-end cars on aerodynamics, quietness, top speed, and fuel efficiency.

△ Volvo 760GLE 1982

Origin Sweden

Engine 2,849 cc, straight-four

Top speed 118 mph (190 km/h)

Aimed at the US luxury car market, the 760GLE helped the 700 series sell over a million. In 1984 it became turbocharged and intercooled, which greatly improved its performance.

△ Ferrari 412 1986

Origin Italy

Engine 4,942 cc, V12

Top speed 158 mph (254 km/h)

Ferrari's executive family car came with comfortable seats, leather trim, air conditioning, and anti-lock brakes. Vitally, it was still as exciting to drive as a Ferrari should be.

▷ Mercedes-Benz 190 1982

Origin Germany

Engine 1,997 cc, straight-four

Top speed 117 mph (188 km/h)

Mercedes' entry-level model for the 1980s was very well equipped and extremely durable. It easily ran for 300,000 miles (480,000 km) or so without needing major attention.

◁ Mercedes-Benz 560 SEC 1985

Origin Germany

Engine 5,547 cc, V8

Top speed 156 mph (251 km/h)

The 560 SEC was at the top of Mercedes' quality-laden range. Very expensive when new, it had 300 bhp from its big V8 engine and 6.8-second 0–60 mph acceleration.

Modern Roadsters

The 1990s saw the resurgence of sports cars, as fears that legislation would ban open cars receded. Manufacturers were divided on whether the best sporting solution was the traditional front-engine rear-drive, mid-engine rear-drive, or front-engine front-drive. Rounded styling returned, along with the arrival of retro – and luxury, including folding hardtop roofs.

△ **Nissan Figaro 1989**

Origin Japan

Engine 987 cc, straight-four

Top speed 106 mph (171 km/h)

Nissan popularized retro styling with this Micra-based two-seater with roll-back sunroof and three-speed automatic transmission. It was fun, but not sporting.

△ **Porsche 944 S2 Cabriolet 1989**

Origin Germany

Engine 2,990 cc, straight-four

Top speed 149 mph (240 km/h)

The final development of the 1976 Porsche 924 was the 944 S2, which was also at last available as a cabriolet – but production ended in 1991.

△ **Porsche Boxster 1996**

Origin Germany

Engine 2,480 cc, flat-six

Top speed 152 mph (245 km/h)

Almost 50 years after its first mid-engined prototype, Porsche finally introduced a mid-engined road sports car, which became its fastest-selling sports car ever.

△ **Mazda MX-5 (MkI) 1989**

Origin Japan

Engine 1,597 cc, straight-four

Top speed 114 mph (183 km/h)

Inspired by the 1960s Lotus Elan, Mazda reintroduced the world to traditional sports-car fun with the twin-cam, front-engined, rear-wheel drive MX-5 (also called Miata/Eunos).

△ **BMW Z3 1996**

Origin Germany

Engine 1,895 cc, straight-four

Top speed 123 mph (198 km/h)

BMW's first ever volume sports car had retro looks, rear-wheel drive, and an uncompromised roadster feel. The Z3 was fitted with 1.8, 1.9, 2.0, 2.2, 2.8, 3.0, or 3.2-litre engines.

◁ **Morgan Plus 8 1990**

Origin UK

Engine 3,946 cc, V8

Top speed 121 mph (195 km/h)

The ultra-traditional Morgan with its wood-framed body and separate chassis started using Rover's 3.5-litre V8 engine in 1968. It got the 3.9-litre version in 1990.

△ **Suzuki Cappuccino 1991**

Origin Japan

Engine 657 cc, straight-three

Top speed 85 mph (137 km/h)

Restricted to 85 mph, the Cappuccino was designed to give fun motoring within Japan's *Kei* car tax regulations. Front-engined and rear-driven, it is a proper mini-sports car.

▷ **TVR Griffith 400 1992**

Origin UK

Engine 3,948 cc, V8

Top speed 148 mph (238 km/h)

The best British sports car of the 1990s had stunning lines and effortless Rover V8 power (with the ultimate soundtrack), but reliability issues dogged it, like all TVRs.

▽ **Renault Sport Spider 1995**

Origin France

Engine 1,998 cc, straight-four

Top speed 131 mph (211 km/h)

Renault wanted to inject some sporty excitement into the brand, so it commissioned this roofless, mid-engine, aluminium-chassis roadster for road and track use.

△ **Alfa Romeo Spider 1995**

Origin Italy

Engine 2,959 cc, V6

Top speed 140 mph (225 km/h)

Available with 2-litre or 3-litre engines, Alfa's Spider for the 1990s was a striking front-wheel-drive sports car designed by Pininfarina, with a high tail but small boot.

◁ **MGF 1995**

Origin UK

Engine 1,796 cc, straight-four

Top speed 130 mph (209 km/h)

The first serious, new MG sports car for over 30 years was a pretty mid-engined two-seater with clever packaging and good handling from its hydragas suspension system.

△ **MG RV8 1992**

Origin UK

Engine 3,946 cc, V8

Top speed 136 mph (219 km/h)

The car MG should have built 25 years earlier finally entered limited production in the 1990s, with a pumped-up MGB bodyshell, Rover V8 engine, and leather trim.

△ **Lotus Elise 1996**

Origin UK

Engine 1,796 cc, straight-four

Top speed 124 mph (200 km/h)

Using a Rover K-series engine in an extruded aluminium chassis with glassfibre body, the Elise weighs just 725 kg (1,599 lb), giving superb handling and performance.

△ **De Tomaso Guarà Spider 1994**

Origin Italy

Engine 3,982 cc, V8

Top speed 170 mph (274 km/h)

More commonly sold as the Coupé or Barchetta (just five Spiders were built), this was the last project of founder Alejandro de Tomaso and used BMW running gear.

◁ **Mercedes SLK 230K 1997**

Origin Germany

Engine 2,295 cc, straight-four

Top speed 148 mph (238 km/h)

Mercedes' answer to the BMW Z3 and Porsche Boxster was a more civilized sports car (almost all those sold were automatics) with an electric hardtop and a supercharger.

▷ **Honda S2000 1999**

Origin Japan

Engine 1,997 cc, straight-four

Top speed 150 mph (241 km/h)

This rear-wheel-drive sports car was built to the highest standards to mark Honda's 50th birthday celebration. It had the world's highest-revving production car engine.

△ **Audi TT Roadster 1999**

Origin Germany

Engine 1,781 cc, straight-four

Top speed 138 mph (222 km/h)

Built in Hungary with either 4X2 or 4X4, Audi's TT uses Volkswagen Golf technology. It suffered bad press due to high speed instability, prompting recall modifications.

◁ **Fiat Barchetta 1995**

Origin Italy

Engine 1,747 cc, straight-four

Top speed 118 mph (190 km/h)

Fiat built the Barchetta on the Punto platform but, with a brand new twin-cam engine and beautiful, in-house-designed body, it's a far better sports car than many expect.

Competition Machines

This was the decade of technology, as manufacturers strove to achieve more performance than ever before. Restricted by regulations, they designed to reduce speeds and danger. Active suspension, active differentials, traction control, and semi-automatic transmissions were among the developments aimed at helping drivers get the most from cars, while twin turbochargers and their intercoolers helped get the most out of the engines.

△ **Porsche 962 1984**

Origin Germany

Engine 2,995 cc, flat-six

Top speed 200 mph (322 km/h)

A sports prototype designed for races such as Le Mans and the IMSA GTP series, the aluminium-chassis 962 was winning races well into the 1990s.

△ **Benetton-Ford B193 1993**

Origin UK

Engine 3,493 cc, V8

Top speed 200 mph (322 km/h)

Benetton's answer to the high-tech revolution in Formula 1, the B193 had active suspension and traction control. Michael Schumacher used one to win the Portuguese GP in 1993.

◁ **BMW V12 LMR 1998**

Origin Germany

Engine 6,100 cc, V12

Top speed 214 mph (344 km/h)

This striking roadster was built to win the Le Mans 24-hour race in France. It became the first BMW ever to do so in 1999, and won the Sebring 12 Hours in the US that same year.

△ **Leyton House-Judd CG901B 1990**

Origin UK

Engine 3,496 cc, V8

Top speed 205 mph (330 km/h)

Leading Formula 1 designer Adrian Newey tried out some advanced aerodynamic ideas on this Formula 1 racer; it had little success, though it did lead for most of the French GP in 1990.

△ **Sauber-Mercedes C11 1990**

Origin Switzerland

Engine 4,973 cc, V8

Top speed 240 mph (386 km/h)

With 950 bhp from its twin-turbocharged Mercedes V8 engine, the C11 dominated the 1990 World Sportscar Championship and continued winning into 1991.

Subaru

Subaru was a little-known Japanese car maker producing anonymous road cars that happened to have four-wheel drive and "boxer" engines – until it started rallying. After showing potential with the Legacy, Subaru engaged British motorsport company Prodrive to prepare Imprezas for the World Rally Championship. With top drivers such as Colin McRae, Richard Burns, Carlos Sainz, and Juha Kankkunen, their spectacular success made Subaru world famous.

▽ **Subaru Impreza WRC 1993**

Origin Japan

Engine 1,994 cc, flat-four

Top speed 135 mph (217 km/h)

Prodrive began fielding Imprezas in 1993, won its first rally with Carlos Sainz in 1994, and took the World Driver's title with Colin McRae in 1995.

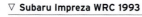

◁ **Ferrari F300 1998**

Origin Italy

Engine 2,997 cc, V10

Top speed 210 mph (338 km/h)

The F300 was the first Ferrari built under the highly successful pairing of Ross Brawn and Rory Byrne: it gave Michael Schumacher six wins in 1998.

◁ **Audi R8R 1999**

Origin Germany

Engine 3,596 cc, V8

Top speed 208 mph (335 km/h)

Audi's first Le Mans racer, with twin-turbo 600 bhp V8, proved reliable from the start but needed development to match the pace of rivals Toyota and BMW.

△ **Chevrolet Monte Carlo "T-Rex" 1997**

Origin USA

Engine 5,850 cc, V8

Top speed 215 mph (346 km/h)

Known by the dinosaur painted on the roof, Jeff Gordon's car won the 1997 NASCAR All Star race so easily that, even though it was legal, officials asked him not to bring it back.

▷ **Williams-Renault FW16B 1994**

Origin UK

Engine 3,493 cc, V10

Top speed 210 mph (338 km/h)

Damon Hill won six Grands Prix in 1994 in the FW16B; he would have won the World Championship if a brush with Michael Schumacher hadn't taken him out of the last race.

▽ **Chevrolet Monte Carlo 2000**

Origin USA

Engine 5,850 cc, V8

Top speed 215 mph (346 km/h)

The US's hugely popular NASCAR racing series features composite silhouette bodies resembling road cars, such as this Chevy, mounted on full race chassis with tuned V8s.

▽ **Williams-Renault FW18 1996**

Origin UK

Engine 3,000 cc, V10

Top speed 210 mph (338 km/h)

The dream team of Patrick Head and Adrian Newey developed another world beater in the FW18, giving Damon Hill a World Championship title in 1996.

▷ **Subaru Impreza WRC 2000**

Origin Japan

Engine 1,994 cc, flat-four

Top speed 140 mph (225 km/h)

Richard Burns and Juha Kankkunen led the Subaru comeback in 2000 with the intercooled and turbocharged Impreza, Burns taking four wins in the season.

△ **Subaru Impreza WRC 1999**

Origin Japan

Engine 1,994 cc, flat-four

Top speed 140 mph (225 km/h)

The Impreza was steadily redesigned to make full use of rule changes in World Rallying, with active differentials and semi-automatic transmission in place for 1999.

◁ **Subaru Impreza WRX 2000**

Origin Japan

Engine 1,994 cc, flat-four

Top speed 137 mph (220 km/h)

From its launch, Subaru included a turbocharged, intercooled version of its new saloon car with racing and rallying in mind: it proved extremely successful in motorsport.

US Design Reinvigorated

In the 1970s and 80s, other than a few notable exceptions, North American car design seemed to lag behind Europe. US car manufacturers were mildly updating their over-large, slab-like saloons, while smaller Japanese cars picked away at the US's market share. Finally, in the 1990s US designers found new life with retro-inspired models and striking pick-up trucks that all of the US wanted to buy.

△ Buick Park Avenue 1990

Origin USA

Engine 3,791cc, V6

Top speed 108mph (174km/h)

This big saloon, made until 1996, was the last Buick officially sold in Europe. US customers had the option of a supercharged version capable of close to 130mph (209km/h).

▷ Cadillac Eldorado 1991

Origin USA

Engine 4,893cc, V8

Top speed 130mph (209km/h)

This last incarnation of the US's longest-running personal luxury car model ended in 2002 – despite modern styling, large space-wasting cars had become unfashionable.

▷ Chevrolet Camaro 1993

Origin USA

Engine 5,733cc, V8

Top speed 155mph (249km/h)

The fourth-generation Camaro was built in Canada with V6 or V8 power, a six-speed gearbox being optional on the V8. It was good value against Ford's Mustang.

△ Saturn SL 1990

Origin USA

Engine 1,901cc, straight-four

Top speed 121mph (195km/h)

GM founded the Saturn brand in 1985 to counter Japanese imports. Stylish and aerodynamic, the S-Series was among the most fuel-efficient cars in the US at the time.

◁ Dodge Neon 1994

Origin USA

Engine 1,996cc, straight-four

Top speed 121mph (195km/h)

The Neon marked a move by Chrysler to sell worldwide, even in Japan and UK in right-hand-drive form. It was a compact front-wheel-drive saloon with a 2-litre engine.

△ Dodge Intrepid 1993

Origin USA

Engine 3,301cc, V6

Top speed 112mph (180km/h)

Closely related to the Chrysler New Yorker, the Dodge had more success, as it was built until 1997 and was followed by a second generation. Engines were 3.3 or 3.5 litre.

△ Oldsmobile Aurora 1994

Origin USA

Engine 3,995cc, V8

Top speed 140mph (225km/h)

GM revitalised the Oldsmobile brand with this striking, new, low-drag sports saloon. Well built, fast, and immensely strong, the Aurora's downfall was its high price.

▷ Dodge Ram 1994

Origin USA

Engine 7,886cc, V10

Top speed 113mph (180km/h)

Styled to look like a semi-trailer truck, the Ram was unsubtle, with engines from a 3.9-litre V6 to a Viper's 8-litre V10. It was what the US wanted, and sold rapidly.

◁ Plymouth Prowler 1997

Origin USA

Engine 3,528cc, V6

Top speed 118mph (190km/h)

A brave and truly American concept, the Prowler was based on a design by Chip Foose and boasted 5.9-second 0–62mph (0–100km/h) acceleration to match its exterior.

△ Ford Mustang GT 1994
Origin USA
Engine 4,942 cc, V8
Top speed 136 mph (219 km/h)

This successful restyle by Patrick Schiavone retained hints of the original Mustang, and also saw the return of a convertible to the Mustang range. Engines were 3.8-litre V6, or V8 like this model.

△ Ford Windstar 1994
Origin USA
Engine 3,797 cc, V6
Top speed 116 mph (187 km/h)

Ford's first front-wheel-drive, seven-seat MPV beat US rivals with its smoother performance and handling. It guaranteed Ford a big slice of the minivan market in the US.

▽ Ford Taurus 1996
Origin USA
Engine 2,967 cc, V6
Top speed 130 mph (209 km/h)

Jack Telnack's dramatic 1996 restyle of the Taurus did not prove popular, and it lost its place as the US's best-selling car after the first year, despite its user-friendly interior.

△ Mercury Villager 1993
Origin USA
Engine 2,960 cc, V6
Top speed 112 mph (180 km/h)

A joint project with Nissan, which sold it as the Quest, this car could seat seven, with a removable two-seat bench in the middle and a sliding/folding bench for three at the back.

▷ Mercury/Ford Cougar 1999
Origin USA
Engine 2,540 cc, V6
Top speed 140 mph (225 km/h)

Ford's second attempt – after the Probe – to emulate the sales success of its 1970s Capri was built in the US, and was too large for most customers in the rest of the world.

◁ Chrysler New Yorker 1993
Origin USA
Engine 3,494 cc, V6
Top speed 134 mph (216 km/h)

This final version of Chrysler's flagship model had just a three-year life in which sales tailed off dramatically, despite its high specification and large, airy cabin.

△ General Motors EV1 1996
Origin USA
Engine electric motor
Top speed 80 mph (129 km/h)

GM's purpose-built electric two-seater had a 55-150 mile (90–240 km) range; just 1,117 were leased to owners, so GM recalled and crushed them in 2002, due to a lack of consumer interest.

▷ Chrysler PT Cruiser 1999
Origin USA/Mexico
Engine 2,429 cc, straight-four
Top speed 121 mph (195 km/h)

Retro-styled and with a resemblance to the Chrysler Airflow, this car sold 1.35 million worldwide in 11 years. The new millennium brought convertible and turbocharged options.

Family-friendly Cars

By the 1990s the everyday family car had been transformed. Improvements had been made in the unsung areas of car development, such as soundproofing, windproofing, heating, and ventilation. Electronics to make engines start instantly and run smoothly through a wide rev band were also introduced. Almost all cars, from the smallest models up, would now run quietly and comfortably at legal speed limits.

△ **Fiat Cinquecento 1991**

Origin Italy/Poland

Engine 903 cc, straight-four

Top speed 83 mph (134 km/h)

Giugiaro styled Fiat's tiny four-seater for the 1990s, abandoning the rear-engined layout that had served Fiat for almost 40 years. It was neat and efficient and sold well.

◁ **Toyota Previa 1990**

Origin Japan

Engine 2,438 cc, straight-four

Top speed 108 mph (174 km/h)

Toyota made this seven or eight-seater exceptionally spacious for its length by placing the engine near-horizontal under the front seats, behind the line of the front axle. 4x4 was optional.

△ **Fiat Multipla 1998**

Origin Italy

Engine 1,581 cc, straight-four

Top speed 106 mph (171 km/h)

Short and wide compared with rival MPVs, the Multipla has two rows of three seats. It was hailed as one of the most innovative cars of its day, though it was also described as ugly.

△ **Citroën Berlingo Multispace 1996**

Origin France

Engine 1,360 cc, straight-four

Top speed 94 mph (151 km/h)

Related to Peugeot's Partner, the Berlingo (shown here after its 2002 facelift) was offered as a van or an adaptable and inexpensive passenger vehicle, with an electric powered option.

▷ **Peugeot 406 TD 2.1 1995**

Origin France

Engine 2,088 cc, straight-four

Top speed 118 mph (190 km/h)

This large family car proved popular. It had engines from 1.6 to 3.0 litres, and in turbodiesel form it enjoyed a 10-year production life until it was replaced by the 407.

△ **Citroën Xsara Picasso 1999**

Origin France/Spain

Engine 1,749 cc, straight-four

Top speed 118 mph (190 km/h)

Taking over from Renault's Scénic as the best-seller in the compact MPV market in most of Europe, the Picasso offered versatile family transport.

◁ **Peugeot 206 XR 1998**

Origin France

Engine 1,124 cc, straight-four

Top speed 98 mph (158 km/h)

By the end of production in 2010, 6.8 million 206s had been made, making it Peugeot's best-seller. Engines ranged from the 1.0- to 2.0-litre GTi.

△ Alfa Romeo 156 TS 2.0 1997
Origin Italy
Engine 1,970 cc, straight-four
Top speed 133 mph (214 km/h)

Alfa achieved class-leading styling with this sporting saloon. Features include concealed rear door handles to give it a coupé look.

◁ Subaru Forester 1997
Origin Japan
Engine 1,994 cc, flat-four
Top speed 111 mph (179 km/h)

Subaru's tough 4x4 estate offered comfortable road driving thanks to its low, flat engine. This made it more versatile than its competitors, though its looks were fairly uninspiring.

△ Rover 25 VVC 1999
Origin UK
Engine 1,796 cc, straight-four
Top speed 127 mph (204 km/h)

Based on engineering from Honda pre-1994, the 25 was well equipped and good value, with engines from 1.1 to 2.0 litres.

◁ Volkswagen Sharan 1995
Origin Germany/Portugal
Engine 1,984 cc, straight-four
Top speed 110 mph (177 km/h)

Also sold as the SEAT Alhambra and produced alongside the similar Ford Galaxy, Volkswagen's people carrier didn't have the best reliability record. Engines ranged from 1.8 to 2.8 litres.

△ Volkswagen Golf GTI Mk4 1997
Origin Germany
Engine 1,781 cc, straight-four
Top speed 138 mph (222 km/h)

The perennial hot hatch continued to sell well in its fourth generation with a turbo option. Volkswagen added a 3.2-litre 4x4 model too.

△ Volvo V70 T5 1997
Origin Sweden
Engine 2,319 cc, straight-five
Top speed 152 mph (245 km/h)

After the success of the 850 T5, Volvo rounded off the angular style and added a high-pressure turbocharger to create this unassuming, high-spec "Q-car".

△ Renault Mégane Scénic 1996
Origin France
Engine 1,598 cc, straight-four
Top speed 106 mph (171 km/h)

Having led the MPV market with the Espace, Renault kickstarted the compact MPV market with the Scénic, based on the small, family-car platform of the Mégane. The Scénic sold far more than expected.

◁ Renault Kangoo 1997
Origin France
Engine 1,390 cc, straight-four
Top speed 97 mph (156 km/h)

Renault's adaptable van/MPV (sold as a Nissan in some markets) boasted sliding side doors and a wide range of options, including 4x4. The model shown is with the facelift from 2003.

△ Volkswagen Beetle 1998
Origin Germany
Engine 1,984 cc, straight-four
Top speed 115 mph (185 km/h)

A bulky front-wheel-drive hatchback based on the Golf platform seemed an unlikely retro successor to the original Beetle, but the Beetle's long-lasting appeal has kept it selling into 2011.

◁ Mercedes-Benz A-class 1997
Origin Germany
Engine 1,598 cc, straight-four
Top speed 113 mph (182 km/h)

Offering a compact hatchback car was a radical step for Mercedes-Benz, forced on it by market trends. Doubts over its roadholding – though challenged by Mercedes-Benz – forced an embarrassing recall.

▷ Audi A2 2000
Origin Germany
Engine 1,390 cc, straight-four
Top speed 107 mph (172 km/h)

Audi brought high technology to the supermini with the aluminium, ultra-economical A2. However, Audi discovered that customers were led more by price and looks than quality and pedigree, and sales were somewhat disappointing.

Executive Saloons

With the continuing popularity of saloon, or touring car, racing around the world, some executive saloons in the 1990s became much more sporty, but others concentrated on comfort and refinement. All were increasingly fitted with complex electronics, gadgets, and driver aids, while multiple camshafts and valves, as well as light alloy construction, helped keep engine power up and weight down.

△ **Saab 900 Carlsson 1990**

Origin Sweden

Engine 1,985 cc, straight-four

Top speed 135 mph (217 km/h)

Built from 1978 and based on the 1967 Saab 99 floorpan, the 900 was still a surprisingly refined and potent front-wheel-drive saloon in ultimate "Carlsson" version.

◁ **BMW 5-Series 1995**

Origin Germany

Engine 2,793 cc, straight-six

Top speed 142 mph (229 km/h)

The E39 5-series was launched with 2-litre straight-six to 4.4-litre V8 engines and developed with electronic and trim options, retaining the model's strong position in the luxury saloon sector.

△ **Audi A4 Quattro 1994**

Origin Germany

Engine 1,781 cc, straight-four

Top speed 137 mph (220 km/h)

Five valves per cylinder and a turbo gave the four-wheel-drive A4 a reliable 150bhp and made it a success on road and track. This car was Frank Biela's BTCC-winner.

△ **Lincoln Continental 1995**

Origin USA

Engine 4,601 cc, V8

Top speed 120 mph (193 km/h)

Ford's top Lincoln model since 1939, the Continental for 1995 had the Mustang Cobra twin-cam V8 and many luxury fittings, including air-ride suspension.

△ **Holden VR Commodore SS 1993**

Origin Australia

Engine 4,987 cc, V8

Top speed 143 mph (230 km/h)

Australia's native car maker added anti-lock brakes and independent rear suspension to its big saloon's refinements. This is the 1995 Bathurst Great Race winner.

△ **Audi A8 1994**

Origin Germany

Engine 4,172 cc, V8

Top speed 155 mph (249 km/h)

Audi's flagship saloon used the world's first production aluminium monocoque, keeping weight down and performance up. It sold with two- or four-wheel drive and 2.8-litre V6 to 4.2-litre V8 engines.

△ **Mercedes-Benz S-Class 1991**

Origin Germany

Engine 5,987 cc, V12

Top speed 155 mph (249 km/h)

Mercedes' 1990s flagship car was not the most elegant, but it was one of the biggest and was technically magnificent, with double glazing, and engines from 2.8-litre straight-six to 6-litre V12.

△ **Mercedes-Benz C220 1993**

Origin Germany

Engine 2,199 cc, straight-four

Top speed 130 mph (209 km/h)

The C-class was the entry-level saloon from Mercedes for the 1990s. Engines ranged from 1.8-litre four-cylinder to 2.8-litre six-cylinder - or 4.3-litre V8 in the 1998 AMG models.

▷ **Mercedes-Benz S-Class 1999**

Origin Germany

Engine 5,786 cc, V12

Top speed 155 mph (249 km/h)

The new S-class was lighter, smaller, and more elegant than before, with more interior space, but proved to be less well built. Engines ranged from 3.2-litre V6 to 6.3-litre V12.

△ Chrysler LHS 1994

Origin USA

Engine 3,518 cc, V6

Top speed 136 mph (219 km/h)

Eight years in development and via various show cars, the LHS was a radical move for Chrysler, with a large cabin in overall compact dimensions, and a new overhead-cam V6.

△ Lexus GS300 1997

Origin Japan

Engine 2,997 cc, V6

Top speed 143 mph (230 km/h)

High on technology, the GS sports saloon could be ordered with twin turbos, electronic four-wheel steering, and stability control. The US had a 4-litre V8 GS400 option.

△ Bentley Arnage 1998

Origin UK

Engine 4,398 cc, V8

Top speed 150 mph (241 km/h)

Developed under Vickers' ownership of Rolls-Royce/Bentley and visually reminiscent of earlier models, the all-new Arnage featured a Cosworth-tuned BMW engine.

△ Cadillac Seville STS 1998

Origin USA

Engine 4,565 cc, V8

Top speed 150 mph (241 km/h)

The first Cadillac engineered for both left- and right-hand drive was also the most powerful front-wheel-drive car on the market at its launch, with 300 bhp in STS form.

△ Jaguar S-type 1999

Origin UK

Engine 3,996 cc, V8

Top speed 149 mph (240 km/h)

For the new millennium Jaguar tried retro styling echoing the 1963 S-type for its executive sporting saloon. Offered with 2.5-litre V6 to 4.2-litre V8 engines, it sold well.

Hyper-performance Cars

Extreme performance cars came to the fore in the 1990s with models that broke both styling conventions and speed records. Manufacturers used technology and materials from Formula 1 to set new benchmarks for what production models could look like and how they behaved on the road. Some marques created race-tuned models; others added extra horsepower to their existing designs.

△ Jaguar XJS 1991
Origin UK
Engine 3,980 cc, straight-six
Top speed 143 mph (230 km/h)

First seen in 1976, the XJ-S was re-engineered and relaunched in 1991 (minus the hyphen). In 1993 it was offered with a 6.0-litre, V12 engine. Production of the XJS ended in 1996.

△ Jaguar XK8 1996
Origin UK
Engine 3,996 cc, V8
Top speed 155 mph (249 km/h)

Released in 1996 to critical acclaim, Jaguar's all-new XK8 model was available either as a handsome coupé or a stylish convertible.

△ Jaguar XKR 1998
Origin UK
Engine 3,996 cc, V8
Top speed 155 mph (249 km/h)

As a high-performance variant of the XK8, Jaguar's XKR boasted faster acceleration and superior road-handling qualities over the standard model.

△ Bentley Continental R 1991
Origin UK
Engine 6,750 cc, V8
Top speed 150 mph (241 km/h)

This gentleman's express was styled by British designers John Heffernan and Ken Greenley. The turbocharged engine gave about 325 bhp, although no official figure was ever revealed.

△ Ferrari 456GT 1992
Origin Italy
Engine 5,474 cc, V12
Top speed 186 mph (300 km/h)

The Pininfarina styling of the highly popular 456 emphasized refinement and comfort. This exceptionally fast 2+2 coupé remained in production for more than a decade.

△ McLaren F1 GTR 1995
Origin UK
Engine 6,064 cc, V12
Top speed 230 mph (370 km/h)

In 1995 McLaren's F1 road model was developed for competition use. Equipped with a tuned BMW engine, the F1 GTR won the 1995 Le Mans 24-hour race in France.

▷ Ferrari 355 1994
Origin Italy
Engine 3,495.5 cc, V8
Top speed 183 mph (295 km/h)

The first Ferrari road model to feature semi-automatic paddle gearshifters, the 355 is one of the most beautiful recent offerings from the famous Italian marque.

△ Aston Martin DB7 Volante 1996
Origin UK
Engine 3,228 cc, straight-six
Top speed 165 mph (266 km/h)

The soft-top Volante was launched about three years after the sublime DB7 Coupé. With its supercharged engine giving 335 bhp, it was a firm favourite among Aston Martin fans.

◁ Ferrari 348GTB 1994
Origin Italy
Engine 3,405 cc, V8
Top speed 174 mph (280 km/h)

Launched in 1989, the 348 was uprated five years later to GTB specification. Tuned versions were quick enough to compete in top-class race series.

△ Ferrari F50 1995
Origin Italy
Engine 4,698.5 cc, V12
Top speed 202 mph (325 km/h)

The F50, Ferrari's 50th anniversary model, utilized technology and materials derived from the marque's Formula 1 team to create one of the most desirable cars ever produced.

△ Bugatti EB110 1991

Origin Italy

Engine 3,499 cc, V12

Top speed 213 mph (343 km/h)

After an absence of more than 30 years, the fabled Bugatti marque returned in the early 1990s with this 560 bhp supercar, of which just 139 examples were built.

△ Lotus Esprit V8 1996

Origin UK

Engine 3,500 cc, V8

Top speed 175 mph (282 km/h)

Thirty years after the Lotus Esprit was unveiled as a concept car, the model was still going strong, with this V8 version boasting scintillating performance figures.

△ Alfa Romeo 155 DTM 1993

Origin Italy

Engine 2,498 cc, V6

Top speed 186 mph (300 km/h)

This highly tuned 155 participated in the German DTM (Deutsche Tourenwagen Meisterschaft) touring-car series, winning the competition in both 1993 and 1996.

△ Mercedes-Benz C-Class DTM 1994

Origin Germany

Engine 2,500 cc, V6

Top speed 186 mph (300 km/h)

Mercedes-Benz launched its new C-Class compact executive car in 1993. The following year this tuned version of the car secured immediate success by winning the DTM touring-car series in Germany.

△ Lamborghini Diablo VT Roadster 1995

Origin Italy

Engine 5,709 cc, V12

Top speed 208 mph (335 km/h)

Replacing Lamborghini's legendary Countach, the all-new Diablo earned its supercar status by briefly laying claim to being the fastest production car in the world.

△ Lister Storm 1993

Origin UK

Engine 6,996 cc, V12

Top speed 208 mph (335 km/h)

The tuning company Lister Cars' first foray into the supercar market was the impressive Storm, which had one of the largest engines ever fitted to a production car.

△ Renault Clio V6 2001

Origin France/UK

Engine 2,946 cc, V6

Top speed 146 mph (235 km/h)

To transform the performance of its Clio hatchback, Renault enlisted the help of the British company TWR. The result was this stunningly quick, mid-engined, 230 bhp racer.

◁ Porsche 911 1998

Origin Germany

Engine 3,600 cc, flat-six

Top speed 170 mph (274 km/h)

In 1998 a water-cooled engine was fitted into the Porsche 911, replacing the air-cooled unit that had powered the 911 since the model's inception in 1963.

Famous Marques Reinvented

After building cars for more than a century, the motor industry discovered the power of its heritage in public perception. Today, every manufacturer who is able to, draws heavily on its past with evocative model names and styling cues. For other manufacturers, there is a need to create new brands that distance them from any negative associations with the parent brand or its past.

△ Dodge Challenger 2008

Origin USA

Engine 6,059 cc, V8

Top speed 145 mph (233 km/h)

Fans of the 1971 film *Vanishing Point* will recognize the lines of its four-wheeled star in this latest version of the model, despite the four-decade gap since the original.

△ MG ZT 260 2001

Origin UK

Engine 4,601 cc, V8

Top speed 155 mph (249 km/h)

Based on Rover's 75 saloon, MG put in a Ford V8 and converted it to rear-wheel drive, creating a car with big performance under a subtle exterior.

△ Maybach 57 2002

Origin Germany

Engine 5,980 cc, V12

Top speed 155 mph (249 km/h)

Having not built cars since 1940, this marque had been long dead until it was revived by Daimler-Benz as its hyper-luxury brand in 2002.

△ Mercedes-Benz CLK 320 2002

Origin Germany

Engine 3,199 cc, V6

Top speed 155 mph (249 km/h)

Based on the company's C-Class models, this car is closer to the E-Class in price. It keeps alive Mercedes-Benz's tradition of offering convertibles.

△ Cadillac STS 2005

Origin USA

Engine 4,371 cc, V8

Top speed 155 mph (249 km/h)

Sharp-suited styling and taut handling are at odds with the ungainly, fin-tailed Cadillacs of old. Fitting a supercharger to the Northstar V8 produced 469 bhp for the STS-V model.

◁ Ford Mustang GT convertible 2004

Origin USA

Engine 4,951 cc, V8

Top speed 149 mph (240 km/h)

The Mustang's design team took styling cues from the very first Mustang for the 2004 model – these included the scallops down the sides and the set-back headlights.

▷ Maserati Quattroporte 2004

Origin Italy

Engine 4,691 cc, V8

Top speed 174 mph (280 km/h)

The name simply means "four doors", but it sounds so much more exciting in Italian. The Quattroporte's 434 bhp V8 delivers performance to match.

△ BMW Alpina B7 Bi-Turbo 2010

Origin Germany

Engine 4,395 cc, V8

Top speed 188 mph (302 km/h)

Officially registered as a manufacturer, Alpina creates high-performance versions of BMWs, such as this polished 7 Series that delivers 500 bhp.

▷ Lexus IS-F 2005

Origin Japan

Engine 4,969 cc, V8

Top speed 155 mph (249 km/h)

Japanese team Gazoo Racing prepared this Lexus to compete in a 24-hour race at the challenging Nürburgring Nordschleife circuit in Germany.

△ **Rolls-Royce Phantom 2003**

Origin UK

Engine 6,750 cc, V12

Top speed 155 mph (249 km/h)

When BMW took control of Rolls-Royce, it built a new factory near Goodwood and created a car that captured the marque's legendary presence.

△ **Rolls-Royce Phantom drophead 2007**

Origin UK

Engine 6,750 cc, V12

Top speed 155 mph (249 km/h)

The drophead's styling remained remarkably faithful to the 100EX, a concept car unveiled to mark the centenary of the company in 2006.

▷ **Infiniti G37 convertible 2009**

Origin Japan

Engine 3,696 cc, V6

Top speed 155 mph (249 km/h)

The Infiniti brand was created by Nissan to overcome resistance in the US market to Japanese cars and is reserved for prestige models.

◁ **Audi A5 Coupé 2007**

Origin Germany

Engine 2,967 cc, V6

Top speed 155 mph (249 km/h)

Reviving Audi's stylish 1970s coupé, the A5's shape was drawn from the Nuvolari quattro concept car exhibited at the 2003 Geneva Motor Show.

△ **Porsche Panamera 4S 2009**

Origin Germany

Engine 4,806 cc, V8

Top speed 175 mph (282 km/h)

Despite putting the engine up front and adding two extra doors, the Panamera manages to retain styling cues that date back to the 911 of the 1960s.

△ **Chevrolet Camaro 2SS 2010**

Origin USA

Engine 6,162 cc, V8

Top speed 155 mph (249 km/h)

Blending 1960s styling with 21st-century film culture, the fifth-generation Chevrolet Camaro is also available in a *Transformers* special edition.

▽ **Aston Martin Rapide 2010**

Origin UK

Engine 5,935 cc, V12

Top speed 184 mph (296 km/h)

Offering four doors in a supercar package, the Rapide takes its name from the 1930s Lagonda model, a famous marque Aston Martin acquired in 1947.

△ **Jaguar XJ 2009**

Origin UK

Engine 5,000 cc, V8

Top speed 155 mph (249 km/h)

The all new XJ has an aerospace-inspired aluminium frame made from 50 per cent recycled material. This is about 150 kg (330 lb) lighter than its steel rivals.

△ **Jaguar XF 2008**

Origin UK

Engine 5,000 cc, V8

Top speed 155 mph (249 km/h)

With this model, Jaguar aimed to re-create the appeal of its mid-sized S-Type model from the 1960s and make Jaguar quality more affordable.

Crossovers and Off-roaders

For 50 years the trend had been to build cars lower and sleeker, but designers realized that people were increasingly buying four-wheel-drive vehicles because they wanted higher, safer-feeling cars. A surge in production of "crossover" vehicles followed, some with only limited off-road ability.

△ **Land Rover Discovery Series II 1998**
Origin UK
Engine 2,495 cc, straight-five
Top speed 98 mph (158 km/h)

Launched in 1989 for a new market segment where style and comfort were important, the Discovery retained exceptional off-road ability and sold strongly.

△ **Land Rover Discovery 3 2004**
Origin UK
Engine 4,394 cc, V8
Top speed 121 mph (195 km/h)

Sold as the LR3 in North America, this model has a completely new design with monocoque construction and an all-independent air suspension. It has exceptional off/on-road ability.

△ **Honda CR-V 2001**
Origin Japan
Engine 1,998 cc, straight-four
Top speed 110 mph (177 km/h)

The CR-V was one of the first two- or four-wheel-drive option SUVs when launched in 1996. It saw the market niche grow dramatically, and frequent upgrades (this one in 2001) kept it popular.

△ **Renault Avantime 2001**
Origin France
Engine 2,946 cc, V6
Top speed 137 mph (220 km/h)

Designed and built by Matra, this innovative crossover between a two-door coupé and an MPV failed to find a market niche; just 8,557 were sold in 2001–03.

◁ **Subaru Tribeca 2005**
Origin Japan
Engine 2,999 cc, flat-six
Top speed 121 mph (195 km/h)

Based on the Legacy car platform, the Tribeca benefits from Subaru's long four-wheel-drive and rallying heritage. The lightweight, flat engine gives it a low centre of gravity.

△ **Chevrolet Tahoe 2005**
Origin USA
Engine 5,300 cc, V8
Top speed 123 mph (198 km/h)

A full-size SUV from General Motors, this car is also sold as GMC Yukon and LWB Chevy Suburban. It is available as a two- or four-wheel drive, or as a hybrid.

▷ **Chevrolet HHR 2005**
Origin USA
Engine 2,130 cc, straight-four
Top speed 110 mph (177 km/h)

HHR stands for "Heritage High Roof", referring to styling inspired by the 1949 Chevrolet Suburban. The HHR is also available as a panel van, or turbocharged.

◁ **BMW X3 2004**
Origin Germany/Austria
Engine 2,494 cc, straight-six
Top speed 129 mph (208 km/h)

Designed and built by Magna Steyr of Austria, the X3 was based on the four-wheel-drive 3-Series saloon, and so lacked optimum off-road ability.

▷ **Mazda CX-7 2006**
Origin Japan
Engine 2,260 cc, straight-four
Top speed 130 mph (209 km/h)

Unlike most opposition, Mazda's mid-size crossover SUV is built on an all-new platform. It is clearly primarily a luxury road car, with two- or four-wheel-drive options.

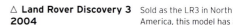

△ Toyota Highlander 2000

Origin Japan

Engine 2,995 cc, V6

Top speed 125 mph (201 km/h)

The first car-based mid-size crossover SUV, based on the Camry platform, this was Toyota's best-selling SUV for the first half of the decade.

▷ Toyota Sienna 2006

Origin Japan

Engine 3,310 cc, V6

Top speed 111 mph (179 km/h)

A family mini van, or MPV, the front-wheel-drive Sienna was launched in 1997. Four-wheel drive became an option in 2004, but this is not an off-road vehicle.

▷ Nissan Qashqai 2006

Origin Japan/UK

Engine 1,997 cc, straight-four

Top speed 119 mph (192 km/h)

The Qashqai sold 100,000 units in its first year. Primarily a road car with two- or four-wheel drive, it has fair off-road ability.

▽ Nissan Rogue 2007

Origin Japan

Engine 2,488 cc, straight-four

Top speed 120 mph (193 km/h)

The North American equivalent of the Qashqai is a compact crossover SUV with constantly variable transmission, and front- or four-wheel drive.

△ Saturn Outlook 2006

Origin USA

Engine 3,600 cc, V6

Top speed 120 mph (193 km/h)

General Motors launched Saturn in 1987 and closed it in 2010. The Outlook was a full-size crossover SUV with eight seats and front- or four-wheel drive.

▷ Volkswagen Touran 2003

Origin Germany

Engine 1,968 cc, straight-four

Top speed 122 mph (196 km/h)

Based on the four-wheel-drive VW Golf, the Touran was a compact SUV that was offered with petrol, diesel, or LPG engines from 1.2 to 2.0 litre, hybrid or battery-only.

△ Ford Kuga 2008

Origin Germany

Engine 2,522 cc, straight-five

Top speed 129 mph (208 km/h)

Based on the Focus platform with front- or four-wheel-drive options, the Kuga is aimed at the on-road premium market with performance engines and a high standard of trim.

△ Jeep Patriot 2007

Origin USA

Engine 1,968 cc, straight-four

Top speed 117 mph (188 km/h)

Jeep's entry into the compact SUV market, the Patriot is sold with completely different choices of engine and drive packages in Europe and in the US.

▷ Ford Escape Hybrid 2009

Origin USA

Engine 2,488 cc, straight-four

Top speed 102 mph (164 km/h)

Launched in 2004, the Escape was the first hybrid (petrol and electric) SUV on the market. It was also the first US-built hybrid from a US manufacturer.

City Cars

As manufacturers worldwide strove to meet legislation that demanded reduced emissions and greater fuel efficiency, interest turned again to tiny city cars with two, or at most four, seats. Some manufacturers produced tiny, sub-1,000cc, two- or three-cylinder cars designed for city use. Others made small cars that could still be comfortable on motorways, and had efficient-running, lightly stressed, four-cylinder engines.

◁ **REVA/G-Wiz i 2001**

Origin India

Engine Electric motor

Top speed 50 mph (80 km/h)

The world's best-selling electric car of the decade was this 2+2 Indian model with a 75-mile (120-km) range. A larger and safer model was planned for the next decade.

△ **Smart City-Coupé 1998**

Origin Germany/France

Engine 599 cc, straight-three

Top speed 84 mph (135 km/h)

The most popular two-seat city car yet was the vision of Swatch creator Nicolas Hayek. Features included rear-wheel drive, electronic stability control, and anti-lock braking.

▷ **Ligier Ambra 2000**

Origin France

Engine 505 cc, straight-two

Top speed 65 mph (105 km/h)

Former F1 racing-car maker Ligier has long catered for the two-seat "quadricycle" market. The car has tax and regulatory advantages, but is limited to 550 kg (1,212 lb) and 20 bhp.

△ **Fiat Panda 2003**

Origin Italy/Poland

Engine 1,108 cc, straight-four

Top speed 93 mph (150 km/h)

The Panda of 2003 proved a worthy successor to the name. It was voted European Car of the Year in 2004 and sold 1.5 million in its first six years. It had 1.1-1.4-litre engines.

▷ **Subaru R1 2005**

Origin Japan

Engine 658 cc, straight-four

Top speed 85 mph (137 km/h)

Not widely marketed outside Japan, the R1 was a short, 2+2, upmarket sporty model in the Japanese *kei car* cheap tax bracket. The R1 had leather trim and optional supercharger.

◁ **Opel/Vauxhall Agila 2000**

Origin Poland

Engine 973 cc, straight-three

Top speed 88 mph (142 km/h)

Badged as a Vauxhall in the UK, the Opel was a version of Suzuki's Wagon-R or Splash. It had five doors and good interior space.

▷ **Kia Picanto 2005**

Origin South Korea

Engine 999 cc, straight-four

Top speed 93 mph (150 km/h)

Built on a Hyundai Getz platform, the Picanto had 1.0- or 1.1-litre petrol engines, or a 3-cylinder direct-injection turbodiesel engine. In Europe it sold as a budget car.

▷ Toyota Yaris/Vitz 2005
Origin France
Engine 1,364 cc, straight-four
Top speed 109 mph (175 km/h)

Designed in Toyota's European studios and sold worldwide with engines from 1.0- to 1.8-litre, this second generation Yaris was the first in its class to have nine airbags.

◁ Toyota iQ 2008
Origin Japan
Engine 1,329 cc, straight-four
Top speed 106 mph (171 km/h)

The ultra-compact iQ had four seats, good performance, and a five-star European crash safety rating. Stability control, anti-lock brakes, and brake assist were all standard.

△ Peugeot 1007 2004
Origin France
Engine 1,360 cc, straight-four
Top speed 107 mph (172 km/h)

This was a brave attempt to market an unconventional city car with powered sliding doors and semi-automatic gears. Sales were poor, however, due to its high price.

△ Fiat 500 2007
Origin Italy/ Poland
Engine 1,242 cc, straight-four
Top speed 99 mph (159 km/h)

Retro-styling gave Fiat a new best-seller with this well-engineered four-seater. It had 1.2–1.4-litre engines at its launch; more options were added later.

△ Toyota Aygo 2005
Origin Japan/Czech Republic
Engine 998 cc, straight-three
Top speed 98 mph (158 km/h)

Built alongside the identical Peugeot 107 and Citroën C1, the Aygo had three- or five-door options and a 1.0-litre petrol or 1.4-litre diesel engine.

△ Tata Nano 2009
Origin India
Engine 624 cc, straight-two
Top speed 65 mph (105 km/h)

This home-market Indian car has attracted worldwide interest due to its price (under $3,000). Stripped of all extras, it is potentially the Ford Model T of the 21st century.

◁ Secma F16 Sport 2008
Origin France
Engine 1,598 cc, four-cylinder
Top speed 110 mph (177 km/h)

Weighing just half a tonne, the F16 promises fun but little practicality, even with its optional gullwing doors. It has a rear-mounted, fuel-injected 16-valve Renault engine.

Towards 200 mph

After the Ferrari F40 road car passed the 200 mph mark in 1987, this figure became the badge of honour for any supercar to aspire to. Some machines, German ones especially, had factory-fitted speed limiters to bridle owners' enthusiasm. The 250 mph Bugatti Veyron went a step further in 2005 with its technical magnificence.

△ Lamborghini Murcièlago Roadster 2004

Origin Italy

Engine 6,496 cc, V12

Top speed 200 mph (322 km/h)

Fighter aircraft, Spanish architecture, and mega-yachts were among the things that inspired the styling of this awesome, soft-top Lamborghini, with its low-tech manually-operated roof.

△ Pagani Zonda 1999

Origin Italy

Engine 7,291 cc, V12

Top speed 220 mph (354 km/h)

Some early development was done on the Zonda by five-time Formula 1 champion Juan Manuel Fangio. With just 10 cars built each year, it is a rare delicacy.

◁ Lamborghini Murcièlago 2001

Origin Italy

Engine 6,496 cc, V12

Top speed 213 mph (343 km/h)

The first new model under Volkswagen ownership, the Murcièlago was named after a famous fighting bull that survived 28 sword strokes in Spain in 1879.

◁ Bentley Continental Supersport 2003

Origin UK

Engine 5,998 cc, W12

Top speed 204 mph (328 km/h)

An attempt to unleash the performance potential of this luxury coupé, cued a stripped-out interior, no rear seat, pumped-up suspension, and 630 bhp.

△ Aston Martin V12 Vantage 2009

Origin UK

Engine 5,935 cc, V12

Top speed 190 mph (306 km/h)

The V12 engine shoehorned into the V8 Vantage and pumped up to give more than 500 bhp produces an irresistible combination of performance and agility.

△ Caparo T1 2007

Origin UK

Engine 3,496 cc, V8

Top speed 205 mph (330 km/h)

Inspired by racing cars, the T1 was designed by Formula 1 engineers and is powered by an engine descended from Indianapolis racers.

◁ Ferrari Enzo 2002

Origin Italy

Engine 5,998 cc, V12

Top speed 226 mph (363 km/h)

The ultimate Ferrari road car when it was released, just 400 models were produced for the most wealthy and discerning customers.

△ Ferrari 599 GTB Fiorano 2006

Origin Italy

Engine 5,999 cc, V12

Top speed 205 mph (330 km/h)

The archetypal Ferrari for the modern age, this civilized coupé with the classic V12 engine up front is blisteringly quick.

△ **Bristol Fighter 2004**

Origin UK

Engine 7,996 cc, V10

Top speed 225 mph (362 km/h)

Produced in very small numbers, strictly to order, the top-of-the-range Fighter T extracts more than 1,000 bhp from its Chrysler Viper engine.

▷ **Bugatti Veyron Grand Sport 2005**

Origin France

Engine 7,993 cc, W16

Top speed 253 mph (407 km/h)

Rumour has it that the company loses money on every car it builds, but the prestige and technology benefits to the parent company Volkswagen are worth it.

▷ **Koenigsegg CCX-R 2006**

Origin Sweden

Engine 4,719 cc, V8

Top speed 250 mph (402 km/h)

This car's engine is based on Ford's V8, but with almost every component, including the block, modified or re-manufactured to give 800 bhp.

▷ **Nissan GT-R Spec V 2007**

Origin Japan

Engine 3,799 cc, V6, twin-turbo

Top speed 193 mph (311 km/h)

A stripped-out version of the standard GT-R, the Spec V features racing front seats, no rear seat, and carbon-fibre, aerodynamic bodywork trim.

△ **Mercedes-McLaren SLR 722S 2003**

Origin UK

Engine 5,439 cc, V8

Top speed 209 mph (336 km/h)

The 722 in the name is a tribute to the race number of the Mille Miglia-winning Mercedes driven by Sir Stirling Moss in 1955.

△ **Mercedes-Benz SLS AMG 2010**

Origin Germany

Engine 6,208 cc, V8

Top speed 197 mph (317 km/h)

An attempt to recapture the spirit of the 1950s 300SL Gullwing, the SLS was designed in-house by AMG and saw action as Formula 1's safety car.

△ **Mercedes-Benz SL65 Black 2008**

Origin Germany

Engine 5,980 cc, V12

Top speed 155 mph (249 km/h)

Produced in limited numbers, this ultimate version of the SL roadster would exceed 200 mph (322 km/h) if there was no electronic speed limiter fitted in it.

△ **RUF Porsche CTR3 2007**

Origin Germany

Engine 3,746 cc, flat-six

Top speed 233 mph (375 km/h)

The highly respected German tuner RUF is famous for its uncompromising versions of Porsches. This one features weight-saving, carbon-fibre bodywork, and a 691 bhp engine.

◁ **Lexus LFA 2010**

Origin Japan

Engine 4,805 cc, V10

Top speed 203 mph (327 km/h)

The pearl in this oyster is the 1LR-GUE V10 engine that is smaller than most V8s and will rev from tickover to 9,500 rpm in just 0.6 seconds.

△ **Noble M600 2009**

Origin UK

Engine 4,439 cc, V8

Top speed 225 mph (362 km/h)

From the company founded by the highly respected maverick car designer Lee Noble, the M600 is thought by some to be one of the finest-handling current supercars.

Motor Sports Contenders

At the start of the 21st century the biggest impact on the design and manufacture of racing cars was created by computers. Their influence was so great that they had to be severely limited within the car to stop them from taking over the driving. Now the typical racing car has fewer computer systems than the average road car, but they still have a huge impact on the way these machines are designed and operated.

△ **Aston Martin DBR9 2005**

Origin UK

Engine 6,000 cc, V12

Top speed 186 mph (299 km/h)

Winning on its debut at Sebring in the US in 2005, the future looked bright for the DBR9, and it bagged a Le Mans class win in France in 2007.

▷ **Lola Aston Martin LMP1 2009**

Origin UK

Engine 6,000 cc, V12

Top speed 209 mph (336 km/h)

Having conquered GT racing with its DBR9, Aston Martin transferred its V12 engine into a Lola chassis to tackle the GT1 Prototype class.

△ **Bentley Speed 8 2001**

Origin UK

Engine 4,000 cc, V8

Top speed 205 mph (330 km/h)

Returning to Le Mans 73 years after its glory days in the 1920s, it took Bentley three attempts before winning once again in 2003.

◁ **BAR Honda 2004**

Origin UK

Engine 3,000 cc, V10

Top speed 200 mph (322 km/h)

Engine supplier Honda bought the BAR team, but only managed one win before pulling out at the end of 2008. The team then became Brawn.

△ **Mercedes-Benz CLK DTM 2003**

Origin Germany

Engine 4,000 cc, V8

Top speed 180 mph (290 km/h)

Based on a tubular-steel chassis and powered by V8 engines, German Touring Cars have only a passing resemblance to the production models they represent.

△ **McLaren-Mercedes MP4/23 2008**

Origin UK

Engine 2,400 cc, V8

Top speed 200 mph (322 km/h)

In only his second season of Formula 1 Grand Prix racing, Lewis Hamilton became the youngest world champion ever at the wheel of this car.

◁ **Chevrolet Monte Carlo 2001**

Origin USA

Engine 5,860 cc, V8

Top speed 190 mph (306 km/h)

Prepared for North American Stock Car racing, this one was raced by the late NASCAR legend Dale Earnhardt, known to his fans as the "Intimidator".

△ **Dodge Charger 2005**

Origin USA

Engine 5,860 cc, V8

Top speed 190 mph (306 km/h)

Although branded a Charger, very little of the road car is used in NASCAR; just the engine within a purpose-built tubular chassis and sheet metal body.

Audi R Series

The Le Mans 24-hour race in France is one of the three biggest races in the world and renowned for being one of the toughest challenges in motor sport. For the first decade of this century the race has been dominated by Audi, which won 9 times out of 11 races between 2000 and 2010; a remarkable achievement.

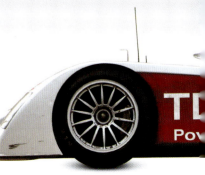

△ **Audi R8 2000**

Origin Germany

Engine 3,600 cc, V8

Top speed 211 mph (339 km/h)

One of the most successful endurance racing cars ever, the R8 won Le Mans five times over six years, only losing out to Audi-owned Bentley in 2003.

▷ Red Bull-Cosworth STR1 2006

Origin UK

Engine 3,000 cc, V10

Top speed 200 mph (322 km/h)

In 2004 when Red Bull was sponsoring the Sauber team, it bought Jaguar Racing from Ford for a symbolic $1 and is now a front runner in Formula 1.

▽ Toyota TF108 2008

Origin Germany

Engine 2,400 cc, V8

Top speed 200 mph (322 km/h)

Entering Formula 1 in 2002, Toyota had moments of promise but never won a race. It eventually pulled out after the 2009 season.

△ Ferrari F2008 2008

Origin Italy

Engine 2,400 cc, V8

Top speed 200 mph (322 km/h)

Having impressed in the F2007, Kimi Räikkönen, in the heavier F2008, helped Felipe Massa deliver F1 team championship honours for the 2008 season.

△ Toyota Camry, NASCAR Nextel Cup 2007

Origin Japan

Engine 5,860 cc, V8

Top speed 190 mph (306 km/h)

To take part in NASCAR, Toyota had to produce a push-rod V8 engine, an archaic design it would never have contemplated otherwise.

◁ BMW M3 GT2 2008

Origin Germany

Engine 3,999 cc, V8

Top speed 180 mph (290 km/h)

Introduced for the American Le Mans series in 2009, this car raced at Le Mans in 2010 and was the cover car for the racing game *Need for Speed*.

△ Peugeot 908 HDI FAP 2009

Origin France

Engine 5,500 cc, V12

Top speed 212 mph (341 km/h)

Peugeot entered Le Mans in France with the diesel 908 in 2009 and won the race – breaking Audi's dominance in the process.

◁ Audi R10 TDI 2006

Origin Germany

Engine 5,500 cc, V12

Top speed 211 mph (339 km/h)

Following on from a string of successes with the petrol-engined R8, the R10 became the first diesel-engined car to win Le Mans.

△ Audi R15 TDI 2009

Origin Germany

Engine 5,500 cc, V10

Top speed 205 mph (330 km/h)

Although the R10 was fast, its handling was compromised by a heavy V12 engine. Changing to a V10 design made the engine lighter and the car faster.

Compact Genius

Ever-shrinking microchip technology has allowed more and more functionality to be added to cars, putting paid to the idea that the smallest vehicles must be stripped of all extra features. Engineers know that lighter cars are the most fuel-efficient, but legislators – and the driving public – insist on the latest safety systems, and these naturally add weight. Designers wrestle with these requirements as they create the latest models, ensuring that size is no barrier to safety, comfort, and efficiency.

▷ Honda Fit/Jazz MkI 2001

Origin Japan
Engine 1,497 cc, four-cylinder
Top speed 106 mph (171 km/h)

As the Civic became larger, Honda attacked the supermini sector anew with the Honda Fit (or Jazz in Europe). It became an instant class benchmark.

◁ BMW 1 series 2004

Origin Germany
Engine 1,599 cc, four-cylinder
Top speed 138 mph (222 km/h)

BMW's 1 Series reworked the 3 Series in a tighter package. As well as this five-door model, there was a three-door version, a coupé, and a convertible.

◁ Mercedes-Benz A-Class MkII 2004

Origin Germany
Engine 2,034 cc, four-cylinder
Top speed 114 mph (183 km/h)

The 1997 Mercedes-Benz A-Class was a small car designed so that its engine diverted below the cabin in the event of a crash. This is the more mature, second-generation model.

▷ Toyota Prius MkII 2004

Origin Japan
Engine 1,496 cc, four-cylinder
Top speed 104 mph (167 km/h)

With a 76 bhp petrol engine augmented by a 68 bhp electric motor – plus on-the-move battery recharging – the Prius MkII offered minimal fuel consumption.

▷ Toyota iQ 2008

Origin Japan
Engine 1,329 cc, three-cylinder
Top speed 106 mph (171 km/h)

This is Toyota's upmarket city car. Clever features abound, including a three-cylinder engine, slimline seats, nine airbags, and electronic stability control.

▽ MCC Smart Crossblade 2002

Origin France
Engine 599 cc, three-cylinder
Top speed 84 mph (135 km/h)

The Smart City-Cabrio was a tiny car, but the Crossblade (of which 2,000 were built) was pared down even further. It had no doors, no windscreen, and no roof.

◁ MCC Smart Roadster 2003

Origin France
Engine 698 cc, three-cylinder
Top speed 109 mph (175 km/h)

This tiny two-seater extended the Smart city car philosophy to create a latterday Frogeye Sprite. It was fun to drive, and economical.

▷ **Renault Megane MkII 2002**

Origin France

Engine 1,998 cc, four-cylinder

Top speed 149 mph (240 km/h)

Designers at Renault caused a stir with the upright rear window of this second-generation Megane. As before, the five-door family car was only one of many Megane incarnations.

△ **Citroën DS3 2009**

Origin France

Engine 1,598 cc, four-cylinder

Top speed 133 mph (214 km/h)

There is nothing retro about the neat DS3 – nothing links it to the famous DS of old – but the short length and massive cabin make it an intriguing Mini alternative.

▷ **Opel/Vauxhall Astra 2004**

Origin Germany/UK

Engine 1,998 cc, four-cylinder

Top speed 152 mph (245 km/h)

The Astra, from General Motors Europe, took a quantum leap forwards in its design in 2004. This three-door car, called the GTC, introduced a panoramic windscreen stretching into the roof panel.

▽ **Peugeot RCZ THP 200 2010**

Origin France/Austria

Engine 1,997cc, four-cylinder

Top speed 146 mph (235 km/h)

This coupé, which is similar in size to Audi's TT, began life as a motor show concept car, but huge public demand pushed it into showrooms. It has two small seats in the back.

△ **Volvo C70 MkII 2006**

Origin Sweden

Engine 2,521cc, five-cylinder

Top speed 130 mph (209 km/h)

This four-seater is not small, but the all-steel, three-part roof mechanism that converts it from snug saloon to open convertible is a masterpiece of space-efficiency.

▷ **Ford Streetka 2003**

Origin Spain/Italy

Engine 1,597 cc, four-cylinder

Top speed 108 mph (174 km/h)

Ford based this tiny two-seat roadster on its Ka hatchback. Designed and built in Italy, it was given a traditional fabric hood, and launched by diminutive pop star Kylie Minogue.

◁ **Ford Focus Mk2 RS 2009**

Origin Germany

Engine 2,522 cc, five-cylinder

Top speed 163 mph (262 km/h)

With over 300 bhp of power going through the front wheels of what is essentially a family hatchback, the Mk2 has bespoke limited-slip differential and front suspension.

◁ **Alfa Romeo MiTo 2008**

Origin Italy

Engine 1,593 cc, four-cylinder

Top speed 136 mph (219 km/h)

Sharing its underpinnings with the Fiat Grande Punto, this was the first ever really small Alfa. MiTo stands for Milan, where it was designed, and Turin, where it is built.

△ **Scion xB 2007**

Origin Japan

Engine 2,362 cc, four-cylinder

Top speed 109 mph (175 km/h)

To target younger US buyers, Toyota introduced its Scion sub-brand in 2004. The chunky xB, now in its second incarnation, is the mainstay.

▽ **Cadillac CTS-V coupé 2010**

Origin USA

Engine 6,162 cc, V8

Top speed 191 mph (307 km/h)

The stocky CTS-V saloon holds the production car record for lapping Germany's Nürburgring, at 7min 59.3sec. This coupé shares its 556 bhp power unit.

▷ **Mini Clubman 2008**

Origin UK

Engine 1,598 cc, four-cylinder

Top speed 125 mph (201 km/h)

BMW's reinvention of the Mini saw the production of this estate car. It has twin, van-style doors at the rear, and a small "clubdoor" on the driver's side.

High-performance Sports Cars

In the last couple of decades, a whole new tier of cars has emerged that bridges the gap between sports cars and supercars. They range from hot versions of affordable coupés and roadsters to entry-level models from prestige manufacturers. Stylish and exciting, their existence proves that demand for performance has never been stronger – and the choice has never been wider.

△ **Ferrari F430 2004**

Origin Italy

Engine 4,308 cc, V8

Top speed 196 mph (315 km/h)

The first Ferrari road car to use an electronically-controlled differential, derived directly from the company's F1 traction, the F430 was aerodynamically designed underneath as well as on top.

△ **Morgan Aero 8 2001**

Origin UK

Engine 4,398 cc, V8

Top speed 150 mph (241 km/h)

The overall profile may have been familiar, but the Aero 8 was a radical car for Morgan, the first with an aluminium chassis and a BMW V8 engine.

△ **Ferrari California 2008**

Origin Italy

Engine 4,297 cc, V8

Top speed 193 mph (311 km/h)

This is the first time Ferrari has put a V8 engine in the front of one of its road cars; the shape is the result of 1,000 hours in the wind tunnel.

△ **Aston Martin DB9 2003**

Origin UK

Engine 5,935 cc, V12

Top speed 190 mph (306 km/h)

Sporting the company's new V12 engine, the DB9 was the car that ushered in a new era of Aston Martin under Ford ownership.

◁ **Aston Martin Vanquish 2001**

Origin UK

Engine 5,935 cc, V12

Top speed 196 mph (315 km/h)

This car re-created the link with James Bond when Pierce Brosnan was issued with one in the film *Die Another Day*.

△ **Ferrari 458 Italia 2009**

Origin Italy

Engine 4,499 cc, V8

Top speed 202 mph (325 km/h)

This car received input from former world champion Michael Schumacher, and it features winglets that drop at speed to reduce drag.

◁ **Aston Martin V8 Vantage convertible 2005**

Origin UK

Engine 4,735 cc, V8

Top speed 180 mph (290 km/h)

With a V8 from Ford-owned Jaguar, it may be a smaller car than the DB9, but there is plenty of performance and nimble handling.

△ **Mercedes-Benz SL 2008**

Origin Germany

Engine 5,513 cc, V12

Top speed 155 mph (249 km/h)

Back in 1954 the 300SL Gullwing was a genuine supercar. The latest version retains that tradition with more than 500 bhp on tap.

▷ **Audi R8 2006**

Origin Germany

Engine 5,204 cc, V10

Top speed 196 mph (315 km/h)

Inspired by the company's multiple Le Mans-winning car of the same name, this is a fully fledged, Porsche-rivalling supercar with performance to match.

△ **Spyker C8 Laviolette 2001**

Origin Holland

Engine 4,172 cc, V8

Top speed 187 mph (301 km/h)

The Laviolette's design draws heavily from the company's aviation past, and even the spokes of the steering wheel look like propeller blades.

△ **Porsche 911 Turbo 2006**

Origin Germany

Engine 3,600 cc, flat-six

Top speed 198 mph (319 km/h)

Unofficially referred to as the 997, this is the spiritual descendant of the original 911 and still has its engine hanging out the back.

△ **Chevrolet Corvette C6 2005**

Origin USA

Engine 5,967 cc, V8

Top speed 198 mph (319 km/h)

Originally known as a car that had looks and power but little else, this Corvette can also boast of handling to match.

◁ **Nissan 350Z 2008**

Origin Japan

Engine 3,498 cc, V6

Top speed 156 mph (251 km/h)

Following an online contest in the computer game *Gran Turismo*, the quickest drivers competed for the prize of a real race drive with the Nissan team.

△ **Artega GT 2009**

Origin Germany

Engine 3,597 cc, V6

Top speed 170 mph (274 km/h)

Styled by Henrik Fisker, also responsible for the Aston Martin Vantage, the Artega is focused on low weight. At just 1,100 kg (2,205 lb), it is light for a supercar.

◁ **Maserati Coupé 2002**

Origin Italy

Engine 4,244 cc, V8

Top speed 177 mph (285 km/h)

Being part of the Fiat stable alongside Ferrari, Maserati concentrates on grand tourers rather than outright sports cars.

△ **Alfa Romeo 8C Competizione 2007**

Origin Italy

Engine 4,691 cc, V8

Top speed 181 mph (292 km/h)

Few believed that the design study exhibited at the 2003 Frankfurt Motor Show would ever make it into production, but Alfa built 500 coupés.

▷ **Maserati Granturismo S 2007**

Origin Italy

Engine 4,691 cc, V8

Top speed 183 mph (295 km/h)

Although based on the floorpan of the Quattroporte saloon, the Granturismo S is a very fast GT with the bonus of two extra rear seats.

△ **Jaguar XKR 75 2010**

Origin UK

Engine 5,000 cc, V8

Top speed 174 mph (280 km/h)

To celebrate the company's 75th anniversary, Jaguar built 75 of these special edition XKRs with improved handling and engines updated to 530 bhp.

Sports Cars

In the 1980s many thought the sports car could become extinct, but they are now back with a vengeance. Every major car manufacturer today has its own interpretation of the sports car, and legions of small specialists build nothing else. Ranging from cutting-edge concepts to shameless attempts at evoking the past, the golden rule is that they should always be fun.

△ Ariel Atom 1996

Origin UK

Engine 1,998 cc, straight-four

Top speed 140 mph (225 km/h)

This is as stripped down as a car gets: a steel frame hung with the bare essentials, and bodywork positively prohibited. The Atom is still in production.

▷ Vauxhall VX220 2000

Origin UK

Engine 1,998 cc, straight-four

Top speed 150 mph (241 km/h)

Also branded as an Opel and a Daewoo, the VX220 was developed by Lotus Cars and based on the Elise chassis, but with a GM engine.

△ Lotus Elise 340R 2000

Origin UK

Engine 1,795 cc, straight-four

Top speed 130 mph (209 km/h)

The car was designed in collaboration with *Autocar* magazine and developed from the Elise. Just 340 examples of this were produced, all finished in black and silver.

△ Lotus Elise 2000

Origin UK

Engine 1,792 cc, straight-four

Top speed 145 mph (233 km/h)

Praised for its extreme light weight and wonderful handling, the Elise exceeded all expectations. In 2000 Lotus introduced a restyled version of its Elise to meet European crash regulations.

▷ Lotus Evora 2009

Origin UK

Engine 3,456 cc, V6

Top speed 162 mph (261 km/h)

With legendary Lotus handling and 2+2 accommodation, Lotus hoped this car would find fans among performance-loving drivers with young families.

◁ Ginetta/Farbio F400 2002

Origin UK

Engine 2,967 cc, V6

Top speed 185 mph (298 km/h)

From Farboud to Farbio to Ginetta, this car had a difficult birth but has always been impressive. With its carbon-fibre chassis, it weighs just 1,046 kg (2,205 lb).

△ Ginetta G50 EV 2009

Origin UK

Engine Electric motor

Top speed 120 mph (193 km/h)

Shattering the illusion that electric power is for milk floats, the G50 EV is a low-carbon vehicle that also delivers a thrilling drive.

▽ MG TF 2002

Origin UK

Engine 1,795 cc, straight-four

Top speed 127 mph (204 km/h)

Re-engineered to improve its stiffness and crash protection, and then relaunched in 2002, the MG F was renamed the TF in tribute to the 1950s MG.

△ BMW Z4 2002

Origin Germany

Engine 2,996 cc, straight-six

Top speed 155 mph (249 km/h)

With a straight-six engine up front and rear-wheel drive, this is a rare chance to experience the thrill of a classic 1950s-style sports car.

△ Mercedes-Benz SLK 2004
Origin Germany
Engine 5,439 cc, V8
Top speed 155 mph (249 km/h)

The SLK was revised in 2004 to update its styling and improve its performance. This Mark II R171 version was named one of the "Ten Best" by a US car magazine.

▷ Pontiac Solstice 2005
Origin USA
Engine 2,376 cc, straight-four
Top speed 120 mph (193 km/h)

This European-style roadster from General Motors was a hit when launched but production ended just four years later when the Wilmington factory closed.

▷ Mazda MX-5 2005
Origin Japan
Engine 1,999 cc, straight-four
Top speed 131 mph (211 km/h)

This Mark III MX-5 is perhaps the most perfect mass-production sports car ever conceived; even beyond its 20th birthday it still sells well.

△ Porsche Cayman 2006
Origin Germany
Engine 3,436 cc, flat-six
Top speed 171 mph (275 km/h)

More than just a Boxster with a roof, the Cayman captures the spirit of the original 911 and arguably offers all the performance you could need.

△ Audi TT 2006
Origin Germany
Engine 2,480 cc, straight-five
Top speed 155 mph (249 km/h)

In its original form, the TT captured attention with its striking retro look and the latest version remains faithful to that classic coupé style.

▷ Caterham Superlight 300 2007
Origin UK
Engine 1,999 cc, straight-four
Top speed 140 mph (225 km/h)

Descended from the 1950s Lotus Seven that inspired a legion of imitators, the Caterham is the rightful heir to the original. It had the fastest 0–60 mph acceleration when launched.

△ Alfa Romeo Spider 2006
Origin Italy
Engine 3,195 cc, V6
Top speed 144 mph (232 km/h)

With a direct lineage going back to the 1950s, the Spider is an icon, even though the latest version has given in to front-wheel drive.

△ KTM X-Bow 2008
Origin Austria
Engine 1,984 cc, straight-four
Top speed 136 mph (219 km/h)

The first car to be produced by this motorcycle manufacturer offers little more comfort than a two-wheeler, but it provides just as much of a thrill.

▽ Tramontana 2007
Origin Spain
Engine 5,513 cc, V12, twin-turbo
Top speed 202 mph (325 km/h)

A monster in all respects, the passenger seat is an optional extra and is mounted directly behind the driver. Just 12 cars are built each year.

Off-road Luxury and Power

The 1990s trend for using big 4x4s as road cars developed into large-scale production of big, fast, luxuriously equipped vehicles with four-wheel drive. Some of these "crossover" cars were still good off-road, though many were not. Criticism of "gas-guzzling" sport-utility vehicles (SUVs) eventually led manufacturers to produce hybrid powertrains.

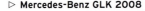

▷ **Mercedes-Benz GLK 2008**

Origin Germany

Engine 3,498 cc, V6

Top speed 143 mph (230 km/h)

A compact and luxurious road car that retains useful off-road ability, the GLK is more upright than its rivals but moves well, aided by a seven-speed automatic gearbox.

△ **Volvo XC90 2002**

Origin Sweden

Engine 2,922 cc, straight-six

Top speed 130 mph (209 km/h)

Volvo's best-selling car in 2005 with 85,994 sold worldwide in that year alone, is a mid-size SUV with turbo engines (or a 4.4 Ford V8), and either front or four-wheel drive.

◁ **Lexus RX 400h 2005**

Origin Japan/USA

Engine 3,311 cc, V6, two electric motors

Top speed 124 mph (200 km/h)

Since its introduction in 1997, the RX has been the best-selling luxury crossover car in the US. The 400h was the world's first luxury hybrid – successful despite its still-heavy fuel economy.

△ **Audi Q7 2005**

Origin Germany/Slovakia

Engine 4,163 cc, V8

Top speed 154 mph (248 km/h)

The Q7 combines good performance with spacious comfort. It has four-wheel drive, not for driving across ploughed fields but for superb road grip.

▷ **Range Rover 2002**

Origin UK

Engine 4,398 cc, V8

Top speed 130 mph (209 km/h)

Fitted with BMW V8 engines (more recently Jaguar/Ford units) the Range Rover has come a long way from its luxury off-roader origins, but it still does both jobs well.

◁ **Range Rover Sport 2005**

Origin UK

Engine 4,197 cc, V8

Top speed 140 mph (225 km/h)

Using a supercharged Jaguar engine on the Discovery 3 platform with added adjustable air suspension, the Sport has good off-road and excellent on-road performance.

▷ **Chrysler Pacifica 2004**

Origin USA

Engine 3,518 cc, V6

Top speed 131 mph (211 km/h)

A two/four-wheel-drive crossover marketed as a "sports tourer", the Pacifica was engineered with Daimler-Benz. However, its sales were poor and it was discontinued in 2008.

◁ **Lincoln Mk LT 2005**

Origin USA

Engine 5,408 cc, V8

Top speed 110 mph (177 km/h)

Lincoln's luxury pick-up with optional four-wheel drive is based on the Ford F-150. It had to be heavily discounted to achieve good sales figures, and production ended in 2008.

△ **Toyota Sequoia 2007**

Origin Japan/USA

Engine 5,670 cc, V8

Top speed 120 mph (193 km/h)

Toyota's full-size SUV for the US market is based on the Tundra pick-up but with independent rear suspension, two- or four-wheel drive, and 4.6–5.7 V8 engines.

◁ **Nissan Armada 2004**

Origin Japan/USA

Engine 5,552 cc, V8

Top speed 120 mph (193 km/h)

Nissan's full-size SUV shared its platform with the Titan pick-up and was built only in Canton, Mississippi, for the US market. Rear- or four-wheel drive was produced.

▷ **Cadillac Escalade EXT 2002**

Origin USA/Mexico

Engine 5,327 cc, V8

Top speed 108 mph (174 km/h)

Cadillac's first Sport Utility Vehicle appeared in 1998, and by 2002 offered eight seats, except for the five-seat EXT pick-up. A 345 bhp, 6-litre V8 engine was optional.

▽ **BMW X6 2008**

Origin Germany/USA

Engine 4,395 cc, V8

Top speed 155 mph (249 km/h)

Marketed as a "sports activity coupé", the X6 combined high ground clearance, all-wheel drive, and large wheels, with coupé styling and a twin-turbocharged six or V8 engine.

△ **Jeep Commander 2006**

Origin USA

Engine 3,701 cc, V6

Top speed 113 mph (182 km/h)

The Commander was a mid-size SUV based on the Grand Cherokee but was more like earlier Jeeps, with its angular, rugged lines. There was also a high performance V8 version.

△ **Jeep Grand Cherokee 2004**

Origin USA

Engine 6,059 cc, V8

Top speed 152 mph (245 km/h)

The all-new WK-series Grand Cherokee used Jeep's sophisticated Quadra-drive II system for excellent off-road performance. It came with 3.1-litre V6 to 6.1-litre V8 engines.

◁ **Porsche Cayenne Hybrid 2010**

Origin Germany

Engine 2,995 cc, V6 + electric motor

Top speed 145 mph (233 km/h)

Sports-car builder Porsche scored remarkable success with its 4x4 Cayenne soft-roader. A 325 bhp petrol engine was joined by a token 47 bhp electric motor on the Hybrid.

△ **Infiniti FX50 2008**

Origin Japan

Engine 5026 cc, V8

Top speed 155 mph (249 km/h)

Nissan's premium brand Infiniti, which is unknown in Japan, appeared in the US in 1989, then in Europe in 2008. This top performance SUV is very fast and well equipped.

▷ **Hummer H3 2005**

Origin USA

Engine 3653 cc, straight-five

Top speed 113 mph (182 km/h)

Derived from the US army vehicle called a Hummer, this large 4x4 is great off-road but compared with purpose-built road 4x4s, it is rather crude and cramped.

Hybrid and Electric Cars

Exotic materials and hybrid powertrains are the hallmarks of today's pioneering car designs. The challenge is to produce a car that is environmentally friendly, but can travel further than a battery-only vehicle, which is usually limited to a range of under 300 miles (480 km). The current solution is a car with both lithium-ion batteries and an on-board engine. The engine engages at a certain speed and charges the batteries as it powers the car.

△ Tesla Roadster 2007

Origin USA/UK

Engine Electric motor

Top speed 125 mph (201 km/h)

A huge step forward in electric vehicle manufacture, the Roadster entered production in 2008. It has batteries with a 300-mile (480-km) range and a Lotus Elise shell.

▷ Toyota Prius 2009

Origin Japan

Engine Hybrid

Top speed 62 mph (100 km/h) under electric power

Toyota ignited the hybrid petrol-electric trend with its original Prius in 1998. This third-generation model now comes in plug-In hybrid form, which allows it to be run as a purely electric car rechargeable at the mains.

◁ Frazer Nash Namir 2009

Origin UK/Italy

Engine 814 cc, rotary/four electric motors

Top speed 187 mph (301 km/h)

The reborn Frazer Nash company worked with Italdesign to produce this striking concept car to showcase its hybrid rotary and electric powertrains.

▷ Audi e-tron 2009

Origin Germany

Engine Four electric motors

Top speed 124 mph (200 km/h)

Unveiled at the 2009 Frankfurt Show, this R8-based electric supercar has four-wheel drive, using a motor for each wheel. Limited production is promised.

◁ Peugeot bb1 2009

Origin France

Engine Two electric motors

Top speed 80 mph (129 km/h)

Powered by lithium-ion batteries, the bb1 is a city car with bike-style handlebars, a double-bubble roof, and a 75-mile (120-km) range.

▷ Renault Twizy 2012

Origin Spain

Engine Electric motor

Top speed 28 mph (45 km/h)

First revealed as a concept car in 2009, the zero-emission Twizy has tandem seating. At about 1-m (3-ft) wide and 2.3-m (7.5-ft) long, its tiny "footprint" has endeared it to chic city dwellers across Europe.

△ Honda P-NUT 2009

Origin Japan/USA

Engine Petrol/hybrid/electric options

Top speed Undetermined

Designed in Honda's US Advanced Design Studio, the Personal-Neo Urban Transport concept car has a central driving seat with two rear seats and a rear power unit.

◁ Mercedes-Benz F800 Style 2010

Origin Germany

Engine 3,498 cc, V6/electric motor

Top speed 155 mph (249 km/h)

Mercedes showcased its new technology in the front-wheel-drive F800. It has sliding rear doors, state-of-the-art electronics, and hybrid or fuel cell power options.

△ **Opel Flextreme GT/E 2010**

Origin Germany/USA

Engine Hybrid

Top speed 124 mph (200 km/h)

Derived from General Motors' Volt hybrid, the Flextreme is powered by an electric motor. Its battery lasts for 37 miles (60 km) before a 1.4-litre diesel engine starts to charge it.

◁ **Opel/Vauxhall Ampera 2010**

Origin USA

Engine Hybrid

Top speed 100 mph (161 km/h)

General Motors' electric car will be sold as the Chevrolet Volt, or the Opel/Vauxhall Ampera. It has a 1.4-litre petrol engine, which drives a generator to boost electric charge.

◁ **Nissan Leaf 2010**

Origin Japan

Engine Electric motor

Top speed 93 mph (150 km/h)

The Leaf is assembled in Japan, the USA, and the UK, and by January 2014 around 100,000 examples of this genuinely zero-emission family hatchback saloon had been sold in 35 countries.

△ **Peugeot 3008 Hybrid4 2012**

Origin France

Engine Hybrid

Top speed 118 mph (190 km/h)

Peugeot broke new ground with this compact crossover, the first hybrid to mix diesel and electric power. Its four driving modes include auto, electric-only, four-wheel drive, and sport.

◁ **Volkswagen XL1 2013**

Origin Germany

Engine Hybrid

Top speed 99 mph (158 km/h)

Never mind the speed, be awed at this diesel-electric car's 313 mpg (0.9 litres/100 km) fuel economy, partly facilitated by the world's sleekest production car aerodynamics. Just 250 examples have been built.

◁ **BMW i3 2013**

Origin Germany

Engine Electric motor

Top speed 93 mph (150 km/h)

The radical carbon-fibre-reinforced plastic body keeps weight down, to compensate for the lithium-ion battery pack. An optional on-board petrol-powered generator can extend the i3's range beyond its standard 100 miles (160 km).

◁ **Detroit Electric SP-01 2013**

Origin USA/UK

Engine Electric motor

Top speed 155 mph (249 km/h)

When manufacture begins, this is likely to be the fastest pure electric production car in the world. It is said to reach 62 mph (100 km/h) from rest in 3.7 seconds. Lotus provides the ultra-light two-seater body/chassis.

▷ **Porsche 918 Spyder 2013**

Origin Germany

Engine Hybrid

Top speed 214 mph (345 km/h)

By combining a 4.6-litre V8 engine with twin electric motors, Porsche has created a phenomenally capable supercar that can also whisper its way around city streets while achieving unheard-of levels of fuel efficiency.

Aircraft
Before 1929

Lighter than Air

Man's first forays into the air were made not in aeroplanes, but in lighter-than-air vehicles: engineless balloons made buoyant by light gases (such as hot air or hydrogen), or bigger, streamlined, powered airships, often known as dirigibles (meaning steerable). In the early years France led the way, as these pages show; but, as World War I approached, Germany rapidly worked out how to make the airship into a weapon.

◁ J. A. C. Charles & The Robert Brothers "la Charlière" 1783

Origin	France
Engine	None
Top speed	N/A

On 1 December 1783, Jacques Charles and Nicolas-Louis Robert made the second-ever manned balloon flight, from Paris. Hydrogen-filled, it flew for 2 hours 5 minutes, over 22 miles (36 km), and reached 1,800 ft (550 m).

▷ Montgolfier Hot-air Balloon 1783

Origin	France
Engine	None
Top speed	N/A

Built by the Montgolfier brothers in Paris, this made the first-ever manned balloon flight, on 21 November 1783, piloted for 25 minutes by Jean-François Pilâtre de Rozier and the Marquis d'Arlandes.

◁ Javel "Steerable" Balloon 1785

Origin	France
Engine	None
Top speed	N/A

Built by Messrs Alban and Vallet at Javel in western Paris, this balloon had hand-cranked windmill-like propellers designed to move it in any desired direction – they did not work.

▷ Godard Balloon, Siege of Paris 1870-71

Origin	France
Engine	None
Top speed	N/A

During the Prussian Siege of Paris in 1870-71, balloonist Eugène Godard built a fleet of hydrogen balloons that transported mail and dispatches out of the besieged city.

◁ Jean-Pierre Blanchard's "Steerable" Balloon 1784

Origin	France
Engine	None
Top speed	N/A

Equipped with oars and rudder (in a hopeless attempt to provide propulsion and steering), plus a parachute, Blanchard's balloon flew in Paris on 2 March 1784, drifting over the River Seine and back.

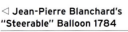

L 49

▽ Santos Dumont No.1 1898

Origin	France
Engine	De Dion Bouton
Top speed	N/A

Wealthy Brazilian Alberto Santos Dumont arrived in Paris in 1897 and began experiments with balloons and airships. His airship No.1 ended its first flight in a tree.

△ Lebaudy No.1 "le Jaune" 1902

Origin	France
Engine	40 hp Mercedes-Benz
Top speed	N/A

Nicknamed "The Yellow One", and distinctive not only for its colour but also its pointed-at-both-ends envelope fixed to an open keelframe, Lebaudy airship No.1 was the world's first successful airship.

▷ Severo Airship Pax 1902

Origin	France
Engine	24 hp Buchet driving tractor screw, 16 hp Buchet driving pusher screw
Top speed	N/A

As well as propulsion screws, the Pax had lifting screws to control trim. Sadly, during its trials over Paris, it caught fire and exploded, killing its creator-pilot and his mechanic.

△ HMA No.1 1909

Origin	UK
Engine	2 x 160 hp Wolseley
Top speed	N/A

His Majesty's Airship No.1, built for the Royal Navy, was named "Mayfly" – but unfortunately it did not: a gust broke its back on the ground before its first test flight.

△ Clément-Bayard Airship Adjudant Vincenot 1911

Origin	France
Engine	2 x 120 hp Clément-Bayard
Top speed	N/A

The Adjudant Vincenot was 289 ft (88 m) long and had a boxkite-type tail. A month before the outbreak of WWI, on 28 June 1914, it made a record endurance flight lasting 35 hours 19 minutes.

△ Chalais-Meudon Type T Airship 1916

Origin	France
Engine	2 x 150 hp Salmson
Top speed	50 mph (80 km/h)

Built at the military engineering establishment and army balloon school of the same name in south-western Paris, the Chalais-Meudon series of nonrigid airships were used in WWI for anti-submarine patrols.

△ Submarine Scout Zero Airship 1916

Origin	UK
Engine	75 hp Rolls-Royce
Top speed	N/A

Conceived by the Royal Naval Air Service as an inexpensive weapon against the urgent threat of German submarines, the SS "blimps" (nonrigids) proved very successful, and 158 were built.

◁ Zeppelin LZ 96 1917

Origin	Germany
Engine	5 x 240 hp Maybach
Top speed	66 mph (106 km/h)

Wearing the serial L49, Zeppelin LZ 96 - a typical large German rigid airship - flew two North Sea reconnaissance missions and one bombing raid on England before it was captured in France.

Pioneers

It was not until 1799 that a British engineer, Sir George Cayley, understood the principles of flight and applied science to the design of a heavier-than-air flying machine. The early pioneers journeyed down many dead ends, designing aircraft with the emphasis more on stability than control, before the Wright brothers finally conquered the air in 1903.

◁ **Henson & Stringfellow Aerial Carriage model 1843**

Origin UK

Engine Steam engine

Top speed N/A

Patented in 1842 the Aerial (as it was known) was designed to be a monoplane with an impressive 148-ft (45-m) wingspan. It was doomed by its poor power-to-weight ratio.

Frame for wing

◁ **Cayley Glider 1849**

Origin UK

Engine None

Top speed N/A

Sir George Cayley designed, built, and flew his man-powered glider in 1853. A replica was successfully flown by famous glider pilot Derek Piggott in 1973, and also by Sir Richard Branson in 2003, proving that the design was essentially airworthy.

▽ **Biot-Massia Planeur 1879**

Origin France

Engine None

Top speed N/A

Early pioneers often applied either maritime principles to their designs, or looked to ornithology. The Biot-Massia Planeur was an attempt to combine the features of a bird with those of a boat – it did not work.

△ **Ader Éole 1890**

Origin France

Engine 20 hp Ader alcohol-burning steam engine

Top speed N/A

This early aircraft was powered by a steam engine. It allegedly achieved a short hop in 1890, but it cannot be considered a successful aeroplane. The pilot had no directional controls and the heavy power-to-weight ratio ensured it was a technological dead end.

△ **Pilcher Bat 1895**

Origin UK

Engine None

Top speed N/A

Built by British aviation pioneer Percy Pilcher in 1895 the Bat was essentially a very crude hang-glider. It did fly, albeit poorly, controlled by weight shifting.

◁ **Pilcher Hawk 1897**

Origin UK

Engine None

Top speed N/A

The Hawk leant heavily on input from German pioneer Otto Lilienthal. Pilcher was killed on 30 September 1899, when the tailplane failed while he was demonstrating the Hawk to investors.

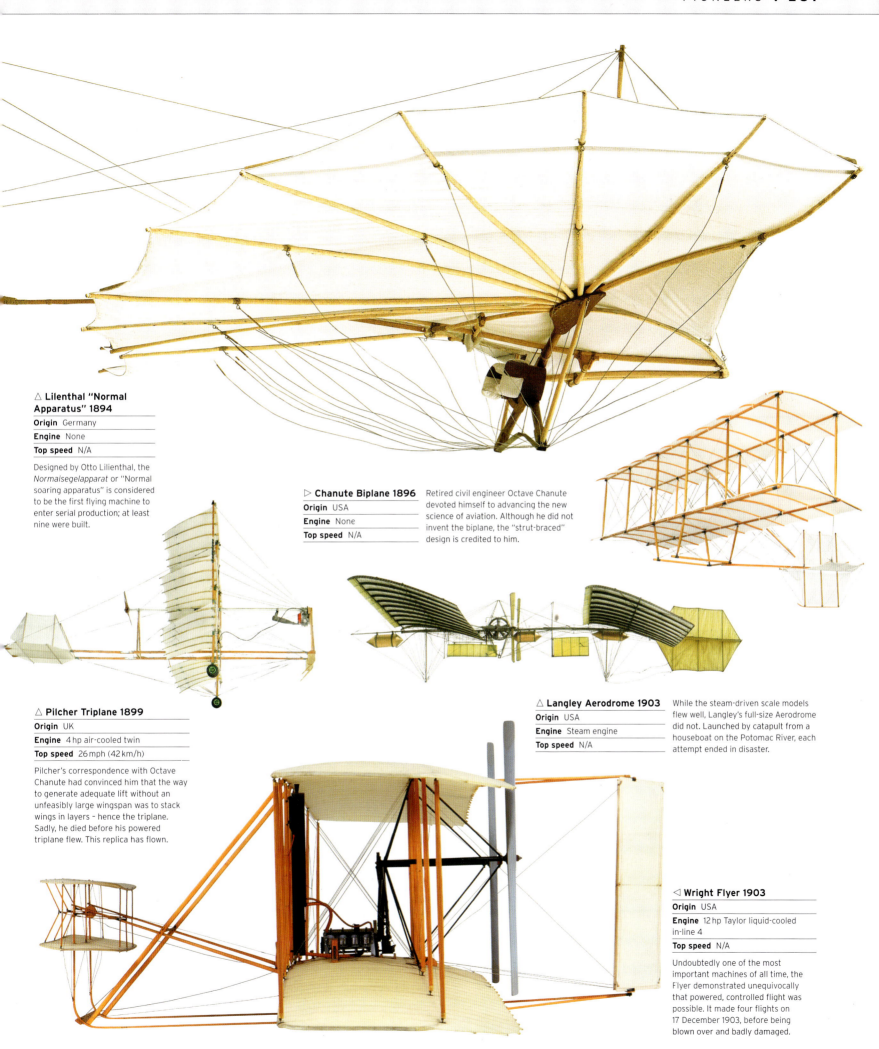

△ **Lilenthal "Normal Apparatus" 1894**

Origin Germany

Engine None

Top speed N/A

Designed by Otto Lilienthal, the *Normalsegelapparat* or "Normal soaring apparatus" is considered to be the first flying machine to enter serial production; at least nine were built.

▷ **Chanute Biplane 1896**

Origin USA

Engine None

Top speed N/A

Retired civil engineer Octave Chanute devoted himself to advancing the new science of aviation. Although he did not invent the biplane, the "strut-braced" design is credited to him.

△ **Pilcher Triplane 1899**

Origin UK

Engine 4hp air-cooled twin

Top speed 26mph (42km/h)

Pilcher's correspondence with Octave Chanute had convinced him that the way to generate adequate lift without an unfeasibly large wingspan was to stack wings in layers – hence the triplane. Sadly, he died before his powered triplane flew. This replica has flown.

△ **Langley Aerodrome 1903**

Origin USA

Engine Steam engine

Top speed N/A

While the steam-driven scale models flew well, Langley's full-size Aerodrome did not. Launched by catapult from a houseboat on the Potomac River, each attempt ended in disaster.

◁ **Wright Flyer 1903**

Origin USA

Engine 12hp Taylor liquid-cooled in-line 4

Top speed N/A

Undoubtedly one of the most important machines of all time, the Flyer demonstrated unequivocally that powered, controlled flight was possible. It made four flights on 17 December 1903, before being blown over and badly damaged.

Successful Pioneers

By 1910 aviation pioneers in Europe were competing strongly with the US, where the Wright brothers' legal battles with competitors had delayed progress. There were triplanes, biplanes, and especially light, manoeuvrable monoplanes. Louis Blériot's successful crossing of the English Channel in 1909 brought a sea change in the popular perception of aviation as a practical possibility, rather than just a dangerous adventure for wealthy eccentrics.

▷ Santos-Dumont Demoiselle Type 20 1908

Origin France

Engine 35 hp Darracq water-cooled flat-twin

Top speed 56 mph (90 km/h)

Brazilian aviator Alberto Santos-Dumont developed the ultra-light, bamboo-fuselage Demoiselle (Damselfly) and released the plans for free; it was claimed one could be built for under 500 French francs.

△ Blériot Type XI 1909

Origin France

Engine 24 hp Anzani air-cooled 3-cylinder fan

Top speed 47 mph (76 km/h)

On 25 July 1909 Louis Blériot and this aircraft made the first heavier-than-air flight over the English Channel, taking 36.5 minutes. Within two months he had taken 103 orders for Type XIs.

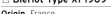

△ Rumpler Taube 1910

Origin Austria/Germany

Engine 100 hp Mercedes D1 water-cooled 6-cylinder in-line

Top speed 60 mph (97 km/h)

Derived from Austrian Igo Etrich's 1907 glider, the birdlike wing tips were warped for flight control. Built by many companies worldwide, the Taube (Dove) was used for reconnaissance and training in WWI.

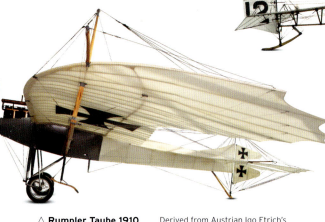

△ Voisin Biplane 1907

Origin France

Engine 50 hp Antoinette water-cooled V8

Top speed 35 mph (56 km/h)

Gabriel Voisin built aircraft from 1904. Henry Farman flew a Voisin biplane to win the prize for the first 0.62 miles (1 km) circular flight on 13 January 1908. Some 60 more were built; this is a replica.

△ Avro Triplane IV 1910

Origin UK

Engine 35 hp Green water-cooled 4-cylinder in-line

Top speed 45 mph (72 km/h)

Alliott Verdon Roe built triplanes from 1907, culminating in a simpler single-tailplane, wing-warping trainer for the Avro Flying School at Brooklands, UK; this is a 1960s replica.

△ Wallbro Monoplane 1910

Origin UK

Engine 25 hp JAP air-cooled V4

Top speed N/A

The motorcycle-racing Wallis brothers built the first all-British aircraft, with a steel-tube fuselage. It was damaged beyond repair before it flew any distance, but this 1970s replica is flyable.

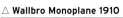

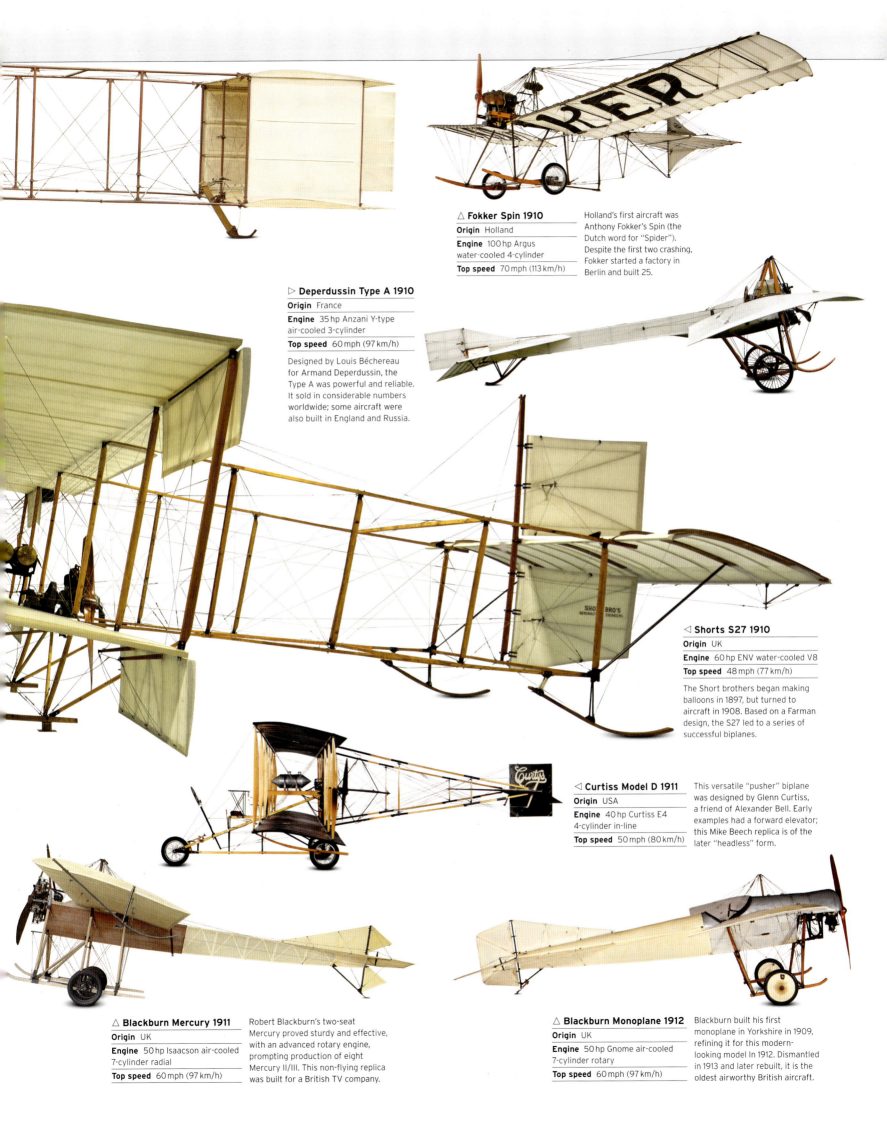

△ **Fokker Spin 1910**

Origin Holland

Engine 100 hp Argus water-cooled 4-cylinder

Top speed 70 mph (113 km/h)

Holland's first aircraft was Anthony Fokker's Spin (the Dutch word for "Spider"). Despite the first two crashing, Fokker started a factory in Berlin and built 25.

▷ **Deperdussin Type A 1910**

Origin France

Engine 35 hp Anzani Y-type air-cooled 3-cylinder

Top speed 60 mph (97 km/h)

Designed by Louis Béchereau for Armand Deperdussin, the Type A was powerful and reliable. It sold in considerable numbers worldwide; some aircraft were also built in England and Russia.

◁ **Shorts S27 1910**

Origin UK

Engine 60 hp ENV water-cooled V8

Top speed 48 mph (77 km/h)

The Short brothers began making balloons in 1897, but turned to aircraft in 1908. Based on a Farman design, the S27 led to a series of successful biplanes.

◁ **Curtiss Model D 1911**

Origin USA

Engine 40 hp Curtiss E4 4-cylinder in-line

Top speed 50 mph (80 km/h)

This versatile "pusher" biplane was designed by Glenn Curtiss, a friend of Alexander Bell. Early examples had a forward elevator; this Mike Beech replica is of the later "headless" form.

△ **Blackburn Mercury 1911**

Origin UK

Engine 50 hp Isaacson air-cooled 7-cylinder radial

Top speed 60 mph (97 km/h)

Robert Blackburn's two-seat Mercury proved sturdy and effective, with an advanced rotary engine, prompting production of eight Mercury II/III. This non-flying replica was built for a British TV company.

△ **Blackburn Monoplane 1912**

Origin UK

Engine 50 hp Gnome air-cooled 7-cylinder rotary

Top speed 60 mph (97 km/h)

Blackburn built his first monoplane in Yorkshire in 1909, refining it for this modern-looking model In 1912. Dismantled in 1913 and later rebuilt, it is the oldest airworthy British aircraft.

Military Two-seaters

Two-seaters were built in large numbers, enabling the pilot to concentrate on flying while the observer fired on enemy targets, dropped bombs, or carried out reconnaissance of enemy activity. At first, basic, unarmed aircraft were used, but as fighters and anti-aircraft guns became more effective, more powerful engines were fitted, and personal sidearms gave way to machine guns. Some aircraft even had heated flying suits and radio communications.

△ Royal Aircraft Factory B.E.2c 1912

Origin UK

Engine 90 hp Royal Aircraft Factory 1a air-cooled V8

Top speed 75 mph (120 km/h)

Some 3,500 of this slow but stable reconnaissance and light bombing machine were built. In 1914 the observer gained a machine gun, but by 1916 the aircraft was dangerously outdated.

△ Avro 504 1913

Origin UK

Engine 80 hp Gnome et Rhône Lambda air-cooled 7-cylinder rotary

Top speed 90 mph (145 km/h)

The highest-production WWI aircraft, the wood-framed 504s served as light bombers, fighters, and trainers, becoming popular post war for civil flying and also serving in Russia and China.

◁ Royal Aircraft Factory F.E.2 1915

Origin UK

Engine 120-160 hp Beardmore water-cooled 6-cylinder in-line

Top speed 92 mph (147 km/h)

Originally intended as a fighter, the "pusher" F.E.2 was technically obsolete from the start. However, its observer had a wide field of fire and it was a success as a light bomber. More than 2,000 were built.

◁ Caudron G.3 1914

Origin France

Engine 80 hp Le Rhône 9C air-cooled 9-cylinder rotary

Top speed 68 mph (106 km/h)

Though of primitive design, using wing warping, the Caudron had a good rate of climb and was useful for reconnaissance. It was later used for training purposes.

◁ Anatra Anasal DS 1916

Origin Russia

Engine 150 hp Salmson 9U water-cooled 9-cylinder radial

Top speed 90 mph (145 km/h)

Manufactured in Odessa with a French Salmson engine built under licence, the Anasal was used mostly for reconnaissance by Ukraine, Russia, Austro-Hungary (later Austria and Hungary), and Czechoslovakia.

▷ Bristol F.2B Fighter 1916

Origin UK

Engine 275 hp Rolls-Royce Falcon III water-cooled V12

Top speed 123 mph (198 km/h)

Perfected in this F.2B version, the lively Bristol Fighter held its own against single-seaters and served into the 1930s; shortage of Rolls-Royce engines held back production in WWI.

▷ Sopwith 1½ Strutter 1916

Origin UK

Engine 130 hp Clerget air-cooled 9-cylinder rotary

Top speed 100 mph (161 km/h)

Named after its oddly shaped centre section struts, this was an effective fighter and bomber. It was the first British aircraft with a synchronized machine gun for the pilot. It was also built in France.

△ **Royal Aircraft Factory R.E.8 1916**
Origin UK
Engine 140 hp Royal Aircraft Factory 4a air-cooled V12
Top speed 103 mph (166 km/h)

Slow, cumbersome, and difficult to fly, the R.E.8 was better armed and carried a greater payload than its B.E.2c predecessor. More than 4,000 were built, and they performed well in skilled hands.

◁ **Junkers J4 (JI) 1917**
Origin Germany
Engine 200 hp Benz Bz.IV water-cooled 6-cylinder in-line
Top speed 97 mph (155 km/h)

Dr Hugo Junkers pioneered this all-metal aircraft. The ground-attack machine's 0.2 in (5 mm) thick steel "bathtub" was both structure and armour protection; 227 were built. Most served on the Western Front.

◁ **LVG C.VI 1917**
Origin Germany
Engine 200 hp Benz Bz.IV water-cooled 6-cylinder in-line
Top speed 103 mph (166 km/h)

Designed by Willy Sabersky-Müssigbrodt, the C.VI had a semi-monocoque wooden fuselage. Chiefly used for reconnaissance, it continued in service as late as 1940 in Lithuania.

▷ **Vickers F.B.5 Gunbus 1914**
Origin UK
Engine 100 hp Gnome Monosoupape 9-cylinder rotary
Top speed 70 mph (113 km/h)

The F.B.5 was one of the first aircraft designed for air-to-air combat. Its weight and inefficient pusher design with wing-warping control meant that it rapidly became outdated.

◁ **Airco DH9A "Ninak" 1918**
Origin UK
Engine 400 hp Packard Liberty 12A water-cooled V12
Top speed 123 mph (198 km/h)

Airco struggled to find a powerful enough engine for the DH9, but with the US-built Liberty engine it was a great success, staying in service until 1931. Many replicas were built in Russia too.

Single-seat Fighters

World War I saw tremendously rapid progress in airframe and engine technology, and in every aspect of aircraft design. As each side struggled for aerial supremacy, first one then another aircraft would briefly flourish, then wither as its leading features were either copied or beaten. Speed, agility, armaments, and strength were the key factors in successful single-seat fighter design.

△ Fokker E.II Eindecker 1915

Origin Germany

Engine 100 hp Oberursel U.19 air-cooled 9-cylinder rotary

Top speed 87 mph (140 km/h)

Dutchman Anthony Fokker's monoplane was an improved version of the Morane-Saulnier. Fitted with a synchronizing interrupter gear for its gun, it gave Germany air superiority in late 1915.

◁ Morane-Saulnier Type N 1915

Origin France

Engine 80 hp Gnome et Rhône air-cooled 9-cylinder rotary

Top speed 89 mph (144 km/h)

The Type N was fitted with Roland Garros's pioneering machine gun, which fired through a propeller with steel deflector plates to prevent damage. Although effective when first built, the wing-warping aircraft was soon obsolete.

▷ Nieuport 17 1916

Origin France

Engine 110-130 hp Gnome et Rhône 9Ja air-cooled 9-cylinder rotary

Top speed 110 mph (177 km/h)

Developed from the agile Type 11, the Nieuport 17 was the best fighter of 1916 and widely used by the Allies: it offered superior performance and agility, plus a synchronized machine gun.

◁ Sopwith Triplane 1916

Origin UK

Engine 130 hp Clerget 9B air-cooled 9-cylinder rotary

Top speed 117 mph (188 km/h)

Developed from the "Pup", the Triplane was very agile and scored many victories in 1916-17, inspiring the Germans to build the Fokker Dr.1. Just 147 were built before the Camel took over.

▷ Sopwith Pup 1916

Origin UK

Engine 80 hp Gnome et Rhône 9c air-cooled 9-cylinder rotary

Top speed 112 mph (180 km/h)

Compact, with a large wing area, the Sopwith Scout, as it was officially known, could "almost land on a tennis court". It enjoyed brief superiority but was soon overtaken by new designs; 1,770 were built.

▽ Sopwith F.1 Camel 1917

Origin UK

Engine 130 hp Clerget 9B/150 hp Bentley BR1 air-cooled 9-cylinder rotary

Top speed 115 mph (185 km/h)

Though difficult to fly, the highly manoeuvrable Camel, armed with twin machine guns, shot down more enemy aircraft than any other in WWI. Some 5,490 were built, giving Allied forces air superiority.

△ Sopwith 5F.1 Dolphin 1917

Origin UK

Engine 200 hp Hispano-Suiza 8B water-cooled V8

Top speed 131 mph (211 km/h)

Fast, manoeuvrable, and easy to fly, Herbert Smith's new fighter for 1917 was outstanding at high altitude, though its unusual forward-lower-wing design led to it being mistaken for a German fighter.

△ Fokker Dr.1 1917

Origin Germany

Engine 110 hp Oberursel Ur.II air-cooled 9-cylinder rotary

Top speed 115 mph (185 km/h)

Famous as the favourite mount of Manfred von Richthofen (the Red Baron), the "Dreidecker" was Fokker's effective response to the highly manoeuvrable Sopwith Triplane; 320 were built.

◁ Albatros DVa 1916

Origin Germany

Engine 180 hp Mercedes-Benz D. IIIa water-cooled 6-cylinder in-line

Top speed 116 mph (186 km/h)

The Albatros D-series (this is a late Va) won back air domination for Germany in 1917. With light, strong semi-monocoque plywood fuselage, it was fast and had good firepower, but was not very manoeuvrable.

△ Fokker D.VII 1918

Origin Germany

Engine 180 hp Mercedes-Benz D.IIIaü water-cooled 6-cylinder in-line

Top speed 118 mph (190 km/h)

The last of the Fokker fighters of WWI, the Reinhold Platz-designed D.VII was judged the best German fighter aircraft in early 1918. Its steel-tube fuselage and cantilever wings were ahead of their time.

△ Royal Aircraft Factory S.E.5a 1916

Origin UK

Engine 200 hp Hispano-Suiza/Wolseley Viper water-cooled V8

Top speed 138 mph (222 km/h)

Once shortage of its French-built engine was overcome by Wolseley building them, the stable, fast, and strong S.E.5a helped the Allies regain air superiority in mid-1917 and keep it to the end of the war.

△ SPAD SVII 1916

Origin France

Engine 220 hp Hispano-Suiza water-cooled V8

Top speed 135 mph (218 km/h)

Designed by Louis Béchéreau, and armed with one gun, this was one of the most capable fighters of WWI. Strength and speed from its powerful V8 engine made up for its limited agility.

▽ Pfalz D.III 1917

Origin Germany

Engine 180 hp Mercedes D.IIIa water-cooled 6-cylinder in-line

Top speed 103 mph (166 km/h)

Rudolph Gehringer developed the plywood monocoque D.III from the Roland D.II. It was slower than rivals but strong, so useful in dive attacks. It was in service to the end of WWI; more than 1,000 were built.

Racers and Record Breakers

The speed of development in these early years was astonishing. At the start of the 20th century, only an airship could set a powered flight record, but in the first decade heavier-than-air craft went from their first staggering hops to flying 26 miles (42 km) across the English Channel at almost 50 mph (80 km/h). A decade later speeds had more than trebled and the first non-stop flight across the Atlantic had been achieved.

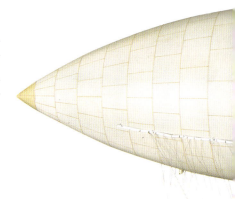

▷ Santos-Dumont No.6 1901

Origin France

Engine 20 hp Buchet water-cooled 4-cylinder in-line

Top speed 23 mph (37 km/h)

Alberto Santos-Dumont won the 100,000 French franc Deutsche prize by flying from Parc Saint Cloud to the Eiffel Tower and back in under 30 minutes with this hydrogen-filled airship, on 19 October 1901.

◁ Voisin-Farman Biplane No.1 1907

Origin France

Engine 50 hp Antoinette water-cooled V8

Top speed 56 mph (90 km/h)

Gabriel Voisin's first successful aircraft was flown by Henri Farman to achieve the inaugural 0.6-mile (1-km) closed circuit flight, the earliest 1.2-mile (2-km), and then a 17-mile (27-km) cross-country flight in 20 minutes, all in 1908.

△ Antoinette VII 1909

Origin France

Engine 50 hp Antoinette V8

Top speed 44 mph (70 km/h)

Brilliant engineer Léon Levavasseur patented V8 engines for light aircraft engines in 1903. He went on to build this prize-winning aircraft for Hubert Latham, and even a flight simulator for training.

△ Morane-Saulnier H 1913

Origin France

Engine 80 hp Le Rhône 9C air-cooled 9-cylinder radial

Top speed 75 mph (120 km/h)

This single-seat sporting aircraft won a precision landing contest in 1913 piloted by Roland Garros. The design was ordered by both France and England for combat use at the start of WWI.

▷ Wright EX Vin Fiz 1911

Origin USA

Engine 35 hp Wright Aero 4-cylinder in-line

Top speed 51 mph (82 km/h)

This was Calbraith Perry Rodgers's mount for the first coast-to-coast crossing of the US in 1911, with 75 stops including 16 crashes and numerous personal injuries. Many parts were replaced en route.

▷ Astra Wright BB 1912

Origin USA/France

Engine 35 hp Barriquand et Marre 4-cylinder in-line

Top speed 37 mph (60 km/h)

Dating from 1912 this French-built aircraft was based closely on the record-setting Wright Brothers Baby. The Baby flew from Springfield to St Louis in 1910, a distance of 95 miles (153 km), and in 1911 crossed the US in only 83 hours' flying time.

△ Morane-Saulnier A1 Type XXX 1917

Origin France

Engine 150 hp Gnome Monosoupape 9N air-cooled 9-cylinder radial

Top speed 140 mph (225 km/h)

This WWI single-seat fighter had aerobatic ability because of its compact dimensions and sweptback parasol wings. After war service it became a trainer, 51 going to the US Expeditionary Force.

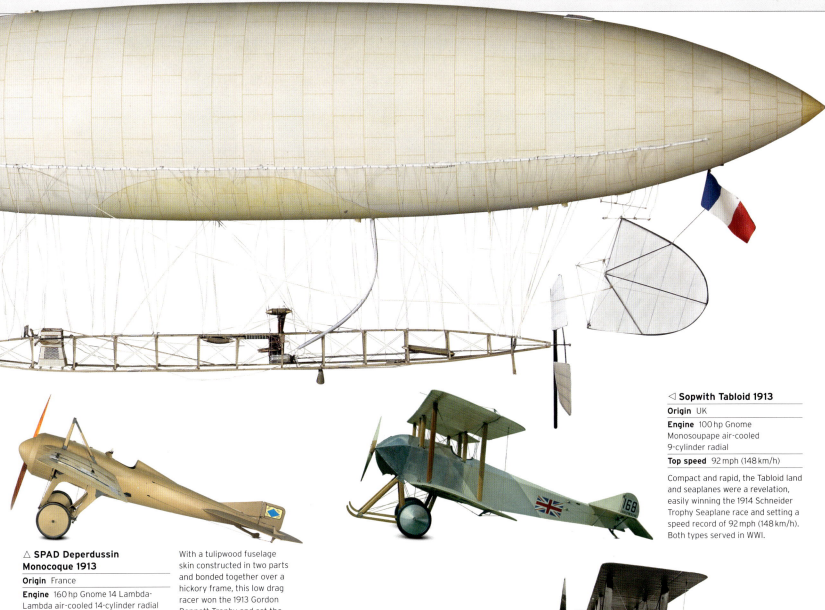

▷ Sopwith Tabloid 1913

Origin UK

Engine 100 hp Gnome Monosoupape air-cooled 9-cylinder radial

Top speed 92 mph (148 km/h)

Compact and rapid, the Tabloid land and seaplanes were a revelation, easily winning the 1914 Schneider Trophy Seaplane race and setting a speed record of 92 mph (148 km/h). Both types served in WWI.

△ SPAD Deperdussin Monocoque 1913

Origin France

Engine 160 hp Gnome 14 Lambda-Lambda air-cooled 14-cylinder radial

Top speed 130 mph (209 km/h)

With a tulipwood fuselage skin constructed in two parts and bonded together over a hickory frame, this low drag racer won the 1913 Gordon Bennett Trophy and set the world speed record.

◁ Vickers Vimy 1918

Origin UK

Engine 2 x 360 hp Rolls-Royce Eagle VIII water-cooled V12

Top speed 100 mph (161 km/h)

Though it just missed WWI service, the Vimy became Britain's lead bomber until 1925. John Alcock and Arthur Whitten Brown made the first non-stop Atlantic crossing in a Vimy in 1919.

△ Sopwith Schneider 1919

Origin UK

Engine 450 hp Cosmos Jupiter air-cooled 9-cylinder radial

Top speed 170 mph (274 km/h)

Built to contest the 1919 Schneider Trophy race, which was cancelled because of fog, this seaplane was rebuilt as a land racer, finishing second in the 1923 Aerial Derby, but destroyed in a crash a month later.

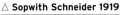

△ Nieuport II N 1910

Origin France

Engine 28 hp Nieuport air-cooled flat-twin

Top speed 71 mph (115 km/h)

Edouard Nieuport made ignition equipment for cars before experimenting with aircraft. In 1910 he took the world speed record up to 62 mph (100 km/h) with his light and efficient flat-twin engined monoplane.

Multi-engine Giants and Seaplanes

Lack of firm, smooth runways made seaplanes popular: they could be landed almost anywhere, provided the seas were calm. Designers, especially Sikorsky in Russia, had already conceived luxury airliners with insulated, heated cabins. World War I brought the need for heavy bombers, which led to vast aircraft with up to six engines, flying at high altitude for hundreds of miles to drop tonnes of bombs on enemy cities.

△ Benoist XIV 1913

Origin USA

Engine 75 hp Roberts water-cooled 6-cylinder in-line

Top speed 64 mph (103 km/h)

After airships, the world's first airline service used the two Benoist XIV seaplanes, first over Duluth harbour in Minnesota, then over Tampa Bay in Florida; it was not a commercial success.

▷ Sikorsky S22 Ilya Murometz 1913

Origin USSR

Engine 4 x 148 hp Sunbeam Crusader water-cooled V8

Top speed 68 mph (109 km/h)

Igor Sikorsky had designed the first four-engined aircraft; he built this as a luxury airliner with heating and toilet, but swiftly redesigned it as the first heavy bomber. Of 73 built, only one was shot down.

△ Caproni Ca36 1916

Origin Italy

Engine 3 x 150 hp Isotta-Fraschini V4B water-cooled 6-cylinder in-line

Top speed 85 mph (137 km/h)

Armed with two machine guns and able to carry 1,764 lb (800 kg) of bombs, the Ca36 was a potent heavy bomber from the final years of WWI, operated by the Italian Army and Air Force; 153 were built.

△ Caudron G.4 1915

Origin France

Engine 2 x 80 hp Le Rhône 9C air-cooled 9-cylinder radial

Top speed 77 mph (124 km/h)

Caudron enlarged the G.3 and fitted twin engines to turn it into a practical bomber. It carried 220 lb (100 kg) of bombs into the heart of Germany in WWI, often at night, though it soon suffered heavy losses.

△ Shorts 184 1915

Origin UK

Engine 260 hp Sunbeam Maori water-cooled V12

Top speed 89 mph (143 km/h)

Designed to drop torpedos on enemy shipping, the 184 was the first – on 12 August 1915 – to sink a ship with an air-launched torpedo and was the only plane to participate in the Battle of Jutland.

△ Sopwith Baby 1915

Origin UK

Engine 110 hp Clerget air-cooled 9-cylinder radial

Top speed 100 mph (161 km/h)

Developed from Sopwith's 1914 Schneider Trophy winner, the Baby was built to intercept Zeppelin raids, fitted with explosive darts or two 66-lb (30-kg) bombs; 286 were built, seeing service worldwide.

△ B & W Seaplane 1916

Origin USA

Engine 125 hp Hall-Scott A5 water-cooled 6-cylinder in-line

Top speed 75 mph (121 km/h)

William Boeing and Conrad Westervelt built the first Boeing of wood, linen, and wire, improving on a Martin trainer that Boeing owned. Two were sold to New Zealand, to be used for Airmail deliveries.

▷ Handley Page 0/400 1917

Origin UK

Engine 2 x 360 hp Rolls-Royce Eagle VIII water-cooled V12

Top speed 98 mph (158 km/h)

Production difficulties delayed Britain's heavy bomber, the largest UK aircraft of its day. In its second, 0/400 form, it could carry 2,000 lb (907 kg) of bombs. Post-war, a handful were used for civil transport.

▷ AEG G.IV 1916

Origin Germany

Engine 2 x 260 hp Daimler-Benz D.IVa water-cooled 6-cylinder in-line

Top speed 103 mph (165 km/h)

The AEG boasted a welded steel tube frame, onboard radios, and heated suits, but lacked power and range. It was used mainly as a tactical bomber attacking battlefield targets and nearby cities.

△ Handley Page V/1500 1918

Origin UK

Engine 4 x 375 hp Rolls-Royce Eagle VIII water-cooled V12

Top speed 99 mph (159 km/h)

Just too late for WWI, this large long-range bomber carried 3,086 lb (1,400 kg). One made the first flight from England to India in 1918–19; another bombed the Royal Palace to end the Anglo-Afghan War in 1919.

△ Gotha GV 1917

Origin Germany

Engine 2 x 260 hp Mercedes D.IVa water-cooled 6-cylinder in-line

Top speed 87 mph (140 km/h)

Although they could carry just six 110-lb (50-kg) bombs per raid, Germany's Gotha heavy bombers dropped some 85 tonnes of bombs on England in 1917–18 for the loss of 24 aircraft, flying at over 15,000 ft (4,572 m).

△ Zeppelin Staaken R.IV 1915

Origin Germany

Engine 6 x 160 hp Mercedes D.III/ 220 hp Benz Bz.IV water-cooled 6-cylinder in-line

Top speed 84 mph (135 km/h)

Based, ironically, on a civil aircraft designed for a competition sponsored by the *Daily Mail*, Zeppelin *Staaken Riesenflugzeuge* (giant aircraft) bombers proved capable of operating over England with near impunity.

◁ Bristol Type 24 Braemar I 1918

Origin UK

Engine 2 x 230 hp Siddeley Puma water-cooled 6-cylinder in-line

Top speed 106 mph (171 km/h)

This prototype heavy bomber was capable of bombing as far away from England as Berlin. Just two prototypes (of which this is the first) were built, followed by one 14-passenger civil transport.

Mailplanes and Barnstormers

With thousands of trained pilots and surplus aircraft available from the war, aviation really began to gain momentum in the 1920s. Barnstorming pilots giving joyrides brought it to the general public's attention and Hollywood made flying films using any old planes it could find. Governments increasingly moved mail by air, which led to the production of dedicated mailplanes.

◁ **Curtiss JN-4 Jenny 1920**

Origin USA

Engine 90 hp Curtis OX-5 liquid-cooled V8

Top speed 75 mph (121 km/h)

First introduced into the US Army in 1915 the Jenny was probably the most famous US aircraft of WWI. Thousands were sold as surplus when the war ended, some still in their packing cases, and for as little as $50. The aircraft is considered to have played a pivotal role in the emergence of civil aviation in the US.

◁ **de Havilland DH4B mailplane 1918**

Origin UK/USA

Engine 400 hp Liberty L-2 liquid-cooled V8

Top speed 143 mph (230 km/h)

Considered to be the best single-engine British bomber of WWI, the DH4 flew with the US Army in 1918. After the war many were converted for use as mailplanes in Europe, Australia, and the US.

◁ **Nieuport 28 C1 1926**

Origin France

Engine 160 hp Gnome 9-N Monosoupape air-cooled 9-cylinder rotary

Top speed 122 mph (196 km/h)

Although not an especially successful fighter, the Nieuport 28's place in history is assured, as it was the first fighter to be flown in combat by an American fighter squadron. Sold off to civilians in 1926 a small fleet of surplus 28s appeared in early Hollywood films, including *The Dawn Patrol*.

◁ **Thomas-Morse MB-3 1920**

Origin USA

Engine 300 hp Wright-Hisso liquid-cooled V8

Top speed 141 mph (228 km/h)

Built by both the Thomas-Morse Company and Boeing, the MB-3 entered service too late to see combat in WWI, and had a relatively short service life. At least one MB-3 was used in the classic aviation film *Wings*.

▷ **Douglas M-2 1926**

Origin USA

Engine 400 hp Liberty L-2 liquid-cooled V8

Top speed 140 mph (225 km/h)

When the US Post Office decided it could no longer rely on converted army-surplus DH4s to operate on the mail runs, it contracted Douglas to produce a dedicated mailplane.

△ **Pitcairn Mailwing 1927**

Origin USA

Engine 220 hp Wright J-5 Whirlwind air-cooled 9-cylinder radial

Top speed 131 mph (211 km/h)

Another type that was specifically designed for the expanding US Air Mail system. Pitcairn produced over 100 Mailwings, with some being built as three-seat sportplanes. Howard Hughes is alleged to have owned one.

△ **Boeing B-40 1927**

Origin USA

Engine 420 hp Pratt & Whitney Wasp air-cooled 9-cylinder radial

Top speed 128 mph (206 km/h)

Built to service the US Air Mail routes, the B-40 incorporated a small cabin, which allowed it to carry two passengers as well as the mail. The type was originally fitted with a liquid-cooled Liberty engine.

▽ **Travel Air 4000 1929**

Origin USA

Engine 300 hp Wright J-6 Whirlwind air-cooled 9-cylinder radial

Top speed 155 mph (250 km/h)

Established in Wichita, Kansas by Clyde Cessna, Walter Beech, and Lloyd Stearman, Travel Air produced some of the most famous biplanes of the 1920s. The 4000 starred as a Wichita Fokker in Hollywood films.

△ **Stearman 4DM Junior 1929**

Origin USA

Engine 300 hp Pratt & Whitney Wasp Junior air-cooled 9-cylinder radial

Top speed 158 mph (256 km/h)

Allegedly described by designer Lloyd Stearman as "the best airplane I ever designed", the Stearman Model 4 was an extremely rugged aeroplane and several different variants were produced, powered by a variety of engines.

◁ **New Standard D-25 1929**

Origin USA

Engine 220 hp Wright J-5 Whirlwind air-cooled 9-cylinder radial

Top speed 110 mph (176 km/h)

The D-25's wings are arranged in the sesquiplane configuration – the upper wing being much larger than the lower. It was popular with barnstormers for "hopping" joyrides.

△ **Fairchild FC-2 1929**

Origin USA

Engine 220 hp Wright J-5 Whirlwind air-cooled 9-cylinder radial

Top speed 122 mph (196 km/h)

Originally designed as a camera aircraft for parent company Fairchild Aerial Surveys, the FC-2 was a rugged, reliable bushplane that was used extensively in the Canadian bush, and also by the Royal Canadian Air Force.

▷ **Waco ASO 1929**

Origin USA

Engine 220 hp Wright J-5 Whirlwind air-cooled 9-cylinder radial

Top speed 97 mph (156 km/h)

Waco ASO, or the Waco 10, was a handsome three-seat biplane that was popular with barnstormers. It was the most produced Waco biplane, with over 1,600 being made. There were around 17 different versions, all powered by a wide variety of engines, including V8s, and even a diesel.

Private Flying Begins

The 1920s saw designers start to produce machines specifically for the private owner. Although there were still surplus military aircraft available, none was particularly economical to operate. Flying competitions were held to encourage companies to build light, more affordable planes, and develop interest in aviation.

◁ **Farman FF65 Sport 1920**

Origin France

Engine 80 hp Anzani air-cooled 6-cylinder 2-row radial

Top speed 87 mph (140 km/h)

Farman was well known for its military aircraft and airliners. The FF65 Sport is notable in that it was one of the first aircraft to be powered by a two-row radial engine.

△ **ANEC II 1923**

Origin UK

Engine 30 hp ABC Scorpion air-cooled flat-twin

Top speed 74 mph (119 km/h)

One of the earliest ultralight aircraft, the ANEC II was a slightly larger two-seat version of the original ANEC I. Designed for the 1924 Lympne trials, only one was built. It survives in the Shuttleworth Collection at Old Warden, UK.

△ **English Electric Wren 1921**

Origin UK

Engine 8 hp ABC air-cooled flat-twin

Top speed 50 mph (80 km/h)

This very light machine, powered by a motorcycle engine, shared first prize at the Lympne aircraft trials, when it flew 87 miles (140 km) on 1 gallon (4.5 litres) of petrol.

△ **de Havilland DH53 Humming Bird 1923**

Origin UK

Engine 26 hp Blackburne Tomtit air-cooled inverted V-twin

Top speed 73 mph (118 km/h)

Another aircraft that was designed for the Lympne trials, the prototype Humming Bird was powered by a 750 cc Douglas aircraft engine, although production aircraft were fitted with a 26 hp Blackburne Tomtit inverted V-twin.

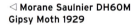

◁ **Morane Saulnier DH60M Gipsy Moth 1929**

Origin UK design/French Built

Engine 100 hp de Havilland Gipsy I air-cooled in-line 4

Top speed 105 mph (169 km/h)

The Gipsy Moth was the affordable, folding-wing aircraft that made private flying possible in Britain and was popular across the globe. The DH60M was a metal-frame version intended for hostile climates.

△ **Hawker Cygnet 1924**

Origin UK

Engine 34 hp Bristol Cherub III air-cooled flat-twin

Top speed 82 mph (132 km/h)

Designed by the great British designer, Sidney Camm, the Cygnet competed at the famous Lympne trials. Only two were built, and both were always well placed. They came first and second in 1926.

△ Westland Widgeon MkII 1924

Origin UK

Engine 60 hp Armstrong Genet air-cooled 5-cylinder radial

Top speed 104 mph (167 km/h)

The parasol-winged Widgeon was Westland's competitor to the DH60 Gipsy Moth biplane. It was more expensive to produce than its competitors and only 26 (of all Marks) were built.

▷ Ryan M-1 1926

Origin USA

Engine 200 hp Wright J-4 Whirlwind air-cooled 9-cylinder radial

Top speed 125 mph (200 km/h)

The first craft by San Diego-based Ryan Aircraft, the M-1 was a parasol design. Although the prototype was fitted with a Hispano-Suiza liquid-cooled V8 of 150 hp, production aircraft were powered by an air-cooled radial.

▽ Zogling 1926

Origin Germany

Engine None

Top speed 80 mph (129 km/h)

Designed by famous aerodynamicist Alexander Lippisch, the Zogling was designed to be bungee launched from slopes and was used for (very) basic glider training.

△ Fairchild 71 1926

Origin USA

Engine 420 hp Pratt & Whitney Wasp air-cooled 9-cylinder radial

Top speed 128 mph (206 km/h)

Developed from the successful FC-2, the Fairchild 71 was slightly larger and had an extra 200 hp. Some were also built in Canada specifically for aerial photography.

◁ Brunner-Winkle Bird Model A-T 1929

Origin USA

Engine 115 hp Milwaukee Tank V-502 liquid-cooled V8

Top speed 105 mph (169 km/h)

Originally powered by a Curtis OX-5, a wide variety of engines powered the Brunner-Winkle Bird, with the most successful version having a Kinner B-5 radial. The Milwaukee engine in this aircraft was derived from the OX-5.

▷ Great Lakes Sports Trainer 1929

Origin USA

Engine 85 hp Cirrus air-cooled in-line 4

Top speed 153 mph (246 km/h)

The Great Lakes won many aerobatic aircraft competitions over several decades. In fact, the basic design was so sound that the type was returned to production in 1973.

◁ Travel Air 4D 1929

Origin USA

Engine 220 hp Wright J-5 Whirlwind air-cooled 9-cylinder radial

Top speed 125 mph (200 km/h)

Popular with the barnstormers who roamed the American Midwest in the 1920s, the Travel Air 4000 was a rugged, reliable biplane. It was often used in war films as "stand-ins" for the Fokker DVII.

Setting Speed Records

The 1920s was a great era for racing and record breaking, with contests like the Schneider Trophy for seaplanes really capturing public interest. An international contest, it was won by Italian, British, and American aircraft in the 1920s and racing definitely improved the breed. Reginald Mitchell's Supermarine racers clearly inspired the Spitfire; while in the US Alfred Verville built the first fighter monoplane with a retractable undercarriage.

▷ **Gloster Bamel/Mars I 1921**

Origin UK

Engine 450 hp Napier Lion II water-cooled Broad Arrow

Top speed 212 mph (341 km/h)

Designed by Henry Folland based on his Nieuport Nighthawk fighter, Mars I (or Bamel) was modified to reduce drag, setting a British speed record of 212.15 mph (341.42 km/h), just above the world record.

▷ **Verville-Sperry R-3 1922**

Origin USA

Engine 443 hp Curtiss D12 water-cooled V12 (earlier, 300 hp Wright H3)

Top speed 233 mph (375 km/h)

Alfred Verville's streamlined cantilever-wing monoplane racer was even fitted with fully retractable landing gear. Three were built, contesting the Pulitzer Prize from 1922 to 1924, when it won.

△ **Nieuport-Kirsch 1921**

Origin France

Engine 300 hp Hispano-Suiza 8Fb water-cooled V8

Top speed 173 mph (278 km/h)

After winning the Coupe Deutsch de la Meurth in October 1921 at 172.96 mph (278.36 km/h), Georges Kirsch fitted a 400 hp Wright H3 engine and, in October 1923, set a world speed record at 233.096 mph (375.132 km/h).

△ **Supermarine Sea Lion II 1922**

Origin UK

Engine 450 hp Napier Lion II water-cooled Broad Arrow

Top speed 160 mph (258 km/h)

Supermarine modified its Sea King fighter to contest the 1922 Schneider Trophy, fitting a Napier Lion engine for the race. Despite its bulky appearance, it won at 145.7 mph (234.48 km/h), flown by Henri Biard.

△ **Supermarine S6A 1928**

Origin UK

Engine 1,900 hp Rolls-Royce R supercharged water-cooled V12

Top speed 329 mph (529 km/h)

For 1928 Reginald Mitchell refined his superb S5, swapping the 900 hp Napier Lion engine for a 1,900 hp Rolls-Royce unit, adding extra radiators in the floats. H. R. D. Waghorn won, at 328.63 mph (528.88 km/h).

▷ **Supermarine S5 1927**

Origin UK

Engine 900 hp Napier Lion VIIA water-cooled Broad Arrow

Top speed 320 mph (515 km/h)

Brilliant designer R. J. Mitchell built an all-metal semi-monocoque for the 1927 Schneider Trophy race. Napier Lion-engined, it looked right – and was. Lt S. N. Webster won the race at 281.66 mph (453.28 km/h).

△ **Curtiss CR1/CR2/R6 1921**

Origin Italy

Engine 619 hp Curtiss V-1400 water-cooled V12

Top speed 138 mph (222 km/h)

Curtiss developed this racer for the US services. The Navy's CR1 and CR2 competed against Army's R6s for the Pulitzer Prize – the Navy winning in 1921 and the Army in 1922. R6s set world speed records in 1922-23.

△ **Curtiss R3C-2 1925**

Origin USA

Engine 619 hp Curtiss V-1400 water-cooled V12

Top speed 246 mph (396 km/h)

Jimmy Doolittle won the 1925 Schneider Trophy race in the R3C-2 seaplane. The next day he set a world record speed of 245.7 mph (395.4 km/h). The R3C-1 landplane version won the 1925 Pulitzer Prize at 248.9 mph (400.6 km/h).

△ **Macchi M39 1926**

Origin Italy

Engine 800 hp Fiat AS.2 water-cooled V12

Top speed 259 mph (417 km/h)

Mario Castoldi chose a low-wing monoplane layout to win the 1926 Schneider Trophy. The plane was flown by Major Mario de Bernardi at 247 mph (397 km/h) – a new world record – which he raised to 258 mph (416 km/h) four days later.

◁ **Travel Air Type R "Mystery Ship" 1929**

Origin USA

Engine 300-425 hp Wright J-6-9 supercharged air-cooled 9-cylinder radial

Top speed 235 mph (378 km/h)

Determined to beat their all-conquering military rivals, Herb Rawdon and Walter Burnham built racers in secret. Doug Davis won the 1929 Thomson Cup race in one, beating all the military entries, and went on to win many more races.

▷ **Supermarine S6B 1930**

Origin UK

Engine 2,350 hp Rolls-Royce R water-cooled V12

Top speed 408 mph (657 km/h)

R. J. Mitchell's final racing seaplane won the 1931 Schneider Trophy flown by J. N. Boothman, then G. Stainforth took the world airspeed record to 407.41 mph (655.67 km/h). The S6B was the inspiration for the Spitfire.

Outstanding Achievements

The world became a smaller place after Alcock and Brown's 1919 transatlantic flight. During the 1920s long-distance flights attracted huge public attention, inspiring newspapers and governments to sponsor ever more ambitious journeys. Many intrepid pilots died, but those who survived clocked up remarkable feats of endurance. Piston-engined aircraft were now powerful and reliable, but the most impressive trips were achieved by vast, luxurious airships.

▽ Avro Avian 1926

Origin UK

Engine 90 hp ADC Cirrus air-cooled 4-cylinder in-line

Top speed 105 mph (169 km/h)

The Avian was a sound late 1920s tourer popular for record flights. In 1927 Bert Hinkler flew solo from Croydon, UK to Darwin, Australia in 15½ days and in 1928 Amelia Earhart crossed the US and back in one.

△ Douglas World Cruiser 1923

Origin USA

Engine 423 hp Liberty L-12 water-cooled V12

Top speed 103 mph (166 km/h)

Five World Cruisers were built for the US Army Air Service, based on a torpedo bomber. In April to Sept 1924 "Chicago" and "New Orleans" flew 27,533 miles (44,310 km) around the world in 371 hours, 11 minutes flying time, averaging 70 mph (113 km/h).

▷ Junkers W.33 Bremen 1926

Origin Germany

Engine 310 hp Junkers L.5 water-cooled 6-cylinder in-line

Top speed 120 mph (193 km/h)

An advanced all-metal cantilever monocoque freighter, "Bremen" made the first east-west heavier-than-air nonstop Atlantic crossing in 1928. Another W.33 set a 52-hour 22-minute endurance record in 1927.

△ Ryan NYP Spirit of St Louis 1927

Origin USA

Engine 223 hp Wright R-790 Whirlwind J-5C air-cooled 9-cylinder radial

Top speed 133 mph (214 km/h)

Based on Ryan's M-2 mailplane, the NYP was designed and built in 60 days by Donald A. Hall. Charles Lindbergh made the first nonstop solo Atlantic crossing and first New York to Paris flight in this aircraft in 1927.

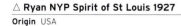

△ Bernard 191GR Oiseau Canari 1928

Origin France

Engine 600 hp Hispano-Suiza 12 Lb water-cooled V12

Top speed 134 mph (216 km/h)

Three record breakers were based on the enclosed-cockpit 190. This one made the first French North Atlantic crossing, piloted by Jean Assolant, René Lefèvre, Armand Lotti, and a stowaway, in June 1929.

△ Fairey Long-range Monoplane 1928

Origin UK

Engine 570 hp Napier Lion XIa water-cooled V12

Top speed 110 mph (177 km/h)

Built for the RAF to set nonstop distance records, one, with a bed for the copilot, made the first nonstop flight from Britain to India in 1929. The second flew a record 5,410 miles (8,707 km) to south-west Africa in 1933.

△ **Graf Zeppelin D-LZ 127 1928**

Origin Germany

Engine 5 x 550 hp Maybach VL-2 water-cooled V12

Top speed 80 mph (129 km/h)

This successful, hydrogen-filled, gas/petrol-fuelled airship was the first aircraft to fly 1 million miles (1.6 million km) and made the first nonstop crossing of the Pacific when flying around the world in 1929.

△ **Breguet XIX TF Super Bidon Point d'Interrogation 1929**

Origin France

Engine 600 hp Hispano-Suiza 12 Lb water-cooled V12

Top speed 133 mph (214 km/h)

Based on a light bomber, the "Point d'Interrogation" (Question Mark) had a 1,419-gallon (5,370-litre) fuel tank. Dieudonne Costes and Maurice Bellonte flew it nonstop from Paris to New York in September 1930.

△ **Lockheed Model 8 Sirius 1929**

Origin USA

Engine 710 hp Wright SR-1820 Cyclone supercharged air-cooled 9-cylinder radial

Top speed 185 mph (298 km/h)

Charles and Anne Lindbergh set a US coast-to-coast speed record on 20 April 1930 in a Model 8. Its most significant flights were in 1931, to the Far East, and in 1933, 30,000 miles (48,280 km) scouting air routes worldwide.

△ **Stinson SM-8A Detroiter 1926**

Origin USA

Engine 215 hp Lycoming R-680

Top speed 135 mph (217 km/h)

Ahead of its time with an enclosed heated cabin, the Detroiter was used for North Pole and Atlantic record attempts. In 1928, working with Packard, one became the first diesel-engined aircraft to fly.

◁ **de Havilland DH60 Gipsy Moth 1928**

Origin UK

Engine 100 hp de Havilland Gipsy I air-cooled 4-cylinder in-line

Top speed 102 mph (164 km/h)

The Gipsy Moth was a popular choice among those bent on setting records. Amy Johnson was the first woman to fly solo from Britain to Australia in one. She flew 11,000 miles (17,703 km) from Croydon to Darwin, in 1930.

Biplanes Dominate

Lessons learned from World War I were consolidated into stronger, faster, and more efficient military aircraft. Britain and the US still favoured biplanes, but now with steel frames and innovations including supercharged engines, hydraulic wheel brakes, and landing flaps. France preferred monoplanes, and built effective aircraft still with wood frames. Aircraft would be increasingly important in future conflict, as messengers and troop transports, not just fighters and bombers.

△ **Sopwith 7F.1 Snipe 1919**

Origin UK

Engine 230 hp Bentley BR2 air-cooled 9-cylinder radial

Top speed 121 mph (195 km/h)

Introduced a few weeks before the end of WWI, the Snipe became the RAF's main post-war single-seat fighter, finally retired in 1926. Its agility and rate of climb made up for a low top speed.

△ **Verville-Sperry M-1 Messenger 1920**

Origin USA

Engine 60 hp Lawrance L-3 air-cooled 3-cylinder radial

Top speed 97 mph (156 km/h)

Small, simple, cheap, and designed by Alfred Verville to replace motorcycles carrying messages for the US Army Air Service, the M-1 was also used for research, including airship hook-up.

▽ **Fairey Flycatcher 1923**

Origin UK

Engine 400 hp Armstrong Siddeley Jaguar IV air-cooled 14-cylinder radial

Top speed 133 mph (214 km/h)

Designed for aircraft carrier use with flaps running the full length of both wings and hydraulic wheel brakes, the pioneering Flycatcher could land or take off on just 151 ft (46 m) of deck; 192 were built.

△ **Vickers Type 56 Victoria 1922**

Origin UK

Engine 2 x 570 hp Napier Lion XI liquid-cooled Broad Arrow

Top speed N/A

WWI showed that getting troops into place before the enemy would be crucial in future conflicts, so the RAF ordered these troop transports. They served until 1944, with new engines fitted in the 1930s.

△ **Boeing Model 15 FB-5 Hawk 1923**

Origin USA

Engine 520 hp Packard 2A-1500 liquid-cooled V12

Top speed 159 mph (256 km/h)

Boeing analysed WWI Fokker DVIIs before building the Model 15 pursuit fighter, which served with the USAAF and with the US Navy. The FB-5 was the production carrier-borne variant.

△ **Boeing F4B-4 1928**

Origin USA

Engine 550 hp Pratt & Whitney 9-cylinder radial

Top speed 189 mph (304 km/h)

A compact, light, and agile fighter for the US Navy, the F4B (or P-12) flew from the USS Lexington from 1929 and served as a pursuit fighter until the mid-1930s, then on training duties until 1941.

△ **Armstrong Whitworth Siskin III 1923**

Origin UK

Engine 400 hp Armstrong Siddeley Jaguar IV supercharged 14-cylinder radial

Top speed 156 mph (251 km/h)

Lessons learned from WWI produced the aerobatic Siskin biplane fighter for the RAF. In IIIA form it was the RAF's first all-steel framed fighter – and very rapid when fitted with a supercharger.

◁ **Morane-Saulnier MS138 1927**

Origin France

Engine 80 hp Le Rhône 9Ac air-cooled 9-cylinder radial

Top speed 88 mph (142 km/h)

France had always tended to prefer monoplanes, so its primary training two-seater was this light monoplane with slightly sweptback parasol wings and fabric-covered, wood-framed fuselage.

△ **Fairey IIIF 1926**

Origin UK

Engine 570 hp Napier Lion XI liquid-cooled Broad Arrow

Top speed 120 mph (192 km/h)

Versions of Fairey III served in both WWI and WWII on reconnaissance duty: conceived as a carrier-borne seaplane, it was built with three seats for the Fleet Air Arm and two for the RAF.

△ **Hawker Tomtit 1928**

Origin UK

Engine 150 hp Armstrong Siddeley Mongoose IIIc air-cooled 5-cylinder radial

Top speed 124 mph (200 km/h)

The RAF disliked wood-framed aircraft, so Sydney Camm designed the Tomtit trainer with steel/duralumin frame and an all-fabric covering. It did not win the contract, so only 35 were built.

△ **Hawker Hart 1928**

Origin UK

Engine 525 hp Rolls-Royce Kestrel 1B liquid-cooled V12

Top speed 185 mph (298 km/h)

Sleek and aerodynamic, the Hart was the most prolific British military aircraft of the interwar years with 992 built. A light bomber, it was faster than contemporary fighters, carrying 529 lb (240 kg) of bombs.

◁ **Morane-Saulnier MS230 1929**

Origin France

Engine 230 hp Salmson 9AB air-cooled 9-cylinder radial

Top speed 127 mph (204 km/h)

Much faster than the MS138, this would be the main elementary trainer for the French Armée de l'Air throughout the 1930s and over 1,000 were built. It was very easy to fly, and sold worldwide.

Airliners Emerge

During the 1920s the airliner began to emerge as a viable means of transport. Although initial designs were loosely based on World War I strategic bombers, such as the Farman F4X, by the mid-1920s there were many purpose-built airliners operating all over the world. This decade also saw some fantastic, but unsuccessful, flying machines, such as the giant Junkers G38 and the 12-engine Dornier Do-X flying boat.

△ de Havilland DH18 1920

Origin UK

Engine 450 hp Napier Lion liquid-cooled 12-cylinder broad arrow

Top speed 125 mph (200 km/h)

This large single-engine biplane was mostly used on the Croydon to Paris run. The type has the dubious distinction of being involved in the first airliner-to-airliner mid-air collision, when one collided with a Farman Goliath over northern France.

◁ Fokker FII 1920

Origin Germany/Netherlands

Engine 250 hp Armstrong Siddeley Puma liquid-cooled in-line 6

Top speed 93 mph (150 km/h)

The Fokker FII drew heavily on the experience that Fokker gained with the DVIII monoplane fighter. At a time when most aeroplanes were biplanes, the FII looked very modern. An unusual feature is the lack of a vertical stabilizer or fin, with directional stability being provided solely by the deep, slab-sided fuselage.

▽ Fokker FVIIa 1925

Origin Netherlands

Engine 400 hp Liberty L-12 liquid-cooled V-12

Top speed 115 mph (185 km/h)

The predecessor to the successful Fokker Trimotor, 40 FVIIas were built. Although the original aircraft was powered by a Liberty engine, all subsequent machines were fitted with either Bristol Jupiter or Pratt & Whitney Wasp radial engines.

▷ Fokker FVIIb/3M/FX 1925

Origin Netherlands design/US built

Engine 3 x 220 hp Wright J-5 Whirlwind air-cooled 9-cylinder radial

Top speed 115 mph (185 km/h)

Known as the Fokker Trimotor, this was a very popular airliner. Of Dutch design but powered by American engines; this is enlarged FX version built in the US. The aircraft Sir Charles Kingsford-Smith flew for the the first crossings of the Pacific Ocean and Tasman Sea, was an FVIIb.

◁ Handley Page Type W8 1921

Origin UK

Engine 2 x 450 hp Napier Lion liquid-cooled 12-cylinder broad arrow

Top speed 103 mph (166 km/h)

Handley Page's first purpose-built civil transport aircraft, is notable for being the first airliner to be designed with an integral toilet. As with many aircraft of the 1920s, it was somewhat underpowered with only two engines, and later models had an additional 360 hp Rolls-Royce Eagle V12 mounted in the nose.

△ **de Havilland DH34 1922**

Origin UK

Engine 450hp Napier Lion liquid-cooled 12-cylinder broad arrow

Top speed 128mph (206km/h)

Essentially a larger version of the DH18, an unusual feature of this aircraft was the ability to carry a spare engine in the cabin, as both the door and fuselage were specifically designed to allow this. However, the spare greatly reduced the payload.

△ **de Havilland DH50J 1923**

Origin UK

Engine 450hp Bristol Jupiter IV air-cooled radial

Top speed 112mph (180km/h)

Designed to replace the war-surplus DH9, the DH50 enjoyed an excellent start to its career when aviation pioneer Alan Cobham (later Sir Alan) won a reliability trial in the prototype, only four days after its maiden flight.

△ **Boeing 80 1928**

Origin USA

Engine 3 x 450hp Pratt & Whitney Wasp air-cooled 9-cylinder radial

Top speed 138mph (222km/h)

This three-engine biplane was used by Boeing's own airline, Boeing Air Transport. Other trimotor airliners were monoplanes. Boeing opted for a biplane configuration for improved takeoff and landing performance.

△ **Ford 5-AT Trimotor 1928**

Origin USA

Engine 3 x 420hp Pratt & Whitney Wasp air-cooled 9-cylinder radial

Top speed 150mph (241km/h)

Although the Ford Trimotor strongly resembled the contemporary Fokker, it was an all-metal machine, with more powerful engines. Nicknamed the "Tin Goose", Ford built 199 Trimotors, and several are still airworthy today.

◁ **Sikorsky S38 1928**

Origin USA

Engine 2 x 400hp Pratt & Whitney Wasp air-cooled 9-cylinder radial

Top speed 120mph (192km/h)

Sikorsky's first amphibian to sell in large numbers, the S38 was particularly popular with explorers and adventurers, although it was also operated by many airlines and the armed forces of several countries.

△ **Junkers G38 1929**

Origin Germany

Engine 2 x 690hp Junkers L55 liquid-cooled V12 inboard, 2 x 413hp Junkers L8a liquid-cooled in-line 6 outboard

Top speed 140mph (225km/h)

Junkers only built two G38s, but at the time they were the largest aircraft in the world. The wings were so thick that there was room for passengers in the leading edges.

◁ **Dornier Do-X 1929**

Origin Germany

Engine 12 x 610hp Curtis Conqueror liquid-cooled V12

Top speed 131mph (211km/h)

A truly remarkable machine, the Do-X set many records, including being the heaviest and largest aircraft of its time, and also carrying the greatest number of passengers – an incredible 169.

Aircraft
1930–1949

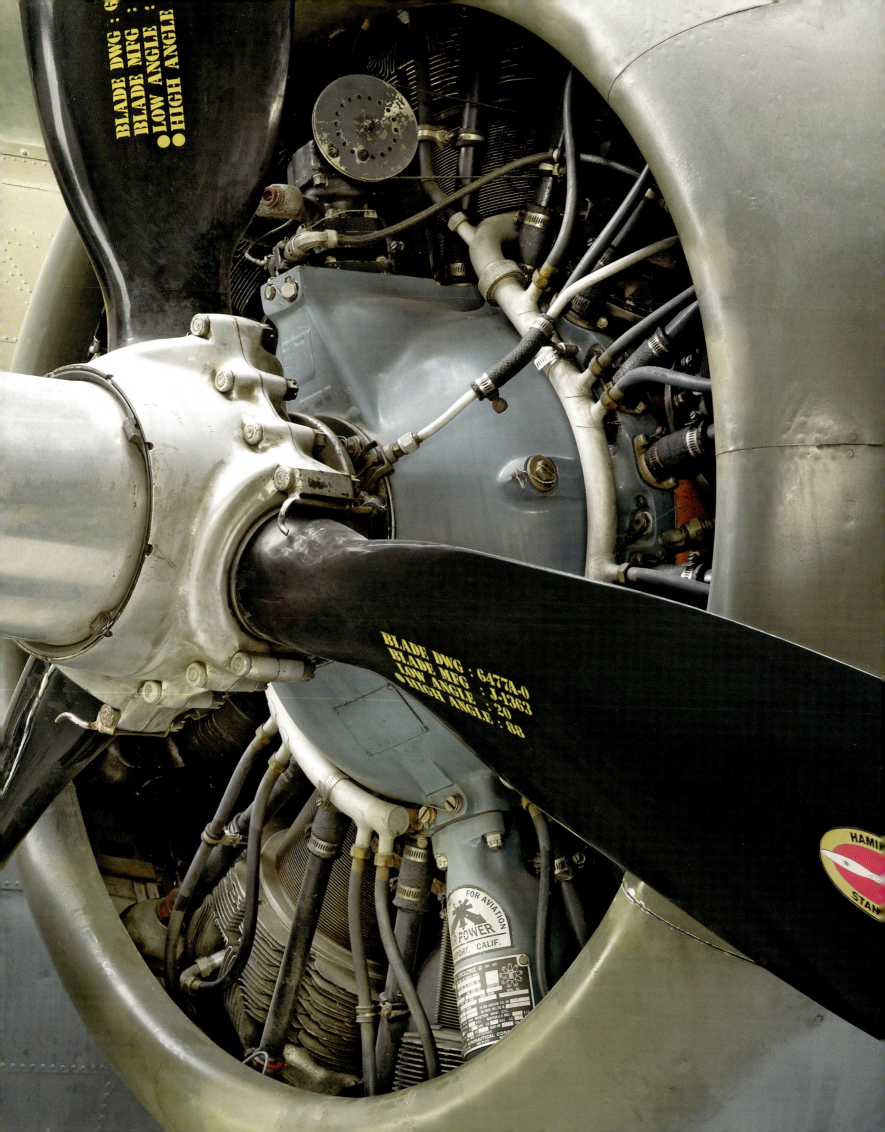

Private Aircraft For All

During the 1930s General Aviation really began to gather momentum. Inspired by events such as Sir Alan Cobham's National Aviation Day displays and films like *Hell's Angels* and *The Dawn Patrol*, interest in sport flying grew exponentially, and manufacturers on both sides of the Atlantic strove to produce suitable machines for this expanding market.

▽ **Taylor E2 Cub (converted) 1930**

Origin USA

Engine 35 hp Szekely air-cooled 3-cylinder radial

Top speed 70 mph (113 km/h)

The E2 was the first Taylor/Piper aircraft to bear the Cub name. Originally fitted with a 37 hp Continental A40 flat-4, this aircraft was converted to the H2 specification with the Szekely engine. Around 350 were built.

△ **de Havilland DH82A Tiger Moth 1931**

Origin UK

Engine 130 hp de Havilland Gipsy Major I air-cooled inverted in-line 4

Top speed 109 mph (175 km/h)

Based on the DH Gipsy Moth, the DH Tiger Moth was designed as a military trainer. The type was very successful, with over 8,800 being built. Many survivors remain airworthy today.

▷ **Stampe SV4C 1933**

Origin Belgium/France

Engine 145 hp de Havilland Gipsy Major X air-cooled in-line 4

Top speed 116 mph (186 km/h)

Designed as an improvement on the DH Tiger Moth, the Stampe offered a slightly more modern design, much better handling, and superior aerobatic capabilities. Eventually almost 1,000 would be built, many in France and mostly for the French Air Force.

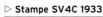

△ **de Havilland DH87B Hornet Moth 1934**

Origin UK

Engine 130 hp de Havilland Gipsy Major I air-cooled inverted in-line 4

Top speed 124 mph (200 km/h)

Another of de Havilland's series of Moth biplanes, the Hornet Moth featured a fully enclosed cockpit and side-by-side seating. Popular with private owners, of the 164 built several still survive, being much prized by collectors.

△ **Stinson V.77 Reliant 1933**

Origin USA

Engine 300 hp Lycoming R-680 air-cooled 9-cylinder radial

Top speed 177 mph (285 km/h)

The Stinson Reliant was produced over a ten-year period, in literally dozens of versions and powered by many different radial engines. Operated by the USAAF, RAF, and RN, later models are easily identified by the gull-wing configuration.

△ **de Havilland DH94 Moth Minor 1939**

Origin UK

Engine 90 hp de Havilland Gipsy Minor air-cooled inverted in-line 4

Top speed 118 mph (190 km/h)

The last de Havilland design to be called Moth, the DH94 Moth Minor was an elegant monoplane that was descended from the earlier Swallow Moth. Aimed directly at the flying club market it initially sold well, although the outbreak of WWII caused production to cease after barely 140 had been produced.

△ Taylor/Piper J2 1935

Origin USA

Engine 40 hp Continental A-40-4 air-cooled flat-4

Top speed 80 mph (129 km/h)

Based on the E2, the J2 established the definitive Cub configuration, with enclosed cabin, and rounded wing tips and tail surfaces. Some 1,158 J2s were built by Taylor and, from November 1937, Piper Aircraft.

△ Piper J3C-65 Cub 1939

Origin USA

Engine 65 hp Continental A-65 air-cooled flat-4

Top speed 87 mph (140 km/h)

One of the great all-time general aviation aircraft, the Piper J3 Cub is an aviation icon. Piper produced almost 20,000 (many as L-4 "Grasshoppers" for the US military) during its ten-year production run.

▷ Mignet HM14 Pou du Ciel (Flying Flea) 1933

Origin France

Engine 17 hp Aubier-Dunne 500 cc air-cooled 3-cylinder 2-stroke motorcycle engine

Top speed 85 mph (138 km/h)

This aircraft sparked the home-building craze of the 1930s. Its tandem wing design contained a dangerous aerodynamic flaw and many Fleas crashed. Hundreds were built, consisting of many variants and powered by a variety of engines before the type was grounded.

▷ Miles M.3A Falcon Major 1936

Origin UK

Engine 130 hp de Havilland Gipsy Major I air-cooled inverted in-line 4

Top speed 150 mph (241 km/h)

This is a sleek monoplane of mostly wood-and-fabric construction. Its two distinguishing features are the forward-swept windscreen and the "trousered" undercarriage. In its time it was a popular machine.

◁ Blackburn B2 1936

Origin UK

Engine 120 hp de Havilland Gipsy III air-cooled in-line 4

Top speed 112 mph (180 km/h)

Derived from Blackburn's Bluebird IV trainer, the principal difference over the earlier aircraft was that it had a metal semi-monocoque fuselage. The side-by-side seating arrangement is unusual for an open-cockpit biplane.

◁ Spartan Executive 1936

Origin USA

Engine 450 hp Pratt & Whitney Wasp air-cooled 9-cylinder radial

Top speed 257 mph (414 km/h)

The LearJet of its time, the Spartan Executive was not only very fast but extremely luxurious. At a time when most air forces operated biplanes with fixed undercarriages, this sleek, powerful, retractable monoplane was – and still is – a much-desired machine.

▷ Aeronca 100 1937

Origin USA/UK

Engine 36 hp J-99 air-cooled flat-twin

Top speed 95 mph (152 km/h)

Not one of the prettiest aircraft ever built, the Aeronca 100 was a version of the Aeronca C-3 built under licence in Britain. Increasingly stringent airworthiness requirements (which the C-3 could not meet) caused production to cease in 1937. Only 24 were built in the UK.

Quest for Speed

The 1930s brought a new thirst for speed among pilots, with ever more extreme aircraft being built. In the US huge engines were put into tiny, stubby aircraft that were incredibly difficult to fly. European enthusiasts were just as competitive, but their sporting aircraft tended to be a little slower and more practical, having been built for long-distance contests, such as from England to South Africa and back, where reliability was critical.

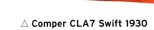

△ Comper CLA7 Swift 1930

Origin UK

Engine Original 70 hp R/now 90 hp Niagara II Pobjoy air-cooled 7-cylinder radial

Top speed 140 mph (225 km/h)

Small and light, constructed of fabric-covered spruce, Flight Lieutenant Nicholas Comper's Swift was built with increasingly powerful engines, making it an effective racing and sporting aeroplane.

△ Northrop Alpha 1930

Origin USA

Engine 420 hp Pratt & Whitney Wasp R-1340-SC1 air-cooled 9-cylinder radial

Top speed 177 mph (285 km/h)

Jack Northrop's brilliant and very fast Alpha combined all-metal, semi-monocoque fuselage with multi-celled cantilever wings and wing fillets. It was built either with seating for six passengers inside or a cargo hull.

△ Gee Bee Model Z Super Sportster 1931

Origin USA

Engine 535 hp Pratt & Whitney R-985 Wasp Jr air-cooled 9-cylinder radial

Top speed 267 mph (430 km/h)

Granville Brothers crammed the largest possible engine into the smallest possible aircraft to win the 1931 Thompson Trophy in a new record speed. Fitted later with a 750 hp engine, it crashed during a record attempt.

△ Gee Bee R-2 1932

Origin USA

Engine 800 hp Pratt & Whitney R-1340 Wasp air-cooled 9-cylinder radial

Top speed 296 mph (476 km/h)

Gee Bees are the most evocative aircraft of the golden age of American air racing in the 1930s. After the success of the Sportster, true racers like this were built to break records. Its wingspan was 25 ft (8 m).

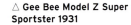

◁ Arrow Active 2 1932

Origin UK

Engine 120 hp de Havilland Gipsy III air-cooled inverted 4-cylinder in-line

Top speed 144 mph (230 km/h)

Only two Actives were built, of which this is the second. Failing to get military orders, they were flown as sports planes. Active 2 competed in the King's Cup in 1932–33, recording 137 mph (220 km/h).

◁ **Beechcraft Model 17 Staggerwing 1933**

Origin USA

Engine 450 hp Pratt & Whitney R985 AN-1 Wasp Junior air-cooled 9-cylinder radial

Top speed 212 mph (341 km/h)

Walter Beech conceived the Staggerwing (upper wing rearward of lower) as a luxury, high-speed cabin plane. Spacious and rapid, it was popular in wartime; 785 were built.

▷ **Hughes H-1 1935**

Origin USA

Engine 1,000 hp Pratt & Whitney R-1535 twin-row 14-cylinder radial

Top speed 352 mph (566 km/h)

Howard Hughes used streamlining and fully retracting undercarriage to squeeze record speeds out of the H-1. He also set a new transcontinental record, but failed to achieve military orders.

△ **Percival P10 Vega Gull 1935**

Origin UK

Engine 205 hp de Havilland Gipsy Six Series II air-cooled inverted 6-cylinder in-line

Top speed 174 mph (280 km/h)

Despite being an enlarged, four-seater version of the earlier Gull, the Vega Gull was still an efficient design, winning the King's Cup and Schlesinger races in 1936; 90 were built.

▽ **Percival Mew Gull 1936**

Origin UK

Engine 200 hp de Havilland Gipsy Six air-cooled 6-cylinder inverted

Top speed 245 mph (394 km/h)

Captain Edgar Percival's Mew Gull was a highly effective racer of which six were built, ultimately reaching 265 mph (426 km/h) and winning many races, including the King's Cup in 1937–38 and 1955.

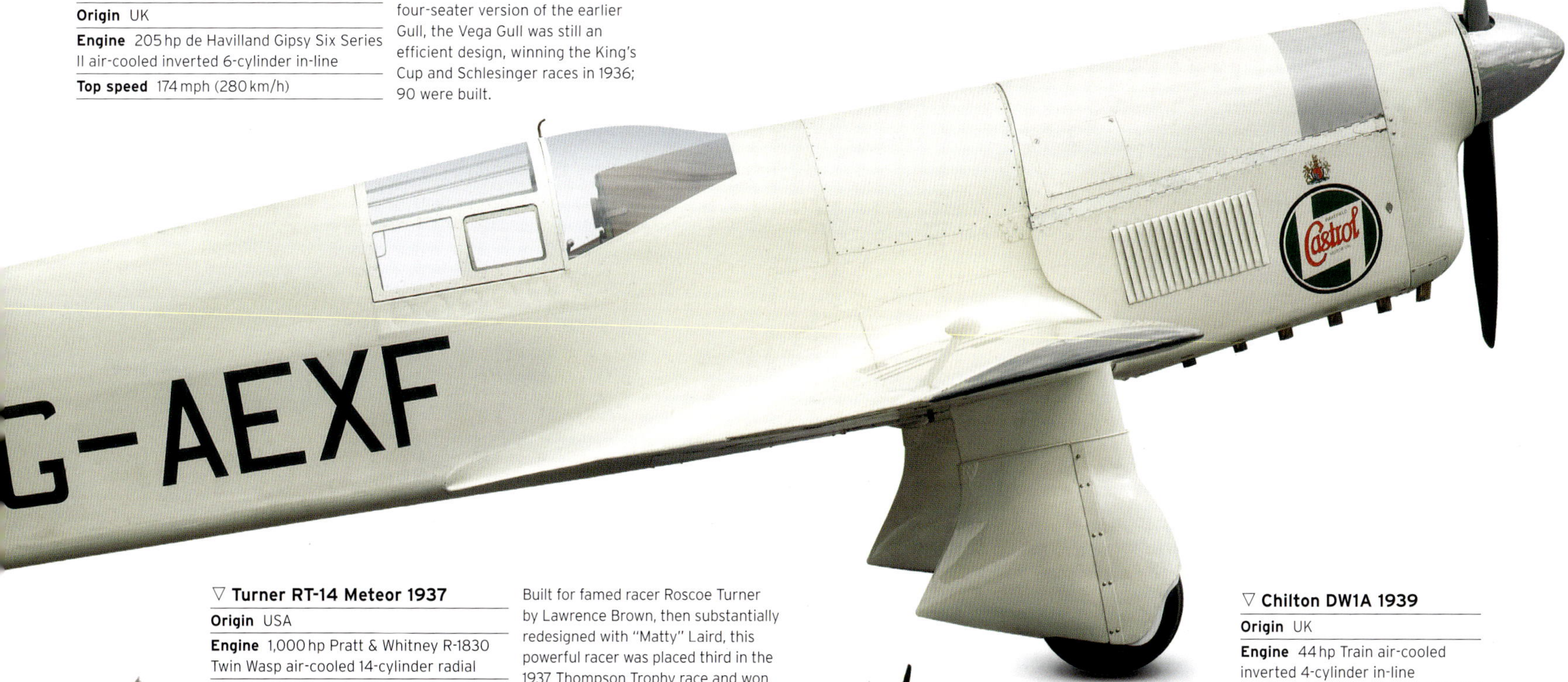

▽ **Turner RT-14 Meteor 1937**

Origin USA

Engine 1,000 hp Pratt & Whitney R-1830 Twin Wasp air-cooled 14-cylinder radial

Top speed 350 mph (563 km/h)

Built for famed racer Roscoe Turner by Lawrence Brown, then substantially redesigned with "Matty" Laird, this powerful racer was placed third in the 1937 Thompson Trophy race and won in 1938 and 1939.

▽ **Chilton DW1A 1939**

Origin UK

Engine 44 hp Train air-cooled inverted 4-cylinder in-line

Top speed 135 mph (217 km/h)

Wealthy de Havilland students Andrew Dalrymple and Alex Ward founded Chilton Aircraft to build the DW1 in 1936 with a 1,172 cc Ford car engine, soon upgraded to this model. This is a replica.

Setting Records

Public interest and government enthusiasm for setting aerial world records continued throughout the 1930s, with the US, Soviet Union, and European nations in particular competing to send pilots to ever greater altitudes, speeds, and distances. Some of the records set in this decade are still unbroken over 70 years later, including the world speed record for seaplanes and the longest nonstop flight for a single-engined aircraft.

△ **de Havilland DH80A Puss Moth 1930**

Origin UK

Engine 120 hp de Havilland Gipsy III air-cooled inverted 4-cylinder in-line

Top speed 128 mph (206 km/h)

This modern and rapid three-seater with enclosed cockpit made many record attempts, notably with Jim Mollison (first solo east-west Atlantic) and his wife Amy Johnson (UK to Cape Town, and Tokyo).

△ **de Havilland DH88 Comet Racer 1934**

Origin UK

Engine 223 hp de Havilland Gipsy Six R air-cooled inverted 6-cylinder in-line

Top speed 255 mph (410 km/h)

The Comet was light, fast, and built to win the 1934 MacRobertson Air Race from London, UK to Melbourne, Australia. C. W. A. Scott and Tom Campbell Black arrived in 71 hours – 19 hours ahead of the next competitor.

◁ **Blériot 110 1930**

Origin France

Engine 600 hp Hispano-Suiza 12L water-cooled V12

Top speed 137 mph (220 km/h)

Built for the government, it had mirrors for takeoff and landing and carried 1,320 gallons (6,000 litres) of fuel. Its 1932 closed-circuit record was 76 hours and 34 minutes for 5,658 miles (9,106 km) and, in 1933, New York to Rayak, Syria, 6,587 miles (10,600 km).

△ **Curtiss Robin J-1 1928**

Origin USA

Engine 165 hp Wright Whirlwind J-6-5 radial

Top speed 110 mph (177 km/h)

Supported by in-flight refuelling, Dale Jackson and Forest O'Brine took the world endurance record to 17 days, 12 hours, and 17 minutes from 13 to 30 July 1929; in 1935 Fred and Algene Key raised it to 27 days in the same aircraft type.

▷ **Macchi Castoldi MC72 1931**

Origin Italy

Engine 2,850 hp Fiat AS.6 supercharged water-cooled V24

Top speed 441 mph (709 km/h)

The fastest seaplane ever, the tandem-engined MC72 was the holder of the outright world airspeed record for five years. Francesco Agello averaged 441 mph (710 km/h) on 23 October 1934.

▽ **Franklin PS-2 Texaco Eaglet 1931**

Origin USA

Engine None

Top speed 125 mph (201 km/h)

Frank Hawks flew the Eaglet glider across the US from Los Angeles to New York in 1930, towed by a Waco 10 biplane and sponsored by Texaco. He attracted huge crowds at every refuelling stop.

▷ Lockheed Vega 5B 1927

Origin USA

Engine 500 hp Pratt & Whitney Wasp R1340C supercharged air-cooled 9-cylinder radial

Top speed 185 mph (298 km/h)

A long-range passenger transport for Lockheed, this rugged aircraft was ideal for records. On 20–21 May 1932, Amelia Earhart became the first woman to fly solo, nonstop across the Atlantic in this aircraft.

▽ Tupolev ANT-25 1933

Origin USSR

Engine 750 hp Mikulin M-34 water-cooled V12

Top speed 153 mph (246 km/h)

ANT-25 made many remarkable, long-distance flights, including a world record 56 hours and 20 minutes, 5,825 miles (9,374 km), from Moscow to the Far East in July 1936, and 7,146 miles (11,500 km) Moscow to California in July 1937.

◁ Howard DGA-6 "Mister Mulligan" 1934

Origin USA

Engine 850 hp Pratt & Whitney Wasp supercharged air-cooled 9-cylinder radial

Top speed 260 mph (418 km/h)

Designed by Ben Howard and Gordon Israel to win the trans-US Bendix Trophy race, which they did in 1935 by flying non-stop at high altitude with oxygen masks. The DGA-6 went on to win the Thompson Trophy in the same year.

▽ Bristol Type 138A 1936

Origin UK

Engine 500 hp Bristol Pegasus P.E.6S supercharged air-cooled 9-cylinder radial

Top speed 123 mph (198 km/h)

The UK Air Ministry sponsored this light wooden monocoque with two-stage supercharged Pegasus engine. With oxygen and a pressure suit for the pilot, it reached 49,967 ft (15,230 m) in 1936 and 53,937 ft (16,440 m) in 1937.

△ Vickers Wellesley Type 292 1937

Origin UK

Engine 950 hp Bristol Pegasus XXII supercharged air-cooled 9-cylinder radial

Top speed 228 mph (367 km/h)

In November 1938 three Wellesleys flew a world record 7,161 miles (11,525 km) from Egypt to Australia, still the longest single-engined flight. Remarkably, the aircraft were modified bombers, not purpose-built.

◁ Bücker Bü133C Jungmeister 1936

Origin Germany

Engine 160 hp Siemens-Bramo SH14A-4 air-cooled 7-cylinder radial

Top speed 137 mph (220 km/h)

The 1936 Olympics in Berlin featured the first and only aerobatic competition. It was won by German pilot Graf von Hafenburg in a Jungmeister. At an international competition a year later, nine out of 13 competitors flew the type; Jungmeisters took the first three places.

Airliners Win Through

By the 1930s aviation had become part of many industrialized countries' transportation systems. Having demonstrated that air travel was viable, the aircraft manufacturers had to demonstrate that it was also safe and comfortable. Fully enclosed, insulated, and heated cabins became the norm, and twin-engine aircraft that could safely fly on one motor began to enter service.

△ Handley Page HP-42 1931

Origin UK

Engine 4 x 500 hp Bristol Jupiter XIF air-cooled 9-cylinder radial

Top speed 120 mph (193 km/h)

Designed to an Imperial Airways specification, eight were built (four long-range HP-42s, four HP-45s) and all had names beginning with the letter "H". Although slow, none of them was ever involved in a fatal accident while in civilian service, making the type unique among its peers.

△ Armstrong Whitworth AW15 Atlanta 1931

Origin UK

Engine 4 x 340 hp Armstrong Whitworth Serval III air-cooled 10-cylinder 2-row radial

Top speed 174 mph (280 km/h)

In 1930 Armstrong Whitworth designed an aircraft to service Imperial Airways' African routes. As the engines of the time were notoriously unreliable, Imperial Airways specified that four engines would be required.

◁ Fokker FXVIII 1932

Origin Netherlands

Engine 3 x 420 hp Pratt & Whitney Wasp C air-cooled 9-cylinder radial

Top speed 150 mph (241 km/h)

The FXVIII was essentially an enlarged and improved variant of the Fokker Trimotor. However, questions over structural integrity and the drag penalty of the fixed undercarriage ensured it could not compete with more modern designs such as the DC-2.

△ Junkers Ju52/3m 1932

Origin Germany

Engine 3 x 715 hp BMW 132 air-cooled 9-cylinder radial

Top speed 168 mph (270 km/h)

Known as "Tante Ju" and "Iron Annie", the Ju52 had a long and illustrious career as both a commercial airliner and military transport. Notable for its corrugated skin (which stiffened the fuselage and wings), around 4,800 were built. Most were fitted with BMW engines, although the prototype was powered by Pratt & Whitney Hornets.

△ Koolhoven Fokker FK 48 1934

Origin Netherlands

Engine 2 x 130 hp de Havilland Gipsy Major air-cooled inverted in-line 4

Top speed 129 mph (207 km/h)

Outdated even before it entered service, the FK 48 was not a success. Only one was built, and it was in service with KLM for only two years.

△ **Boeing 247 1933**

Origin USA

Engine 2 x 550 hp Pratt & Whitney Wasp
air-cooled 9-cylinder radial

Top speed 200 mph (322 km/h)

This very advanced machine for its time
incorporated many modern features, including
an all-metal semi-monocoque fuselage and
cantilever wing, retractable undercarriage,
autopilot, variable pitch propellers, and a de-icing
system. It was the first twin-engine transport
capable of sustained flight on one engine, and
was faster than most fighters of the time.

◁ **de Havilland DH89 Dragon
Rapide 6 1934**

Origin UK

Engine 2 x 200 hp de Havilland Gipsy
6 air-cooled inverted in-line 6

Top speed 157 mph (254 km/h)

Possibly the best British short-haul
aircraft of the 1930s, the Dragon
Rapide was a rugged and reliable
aircraft that replaced the earlier DH84
Dragon. The biplane configuration
ensured that takeoff and landing
speeds were low, making it ideal for
operating from small grass runways.

△ **de Havilland DH91
Albatross 1938**

Origin UK

Engine 4 x 525 hp de Havilland Gipsy
Twelve air-cooled inverted V12

Top speed 225 mph (362 km/h)

Originally designed as a long-range
mailplane, of the seven aircraft built five
were constructed as passenger aircraft.
Two notable features are that it was
made from a ply-and-balsa sandwich
(which de Havilland would use to
great effect on its famous Mosquito
fighter-bomber) and that the air-cooled
engines had reverse-flow cowlings.

▷ **de Havilland DH95
Flamingo 1939**

Origin UK

Engine 2 x 930 hp Bristol Perseus
air-cooled 9-cylinder radial

Top speed 239 mph (385 km/h)

The first all-metal aircraft built by de Havilland,
the Flamingo was intended to compete with
contemporary American machines, such as the
Lockheed Electra and Douglas DC-3. Fitted with
slotted flaps, variable pitch propellers, and a
retractable undercarriage it performed well,
but only 14 were built.

▷ **Douglas DC-2 1934**

Origin USA

Engine 2 x 730 hp Wright Cyclone
air-cooled 9-cylinder radial

Top speed 210 mph (338 km/h)

The DC-2 entered service with TWA in 1934.
The Dutch airline KLM entered one in the
MacRobertson air race, between London
and Melbourne the same year. Astonishingly,
it came second, being beaten only by the
purpose-built DH88 racer.

◁ **Lockheed Model 10 Electra 1934**

Origin USA

Engine 2 x 450 hp Pratt & Whitney Wasp
Junior air-cooled 9-cylinder radial

Top speed 202 mph (325 km/h)

Probably best known as the type of aircraft in which
famous aviatrix Amelia Earhart went missing, the
Electra was Lockheed's first all-metal design. Much
of the design work was done by a young student,
Clarence Johnson, who would later lead Lockheed's
famous "Skunk Works".

△ **Beechcraft Model 18 1937**

Origin USA

Engine 2 x 450 hp Pratt & Whitney Wasp
air-cooled 9-cylinder radial

Top speed 264 mph (424 km/h)

Known universally as the "Twin Beech", the
Model 18 was an extremely successful design
with over 9,000 being built over a very long
production run. Available with a variety of
different engines later in trigear form, several
hundred remain airworthy.

Flying Boats and Amphibians

The 1930s was the "Golden Age" for flying boats, with airlines operating large luxurious machines that were fitted with beds and offered silver service dining. Some of the aircraft could touch down on land or water. However, one of the consequences of World War II was that a large number of runways were built all over the world. As a result the faster, more economical landplanes soon rendered the flying boat obsolete.

△ **Saro A.19 Cloud 1930**

Origin UK

Engine 3 x 340 hp Armstrong-Whitworth Serval III air-cooled 10-cylinder 2-row radial

Top speed 118 mph (190 km/h)

Descended from the Saro A.17 Cutty Sark amphibian, 22 A.19 Clouds were built and used mostly by the RAF, although a few were operated as civilian aircraft. One was sold to the Czechoslovakian state airline and its fuselage survives at the Prague Aviation Museum, Kbely.

△ **Savoia-Marchetti S.66 1932**

Origin Italy

Engine 3 x 750 hp Fiat A.24R liquid-cooled V-12

Top speed 164 mph (264 km/h)

A large flying boat notable for its twin-hull design, the S.66 was designed as an airliner, although during the war it was used for search and rescue. Unusually, the flight deck was located in the centre section of the wing, while all the passenger seats were in the hulls.

△ **Martin M130 1935**

Origin USA

Engine 4 x 950 hp Pratt & Whitney Twin Wasp air-cooled 14-cylinder 2-row radial

Top speed 180 mph (290 km/h)

Intended to service Pan Am's Pacific routes, only three M130s were built. Like the later Boeing 314s, all were named "clipper" (China Clipper, Hawaii Clipper, and Philippine Clipper). One flew the first trans-Pacific airmail service, and all were lost in fatal accidents.

▷ **Grumman J2F-6 Duck 1936**

Origin USA

Engine 1,050 hp Wright Cyclone air-cooled 9-cylinder radial

Top speed 190 mph (304 km/h)

Although it may look like a biplane on an amphibious float, the Duck is actually more like a flying boat, as the single float is blended into the fuselage. The Duck was used by all branches of the US military and Coast Guard, and also Argentina, Colombia, Mexico, and Peru.

▽ **Grumman JRF-5 Goose 1937**

Origin USA

Engine 2 x 450 hp Pratt & Whitney Wasp Junior air-cooled 9-cylinder radial

Top speed 264 mph (424 km/h)

Initially intended to be used as a "commuter" aircraft, between Long Island and New York, the Goose proved to be a rugged and reliable amphibian, and was used for both military and civil (as the G-21) applications. Around 340 machines were built.

△ **Consolidated PBY Catalina 1936**

Origin USA

Engine 2 x 1,200 hp Pratt & Whitney Twin Wasp air-cooled 14-cylinder 2-row radial

Top speed 196 mph (314 km/h)

Available as both a pure flying boat and an amphibian, the Catalina had a truly remarkable range, albeit at a relatively slow speed. Catalinas saved thousands of downed aircrew during WWII, and were used as airliners.

△ **Sikorsky JRS-1/S-43 1937**

Origin USA

Engine 2 x 750 hp Pratt & Whitney Hornet air-cooled 9-cylinder radial

Top speed 190 mph (306 km/h)

Sometimes called the "Baby Clipper", its principal operator was Pan Am, although airlines in Brazil and Norway also used them. Two were sold to private owners, and the example once owned by Howard Hughes remains airworthy.

△ **Shorts S25 Sunderland 1938**

Origin UK

Engine 4 x 1,065 hp Bristol Pegasus air-cooled 9-cylinder radial

Top speed 213 mph (343 km/h)

Although loosely based on Short's S23 Empire Class flying boat, the Sunderland was significantly different from its civilian ancestor. The aircraft sank many U-boats during WWII.

Airmail floatplane, S20 Mercury

Carrier flying boat

◁ **Shorts Mayo Composite 1938**

Origin UK

Engine S21 Maia, 4 x 919 hp Bristol Pegasus air-cooled radial; S20 Mercury, 4 x 365 hp Napier Rapier air-cooled H-16

Top speed 212 mph (341 km/h)

This unusual machine was built to carry airmail. The smaller S20 Mercury floatplane was launched from the roof of a dedicated carrier aircraft, the S21 Maia. It did work, but advances in design soon rendered it redundant.

△ **Boeing 314 clipper 1939**

Origin USA

Engine 4 x 1,600 hp Wright Twin Cyclone air-cooled 14-cylinder 2-row radial

Top speed 210 mph (340 km/h)

Built by Boeing especially for Pan Am's Atlantic and Pacific services, at one point the 314 was the largest aircraft in the world. Only 12 of these magnificent aircraft were built, with three being operated by British Overseas Airways (BOAC) during WWII. None survive.

◁ **Supermarine Walrus 1939**

Origin UK

Engine 750 hp Bristol Pegasus VI air-cooled 9-cylinder radial

Top speed 135 mph (215 km/h)

The Walrus was designed to be launched by a warship's catapult, and was consequently much stronger than it looked. Rugged and reliable, the Walrus saved countless lives as a search-and-rescue aircraft. Its wings folded for carrier storage.

Rotorcraft Emerge

A worldwide race was under way in the 1930s to perfect the helicopter, but it was only when disparate touches of genius were brought together that progress was made. Spain's Juan de la Cierva invented the hinge systems that made rotors practical; Austrian Raoul Hafner came up with the cyclic system that made them controllable; Frenchman Louis Breguet created coaxial contra-rotating blades that prevented the rotor blades and the helicopter fuselage rotating in opposite directions (torque reaction); and Russian-American Igor Sikorsky made the important steps that turned the autogyro into a true helicopter.

△ Cierva C19 1930

Origin Spain/UK

Engine 80 hp Armstrong Siddeley Genet II radial

Top speed N/A

A method of spinning the main rotor by deflecting the propeller wash allowed the C19 to "spin up" while stationary. In the MkVI, the rotor was "pre-spun" directly by the engine.

▽ Cierva C8 MkIV Autogiro 1930

Origin UK

Engine 200 hp Armstrong Siddeley Lynx IVC 7-cylinder radial

Top speed 100 mph (161 km/h)

Cierva's "articulated" rotor is now used on almost all helicopters. The C8 added drag dampers to limit blade movement and successfully completed a 3,000-mile (4,828-km) tour of Britain.

△ Cierva C30A Autogiro 1934

Origin Spain/UK

Engine Armstrong Siddeley Genet Major 1A radial

Top speed 110 mph (177 km/h)

Cierva's autogyros were rightly described in their time as "the most important step in aeronautics since the Wright Brothers". Tragically Cierva was killed in a plane crash in 1936.

△ D'Ascanio D'AT3 1930

Origin Italy

Engine 95 hp Fiat A-505 piston

Top speed N/A

This early coaxial twin rotor machine set height (59 ft/18 m) and distance (3,537 ft/1,078 m) records, but designer Corradino D'Ascanio's potential was unfulfilled. He went on to invent the first scooter.

◁ de Havilland/Cierva C24 Autogiro 1931

Origin UK

Engine 120 hp de Havilland Gipsy III in-line

Top speed 115 mph (185 km/h)

The sole venture of de Havilland into autogyros "married" a Cierva rotor to a DH Puss Moth fuselage. Designed for three people, it could barely lift two, and only one was made.

△ Herrick HV-2A Verta 1933

Origin USA

Engine 125 hp Kinner B-5 radial

Top speed 99 mph (159 km/h)

The Verta was an inspired biplane design with a conventional lower wing and an upper wing that rotated, autogyro style, for low-speed flight or landings. It was too heavy to develop successfully.

△ Florine Tandem Motor 1933

Origin Belgium

Engine 180 hp Hispano-Suiza piston

Top speed N/A

Russian émigré Nicolas Florine built the first flyable twin tandem rotor helicopter. Rather than contra-rotating, the rotors were tilted 10 degrees in relation to each other to counter torque.

△ Breguet-Dorand Gyroplane 1936

Origin France

Engine 240 hp Hispano-Suiza radial

Top speed 62 mph (100 km/h)

This worthy claimant to the title of "first successful helicopter", flew at 70 mph (113 km/h) and stayed airborne for an hour in 1936. It was destroyed by the Allied bombing of Villacoublay airfield, France in 1943.

▷ Focke-Wulf Fa61 1936

Origin Germany

Engine 160 hp BMW-Bramo Sh.14A radial

Top speed 70 mph (112 km/h)

The Fa61 was a milestone in helicopter design. It was famously demonstrated by German test pilot Hanna Reitsch indoors in the Deutschlandhalle, Berlin in 1938.

△ Sikorsky VS-300 1939

Origin USA

Engine 75 hp Lycoming

Top speed 64 mph (103 km/h)

Igor Sikorsky's single, powered rotor with anti-torque tail rotor – known by the company as "Igor's Nightmare" – established the template for the successful helicopter, which made the autogyro obsolete.

▽ SNCASE Liore et Olivier LeO C302 1939

Origin France

Engine 175 hp Salmson 9Ne radial

Top speed 112 mph (180 km/h)

LeO, in 1937 nationalized as SNCASE – also known as Sud Est – held Cierva's rotor patent for France and created a machine with improved jump-takeoff ability and better landing characteristics.

The Warplane Evolves

The 1930s saw rapid development in warplanes, especially from 1935 as the threat of war loomed. At the start of the decade, basic bombers and trainers looked much like late World War I aircraft, but soon monocoque fuselages, enclosed cockpits, all-metal construction, and advanced monoplane wing designs were the norm.

△ Polikarpov Po-2 1930

Origin USSR

Engine 125 hp Shvetsov M-11D air-cooled 5-cylinder radial

Top speed 94 mph (152 km/h)

The Soviets claimed that over 40,000 of Nikolai Polikarpov's Po-2s were built. Being surprisingly difficult to shoot down, in WWII they were used as trainers, night bombers, and reconnaissance and liaison aircraft.

▷ Bristol Bulldog 1929

Origin UK

Engine 440-490 hp Bristol Jupiter VII supercharged air-cooled 9-cylinder radial

Top speed 178 mph (287 km/h)

Frank Barnwell's design was the RAF's main day/night fighter between the wars. Cheap to maintain, it offered good speed, twin guns, and light bomb capability.

◁ Dewoitine D27 1930

Origin France

Engine 425hp Gnome-Rhone Jupiter VII air-cooled 9-cylinder radial

Top speed 194 mph (312 km/h)

French aero-builder Émile Dewoitine moved to Switzerland in 1927 and designed this parasol-wing monoplane. Also built in Romania and Yugoslavia, 66 served with the Swiss Air Force.

▷ Martin B-10 1933

Origin USA

Engine 2 x 775 hp Wright R-1820 Cyclone air-cooled 9-cylinder radial

Top speed 213 mph (343 km/h)

The B-10 began a revolution in bomber design: it was the first US all-metal bomber, had the first gun turret, and was faster than fighters. It remained in production until 1937.

◁ Seversky P-35/AT-12 Guardsman 1935

Origin USA

Engine 1,050 hp Pratt & Whitney R-1830-45 Twin Wasp air-cooled 14-cylinder radial

Top speed 290 mph (467 km/h)

All-metal with retractable undercarriage and enclosed cockpit, the single-seat P-35 fighter was top of its class in 1935, but was soon outmoded. The two-seat AT-12 was a trainer development.

▷ Hawker Hurricane Mk1 1936

Origin UK

Engine 1,030 hp Rolls-Royce Merlin supercharged liquid-cooled V12

Top speed 328 mph (528 km/h)

Sydney Camm's Hurricane was an interceptor, fighter-bomber, night fighter, and ground-attack aircraft. It scored 60 per cent of the victories in WWII's Battle of Britain.

◁ **Savoia-Marchetti SM79 "Sparviero" 1936**

Origin Italy

Engine 3 x 1,000 hp Piaggio P.XI RC 40 air-cooled 14-cylinder radial

Top speed 286 mph (460 km/h)

Conceived as a fast, eight-passenger transport and for air racing, the "Sparrowhawk" made an ideal medium bomber, first in the Spanish Civil War and then as Italy's most effective torpedo bomber in WWII.

△ **Messerschmitt Bf 109E 1938**

Origin Germany

Engine 1,000 hp DB601A supercharged liquid-cooled inverted V12

Top speed 355 mph (572 km/h)

First flown in 1935, the all-metal Bf 109E was Germany's key fighter aircraft of its day. Tricky in takeoff, it was nevertheless light, fast, and agile in flight. Early models saw action in the Spanish Civil War.

◁ **Gloster Gladiator 1936**

Origin UK

Engine 830 hp Bristol Mercury IX air-cooled 9-cylinder radial

Top speed 255 mph (410 km/h)

Technically outdated, the Gladiator was the RAF's last biplane fighter in front-line service, including the 1940 siege of Malta. It was deployed by numerous other countries, such as China and Finland.

▷ **Westland Lysander 1936**

Origin UK

Engine 810 hp Bristol Mercury XX supercharged air-cooled 9-cylinder radial

Top speed 212 mph (341 km/h)

The Lysander was used for WWII army operations, most famously to insert and recover agents in enemy-occupied territory, for which it would land in fields at night; 1,786 were built.

△ **Supermarine Spitfire MK1a 1936**

Origin UK

Engine 1,030–1,175 hp Rolls-Royce Merlin supercharged liquid-cooled V12

Top speed 360 mph (580 km/h)

R.J. Mitchell's Spitfire first flew in 1936. Subject to continuous development (20,351 were built in 13 main variants), it made a huge contribution to the Allied success in WWII.

▷ **Curtiss P-40 Warhawk 1938**

Origin USA

Engine 1,040 hp Allison V-1710 supercharged liquid-cooled V12

Top speed 360 mph (580 km/h)

The Warhawk would be used by the air forces of 28 nations and was in service throughout WWII; 13,738 were built. Though not as fast as some, it was agile, durable, and cheap to build.

Trainers, Parasites, and Parasols

While both biplane and monoplane training aircraft introduced in this decade would for the most part be still serving faithfully over 50 years later – and some still in active service rather than retired to leisure use – the 1930s also saw the final grand fling of the airships, vast lighter-than-air craft that in the end proved unable to withstand the full forces of nature and were retired after tragic crashes.

△ de Havilland DH82 Tiger Moth 1931

Origin UK

Engine 130 hp de Havilland Gipsy Major I air-cooled inverted 4-cylinder in-line

Top speed 109 mph (175 km/h)

This highly successful tandem-seat dual-control trainer of which 8,868 were built, was used by the RAF and many other air forces. Still sometimes flown for training it is now principally a leisure aircraft.

△ Bücker Bü131/CASA 1-131 1934

Origin Germany/Spain

Engine 150 hp Enma Tigre G-IV-B inverted air-cooled 4-cylinder in-line

Top speed 125 mph (201 km/h)

Originating in Germany but built in big numbers in Spain (about 530, including this one) and Japan (1,376), this tandem biplane was the primary trainer for the Luftwaffe and many other air forces worldwide.

Hook for attaching aircraft to airship

◁ Curtiss F9C-2 Sparrowhawk 1931

Origin USA

Engine 415 hp Wright R-975-E3 air-cooled 9-cylinder radial

Top speed 176 mph (283 km/h)

This was a "parasitic" aircraft operated from US Navy airships such as the USS *Akron* for reconnaissance and defence. There were up to four on an airship; they were deployed and recovered in midair.

△ Morane-Saulnier MS315 1932

Origin France

Engine 135 hp Salmson 9Nc air-cooled 9-cylinder radial

Top speed 106 mph (171 km/h)

The 315 was a primary-training parasol-wing monoplane of which 356 were built for the French air force and navy through WWII. In the 1960s, 40 were fitted with 220 hp Continental engines and renamed 317.

▷ Naval Aircraft Factory N3N-3 Canary 1935

Origin USA

Engine 235 hp Wright R-760-2 Whirlwind air-cooled 7-cylinder radial

Top speed 126 mph (203 km/h)

Designed and built (including licence-built engines) by a factory wholly owned by the US government, the yellow Canary was in service with the US Navy as a primary trainer until 1961.

Age of Airship

In the 1920s and 30s airships seemed a far more safe, luxurious, and reliable form of air travel than heavier-than-air craft. They could travel vast distances, smoothly and comfortably, with spacious passenger accommodation, and for war they made stable platforms for surveying the enemy. The US Navy developed airships with integral "hangars" that small aircraft could fly in and out of.

▽ USS Akron ZRS-4 1931

Origin USA

Engine 8 x Maybach VL2

Top speed 83 mph (134 km/h)

Built from 1929 with German help, the duralumin-framed *Akron* and its sister *Macon* were the largest ever helium-filled airships, each carrying four parasite aircraft. *Akron* crashed in severe weather in 1933.

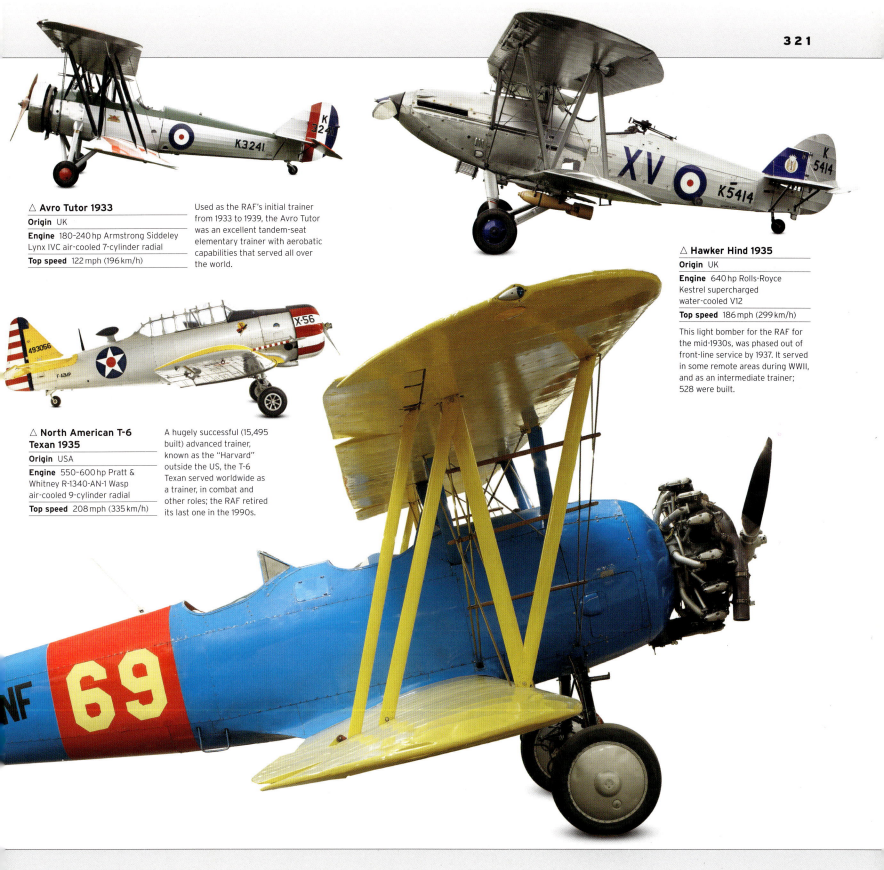

△ **Avro Tutor 1933**

Origin UK

Engine 180-240 hp Armstrong Siddeley Lynx IVC air-cooled 7-cylinder radial

Top speed 122 mph (196 km/h)

Used as the RAF's initial trainer from 1933 to 1939, the Avro Tutor was an excellent tandem-seat elementary trainer with aerobatic capabilities that served all over the world.

△ **Hawker Hind 1935**

Origin UK

Engine 640 hp Rolls-Royce Kestrel supercharged water-cooled V12

Top speed 186 mph (299 km/h)

This light bomber for the RAF for the mid-1930s, was phased out of front-line service by 1937. It served in some remote areas during WWII, and as an intermediate trainer; 528 were built.

△ **North American T-6 Texan 1935**

Origin USA

Engine 550-600 hp Pratt & Whitney R-1340-AN-1 Wasp air-cooled 9-cylinder radial

Top speed 208 mph (335 km/h)

A hugely successful (15,495 built) advanced trainer, known as the "Harvard" outside the US, the T-6 Texan served worldwide as a trainer, in combat and other roles; the RAF retired its last one in the 1990s.

◁ **Zodiac V-II 1935**

Origin France

Engine 2 x 120 hp Salmson 9Ac radial

Top speed 62 mph (100 km/h)

Operated as a maritime patrol airship by France's Aéronavale, the V-II was reinforced at its bow (note the radial battens to stiffen the envelope) to allow it to dock to a mooring-mast.

△ **Zodiac Eclaireur E8 1931**

Origin France

Engine 2 x 175 hp Hispano-Suiza

Top speed 70 mph (113 km/h)

Zodiac built 63 dirigibles from 1908. With two powerful engines, the semirigid E8 "Scout" was the fastest. It had three balloons of air located inside its 359,150 cu ft (10,170 cu m) hydrogen envelope.

Bombers

As soon as the threat of World War II was apparent, both sides knew that bomber aircraft could have a huge impact on the outcome of the war – by demoralizing the people, destroying the factories, disrupting army supplies, and attacking ground troops, tanks, and warships. Huge, multi-engined aircraft were developed to carry ever-greater loads. Some bristled with gunners to counter fighter attack, while lighter, high-speed aircraft were built for more specific targeting.

△ Boeing B-17G Flying Fortress 1940
Origin USA
Engine 4 x 1,200 hp Wright R-1820-97 Cyclone turbocharged air-cooled 9-cylinder radial
Top speed 287 mph (462 km/h)

First flown in 1935, the B-17 was the USAAF's main precision daytime bomber in WWII. It was well defended and able to survive much damage, but it had only half the bomb capacity of an Avro Lancaster.

◁ Heinkel He111 1940
Origin Germany
Engine 2 x 1,340 hp Junkers Jumo 211 F-2 supercharged liquid-cooled inverted V12
Top speed 270 mph (434 km/h)

Disguised as a fast transport plane, when Germany was not allowed to build military aircraft, the He111 was an effective medium bomber. Introduced in 1935, it was progressively developed throughout WWII.

△ Junkers Ju88 1940
Origin Germany
Engine 2 x 1,677 hp BMW 801 supercharged air-cooled 14-cylinder radial
Top speed 342 mph (550 km/h)

Introduced in 1939 Germany's most successful medium bomber proved exceptionally versatile, serving as fighter, dive bomber, night-fighter, reconnaissance aircraft, trainer, and long-range escort. More than 15,000 were built.

△ Vickers Wellington X 1940
Origin UK
Engine 2 x 1,050–1,735 hp Bristol Pegasus/Hercules supercharged air-cooled 14-cylinder radial
Top speed 270 mph (434 km/h)

Britain's most effective night bomber in the early years of WWII was introduced in 1938. It had a fabric-covered geodesic structure that could fly after severe damage. The Wellington was later adapted to other roles; 11,461 were built.

△ Fairey Albacore 1940
Origin UK
Engine 1,065–1,130 hp Bristol Taurus II/XII supercharged air-cooled 14-cylinder radial
Top speed 172 mph (277 km/h)

This three-seat reconnaissance aircraft and torpedo bomber was to be the Fleet Air Arm's successor to the Swordfish. Although it had a larger engine, enclosed cockpit, and heating, it would ultimately be retired first.

△ Shorts S29 Stirling 1941
Origin UK
Engine 4 x 1,500–1,635 hp Bristol Hercules supercharged air-cooled 14-cylinder radial
Top speed 270 mph (434 km/h)

The first four-engined bomber to enter RAF service, with a then-exceptional 14,000-lb (6,350-kg) payload, was superseded by 1943 when its performance and range were outstripped by later designs.

◁ Douglas A-20 Havoc 1941

Origin USA

Engine 2 x 1,700 hp Wright R2600-A win Cyclone supercharged air-cooled 14-cylinder radial

Top speed 340 mph (549 km/h)

A favourite of pilots because of its fighter-like handling, this light bomber was also known as the DB-7 Boston. It doubled as a night-fighter and was operated by many Allied air forces; 7,478 were built.

△ Consolidated B-24 Liberator 1941

Origin USA

Engine 4 x 1,200 hp Pratt & Whitney R-1830-65 Twin Wasp turbosupercharged air-cooled 14-cylinder radial

Top speed 290 mph (467 km/h)

The B-24 Liberator was lighter, faster, with a greater range and bomb load than the B-17. However, it was also harder to fly and more liable to catch fire or crash if hit. More than 18,400 of this prolific WWII Allied bomber were built.

△ Handley Page Halifax 1940

Origin UK

Engine 4 x 1,615–1,800 hp Bristol Hercules XVI/100 supercharged air-cooled 14-cylinder radial

Top speed 282 mph (454 km/h)

First flown in 1939 and progressively uprated from its original Rolls-Royce Merlin to Bristol engines, the Halifax was an effective heavy bomber used widely in WWII. It was later adapted for use as a civilian freighter.

▷ North American B-25 Mitchell 1940

Origin USA

Engine 2 x 1,700 hp Wright R-2600-92 supercharged air-cooled 14-cylinder radial

Top speed 272 mph (438 km/h)

Some 9,984 were built, in numerous variants, of this successful medium bomber and ground-attack aircraft. It operated in many arenas of WWII and was used by air forces worldwide until as late as 1979.

△ Ilyushin Il-2 "Shturmovik" 1940

Origin USSR

Engine 1,700 hp Mikulin AM-38F supercharged liquid-cooled V12

Top speed 257 mph (414 km/h)

Built around a 1,543-lb (700-kg) armoured shell that protected the crew, engine, radiator, and fuel tank, the "flying tank" was a pure ground-attack aircraft. Over 38,000 of this machine were built.

△ Yokosuka D4Y3 Model 33 "Judy" 1940

Origin Japan

Engine 1,075 hp Mitsubishi Kinsei air-cooled 14-cylinder radial

Top speed 342 mph (550 km/h)

A carrier-based aircraft, this was one of the fastest dive bombers of WWII. It was also used for reconnaissance and Kamikaze missions. Development issues delayed production and only 2,038 were constructed.

△ Avro Lancaster 1941

Origin UK

Engine 4 x 1,280 hp Rolls-Royce Merlin XX supercharged liquid-cooled V12

Top speed 285 mph (460 km/h)

With four Rolls-Royce Merlin engines, the RAF's main heavy bomber had huge capacity. A phenomenally successful night bomber, the Lancaster carried its huge 14,000-lb (6,350-kg) bomb load to targets in Germany and beyond.

Wartime Fighters

Fighters were built in huge numbers in World War II. Tens of thousands of the most successful types were built, including almost 34,000 Bf 109s. Nations and lives depended on constant development, and Germany, Britain, the US, Japan, and the USSR all built aircraft that excelled in their own ways. Some were so good that they continued in service with smaller nations as late as the 1980s.

△ Messerschmitt Bf 110G 1943

Origin Germany

Engine 2 x 1,085/1,455 hp Daimler-Benz DB 601/605 liquid-cooled inverted V12

Top speed 348 mph (560 km/h)

In production ahead of WWII, this twin-engined fighter-bomber was effective in early engagements but lacked agility, changing to ground support and night fighting with radar, at which it excelled.

▽ Messerschmitt Bf 109G 1942

Origin Germany

Engine 1,455 hp Daimler-Benz DB 605A-1 supercharged liquid-cooled inverted V12

Top speed 386 mph (621km/h)

The Bf, or Me109, was progressively developed throughout WWII, becoming the most-produced fighter aircraft in history, with 33,984 built. Very successful, it remained in service in Spain until 1965.

△ Hawker Hurricane MkIIB 1942

Origin UK

Engine 1,185 hp Rolls-Royce Merlin XX supercharged liquid-cooled V12

Top speed 340 mph (547 km/h)

Simpler, cheaper, and easier to build and repair than Spitfires, Hurricanes were turned out in large numbers (14,533 total) across several variants. This MkIIB could carry two 500-lb (227-kg) bombs.

▷ Fiat CR.42 Falco 1940

Origin Italy

Engine 840 hp Fiat A.74 RC38 supercharged air-cooled 14-cylinder radial

Top speed 274 mph (441km/h)

The ultimate biplane fighter, the Falco (Falcon) was the most-produced Italian fighter of WWII, with 1,818 built. Against monoplanes, it made up in agility what it lacked in speed.

▽ Lockheed P-38 Lightning 1941

Origin USA

Engine 2 x 1,725 hp Allison V-1710-111/113 turbo-supercharged liquid-cooled V12

Top speed 420 mph (676 km/h)

This distinctive twin-boom, long-range, high-altitude interceptor fighter-bomber was fast and forgiving, but not very agile. In production throughout the US involvement in WWII; 10,037 were built.

◁ Mitsubishi A6M5 Zero 1943

Origin Japan

Engine 940-1,130 hp Nakajima Sakae 12/21 supercharged air-cooled 14-cylinder radial

Top speed 340 mph (547 km/h)

This was Japan's most plentiful fighter with 10,939 built. The Zero was the most capable carrier-based fighter of its day, with excellent agility and range; not until 1943 did Allied aircraft overhaul it.

▽ Focke-Wulf Fw 190 1941

Origin Germany

Engine 1,940 hp BMW 801S supercharged air-cooled 14-cylinder radial

Top speed 408 mph (658 km/h)

Kurt Tank conceived a radial-engined fighter to beat in-line engined rivals: the Fw 190 retained air superiority over the Allies from mid-1941 to mid-1942. More than 20,000 of all variants were built.

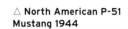

△ North American P-51 Mustang 1944

Origin USA

Engine 1,720 hp Packard V-1650-7 supercharged liquid-cooled V12

Top speed 437 mph (703 km/h)

This highly aerodynamic long-range fighter-bomber had a huge impact on Allied air success, aided latterly by Packard-built Rolls-Royce Merlin engines. It served into the 1980s, with 15,000 built.

◁ Supermarine Spitfire MkII 1940

Origin UK

Engine 1,440–1,585 hp Rolls-Royce Merlin 45 supercharged liquid-cooled V12

Top speed 357 mph (575 km/h)

Combat superiority from its light weight and aerodynamics made the Spitfire hugely important. The MkII played a key role in the Battle of Britain.

△ Republic P-47 Thunderbolt 1944

Origin USA

Engine 2,535 hp Pratt & Whitney R-2800-59W Double Wasp supercharged air-cooled 18-cylinder radial

Top speed 435 mph (700 km/h)

Large, heavy, and expensive, Alexander Kartveli's "Jug" (named for its shape) proved extremely effective as a high-altitude fighter and ground-attack fighter-bomber; 15,678 were built.

△ Grumman F6F Hellcat 1943

Origin USA

Engine 2,200 hp Pratt & Whitney R-2800-10W Double Wasp supercharged air-cooled radial

Top speed 391 mph (629 km/h)

This was a powerful and effective carrier-based fighter of which 12,275 were built. The Hellcat was designed to outperform the Mitsubishi Zero, which was faster than its predecessor, the Wildcat.

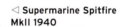

▷ Chance Vought F4U Corsair 1944

Origin USA

Engine 2,000–2,325 hp Pratt & Whitney Type R-2800 Double Wasp air-cooled 18-cylinder radial

Top speed 417 mph (671 km/h)

When first flown, Rex Beisel's Corsair had the most powerful engine and largest propeller of any fighter. The most capable carrier-based fighter-bomber of its time, 12,571 were built.

△ Yakovlev Yak-3 1944

Origin USSR

Engine 1,300 hp Klimov VK-105PF-2 supercharged liquid-cooled V12

Top speed 407 mph (655 km/h)

Conceived in 1941 the Yak-3 was smaller and lighter than its contemporaries. With a good power-to-weight ratio that made it formidable in aerial combat, it was also easy and cheap to maintain.

Military Support Aircraft

While the wartime news was filled with tales of the fighters and bombers behind the front line (and sometimes ahead of it) a multitude of workhorse aircraft performed vital roles from training pilots to transporting equipment, ground troops, and parachutists. In most cases, these were civilian models from the 1930s, usually strengthened and fitted with more powerful engines to withstand the rigours of military service.

▽ Douglas C-47 Skytrain 1940

Origin USA

Engine 2 x 1,200 hp Pratt & Whitney R-1830-90C Twin Wasp air-cooled 14-cylinder radial

Top speed 224 mph (360 km/h)

The commercial DC-3 airliner entered military service as the much-loved C-47 Skytrain, or Dakota. Over 10,000 were built, with a cargo door and strengthened floor to carry troops and equipment.

△ Junkers Ju52 1940

Origin Germany

Engine 3 x 720 hp BMW 132T air-cooled 9-cylinder radial

Top speed 165 mph (265 km/h)

After both commercial and military roles pre war, the Ju 52 – with its distinctive corrugated metal skin – was a crucial transport aircraft for German forces in WWII despite its vulnerability to fighter attack.

△ Douglas C-54 Skymaster 1942

Origin USA

Engine 4 x 1,450 hp Pratt & Whitney R-2000-9 Twin Wasp air-cooled 14-cylinder radial

Top speed 275 mph (442 km/h)

The Skymaster was the first aircraft type to carry the US President. It was a civilian DC-4 in military guise, and was used for many roles from transport and research to missile tracking and recovery. The C-54 was in service until 1975.

◁ Boeing Stearman Model 75 1940

Origin USA

Engine 220 hp Continental 670 air-cooled 7-cylinder radial

Top speed 135 mph (217 km/h)

Flown solo from the rear seat, the remarkably sturdy Stearman first appeared in 1934 but performed well as a trainer for US and Canadian military pilots in WWII; over 8,000 were built.

▷ Miles M14 Magister 1940

Origin UK

Engine 130 hp de Havilland Gipsy Major I air-cooled 4-cylinder in-line

Top speed 132 mph (212 km/h)

Based on the civilian Hawk Trainer, the Magister first flew in 1937. It was the first monoplane designed as a trainer for the RAF, ideal for familiarizing pilots with the low-wing monoplane front-line aircraft then coming into service.

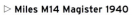

◁ Ryan PT-22 Recruit 1941

Origin USA

Engine 160 hp Kinner R540 air-cooled 5-cylinder radial

Top speed 125 mph (200 km/h)

Claude Ryan's ST first flew in 1934. When war came, the military version – designated the PT – proved an ideal trainer for low-wing monoplanes and was also used for reconnaissance.

▽ **Fairchild Argus 1941**

Origin USA

Engine 165 hp Warner Super Scarab air-cooled 7-cylinder radial

Top speed 130 mph (209 km/h)

Based on the Model 24, which dated back to 1932, the Argus served in both US and British forces in WWII. It was used by the RAF Air Transport Auxiliary to ferry aircrew between bases and to collect aircraft.

◁ **Taylorcraft Auster MkV 1942**

Origin UK

Engine 130 hp Lycoming 0-290-3 air-cooled flat-4

Top speed 130 mph (209 km/h)

Derived from US-built Taylorcraft aircraft, and with armour plate for the pilot, the Auster V was used for light liaison and observation by the RAF in WWII. Eventually, helicopters took over this role in the 1960s.

△ **Fairchild C-82A Packet 1944**

Origin USA

Engine 2 x 2,100 hp Pratt & Whitney R-2800-85 Double Wasp air-cooled 18-cylinder radial

Top speed 248 mph (399 km/h)

Designed during WWII as a heavy-lift cargo aircraft for carrying troops and equipment, the Packet entered service post war. It proved capacious but underpowered, resulting in a short service life.

△ **Focke-Wulf Fw190 S-8 1944**

Origin Germany

Engine 1,540 hp BMW 801 D-2 supercharged air-cooled 14-cylinder radial

Top speed 408 mph (657 km/h)

Around 58 examples of this successful WWII German fighter were converted or built as two-seat "Schulflugzeug" trainers late in the war to ease the transition to the more powerful fighter aircraft.

▷ **Piper L-4H Grasshopper 1944**

Origin USA

Engine 65 hp Continental A-65

Top speed 85 mph (137 km/h)

US forces used this military liaison aircraft based on the Piper Cub for artillery spotting, short-range reconnaissance, and transport during WWII, alongside types from other light plane manufacturers. It proved to be a rugged workhorse.

Civil Transport

Civilian aircraft in the 1940s were a mix of the best prewar designs and "brave new world" concepts influenced by wartime developments. Powered flight controls supplemented the traditional manual flight controls, and cabin pressurization became commonplace. While the best machines of this decade saw long, reliable service – some were still flying commercially in the 21st century – others were stillborn or made in tiny numbers, because of over-ambitious ideas of what the post-war market wanted – or could afford.

△ **Douglas DC-3 1940**

Origin USA

Engine 2 x 1,200 hp Pratt & Whitney R-1830-S1C3G Twin Wasp aircooled 14-cylinder radial

Top speed 230 mph (370 km/h)

First flown in 1935 the DC-3 revolutionized air transport in the 1930s and 1940s, as well as serving vital roles in WWII. Built in the Soviet Union and Japan as well as the US, many are still in use.

△ **Boeing 314A Clipper 1941**

Origin USA

Engine 4 x 1,600 hp Wright R-2600-3 Twin Cyclone air-cooled 14-cylinder radial

Top speed 210 mph (340 km/h)

One of the largest aircraft of its day, the 1939 Clipper was upgraded in performance, range, and comfort in 1941. Providing transatlantic luxury for the wealthy, just 12 were built; all had gone by 1951.

△ **Boeing C-97 1947**

Origin USA

Engine 4 x 3,500 hp Pratt & Whitney R-4360-B6 Wasp Major air-cooled 28-cylinder radial

Top speed 375 mph (603 km/h)

Derived from the Superfortress this machine had an enlarged upper fuselage to give it two decks. The pressurized civilian 377 Stratocruiser made transatlantic travel easy, though poor reliability brought just 56 sales.

▷ **Lockheed Constellation 1943**

Origin USA

Engine 4 x 3,250 hp Wright R-3350-DA3 Turbo Compound supercharged 18-cylinder radial

Top speed 377 mph (607 km/h)

Commissioned by TWA in 1939 for transcontinental service, the Constellation entered production as a military transport aircraft during WWII. This first widely used pressurized airliner was exceptionally fast for its time.

△ **Ilyushin Il-12 1945**

Origin USSR

Engine 2 x 1,850 hp ASh-82FNV air-cooled 14-cylinder radial

Top speed 253 mph (407 km/h)

Developed to replace licence-built DC-3s, the Il-12's tricycle landing gear aided ground handling. Briefly fitted with diesel engines, 663 of this unpressurized transport were built with radial engines.

▷ Sud-Ouest SO30P Bretagne 1945

Origin France

Engine 2 x 2,400 hp Pratt & Whitney R-2800-CA18 air-cooled 18-cylinder radial

Top speed 263 mph (422 km/h)

Designed during WWII by a group of designers based at Cannes after the invasion of France, this all-metal transport aircraft was operated both as an airliner and a troop carrier; 45 were built.

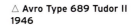

△ Douglas DC-6 1946

Origin USA

Engine 2 x 2,400 hp Pratt & Whitney R-2800-CB16 "Double Wasp" air-cooled 18-cylinder radial

Top speed 315 mph (507 km/h)

Planned as a WWII military transport, the DC-6 was ideal for use on long-range commercial flights and 804 were built. Some of these machines are still flying on wildfire control, cargo, and military missions.

△ Avro Type 689 Tudor II 1946

Origin UK

Engine 4 x 1,770 hp Rolls-Royce Merlin 100 liquid-cooled V12

Top speed 320 mph (515 km/h)

Based on the Lancaster bomber, Britain's first pressurized airliner was stretched 25 ft (7.62 m) and widened 1 ft (30 cm) to take 60 passengers instead of 24, making it Britain's biggest, in this rare Tudor II form.

◁ Avro 652A Anson C19 Series 2 1946

Origin UK

Engine 2 x 385 hp Armstrong Siddeley Cheetah XVII 7-cylinder radial

Top speed 188 mph (303 km/h)

First introduced in 1936, 11,020 Ansons were built, being used for many roles from maritime reconnaissance to aircrew training. The RAF used C19s for communications and transport during WWII.

▷ Breguet 761 "Deux-Ponts" 1949

Origin France

Engine 4 x 2,020 hp Pratt & Whitney R-2800-B31 air-cooled 18-cylinder radial

Top speed 242 mph (389 km/h)

Design began on the capacious double-deck 761 in 1944, before WWII ended. It had an elevator between the two decks. Though rapidly outdated and just 20 were built, it had an excellent safety record.

◁ Antonov An-2 1947

Origin USSR

Engine 1,000 hp Shvetsov ASh-62IR 9-cylinder supercharged radial

Top speed 160 mph (258 km/h)

A utility/agricultural aircraft with an incredible 45-year production run, the slow-flying An-2 proved remarkably rugged and able to operate out of small airfields. More than 18,000 were built.

△ Sud-Est SE2010 Armagnac 1949

Origin France

Engine 4 x 3,500 hp Pratt & Whitney R-4360-B13 Wasp Major air-cooled 28-cylinder radial

Top speed 308 mph (495 km/h)

One of the largest civil aircraft built at the time, its huge fuselage was designed for three-tier sleeping but was never used in that format. Underpowered with limited range, just nine were built.

▷ Bristol Brabazon Mk1 1949

Origin UK

Engine 8 x 2,650 hp Bristol Centaurus air-cooled 18-cylinder radial

Top speed 300 mph (482 km/h)

This super-luxury plane needing extra-long runways was not what the market wanted; just one was built. It had the first all-powered flying systems, electric engine controls, and high-pressure hydraulics.

Post-war Light Aircraft

Despite World War II shutting down civilian production for five years, the light aircraft that were built in the 1940s set the pattern for the next 60 years. They featured a light, simple, monocoque fuselage; increasingly metal construction; and efficient, horizontally opposed air-cooled engines. Many 1940s aircraft remain in use in the 21st century, while others have been mildly modified and put back into production.

◁ Boeing-Stearman PT-17/N2S Kaydet 1940

Origin USA

Engine 450 hp Pratt & Whitney R-985 Wasp Junior air-cooled 9-cylinder radial

Top speed 140 mph (225 km/h)

Designed in 1934 and built in thousands in WWII, many Stearmans were sold off post war. They were fitted with more powerful engines and used for agricultural duties like crop-dusting, as well as aerobatic shows.

▷ Luscombe 8A Silvaire Ragwing 1941

Origin USA

Engine 65 hp Continental A-65 air-cooled flat-4

Top speed 128 mph (206 km/h)

Don Luscombe's Model 8 was radical in 1937 for its monocoque fuselage and all-metal structure. With its new horizontally opposed engine, it was an early post-war pacesetter.

△ Aeronca Champion 1944

Origin USA

Engine 65-90 hp Continental A65-C90 air-cooled flat-4

Top speed 100 mph (160 km/h)

The tandem-seat "Champ" was such an effective design that it re-entered production in 2007. Speedier than the rival Piper Cub, it could be flown solo from the front seat, giving better visibility.

△ Auster J/1 Autocrat 1945

Origin UK

Engine 100 hp Blackburn Cirrus Minor or 145 hp de Havilland Gipsy Major air-cooled 4-cylinder inverted in-line

Top speed 120 mph (193 km/h)

The Autocrat was a successful three-seater light aircraft derived from a wartime observation design. It is still flown widely for leisure in the 21st century. This example is fitted with a long-range belly tank.

▷ Fairchild UC-61K Argus Mk3 1944

Origin USA

Engine 200 hp Fairchild Ranger air-cooled 6-cylinder inverted in-line

Top speed 124 mph (200 km/h)

Popular as personal transport post war, 306 of this rugged development of the 1932 Fairchild F-24 were built for the RAF Air Transport Auxiliary. They had the powerful Ranger engine and four seats.

◁ Cessna 140 1946

Origin USA

Engine 85 hp Continental C-85-12 air-cooled flat-4

Top speed 125 mph (201 km/h)

Cessna leapt ahead of the competition after WWII with this modern, all-metal, light two-seater that was economical, practical, and easy to operate; 7,664 were built and many are still flying.

△ Miles Gemini 1947

Origin UK

Engine 2 x 100 hp Blackburn Cirrus Minor air-cooled 4-cylinder inverted in-line

Top speed 145 mph (233 km/h)

Built of plastic-bonded plywood, this was the last Miles aircraft to be built in quantity, proving very popular for private transport in the immediate post-war years; 170 were built, most in 1945-46.

△ Cessna 195 Businessliner 1947

Origin USA

Engine 300 hp Jacobs R-755 air-cooled 7-cylinder radial

Top speed 185 mph (298 km/h)

Cessna's 195 prototype flew in 1945, and this speedy all-metal five-seater entered production two years later. It could also be equipped with floats. Including the military version, 1,180 were built.

△ de Havilland DH104 Dove 1947

Origin UK

Engine 2 x 380 hp Gipsy Queen air-cooled 6-cylinder inverted in-line

Top speed 230 mph (370 km/h)

One of Britain's most successful post-war civil aircraft, 542 examples of this short-haul airliner were built and some still operate commercially. This Dove was first registered to the Dunlop Rubber Company.

△ Piper PA-12 Super Cruiser 1946

Origin USA

Engine 108-115 hp Lycoming O-235-C1 air-cooled flat-4

Top speed 115 mph (185 km/h)

An update of the post-war era 1940 J5 Cub Cruiser, this three-seat PA-12 was sturdy, sleek, and approved for wheels, skis, and floats. It continues to be very popular for personal use today.

▷ Piper PA-17 Vagabond 1948

Origin USA

Engine 65 hp Continental A-65-8

Top speed 102 mph (164 km/h)

The PA-17 was a development of the Lycoming-engined 1947 PA-15, Piper's first post-war design. Based on the Cub with a shorter wing, it was simple, rugged, and cheap to build.

Piston Perfection

By the mid-1940s it was clear that jet engines were going to revolutionize aircraft design and take over in many arenas, but piston engines continued to be refined and to excel in specific fields. With lower fuel consumption than early jets, they remained ideal for ultra-long-range aircraft; they were also better suited to naval carrier operations, and for seaplanes.

△ **de Havilland DH98 Mosquito 1940**

Origin UK

Engine 2 x 1,480 hp Rolls-Royce Merlin 21/21 + 23/23 water-cooled V12 (later 2 x 1,690 hp 113 + 114)

Top speed 366-415 mph (589-670 km/h)

Built entirely of wood, the "Wooden Wonder" was the world's fastest military aircraft in 1941. Conceived as an unarmed fast bomber, it fulfilled many roles from photo reconnaissance to fighter.

◁ **Supermarine Seafire F MkXVII 1941**

Origin UK

Engine 1,850-2375 hp Rolls-Royce Merlin/Griffon supercharged liquid-cooled V12

Top speed 387 mph (623 km/h)

Conceived in 1939, the seaborne Spitfire was delayed at first. Progressively improved with rocket-assisted take off, folding wings, and ever more power, it remained fragile for carrier use.

△ **Lavochkin La-5 1942**

Origin USSR

Engine 1,850 hp ShvetsovASh-82FN air-cooled 14-cylinder radial

Top speed 403 mph (650 km/h)

This effective Russian WWII combat aircraft, despite its largely wooden construction, became a match for German fighters at low altitude once fuel injection was added; 9,920 were built.

△ **Yakovlev Yak-9 1942**

Origin USSR

Engine 1,650 hp Klimov VK-107A supercharged liquid-cooled V12

Top speed 435 mph (700 km/h)

Light, fast, easy to fly, and progressively updated, this was the most-produced Soviet fighter with 16,769 built. Its main weakness was that the engine was too powerful for the weight of the aircraft.

△ **Northrop P-61 Black Widow 1943**

Origin USA

Engine 2 x 2,250 hp Pratt & Whitney R-2800-5W Double Wasp air-cooled 18-cylinder radial

Top speed 366 mph (589 km/h)

The first US purpose-built night-interceptor, and the first aircraft specifically designed to carry radar, the "Black Widow" could stay aloft for up to eight hours. It operated extensively in WWII.

△ **Grumman F7F-3 Tigercat 1944**

Origin USA

Engine 2 x 2,100 hp Pratt & Whitney R-2800-34W Double Wasp air-cooled 18-cylinder radial

Top speed 460 mph (740 km/h)

The US Navy's first twin-engined fighter entered service at the end of WWII. One of the fastest piston-engined fighters, it served widely in Korea, both in land-based and carrier operations.

◁ **Grumman F8F Bearcat 1944**

Origin USA

Engine 2,100 hp (later 2,250 hp) Pratt & Whitney R-2800 "Double Wasp" air-cooled 18-cylinder radial

Top speed 421 mph (678 km/h)

The last of the piston-engined "Cats", the F8F was 20 per cent lighter than the F6F Hellcat, climbed 30 per cent quicker, and was 40 mph (64 km/h) faster. It served in Korea and holds piston-engined speed records.

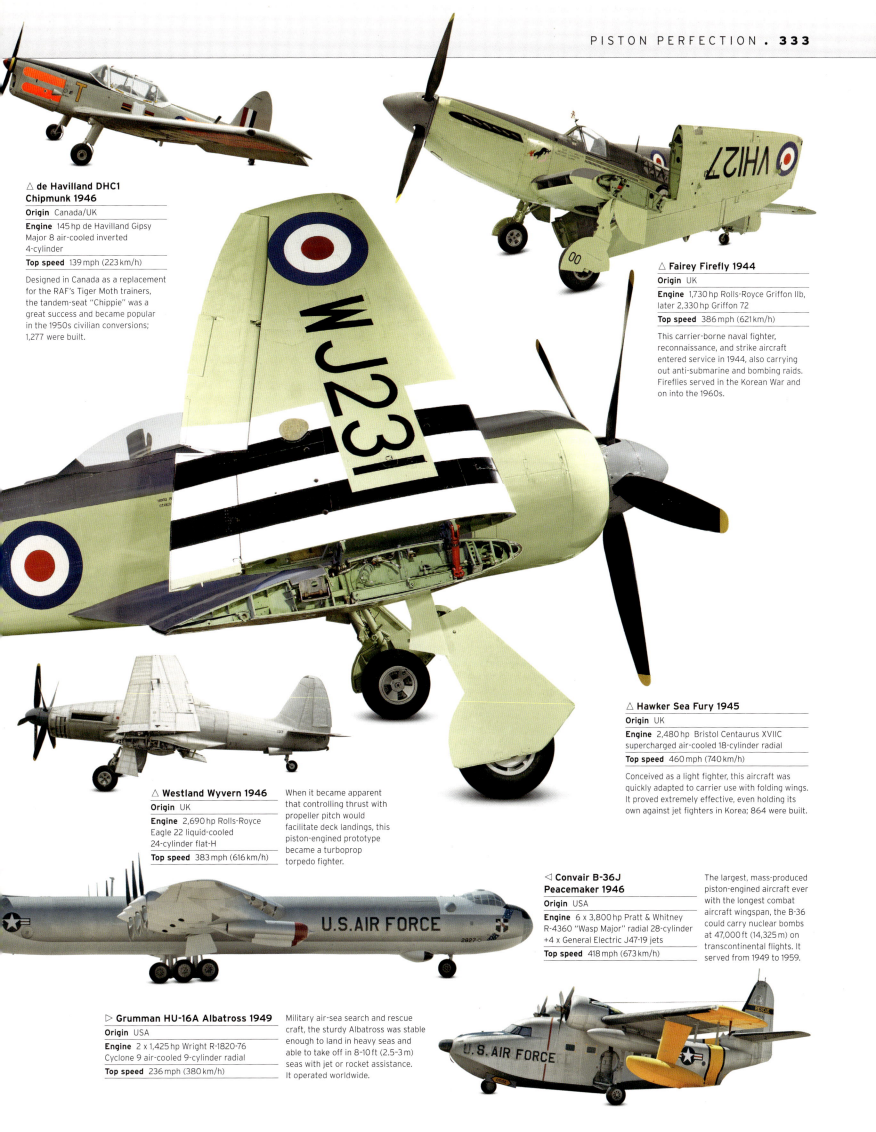

△ de Havilland DHC1 Chipmunk 1946

Origin Canada/UK

Engine 145 hp de Havilland Gipsy Major 8 air-cooled inverted 4-cylinder

Top speed 139 mph (223 km/h)

Designed in Canada as a replacement for the RAF's Tiger Moth trainers, the tandem-seat "Chippie" was a great success and became popular in the 1950s civilian conversions; 1,277 were built.

△ Fairey Firefly 1944

Origin UK

Engine 1,730 hp Rolls-Royce Griffon IIb, later 2,330 hp Griffon 72

Top speed 386 mph (621 km/h)

This carrier-borne naval fighter, reconnaissance, and strike aircraft entered service in 1944, also carrying out anti-submarine and bombing raids. Fireflies served in the Korean War and on into the 1960s.

△ Hawker Sea Fury 1945

Origin UK

Engine 2,480 hp Bristol Centaurus XVIIC supercharged air-cooled 18-cylinder radial

Top speed 460 mph (740 km/h)

Conceived as a light fighter, this aircraft was quickly adapted to carrier use with folding wings. It proved extremely effective, even holding its own against jet fighters in Korea; 864 were built.

△ Westland Wyvern 1946

Origin UK

Engine 2,690 hp Rolls-Royce Eagle 22 liquid-cooled 24-cylinder flat-H

Top speed 383 mph (616 km/h)

When it became apparent that controlling thrust with propeller pitch would facilitate deck landings, this piston-engined prototype became a turboprop torpedo fighter.

◁ Convair B-36J Peacemaker 1946

Origin USA

Engine 6 x 3,800 hp Pratt & Whitney R-4360 "Wasp Major" radial 28-cylinder +4 x General Electric J47-19 jets

Top speed 418 mph (673 km/h)

The largest, mass-produced piston-engined aircraft ever with the longest combat aircraft wingspan, the B-36 could carry nuclear bombs at 47,000 ft (14,325 m) on transcontinental flights. It served from 1949 to 1959.

▷ Grumman HU-16A Albatross 1949

Origin USA

Engine 2 x 1,425 hp Wright R-1820-76 Cyclone 9 air-cooled 9-cylinder radial

Top speed 236 mph (380 km/h)

Military air-sea search and rescue craft, the sturdy Albatross was stable enough to land in heavy seas and able to take off in 8-10 ft (2.5-3 m) seas with jet or rocket assistance. It operated worldwide.

Early Jets

With the advent of the jet engine, entirely new types of combat aircraft began to appear. Radically different in appearance, and with top speeds significantly faster than their piston-powered predecessors, these new fighters and bombers would change the course of aerial combat forever.

▷ **Gloster Whittle E28/39 1941**

Origin UK

Engine 868 lb (394 kg) thrust Power Jets W.1 turbojet

Top speed 338 mph (544 km/h)

Although only two of these little jets were built, the E28/39 has tremendous historic significance, as it was Britain's first jet aircraft. Although intended purely as an engine testbed it was by all accounts a pleasant aircraft to fly, with reasonable performance.

△ **Gloster Meteor prototype DG202G 1943**

Origin UK

Engine 2 x 3,500 lb (1,588 kg) thrust Rolls-Royce Derwent turbojets

Top speed 415 mph (668 km/h)

This was the only Allied jet to see combat in WWII. The Meteor had a long military career, as it remained in production until the mid-1950s, and set several speed records. The type was sold to many foreign air forces, and even today two Meteors are used as test-beds for ejection-seat manufacturer Martin-Baker.

△ **Messerschmitt Me262 Schwalbe 1942**

Origin Germany

Engine 2 x 1,980 lb (898 kg) thrust Junkers Jumo 004 B-1 turbojets

Top speed 559 mph (900 km/h)

This very advanced aircraft was the world's first operational jet fighter. Although much faster than any piston machine, it was hampered by the lack of dive brakes, and also the short life and inherent unreliability of its Jumo turbojets.

△ **de Havilland DH100 Vampire FB 6 1943**

Origin UK

Engine 3,350 lb (1,520 kg) thrust de Havilland Goblin 3 turbojet

Top speed 548 mph (882 km/h)

Designed and built by famed British aircraft manufacturer de Havilland, the Vampire was the RAF's second jet fighter, and the company's first jet. Two unusual facets of the aircraft are that a lot of wood (plywood and balsa) was used in its construction, and that both engine and airframe were built by the same company.

△ **Bell P-59A Airacomet 1944**

Origin USA

Engine 2 x 2,000 lb (907 kg) thrust General Electric J31-GE-3 turbojets

Top speed 413 mph (665 km/h)

The Airacomet was America's first jet aircraft. It was deemed a most unsatisfactory machine by all that flew it as it was not only slower than most contemporary piston fighters but also had poor handling and stability. It is notable for being the first jet to have two engines integrated into the fuselage.

▷ **Heinkel He162 1944**

Origin Germany

Engine 1,760 lb (798 kg) thrust BMW 003 turbojet

Top speed 562 mph (905 km/h)

Known as the "Volksjager" (People's Fighter) the He162 was intended to be a cheap, simple aircraft that could be flown by relatively inexperienced pilots. Unfortunately, because it was rushed into production it had many design flaws, and the prototype crashed on only its second flight.

◁ **Arado Ar 234B-2 1944**

Origin Germany

Engine 2 x 1,103 lb (500 kg) thrust Junkers Jumo 004B-1 turbojets

Top speed 461 mph (742 km/h)

The Ar 234 was the world's first jet bomber. Designed for long-range reconnaissance, it was so fast that few Allied aircraft could catch it. Initially it had a dolly and skid type undercarriage (to save weight). This proved impractical in service and most were fitted with wheels.

▷ **Lockheed P-80A Shooting Star 1944**

Origin USA

Engine 4,600 lb (2,087 kg) thrust Allison J33-9 turbojet

Top speed 558 mph (898 km/h)

The Shooting Star was America's first operational American jet fighter, and, although it arrived in Europe too late to see action during WWII, it was used extensively in Korea as the F-80. It quickly became obsolete as a fighter, but evolved into the T-33 jet trainer, which remained in service with both the US Air Force and Navy until the 1970s.

△ **Republic F-84C Thunderjet 1946**

Origin USA

Engine 5,560 lb (2,522 kg) thrust Allison J-35 turbojet

Top speed 622 mph (1,000 km/h)

Republic's first jet fighter, this aircraft was intended as a jet-powered replacement for their P-47 Thunderbolt. After a long and troubled gestation period, it evolved into a highly capable fighter-bomber that saw extensive service in the Korean War. The Thunderjet was also the first aircraft flown by the USAF aerobatic team, the Thunderbirds.

◁ **Grumman F9F-2 Panther 1947**

Origin USA

Engine 5,000 lb (2,268 kg) thrust Pratt & Whitney J42-2 turbojet

Top speed 575 mph (926 km/h)

Grumman's first jet fighter, the Panther, was one of the first jets operated by the US Navy and to see combat in Korea. It was also the first navy jet to score a "kill" during this conflict. The straight-wing Panther was deemed inferior to the sweptwing MiG-15, and a sweptwing version called the Cougar was built later.

▷ **McDonnell F2H-2 Banshee 1947**

Origin USA

Engine 2 x 3,250 lb (1,474 kg) thrust Westinghouse J-34 turbojets

Top speed 580 mph (933 km/h)

Derived from the woefully underpowered FH-1 Phantom, the Banshee was fitted with much more powerful engines and soon became an effective fighter-bomber. It also had excellent performance at high altitude, and was often used for photo-reconnaissance. It was the only jet fighter operated by the Royal Canadian Navy.

Early Rotorcraft

War set back helicopter development in Europe; Germany built several dozen helicopters of different types in the 1940s but production was limited by lack of resources. In America pioneers like Igor Sikorsky, Frank Piasecki, Arthur Young, and Stanley Hiller drove progress, producing the forerunners of the machines flown today. The first ever helicopter winch rescue took place in 1945 when a Sikorsky R5 flown by Igor's son-in-law lifted two men off a sinking barge in a storm.

▷ Sikorsky R-4 1942

Origin USA

Engine 1 x 200 hp Warner R-500-3 Super Scarab radial

Top speed 75 mph (121 km/h)

This was the breakthrough machine. Sikorsky's R4, developed from the VS-300, was the first truly practical helicopter and was mass-produced for the American and British armed forces towards the end of WWII.

△ Kellett XO-60 autogyro 1943

Origin USA

Engine 1 x 330 hp Jacobs R-915-3 radial

Top speed 125 mph (201 km/h)

The last gasp of the autogyro before the helicopter eased it out, the XO-60 had a rotor that could be driven by the engine for jump takeoffs but was demanding to fly and suffered several accidents.

△ Sikorsky S51/H-5 1945

Origin USA

Engine 1 x 450 hp Pratt & Whitney R-985 Wasp Junior radial

Top speed 106 mph (171 km/h)

This was the second-generation Sikorsky, designed with post-war civilian uses in mind. It was too complex and expensive for the nonmilitary market; the US Navy remained the largest customer.

△ Kellett XR-10 1947

Origin USA

Engine 2 x 415 hp Continental R-975-15 radial

Top speed 100 mph (161 km/h)

Kellett's 5-tonne twin-engined transport helicopter was ambitious, but mechanical failure of the intermeshing rotors killed the company's test pilot and the project was abandoned.

△ P-V Engineering Forum PV-2 1943

Origin USA

Engine 1 x 90 hp Franklin air-cooled opposed

Top speed 100 mph (161 km/h)

P-V eventually morphed into Boeing Vertol, makers of the mighty Chinook; Frank Piasecki's experimental PV-2 had full cyclic and collective rotor pitch control and tail rotor anti-torque.

◁ Focke Achgelis Fa-330 1943

Origin Germany

Engine None

Top speed 25 mph (40 km/h)

Heinrich Focke was sacked from Focke-Wulf for being politically suspect, but the Nazis allowed him to work on helicopters. The Fa-330 was an unpowered submarine-towed rotary kite used for ship-spotting.

▷ Hiller UH-12B (Hiller 360) 1947

Origin USA

Engine 1 x 178 hp Franklin O-335-4 air-cooled opposed

Top speed 95 mph (153 km/h)

Stanley Hiller was one of the great aviation innovators of the 20th century. His 360 Model UH-12 followed the XH-44 Hiller-Copter that he built for the US Army when he was just 17 years old.

▽ Westland Dragonfly HR3 1947

Origin UK

Engine 1 x 540 hp Alvis Leonides 50 radial

Top speed 105 mph (169 km/h)

Based on the Sikorsky S-51 but substantially modified with all-British components for want of dollars to pay for US parts, the Dragonfly was Westland's first helicopter.

△ Bell 47B 1945

Origin USA

Engine 1 x 157 hp Franklin O-335-1 air-cooled opposed

Top speed 105 mph (169 km/h)

The first helicopter in the world to be officially certified for civilian use, the Bell 47 was designed to meet overoptimistic forecasts for personal '"flying cars" post-war. Many are still flying today.

◁ Breguet GIII 1949

Origin France

Engine 1 x 450 hp Pratt & Whitney Wasp Junior radial

Top speed 134 mph (215 km/h)

The French-built Breguet GIII, with contra-rotating coaxial rotors, carried five people at a fast cruise speed. Although it was promising, development work ceased after it ran into funding problems.

△ Mil Mi-1M 1948

Origin Soviet Union

Engine 1 x 575 hp Ivchenko AI-26V radial

Top speed 118 mph (190 km/h)

Mikhail Mil ranks with Igor Sikorsky as a helicopter pioneer. His Mi-1 utility helicopter was the first Russian rotorcraft to go into volume production, and more than 2,500 were built.

Towards the Sound Barrier

World War II saw huge resources poured into aircraft development, as having faster machines than the other side could make a significant difference. Rocket-powered interceptors flew at previously unknown speeds, and piston-engined planes approached the speed of sound when diving. Post-war, the research was not wasted as swept wings, jet engines, ramjets, and rockets all took their place and the speed of sound (Mach 1) was easily exceeded.

▷ Supermarine Spitfire PR MkX 1944

Origin UK

Engine 1,655 hp Rolls-Royce Merlin 77 supercharged liquid-cooled V12

Top speed 417 mph (671 km/h)

The thin-winged Spitfire had the highest-limiting mach number of any WWII piston-engined aircraft. A fully instrumented MkXI, similar to the aircraft shown, reached speeds of 606 mph (975 km/h), or Mach 0.891 – nearly nine-tenths the speed of sound – in a dive.

▷ Supermarine Spiteful 1944

Origin UK

Engine 2,375 hp Rolls-Royce Griffon 69 liquid-cooled V12

Top speed 483 mph (778 km/h)

This aircraft was based on the Spitfire but with new laminar-flow wings and a new fuselage to combat instability. The Spiteful was overtaken by jet fighters; 19 were built (2 prototypes and 17 production).

▽ Messerschmitt Me163 Komet 1944

Origin Germany

Engine 3,750 lb (1,701 kg) Walter HWK 109-509A-2 liquid-fuel rocket

Top speed 596 mph (960 km/h)

This was the only rocket-powered aircraft to see active service, relying on its ability to overtake high-altitude bombers and make one or two diving passes before its engine cut out. In a dive it reached 698 mph (1,123 km/h).

△ Gloster Meteor F4 1944

Origin UK

Engine 2 x 3,500 lb (1,588 kg) thrust Rolls-Royce Derwent V turbojet

Top speed 616 mph (991 km/h)

The world's first production jet set new world speed records after WWII, raising it from 469 mph (755 km/h) to 606 mph (975 km/h) in 1945 and on to 616 mph (991 km/h) in 1946. It also set rate of climb and endurance records.

△ de Havilland DH108 Swallow 1946

Origin UK

Engine 3,738 lb (1,696 kg) thrust de Havilland Goblin 4 centrifugal compressor jet

Top speed 605 mph (974 km/h)

Three 108s were built (based on the Vampire jet fighter) to test tailless swept-wing handling: all three crashed fatally, but not before this final example had set a new world speed record for a 62-mile (100-km) circuit.

▷ **Supermarine 510 1948**

Origin UK

Engine 5,000 lb (2,268 kg) thrust Rolls-Royce Nene 2 turbojet

Top speed 630 mph (1,014 km/h)

This was the first British aircraft with swept wings and tail, and the first swept-wing aircraft to operate from an aircraft carrier. The 510 prototype lacked stability, but it helped to develop the Swift jet fighter.

▷ **Bell X-1 1946**

Origin USA

Engine 6,000 lb (2,722 kg) thrust Reaction Motors XLR11-RM3 liquid-fuelled rocket

Top speed 967 mph (1,556 km/h)

The first aircraft to exceed the speed of sound in level flight, X-1 was powered by a rocket with very limited burn time. Air-launched to maximize flying time, Chuck Yeager hit Mach 1.06 on 14 October 1947.

△ **Leduc 0.10 1946**

Origin France

Engine 3,520 lb (1,474 kg) thrust Leduc ramjet

Top speed 500 mph (800 km/h)

René Leduc's remarkable pioneering work on ramjets was carried out under the nose of German occupiers during WWII, finally reaching fruition post war. Launched from the air, it reached Mach 0.85.

▷ **Douglas D-558-2 Skyrocket 1948**

Origin USA

Engine 3,000 lb (1,361 kg) thrust Westinghouse J34-40 turbojet + 6,000 lb (2,722 kg) thrust Reaction Motors LR8-RM-6 rocket

Top speed 1,160 mph (1,867 km/h)

With both jet and rocket power, D-558-2 carried out much research into high-speed handling and stability before Scott Crossfield flew one to Mach 2 for the first time ever on 20 November 1953.

◁ **Hawker P1052 1948**

Origin UK

Engine 5,000 lb (2,268 kg) thrust Rolls-Royce Nene R.N.2 turbojet

Top speed 683 mph (1,098 km/h)

The P1052 was a test aircraft with 35 degree swept wings, of which two were completed for research into swept-wing aircraft characteristics. Several changes were made to the tailplane during the test programme.

▷ **Saab J 29 Tunnan 1948**

Origin Sweden

Engine 6,070 lb (2,753 kg) thrust Volvo Aero RM2B turbojet

Top speed 607 mph (977 km/h)

Nicknamed the "Flying Barrel", the J 29 formed part of Sweden's robust post-war air defence. Influenced by German WWII research, it was one of the first swept-wing fighters: fast, agile, but not quite supersonic.

Ahead of their Time

War brought innovation: sometimes brilliant, sometimes clutching at straws, always desperate to win an advantage. A recurring theme on both sides of the conflict (and of the Atlantic) was the "flying wing": designers attempts to incorporate the "dead" weight of fuselage and tail into a thick wing section, so that the whole aircraft contributed to its lift and aerodynamic efficiency. The ultimate example, the B-2 Spirit "Stealth Bomber", would not be revealed until 40 years later.

△ **Northrop N9M Flying Wing 1942**

Origin USA

Engine 2 x 300 hp Franklin XO-540-7 supercharged air-cooled flat-8

Top speed 258 mph (415 km/h)

Jack Northrop built four one-third scale models of his proposed flying-wing heavy bombers in order to test their flying characteristics and familiarize pilots with the design. The project finally came to fruition in form of the "Stealth Bomber" in 1989.

△ **Northrop XP-56 Black Bullet 1943**

Origin USA

Engine 2,000 hp Pratt & Whitney R-2800-29 air-cooled 18-cylinder radial

Top speed 465 mph (749 km/h)

This revolutionary fighter-interceptor was conceived in 1939 as a way to minimize drag with minimal fuselage, diminutive tail, magnesium alloy construction, and an H-24 layout engine. It was unstable.

▷ **Northrop YB-49 1947**

Origin USA

Engine 8 x 4,000 lb (1,814 kg) thrust Allison/ General Electric J35-A-5 turbojet

Top speed 495 mph (797 km/h)

Jack Northrop worked tirelessly on the flying wing concept, making full-size prototype fast bombers with propeller and then, here, jet engines, but the US government would not progress the project.

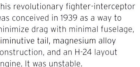

◁ **Miles M.39B Libellula 1943**

Origin UK

Engine 2 x 140 hp de Havilland Gipsy Major IC air-cooled 4-cylinder inverted in-line

Top speed 102 mph (164 km/h)

Innovative manufacturer Miles built this $^5/_8$ scale aircraft to test its revolutionary bomber design (which would have had Merlins or turbojets), with a supplementary low front wing as well as the main one: it flew well.

▽ **Handley Page HP75 Manx 1943**

Origin UK

Engine 2 x 140 hp de Havilland Gipsy Major air-cooled 4-cylinder inverted in-line

Top speed 150 mph (241 km/h)

First conceived in the 1930s the Manx had part-swept wings, two "pusher" engines, and wing-tip rudders. It was poorly constructed by Dart Aircraft and unable to fly until 1943; tests ended in 1946.

△ **Westland Welkin MkI 1944**

Origin UK

Engine 2 x 1,233 Rolls-Royce Merlin 76/77 supercharged liquid-cooled V12

Top speed 385 mph (620 kph)

The Welkin had a pressurized cabin, heated screen, oxygen, and huge wings, to fly interceptor missions at 45,000 ft (13,716 m). It was made in small numbers as high altitude bombing was no longer a great threat.

△ **Horten HVI V2 1944**

Origin Germany

Engine None

Top speed 124 mph (200 km/h)

Reimar Horten experimented with swept-wing aircraft that had no fuselage or tail. This glider's pilot had to kneel semi-prone, and needed oxygen, pressurization, and heated gloves to fly at high altitude.

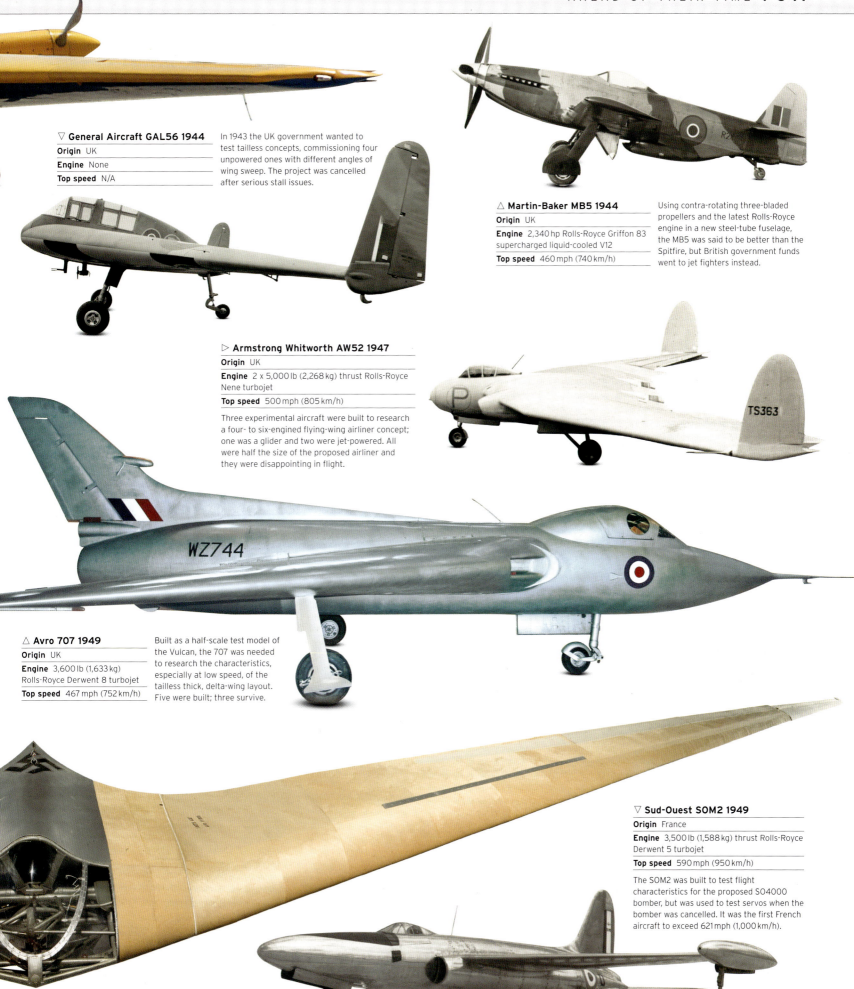

▽ **General Aircraft GAL56 1944**

Origin UK

Engine None

Top speed N/A

In 1943 the UK government wanted to test tailless concepts, commissioning four unpowered ones with different angles of wing sweep. The project was cancelled after serious stall issues.

△ **Martin-Baker MB5 1944**

Origin UK

Engine 2,340 hp Rolls-Royce Griffon 83 supercharged liquid-cooled V12

Top speed 460 mph (740 km/h)

Using contra-rotating three-bladed propellers and the latest Rolls-Royce engine in a new steel-tube fuselage, the MB5 was said to be better than the Spitfire, but British government funds went to jet fighters instead.

▷ **Armstrong Whitworth AW52 1947**

Origin UK

Engine 2 x 5,000 lb (2,268 kg) thrust Rolls-Royce Nene turbojet

Top speed 500 mph (805 km/h)

Three experimental aircraft were built to research a four- to six-engined flying-wing airliner concept; one was a glider and two were jet-powered. All were half the size of the proposed airliner and they were disappointing in flight.

△ **Avro 707 1949**

Origin UK

Engine 3,600 lb (1,633 kg) Rolls-Royce Derwent 8 turbojet

Top speed 467 mph (752 km/h)

Built as a half-scale test model of the Vulcan, the 707 was needed to research the characteristics, especially at low speed, of the tailless thick, delta-wing layout. Five were built; three survive.

▽ **Sud-Ouest SOM2 1949**

Origin France

Engine 3,500 lb (1,588 kg) thrust Rolls-Royce Derwent 5 turbojet

Top speed 590 mph (950 km/h)

The SOM2 was built to test flight characteristics for the proposed SO4000 bomber, but was used to test servos when the bomber was cancelled. It was the first French aircraft to exceed 621 mph (1,000 km/h).

Aircraft
1950–1979

Jet Fighters

The legacy of World War II was a tremendous advance in jet development. Fighters now had to be jet-powered to be competitive, and able to reach supersonic speeds. In the UK there were only a few manufacturers trying to build the aircraft, while US and Soviet fighters were honed in the skies above Korea. As building costs soared, 1950s fighters remained in service with smaller nations' air forces for decades.

◁ **North American F-86A Sabre 1949**

Origin USA

Engine 5,200 lb (2,359 kg) thrust General Electric J47-GE-7 turbojet

Top speed 685 mph (1,102 km/h)

The only US swept-wing fighter able to combat the Soviet MiG-15s, the transonic Sabre used research seized from German aerodynamicists after WWII. First flown in 1947, the "A" began service during 1949.

△ **North American F-86H Sabre 1953**

Origin USA

Engine 5,910 lb (2,681 kg) thrust General Electric J47-GE-27 turbojet

Top speed 693 mph (1,115 km/h)

Progressive development kept the Sabre competitive against updated MiGs. It had an uprated engine, more adaptable wings, a low-altitude bombing system, and provision to carry nuclear weapons.

◁ **de Havilland DH112 Venom Mk4 1952**

Origin UK

Engine 4,850–5,150 lb (2,200–2,336 kg) thrust de Havilland Ghost 103/105 turbojet

Top speed 640 mph (1,030 km/h)

Developed from the Vampire with a more powerful engine and slimmer wings, the Venom was first built as a single-seat fighter-bomber, then as a two-seat night-fighter; both were successful.

▷ **de Havilland DH115 Vampire T11 1952**

Origin UK

Engine 3,500 lb (1,588 kg) thrust de Havilland Goblin 35 turbojet

Top speed 548 mph (882 km/h)

Continued development of this succesful early jet, first introduced in 1945, brought this two-seat trainer version. The aircraft remained in use until 1966. Total Vampire production was 3,268.

△ **Gloster Meteor F Mk8 1949**

Origin UK

Engine 2 x 3,500 lb (1,588 kg) thrust Rolls-Royce Derwent 8 turbojet

Top speed 616 mph (991 km/h)

The first British jet fighter was built in thousands. A new tail and stretched fuselage came with the definitive F.8, which served with the RAAF in Korea and with many air forces worldwide.

△ **Gloster Meteor NF.14 1953**

Origin UK

Engine 2 x 3,800 lb (1,723 kg) thrust Rolls-Royce Derwent 9 turbojet

Top speed 585 mph (941 km/h)

The Meteor's night-fighter variant was developed from 1950, with longer wings and an extended nose that contained Air Intercept Radar. Early versions served in the Suez crisis; this is the final version.

◁ Mikoyan-Gurevich MiG-17 1951

Origin USSR

Engine 5,046–7,423 lb (2,289–3,367 kg) thrust Klimov VK-1F afterburning turbojet

Top speed 711 mph (1,145 km/h)

Developed from the MiG-15, this was one of the most successful transonic fighters. It was still effective in the 1960s thanks to the addition of an afterburner; China built some from 1966 to 1986.

△ Supermarine Attacker F.1 1951

Origin UK

Engine 5,000 lb (2,268 kg) thrust Rolls-Royce Nene turbojet

Top speed 590 mph (950 km/h)

Test-flown as a land-based fighter in 1946, the Attacker became the Royal Navy's first jet fighter, but was poorly suited to carrier use due to its tail-wheel undercarriage: 185 were built.

▽ Armstrong Whitworth Sea Hawk 1953

Origin UK

Engine 5,200 lb (2,359 kg) thrust Rolls-Royce Nene 103 turbojet

Top speed 600 mph (965 km/h)

Hawker's first jet flew in prototype form in 1947. It was adapted with folding wings for the Royal Navy for carrier launching, commencing service in 1953 and performing well in the Suez crisis.

◁ Supermarine Scimitar F.1 1957

Origin UK

Engine 2 x 11,250 lb (5,103 kg) thrust Rolls-Royce Avon 202 turbojet

Top speed 736 mph (1,185 km/h)

This large twin-engined naval fighter was really too big for the Royal Navy's aircraft carriers and suffered many mechanical problems: more than half of the 76 built were lost in accidents.

▷ Hawker Hunter F Mk1 1954

Origin UK

Engine 7,600 lb (3,447 kg) thrust Rolls-Royce Avon 113 turbojet

Top speed 702 mph (1,130 km/h)

Sydney Camm's Hunter was one of the best and longest-serving early jet fighters, aided by its compact Rolls-Royce Avon engine. First flown in 1951, the prototype set a world air speed record in 1953 of 727 mph (1,171 km/h).

◁ Folland Gnat F1 1955

Origin UK

Engine 4,705 lb (2,134 kg) thrust Bristol Orpheus 701 turbojet

Top speed 695 mph (1,120 km/h)

Designed as a lightweight fighter, "Teddy" Petter's single-seat F1 was sold to India, Finland, and Yugoslavia. The RAF ordered two-seat T1 trainers. They were used by their Red Arrows aerobatic team.

▷ Gloster Javelin FAW.5 1956

Origin UK

Engine 2 x 8,300 lb (3,765 kg) thrust Armstrong Siddeley Sapphire SA.6 turbojet

Top speed 704 mph (1,133 km/h)

With broad delta wings and a large finned "T" tail, this distinctive all-weather interceptor first flew in 1951. After lengthy development to overcome stall issues, it served with the RAF from 1956 to 1968.

Bombers, Attack Aircraft, and Trainers

With Cold War tension at its peak, World War II experiments with jet engines and supersonic wing profiles were exploited to produce some truly impressive aircraft, such as the Avro Vulcan with its electro-hydraulic-powered flying controls, the ultra-high-altitude Canberra, and the double-delta-wing Saab Draken. The Soviets lagged behind at first, finding that only turboprop engines had the range to reach the US and return.

△ **Fokker 4 S.11 "instructor" 1950**

Origin Netherlands

Engine 190 hp Lycoming O-435 A air-cooled flat-8

Top Speed 130 mph (209 km/h)

This tandem-seat military trainer was developed by Fokker immediately after WWII and was adopted by air forces from South America to Israel. It was also built in Italy and Brazil.

▷ **Lockheed T33 Shooting Star 1950**

Origin USA

Engine 5,400 lb (2,466 kg) thrust Allison J33-A-35 turbojet

Top speed 600 mph (970 km/h)

First flown in 1948, used by air forces worldwide, and still in service in Bolivia, 6,557 of this US two-seat jet trainer were built. This is a stretched version of the US's first jet fighter, the F-80 Shooting Star.

▷ **English Electric Canberra 1951**

Origin UK

Engine 2 x 7,400 lb (3,352 kg) thrust Rolls-Royce Avon 109 turbojet

Top speed 580 mph (933 km/h)

Britain's first jet bomber, the Canberra, first flew in 1949. It was highly adaptable and served with many air forces – on both sides in some wars. It set a world altitude record in 1957.

◁ **Percival Pembroke 1952**

Origin UK

Engine 2 x 540 hp Alvis Leonides Mk 127 supercharged air-cooled 9-cylinder radial

Top speed 186 mph (299 km/h)

A light military transport, with a longer wing than its civil counterpart to increase its load capacity, the Pembroke served with the RAF until 1988; 128 were built, some serving in Europe and Africa.

▷ **Vickers Valiant 1953**

Origin UK

Engine 4 x 9,500 lb (4,304 kg) thrust Rolls-Royce Avon RA28 Mk 204 turbojet

Top speed 567 mph (913 km/h)

First of the RAF's nuclear force V-bombers, the sweptwing Valiant high-level strategic bomber was soon reduced to support roles, such as refuelling and reconnaissance, and was retired in 1965.

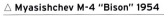

△ **Myasishchev M-4 "Bison" 1954**

Origin USSR

Engine 4 x 19,280 lb (8,734 kg) thrust Mikulin AM-3A turbojet

Top speed 588 mph (947 km/h)

The Soviet Union's first strategic jet bomber had sufficient range to attack North America, though not to return home. It was steadily uprated, but only 93 were built and none saw use in combat.

◁ **Tupolev Tu-95 "Bear" 1955**

Origin USSR

Engine 4 x 14,800 lb (6,704 kg) thrust Kuznetsov NK-12M turboprop

Top speed 562 mph (905 km/h)

Combining unusually sweptback wings and contra-rotating propellers, the Tu-95 has an exceptional range (laden) of 9,320 miles (15,000 km) without refuelling. It is likely to be in service until 2040.

△ **Saab J35E Draken 1955**

Origin Sweden

Engine 12,787–17,637 lb (5,793–7,990 kg) thrust Volvo Flygmotor RM 6C afterburning turbojet

Top speed 1,340 mph (2,150 km/h)

An effective supersonic Cold War fighter, the Draken's unusual double-delta wing gave good speed and agility. It was designed to take off from public roads and be rearmed in 10 minutes; 644 were built.

△ **Avro 698 Vulcan 1956**

Origin UK

Engine 4 x 17,000 lb (7,701 kg) thrust Bristol Siddeley Olympus Mk202 turbojet

Top speed 708 mph (1,139 km/h)

Powered by the world's first two-spool axial flow turbojets, Avro's radical delta-wing Vulcan spearheaded Britain's nuclear deterrent. It had a high payload and was difficult to detect with radar.

△ **Fouga CM-170R Magister 1956**

Origin France

Engine 2 x 880 lb (399 kg) thrust Turbomeca Marboré IIA turbojet

Top speed 444 mph (715 km/h)

One of the first turbojet-powered two-seat trainers, the distinctive V-tail Magister was used by air forces worldwide and 929 were built. From 1960 it was fitted with the more powerful Marboré engine.

△ **Douglas A-4 Skyhawk 1956**

Origin USA

Engine 8,200 lb (3,715 kg) thrust Wright J65 turbojet

Top speed 673 mph (1,077 km/h)

This was a frontline jet that achieved performance through reduced size and weight rather than sheer engine power. Ed Heinemann's design for the US Navy had such a small delta wing it had no need to fold for carrier use.

◁ **Sukhoi Su-7B 1959**

Origin USSR

Engine 14,980–22,148 lb (6,786–10,034 kg) thrust Lyulka AL-7F afterburning turbojet

Top speed 1,335 mph (2,150 km/h)

First flown in 1955 as a fighter, with all-moving tailplane and movable-cone air intake, the Su-7 was refined for ground attack in 1959 as the Su-7B; 1,847 aircraft were built.

Rotorcraft Mature

The adoption of the turbine engine in the 1950s revolutionized the helicopter industry. Small, light, and powerful turbines displaced less-reliable piston engines and allowed a step change in size, speed, and lifting capacity. Helicopters began to be used on scheduled services in the expectation that they would become more cost-effective with time.

△ Westland Dragonfly HR5 1952
Origin UK/USA

Engine 520 hp Alvis Leonides 50 radial

Top speed 105 mph (169 km/h)

The HR5, a refined, winch-equipped version of the earlier HR3, was used by the Royal Navy and tested unsuccessfully on commercial routes in England and Wales by state-owned airline BEA (British European Airways).

△ Piasecki HUP-2 Retriever 1952
Origin USA

Engine 550 hp Continental R975-46 radial

Top speed 105 mph (169 km/h)

Piasecki's HUP-2, produced for the US Navy, was the first helicopter to feature an autopilot but suffered from poor engine reliability; at least 10 HUP-2s were lost at sea.

△ Westland Whirlwind HAR 10 1959
Origin UK

Engine 1,050 shp Bristol Siddeley Gnome turbine

Top speed 109 mph (175 km/h)

Tests with a Gnome turbine in a Whirlwind during 1959 were so encouraging that the RAF placed an order for 68 HAR 10s, and 45 older piston Whirlwinds were converted.

▷ Mil Mi-6A 1957
Origin USSR

Engine 2 x 5,500 shp Soloviev D-25V turboshaft

Top speed 186 mph (299 km/h)

The Soviet Union's first turbine machine, the Mi-6 heavy transport was the largest and fastest helicopter in the world when it appeared. Its many record feats included lifting a 44,350 lb (20,117 kg) load.

▽ Mil Mi-4 1952
Origin USSR

Engine 1,675 hp Shvetsov ASh 82 14 cylinder radial

Top speed 116 mph (186 km/h)

Rushed out in response to the US deployment of helicopters in Korea, the Mi-4 has served in virtually every military and civil role from gunship to crop sprayer.

▽ NHI Sobeh H.2 Kolibri 1955
Origin Netherlands

Engine 2 x 100 hp NHI TJ5 ramjets

Top speed 100 mph (160 km/h)

Thirst for fuel conspired against the use of ramjets on rotor tips. The H.2 was trucked between revenue flights in a special "helicar" to try to make it pay.

◁ Fairey Ultra Light 1955
Origin UK

Engine Turbomeca Palouste turbojet

Top speed 98 mph (158 km/h)

Tip-jets driving the main rotor made the two-seat Ultra Light thirsty and noisy, and despite its agility - it could climb at almost 1,400 ft (427 m) per minute - it was abandoned after only six were made.

△ **Bristol Sycamore HR14 1953**

Origin UK

Engine 520 hp Alvis Leonides 173 9-cylinder

Top speed 127 mph (204 km/h)

The HR14 was the first British-designed commercial helicopter. A total of 177 were built before production ceased in 1959, including 85 HR14s for the RAF. Its crews pioneered search and rescue and medical evacuation techniques.

◁ **Sud-Ouest SO1221S Djinn 1953**

Origin France

Engine 240 hp Turbomeca Palouste IV turbo-compressor

Top speed 81 mph (130 km/h)

Powered by cold, compressed air fed to nozzles on the tips of the rotor blades, the Djinn's directional control was achieved via a "rudder" positioned in the jet efflux.

◁ **Bell 47 G 1953**

Origin USA

Engine 280 hp Lycoming O-540

Top speed 105 mph (169 km/h)

In production for 21 years, the Bell 47 G was manufactured under licence in Italy, Japan, and the UK. In all, 6,221 Bell 47s were built.

▷ **Saro Skeeter Mk7A (AOP-12) 1956**

Origin UK

Engine 215 hp de Havilland Gipsy Major

Top speed 101 mph (162 km/h)

A Cierva design inherited by Saunders Roe, the Skeeter suffered major development problems; 64 examples of its 12th incarnation were bought by the British Army and designated AOP-12.

◁ **Brantly B2 1959**

Origin USA

Engine 180 hp Lycoming IVO 360 A

Top speed 100 mph (161 km/h)

Knitting machine inventor Newby O. Brantly designed the B2 in 1953 as personal transport, although it was not certificated until 1959. The more capable B2-B followed in 1963.

The End of Piston-engined Transport

By the late 1940s air travel was relatively safe and comfortable, with many airlines offering a regular and reliable transatlantic service. However, the piston-engine had peaked, with engines such as the Pratt & Whitney Wasp Major that had 28 cylinders and 56 spark plugs. Although powerful and reasonably reliable, these very complicated motors required a lot of maintenance, and the introduction of the turbojet and turboprop completely eclipsed them.

△ de Havilland DH114 Heron 1950

Origin UK

Engine 4 x 250 hp de Havilland Gipsy Queen 30Mk2 air-cooled 6-cylinder inverted in-line

Top speed 183 mph (294 km/h)

Descended from the earlier Dove, the Heron is notable for having four engines on a relatively small airframe. Despite this, the aircraft was still relatively slow, although it was structurally sound. Consequently, many were later fitted with more powerful American engines, including PT-6 turboprops.

△ Fairchild C-119G Flying Boxcar 1950

Origin USA

Engine 2 x 3,500 hp Pratt & Whitney Wasp Major air-cooled 28-cylinder 4-row radial

Top speed 296 mph (476 km/h)

Fairchild's previous design for a tactical transport, the C-82, was not very successful. However, Fairchild learned from its mistakes and the C-119 addressed all of the C-82's failures successfully. Almost 1,200 were produced, and the aircraft saw active service in many conflicts, including Korea and Vietnam.

△ Boeing C-97G Stratofreighter 1950

Origin USA

Engine 4 x 3,500 hp Pratt & Whitney Wasp Major air-cooled 28-cylinder 4-row radial

Top speed 375 mph (603 km/h)

Based on the B-50 bomber, the Stratofreighter's introduction to service coincided with the USAF making aerial refuelling top priority, as its first generation jet fighters and bombers all had very short range and endurance. Consequently, of the 888 C-97s built, only 60 were Stratofreighters, with the majority being tankers.

△ Douglas C-124C Globemaster II 1950

Origin USA

Engine 4 x 3,800 hp Pratt & Whitney Wasp Major air-cooled 28-cylinder 4-row radial

Top speed 320 mph (515 km/h)

The design of the Globemaster drew heavily on lessons learned during the Berlin Airlift (1948-49). There was a cargo lift at the rear, while the nose featured large clamshell doors and a hydraulic ramp. It carried bulky payloads.

△ Nord Noratlas 1950

Origin France

Engine 2 x 2,090 hp Bristol/SNECMA Hercules air-cooled 14-cylinder 2-row radial

Top speed 273 mph (440 km/h)

Designed to replace France's fleet of WWII-surplus transports, the Noratlas was operated by several other air forces, including Germany, Greece, Portugal, and Israel. Over 400 were built, but unlike many other military transports, it was not a success in the civil market.

▷ de Havilland Canada DHC2 Beaver 1952

Origin Canada

Engine 450 hp Pratt & Whitney Wasp Junior air-cooled 9-cylinder radial

Top speed 158 mph (254 km/h)

One of the top Canadian engineering achievements of the 20th century, the Beaver was designed by bush pilots, for bush pilots. With fine short takeoff and landing performance, the Beaver was equally popular with the military.

△ Lockheed L1049 G Super Constellation 1951

Origin USA

Engine 4 x 3,250 hp Wright R3350 air-cooled 18-cylinder 2-row radial

Top speed 330 mph (531 km/h)

One of the most elegant airliners ever built, the piston-powered Super Constellations had a relatively short service life with the major airlines, as the type was soon eclipsed by jets. However, Constellations served for many years in South and Central America.

△ de Havilland Canada DHC3 Otter 1953

Origin Canada

Engine 600 hp Pratt & Whitney Wasp air-cooled 9-cylinder radial

Top speed 160 mph (258 km/h)

Descended from its slightly smaller stablemate the Beaver, the Otter played an important role in opening up the vast interior of the Canadian bush, being equally capable on wheels, floats, or skis.

▷ Martin 4-0-4 Silver Falcon 1952

Origin USA

Engine 2 x 2,100 hp Pratt & Whitney Double Wasp air-cooled 18-cylinder 2-row radial

Top speed 312 mph (502 km/h)

Called the Silver Falcon by Eastern and the Skyliner by TWA, the 4-0-4 was yet another piston-powered airliner that was soon displaced from the major airlines by the introduction of the turbine engine. However, many were operated by "second level" airlines as a replacement for the DC-3.

△ Ilyushin Il-14 1954

Origin USSR

Engine 2 x 1,900 hp Shvetsov Ash-82T air-cooled 14-cylinder 2-row radial

Top speed 259 mph (417 km/h)

Similar in appearance to the Martin 4-0-4, the Il-14 was not as sophisticated as its capitalist counterpart. It was rugged and reliable, making it ideal to operate from the many relatively rough rural airfields served by Aeroflot.

▷ Blackburn Beverley C1 1955

Origin UK

Engine 4 x 2,850 hp Bristol Centaurus air-cooled 18-cylinder 2-row radial

Top speed 238 mph (383 km/h)

Although its fixed undercarriage made it look old-fashioned, the rugged Beverley was very good at dropping supplies and for operating from rough airstrips. Blackburn produced 49 C1s, and the type was retired in 1967.

Civil Jets and Turboprops

The use of the turbine engine for airliners revolutionized air travel. Not only were journey times slashed by over 50 per cent, but also the ability to fly above most of the bad weather and the much quieter cabins made travelling a considerably more pleasant experience. Furthermore, as the turbine was more reliable than the hugely complex giant radial engines that powered the last of the piston airliners, dispatch rates improved exponentially.

△ **Bristol Britannia 312 1952**
Origin UK
Engine 4 x 4,450 hp Bristol Proteus 765 turboprop
Top speed 397 mph (639 km/h)

Known as the "Whispering Giant", when the Britannia made its maiden flight it offered a significant increase in performance over the other airliners of the time. Unfortunately, only 85 were built.

▷ **de Havilland DH106 Comet 1 1952**
Origin UK
Engine 4 x 5,000 lb (2,268 kg) thrust de Havilland Ghost turbojet
Top speed 460 mph (740 km/h)

The first production jetliner, the Comet caused a sensation when it entered service. Flying at twice the speed of the propliners with significant flaws in both design and construction resulted in several fatal crashes, causing a loss of confidence in the aircraft.

△ **Sud Aviation Caravelle 1 1955**
Origin France
Engine 2 x 11,400 lb (5,171 kg) thrust Rolls-Royce Avon Mk527 turbojet
Top speed 500 mph (805 km/h)

This first French jetliner was also the first to have engines mounted on the rear of the fuselage. Popular with pilots and passengers, the Caravelle entered service in 1959, the last few retiring as recently as 2004.

△ **Saunders Roe SR45 Princess 1952**
Origin UK
Engine 10 x 2,250 hp Bristol Proteus 600 tuboprop
Top speed 380 mph (610 km/h)

Obsolete before it even flew, the designers of the Princess failed to to take into account several significant factors. These included the number of runways built during WWII, the improved performance of land-based aircraft, and the problems caused by saltwater corrosion.

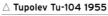

△ **Tupolev Tu-104 1955**
Origin USSR
Engine 2 x 21,400 lb (9,707 kg) thrust Mikulin AM-3M-500 turbojet
Top speed 497 mph (800 km/h)

This was the USSR's first jetliner. Its appearance in London in 1956 carrying Nikita Khrushehev on a State visit caused a stir among Western observers, who were unaware the Soviet aviation industry was so advanced.

△ **Lockheed L188 Electra 1957**
Origin USA
Engine 4 x 3,750 hp Allison 501-D13 turboprop
Top speed 448 mph (721 km/h)

The Constellation had earned Lockheed's commercial aircraft division a fine reputation, and initially the Electra (which was also the first turboprop airliner produced in the US) sold well. However, a fatal design flaw caused two early crashes and only 170 were built.

▷ **Boeing 707 1958**
Origin USA
Engine 4 x 17,000 lb (7,711 kg) thrust Pratt & Whitney JT3-D turbofan
Top speed 621 mph (1,000 km/h)

One of the most important aircraft of all time, the 707 was the West's first successful jetliner. In many ways a civil development of the KC-135 Stratotanker, more than 1,000 would be built in a number of different versions and powered by a variety of engines.

◁ **Fokker F27-100 Friendship 1958**

Origin Netherlands

Engine 2 x 2,250 hp Rolls-Royce Dart Mk528 turboprop

Top speed 282 mph (454 km/h)

In the early 1950s a number of aircraft manufacturers were planning a replacement for the DC-3, and Dutch airframer Fokker opted for a high-wing turboprop design. Called the F27, it was also produced in the US by Fairchild and would eventually become the bestselling Western turboprop airliner.

△ **Douglas DC-8 1959**

Origin USA

Engine 4 x 17,000 lb (7,711 kg) thrust Pratt & Whitney JT3-D turbofan

Top speed 588 mph (946 km/h)

Although Douglas dominated the American airliner market in the 1950s, Boeing got its 707 to market first. However, in many respects the DC-8 was better designed (for example, it had six-abreast seating from the start, whereas the 707 was redesigned). More than 500 were built. A handful are still in operation as freighters.

△ **Ilyushin Il-18 1959**

Origin USSR

Engine 4 x 4,250 hp Ivchenko AI-20M turboprop

Top speed 419 mph (675 km/h)

First flown in 1957, the Il-18 (known to NATO as the "Coot") soon earned a reputation for being an extremely rugged and durable aircraft, capable of operating from unpaved airfields. Many Il-18s remain operational in Africa.

△ **Handley Page Dart Herald 1959**

Origin UK

Engine 2 x 1,910 hp Rolls-Royce Dart Mk527 turboprop

Top speed 275 mph (442 km/h)

The Herald was another contender for a "DC-3 replacement", but Handley-Page's board made an error of judgement by initially specifying that it should be powered by piston engines, not turboprops.

△ **Vickers Viscount 1953**

Origin UK

Engine 2 x 1,990 hp Rolls-Royce Dart Mk525 turboprop

Top speed 352 mph (566 km/h)

The first turboprop airliner to enter service, the Viscount was a quantum jump in air transport design. It was particularly popular with passengers, who loved the large windows, smooth ride (flying above most of the weather), and quiet cabin.

△ **Antonov An-12 1959**

Origin USSR

Engine 4 x 4,000 hp Progress AI-20M turboprop

Top speed 482 mph (775 km/h)

Sometimes described as "the Soviet C-130", the An-12 Cub was a tactical transport that was similar in both design and construction to its capitalist counterpart, the Lockheed Hercules. First flown in 1957, over 1,200 were built and many still remain in service as freighters, particularly in Africa, India, and the former states of the USSR.

Modern Classics

After World War II had broadened horizons for millions of people worldwide and thousands had learned to fly, it was inevitable that, as peace was established and prosperity returned, more and more would take up flying as a leisure activity. Stylish and sporty aircraft flooded the market to cater for this demand, along with simple, cheap amateur-build options, and there was also a steady increase in the popularity of gliding.

△ Piper PA-18 Super Cub 1950

Origin USA

Engine 150 hp Lycoming O-320 air-cooled flat-4

Top speed 153 mph (246 km/h)

Derived from the Taylor Cub of 1930, this is a 1993-built aircraft of a type that went into production in 1949-50. It was capable of operating from small fields; around 15,000 were built and many are still flying.

△ Gardan GY-201 Minicab 1950

Origin France

Engine 65 hp Continental A65-8F air-cooled flat-4

Top speed 123 mph (198 km/h)

First flown in 1949 this inexpensive, lightweight two-seater was designed by Yves Gardan for Constructions Aéronautiques du Béarn, which built 22. Around 140 more were kit-built worldwide.

△ Piper PA-23 Apache 1953

Origin USA

Engine 2 x 150 hp Lycoming O-320-A air-cooled flat-4

Top speed 215 mph (346 km/h)

Popular for its spacious four- to six-seat interior and high weight-carrying ability, this was the first twin-engined Piper. Designed by Stinson, 6,976 were built, in various forms, up to 1981.

△ Cessna 170B 1952

Origin USA

Engine 145 hp Continental O-300-A air-cooled flat-6

Top speed 143 mph (230 km/h)

In 1952 the successful Cessna 170 was updated with a wing design that continued on small Cessnas well into the 21st century, with modified Fowler wing flaps and a new tailplane.

△ Stits SA-2A Sky Baby 1952

Origin USA

Engine 112 hp Continental C-85 flat-4

Top speed 220 mph (354 km/h)

Designed by WWII fighter pilot Ray Stits to be the "world's smallest" aircraft, this tiny biplane required a 170-lb (77-kg) pilot to maintain its centre of gravity. It did 25 hours of display flying before retirement.

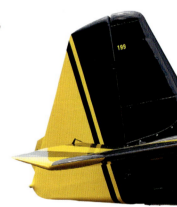

△ Cessna 180 Skywagon 1952

Origin USA

Engine 225 hp Continental O-470-A air-cooled flat-6

Top speed 170 mph (274 km/h)

A more spacious and powerful alternative to the 170, the all-metal framed semi-monocoque 180 was produced in updated forms until 1981, by which time 6,193 had been built.

△ Focke-Wulf FwP149 1953

Origin Italy

Engine 190 hp Lycoming GO-435-A air-cooled flat-6

Top speed 145 mph (233 km/h)

The German Focke-Wulf FwP149D is the licence-built version of the Italian Piaggio P149 four- to five-seat touring aircraft, which was used by the German Air Force for training and utility purposes.

◁ **Cessna 310 1953**

Origin USA

Engine 2 x 240 hp Continental O-470-B air-cooled flat-6

Top speed 220 mph (354 km/h)

Cessna's first post-war twin-engined aircraft was a sleek, aerodynamic six-seater that would continue in production until 1980; the model shown was built in 1973. A popular air taxi, it could fly high loads off short runways.

△ **Schleicher K8 1957**

Origin Germany

Engine None

Top speed 118 mph (190 km/h)

Rudolf Kaiser designed the K8 as a simple single-seat glider with dive brakes and straightforward construction that would lend itself to amateur building from kits. More than 1,100 were made.

△ **Schleicher K4 Rhönlerche 1952**

Origin Germany

Engine None

Top speed 106 mph (171 km/h)

This rather heavy two-seat aircraft could be challenging to fly, but became a popular training glider because of its forgiving flight characteristics and ability to fly very slowly.

△ **Moravan Národní Podnik Zlín Z.226T 1956**

Origin Czechoslovakia

Engine 160 hp Walter Minor 6-III inverted air-cooled straight-6

Top speed 137 mph (220 km/h)

Established in the 1930s, Zlín made highly respected sports/aerobatic aircraft, in a range that included this trainer. Around 250 of these aircraft were built from 1956 and 1961, based on the 1947 Z.26 trainer.

△ **Jodel D117A 1958**

Origin France

Engine 90 hp Continental C90-14F air-cooled flat-4

Top speed 130 mph (209 km/h)

Édouard Joly and Jean Délémontez designed their D11 for flying club use, based on earlier 1940s designs. In initial form it had a 45 hp engine, doubled for the D117, of which 223 were built by the Société Aéronautique Normande (SAN).

△ **Beechcraft 33 Debonair 1959**

Origin USA

Engine 225 hp Continental IO-470-J air-cooled flat-6

Top speed 196 mph (315 km/h)

Ralph Harmon's streamlined all-metal low-wing V-tail monoplane, exceptionally advanced in 1947, was still built in developed form 65 years on. This conventional-tail version was launched in 1959.

Experimental Aircraft

These were exciting times, as European nations and the US experimented with supersonic flight, delta-wing layouts, extreme wing sweeps, vertical takeoff and landing (VTOL), and alternative power from ramjets and rockets. Some sensational prototypes were built and many valuable lessons learned. However, the life of a test pilot in this world was fraught with danger: many lost their lives in testing accidents.

△ **Boulton Paul P.111 1950**

Origin UK

Engine 5,100 lb (2,313 kg) thrust Rolls-Royce Nene R3N2 turbojet

Top speed 649 mph (1,045 km/h)

Designed by Dr S. C. Redshaw for the UK Air Ministry, to test tailless delta-wing characteristics, the P.111 had fully powered controls and tested a selection of glass-fibre wing extensions.

△ **Shorts SB5 1952**

Origin UK

Engine 4,850 lb (2,200 kg) thrust Bristol BE26 Orpheus turbojet (earlier, 3,500 lb/ 1,588 kg thrust Rolls-Royce Derwent 8)

Top speed 403 mph (650 km/h)

Built to check ideal wing angles and tailplane positions for low-speed handling of the proposed Lightning fighter, the SB5's wooden wings could be set at 50 degrees, 60 degrees, or 69 degrees, the greatest sweep yet tried.

▽ **Shorts SC1 1957**

Origin UK

Engine 5 x 2,130 lb (966 kg) thrust Rolls-Royce RB108 turbojet

Top speed 246 mph (396 km/h)

The first British vertical takeoff aircraft with fly-by-wire controls, the SC1 had four engines for vertical operation and a fifth for forward propulsion. Nose, tail, and wing-tip bleeds from the four lift engines gave it low-speed stability.

▷ **Lockheed XFV-1 1954**

Origin USA

Engine 5,332 hp Allison XT40-A-14 double-turboprop

Top speed 580 mph (933 km/h)

The US Navy requested a vertical takeoff aircraft to operate from small platforms on normal ships. The XFV-1, known as the "Pogo" actually flew vertically and did transition to level flight in tests, but it was too slow.

△ **Sud-Ouest SO9000-01 Trident 1953**

Origin France

Engine 2 x 1,654 lb (750 kg) thrust MD 30 Viper ASV.5 turbojet + 8,325 lb (3,776 kg) thrust SEPR 481 3-chamber liquid fuel rocket

Top speed 1,060 mph (1,706 km/h)

Development began in 1948 for France's supersonic interceptor, using wingtip-mounted turbojets plus a three-chamber rocket; 10 pre-production aircraft followed the two prototypes, but no more.

▷ **Rolls-Royce Thrust Measuring Rig "Flying Bedstead" 1953**

Origin UK

Engine 2 x 4,050 lb (1,837 kg) thrust Rolls-Royce Nene turbojet

Top speed N/A

Rolls-Royce engineers under Dr Alan Arnold Griffith built two rigs to test the use of jet engines for vertical takeoff and to develop means of controlling them and keeping them stable when hovering.

◁ Ryan X-13 Vertijet 1955

Origin USA

Engine 10,000 lb (4,536 kg) thrust Rolls-Royce Avon turbojet

Top speed 350 mph (563 km/h)

Built to test vertical takeoff, and horizontal to vertical (and back) flight transition, the successful X-13 might have been launched from submarines, but the US Navy never ordered any.

△ Leduc 022 1955

Origin France

Engine 7,040 lb (3,193 kg) thrust SNECMA Atar 101D-3 turbojet + 14,300 lb (6,486 kg) thrust Leduc ramjet

Top speed 750 mph (1,207 km/h)

René Leduc worked through WWII on ramjet-powered designs; his first one – the Leduc 0.10 – flew, launched from a mother aircraft, in 1946. The 022 had a turbojet as well for takeoff, but drag restricted its top speed.

▽ Nord 1500 Griffon 1955

Origin France

Engine 7,710 lb (3,497 kg) thrust ATAR 101E-3 turbojet + 15,290 lb (6,935 kg) thrust Nord Stato-Réacteur ramjet

Top speed 1,450 mph (2,333 km/h)

Using a turbojet for takeoff supplemented by a ramjet for sensational high-speed performance proved successful for the 1500. It was excessively expensive compared to simpler afterburning turbojets.

△ Fairey FD2 1954

Origin UK

Engine 9,300–13,100 lb (4,218–5,942 kg) thrust Rolls-Royce RA28 Avon afterburning turbojet

Top speed 1,147 mph (1,846 kph)

Built for the UK Ministry of Supply as a supersonic research aircraft, the tailless delta-winged FD2 was the first aircraft to exceed 1,000 mph (1,609 km/h). To aid vision, it had a tilting nose like Concorde.

△ Saunders-Roe SR53 1957

Origin UK

Engine 1,640 lb (744 kg) thrust Armstrong Siddeley Viper 8 turbojet + 8,000 lb (3,629 kg) thrust de Havilland Spectre rocket

Top speed 1,632 mph (2,626 km/h)

The UK Air Ministry wanted an ultra-rapid-climb interceptor to counter the Cold War bomber threat: this rocket/jet-powered prototype flew well, but ground-to-air missiles were chosen instead.

◁ SNECMA C.450 Coléoptère 1959

Origin France

Engine 8,140 lb (3,692 kg) thrust SNECMA Atar 101-EV turbojet

Top speed N/A

French experiments with vertical takeoff centred on this innovative "tail-sitter", which used a 10½ ft (3.2 m) diameter annular wing. It hovered successfully, but crashed when attempting transition to horizontal flight.

△ Payen Pa49 Katy 1957

Origin France

Engine 300 lb (136 kg) thrust Turbomeca Palas turbojet

Top speed 311 mph (500 km/h)

Roland Payen championed tailless, delta-winged aircraft. He built several prototypes of which the wood-framed Katy was the first of its kind in France. It was the smallest jet-powered aircraft of its day.

Supersonic Fighters

The 1950s was a time of tremendous change in the fighter world. Ever more powerful engines and an increasing understanding of supersonic aerodynamics, fuelled by Cold War paranoia and big research and development budgets, saw top speeds rise from barely breaking the sound barrier in a dive to greater than Mach 2 – twice the speed of sound – in level flight.

▽ Dassault MD-452 Mystere IVA 1952

Origin France

Engine 7,716 lb (3,500 kg) thrust Hispano-Suiza Verdon 350 turbojet

Top speed 695 mph (1,120 km/h)

Although descended from the Mystere II, the IVA fighter-bomber was capable of supersonic flight. Originally powered by a Rolls-Royce Tay turbojet, most production aircraft were fitted with an engine built under licence by Hispano-Suiza.

△ Convair F-102A Delta Dagger 1953

Origin USA

Engine 16,000 lb (7,257 kg) thrust Pratt & Whitney J-57 turbojet

Top speed 824 mph (1,328 km/h)

A bold, innovative design, this tailless delta-wing interceptor was initially a huge disappointment as the prototype was incapable of supersonic flight. The improved F102A was given an area-ruled "coke-bottle" shaped fuselage and reached Mach 1.22 in flight.

▽ Convair F-106 Delta Dart 1959

Origin USA

Engine 24,500 lb (11,113 kg) thrust Pratt & Whitney J-75 turbojet

Top speed 1,265 mph (2,035 km/h)

Originally known as F-102B, this aircraft became the F-106, as it was significantly different from the F-102. It was given the, by now proven, coke-bottle shape necessary for supersonic flight, but it also had a more powerful engine and advanced avionics.

△ Mikoyan-Gurevich MiG-19 1955

Origin USSR

Engine 2 x 7,178 lb (3,256 kg) thrust Tumansky RD-9B turbojets

Top speed 909 mph (1,455 km/h)

Known by NATO as the "Farmer", the MiG-19 was the first Soviet fighter to be capable of sustained supersonic flight. Although around 5,500 were produced, it was not as popular as the MiG-17, which it replaced, or the MiG-21, which superseded it.

◁ Grumman F11F-1 Tiger 1956

Origin USA

Engine 10,500 lb (4,763 kg) thrust Wright J-65 turbojet

Top speed 727 mph (1,170 km/h)

The poor range and endurance of the US Navy's second supersonic fighter meant that it had a short career with the fleet, being phased out of operations by 1961. However, the Tiger was flown by the Navy's aerobatic team, the Blue Angels, until 1968.

△ Mikoyan-Gurevich MiG-21 1959

Origin USSR

Engine 12,655 lb (5,740 kg) thrust Tumansky R-11F-300 turbojet

Top speed 1,385 mph (2,230 km/h)

Lighter than its Western contemporaries, the "Fishbed" was designed by the Mikoyan-Gurevich design bureau and nicknamed the "balalaika" because the planform view resembled the instrument. It flew at speeds in excess of Mach 2.

◁ **North American F-100D Super Sabre 1956**

Origin USA

Engine 16,000 lb (7,257 kg) thrust Pratt & Whitney J-57 turbojet

Top speed 864 mph (1,390 km/h)

Nicknamed the "Hun", the F-100 was the first of the USAF's "Century Series" fighters. Although highly advanced when introduced, the F-100C had a dangerous design flaw – the fin was too small. This was rectified with the D model seen here. Designed as a fighter, most F-100Ds were used as fighter-bombers in Vietnam.

△ **North American F-100F Super Sabre 1957**

Origin USA

Engine 16,000 lb (7,257 kg) thrust Pratt & Whitney J-57 turbojet

Top speed 864 mph (1,390 km/h)

Originally intended as a two-seat trainer, the F-100F saw extensive combat in Vietnam, where it was used as a "Fast FAC" (Forward Air Controller). The most notable difference in the F model was that its internal armament was reduced from four to two 20 mm cannon.

△ **McDonnell F-101 Voodoo 1957**

Origin USA

Engine 2 x 16,900 lb (7,666 kg) thrust Pratt & Whitney J-57 turbojet

Top speed 1,134 mph (1,825 km/h)

Originally designed as a single-seater, later Voodoos had a two-crew cockpit and could be armed with nuclear missiles. Although very fast, the slow-speed handling was poor, with unsatisfactory characteristics such as a tendency to "pitch-up" at the stall. This was never fully rectified.

△ **Vought (F-8E) F8U-1 Crusader 1957**

Origin USA

Engine 16,200 lb (7,348 kg) thrust Pratt & Whitney J-57 turbojet

Top speed 1,225 mph (1,975 km/h)

Unusual in that it had a variable-incidence wing to reduce takeoff and landing speeds, the F-8 Crusader was the US Navy's principal fleet defence fighter of the late 1950s. This French F-8E is shown with the wing pivoted upward.

▷ **Lockheed F-104G Starfighter 1958**

Origin USA

Engine 16,500 lb (7,484 kg) thrust General Electric J-79 turbojet

Top speed 1,328 mph (2,125 km/h)

The aircraft was known as "the missile with a man in it". The Starfighter was the first fighter capable of sustained flight at speeds in excess of Mach 2.

△ **Republic F-105D Thunderchief 1958**

Origin USA

Engine 24,500 lb (11,113 kg) thrust Pratt & Whitney J-75 turbojet

Top speed 1,372 mph (2,208 km/h)

Often referred to as the "Thud", the Thunderchief is the largest single-seat, single-engine fighter ever made. Capable of flying supersonic at sea level, and Mach 2 at altitude, it bore the brunt of the fighting in the first half of the Vietnam War.

America Dominates

The 1960s saw a major change in the design of light aircraft. The fabric-covered taildragger gave way to all-metal machines with tricycle undercarriages. Engines changed too – the radial and inverted in-line configuration being superseded by air-cooled, horizontally opposed motors of four, six, or eight cylinders. The introduction of the solid-state VHF omnidirectional receivers (VOR) also made navigation in poor weather easier.

▷ **Cessna 150A 1961**

Origin USA

Engine 100 hp Continental O-200 air-cooled flat-4

Top speed 162 mph (259 km/h)

One of the most famous trainers of all time, the 150/152 series is still in use all over the world, 45 years after the prototype first flew.

▽ **Cessna 172E Skyhawk 1964**

Origin USA

Engine 145 hp Continental O-300 air-cooled flat-6

Top speed 125 mph (201 km/h)

Quite simply the most produced light aircraft in history, the Cessna 172 was the logical progression for any pilot who had learned to fly in either a C150 or C152. The type first flew in 1957, and remains in production today.

△ **Beech S35 Bonanza 1965**

Origin USA

Engine 285 hp Continental O-520 air-cooled flat-6

Top speed 175 mph (281 km/h)

Instantly recognizable by its V-tail, the Bonanza first flew in 1947. More than 17,000 Bonanzas have been built (not all V-tails), and the aircraft has the longest unbroken production run of any aeroplane in history.

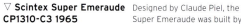

▽ **Scintex Super Emeraude CP1310-C3 1965**

Origin France

Engine 100 hp Continental O-200 air-cooled flat-4

Top speed 115 mph (185 km/h)

Designed by Claude Piel, the Super Emeraude was built by both homebuilders and factories in France, England, and South Africa. The type of engines fitted also varied, with Continental, Lycoming, and Potez motors being used.

△ **Cessna 401 1966**

Origin USA

Engine 2 x 325 hp Continental TSIO-520 turbocharged air-cooled flat-6

Top speed 224 mph (360 km/h)

Developed from the Cessna 411, the 401 was unpressurized and thus easier to maintain than pressurized machines. It proved to be popular with small airlines as a "feeder-liner".

△ **Alon A-2 Aircoupe 1966**

Origin USA

Engine 95 hp Continental C-90 air-cooled flat-4

Top speed 95 mph (152 km/h)

The Alon A-2 was descended from the classic 1941 Ercoupe, although (unlike the Ercoupe) it was fitted with a conventional three-axis control system. A four-seat version was built, but never entered production.

▷ **Piper PA-28 Cherokee 1966**

Origin USA

Engine 150 hp Lycoming O-320 air-cooled flat-4

Top speed 124 mph (200 km/h)

Piper's counterpoint to Cessna's 172, the PA-28 went into production in 1960 and is still being built today. It eventually spawned a wide range of aircraft, from two-seat trainers to turbocharged four-seat tourers.

▷ **Bolkow BO-208C Junior 1966**

Origin Sweden/Germany

Engine 100 hp Continental O-200 air-cooled flat-4

Top speed 100 mph (160 km/h)

This Swedish design was built in Germany, although a primary trainer of the Swedish version (the Malmo MFI-9) saw combat during the Biafran War, where it was fitted with rocket launchers and flown by mercenaries.

◁ **Schleicher ASK 13 1966**

Origin Germany

Engine None

Top speed 125 mph (201 km/h)

One of the most popular glider trainers ever made, the ASK-13 remains the backbone of many gliding clubs' fleets. Its rugged fabric-covered steel tube fuselage and wooden wings ensure easy repair of minor damage.

△ **Glasflugel H201B Standard Libelle 1967**

Origin Germany

Engine None

Top speed 160 mph (250 km/h)

An early composite Standard Class sailplane, the Libelle was particularly popular with pilots as it was very light and easy to rig. However, although both the handling and performance were good, it was under-braked, which made landing in small fields challenging.

△ **Lake LA-4 1967**

Origin USA

Engine 200 hp Lycoming O-360 air-cooled flat-4

Top speed 150 mph (241 km/h)

Commonly referred to as the Buccaneer, the LA-4 amphibian features a tricycle undercarriage carried within a single-step hull. The pylon-mounted "pusher" configuration was chosen to prevent spray causing damage to the prop.

◁ **CEA DR-221 Dauphin 1968**

Origin France

Engine 115 hp Lycoming O-235 air-cooled flat-4

Top speed 137 mph (220 km/h)

The Dauphin used the very efficient cranked wing, which was first seen on the Jodel series of homebuilts. Originally a taildragger, the basic design evolved into the tricycle undercarriage DR400.

▷ **Beagle B-121 Pup Series 2 1969**

Origin UK

Engine 150 hp Lycoming O-320 air-cooled flat-4

Top speed 105 mph (169 km/h)

Although the original 100 hp Pup was woefully underpowered, increasing the power available by 50 per cent transformed it into a fine light aircraft. Unfortunately, at one point Beagle were selling them at below cost, and the company went into receivership after barely 150 had been produced.

◁ **Morane-Saulnier Rallye 180T Galérien 1969**

Origin France

Engine 180 hp Lycoming O-360 air-cooled flat-4

Top speed 135 mph (217 km/h)

Produced by French airframer Morane-Saulnier, the Galérien is a dedicated glider-tug version of the MS880 Rallye. An unusual feature of the Rallye series is the leading edge slats. These give the type excellent short takeoff and landing (STOL) characteristics.

Jet and Propeller Transport

At the start of the 1960s many airlines were convinced that the future was jet-powered, and began replacing all of their propeller-driven aircraft with jets. However, these second-generation turbojets were not only very noisy but also very fuel-inefficient, and – particularly on shorter routes – it soon became apparent that turboprops were actually superior. Consequently, machines such as the Fokker F27 had much longer production runs and recorded better sales than their jet contemporaries.

△ de Havilland DH106 Comet 4C 1960

Origin UK

Engine 4 x 10,500 lb (4,763 kg) thrust Rolls-Royce Avon Mk524 turbojet

Top speed 520 mph (840 km/h)

After several fatal accidents the Comet 1 was withdrawn from service and significantly redesigned. The Comet 4 was larger and more powerful, and gave sterling service with both airlines and the RAF for many years, as well as being the basis for the Nimrod maritime patrol aircraft.

◁ Fokker F27 Mk200 Friendship 1962

Origin Netherlands

Engine 2 x 2,250 hp Rolls-Royce Dart Mk532 turboprop

Top speed 248 mph (399 km/h)

Probably the most successful European turboprop airliner, the F27 was in production between 1958 and 1987, and was also produced in the US by Fairchild. Almost 800 were built many were converted to freighters.

▷ Vickers VC10 1964

Origin UK

Engine 4 x 22,500 lb (10,206 kg) thrust Rolls-Royce Conway Mk301 turbofan

Top speed 580 mph (933 km/h)

Capable of operating from shorter runways than the DC-8 or 707, the VC10 was also faster. However, it had a much larger wing than either, and consequently generated more drag so was less fuel efficient. Only 56 were built, although the RAF also operated the type as a tanker until quite recently.

◁ Transall C-160D 1965

Origin France/Germany

Engine 2 x 6,100 hp Rolls-Royce Tyne Mk22 turboprop

Top speed 319 mph (513 km/h)

Intended to replace the French and German air force's fleets of Noratlas tactical transports, the C-160D was also operated by the South African Air Force. Air France converted four into dedicated airmail aircraft, designated C-160F.

△ BAC 1-11 475 1965

Origin UK

Engine 2 x 12,550 lb (5,692 kg) thrust Rolls-Royce Spey Mk512 turbojet

Top speed 541 mph (871 km/h)

Intended to replace the Vickers Viscount, the 1-11 was the second short-range jetliner to enter service. Despite the prototype being lost in a fatal crash it sold well, particularly in the US. It was, however, very noisy, and although it was one of the most successful British jetliners none remains in service.

△ Dornier Do28D2 Skyservant 1966

Origin Germany

Engine 2 x 380 hp Lycoming IGSO-540 air-cooled flat-6

Top speed 201 mph (323 km/h)

Based on the wing and fuselage of the single-engine Do 27, the Skyservant was a rugged, low-cost utility transport with large doors and big cabin. Mostly used by the German military, two were operated by the UN during the first Gulf War.

▽ **Boeing 727-200 1967**

Origin USA

Engine 3 x 14,500 lb (6,577 kg) thrust Pratt & Whitney JT8-D turbofan

Top speed 541 mph (871 km/h)

The 727 is notable for being the only Boeing trijet, as well as the only one to have a T-tail. A very popular machine on the US's domestic routes, it was also operated on short- and medium-range international flights.

△ **BAe Jetstream TMk2 1967**

Origin UK

Engine 2 x 940 hp Garrett TPE331 turboprop

Top speed 303 mph (488 km/h)

Although originally designed by Handley Page as a small commuter airliner, the Royal Navy operated several Jetstream 31s as the TMk2 navigation trainer.

◁ **Antonov An-26 1967**

Origin USSR

Engine 2 x 2,820 hp Progress AI-24VT turboprop

Top speed 335 mph (540 km/h)

Known by NATO as the "Curl", the An-26 was operated by both the military and civil airlines. As it was a product of the Cold War, emphasis was given to its use for tactical transport.

▷ **Fairchild C-123K Provider 1967**

Origin USA

Engine 2 x 2,500 hp Pratt & Whitney Double Wasp air-cooled 18-cylinder 2-row radial, plus 2 x 2,850 lb (1,293 kg) thrust General Electric J85 turbojet

Top speed 288 mph (463 km/h)

Allegedly based on a design for a WWII assault glider, the C-123 was a rugged machine. The type was also used to spray Agent Orange over Vietnam, during the infamous Operation Ranch Hand.

◁ **Tupolev Tu-154 1969**

Origin USSR

Engine 3 x 23,148 lb (10,500 kg) thrust Soloviev D-30KU turbofan

Top speed 590 mph (950 km/h)

Although the Tu-154 was one of the fastest civil airliners, it also had the ability to operate from unpaved runways. Aeroflot retired its fleet of Tu-154s in 2009, after 40 years of service.

▷ **Tupolev Tu-134A 1969**

Origin USSR

Engine 2 x 14,990 lb (6,799 kg) thrust Soloviev turbofan

Top speed 558 mph (898 km/h)

One of the mainstays of Aeroflot's jet fleet, the Tu-134 was similar in appearance to the Caravelle and DC-9, although early models had a fully glazed nose. In common with many other Soviet designs (and unlike most western jetliners) the Tu-134 could operate from unpaved runways.

Business, Utility, and Firefighting

Manufacturers worldwide stepped up to meet the burgeoning demand for business jets: swept wings and rear-mounted fuselage engines became almost essential for the type. Turboprops played their own role, offering short takeoff and landing (STOL) ability for more rugged terrain. Radial piston engines still had their place for glider towing and the like. Many aircraft of this decade remained in production for 40 to 50 years.

△ Pilatus PC-6/A Turbo-Porter 1961

Origin Switzerland

Engine 523 hp Turboméca Astazou IIE turboprop

Top speed 144 mph (232 km/h)

Also built in the US, the PC-6 first flew in 1959 with a piston engine. The turbine increased its power to 680 hp. Ideal for mountain use, its STOL performances include landing at 18,865 ft (5,750 m) on a glacier in Nepal.

△ LET Z-37 Cmelák 1963

Origin Czechoslovakia

Engine 315 hp Walter M 462RF supercharged air-cooled 9-cylinder radial

Top speed 130 mph (209 km/h)

This powerful agricultural aircraft can carry 1,323 lb (600 kg) of chemicals or cargo, and was widely used in the Eastern Bloc for crop spraying. Later it became popular as a glider tug because it could tow several gliders at once.

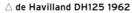

△ de Havilland DH125 1962

Origin UK

Engine 2 x 3,000 lb (1,361 kg) thrust Bristol Siddeley Viper 520 turbojet

Top speed 522 mph (840 km/h)

Renamed Hawker Siddeley HS125, now BAe 125, this highly successful midsize business jet set the standard for its type and has been in production for over 50 years, with more than 1,000 built.

△ de Havilland DHC6 Twin Otter 1965

Origin Canada

Engine 2 x 550 hp Pratt & Whitney PT6A-20 turboprop

Top speed 185 mph (298 km/h)

The DHC6 aircraft was available with floats, skis, or tricycle landing gear. A versatile short takeoff and landing aircraft it re-entered production in 2008 in developed form, being unbeatable for its ease of operation in remote territories.

△ PZL-104 Wilga 35 1963

Origin Poland

Engine 260 hp Ivchenko AI-14RA air-cooled 9-cylinder radial

Top speed 121 mph (195 km/h)

With over 1,000 built in a 43-year production run, the Wilga was progressively improved. Popular for both its STOL and climb performances, it was widely used for glider towing and parachute training.

△ Dassault Mystère 20 1963

Origin France

Engine 2 x 4,180 lb (1,894 kg) thrust General Electric CF700 turbofan

Top speed 536 mph (862 km/h)

Dassault's first business jet, also known as the Falcon 20, followed the ideal layout, with rear-mounted engines to keep the interior quiet and swept wings for speed; 508 were sold.

▷ Mitsubishi MU-2 1963

Origin Japan

Engine 2 x 575 hp Garrett TPE331-25A turboprop

Top speed 311 mph (500 km/h)

One of Japan's most successful post-war aircraft, also built in the US, the MU-2 offered high performance at low cost. Specific pilot training was required to reduce accident rates.

△ Beechcraft King Air 90 1963

Origin USA

Engine 2 x 500 hp Pratt & Whitney Canada PT6A-6 turboprop

Top speed 280 mph (450 km/h)

This market-leading eight-seat twin-turboprop entered production in 1964. The King Air 90 looked exceptionally modern for its day and has kept its lead through progressive development.

ROLLS-ROYCE

BRISTOL ENGINE DIVISION

△ Hamburger Flugzeugbau HFB320 Hansa 1964

Origin Germany

Engine 2 x 2,950 lb (1,338 kg) thrust General Electric CJ610-5 turbojet

Top speed 513 mph (825 km/h)

This was the only civilian jet with a forward-swept wing (so the wing spar passed through the cabin behind the main seating area). Most of the 47 built went to the Luftwaffe for training and VIP transport.

△ Grumman Gulfstream GII 1966

Origin USA

Engine 2 x 11,400 lb (5,171 kg) thrust Rolls-Royce Spey RB.168 Mk511-8 turbofan

Top speed 581 mph (935 km/h)

Grumman joined the business jet market with the state-of-the-art Gulfstream GII, using greater sweep angles on its wings than its competitors to achieve higher top speeds. The aircraft was chosen by NASA and other organizations for special missions.

△ Learjet 25 1966

Origin USA

Engine 2 x 2,950 lb (1,337 kg) thrust General Electric CJ610-6 turbojet

Top speed 534 mph (859 km/h)

Learjet simply stretched the successful 23/24 series to make an eight- to ten-seat business jet. The Learjet 25 has the marque's distinctive wingtip tanks for its extended range of 1,767 miles (2,844 km); it can fly at up to 45,000 ft (13,716 m).

F-ZBAY

SECURITE CIVILE

23

△ Canadair CL-215 1967

Origin Canada

Engine 2 x 2,100 hp Pratt & Whitney R-2800-83AM 18-cylinder radial

Top speed 181 mph (291 km/h)

Though also sold for passenger transport, the CL-215 was designed as a firefighting aircraft, scooping up to 1,412 gallons (6,419 litres) of water (or filled with 6 tonnes of chemicals) to drop on forest fires.

N5VP

▷ Cessna Citation I 1969

Origin USA

Engine 2 x 2,200 lb (997 kg) thrust Pratt & Whitney Canada JT15D-1B turbofan

Top speed 465 mph (749 km/h)

Cessna's ultimately successful bizjet series got off to a shaky start with the Citation I, which was slower than its rivals and required one more crew member than competing turboprops.

Military Developments

The 1960s saw startlingly fast and effective fighters capable of flying at more than twice the speed of sound. In contrast, there were aircraft in supporting roles that had soldiered on reliably since the 1940s. The ultimate 1960s fighters and bombers remain in front-line service worldwide, steadily updated and scheduled to serve until 2045 or beyond.

▽ Boeing B-52 Stratofortress 1960

Origin USA

Engine 8 x 11,400 lb (5,164 kg) thrust Pratt & Whitney J57 turbojet (later, 17,000 lb (7,701 kg) thrust turbofans)

Top speed 650 mph (1,047 km/h)

Designed to carry nuclear warheads across continents, the huge B-52 has served with the USAF since 1955 (extensively in Vietnam) and is still in service. With current upgrades it is expected to serve into the 2040s.

△ Chance Vought (F-8K) F8U-2 Crusader 1960

Origin USA

Engine 10,700-18,000 lb (4,847-8,154 kg) thrust Pratt & Whitney J57 afterburning turbojet

Top speed 1,225 mph (1,975 km/h)

First flown in 1955, this carrier-borne supersonic fighter enjoyed a long service. It was the last US fighter with guns as the primary weapon. Its wings tilted upwards for takeoff and landing.

△ Fairey Gannet AEW.3 1960

Origin UK

Engine 3,875 hp Armstrong Siddeley Double Mamba ASMD 4 turboprop

Top speed 250 mph (402 km/h)

First flown in 1949, the Gannet was adapted in 1958 to provide an airborne early warning service from carriers, serving until 1978. It had two turbines, each driving one of the contra-rotating propellers.

△ Dassault Mirage III 1960

Origin France

Engine 9,436-13,668 lb (4,275-6,192 kg) thrust SNECMA Atar 9C afterburning turbojet

Top speed 1,460 mph (2,350 km/h)

Developed in the late 1950s, the delta-wing Mirage III was a successful light interceptor that, along with this stretched IIIE fighter-bomber variant, still serves with many smaller air forces.

△ McDonnell Douglas F-4 Phantom II 1960

Origin USA

Engine 2 x 11,905-17,844 lb (5,400-8,094 kg) thrust General Electric J79-GE-17A turbojets

Top speed 1,697 mph (2,732 km/h)

This tandem-seat fighter-bomber using titanium extensively in its airframe set outright speed and altitude records. The Phantom II was a successful combat aircraft for decades; 5,195 were built.

▷ English Electric Lightning F6 1968

Origin UK

Engine 2 x 12,530-16,000 lb (5,684-7,257 kg) thrust Rolls-Royce Avon 301R turbojets

Top speed 1,500 mph (2,400 km/h)

"Teddy" Petter's stacked-engine design was the only British-made Mach 2 fighter. The original F1 version was the RAF's first true supersonic fighter. The F6 had more thrust than the F1 and carried more fuel.

△ Mikoyan-Gurevich MiG-21PF 1960

Origin USSR

Engine 8,380–14,550 lb (3,796–6,591 kg) thrust Tumansky R-13-300 afterburning turbojet

Top speed 1,385 mph (2,230 km/h)

The most-produced supersonic aircraft ever, operated by 50 countries, is an extremely effective light fighter-interceptor, also used for reconnaissance. More than 10,000 have been built. Its weaknesses are range and agility.

△ Aero L-29 Delfin 1961

Origin Czechoslovakia

Engine 1,960 lb (888 kg) thrust Motorlet M-701C 500 turbojet

Top speed 407 mph (655 km/h)

Czechoslovakia's first locally designed and built jet aircraft was a tandem-seat trainer for all Eastern Bloc countries. Simple, rugged, and easy to fly, it earned an excellent safety record.

▷ de Havilland FAW2 Sea Vixen 1966

Origin UK

Engine 2 x 11,000 lb (4,983 kg) thrust Rolls-Royce Avon Mk208 turbojet

Top speed 690 mph (1,110 km/h)

Developed during the 1950s, when it proved exceptionally fast, the Vixen was updated to this FAW2 spec in 1962. Equipped with missiles, rockets, and bombs, it was an effective seaborne fighter.

△ Convair B-58 Hustler 1960

Origin USA

Engine 4 x 15,020 lb (6,804 kg) thrust General Electric J79-GE-5A/B/C afterburning turbojet

Top speed 1,319 mph (2,123 km/h)

This ambitious delta-wing Mach 2-capable supersonic nuclear bomber boasted many of the latest advances in technology, but accurate surface-to-air missiles made it highly vulnerable.

▽ Douglas EA-1F Skyraider 1962

Origin USA

Engine 2,700 hp Wright R-3350-26WA supercharged air-cooled 18-cylinder radial

Top speed 322 mph (518 km/h)

First designed during WWII, Skyraiders continued to be recommissioned and serve with distinction into the 1960s and beyond. They were used on the front line as carrier-borne attack aircraft in Vietnam.

◁ Douglas A-4 Skyhawk 1962

Origin USA

Engine 8,200 lb (3,715 kg) thrust Wright J65 or 8,400–9,300 lb (3,805–4,213 kg) thrust Pratt & Whitney J52 turbojet

Top speed 673 mph (1,077 km/h)

Although a 1950s design, the ultra-light Skyhawk was flying well into the 1960s and beyond. It served with distinction as fighter and ground attack in Vietnam, Yom Kippur, and Falklands wars.

▽ Cessna O-2 Skymaster 1967

Origin USA

Engine 2 x 210 hp Continental IO-360-D air-cooled flat-6

Top speed 200 mph (322 km/h)

Based on the civilian Skymaster, the O-2's low-cost twin-engined configuration was ideal for military observation and forward control duties. It was used in the Vietnam War and subsequently up to 2010.

Extremes in Speed

This was a glorious decade for aircraft development, as world optimism for widespread supersonic air travel peaked and experimental aircraft were built to test all the complex issues involved in achieving that safely. Vertical-takeoff-and-landing (VTOL) fighter jets went from calculation and experimentation to flying reality and a rocket-powered prototype aircraft set an enduring world manned speed record.

△ Bell X-14 VTOL Test Bed 1960

Origin USA

Engine 2 x 2,950 lb (1,338 kg) thrust General Electric J85 turbojet

Top speed 186 mph (299 km/h)

First flown in 1957 with Armstrong Siddeley Viper turbojets, the X-14 was transferred to NASA in 1959 for further VTOL research including moon landing tests, flown by astronaut Neil Armstrong.

▷ North American X-15 1960

Origin USA

Engine 70,400 lb (31,933 kg) thrust Reaction Motors Thiokol XLR99-RM-2 liquid-fuel rocket

Top speed 4,520 mph (7,274 km/h)

First flown in 1959 this remarkable rocket-powered research aircraft, released from a B-52, reached outer space (over 62 miles /100 km above the Earth) and still holds the world manned aircraft speed record.

◁ Hawker Siddeley P.1127 1960

Origin UK

Engine 15,000 lb (6,804 kg) thrust Bristol Siddeley Pegasus 5 vectored-thrust turbofan

Top speed 710 mph (1,142 km/h)

Privately funded development by Bristol Engines and Hawker Siddeley in the late 1950s led to the first flight in 1960 of what would become the Harrier "Jump Jet": the first successful VTOL fighter.

△ Bristol 188 1962

Origin UK

Engine 2 x 14,000 lb (6,350 kg) thrust de Havilland Gyron Junior DGJ 10 afterburning turbojet

Top speed 1,345 mph (2,165 km/h)

Conceived in the 1950s for advanced Mach 3 research, the 188 used new materials such as a chromium stainless steel skin and fused-quartz windscreen. It never reached its design speed.

△ Handley Page HP115 1961

Origin UK

Engine 1,900 lb (862 kg) thrust Bristol Siddeley Viper BSV.9 turbojet

Top speed 248 mph (399 km/h)

Tested successfully over 12 years, this aircraft was part of the Concorde development project to test low speed handling of delta wings. Despite wings with a low aspect ratio (75 degrees), it could fly as slow as 69 mph (111 km/h).

△ Dassault Balzac V 1962

Origin France

Engine 4,850 lb (2,200 kg) thrust Bristol Siddeley Orpheus BOr 3 Cruise turbojet, plus 8 x 2,160 lb (980 kg) thrust Rolls-Royce RB108-1A lift turbojet

Top speed 686 mph (1,104 km/h)

Dassault converted a Mirage III fighter for vertical takeoff and landing, with eight lift engines around the main propulsion engine. Only one was built. It flew successfully, but had two fatal crashes when hovering and was not repaired after the second incident.

◁ **EWR VJ 101C 1963**

Origin Germany

Engine 6 x 2,750 lb (1,247 kg) thrust Rolls-Royce RB145 turbojet

Top speed 792 mph (1,275 km/h)

With twin rotating engines in wing-tip nacelles and two extra lift engines in the fuselage, Germany's V/STOL prototype was the first VTOL aircraft to fly supersonic, but it never entered production.

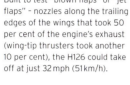

▷ **Hunting H126 1963**

Origin UK

Engine 4,000 lb (1,814 kg) thrust Bristol Siddeley Orpheus BOr.3 Mk805 turbojet

Top speed N/A

Built to test "blown flaps" or "jet flaps" – nozzles along the trailing edges of the wings that took 50 per cent of the engine's exhaust (wing-tip thrusters took another 10 per cent), the H126 could take off at just 32 mph (51 km/h).

△ **BAC 221 1964**

Origin UK

Engine 11,000 lb (4,990 kg) thrust Rolls-Royce Avon RA.28 afterburning turbojet

Top speed 1,061 mph (1,708 km/h)

BAC rebuilt the prototype Fairey Delta (a 1950s supersonic research aircraft, first to reach 1,000 mph/1,609 km/h) with ogee-ogive wing form and other details to provide research data for Concorde.

▷ **Custer CCW-5 Channel Wing 1964**

Origin USA

Engine 2 x 260 hp Continental IO-470P air-cooled flat-6

Top speed 220 mph (354 km/h)

Custer built two CCW-5s with "channel wings" around the engines, for low speed flight and very short takeoff – one in 1955 and this one in 1964. Claimed to fly at 11 mph (18 km/h), its top speed was low too.

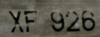

◁ **Dassault Mirage G 1967**

Origin France

Engine Pratt & Whitney/SNECMA TF 306 turbofan

Top speed 1,599 mph (2,573 km/h)

This swing-wing prototype for the French Air Force flew successfully for four years before being lost in an accident. It was never developed for production, though two related prototypes were built.

Rotary-wing Diversity

By the 1960s visions of inexpensive commuter helicopters and scheduled services between city centres had faded as efforts to reduce mechanical complexity were defeated and costs remained stubbornly high. The realization took hold that helicopters would always be specialist machines fit only for tasks no other vehicle could do. The Vietnam War led to the rapid development of helicopters as troop transports, gunships, and rescue aircraft, while offshore oil exploration boosted the civil helicopter industry.

△ **Bell UH-1B Iroquois ("Huey") 1960**

Origin	USA
Engine	960 shp Lycoming YT53-L-5 turboshaft
Top speed	135 mph (217 km/h)

This is the US Army's first turbine helicopter - a prototype flew in 1956. The UH-1B is still in service, larger, heavier, and twice as powerful as the early version; more than 16,000 were built.

△ **Bell AH-1 Cobra 1965**

Origin	USA
Engine	1,400 shp Lycoming T53-13 turboshaft
Top speed	196 mph (315 km/h)

Developed for the Vietnam War using the dynamic components of the Huey allied to a narrow, hard-to-hit fuselage, the agile, heavily armoured Cobra was the first dedicated helicopter gunship.

△ **Westland Scout AH Mk1 1960**

Origin	UK
Engine	1,050 shp Rolls-Royce Nimbus 105 turboshaft (derated to 710 hp)
Top speed	131 mph (211 km/h)

Rugged and robust, the Scout served the British Army in every conflict from Aden to the Falklands, although early Nimbus engines had to be changed after only four to six hours.

▽ **Westland Wessex HAS3 1964**

Origin	UK
Engine	1,600 shp Napier Gazelle 18 Mk165 turboshaft
Top speed	127 mph (204 km/h)

An upgraded anti-submarine version of the original Wessex Mk1, the HAS3 carried a revolutionary Type 195 sonar system that was more expensive than the helicopter itself.

△ **Wallis WA-116 Agile 1961**

Origin	UK
Engine	72 hp McCulloch 4318A
Top speed	120 mph (193 km/h)

Named after music hall star Nellie Wallace, "Little Nellie" appeared in the James Bond film *You Only Live Twice*, flown by its maker Ken Wallis, who has set 30 world autogyro records.

△ **Mil Mi-8 1961**

Origin USSR

Engine 2 x 1,700 shp Izotov TV2-117A turboshaft

Top speed 180 mph (290 km/h)

Successful as a military assault helicopter, the Mi-8 also flew civilian passenger services with Soviet airline Aeroflot. One variant had 32 seats and a lavatory.

△ **Mil Mi-2 1961**

Origin Poland

Engine 2 x 400 shp Isotov GTD-350 turboshaft

Top speed 124 mph (200 km/h)

Although of Russian design, this was Poland's most successful helicopter. More than 5,200 twin-turbine Mi-2s were built in 24 military and civilian variants.

▽ **Hughes OH-6A 1965**

Origin USA

Engine 317 shp Allison T63-A5A turboshaft

Top speed 175 mph (281 km/h)

Successful in military and civilian worlds, the "Loach" was designed as a Vietnam-era light observation helicopter and set 23 world records for speed, endurance, and rate of climb.

△ **Hughes 269C 1969**

Origin USA

Engine 190 hp Lycoming HIO-360-D1A

Top speed 109 mph (175 km/h)

The small piston-engined Hughes, first flown in 1955, reached its zenith with the 269C. Its larger rotor and more powerful engine improved performance by almost 50 per cent.

▽ **Kamov Ka-25PL 1965**

Origin USSR

Engine 2 x 900 shp Glushenkov GTD-3F turboshaft

Top speed 130 mph (209 km/h)

Designed for Soviet Navy anti-submarine work, the Ka-25s folding, coaxial contra-rotating main blades kept dimensions tight to allow for shipboard storage.

▷ **Bensen B-8M Gyroplane 1960**

Origin UK

Engine 72 hp McCulloch 4318 2-stroke

Top speed 85 mph (137 km/h)

Developed from an unpowered rotor-kite, in the 1950s the B-8M set many records for speed, distance, and altitude. Out of production since 1987, the Gyroplane is popular with homebuilders.

US Classics and French Rivals

By the 1970s the light aircraft had become a viable means of reliable transportation. At the start of the decade fuel was still relatively cheap and, when fitted with decent instruments, avionics, and de-ice systems, many of these machines were quite capable of flying reasonable distances in inclement weather.

△ **Piper PA-34-200T Seneca II 1971**

Origin USA

Engine 2 x 200 hp Continental TSIO-360 turbocharged air-cooled flat-6

Top speed 195 mph (314 km/h)

The Seneca first flew in 1971, and the type remains in production. The version shown is the Seneca II, which is fitted with turbocharged engines for improved performance at high altitude. An interesting facet of the Seneca is that the propellers rotate in opposite directions so there is no critical engine.

▽ **Piper PA-28 RT Turbo Arrow IV 1978**

Origin USA

Engine 200 hp Continental TSIO-360 turbocharged air-cooled flat-6

Top speed 161 mph (259 km/h)

A member of Piper's famous PA-28 family, the turbocharged Arrow IV was one of the fastest versions. Although later Arrows – such as the one shown – feature a T-tail, many pilots prefer the handling of earlier models.

△ **Avions Pierre Robin CEA DR400 Chevalier 1972**

Origin France

Engine 160 hp Lycoming O-320 air-cooled flat-4

Top speed 145 mph (233 km/h)

Although the light aircraft market was dominated by the US, French airframer Robin produced a range of fine, two- and four-seat, low-wing aircraft. A distinctive feature of the primarily wooden DR400 is that it shares the same cranked wing as the Jodel homebuilt.

△ **Rockwell International 114A 1972**

Origin USA

Engine 260 hp Lycoming IO-540 air-cooled flat-6

Top speed 191 mph (307 km/h)

Although the Rockwell Commander series were spacious, good-looking machines they never managed to sell in the same numbers as Beechcraft's Bonanza or Piper's Commanche. Although several attempts have been made to resurrect the marque, so far these have not been successful.

△ **Cessna 421B 1973**

Origin USA

Engine 2 x 375 hp Continental GTSIO-520 geared, turbocharged air-cooled flat-6

Top speed 276 mph (444 km/h)

Known as the Golden Eagle, the Cessna 421B was derived from the 411, with the primary difference being that it is pressurized. Over 1,900 were built during an 18-year production run.

▽ **Cessna F177RG Cardinal 1974**

Origin USA design/French built

Engine 200 hp Lycoming IO-360 air-cooled flat-4

Top speed 143 mph (230 km/h)

The 177 was intended to replace the 172, and consequently incorporated several modern features, including a laminar flow aerofoil and a cantilever wing. Although not a great seller at the time, it is now viewed as a fine aircraft.

▽ Bede BD-5J Microjet 1973

Origin USA

Engine 225 lb (102 kg) thrust Microturbo TRS-18 turbojet

Top speed 300 mph (500 km/h)

The Bede BD-5J Microjet is the world's smallest jet. During the 1970s and 1980s it was a popular airshow act, and also appeared in the James Bond film *Octopussy*. However, the type was a demanding machine to fly, and several were lost in accidents.

△ Pitts S-2A 1973

Origin USA

Engine 200 hp Lycoming AEIO-360 air-cooled flat-4

Top speed 155 mph (249 km/h)

A two-seat version of the famous Pitts S-1 aerobatic biplane, the Pitts S-2A dominated the aerobatic scene in the 1970s. Even today it is a fine aircraft with an excellent roll-rate, but it is inferior to the composite monoplane at top-level competitions.

△ Rutan VariEze 1976

Origin USA

Engine 200 hp Continental O-200 air-cooled flat-4

Top speed 165 mph (266 km/h)

The VariEze is notable for making the canard design popular, and also for the extensive use of composites in the home-built market. It was fast and stall-resistant, although it does require a longer runway than conventional two-seaters.

◁ Robin HR-200-120B 1976

Origin France

Engine 118 hp Lycoming O-235 air-cooled flat-4

Top speed 110 mph (177 km/h)

With much better handling and a superior field of view than its American counterparts, the HR-200 is a fine basic trainer although it is interesting to note that – as with so many European light aircraft – it is powered by an American engine.

△ Quickie Q2 1978

Origin USA

Engine 64 hp Revmaster 2100 (Volkswagen conversion) air-cooled flat-4

Top speed 140 mph (225 km/h)

The Quickie was originally designed as a single-seater by prolific aircraft designer Burt Rutan, and then evolved into the two-seat Q2. It had an unusual tandem-wing design and was extremely fast for an aircraft with only 64 hp.

▷ Grumman American AA-5A Cheetah 1978

Origin USA

Engine 150 hp Lycoming O-320 air-cooled flat-4

Top speed 149 mph (240 km/h)

Although never as popular as the four-seaters built by Cessna and Piper, the AA-5 series were generally faster and had better handling than either. Two interesting features were the sliding canopy (very unusual for a four-seater) and that the aircraft's skins were bonded and not riveted.

▷ Socata TB-9 Tampico 1979

Origin France

Engine 160 hp Lycoming O-360 air-cooled flat-4

Top speed 122 mph (196 km/h)

Built by French airframer Socata, the fixed-undercarriage TB-9 is the base model for the TB range. Built in the French city of Tarbes (hence TB) it is noticeably wider than many comparable four-seaters.

Business and Utility Aircraft

Both established and emerging aircraft-manufacturing nations, such as Brazil and Israel, added to the range of business and utility aircraft in the 1970s, with all types, from piston-engined through turboprop and turbofan to turbojet, playing their own roles in providing air travel and transport, from carrying equipment and people into remote areas to ferrying business people across continents in luxury.

△ Britten-Norman Trislander 1970

Origin UK

Engine 3 x 260 hp Avco Lycoming O-540-E4C5 air-cooled flat-6

Top speed 167 mph (268 km/h)

Built on the Isle of Wight (and Romania), John Britten and Desmond Norman enlarged the Islander, increasing its range, to make a versatile, manoeuvrable, and economical island-hopper.

▽ Aero Spacelines Super Guppy 1970

Origin USA

Engine 4 x 4,680 hp Allison 501-D22C turboprop

Top speed 288 mph (463 km/h)

Based on the Boeing 377-derived Stratocruiser, the Super Guppy first flew in 1965 and could carry 24.7 tonnes of outsize cargo: Airbus used four to transport parts from decentralized production.

△ Dassault Falcon 10 1970

Origin France

Engine 2 x 3,230 lb (1,465 kg) thrust Garrett TFE731-2 turbofan

Top speed 556 mph (895 km/h)

Dassault scaled down its successful Falcon 20 to make this compact business jet, in practice an all-new design (with similar high-lift wings, but more swept), of which 226 were built in 19 years.

▷ Aérospatiale SN 601 Corvette 1972

Origin France

Engine 2 x 2,500 lb (1,134 kg) thrust Pratt & Whitney Canada JT15D-4 turbofan

Top speed 472 mph (760 km/h)

Designed by the merging Sud and Nord Aviation, this was Aérospatiale's only business jet and it was not a success, with just 40 of all types made by the time the project ended in 1978.

▽ Ilyushin Il-76 1971

Origin USSR

Engine 4 x 38,367 lb (17,403 kg) thrust Aviadvigatel PS-90-76 turbofan

Top speed 560 mph (901 km/h)

Built as a heavy freighter to deliver machinery to remote parts of the Soviet Union, the Il-76 can operate from unpaved runways and is used for disaster relief worldwide, as well as for airborne refuelling.

△ Embraer EMB110 Bandeirante 1972

Origin Brazil

Engine 2 x 680 hp Pratt & Whitney Canada PT6A-27 turboprop

Top speed 286 mph (460 km/h)

The Brazilian government commissioned the 110 and created a major new manufacturer, Embraer, to build this successful and reliable general-purpose aircraft with low running costs.

▷ Rockwell Sabreliner Model 80A 1973

Origin USA

Engine 2 x 4,500 lb (2,041 kg) thrust General Electric CF7002D2 turbofan

Top speed 563 mph (906 km/h)

A midsized business jet also used for military transport and training, North American's Sabreliner first flew in 1958 and grew progressively in size and power to the ultimate Model 80 of 1973.

△ Beechcraft B200 Super King Air 1972

Origin USA

Engine 2 x 1,015 hp Pratt & Whitney Canada PT6A-41 turboprop

Top speed 339 mph (545 km/h)

With over 3,550 of all variants built in 40 years, this is the longest-production civilian turboprop aircraft in its class. Also popular for military use worldwide, Argentina flew them in the Falklands War.

▷ IAI 1124 Westwind 1976

Origin Israel

Engine 2 x 3,700 lb (1,678 kg) thrust Garrett TFE731-3-1G turbofan

Top speed 539 mph (867 km/h)

Designed in the US by Aero Commander and first flown in 1963, the design was sold to Israeli Aircraft Industries, which launched the much-improved 1124 in 1976. Total production was 442.

◁ Cessna C550 Citation II 1977

Origin USA

Engine 2 x 2,500 lb (1,134 kg) thrust Pratt & Whitney Canada JT15D-4B turbofan

Top speed 464 mph (746 km/h)

Although it used similar turbofan engines to its rivals, the C550 was relatively slow due to its straight wings. However, Cessna boosted performance and seating capacity over the Citation I, also increasing its range.

△ Edgley Optica 1979

Origin UK

Engine 150 hp Textron Lycoming IO-540-V4A5D air-cooled flat-6

Top speed 132 mph (212 km/h)

The Optica was designed as an economical alternative to helicopters for observation work, such as by police forces, with a fully glazed cabin and a flat-6 engine driving a ducted fan. Cruise speed was 80 mph (129 km/h).

△ Canadair Challenger CL600 1978

Origin Canada

Engine 2 x 7,500 lb (3,402 kg) thrust Avco Lycoming ALF-502L turbofan

Top speed 562 mph (904 km/h)

Canadair bought the concept of this aircraft from Bill Lear, securing government support to build it. It featured a wide, "walk-about" cabin and supercritical wing design. Developed versions remain in production.

△ Gates Learjet 55 1979

Origin USA

Engine 2 x 3,700 lb (1,678 kg) thrust Garrett TFE731-3A-2B turbofan

Top speed 541 mph (871 km/h)

Nicknamed "Longhorn" for its cowhorn-shaped NASA-developed winglets, the 50 series was designed around more spacious cabins than previous Learjets. Production began in 1981 and 147 were built.

▷ Gulfstream GIII 1979

Origin USA

Engine 2 x 11,400 lb (5,171 kg) thrust Rolls-Royce Spey RB.163 Mk511-8 turbofan

Top speed 576 mph (927 km/h)

Based on Grumman's Gulfstream GII, enlarged and with longer wings optimized for low aerodynamic drag, the Gulfstream III was popular with the US and other military customers as well as business users.

Diverse Airliners

The age of cooperation between European manufacturers and governments dawned, along with bounding optimism for the future of high-speed air travel. It gave life to some of the most successful airliners ever – the vast Boeing 747 "Jumbo Jet", the wide-body A300 Airbus – and some of the most spectacular: Concorde. But there were also some expensive, and embarrassing, sales flops.

△ VFW-Fokker 614 1971

Origin Germany

Engine 2 x 7,473 lb (3,385 kg) thrust Rolls-Royce/Snecma M45H Mk501 turbofan

Top speed 437 mph (703 km/h)

German-government backed and designed for small regional airlines, the 614's engines were mounted on pylons above the wings. Slow development made it expensive and only 16 were built.

▽ Fokker F28-4000 Fellowship 1976

Origin Netherlands/Germany/N. Ireland

Engine 2 x 9,900 lb (4,485 kg) thrust Rolls-Royce RB183-2 "Spey" Mk555-15P turbofan

Top speed 523 mph (843 km/h)

A short-range jet airliner designed jointly in the 1960s by Dutch, German, and Northern Irish companies and first flown in 1967, the stretched F28-4000 of 1976 proved most successful.

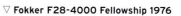

▽ Boeing 747 "Classic" 1970

Origin USA

Engine 4 x 54,750 lb (24,802 kg) thrust Pratt & Whitney JT9D-7R4G2 turbofan

Top speed 594 mph (955 km/h)

The world's first wide-body double-deck airliner, the "Jumbo Jet" had the highest passenger capacity for 37 years. It was a very successful and fast, subsonic airliner, with over 1,435 built so far.

▷ Dassault Mercure 1971

Origin France

Engine 2 x 15,500 lb (7,022 kg) thrust Pratt & Whitney JT8D-15 turbofan

Top speed 578 mph (930 km/h)

A larger, faster rival to the Boeing 737 and Douglas DC-9, this was a commercial failure, largely because of its limited range of just 1,056 miles (1,700 km). Only 11 aircraft were sold, all to Air Inter.

◁ McDonnell Douglas DC-10 1970

Origin USA

Engine 3 x 41,500 lb (18,800 kg) thrust General Electric CF6-6 turbofan

Top speed 610 mph (982 km/h)

Launched in medium-range (domestic US) form and joined in 1972 by long-range variants, this wide-body airliner had a long, successful service, carrying passengers, cargo, fuel, or water.

▷ McDonnell Douglas DC-9 1979

Origin USA

Engine 2 x 18,500 lb (8,381 kg) thrust Pratt & Whitney JT8D-200 series

Top speed 575 mph (925 km/h)

The twin-engined DC-9 was a mid-size, medium-range airliner, highly successful thanks to new features including small, efficient wings and higher-bypass engines; 1,191 were built.

◁ Lockheed L-1011 TriStar 1970

Origin USA

Engine 3 x 42,000 lb (19,026 kg) thrust Rolls-Royce RB.211-22 turbofan

Top speed 605 mph (973 km/h)

Nicknamed "Whisperjet" for its quietness, this efficient medium/long-range jet was the third wide-body airliner built, but sales were affected by Rolls-Royce's bankruptcy.

▽ BAC/Aerospatiale Concorde 1976

Origin UK/France

Engine 4 x 32,000-38,050 lb (14,496-17,259 kg) thrust Rolls-Royce/SNECMA Olympus 593 Mk610 afterburning turbojets

Top speed 1,354 mph (2,179 km/h)

A supreme success for its British/French designers, Concorde was the world's first and only supersonic airliner pioneered fly-by-wire, double-delta wing design, and much more. Its famous "droop snoop nose" was lowered for better pilot visibility on takeoff and landing.

△ Shorts 330 (SD3-30) 1974

Origin UK/N Ireland

Engine 2 x 1,198 hp Pratt & Whitney Canada PT6A-45-R turboprop

Top speed 221 mph (356 km/h)

A low-cost, easy-maintenance transport aircraft based on the "Skyvan", the 330 was unpressurized and slower than its competition, but was sturdy, quiet, and comfortable; 125 were built.

▽ Airbus A300 1972

Origin France/Germany/UK/Spain

Engine 2 x 51,000-61,000 lb (23,103-27,633 kg) thrust General Electric CF6-50C turbofan

Top speed 571 mph (919 km/h)

First product of European group Airbus Industrie, formed in 1970, the advanced A300 boasted high-tech wings, sophisticated autopilot, eight-abreast seating, and soon, an electronic flight engineer.

▷ de Havilland Canada DHC7 Dash 7 1975

Origin Canada

Engine 4 x 1,120 hp Pratt & Whitney Canada PT6A-50 turboprop

Top speed 271 mph (436 km/h)

Creating a new niche for larger, quieter short takeoff and landing aircraft equally suited to city-centre airports and remote, underdeveloped airstrips, the Dash 7 met with limited success; 113 were sold.

Military Support

Though the transport aircraft and trainers may not look like the most advanced aircraft of the 1970s, the decade nevertheless spawned a wide range of new types aimed at military support. Many of them are still in service – and even still in production – 40 years later. Some of the jet trainers were so good that they doubled as light attack aircraft and served well in combat in subsequent decades.

◁ Let L-410 Turbolet 1970
Origin Czechoslovakia
Engine 2 x 740 hp Walter M-601B turboprop
Top speed 227 mph (365 km/h)

A short-range transport aircraft used mostly for passenger transport in Eastern Bloc countries but since re-marketed worldwide. The L-410 is still in service after detailed upgrades in subsequent decades.

◁ BAC Jet Provost T4 1970
Origin UK
Engine 2,500 lb (1,134 kg) thrust Armstrong Siddeley ASVII Viper turbojet
Top speed 440 mph (708 km/h)

Percival developed the Jet Provost in the 1950s. In the 1960s BAC built the more powerful T4, and through the 1970s it was a popular, reliable RAF trainer capable of aerobatics and weapons training.

△ Aero L-39 Albatros 1971
Origin Czechoslovakia
Engine 3,792 lb (1,720 kg) thrust Ivchenko AI-25TL turbofan
Top speed 466 mph (750 km/h)

This is a high-performance two-seat jet trainer with light attack capability, designed by Jan Vlcek. The Czech-built L-39 has served with over 30 air forces, mostly from former Eastern Bloc countries.

△ Aeritalia G.222 1970
Origin Italy
Engine 2 x 3,400 hp General Electric T64-GE-P4D turboprop
Top speed 336 mph (540 km/h)

Designed by Fiat to meet a NATO specification for vertical and/or short takeoff and landing (V/STOL) transport aircraft, G.222 entered production for Italy's armed forces and was adopted by customers worldwide; 111 were built.

◁ AESL CT/4 Airtrainer 1972
Origin New Zealand
Engine 210 hp Teledyne Continental IO-360-HB9 air-cooled flat-6
Top speed 264 mph (424 km/h)

This side-by-side two-seater was designed for basic military training and is fully aerobatic. Popular in service with the New Zealand, Australian, and Thai air forces, it was replaced with an updated model.

◁ Dassault-Breguet/Dornier Alpha Jet 1973
Origin France/Germany
Engine 2 x 2,976 lb (1,350 kg) thrust SNECMA Turbomeca Larzac 04-C5 turbofan
Top speed 621 mph (1,000 km/h)

Developed jointly, primarily as a light attack jet for Germany and an advanced trainer for France, the Alpha Jet was a market competitor to British Aerospace's Hawk; 480 were sold worldwide.

▷ Dassault Falcon 10MER 1975
Origin France
Engine 2 x 3,230 lb (1,465 kg) thrust Garrett TFE731-2 turbofan
Top speed 566 mph (912 km/h)

The French Navy commissioned Dassault to supply a small number of specially adapted business jets for training, electronic countermeasures, communications, and transport services, which emerged as the Falcon 10MER.

△ **Scottish Aviation Jetstream 201 T Mk1 1973**

Origin UK

Engine 2 x 965 hp Turbomeca Astazou XVI turboprop

Top speed 282 mph (454 km/h)

Handley Page folded in 1970 over its slow development, but Scottish Aviation then built what would be the RAF's first multi-engined pilot trainer for 30 years; also used for observer training by the Navy.

△ **Boeing E-3 Sentry 1975**

Origin USA

Engine 4 x 21,500 lb (9,752 kg) thrust Pratt & Whitney TF33-PW-100 turbofan

Top speed 530 mph (855 kph)

Operated by US, UK, French, and Saudi air forces, this aircraft uses an airborne warning and control system (AWACS). A rotating dish antenna is mounted on a converted 707 and it can detect even low-flying aircraft within 245 miles (394 km).

◁ **Yakovlev Yak-52 1976**

Origin USSR/Romania

Engine 360 hp Vedeneyev M-14P supercharged air-cooled 9-cylinder radial

Top speed 177 mph (285 km/h)

This all-metal, radial-engined, tandem-seat primary trainer for Soviet forces, later (as here) built in Romania, was proficient in aerobatics and operable in rugged environments with minimal maintenance.

▽ **British Aerospace Hawk T1 1976**

Origin UK

Engine 5,643 lb (2,560 kg) thrust Rolls-Royce Adour Mk 151 turbofan

Top speed 638 mph (1,028 km/h)

Commissioned from Hawker Siddeley to replace the Folland Gnat as the RAF's fast jet trainer, the Hawk was also sold with lightweight fighter capability. Still in production, with much upgrading, over 900 have been built.

△ **Aermacchi MB-339 1976**

Origin Italy

Engine 4,000 lb (1,814 kg) thrust Rolls-Royce Viper Mk632 turbojet

Top speed 558 mph (898 km/h)

This effective tandem-seat trainer also used for light attack and in production for 40 years, served nine nations, seeing action in the Falklands War and in Ethiopia. At least 213 were built.

▷ **Transall C-160NG 1977**

Origin France/Germany

Engine 2 x 6,100 hp Rolls-Royce Tyne Rty.20 Mk22 turboprop

Top speed 368 mph (593 km/h)

This was a joint Franco-German transport aircraft built for the two countries' air forces, and sold to South Africa. The capable C-160 first flew in 1963 but was updated in 1977 as the NG for the French Air Force.

Front-line Aircraft

This decade saw tremendous advances in warplanes. Building on the great progress in technology through the 1960s and utilizing the immense power of turbojet engines, combat aircraft took to the skies in the 1970s and (with appropriate weapons, engine, and technology upgrades) are still defending major nations 50 years later.

△ Mikoyan-Gurevich MiG-25 "Foxbat" 1970

Origin USSR

Engine 2 x 24,685 lb (11,200 kg) thrust Tumansky R-15B-300 afterburning turbojet

Top speed 2,170 mph (3,600 km/h)

Built around two huge turbojets, MiG-25 set world speed and altitude records in 1967-77, alarming the West. It is the world's fastest combat aircraft, though at Mach 2.7 it damages its engines.

△ Mikoyan-Gurevich MiG-23 1970

Origin USSR

Engine 22,000-27,500 lb (9,979-12,474 kg) thrust Tumansky R-29 afterburning turbojet

Top speed 1,519 mph (2,445 km/h)

This swing-wing interceptor with sophisticated radar targeting and beyond-visual-range missiles effectively fixed the weak points of the MiG-21. It was cheap compared with rivals; 5,047 were built.

△ English Electric Lightning F53 1970

Origin UK

Engine 2 x 12,530-16,300 lb (5,684-7,394 kg) thrust Rolls-Royce Avon RA24 Mk 302C afterburning turbojet

Top speed 1,520 mph (2,446 km/h)

The 1967 F53 Export version added ground-attack capability to this supersonic fighter, with its stacked engines and phenomenal performance; this model was used by the Royal Saudi Air Force.

△ Grumman F-14 Tomcat 1974

Origin USA

Engine 2 x 20,900 lb (9,480 kg) thrust Pratt & Whitney TF-30-P-414A afterburning turbofan

Top speed 1,544 mph (2,485 km/h)

Built to protect US navy ships against enemy aircraft and missiles, the swing-wing Tomcat was in service from 1974 to 2006, with numerous upgrades to its engines, weapons, and radar.

△ Hawker Siddeley Harrier 1970

Origin UK

Engine 21,500 lb (9,752 kg) thrust Rolls-Royce Pegasus 103 turbofan

Top speed 730 mph (1,176 km/h)

Developed in the 1960s the "Jump Jet" was the first successful vertical takeoff and landing fighter. It was highly agile, operable from any small clearing or ship deck, but required a highly skilled pilot.

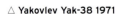

△ Yakovlev Yak-38 1971

Origin USSR

Engine 15,000 lb (6,804 kg) thrust Tumansky R-28 V-300 turbojet, plus 2 x 7,870 lb (3,568 kg) thrust Rybinsk RD-38 turbojet

Top speed 795 mph (1,280 km/h)

The Soviet Navy's only vertical takeoff and landing fighter, guided by its mother ship's computer to land automatically from several miles away, used its two extra engines for takeoff, but was underpowered.

▷ Saab 37 Viggen 1971

Origin Sweden

Engine 16,200-28,110 lb (7,348-12,750 kg) thrust Volvo RM 8A/B afterburning turbofan

Top speed 1,386 mph (2,231 km/h)

The first aircraft with both afterburners and thrust reversers was easy to maintain and operable from a short stretch of road. It had the world's first airborne computer with integrated circuits.

△ Fairchild Republic A-10 Thunderbolt II 1972

Origin USA

Engine 2 x 9,065 lb (4,112 kg) thrust General Electric TF34-GE-100 turbofan

Top speed 439 mph (706 km/h)

This close air support aircraft to back up ground troops is heavily armoured to protect the pilot, and fitted with a 30-mm rotary cannon to destroy tanks. The US military plan to keep it in service until at least 2028.

△ Lockheed S-3 Viking 1972

Origin USA

Engine 2 x 9,275 lb (4,207 kg) thrust General Electric TF34-GE-2 turbofan

Top speed 493 mph (795 km/h)

A carrier-based long-range all-weather aircraft, the Viking was used by the US Navy until 2009 for submarine surveillance, surface warfare, and aerial refuelling.

△ McDonnell Douglas F-15 Eagle 1972

Origin USA

Engine 2 x 17,450-25,000 lb (7,915-11,340 kg) thrust Pratt & Whitney F100-100/-220 afterburning turbofan

Top speed 1,650+ mph (2,660+ km/h)

The Eagle is a highly successful tactical fighter with over 100 dogfight wins and no losses, as a result of its advanced avionics with immense power and performance. Upgraded, the USAF plans to fly it until 2025.

△ SEPECAT Jaguar GR Mk1 1973

Origin UK/France

Engine 2 x 5,115-7,305 lb (2,320-3,313 kg) thrust Rolls-Royce/Turbomeca Adour Mk102 turbofan

Top speed 1,056 mph (1,699 km/h)

A joint French/British project, this successful ground-attack aircraft with nuclear strike ability proved to be very reliable in the Gulf War. It was retired by France and the UK in 2005-07, but it is still in service elsewhere.

△ General Dynamics F-16 Fighting Falcon 1974

Origin USA

Engine 17,155-28,600 lb (7,781-12,973 kg) thrust F110-GE-100 afterburning turbofan

Top speed 1,500 mph (2,414 km/h)

Built as an air superiority day fighter for the USAF, this aircraft is still in production (over 4,500 built) as a multi-role aircraft. Fast and highly manoeuvrable, it is one of the first aircraft to use fly-by-wire controls.

◁ Tupolev Tu-22M3 1978

Origin USSR

Engine 2 x 55,100 lb (24,992 kg) thrust Kuznetsov NK-25 turbofan

Top speed 1,240 mph (2,000 km/h, Mach 1.88)

One of the largest swing-wing aircraft ever, the Tu-22M long-range strategic bomber first flew in 1969. It has been progressively developed and remains in service to this day. This M3 was built in 1978.

Europeans Challenge

The end of the Vietnam War signalled lean times for the helicopter industry. Emphasis shifted to civilian machines, a sector buoyed by the expansion of the North Sea oil industry, but almost all were derivatives of military helicopters. An exception was Enstrom, which made small piston-engined personal helicopters. In Europe manufacturers in five countries competed in a tightening market.

△ **Messerschmitt-Böelkow-Blohm MBB Bo105A 1970**

Origin Germany

Engine 2 x 406 shp Rolls-Royce 250-C20B turboshaft

Top speed 168 mph (270 km/h)

The Bo105A was the first German-designed helicopter to enter production since WWII, and the first four- to five-seat twin-engined utility design with rear loading. Its titanium rigid rotor head and composite main rotor blades gave it remarkable manoeuvrability.

▷ **Mil Mi-24A Hind-A 1971**

Origin USSR

Engine 2 x 2,200 shp Isotov TV3-117 turboshaft

Top speed 168 mph (270 km/h)

The crew of this escort and anti-tank helicopter sit in a glazed cockpit in front of a cabin for soldiers or casualties. Anti-tank missiles and rockets are carried on the wing and there is a gun in the nose.

◁ **Mil Mi-14 BT 1973**

Origin USSR

Engine 2 x 1,900 shp Isotov TV-3 turboshaft

Top speed 143 mph (230 km/h)

The Mil Mi-14 was developed for the Soviet Navy as an amphibious anti-submarine and search and rescue helicopter. A mine-countermeasures version also entered service and was used in other countries including East Germany.

▽ **SA Gazelle 1973**

Origin France

Engine 590 shp Turbomeca Astazou IIIA turboshaft

Top speed 164 mph (263 km/h)

The Gazelle introduced the concept of a fenestron, or fantail – a ducted multi-blade tail rotor. Entering service in 1973, it was used for observation, liaison, and pilot training roles.

armée de TERRE

▽ **Agusta A109BA 1976**

Origin Italy

Engine 2 x 420 shp Rolls-Royce 250-C20 turboshaft

Top speed 193 mph (310 km/h)

Originally a light transport machine, the A109 first flew in 1971 and entered production in 1976. Later versions had military liaison, reconnaissance and anti-tank roles, and paramedic use.

△ **Agusta-Bell AB206C-1 JetRanger 1974**

Origin USA/Italy

Engine 420 shp Allison 250-C20 turboshaft

Top speed 137 mph (220 km/h)

Built under licence in Italy, the AB206 JetRanger found favour with both civil and military for a wide range of missions. The AB206C-1 upgrade can carry specialized equipment under hot and high-altitude conditions.

▷ Enstrom F280C Turbo Shark 1975

Origin USA

Engine 250 hp Lycoming HIO-360-1AD piston engine

Top speed 120 mph (193 km/h)

Certified in 1975 the F280C was an aerodynamically refined development of the F28. For private and corporate use, it was fitted with an upgraded turbocharged engine and featured a three-place cabin layout. Production continued until late 1981.

▷ Westland Lynx 1976

Origin UK

Engine 2 x 1,120 shp Rolls-Royce Gem 41-1 turbine

Top speed 175 mph (281 km/h)

The Lynx AH.1/7 is used for anti-tank and troop support operations and the Lynx HAS 2/4/8 for anti-submarine missions. Both were developed through the Anglo-French Lynx programme of the 1960s.

◁ Westland Sea King HC4 1979

Origin UK

Engine 2 x 1,660 shp Rolls-Royce Gnome H.1400-1 turboshaft

Top speed 129 mph (207 km/h)

The Sea King HC4 is a Sikorsky design built under licence by Westland. This was a modified version of the anti-submarine helicopter. Specialized equipment and reduced weight provided space for up to 21 combat-equipped troops with defensive weapons, armour, and sensors.

▷ Aerospatiale AS350 Squirrel HT1 1977

Origin France

Engine 641 shp Turbomeca Arriel 1D1 turboshaft

Top speed 169 mph (272 km/h)

Launched in the early 1970s as a civil five- to six-seat helicopter, the Squirrel was built using new construction methods and composite plastics. Production began in 1977 and it soon found a military market. This HT1 is a British RAF training helicopter.

◁ Aerospatiale AS365 Dauphin 2 1979

Origin France

Engine 2 x 838 hp Turbomeca 2C Arriel turboshaft

Top speed 174 mph (280 km/h)

Designed to replace the Alouette III, the Dauphin began as an eight-seat single-engined machine but in 1975 was succeeded by a twin-engined version that was further developed into the Dauphin 2.

▷ AS332 Super Puma 1978

Origin France

Engine 2 x 1,742 shp Turbomeca Makila 1A1 turboshaft

Top speed 163 mph (262 km/h)

The soaraway success of the decade, the 18-passenger Super Puma has become the helicopter of choice for offshore oil support and a versatile favourite in the military market.

◁ Sikorsky UH-60 Black Hawk 1978

Origin USA

Engine 2 x 1,543 shp GE T700 turboshaft

Top speed 224 mph (360 km/h)

First designed in the mid-1960s, the UH-60A entered production in 1976 and was deployed with the US Army, mainly in an 11-passenger trooping configuration. The latest version, the UH-60M, will be produced until 2018.

Military Aircraft

As the threat of major international conflict receded and the cost of developing all-new military aircraft increased exponentially because of the hugely complex technology now required, aircraft introductions declined in the 1980s. Many new aircraft were uprated developments of earlier models – with significant exceptions, such as the European Tornado fighter and the radical US F-117 Nighthawk "Stealth Fighter".

△ **Sea Harrier FRS.1 1980**

Origin UK

Engine 21,498 lb (9,751 kg) thrust Rolls-Royce Pegasus-Mk104 turbofan

Top speed 746 mph (1,200 km/h)

The Naval version of Hawker's brilliant Harrier entered service in 1980, providing air defence for carriers - particularly effectively in the Falklands War, where it was Britain's only fixed-wing fighter.

△ **Panavia Tornado GR1 1980**

Origin UK/Germany/Italy

Engine 2 x 15,800 lb (7,167 kg) thrust Rolls-Royce Turbo Union RB199-103 turbofan

Top speed 1,452 mph (2,337 km/h)

Joint European development from the 1970s led to this effective swing-wing multi-role fighter with extensive fly-by-wire technology, designed for low-level penetration of enemy defences.

△ **FMA IA 58 Pucará 1980**

Origin Argentina

Engine 2 x 1,022 hp Turbomeca Astazpu XVIG turboprop

Top speed 310 mph (499 km/h)

First developed in the 1960 and 70s, Argentina's ground-attack counter-insurgency aircraft was extensively used in the Falklands War because of its short take-off and landing (STOL) capability. It remains in service.

▽ **Boeing KC-135R Stratotanker 1980**

Origin USA

Engine 4 x 21,634 lb (9,813 kg) thrust CFM International CFM56 turbofan

Top speed 580 mph (933 km/h)

Developed in the 1950s alongside the 707, this aircraft is still in service for mid-air refuelling of bombers and fighter aircraft. From 1980 turbofan engines were fitted to improve economy and load capacity.

△ **Tupolev Tu-134 UBL 1981**

Origin USSR

Engine 2 x 14,990 lb (6,799 kg) thrust Soloviev D-30-II turbofan

Top speed 534 mph (860 km/h)

First flown in 1963 the Tu-134 was the first Russian airliner to be widely accepted at western airports. This UBL military version was for bomber aircrew training; 90 were built in Ukraine.

▽ **Lockheed F-117 Nighthawk 1981**

Origin USA

Engine 2 x 10,800 lb (4,989 kg) thrust General Electric F404-F1D2 turbofan

Top speed 617 mph (993 km/h)

Kept secret until 1988 the F-117 was designed to be undetectable by radar. Built solely for night attacks it would be flown on instruments alone. The Nighthawk used "smart weapons" for ground attack.

△ Dassault-Breguet Atlantique ATL2 1981

Origin France

Engine 2 x 6,100 hp Rolls-Royce Tyne RTy.20 Mk 21 turboprop

Top speed 402 mph (648 km/h)

This long-range reconnaissance and maritime patrol aircraft with 18-hour endurance was updated in the 1980s, from the original 1960s Atlantique. It gained missile fittings, and improved radar systems.

△ Mikoyan-Gurevich MiG-29 1982

Origin USSR

Engine 2 x 18,300 lb (8,300 kg) thrust Klimov RD-33 afterburning turbofan

Top speed 1,522 mph (2,450 km/h)

Developed to counter F-15s and F-16s via an effective Helmet-mounted Weapons Sight, this light air superiority fighter was designed in the 1970s. It is still in front-line service with more than 1,600 built.

▷ Dassault Mirage 2000 1982

Origin France

Engine 21,385 lb (9,700 kg) thrust SNECMA M53-P2 afterburning turbofan

Top speed 1,500 mph (2,414 km/h, Mach 2.2)

Dassault used computer control to overcome the poor turning ability of tailless delta-wing layouts in this successful, relatively inexpensive interceptor that remains in service worldwide.

▷ Rockwell B-1B Lancer 1983

Origin USA

Engine 4 x General Electric F101-GE-102 afterburning turbofan

Top speed 950 mph (1,530 km/h)

Developed but unused in the early 1970s, then reborn in the 1980s, the swing-wing Lancer is a long-range, low-level bomber with nuclear strike capability. It is likely to remain in service until 2030.

△ Sukhoi Su-27 1984

Origin USSR

Engine 2 x 16,910-27,560 lb (7,670-12,500 kg) thrust Saturn/Lyulka AL-31F afterburning turbofan

Top speed 1,550 mph (2,500 km/h)

The USSR's response to the latest US fighters, the super-manoeuvrable Su-27 had a good range, heavy armament, and sophisticated avionics. It set performance records and remains in production.

△ Lockheed C-5B Galaxy 1985

Origin USA

Engine 4 x 43,300 lb (19,641 kg) thrust General Electric TF39-GE-1C turbofan

Top speed 579 mph (932 km/h)

Among the largest military aircraft, built with special high-bypass turbofan engines to carry the US forces' largest equipment intercontinentally, C-5B joined the 1960s C-5A and will serve until 2040.

▷ McDonnell Douglas F-15E Strike Eagle 1986

Origin USA

Engine 2 x 29,000 lb (13,154 kg) thrust Pratt & Whitney F100-229 afterburning turbofan

Top speed 1,650+ mph (2,660+ km/h, Mach 2.5+)

A multi-role fighter used for deep strike missions, the F-15E is equipped with long-range fuel tanks and a sophisticated Tactical Electronic Warfare System. It can also be flown from the co-pilot seat.

Helicopter Developments

Used increasingly for troop transport, helicopters were also a key part of the air ambulance industry that expanded from small beginnings in the US to become a global phenomena. Research in the UK found that one helicopter could replace 17 ground ambulances. It was calculated that the helicopter had saved its millionth life, in peace and war, towards the end of the 1980s.

△ **Bell 206B JetRanger III 1980**

Origin USA

Engine 450 shp Rolls-Royce 250-C20J turboshaft

Top speed 139 mph (223 km/h)

A development of the 1967 original, the improved JetRanger II was introduced in 1971. By 1977 the first JetRanger IIIs with a larger tail rotor and engine emerged.

◁ **AgustaWestland AW109 1980**

Origin Italy

Engine 2 x 420 shp Rolls-Royce 250-C20 turboshaft

Top speed 193 mph (310 km/h)

First introduced in 1976 several light twin AW109 helicopters were used by Argentina for liaison, transport, and armed escort missions during the Falklands conflict in 1982. Some were later shipped to Britain for display or further operational use.

▷ **Boeing CH-47D Chinook 1982**

Origin USA

Engine 2 x 3,750 shp Honeywell T55-L-712 turboshaft

Top speed 183 mph (294 km/h)

The long-lived CH-47 Chinook heavy-lift helicopter entered service with the US Army in 1962. The CH-47D and the CH-47F remain in service today.

◁ **Hughes MD 500E/Hughes 369 1982**

Origin USA

Engine 420 shp Rolls-Royce 250-CB0B

Top speed 175 mph (281 km/h)

The Hughes MD 500E, derived from the Hughes OH-6/500, is a lightweight utility helicopter, used primarily for private and corporate customers. It has also been purchased for US law enforcement operations.

▽ **Boeing Apache AH-64 1984**

Origin USA

Engine 2 x 1,690 shp General Electric T700-GE-701 turboshaft

Top speed 235 mph (378 km/h)

This heavy attack helicopter introduced an all-weather, day-and-night capability to the battlefield. It was able to engage heavy armour or troop movements at will and had its own defensive protection.

△ **Robinson R22 Beta 1985**

Origin USA

Engine 160 hp Lycoming O-320-B2C piston engine

Top speed 110 mph (177 km/h)

The R22 was introduced in 1979 as a private two-seat light helicopter. It was succeeded by the improved R22B in 1985 with an optional engine speed governor, rotor brake, and auxiliary fuel tank.

▷ **Hughes/McDonnell Douglas MD 520N prototype 1989**

Origin USA

Engine 650 shp Rolls Royce 250-C30 turboshaft

Top speed 175 mph (281 km/h)

The MD 520N features a "notar" system. Instead of a tail rotor, this uses airflow from slots in a pressurized tailboom combining with main rotor downwash to counteract torque.

◁ **Bell-Boeing V22 prototype 1989**

Origin USA

Engine 2 x 6,150 shp Rolls Royce T406 turboshaft

Top speed 316 mph (508 km/h)

The V22 was the first tiltrotor aircraft to enter operational service. It was developed as a multi-mission assault transport for the US Marine Corps for special forces and combat search and rescue operations.

▷ **EH101 Merlin HM1 prototype 1987**

Origin UK/Italy

Engine 3 x 2,100 shp Rolls-Royce Turbomeca RTM322-01

Top speed 167 mph (268 km/h)

The Merlin HM1 aircraft with specified Blue Kestrel radar, dipping sonar, and defensive systems finally started serving the Royal Navy in 2000. A modernized HM2 configuration is due to enter service in 2013.

◁ **Messerschmitt-Böelkow-Blohm MBB Bo108 1988**

Origin Germany

Engine 2 x 450 shp Allison 250-C20R-3 turboshaft

Top speed 158 mph (254 km/h)

In the 1980s Messerschmitt-Böelkow-Blohm began development of a new mid-size helicopter to succeed their successful Bo 105. The resulting five-to six-seat Bo 108 had a choice of power plants and an advanced-technology hingeless main rotor.

△ **Sikorsky HH-60G Pave Hawk 1988**

Origin USA

Engine 2 x 1,630 shp GE T700-GE-701 turboshaft

Top speed 224 mph (360 km/h)

Derived from the US Army UH-60 Black Hawk, this machine was specifically developed for a US Air Force combat search and rescue role, recovering personnel by day or night in hostile environments.

△ **Schweizer 269C 1989**

Origin USA

Engine 190 hp Lycoming HIO-360-D1A piston engine

Top speed 109 mph (175 km/h)

Hughes Helicopters developed a two-seat light helicopter in the 1950s. Military interest in the 1960s resulted in the three-seat 269C, with an uprated engine and increased diameter rotors. The US rights were sold to Schweizer in 1983.

A Scattering of British Types

This decade saw efforts to make aviation more affordable, with a growth in kit aircraft and the arrival of hang-glider-based microlights. Composites were used for fuselage and wings construction and engine tuning was enhanced. At the other end of the market, specialized aircraft such as the Voyager appeared and luxury aircraft were pressurized.

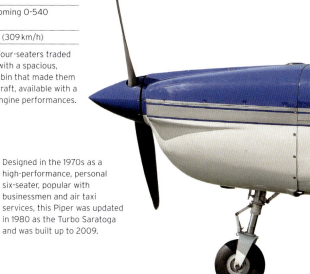

▷ Socata TB-20 Trinidad 1980

Origin France

Engine 250 hp Lycoming O-540 air-cooled flat-6

Top speed 192 mph (309 km/h)

These French-built four-seaters traded speed for comfort, with a spacious, modern, and airy cabin that made them popular touring aircraft, available with a range of different engine performances.

◁ Piper PA-32R-301T Turbo Saratoga 1980

Origin USA

Engine 300 hp Lycoming IO-540-K1G5 turbocharged flat-6

Top speed 215 mph (346 km/h)

Designed in the 1970s as a high-performance, personal six-seater, popular with businessmen and air taxi services, this Piper was updated in 1980 as the Turbo Saratoga and was built up to 2009.

◁ Piper PA-46 Malibu 1982

Origin USA

Engine 310 hp Teledyne Continental Motors TSIO-520BE turbocharged flat-6

Top speed 269 mph (433 km/h)

One of the first pressurized six-seaters, the Malibu was designed to give a range of 1,550 nautical miles (2,871 km). After costly engine failures it was replaced by the Lycoming-engined Malibu Mirage.

△ Slingsby T67A Firefly 1981

Origin UK

Engine 120 hp Lycoming O-235-L2A air-cooled flat-4

Top speed 130 mph (209 km/h)

René Fournier first flew his RF-6 in 1974 and built it in France until 1981, when he sold the design to Slingsby, whose aerobatic training aircraft has proved popular with the US, British, and other armed forces.

◁ Cessna 172Q Cutlass 1983

Origin USA

Engine 180 hp Lycoming O-360-A4N air-cooled flat-4

Top speed 140 mph (225 km/h)

A supremely practical and inexpensive four-seater, the 172 is the world's highest production aircraft, with over 43,000 built. The more powerful 172Q was slightly faster than the standard model.

▷ Rutan Voyager 1984

Origin USA

Engine 130 hp Teledyne Continental O-240/110 hp Teledyne Continental IOL-200

Top speed 122 mph (196 km/h)

Conceived by three enthusiasts and built by volunteers, this ultralight (2,251 lb/1,021 kg unladen) aircraft made the first non-stop flight around the world, covering 26,366 miles (42,432 km) in nine days.

△ Beechcraft A36 Bonanza 1987

Origin USA

Engine 300 hp Continental IO-550-BB air-cooled flat-6

Top speed 203 mph (326 km/h)

Considered by many to be the Rolls-Royce of light aircraft, the beautifully built Bonanza first flew in 1945. It continued in production in the form of the 1980s' A36, which had a fuselage stretched by 10 in (25 cm) and a conventional tailplane.

N5ZY

◁ **Grob G109B/Vigilant T1 1984**

Origin Germany

Engine 95 hp Grob 2500E1
air-cooled flat-4

Top speed 140 mph (225 km/h)

Launched originally in 1980 this
surprisingly rapid (when under power)
motorized glider with a VW car-derived
engine was adopted by the RAF for Air
Cadet training in Vigilant T1 form.

△ **ARV Super2 1985**

Origin UK

Engine 77 hp Hewland AE75 2-stroke
liquid-cooled inverted 3-cylinder in-line

Top speed 118 mph (190 km/h)

World Land Speed record breaker
Richard Noble conceived this
low-cost, two-seat trainer, designed
by Bruce Giddings. Two-stroke
engined, and built from kits,
just 35 were made.

△ **Van's RV-6 1986**

Origin USA

Engine 150–180 hp Lycoming AEIO-360-
A1A air-cooled flat-4

Top speed 210 mph (338 km/h)

Since it was first flown in 1985 almost
2,500 of this all-aluminium two-seater
have been sold in kit form. Designer
Richard VanGrunsven aimed for good
handling, high cruise speed, and STOL.

▷ **Lancair 235 1986**

Origin USA

Engine 118 hp Lycoming
O-235-L2A air-cooled flat-4

Top speed 242 mph (389 km/h)

Lance Neibauer's moulded
composite brainchild was a
high-speed, two-seat private
aircraft sold in kit form. Light
weight and aerodynamics
gave it great performance
and it sold well.

△ **Sequoia Falco F8L 1987**

Origin UK built/Italian design

Engine 160 hp Lycoming O-320-B3B
air-cooled flat-4

Top speed 202 mph (325 km/h)

Designed in Italy in 1955 by Stelio
Frati, the Falco was reborn in the
1980s in the US, selling in kit form.
One of the fastest and most expensive
home-built aircraft, it is renowned
for its fine handling.

▷ **Pegasus XL-R Microlight 1989**

Origin UK

Engine 39 hp Rotax 447/462 2-stroke
liquid-cooled 2-cylinder in-line

Top speed 67 mph (108 km/h)

This flexwing Microlight could be flown solo or
two-up and was well liked, as it was considered
easy to fly if somewhat slow in a headwind,
with a cruise speed of about 45 mph (72 km/h).

Bizjets and Turboprop Rivals

In the 1980s business aircraft really came into their own, with literally dozens of different designs on the market, powered by both jet and turboprop engines. Aircraft such as Beechcraft's King Air series filled a variety of niches within both the military and civil sectors, while air freight companies offering an "overnight service" (such as FedEx) bought the single engine Caravan by the hundreds.

△ BAe Jetstream 31 1980 (Jetstream)

Origin UK

Engine 2 x 940 hp Garrett TPE331 turboprop

Top speed 303 mph (488 km/h)

Although early model Jetstreams were powered by Turbomecca turboprops, the 31 was fitted with more powerful Garrett engines. These had the option of water-methanol injection, which greatly improved performance in "hot-and-high" operations. The aircraft sold well, particularly in the US.

△ Mitsubishi Diamond/Hawker Beechjet 400A 1980

Origin Japan/USA

Engine 2 x 2,950 lb (1,336 kg) thrust Pratt & Whitney Canada JT15D turbofan

Top speed 539 mph (866 km/h)

Originally known as the Mitsubishi Mu-300 Diamond, it was renamed the Beechjet 400 when Beech bought the rights, and then the Hawker 400 when Beech acquired Hawker. Popular with private owners, air-taxi operators, and charter outfits, the USAF also operates around 180 as trainers, called the T.1 Jayhawk.

◁ Dassault Falcon 200 1980

Origin France

Engine 2 x 5,440 lb (2,466 kg) thrust Garrett ATF-3 turbofan

Top speed 536 mph (862 km/h)

Originally called the Dassault-Breguet Mystère 20, this aircraft was known as the Fan Jet Falcon in the US, and then Falcon 20. The 200 was the final version and incorporated a number of improvements, including more powerful engines. Around 500 Falcons in the 20/200 series were built between 1965 and 1988. The USCG operates the type as the HU-25 Guardian.

▽ Cessna 421C Golden Eagle 1981

Origin USA

Engine 2 x 375 hp Continental GTSIO-520 air-cooled flat-6

Top speed 295 mph (475 km/h)

Derived from the earlier Cessna 411 (it shares the same Type Certificate), the principal difference is that the Golden Eagle is pressurized. Popular with small commuter airlines, and also with private owners, more than 1,900 were built before production ceased in 1985.

▷ Cessna 208B Grand Caravan 1984 (208 Caravan)

Origin USA

Engine 677 hp Pratt & Whitney Canada PT6A turboprop

Top speed 197 mph (317 km/h)

An extremely successful aircraft, the Caravan is operated by dozens of air forces, government agencies, and civilian operators all over the world. It can be flown on wheels, skis, or floats, and in a multitude of roles, including short-haul feederliner, freight, air ambulance, and as a parachute drop plane.

▷ Beechcraft King Air 350 1983

Origin USA

Engine 2 x 1,050 hp Pratt & Whitney
Canada PT6A turboprop

Top speed 360 mph (580 km/h)

Originally called Super King Airs (the
"Super" was dropped several years ago),
the 350 is the largest and most powerful
aircraft in the King Air range, which is the
best-selling family of business aircraft
ever produced. Noticeably different from
smaller King Airs as it is fitted with a T-tail.
The 350 remains in production as the 350i.

◁ Beechcraft Model 2000 Starship 1986

Origin USA

Engine 2 x 1,200 hp Pratt &
Whitney Canada PT6A turboprop

Top speed 385 mph (620 km/h)

Innovative in design and striking
to look at, the all-composite, canard
Starship promised much but delivered
little, being heavier and more expensive
than the King Airs it was intended to
replace. Only 53 were built and most
have been brought back and scrapped.

▷ Beechcraft 1900D 1987

Origin USA

Engine 2 x 1,279 hp Pratt & Whitney
Canada PT6A turboprop

Top speed 322 mph (518 km/h)

Based on the King Air series, the
1900D is designed to be flown by
one pilot, although two are
mandatory for airline operations.
It has 19 passenger seats and is the
best-selling aircraft in its class.

△ Gulfstream G-IV 1985

Origin USA

Engine 2 x 13,850 lb (6,274 kg) thrust
Rolls-Royce Tay 611 turbofan

Top speed 581 mph (935 km/h)

Notable for its large cabin and
long range, the G-IV is mostly
used for business, although a
large number of air forces also
operate the type, mostly for
executive/VIP transport.

▷ NDN.6 Fieldmaster 1987

Origin UK

Engine 750 hp Pratt & Whitney
Canada PT6A turboprop

Top speed 165 mph (266 km/h)

One of the first western agricultural
planes to be powered by a turboprop,
the Fieldmaster was designed by
Britten-Norman founder Desmond
Norman. Despite having several innovative
features, the design was not a success.

▽ Socata TBM 700 1988

Origin France

Engine 700 hp Pratt & Whitney
Canada PT6A turboprop

Top speed 344 mph (555 km/h)

Based on a Mooney design and intended
as a joint venture between Socata and
Mooney (the TB stands for Tarbes, where
Socata is located and the M for Mooney)
the TBM 700 has more than twice the
power of the original.

Two-crew Cockpits

By the 1980s air travel had changed once again. Although many industry observers had felt that the propeller had had its day, the 1973 oil crisis made airline executives realize that for short, and even some medium-haul, routes the turboprop still had its part to play. Jets changed too, with even the giant 747 now only needing a two-crew cockpit.

△ BAe 146/Avro RJ 1983

Origin UK

Engine 4 x 6,970 lb (3,157 kg) thrust Textron-Lycoming ALF 502R turbofan

Top speed 498 mph (801 km/h)

The most successful jetliner built in Britain, the 146 is still widely used as a short-haul airliner in Europe. Part of its popularity stems from the fact that it is very quiet, although having four engines (unusual on a jetliner this small) does increase maintenance costs.

△ Boeing 757 1983

Origin USA

Engine 2 x 43,100 lb (19,524 kg) thrust Rolls-Royce RB-211

Top speed 530 mph (853 km/h)

An interesting aspect of the narrow-body 757 is that it was developed concurrently with the wide-body 767 and shares many features, such as the cockpit layout. This allows pilots to operate both aircraft on the same Type Rating.

▷ Boeing 747-400 1989

Origin USA

Engine 4 x 59,500 lb (26,954 kg) thrust Rolls-Royce RB-211-524 turbofan

Top speed 613 mph (988 km/h)

The bestselling version of the original "jumbo jet", the 747-400 is quite different from earlier versions, even though it strongly resembles the 747 "Classic". It has a two-crew cockpit, winglets, and more fuel-efficient engines.

△ CASA C212-300 1984

Origin Spain

Engine 2 x 900 hp Garrett TPE331 turboprop

Top speed 230 mph (370 km/h)

Introduced in 1974 the C212 is still in production today, both in Europe and Indonesia. Unusually for a turbine-powered aircraft, it is non-pressurized and has a fixed undercarriage, making it relatively cheap to buy and maintain, and also very reliable.

◁ EMB120 Brasilia 1985

Origin Brazil

Engine 2 x 1,800 hp Pratt & Whitney Canada PW118 turboprop

Top speed 378 mph (608 km/h)

Having enjoyed considerable success with the Bandeirante, Brazilian airframer Embraer began work on a larger commuter turboprop. Popular with regional airlines, the Brasilia has been described as a modern DC-3.

▷ Dornier Do228-101 1985

Origin Germany

Engine 2 x 770 hp Garrett TPE331 turboprop

Top speed 269 mph (433 km/h)

This twin turboprop utility aircraft benefited from Dornier's experience of short takeoff and landing design with the Do28 Skyservant. Built in Germany and also in India by HAL, around 240 were produced and well over 100 remain in service.

△ Saab Fairchild SF340 1987

Origin Sweden/USA

Engine 2 x 1,750 hp General Electric CT7-9B turboprop

Top speed 288 mph (463 km/h)

Originally a joint venture between Fairchild and Saab, the 340 was designed as a commuter airliner but is also operated as a VIP transport, maritime patrol, and airborne early warning (AEW) aircraft by four different air forces.

△ Shorts 360 1987

Origin UK

Engine 2 x 1,424 hp Pratt & Whitney Canada PT6A turboprop

Top speed 280 mph (450 km/h)

Derived from the earlier, slightly smaller 330, with which it shares many features, the 360 is notable for being extremely quiet. While it is not the fastest turboprop, this rugged aircraft is popular as it can be operated from relatively small airfields.

◁ ATR 72-500 1988

Origin France/Italy

Engine 2 x 2,475 hp Pratt & Whitney PW127F turboprop

Top speed 318 mph (511 km/h)

Essentially a stretched ATR 42, around 400 ATR 72s are in service. An interesting feature is that it does not have an auxiliary power unit (APU). Instead, the starboard propeller is fitted with a brake, so the engine can be left running when the aircraft is on the ground to supply power to its systems.

△ McDonnell Douglas MD-88 1988

Origin USA

Engine 2 x 18,500 lb (8,381 kg) Pratt & Whitney JT8-D turbofan

Top speed 504 mph (811 km/h)

Essentially a "Second-Generation" DC-9, the MD-88 was the last of the MD-80 line to enter production. The principal difference over earlier models was its electronic flight instrument system. The first one was delivered to Delta Airlines in 1987 and production ended 10 years later.

△ Antonov An-225 1988

Origin USSR

Engine 6 x 51,600 lb (23,375 kg) thrust ZMKB Progress D-18 turbofan

Top speed 528 mph (850 km/h)

Designed to carry the Buran space shuttle, the An-225 is a giant six-engine strategic transporter that can carry up to 551,156 lb (250,000 kg) internally. Only one was ever finished – it flies with Antonov Airlines and specializes in carrying oversize freight.

▷ Airbus A320 1988

Origin Multinational

Engine 2 x 27,000 lb (12,231 kg) thrust CFM-56 turbofan

Top speed 537 mph (864 km/h)

Notable for being the first airliner to feature digital fly-by-wire flight controls and side-sticks, the A320 has recorded phenomenal sales since its introduction in 1988.

◁ Fairchild SA227-AC Metro III 1988

Origin USA

Engine 2 x 1,000 hp Garrett TPE331 turboprop with water injection

Top speed 355 mph (572 km/h)

The Metro evolved from the Swearingen Merlin turboprop business aircraft. Originally designed with 19 passenger seats (the maximum allowed by the FAA for operations without a flight attendant) it proved popular with regional airlines and many air forces. The USAF alone ordered more than 50.

Business and Utility

Despite the late 1980s recession, the business aircraft category thrived through the 1990s. Most aircraft represented progressive development from 1970s designs and included every type from relatively inexpensive single-engined aircraft to triple-engined craft. Some machines boasted long ranges, others high cruise altitude; some featured internal luxury, others fuel economy. Similarly targeted aircraft served farmers and high-altitude telecommunications.

▷ Piaggio P180 Avanti 1990

Origin Italy

Engine 2 x 850 hp Pratt & Whitney Canada PT-6A-66 turboprop

Top speed 458 mph (737 km/h)

This unconventional design, with small front wings and conventional tailplane, allowed the main wings and "pusher" turboprops to be mounted far back, giving the Avanti a very quiet cabin and good fuel economy.

△ Air Tractor AT-502 1990

Origin USA

Engine 680 hp Pratt & Whitney Canada PT-6A turboprop

Top speed 140 mph (225 km/h)

The 416-gallon (1,893-litres) AT-502 is the most popular of Leland Snow's big, powerful crop sprayer designs – others carried up to 666 gallons (3,028 litres). First flown in 1986, it is still in production with over 600 built.

△ Bombardier Learjet 60 1991

Origin USA

Engine 2 x 4,600 lb (2,087 kg) thrust Pratt & Whitney Canada PW305A turbofan

Top speed 536 mph (863 km/h)

Bill Lear's very successful business jet family began in the 1960s and was bought by Bombardier in 1990. The 60 added improved aerodynamics and new engines to the 55; 314 were built.

▷ Cessna 525 CitationJet I 1991

Origin USA

Engine 2 x 1,900 lb (862 kg) thrust Williams FJ44 turbofan

Top speed 447 mph (719 km/h)

This light corporate jet was designed to carry six, or up to nine, passengers in luxurious seating. It was intended for single-pilot operation, and had sophisticated avionics; developed versions remain in production.

△ Cessna Citation VII 1991

Origin USA

Engine 2 x Garrett TFE731-4R turbofan

Top speed 552 mph (888 km/h)

Reacting to past snubs of "Slowtations", the VII's powerful engines gave it a maximum cruise speed well above rival Learjets. It was based on the Citation III of the late 1970s; 119 were sold.

△ Cessna Citation X 1993

Origin USA

Engine 2 x 6,442 lb (2,922 kg) thrust Rolls-Royce AE 3007C turbofan

Top speed 700 mph (1,127 km/h)

Though based on the Citation VII, the X had new wing and cabin design, and two powerful Rolls-Royce engines that made it the fastest business jet in the world; over 330 have been sold.

△ Cessna 560 Citation Excel 1996

Origin USA

Engine 2 x 3,952 lb (1,793 kg) thrust Pratt & Whitney Canada PW545 turbofan

Top speed 506 mph (814 km/h)

A more spacious business jet with room to stand upright and space for up to ten passengers, though typically laid out for six to eight, the Excel sold extremely well and had a very good safety record.

▷ Dassault Falcon 900B 1991

Origin France

Engine 3 x 4,750 lb (2,155 kg) thrust Honeywell TFE731-5BR-1C turbofan

Top speed 662 mph (1,065 km/h)

The 900B added more powerful engines and increased range to the 1984-launched corporate jet. It was the only one of its kind (with its sister Falcon X) with three engines. Developed versions are still made.

▽ Pilatus PC-12 1994

Origin Switzerland

Engine 1,200 hp Pratt & Whitney Canada PT-6A-67B turboprop

Top speed 313 mph (504 km/h)

This popular business transport aircraft has been steadily developed and continues in production with over 1,000 made. With a single engine, it was relatively inexpensive.

◁ Gulfstream GV 1995

Origin USA

Engine 2 x 14,750 lb (6,690 kg) thrust Rolls-Royce BR710A1-10 turbofan

Top speed 674 mph (1,084 km/h)

One of the first ultra-long range business jets, able to fly up to 7,456 miles (12,000 km), the GV could cruise at 51,000 ft (16,000 m). It was sold to the US Air Force, Navy, and Coastguard as well as private buyers.

▷ Sino Swearingen SJ30-2 1996

Origin USA

Engine 2 x 2,300 lb (1,243 kg) thrust Williams International FJ44-2A turbofan

Top speed 528 mph (850 km/h)

This little-known business jet has a cramped fuselage but exceptional fuel economy and range, and a high cruise speed. This is aided by class-leading pressurization, which allows it to fly at high altitude.

◁ Scaled Composites Proteus 1998

Origin USA

Engine 2 x 2,293 lb (1,040 kg) thrust Williams FJ44-2 turbofan

Top speed 313 mph (504 km/h)

Innovator Burt Rutan designed this all-composite airframe, high-altitude, high-endurance twin-wing research craft, which could be flown by pilots or remotely. It could orbit at 65,000 ft (19,812 m) for more than 18 hours.

Tradition and Innovation

With mounting use of composites and the increasing dominance of the Rotax 912 engine (which had been launched in 1989), the 1990s saw the emergence of small kitplanes, which totally outperformed the traditional general aviation two-seater. The introduction of the Global Positioning System (GPS) brought a radical change to aircraft communication and navigation capabilities.

△ Commander 114B 1992

Origin USA

Engine 260 hp Lycoming IO-540 air-cooled flat-6

Top speed 165 mph (266 km/h)

Descended from the Rockwell 112, the Commander 114B is a sleek and powerful four-seat retractable tourer. The original Commander was allegedly designed by engineers who also worked on the Space Shuttle. Although the type never sold as well as its main competitor, the Beechcraft Bonanza, it has a loyal following.

△ Robin DR-400-180 Regent 1992

Origin France

Engine 180 hp Lycoming O-360 air-cooled flat-4

Top speed 125 mph (201 km/h)

The installation of a more powerful engine and other improvements ensured that the DR-400 continued to sell well, several decades after it first flew. Probably the most obvious difference from earlier models is that the Regent has an extra row of windows.

△ Sky Arrow 650 TC 1992

Origin Italy

Engine 100 hp Rotax 912S liquid-cooled flat-4

Top speed 116 mph (186 km/h)

This unusual Italian aircraft is a strut-braced high-wing design with tandem seats, and is powered by a Rotax 912 arranged in the "pusher" configuration. It offers an exceptional field-of-view from its fighter-shaped canopy.

△ Maule MXT-7-160 Star Rocket 1993

Origin USA

Engine 10 hp Lycoming O-320 air-cooled flat-4

Top speed 120 mph (193 km/h)

The Star Rocket is unusual for a bushplane in that it has a tricycle undercarriage. It possesses the same fine short takeoff and landing (STOL) characteristics as all Maule aeroplanes.

△ Europa XS 1994

Origin UK

Engine 100 hp Rotax 912S liquid-cooled flat-4

Top speed 145 mph (233 km/h)

Capable of very impressive performance on engines as small as 80 hp, the Europa XS evolved from the Europa Classic. Available with a monowheel or tricycle undercarriage, it is probably the most successful British kitplane.

◁ Maule M-7-235C Orion 1997

Origin USA

Engine 235 hp Lycoming IO-540 air-cooled flat-6

Top speed 164 mph (264 km/h)

Famed for their sparkling short takeoff and landing characteristics, the Maule series make excellent bushplanes. Unlike earlier Maules, which used an Oleo-type undercarriage, the Orion uses a sprung aluminium arrangement, unless it is mounted on floats, such as the example shown.

▷ **Murphy Rebel 1994**

Origin Canada

Engine 115 hp Lycoming O-235 air-cooled flat-4

Top speed 110 mph (177 km/h)

Designed to be a "personal bushplane", the Rebel is a Canadian-designed kitplane. This strut-braced high-wing monoplane taildragger can be powered by a variety of engines and usually has two seats, although a third is an option.

◁ **Piper PA-28R-201 Cherokee Arrow III 1997**

Origin USA

Engine 200 hp Lycoming IO-360 air-cooled flat-4

Top speed 140 mph (225 km/h)

One of Piper's hugely successful Cherokee range, the Arrow III was certified in 1976. Notable differences to the original Arrow I included a longer fuselage, semi-tapered wings, larger fuel tanks, and a more powerful engine.

△ **Cessna 172S 1998**

Origin USA

Engine 180 hp Lycoming IO-360 air-cooled flat-4

Top speed 120 mph (193 km/h)

Production of the Model 172 stopped in the mid-1980s because of the huge cost of product liability insurance, but Cessna began making them again in 1998. The 172S has new features, including a fuel-injected engine and electronic instrument displays.

△ **Zenair CH-601 HDS Zodiac 1999**

Origin Canada

Engine 100 hp Rotax 912S liquid-cooled flat-4

Top speed 161 mph (259 km/h)

Originally designed as a kitplane by Chris Heintz, the CH-601 is available in a number of different versions and powered by several different types of engine. The aircraft shown is a 601 HDS (heavy-duty speed wing) and features a shorter wingspan than earlier 601s.

◁ **Mooney M20R Ovation 1999**

Origin USA

Engine 280 hp Continental IO-550 air-cooled flat-6

Top speed 172 mph (277 km/h)

The M20 prototype first flew in 1955, with the type being the last (and most successful) of Al Mooney's designs. Originally made of wood and fabric, most M20s are of all-metal construction. The Ovation was *Flying* magazine's 1994 single-engine aircraft of the year.

△ **Glasair Super IIS RG 1999**

Origin USA

Engine 180 hp Lycoming IO-360 air-cooled flat-4

Top speed 182 mph (292 km/h)

This sleek composite kitplane was one of the first pre-moulded homebuilts to come to market. It features a retractable tricycle undercarriage and is both a capable aerobatic performer and practical touring machine.

Sports and Sailplanes

Some impressively aerobatic designs dated from the 1940s, but these sports planes were high-risk products for manufacturers in the litigious 1990s. As a result many resorted to selling aircraft as kits or even just sets of plans, so that home builders would hopefully blame themselves if the planes broke up in flight. Gliders became sleeker and faster in this decade, while microlights became more practical for covering longer distances, instead of just local pottering.

△ Stolp SA-300 Starduster Too 1990

Origin USA

Engine 180 hp Lycoming O-360 air-cooled flat-4

Top speed 180 mph (290 km/h)

Lou Stolp's 1960s-designed homebuilt sports biplane, normally with two open cockpits, had wood/metal structure, fabric/glassfibre-covering, and was capable of mild aerobatics.

△ Glaser-Dirks DG-400 1990

Origin Germany

Engine Rotax 505

Top speed 168 mph (270 km/h)

Wilhelm Dirks developed this self-launching variant of his DG-202 glider in 1981; this example was built in 1990. The Rotax engine and propeller rose electrically from behind the pilot, and the wing tips were detachable.

△ Berkut 360 1990

Origin USA

Engine 205 hp Lycoming IO-360 air-cooled flat-4

Top speed 248 mph (399 km/h)

This tandem-seat canard built mostly of carbon fibre and glass fibre bankrupted designer Dave Ronneburg and passed through several makers; in all 20 were built and around 75 were sold as kits.

△ Extra 300 1990

Origin Germany

Engine 300 hp Lycoming AEIO-540 air-cooled flat-6

Top speed 197 mph (317 km/h)

Designed by aerobatic pilot Walter Extra, with a roll-rate of around 400 degrees per second and g-limits of +/-10, the 300 is one of the most potent aerobatic aircraft in the world. It is still a favourite of airshow pilots and aerobatic champions.

◁ Sukhoi Su-29 1991

Origin USSR

Engine 360 hp Vedeneyev M-14P air-cooled 9-cylinder radial

Top speed 183 mph (294 km/h)

This excellent aerobatic performer was based on the single-seat Su-26, and is virtually able to hang on its propellers as well as pull g-limits of +12 to -10. Extensive use of composites made it light and strong.

◁ Pitts Special S-1 1991

Origin USA

Engine 180 hp Lycoming AEIO-360 air-cooled flat-4

Top speed 175 mph (282 km/h)

Based on a 1940s design by Curtis Pitts, the S-1 is still a capable aerobatic machine, now built by Aviat Aircraft of Wyoming. Probably the best-known aerobatic design, it has won many competitions worldwide.

▽ Rolladen Schneider LS8-18 1994

Origin Germany

Engine None

Top speed 175 mph (280 km/h)

Wolf Lemke regained the lead in glider performance with the LS8, deleting the flaps to achieve a lighter, smoother wing that gave the LS8 championship success, while remaining easy and gentle to fly.

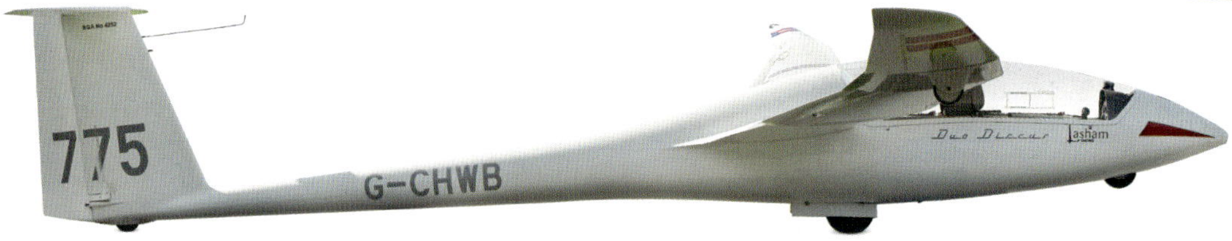

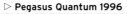

△ Schempp-Hirth Duo Discus 1993

Origin Germany

Engine None

Top speed 164 mph (263 km/h)

A high-performance two-seater capable of competition success as well as long-distance gliding, the Duo Discus wings swept slightly forward to put the rear pilot on the centre of gravity; over 500 have been built.

△ Pegasus XL-Q 1990

Origin UK

Engine 51 hp Rotax 462 liquid-cooled 2-cylinder in-line 2-stroke

Top speed 80 mph (129 km/h)

With a more powerful liquid-cooled two-stroke engine and new wing, the Pegasus XL became a performance microlight with a high rate of climb and was also suitable for pilot training.

▷ Pegasus Quantum 1996

Origin UK

Engine 50 hp Rotax 503-2V air-cooled 2-cylinder in-line two-stroke

Top speed 78 mph (125 km/h)

The Quantum was aimed upmarket for long-distance touring, with tandem seating. In 1998 it was the first microlight to fly around the world and it won the World Microlight Championships.

△ Dyn'Aéro MCR01 1996

Origin French

Engine 80 hp Rotax 912 ULS air/water-cooled flat-4

Top speed 186 mph (300 km/h)

Based on a plan-build aircraft designed by Michel Colomban, this two- to four-seat all-composite plane has proved popular for its high speed, but has also been prone to failures.

Europe Challenges the US

Although for many years the airliner market in the West had been dominated by American manufacturers such as Boeing and McDonnell Douglas, during the 1990s sales of the range of aircraft from Europe's newer Airbus Industrie surged. A significant factor in Airbus's success was the commonality of the various aircraft's cockpits, with the A318, 319, 320, 321, 330, and 340 in particular having very similar layouts.

△ McDonnell Douglas MD-11 1990

Origin USA

Engine 3 x 60,000 lb (27,180 kg) thrust Pratt & Whitney PW4460 turbofan

Top speed 587 mph (945 km/h)

Developed from the DC-10, the MD-11 is in many ways a very different aircraft. Fitted with an electronic digital instrument displays and operated by two pilots, the fuselage is longer than the DC-10's, while the tailplane is smaller.

△ BAe 1000 1990

Origin UK/USA

Engine 2 x 5,200 lb (2,359 kg) thrust Pratt & Whitney PW305 turbofan

Top speed 522 mph (840 km/h)

With a lineage stretching back to the 1962 DH125 Jet Dragon, the BAe 1000 is the intercontinental version of this popular business jet.

△ BAe Jetstream 41 1991

Origin UK

Engine 2 x 1,650 hp Allied Signal TPE331-14 turboprop

Top speed 340 mph (547 km/h)

A "stretched" version of the earlier Jetstream 31, the 41 can carry up to 30 passengers. It is powered by significantly more powerful Allied Signal engines and features an electronic flight instrument system. Around 100 have been built; Eastern Airlines operates the largest fleet of 23 aircraft.

△ Fokker F100 1990

Origin Netherlands

Engine 2 x 13,850 lb (6,274 kg) thrust Rolls-Royce Tay turbofan

Top speed 525 mph (845 km/h)

Having achieved considerable success with its F28, Dutch airframer Fokker took the basic design, stretched it and added upgraded avionics, more powerful engines, and a redesigned wing. The F100 sold well initially, but only 283 were built.

△ Canadair Regional Jet CRJ200 1992

Origin Canada

Engine 2 x 9,220 lb (4,177 kg) thrust General Electric 34 turbofan

Top speed 505 mph (812 km/h)

Based on the Canadair Challenger business jet, the CRJ200 is a regional jetliner manufactured by Canadian airframer Bombardier. The type first flew in 1991, and over 1,000 were built before production ceased.

△ Airbus A340 1993

Origin Multinational

Engine 4 x 34,000 lb (15,402 kg) thrust CFM-56 turbofan

Top speed 563 mph (906 km/h)

The largest aircraft at the time in the Airbus family, the A340 was produced with four different fuselage lengths and powered by a variety of different engines. The aircraft has a phenomenal range, and is used on long-haul flights.

◁ Ilyushin Il-96-300 1992

Origin Russia

Engine 4 x 35,242 lb (15,965 kg) thrust Aviadvigatel PS-90A turbofan

Top speed 559 mph (900 km/h)

A shortened version of the Il-86 (Russia's first wide-body airliner) the Il-96 has many advanced features, including a super-critical wing, winglets, fly-by-wire controls, and electronic flight instrument systems.

△ **Saab 2000 Swordfish MPA 1994**

Origin Sweden

Engine 2 x 4,152 hp Allison AE2100A turboprop

Top speed 424 mph (682 km/h)

Based on the Saab 2000, the Swordfish is a dedicated maritime patrol aircraft. It carries advanced sensor systems and has an endurance of over nine hours.

△ **Boeing 777 1995**

Origin USA

Engine 2 x 93,400 lb (42,310 kg) thrust Rolls-Royce Trent turbofan

Top speed 590 mph (950 km/h)

The first fly-by-wire aircraft built by Boeing, one version of the 777 (the -200LR) has the longest range of any airliner. In production since 1995, more than 1,000 are currently in service.

▽ **Airbus A320-214 1995**

Origin Multinational

Engine 2 x 27,000 lb (12,231 kg) thrust CFM-56 turbofan

Top speed 537 mph (864 km/h)

The A320-200 series is similar to the earlier -100 models, with the most obvious difference being the addition of winglets. It also carries more fuel, and consequently has a greater range.

▽ **Airbus A319 1995**

Origin Multinational

Engine 2 x 27,000 lb (12,231 kg) thrust CFM-56 turbofan

Top speed 537 mph (864 km/h)

Popular with the burgeoning low-cost sector of the airline market, the A319 is a shortened version of the A320. It shares the same design features as other Airbus aircraft, such as common cockpit layout, fly-by-wire, and side-stick controllers.

Upgraded Helicopters

The hiatus between the end of the Cold War and the start of the War on Terror made this a fallow decade for military helicopter sales, especially for Soviet and Eastern Bloc manufacturers. Many 1990s helicopters were upgrades of existing machines for specialist civilian work, such as the oil industry.

△ Robinson R44 1991

Origin USA

Engine Lycoming IO-540-AE1A5 piston

Top speed 149 mph (240 km/h)

With purchase, maintenance, and running costs that were astoundingly low by helicopter standards, the four-place R44 became and remains the world's bestselling helicopter.

◁ AS 555 Fennec 1992

Origin France

Engine 2 x 456 shp Turbomeca TM319 Arrius 1M turboshaft

Top speed 178 mph (287 km/h)

This aircraft was a twin-engined military version of the venerable and globally popular Ecuriel (Squirrel) line. The 1990s upgrades included navigation, radar, autopilot, and weapons systems.

▷ MD900 Explorer 1992

Origin USA

Engine 2 x 550 shp Pratt & Whitney PW206E turboshaft

Top speed 161 mph (259 km/h)

The Explorer's twin-engined transport uses a patented "notar" system that utilized main rotor downwash to create anti-torque force on the tail boom, reducing noise and increasing safety.

△ DragonFly 333 1993

Origin Italy

Engine 110 hp Hirth F30A26AK two-stroke piston

Top speed 83 mph (134 km/h)

This Italian ultralight model, weighing only 622 lb (282 kg) empty, was designed by two Italian brothers – an archaeologist and a film-maker – for their personal use, then put into limited production.

◁ Bell 230 1991

Origin USA

Engine 2 x 700 shp Allison 250-C30G2 turboshaft

Top speed 172 mph (277 km/h)

This was a more powerful variant of the Bell 222, available with skids or wheels. It was superseded by the Bell 430 after four years, with only 38 Bell 230s built.

△ Bell 407 1994

Origin USA

Engine 813 shp Allison 250-C47B turboshaft

Top speed 161 mph (259 km/h)

Designed to supersede the ubiquitous but long-in-the-tooth Bell 206 JetRanger, the 407 had a four-bladed main rotor, better performance, and more internal space.

△ Eurocopter EC135 1994

Origin France

Engine 2 x 434 shp Turbomeca
Arrius B2B turboshaft

Top speed 178 mph (287 km/h)

This successful twin-engined police and
EMS helicopter designed by MBB but
improved by Eurocopter with fenestron
and French turbines, is the bestselling
light twin of modern times.

▷ Eurocopter HH-65 Dolphin 1994

Origin French design/US built

Engine 2 x 853 shp Turbomeca
Arriel 2C2-CG turboshaft

Top speed 190 mph (306 km/h)

This American-built version of Eurocopter
AS365 Dauphin was used by the US Coast
Guard for air-sea rescue. The original
American engines were replaced with
French turbines in 2004.

▷ Eurocopter EC120B Colibri 1998

Origin France

Engine 504 shp Turbomeca Arrius
2F turboshaft

Top speed 172 mph (277 km/h)

Eurocopter's entry-level helicopter,
the Colibri, is renowned for low
noise levels and passenger comfort.
Used as a basic military trainer in
France, it is also manufactured
in Australia and China.

△ Messerschmitt-Boelkow-Blohm MBB Bo105LS A3 Superlifter 1995

Origin Germany

Engine 2 x 650 shp Rolls-Royce 250-C30
turboshaft

Top speed 150 mph (241 km/h)

Forerunner of the EC135,
the 105 was the smallest
and least expensive
twin-turbine helicopter.
The 1995 variant included
more powerful engines
and improved rotor blades.

△ Kamov Ka-52 (Alligator) 1996

Origin Russia

Engine 2 x 2,200 shp Klimov TV3-117VK
turboshaft

Top speed 196 mph (315 km/h)

Designed to replace the Mi-24
gunship, the Ka-52, had distinctive
coaxial contra-rotating rotors.
It was unusual in having an ejector
seat – explosive bolts remove
the rotors.

▽ Westland AH-64D Apache Longbow 1998

Origin UK (under US licence)

Engine 2 x 2,100 shp
Rolls-Royce/Turbomeca
RTM322 01/12 turboshaft

Top speed 182 mph (293 km/h)

As flown by Prince Harry in
Afghanistan, the AH-64
was built in Britain from
Boeing-provided kits. Some
British versions had folding
blades for shipboard operation.

Military Technology

By 1990 there was no benefit in making faster military aircraft; instead efforts concentrated on updating existing models with the latest technology and materials, to increase their efficiency and range, improve their navigation systems, and upgrade their weapons potential. As fuel consumption became a political issue, more efficient transport aircraft were sought. Only the US had the resources to develop a radical, all-new aircraft: the Stealth Bomber.

△ Hawker Siddeley Buccaneer S2 1991

Origin UK

Engine 2 x 11,100 lb (5,035 kg) thrust Rolls-Royce Spey 101 turbofan

Top speed 690 mph (1,110 km/h)

Designed by Blackburn in the 1950s, the nuclear strike-capable Buccaneer was the first Royal Navy aircraft to cross the Atlantic without refuelling. In 1991 it provided guided bombing in the Gulf War.

△ Lockheed MC-130P Combat Shadow 1990

Origin USA

Engine 4 x 4,910 hp Allison T56-A-15 turboprop

Top speed 366 mph (589 km/h)

Aircraft based on the Hercules have supported the US Special Operations forces since the 1960s. The MC-130P provides operation command and support, as well as helicopter inflight refuelling.

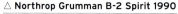

△ Saab JAS 39 Gripen 1990

Origin Sweden

Engine 12,100-18,100 lb (5,488-8,210 kg) thrust Volvo Aero RM12 afterburning turbofan

Top speed 1,372 mph (2,208 km/h, Mach 2)

This lightweight Mach 2 multi-role fighter came with "relaxed stability" delta wings and canards, plus fly-by-wire technology and STOL capability. By 2012, 240 had been delivered to air forces worldwide.

△ Northrop Grumman B-2 Spirit 1990

Origin USA

Engine 4 x 17,300 lb (7,847 kg) thrust General Electric F118-GE110 turbofan

Top speed 630 mph (1,010 km/h)

Just 21 flying-wing "Stealth Bombers" were built, costing over $2 billion each, able to slip undetected to the heart of enemy territory, and drop 80+ tonnes of bombs or 17+ tonnes of nuclear warheads.

△ British Aerospace Harrier II GR7 1990

Origin UK

Engine 21,750 lb (9,866 kg) thrust Rolls-Royce Pegasus 105 vectored-thrust turbofan

Top speed 662 mph (1,065 km/h)

Unique in its V/STOL (Vertical or Short Takeoff and Landing) capability, the Harrier was completely revised in the 1980s with composite fuselage, more power, and improved avionics.

▽ Dassault Mirage 2000D 1991

Origin France

Engine 14,300-21,400 lb (6,486-9,707 kg) thrust SNECMA M53-P2 afterburning turbofan

Top speed 1,453 mph (2,338 km/h)

France's nuclear strike Mirage 2000N was developed into the 2000D for long-range strikes with conventional weapons, being equipped with improved controls, navigation, and defences.

▽ **Lockheed Hercules C-130K Mk3 1992**

Origin USA

Engine 4 x 4,590 hp Allison T56-A-15 turboprop

Top speed 366 mph (589 km/h)

First flown in 1954 the rugged and versatile Hercules has fulfilled vital roles in every major conflict since and is still being updated for the future. This 1990s K-spec is in RAF Gulf War camouflage.

◁ **McDonnell Douglas/Boeing C-17 Globemaster III 1991**

Origin USA

Engine 4 x 40,400 lb (18,325 kg) thrust Pratt & Whitney F117-PW-100 turbofan

Top speed 515 mph (830 km/h)

Designed to replace the Starlifters, this large military transport aircraft began development in the 1980s. It proved to be capable and adaptable, carrying military equipment and troops to and from the battlefield.

△ **Britten-Norman BN-2T-4S Defender 4000 1994**

Origin UK

Engine 2 x 400 hp Rolls-Royce 250-17F/1 turboprop

Top speed 225 mph (362 km/h)

This multi-role military version of the Islander was substantially upgraded in the 1990s for aerial surveillance, with the Trislander's wing, stretched fuselage, and a new nose-mounted radar.

△ **Panavia Tornado GR4 1997**

Origin UK

Engine 2 x 9,850–17,270 lb (4,468–7,833 kg) thrust Turbo Union RB199-34R Mk103 afterburning turbofan

Top speed 1,511 mph (2,431 km/h)

The GR4 was a mid-life update of the Tornado, vastly improving the navigation systems, avionics, and weapons capability following lessons learned in Gulf War use, particularly at medium altitude.

△ **EADS Casa C-295M 1997**

Origin Spain

Engine 2 x 2,645 hp Pratt & Whitney Canada PW127G Hamilton Standard turboprop

Top speed 358 mph (576 km/h)

This compact and relatively low-cost military transport, also capable of maritime patrol or airborne early warning, is in service with the armed forces of 13 countries from Finland to Colombia.

◁ **Pilatus PC-9M 1997**

Origin Switzerland

Engine 1,149 hp Pratt & Whitney Canada PT6A-62 turboprop

Top speed 368 mph (593 km/h)

This Swiss-built military trainer was first flown in 1984 and sold to numerous air forces around the world. Updated in PC-9M form, 60 more were sold to Croatia, Slovenia, Oman, Ireland, Bulgaria, and Mexico.

Europeans Lead

The advent of the 21st century saw many developments in the lighter side of general aviation, including the introduction of diesel and electric engines, ballistic recovery systems (BRS), and the recognition of an entirely new class of aeroplane, the FAA's Light Sport Aircraft (LSA). However, the biggest changes were in avionics, with even small two-seat aircraft being fitted with advanced autopilots, traffic collision avoidance systems (TCAS), and synthetic vision – equipment that would not look out of place in an Airbus or a big Boeing.

△ Cirrus SR22 2000

Origin USA

Engine 310 hp Continental Motors IO-550 turbocharged air-cooled flat-6

Top speed 231 mph (372 km/h)

Derived from the Cirrus SR20, the 22 is a significantly more powerful version as it is fitted with a turbocharged engine. It has the same ballistic recovery systems as the SR20, and features a very powerful avionics suite.

◁ Diamond DA42 Twin Star 2002

Origin Austria

Engine 2 x 165 hp Austro turbocharged liquid-cooled diesel in-line 4-cylinder

Top speed 222 mph (356 km/h)

Made primarily from composite material, the DA42 has very impressive performance, particularly for range and endurance, because of its extremely efficient diesel engines and advanced aerodynamics.

▷ Alpi Pioneer 300 2006

Origin Italy

Engine 100 hp Rotax 912 ULS liquid-cooled flat-4

Top speed 168 mph (270 km/h)

Looking like a scaled-down version of a Siai Marchetti SF-260, Alpi Aviation's sleek, kit-built two-seat retractable boasts an impressive cruise speed for an aircraft that only has a 100 hp engine.

◁ Alpi Pioneer 400 2010

Origin Italy

Engine 115 hp Rotax 914 turbocharged liquid-cooled flat-4

Top speed 184 mph (296 km/h)

Derived from the successful Pioneer 300 two-seater, the retractable tricycle undercarriage and turbocharged engine ensure high cruise speeds. Although a very modern design, the Pioneer 400 is unusual for a 21st-century aircraft as it is constructed primarily from wood.

Light Sport Aircraft

The introduction of the new category of LSA rejuvenated sport aviation in the US. These aircraft could be flown on a new type of licence – the Sport Pilot Certificate – which has less strict medical requirements. These aircraft have an unpressurized cabin, fixed landing gear, and no more than two seats. They are limited to a weight of 1,321 lb (599 kg) and a stall speed of no more than 52 mph (83 km/h).

△ American Legend Cub 2004

Origin USA

Engine 100 hp Continental O-200 air-cooled flat-4

Top speed 108 mph (174 km/h)

The introduction of the LSA class by the FAA saw many new machines come to market, including some "retro" designs. These include this Legend Cub, which is based on the classic Piper J3 Cub, but built using modern materials and methods, and fitted with advanced instruments and avionics.

◁ **Tecnam P2002-EA Sierra 2006**

Origin Italy

Engine 100 hp Rotax 912 ULS liquid-cooled flat-4

Top speed 180 mph (290 km/h)

This all-metal low-wing two-seater is popular with both flight training schools and private owners. It has side-by-side seats and a sliding canopy that can be opened in flight.

▷ **Tecnam P2006T 2007**

Origin Italy

Engine 2 x 100 hp Rotax 912-S3 liquid-cooled flat-4

Top speed 192 mph (309 km/h)

The P2006T is an innovative attempt by Tecnam to produce a light twin with lower operating costs than conventional American aircraft. Powered by a pair of efficient 100 hp Rotax engines, it is the lightest certified multi-engine aircraft currently available.

◁ **Xtreme Sbach 342 2011**

Origin Germany

Engine 315 hp Lycoming AEIO-580 air-cooled flat-6

Top speed 256 mph (412 km/h)

This all-composite, high-performance aerobatic aircraft was derived from the single-seat Xtreme 3000. It is capable of all current aerobatic manoeuvres and has G limits of +/-10.

△ **Van's RV-9A 2011**

Origin USA

Engine 160 hp Lycoming O-320 air-cooled flat-4

Top speed 170 mph (274 km/h)

A product of prolific designer Richard Van Grunsven, the RV-9 was the first of Van Grunsven's line that was not designed to be aerobatic. An all-metal kitplane built using the "matched-hole" system, it can be powered by a variety of engines between 118 hp and 160 hp.

▷ **Lambert Mission M108 2012**

Origin Belgium

Engine 100 hp Rotax 912iS liquid-cooled flat-4

Top speed 130 mph (210 km/h)

The Lambert Mission M108 is a high-wing, side-by-side two-seater that is available with either a tail wheel or tricycle undercarriage. Based on the Avid flyer and Kitfox home builds, it has a redesigned wing.

▽ **Czech Aircraft Works SportCruiser 2005**

Origin Czech Republic

Engine 100 hp Rotax 912 ULS liquid-cooled flat-4

Top speed 160 mph (258 km/h)

This all-metal two-seater aimed at the American market is a popular LSA machine. Powered by the ubiquitous Rotax 912, the SportCruiser performs well for an aircraft that only has a 100 hp engine. It was briefly marketed by Piper as the PiperSport.

△ **Flight Design CTSW 2008**

Origin Germany

Engine 100 hp Rotax 912 ULS liquid-cooled flat-4

Top speed 187 mph (301 km/h)

The Flight Design CTSW is built primarily from composites. Its high wing features advanced aerodynamics (including reflexed flaps), while its very large fuel tanks give it a range of almost 800 miles (1,287 km) when operated as an LSA machine.

Ultra-efficient Civil Transport

The 21st century brought even greater awareness of the need to economize on fossil fuels. One solution was the largest passenger airliner yet, with room for over 850 passengers; another was to use composite construction for light weight and durability for both airliners and business jets that can legally be operated with one pilot (cutting costs and increasing capacity).

▷ Piper PA-46-500TP Malibu Meridian 2000

Origin USA

Engine 500 hp Pratt & Whitney Canada PT6A-42A turboprop

Top speed 301 mph (484 km/h)

Certificated in 2000 the turboprop version of Piper's 1979 piston-engined Malibu, the Meridian, was given larger wing and tail surfaces and a new instrument panel; it sold in 2012 for US $2.13 million.

◁ Beechcraft Premier I 2001

Origin USA

Engine 2 x 2,300 lb (1,043 kg) thrust Williams International FJ44-2A turbofan

Top speed 530 mph (853 km/h)

With a spacious and comfortable cabin, the Premier's carbon-fibre/epoxy honeycomb fuselage construction made it light enough to be operated by a single pilot, and capable of record speeds.

△ Bombadier Learjet 45XR 2004

Origin Canada/USA

Engine 2 x 3,500 lb (1,5868 kg) thrust Honeywell TFE731-20BR turbofan

Top speed 535 mph (861 km/h)

Bombardier upgraded the successful midsized 1990s Learjet 45 to XR specification in 2004, giving it more powerful engines and offering faster climb rate, higher weight capacity, and increased cruise speed.

△ Dassault Falcon 900C 2000

Origin France

Engine 3 x 4,750 lb (2,155 kg) thrust AlliedSignal TFE731-5BR-1C turbofan

Top speed 590 mph (950 km/h)

Dassault's intercontinental business jet for the 21st century boasts three engines, giving excellent performance as well as increased range, enhanced by the latest Honeywell avionics.

▷ Gulfstream G150 2002

Origin USA

Engine 2 x 4,420 lb (2,005 kg) thrust Honeywell TFE731-40AR turbofan

Top speed 631 mph (1,015 km/h)

Gulfstream re-entered the midsize market, giving the G150 a near- square cabin cross-section with more useful space than circular cabins, and major improvement on all fronts over the G100.

△ Airbus A380 2005

Origin European Consortium

Engine 4 x 84,000 lb (38,102 kg) thrust Rolls-Royce Trent 900 or 81,500 lb (36,968 kg) thrust Engine Alliance GP7000 turbofan

Top speed 587 mph (945 km/h)

The world's largest passenger airliner of the early 21st century, the double-deck A380 required airports to enlarge their facilities to cope with it. Singapore Airlines flew the first one in 2007.

◁ Gulfstream G550 2003

Origin USA

Engine 2 x 15,385 lb (6,978 kg) thrust Rolls-Royce BR710 turbofan

Top speed 585 mph (941 km/h)

With range and performance increased over the Gulfstream GV by reducing aerodynamic drag, the 550 has the longest range in its class at 7,767 miles (12,500 km). It also has Enhance Vision for landing in fog.

◁ Eclipse 500 2002

Origin USA

Engine 2 x 900 lb (408 kg) thrust Pratt & Whitney Canada PW610F turbofan

Top speed 425 mph (684 km/h)

The first of the new class of Very Light Jet (VLJ) certified in 2006 the compact, light, six-seat 500 claimed to be "the most efficient jet on the planet". Production stopped in 2008, but restarted in 2012.

△ Cessna Citation Mustang 510 2005

Origin USA

Engine 2 x 1,460 lb (662 kg) thrust FADEC Pratt and Whitney Canada PW615F turbofan

Top speed 391 mph (629 km/h)

Classified as a VLJ and therefore accepted for single-pilot operation, the Mustang is a proper business jet in miniature, with aluminium alloy airframe. Over 400 have been built since 2006.

△ Embraer Phenom 100 2007

Origin Brazil

Engine 2 x 1,695 lb (768 kg) thrust Pratt & Whitney Canada PW617-F turbofan

Top speed 449 mph (723 km/h)

Brazil's entry in the Very Light Jet market was competitively priced and sold well: over 240 worldwide by 2012. Simple, easy to operate, and very durable, it boasted 70 per cent fewer checks than its rivals.

▽ Boeing 787-8 Dreamliner 2009

Origin USA

Engine 2 x 64,000 lb (28,030 kg) thrust General Electric GEnx or Rolls-Royce Trent 1000

Top speed 593 mph (954 km/h)

Entering service in 2011 with All Nippon Airways, this is claimed to be Boeing's most efficient airliner and the world's first to be mostly of composite construction. It also boasts a reduced noise "footprint".

△ SOCATA TBM 850 2006

Origin France

Engine 850 hp Pratt & Whitney Canada PT6A-66D turboprop

Top speed 368 mph (592 km/h)

A collaborative Socata-Mooney design, this top-of-the-range single-engined turboprop is a viable and cost-effective alternative to lower-end business jets and has the Garmin G1000 flight deck.

Extending Rotary Wing Range

Initially, wars in Iraq and Afghanistan consumed military helicopters and the offshore oil industry kept civilian producers in profit. However, the recession of 2008 hit the helicopter industry hard; private buyers vanished, defence budgets were cut, and development plans postponed. Instead, companies concentrated on upgrading existing airframes. With the oil exploration moving further offshore into deeper waters manufacturers extended helicopters' ranges to meet the new demands.

▷ Schweizer 333 2000

Origin USA

Engine 420 shp Allison 250-C20W turboshaft (derated to 220 hp)

Top speed 138 mph (222 km/h)

A definitive version of Schweizer's turbine-powered 330 range, this aircraft offers a 30 per cent increase in useful load. It is now manufactured by parent company Sikorsky.

▷ AgustaWestland AW101 Merlin 2000

Origin Italy/UK

Engine 3 x 2,100 shp Rolls-Royce Turbomeca RTM322-01 turboshaft

Top speed 192 mph (309 km/h)

Few aircraft have had a gestation period as long as the quarter-century of the AW101; nine prototypes were built while Westland went through three owners and a merger.

▷ AgustaWestland AW109E 2005

Origin Italy

Engine 2 x 571 shp Turbomeca Arrius 2K1 turboshaft

Top speed 193 mph (311 km/h)

A stunning Italian design, this aircraft was updated in 2005 as the 109 "Power" with new engines and avionics. It also holds the helicopter circumnavigation record of 11 days.

△ AgustaWestland AW189 2011

Origin UK/Italy

Engine 2 x 2,000 shp General Electric GE CT7-2E1 turboshaft

Top speed 183 mph (294 km/h)

A civilianized version of the military AW149, the AW189 was designed with the oil market in mind and was able to reach oil platforms 230 miles (370 km) offshore with 12 passengers.

△ Eurocopter EC225 Super Puma 2000

Origin France

Engine 2 x 2,382 shp Turbomeca Makila 2A1 turboshaft

Top speed 171 mph (275 km/h)

An improved variant of a successful helicopter, the 5 hour 30 minutes endurance of the EC225 Super Puma brings deepwater oil installations within reach.

◁ Eurocopter UH-72 Lakota 2004

Origin France

Engine 2 x 738 shp Turbomeca Arriel 1E2 turboshaft

Top speed 167 mph (268 km/h)

Eurocopter beat the American manufacturers on their own turf by winning a US Army light utility helicopter competition with this military variant of the EC145.

△ **Magni Gyroplane M16 2006**

Origin Italy

Engine 115 hp Rotax 914 turbo

Top speed 115 mph (185 km/h)

Established for more than 25 years, Magni has developed a reputation for safety and reliability with single-seat gryoplanes and tandem trainers.

▽ **Bell Boeing MV-22B Osprey 2007**

Origin USA

Engine 2 x 6,150 shp Rolls-Royce Allison T406/AE 1107C turboshaft

Top speed 316 mph (508 km/h)

A gallant attempt at a hybrid helicopter/fixed wing aircraft, the Osprey's complexity slowed development and massively increased costs; each V-22 works out at $110 million.

◁ **Robinson R66 2011**

Origin USA

Engine 300 shp Rolls-Royce RR250-C300 turbine

Top speed 144 mph (232 km/h)

With the R66, Frank Robinson aims to do for the turbine helicopter market what he did for the piston world with the R22 and R44 – cut costs and drive new sales.

▷ **Guimbal G2 Cabri 2008**

Origin France

Engine 180 hp Lycoming O-360 piston

Top speed 115 mph (185 km/h)

Former Eurocopter engineer Bruno Guimbal's two-seater has been built with backing from his old company to take on the Robinsons in the personal transport market.

◁ **Sikorsky S-92 2002**

Origin USA

Engine 2 x 2,520 shp General Electric GE CT7-8A turbine

Top speed 190 mph (306 km/h)

A civilian transport manufactured using Black Hawk dynamic components, the S-92 was designed in the 1990s but not produced for 10 years while oil prices were low.

◁ **Sikorsky S-70i Black Hawk 2011**

Origin US design/Polish built

Engine 2 x 2,000 shp General Electric T700-GE-701D turbine

Top speed 183 mph (294 km/h)

This is the latest version of Sikorsky's top-selling Black Hawk built in Poland by PZL Mielec, a company acquired by Sikorsky in 2007, and offered on international markets.

End of the Line for Manned Fighters?

While new superpowers China and India are steadily developing more sophisticated manned fighters of their own, in the West political pressure on costs has seen complete programmes terminated and current fleets scheduled to continue for decades to come. Unmanned aircraft development has continued apace: first used solely for surveillance, such aircraft are expected to fulfil wider roles in future conflicts including air combat.

△ Boeing F/A-18E Super Hornet 2000

Origin USA

Engine 2 x 13,000-22,000 lb (5,8969-9,979 kg) thrust General Electric F414-GE-400 afterburning turbofan

Top speed 1,190 mph (1,915 km/h)

With 50 per cent greater endurance, the larger, more powerful version of the Hornet had long been planned. It finally entered service in 2000 with the US Navy and in 2010 with the Australian Air Force.

▷ BAe Harrier GR.9A 2003

Origin UK

Engine 23,800 lb (10,795 kg) thrust Rolls-Royce Pegasus 107 turbofan

Top speed 662 mph (1,065 km/h)

Fitted with the latest uprated Pegasus engine and avionics and weapons upgrades, the final GR.9A version of BAe's class-leading vertical takeoff aircraft was retired in 2011 on cost grounds.

▽ Sukhoi Su-30 MkI 2000

Origin Russia

Engine 2 x 27,500 lb (12,474 kg) thrust Lyulka AL-31FP vectoring turbofan

Top speed 1,320 mph (2,124 km/h)

This high-performance Su-30 was developed jointly by Russia and India, which makes it for the Indian Air Force. It is highly agile thanks to its canard configuration and more than 150 have been built.

△ Eurofighter Typhoon FGR4 2007

Origin UK, Germany, Italy, Spain

Engine 2 x 20,000 lb (9,071 kg) thrust EJ200 turbojet

Top speed 1,320 mph (2,124 km/h)

The FGR4 – Fighter, Ground attack, and Reconnaissance, Mk4 – was introduced in 2007 when the RAF's Typhoon fighters were upgraded to these two new roles. Some were modified and some newly built.

▷ Lockheed Martin Boeing F-22 Raptor 2005

Origin USA

Engine 2 x 23,500-35,000 lb (10,659-15,876 kg) thrust Pratt & Whitney F119-PW-100 Pitch Thrust vectoring turbofan

Top speed 1,669 mph (2,686 km/h)

Hugely expensive but claimed to be the best fighter in the world, the F-22 combines stealth technology with fighter, ground attack, electronic warfare, and signals intelligence capabilities; 195 were built.

Unmanned Aircraft

Are Unmanned Aerial Vehicles (UAVs), or "drones", the future of aerial warfare? Will they slug it out in dogfights, dash to rescue lost troops, or shoot down enemy bombers? Their use for observation is already widespread and, as technology has advanced, there are vehicles that can carry – and fire – missiles for attack or defence. It is also possible for troops and supplies to be carried to the front line in craft flown only by computers. However, there is still a long way to go before the fighter ace is relegated to the history books.

△ Selex Galileo Falco Evo 2012

Origin Italy

Engine 80 hp UAV petrol, possibly flat-6

Top speed 134 mph (216 km/h)

This compact and light Unmanned Aerial Vehicle was built for Pakistan. In original form, it was only capable of medium-altitude surveillance duties, but the Evo is expected to carry weapons too.

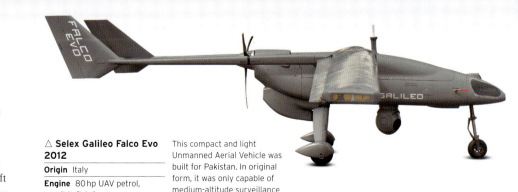

△ Boeing KC-767A 2003

Origin USA

Engine 2 x General Electric CF6-80C2B6F turbofan

Top speed 569 mph (916 km/h)

Based on the 1980s Boeing 767-200, KC-767A was designated in 2002 for military aerial refuelling and transport. Italy and Japan took four each, and the US has ordered the latest KC-46 variant.

△ Boeing C-17 Globemaster III 2012

Origin USA

Engine 4 x 40,440 lb (18,343 kg) thrust Pratt & Whitney F117-PW-100

Top speed 515 mph (830 km/h)

In 2012 Boeing delivered C-17 IIIs to the air forces of the US, UK, and UAE. This brought the total number of this massive, sturdy, long-haul transporter able to operate out of remote airfields to some 220.

▽ Airbus A330 MRTT 2007

Origin Joint European

Engine 2 x 72,000 lb (32,658 kg) thrust Rolls-Royce Trent 772B / General Electric CF6-80E1A4 / Pratt & Whitney PW 4168A turbofan

Top speed 547 mph (880 km/h)

The MRTT (Multi-Role Tanker Transport) is based on commercial A330-200s and can carry airborne refuelling kit, or 380 troops, or 130 standard stretchers. Australia, UK, UAE, and Saudi Arabia have ordered them.

△ Chengdu J-10 2003

Origin China

Engine 25,740 lb (11,675 kg) thrust Lyulka-Saturn AL-31FN turbofan

Top speed 1,632 mph (2,626 km/h, Mach 2.2)

With delta wings and delta-profile canard, the J-10 is highly manoeuvrable at high speeds. Cloaked in secrecy until 2007, it has a Russian engine. An export variant was sold to Pakistan.

◁ Northrop Grumman RQ-4 Global Hawk 2000

Origin USA

Engine 7,050 lb (3,198 kg) thrust Allison Rolls-Royce AE3007H turbofan

Top speed 404 mph (650 km/h)

This unmanned surveillance aircraft has state-of-the-art radar and camera gear. Able to survey through sandstorm and cloud, the Global Hawk was extensively used in Iran and Afghanistan.

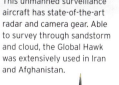

▷ BAE Systems Mantis 2009

Origin UK

Engine 2 x 380 hp Rolls-Royce M250B-17 turboshaft

Top speed 345 mph (556 km/h)

Built to demonstrate and test Unmanned Autonomous Systems, Mantis has 24-hour endurance, flies itself, and plots its own route. It relays observations to its base station via satellites.

Alternative Power

The 21st century brought pollution and fuel use into sharp focus. The industry responded with brilliantly innovative aircraft, from small fuel-efficient petrol and diesel power plants, some running on environmentally friendly biofuels, to a wide range of electric aircraft (even carrying solar panels to maintain charge) and a hydrogen fuel cell-powered light aircraft. One pioneer promises Mach 1 solar flight in a decade.

△ Thruster T600N 450 2002
Origin UK

Engine 85 hp Jabiru 2200A air-cooled flat-4

Top speed 87 mph (140 km/h)

Introduced in the mid-1990s with a two-stroke engine, this is an enclosed-cockpit, side-by-side two-seat ultralight with an efficient, modern four-stroke engine.

△ Diamond DA40 TDI Star 2002
Origin Austria

Engine 135 hp Thielert Centurion 1.7 turbocharged liquid-cooled 4-cylinder in-line diesel

Top speed 144 mph (232 km/h)

Austrian light aircraft-builder Diamond was the first to use this turbodiesel engine, developed from the Mercedes-Benz A-class 170 car unit. It proved unreliable, so Diamond sourced its own unit.

△ Diamond DA42 2009
Origin Austria

Engine 2 x 168 hp Austro AE 300 turbocharged liquid-cooled 4-cylinder in-line diesel

Top speed 222 mph (357 km/h)

Eco-aware Diamond began building its own diesel engines in 2008: the first flew in 2009. The DA42 was the first diesel plane to cross the Atlantic and in 2010 the first to fly on algae-derived biofuel.

△ Lange Antares 20E 2003
Origin Germany

Engine 57 hp Lange EA42 electric motor

Top speed N/A

Lange Aviation offers self-launching gliders capable of taking off and climbing 10,000 ft (3,048 m) on battery power alone, with lithium-ion batteries in the wings and a built-in charging system.

△ Boeing-FCD 2008
Origin Spain

Engine Electric motor plus fuel cell

Top speed N/A

Boeing's Fuel Cell Demonstrator achieved the first fuel cell-powered level flight in February 2008. It was built with the aid of British, Austrian, US, and Spanish companies.

△ Solar Impulse 2009
Origin Switzerland

Engine 4 x 10 hp electric motor

Top speed 43 mph (69 km/h)

Conceived by Bertrand Piccard, this solar-charged craft has four electric motors under its 747-scale wings. It has stayed aloft for 26 hours and is to be flown around the world.

△ Electravia MC15E Cri-Cri 2010

Origin France

Engine 2 x 25 hp Electravia E-Motor GMPE-104 electric motor

Top speed 176 mph (283 km/h)

Using two electric motors and 3 kWh lithium-polymer batteries, Hugues Duval set two world records in his diminutive Colomban Cri-Cri, 163 mph (262 km/h) in 2010 and 176 mph (283 km/h) in 2011, at the Paris Air Show.

▷ Schempp-Hirth Arcus-E 2010

Origin Germany

Engine 42 kW Lange electric motor

Top speed N/A

Germany's electric-powered, two-seat, self-launching glider with flaps shares the electric drive technology of the Lange Antares 20E. It is charged by a hangar-mounted Windreich wind turbine.

△ Robin DR400 Ecoflyer 2008

Origin France

Engine 155 hp Thielert Centurion 2.0 turbocharged liquid-cooled 4-cylinder in-line diesel

Top speed 159 mph (256 km/h)

A fabric-covered wood aircraft first flown in 1972, the Robin came up to date with the turbodiesel Ecoflyer option, in 135 hp or 155 hp options, claimed to be far cheaper to run than Avgas engines.

△ Pipistrel Taurus Electro G2 2008

Origin Slovenia

Engine 40 kW electric motor

Top speed 99 mph (159 km/h)

This was the first electric-powered two-seater, with electric motor on a hinged boom for self-launching. It can be transported in a trailer clad in solar panels to charge the batteries, which allows the pilot to fly "for free".

◁ Luxembourg Spécial Aerotechnics MC30E Firefly 2011

Origin Luxembourg

Engine 26 hp Electravia electric motor

Top speed 119 mph (191 km/h)

Like the Electravia, this electric installation is in a Colomban airframe normally fitted with a small petrol engine. Jean-Luc Soullier's MC30E weighs 249 lb (113 kg) empty, including 4.7 kWh battery pack.

△ Pipistrel Taurus Electro G4 2011

Origin Slovenia

Engine 145 kW electric motor

Top speed 100 mph (161 km/h)

Pipistrel's Taurus won NASA's 2011 Green Flight Challenge (and $1.35 million) with the only electric-powered four-seater – two G2s linked by a central engine/battery nacelle with a 100 kWh battery pack.

Into the Future

Far from seeing the aircraft market collapsing as fossil fuels continue to surge in price, there is a polarization of aircraft manufacture. At one end the giant aircraft-building nations are pouring resources into state-of-the-art, next-generation fighters and light, efficient airliners, while at the other end of the scale small manufacturers are popping up building ultralight electric-powered aircraft charged by solar or wind power.

SpaceShipOne attached to main aircraft

△ White Knight One & SpaceShipOne 2003

Origin USA

Engine White Knight: 2 x 2,400-3,600 lb (1,089-1633 kg) thrust General Electric J85-GE-5 afterburning turbojet

Top speed 445 mph (716 km/h)

Burt Rutan's creation achieved the first manned private spaceflight with SpaceShipOne for astronaut Mike Melville, after airborne launch from its mothership, White Knight. The spacecraft flew at 2,292 mph (3,689 km/h), powered by an N20/HTPB Spacedev hybrid rocket.

▷ Lockheed Martin F-35A Lightning II 2006

Origin USA

Engine 28,000-43,000 lb (12,700-19,500 kg) thrust Pratt & Whitney F135 afterburning turbofan

Top speed 1,200 mph (1,930 km/h)

The advanced-stealth-technology F-35 has three forms: F-35A conventional takeoff and landing; F-35B short takeoff, vertical landing; F-35C carrier-based. It will equip most of the western world.

▷ Airbus A400M Atlas 2009

Origin European consortium

Engine 4 x 11,060 hp Europrop TP400-D6 turboprop

Top speed 485 mph (780 km/h)

Immersed in controversy over delays and overspending, the all-new A400M Atlas doubles the military long-range transport capacity of the C-130 Hercules and boasts state-of-the-art technology.

◁ Airbus A350-800 2014

Origin European consortium

Engine 2 x 84,000 lb (38,102 kg) Rolls-Royce Trent XWB-83 turbofan

Top speed 587 mph (945 km/h)

Customer pressure led Airbus to a radical overhaul for its new family of wide-body jets. They used carbon-fibre reinforced polymer for both fuselage and wings as part of a major efficiency drive.

Helicopter Advances

While cost and relatively high fuel consumption has prevented helicopters becoming mainstream aircraft, their unique vertical takeoff and landing capabilities ensure their popularity. Composite construction has helped reduce weight, while experiments continue with booster engines and propellers to improve maximum speeds, and unmanned models controlled by computers.

◁ Eurocopter X3 2010

Origin France

Engine 2 x 2270 shp Turbomeca RTM332 turboshaft

Top speed 267 mph (430 km/h)

As a less-complex solution to the problems of high-speed helicopter flight than a tilt-rotor, the X3's rotor can be slowed down to keep tip speeds out of the efficiency-sapping transonic range.

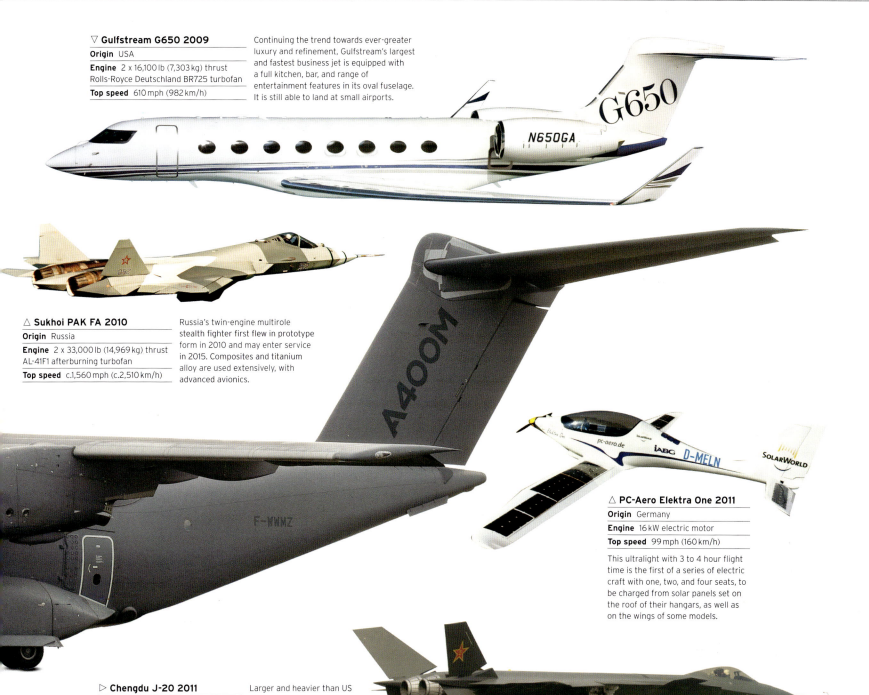

▽ **Gulfstream G650 2009**

Origin USA

Engine 2 x 16,100 lb (7,303 kg) thrust Rolls-Royce Deutschland BR725 turbofan

Top speed 610 mph (982 km/h)

Continuing the trend towards ever-greater luxury and refinement, Gulfstream's largest and fastest business jet is equipped with a full kitchen, bar, and range of entertainment features in its oval fuselage. It is still able to land at small airports.

△ **Sukhoi PAK FA 2010**

Origin Russia

Engine 2 x 33,000 lb (14,969 kg) thrust AL-41F1 afterburning turbofan

Top speed c.1,560 mph (c.2,510 km/h)

Russia's twin-engine multirole stealth fighter first flew in prototype form in 2010 and may enter service in 2015. Composites and titanium alloy are used extensively, with advanced avionics.

△ **PC-Aero Elektra One 2011**

Origin Germany

Engine 16 kW electric motor

Top speed 99 mph (160 km/h)

This ultralight with 3 to 4 hour flight time is the first of a series of electric craft with one, two, and four seats, to be charged from solar panels set on the roof of their hangars, as well as on the wings of some models.

▷ **Chengdu J-20 2011**

Origin China

Engine 2 x 30,000-40,000 lb (13,608-18,144 kg) thrust WS-15 afterburning turbofan

Top speed c.1,430 mph (c.2,300 km/h)

Larger and heavier than US and Russian stealth fighters, China's J-20 has a long, wide fuselage with canard and main delta wings. Its rapid development shows China's determination to catch up.

▽ **Bell Relentless 525 2013**

Origin USA

Engine 2 x 1800 shp General Electric CT7-2F1 turboshaft

Top speed 161 mph (259 km/h)

Composite construction, fly-by-wire controls, state-of-the-art flight deck, and extensive computerization will make the 525 the most technically advanced helicopter yet.

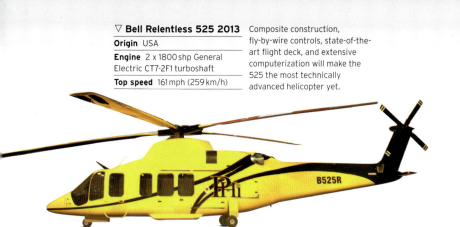

△ **Sikorsky S97 Raider 2014**

Origin USA

Engine c.3000 hp General Electric T700 turboshaft

Top speed 230 mph (370 km/h)

This proposed composite-fuselage, high-speed scout-and-attack army helicopter has a "pusher" propeller as well as main rotors, retractable landing gear, and the potential to fly itself – without a pilot.

Index

All general page references are given in *italics*.

Acknowledgments

Dorling Kindersley would like to thank Tony Streeter, Giles Chapman, and Philip Whiteman for all their time, assistance, and support throughout the making of this book.

Tony Streeter is a journalist and editor who writes across the rail spectrum from steam to modern railways and international light rail. A former long-term editor of UK's *Steam Railway Magazine*, he has travelled by, and written about, rail in Russia, China, India, Canada, and Eastern and Western Europe.

Giles Chapman is an award-winning writer and commentator on the industry, history, and culture of cars. A former editor of *Classic & Sports Car*, the world's best-selling classic car magazine, he has written over 15 books, including *Chapman's Car Compendium* and DK's *Illustrated Encyclopedia of Extraordinary Automobiles*, and has edited or contributed to many more besides.

Philip Whiteman is an award-winning aviation journalist and consulting engineer, specializing in fuel and engine technology. He has contributed to numerous aviation publications and is the Editor of *Pilot*, the UK's longest established and best-selling general aviation magazine. He has flown many of the aircraft featured in *Aircraft* and operates a 1944 Piper L-4H Cub from a farm strip in Buckinghamshire.

Tony Streeter would like to thank the many people who assisted in the making of this book, including: Pip Dunn, Peter Johnson, Anthony Coulls, Tim Bryan, Bernd Seiler, Richard Croucher, Paul Chancellor, Brian Stephenson, Marek Ciesielski, Robin Garn, Jacques Daffis, Uwe Hüttner, and Peter Weißhahn.

Philip Whiteman would like to thank the many aviation writers, historians, and photographers – both named and anonymous – who played a part in preparing *Aircraft*, as well as Dorling Kindersley's fantastically hard-working, patient, and above all good-humored editorial and design team.

The publisher would like to thank the following people for their help with making the book: Mel Fisher, Steve Crozier at Butterfly Creative Solutions, and Tom Morse for colour retouching; Simon Mumford for cartography; Phil Gamble for illustrations; Sonia Charbonnier for technical support; Nicola Hodgson for additional text contributions; Arpita Dasgupta, Dharini Ganesh, Neha Pande, Tejaswita Payal, and Catherine Thomas, and Sonia Yooshing for editorial assistance; Gillian Andrews, Carol Davis, Nicola Erdpresser, Gadi Farfour, Rebecca Guyatt, Francesca Harris, Amit Malhotra, Johnny Pau, Upasana Sharma, and Shruti Singhal for design assistance; Joanna Chisholm and Caroline Hunt for

proofreading; Sue Butterworth and Helen Peters for the index; Jyoti Sachdev, Sakshi Saluja, and Malavika Talukder for arranging the India photoshoot; Peter Cook for the use of his images; Sachin Singh and Anita Yadav at DK Delhi for DTP help. The publishers would also like to extend a special thanks to contributors Keith Fender and Julian Holland, whose assistance throughout the project was invaluable.

The Publisher would also like to thank the following museums, companies, and individuals for their generosity in allowing Dorling Kindersley access to their rail vehicles and equipment for photography:

8 201, Dampf-Plus GmbH
Moosglöckchenweg 10, 80995
München, Germany
www.zugparty.de
With special thanks to Christian Goldschagg

Adrian Shooter
(Owner of DHR B Class No.19 and its carriages)

Ashford Depot
Station Road,
Ashford, TN23 1EZ, UK
With special thanks to Nigel King and Mark Fitzgerald

B&O Railroad Museum
901, West Pratt Street,
Baltimore,
MD 21223, US
www.borail.org
With special thanks to David Shackelford, Ryan McPherson, and Jane Harper

Didcot Railway Centre
Didcot Parkway Station,
Didcot, Oxfordshire,
OX11 7NJ, UK
www.didcotrailwaycentre.org.uk
With special thanks to Roger Orchard, Peter Rance, and Frank Dumbleton

Eisenbahnfreunde Traditionsbahnbettiebwerk Strasssfurt e.V.
Guestener Weg,
39418 Strassfurt, Germany
www.efsft.de
With special thanks to Uwe Hüttner

Ffestiniog & Welsh Highland Railways
Porthmadog,
LL49 9NF, UK
www.festrail.co.uk
With special thanks to Andrew Thomas and Chris Parry

Hitachi Rail Europe Limited
40 Holborn Viaduct,
London, EC1N 2PB, UK
www.hitachirail-eu.com
With special thanks to Daniela Karthaus

HSB, Harzer Schmalspurbahner
Friedrichstrasse 151,
38855, Wernigerode, Germany
www.hsb-wr.de
With special thanks to Bernd Seiler

National Railway Museum (NRM York)
Leeman Road,
York, YO26 4XJ, UK
www.nrm.org.uk
With special thanks to Chris Hanley

National Railway Museum
Chanakyapuri,
New Delhi – 110021, India
With special thanks to
Uday Singh Mina, Director

Northern Railway
D.R.M. Office, State Entry Road,
New Delhi – 110055, India
www.nr.indianrailways.gov.in
With special thanks to Rajesh Kumar,
Sr. DME/Power/Delhi

Palace on Wheels
Rajasthan Tourism Development Corporation Ltd.
Ground floor, Bikaner House,
Pandara Road, New Delhi – 110011, India
www.rtdc.in
www.thepalaceonwheels.com
With special thanks to Pramod Sharma, General Manager, Rajasthan Tourism Development Corporation Ltd., and Pradeep Bohra, General Manager, Palace on Wheels

Railway Board
Rail Bhavan, 1, Raisina Road,
New Delhi - 110001, India
www.indianrailways.gov.in
With special thanks to Seema Sharma, Director, Information & Publicity, Railway Board, and Siddharth Singh, Deputy Director Public Relations, Railway Board

Railroad Museum of Pennsylvania, PHMC
P.O. Box 15,
Strasburg, PA17579
www.rrmuseumpa.org
With special thanks to Dodie Robbins, Nicholas Zmijewski, Charles Fox, and Deborah Reddig

Rewari Steam Loco Shed
Northern Railways, Rewari, Haryana – 123110, India
www.rewaristeamloco.com
With special thanks to Shyam Bihari Gautam, Sr. Section Engineer, Rewari Steam Loco Shed

Ribble Steam Railway Museum
Chain Caul Road,
PR2 2PD, UK
www.ribblesteam.org.uk
With special thanks to Howard Fletcher, Terri Hearty, Jayne Waring, and Chris Mills

SCMG Enterprises Limited
The Science Museum,
Exhibition Road,
London, SW7 2DD, UK
With special thanks to
Sophia Brothers and Wendy Burford

The Merchant Navy Locomotive Preservation Society Ltd
(Owners of 35028 *Clan Line*)
12 Inglewood Avenue,
Camberley,
Surrey, GU15 1RJ, UK

www.clan-line.org.uk
With special thanks to
Mr R.F. Abercrombie, Tim Robbins,
Peter Starks, and Alan French

Venice Simplon-Orient-Express Limited
Shackleton House,
4, Battle Bridge Lane,
London, SE1 2HP, UK
www.orient-express.com
With special thanks to Andrew Cook, Victoria Christie, Jeff Monk, Julian Clark, and Pat Thompson

Virginia Museum of Transportation
303 Norfolk Avenue SW,
Roanoke, VA 24016
www.vmt.org
With special thanks to Beverly Fitzpatrick and Fran Ferguson

Key to museums/contributors
B&O Railroad Museum (BORM)
Didcot Railway Centre (DRC)
Eisenbahnfreunde Traditionsbahnbetriebwerk Stassfurt e.V. (ETS)
Ffestiniog & Welsh Highland Railways (FWHR)
Harzer Schmalspurbahner (HSB)
The National Railway Museum, India (NRMI)
The National Railway Museum, York (NRMY)
Railroad Museum of Pennsylvania, PHMC (RMP)
Rewari Steam Loco Shed (RSLS)
Ribble Steam Railway (RSR)
Virginia Museum of Transportation (VMT)
Brooklands Museum (BM)
City of Norwich Aviation Museum (CNAM)
De Havilland Aircraft Heritage Center (DHAHC)
Early Bird Foundation (EBF)
Fleet Air Arms Museum (FAAM)
Flugausstellung (F)
Golden Apple Operations (GAO)
Midland Air Museum (MAM)
Musée Air + Space (MAS)
Norfolk & Suffolk Aviation Museum (NSAM)
RAF Battle of Britain Memorial Flight (RAFBBMF)
RAF Coningsby (RAFC)
RAF Cranwell (RAFCW)
RAF Museum Cosford (RAFMC)
RAF Museum London (RAFML)
Sarl Salis Aviation (SSA)
Smithsonian's National Air and Space Museum, Archives Division (SNASM)
The Aeroplane Collection Ltd. (TACL)
The Helicopter Museum (THM)
The Museum of Army Flying (TMAF)
The Nationaal Luchvaart-Themapark Aviodrome (TNLTA)
The Real Aeroplane Company (TRAC)
The Shuttleworth Collection (TSC)
Ukraine State Aviation Museum (USAM)
Yorkshire Air Museum (YAM)

Alex Pilkington
Audi UK: www.audi.co.uk
Beaulieu National Motor Museum, Brockenhurst, Hampshire, UK: www.beaulieu.co.uk

Brands Hatch Morgans,
Borough Green, Kent,
UK: www.morgan-cars.com
Chris Williams, The DeLorean Owners Club
UK: www.deloreans.co.uk
Chrysler UK, Slough, Berkshire,
UK: www.chrysler.co.uk
Claremont Corvette, Snodland,
Kent, UK: www.corvette.co.uk
Colin Spong
DK Engineering, Chorleywood,
Hertfordshire, UK: www.dkeng.co.uk
Eagle E-Types, East Sussex,
UK: www.eaglegb.com
Gilbert and Anna East
Haynes International Motor Museum, Yeovil, Somerset, UK:
www.haynesmotormuseum.com
Heritage Motoring Club of India (HMCI), New Delhi, India: Mr. HW Bhatnagar, Mr. Avinash Grewhal, Mr. SB Jatti, Mr. Ashok Kaicker, Mr. Sandeep Katari, Mr. Ranjit Malik, Mr. Bahadur Singh, Mr. Navinder Singh, Mr. Harshpati Singhania, Mr. Diljeet Titus www.hmci.org
Honda Institute, Slough, Berkshire, UK: www.honda.co.uk
Jaguar Daimler Heritage Trust, Coventry, Warwickshire, UK: www.jdht.com
John Mould
P & A Wood, Rolls Royce and Bentley Heritage Dealers, Dunmow, Essex, UK: www.pa-wood.co.uk
Peter Harris
Philip Jones, Byron International, Tadworth, Surrey, UK: www.allastonmartin.com
Porsche Cars (Great Britain) Ltd, Reading, Berkshire, UK: www.porsche.com/uk/
Roger Dudding
Roger Florio
Silver Arrows Automobiles, Classic Mercedes-Benz, London, UK: www.silverarrows.co.uk
Silver Lady Services Ltd, Rolls Royce and Bentley Car Services, Bournemouth, Dorset, UK: www.silverladyservices.co.uk
Tata Motors, Mumbai, India: www.tatamotors.com
Tim Colbert
Timothy Dutton, Ivan Dutton Ltd, Aylesbury, Buckinghamshire, UK: www.duttonbugatti.co.uk
Tuckett Brothers, North Marston, Buckinghamshire, UK: www.tuckettbrothers.co.uk

Bob Morcom for helping arrange photography for several aircraft and locations

Aero Antiques
Durley Airstrip
Hill Farm, Durley
Nr Southampton,
Hants SO32 2BP
email: aeroantiques@unibox.com
With special thanks to Ron Souch, Mike Souch and Roy Palmer

Aero Expo
www.expo.aero

The Aeroplane Collection Ltd.
The Hangers,
South Road,

Ellesmere Port,
Cheshire, CH65 1BQ, UK
www.theaeroplanecollection.org

With special thanks to Michael Davey for allowing us to photograph his Pratt and Whitney Twin Wasp Engine

Air Britain, Classic Fly-in
www.air-britain.com

B17 Preservation
PO Box 92,
Bury St. Edmunds
Suffolk, IP28 8RR, UK
www.sallyb.org.uk

B-17 Flying Fortress G-BEDF *Sally B* is the last remaining airworthy B-17 in Europe. *Sally B* has been operated by Elly Sallingboe of B-17 Preservation with the help of a dedicated team of volunteers. *Sally B* is permanently based at the Imperial War Museum, Duxford, where she is on static display when not flying. However, the aircraft is not part of the Museum's own collection and relies solely on charitable donations.

Brooklands Museum
Brooklands Road,
Weybridge,
Surrey, KT13 0QN, UK
www.brooklandsmuseum.com

City of Norwich Aviation Museum
Old Norwich Road,
Horsham St. Faith,Norwich,
Norfolk, NR10 3JF, UK
www.cnam.co.uk

Early Birds Foundation
Emoeweg 20,
Lelystad, The Netherlands
www.earlybirdsmuseum.nl

Farnborough International Airshow
www.farnborough.com

Fleet Air Arms Museum
RNAS Yeovilton,
Ilchester
Somerset, BA22 8HT, UK
www.fleetairarm.com

Flugausstellung
Habersberg 1
Hunsrückhöhenstr. (B327)
54411 Hermeskeil II
Germany
www.flugausstellung.de

Golden Apple Operations Ltd.
The Aircraft Restoration Company
Imperial War Museum
Duxford Airfield
Cambridge, CB2 4QR, UK
www.goldenappleoperations.org

Hamilyn Jet
Office and Operations:
Hamlin Jet Ltd.
Hangar 125,
London Luton Airport,
LU2 9PA, UK
www.hamlinjet.com

de Havilland Aircraft Heritage Center
Sailsbury Hall,
London Colney,
Hertfordshire, AL2 1BU, UK
www.dehavillandmuseum.co.uk

The Helicopter Museum
Locking Moor Road
Weston-super-Mare
Somerset, BS24 8PP, UK
www.helicoptermuseum.co.uk

Herefordshire Aero Club
Shobdon Airfield,
Leominster,
Herefordshire, HR6 9NR, UK
www.herefordshireaeroclub.com

Herefordshire Gliding Club
Shobdon Airfield,
Leominster,
Herefordshire, HR6 9NR, UK
www.shobdongliding.co.uk

IPMS Scale ModelWorld
www.smwshow.com
with special thanks to
John Tapsell

Lasham Gliding Club
The Avenue,
Lasham Airfield,
Alton,
Hants, GU34 5SS, UK
www.lashamgliding.com

Midland Air Museum
Coventry Airport,
Baginton,
Warwickshire, CV3 4FR, UK
www.midlandairmuseum.co.uk

Musée Air + Space
Aeroport de Paris,
Le Bourget, BP 173, France
www.museeairespace.fr

The Museum of Army Flying
Middle Wallop, Stockbridge,
Hampshire, SO20 8DY, UK
www.armyflying.com

The Nationaal Luchtvaart-Themapark Aviodrome
Aviodrome Lelystad Airport
Pelikaanweg 50
8218 PG Luchthaven Lelystad
The Netherlands
www.aviodrome.nl

Norfolk & Suffolk Aviation Museum
The Street,
Flixton,
Suffolk, NR35 1NZ, UK
www.nasm.flixton@tesco.net

The Real Aeroplane Company
The Aerodrome,
Breighton, Selby,
North Yorkshire, YO8 6DS, UK
www.realaero.com

The Rolls-Royce Heritage Trust
Rolls-Royce plc,
PO Box 31,
Derby, DE24 8BJ, UK
www.rolls-royce.com/about/heritage/heritage_trust

RAF Battle of Britain Memorial Flight
Coningsby,
Lincolnshire, LN4 4SY, UK
www.raf.mod.uk/bbmf

RAF Coningsby
Coningsby,
Lincolnshire, LN4 4SY, UK
www.raf.mod.uk/rafconingsby

RAF Cranwell
RAF Cranwell,
Sleaford,
Lincolnshire, NG34 8HB, UK
www.raf.mod.uk/rafcranwell

RAF Museum Cosford
Shifnal,
Shropshire, TF11 8UP, UK
www.rafmuseum.org.uk/cosford

RAF Museum London
Grahame Park Way,
London, NW9 5LL, UK
www.rafmuseum.org.uk/london

Royal International Air Tattoo
www.airtattoo.com
with special thanks to
Richard Arquati

Sarl Salis Aviation
Aerodrome de La Ferte Alais,
91590 Cerny, France
salis.aviation@free.fr

Skydrive Ltd. (Rotax engines)
Burnside,
Deppers Bridge,
Southam,
Warwickshire, CV47 2SU, UK
www.skydrive.co.uk

The Shuttleworth Collection
Shuttleworth (Old Warden)
Aerodrome,
Nr Biggleswade,
Bedfordshire, SG18 9EP, UK
www.shuttleworth.org

Tiger Helicopters Ltd.
Shobdon Aerodrome
Leominster
Herefordshire, NR6 9NR, UK
www.tigerhelicopters.co.uk

Ukraine State Aviation Museum
1 Medova street,
Kiev, 03048
Ukraine

West London Aero Club
White Waltham Airfield,
Maidenhead,
Berkshire, SL6 3NJ, UK
www.wlac.co.uk

Yorkshire Air Museum
Elvington,
York, YO41 4AU, UK
www.yorkshireairmuseum.org

(Key: a-above; b-below/bottom; c-centre; f-far; l-left; r-right; t-top)

2-3 USAM. 4 Dorling Kindersley: Gary Ombler / Courtesy of NRMY / Science Museum Group. **5 Dorling Kindersley:** Gary Ombler / Courtesy of Adrian Shooter (bl). **7 TNLTA** (bl), BM (br). **8-9 Dorling Kindersley:** Gary Ombler / Courtesy of NRMY / Science Museum Group. **10 Dorling Kindersley:** Mike Dunning / Courtesy of The Science Museum, London (cl). **Science & Society Picture Library:** National Railway Museum (tr). **10-11 Dorling Kindersley:** Mike Dunning / Courtesy of NRMY (tc). **SuperStock:** Science and Society (bc). **11 The Bridgeman Art Library:** Science Museum, London, UK (cb). **Dorling Kindersley:** Mike Dunning / Courtesy of NRMY (br). **Science Museum, London :** (cr). **12 Getty Images:** SSPL / NRM / Pictorial Collection (cra). **Milepost:** (tc). **Smithsonian Institution, Washington, DC, USA:** (bc, cl). **13 Alamy Images:** The Art Gallery (cb). **colour-rail.com:** (tc, br). **Milepost:** Orion Books / Blandford / Clifford & Wendy Meadway (ca, clb). **14 The Bridgeman Art Library:** Peter Newark American Pictures (cr); National Railway Museum, York, Uk (tr). **Dorling Kindersley:** Gary Ombler / Courtesy of RMP (b). **15 Baltimore and Ohio Railroad:** (bc). **Dorling Kindersley:** Gary Ombler / Courtesy of BORM (cl). **Mary Evans Picture Library:** (tr). **TopFoto.co.uk:** ullsteinbild (crb). **16 Dorling Kindersley:** Gary Ombler / Courtesy of BORM (cl, b). **17 Baltimore and Ohio Railroad:** (tr). **Dorling Kindersley:** Gary Ombler / Courtesy of BORM (tl, bl, br). **Masterfile:** (clb). **Wikipedia:** Urmelbeauftragter (c). **18 Corbis:** Bettmann (br). **Dorling Kindersley:** Gary Ombler / Courtesy of BORM (cl, bl). **18-19 Dorling Kindersley:** Gary Ombler / Courtesy of BORM. **19 Dorling Kindersley:** Gary Ombler / Courtesy of BORM (t). **Golden Spike National Historic Site Promontory Summit, Utah :** (bl, br). **20 Mary Evans Picture Library:** (cla). **20-21 Dorling Kindersley:** Gary Ombler / Courtesy of FWHR (bl); Mike Dunning / Courtesy of NRMY (bc). **21 The Bridgeman Art Library:** Ironbridge Gorge Museum, Telford, Shropshire, UK (tr). **Brian Stephenson/RAS:** (ca). **Dorling Kindersley:** Gary Ombler / Courtesy of NRMY / Science Museum Group (cl); Gary Ombler / Courtesy of DRC (cr). **22 Dorling Kindersley:** Gary Ombler / Courtesy of the Verkehrshaus der Schweiz, Luzern, Switzerland (c). **Tobias Koehler:** (tr). **Alex Leroy:** (bl). **22-23 Dorling Kindersley:** (bc). **23 Alamy Images:** Didier Zylberyng (tc). **Getty Images:** SSPL (cra). **Verkehrsmuseum Dresden:** (cl). **24 Alamy Images:** ImagesEurope (cb). **Didcot Railway Centre:** (cl). **24-25 Steam Picture Library:** (tc). **25 Dorling Kindersley:** Gary Ombler / Courtesy of DRC (bl). **Mary Evans Picture Library:** (ca). **Science & Society Picture Library:** NRM / Pictorial Collection (br). **Steam Picture Library:** (clb). **26 Dorling Kindersley:** Mike Dunning / Courtesy of NRMY (bc). **Getty Images:** (cla). **26-27 Dorling Kindersley:** Mike Dunning / Courtesy of NRMY (bc). **Science & Society Picture Library:** NRM / Pictorial Collection (tc). **27 Dorling Kindersley:** Gary Ombler / Courtesy of DRC (c); Gary Ombler / Courtesy of NRMY / Science Museum Group (b). **28 akg-images:** (tr). **NSW Government State Records:** (cla). **29 Dorling Kindersley:** Deepak Aggarwal / Courtesy of NRMI (c). **Mary Evans Picture Library:** (br). **Danie van der Merwe:** (tl). **30-31 colour-rail.com:** (tc). **Dorling Kindersley:** Mike Dunning / Courtesy of NRMY (bc). **30 Brian Stephenson/RAS:** (cla). **John Whiteley:** (crb). **31 Edward Gately:** (c). **32 colour-rail.com:** (tr). **Steam Picture Library:** (cl). **Brian Stephenson/RAS:** (c, clb, bc). **33 colour-rail.com:** (clb, br). **Getty Images:** SSPL / National Railway Museum (cra). **Brian Stephenson/RAS:** (cr). **TfL from the London Transport Museum collection :** (tc, bc). **34 Dorling Kindersley:** Gary Ombler / Courtesy of the Verkehrshaus der Schweiz, Luzern, Switzerland (c); Gary Ombler / Courtesy of FWHR (bl). **Milepost:** (crb). **35 Brian Stephenson/RAS:** (tr). **David Wilcock:** (bc). **Dorling Kindersley:** Gary Ombler / Courtesy of NRMY / Science Museum Group (tl); Gary Ombler / Courtesy of FWHR (c, cb). **36 Dorling Kindersley:** Deepak Aggarwal / Courtesy of NRMI (cl, bl). **36-37 Dorling Kindersley:** Gary Ombler / Courtesy of Adrian Shooter (t); Gary Ombler / Courtesy of RMP (c). **37 colour-rail.com:** (cr). **Dorling Kindersley:** Gary Ombler / Courtesy of FWHR (ca). **Keith Fender:** (cl). **Milepost:** (br). **38-39 Dorling Kindersley:** Gary Ombler / Courtesy of NRMY / Science Museum Group. **40 colour-rail.com:** (tc, bl). **Brian Stephenson/RAS:** (c). **41 Milepost:** (cra, tc, cb). **Brian Stephenson/RAS:** (bl). **42 TfL from the London Transport Museum collection :** (tr). **David Wilcock:** (cla). **Dorling Kindersley:** Gary Ombler / Courtesy of DRC (bc). **42-43 Dorling Kindersley:** Gary Ombler / Courtesy of NRMY / Science Museum Group (b). **43 Milepost:** (tr). **Brian Stephenson/RAS:** (cr). **David Wilcock:** (ca). **Dorling Kindersley:** Gary Ombler / Courtesy of DRC (bl, br). **44 Dorling Kindersley:** Gary Ombler / Courtesy of the DB Museum, Nurnburg, Germany (br); Gary Ombler / Courtesy of the Musee de Chemin de Fer, Mulhouse (tc). **Getty Images:** ND / Roger Viollet (bl). **Brian Stephenson/RAS:** (cla). **44-45 Dorling Kindersley:** Gary Ombler / Courtesy of the Musee de Chemin de Fer, Mulhouse (c). **45 colour-rail.com:** (bl). **Brian Stephenson/RAS:** (br, tr). **46 Milepost:** (tc). **Brian Stephenson/RAS:** (cl). **47 Dorling Kindersley:** Gary Ombler / Courtesy of VMT (tr). **Alamy Images:** John Wingfield (cb). **Milepost:** (cr). **48 Dorling Kindersley:** Deepak Aggarwal / Courtesy of NRMI (cl); Gary Ombler / Courtesy of HSB (c). **Peter Johnson:** (cr). **Milepost:** (bc). **49 Brian Stephenson/RAS** (tr). **Dorling Kindersley:** Deepak Aggarwal / Courtesy of NRMI (cl); Gary Ombler / Courtesy of FWHR (cr); Gary Ombler / Courtesy of RMP (br). **50 Stephen Middleton:** (cl). **Siemens AG, Munich/Berlin:** (tr, cb). **50-51 Dorling Kindersley:** Mike Dunning / Courtesy of NRMY (bc). **51 Alamy Images:** David Askham (cr). **Dorling Kindersley:** Gary Ombler / Courtesy of BORM (tl, tr). **52 Brian Stephenson/RAS:** A.W. Croughton (cl, tc). **David Wilcock:** (bl). **52-53 Dorling Kindersley:** Gary Ombler / Courtesy of HSB. **53 Milepost:** (cra). **Brian Stephenson/RAS:** C.R.L. Coles (br); (tc, cr). **54 Dorling Kindersley:** Gary Ombler / Courtesy of RMP (bl). **Getty Images:** SSPL / National Railway Museum (br). **Milepost:** (tr). **54-55 Dorling Kindersley:** Gary Ombler / Courtesy of DRC. **55 Brian Stephenson/RAS:** F.R. Hebron (tl); T.G. Hepburn (tr). **Dorling Kindersley:** Gary Ombler / Courtesy of DRC (cr). **56 Alexander Turnbull Library, National Library Of New Zealand, Te Puna Matauranga o Aotearoa:** (cl). **colour-rail.com:** (cla). **Brian Stephenson/RAS:** (tr). **56-57 Dorling Kindersley:** Gary Ombler / Courtesy of DRC (b). **57 Didcot Railway Centre:** Frank Dumbleton (c). **Dorling Kindersley:** Gary Ombler / Courtesy of DRC (cra). **Brian Stephenson/RAS:** (cla). **58 colour-rail.com:** (cla). **Dorling Kindersley:** Gary Ombler / Courtesy of RMP (tr, cra); Gary Ombler / Courtesy of RSR / Science Museum Group (bl). **58-59 Dorling Kindersley:** Gary Ombler / Courtesy of FWHR (b). **59 David Wilcock:** (c). **Dorling Kindersley:** Gary Ombler / Courtesy of DRC (tl, tr); Deepak Aggarwal / Courtesy of NRMI (br). **60 Chris Doering:** (cr). **Dorling Kindersley:** Gary Ombler / Courtesy of RMP (tr); Deepak Aggarwal / Courtesy of RSLS (cla); Gary Ombler / Courtesy of DRC (bc). **60-61 Dorling Kindersley:** Gary

Ombler / Courtesy of ETS (c); Gary Ombler / Courtesy of RMP (b). 61 Kevin Andrusia: (tl). colour-rail.com: (cra). Dorling Kindersley: Gary Ombler / Courtesy of DRC (cl). Gary Ombler / Courtesy of RMP (br). 62 Brian Stephenson/RAS: (tr, clb). 62-63 Science & Society Picture Library: National Railway Museum (c). 63 colour-rail.com: (tl). Corbis: Hulton-Deutsch Collection (br). Dorling Kindersley: Gary Ombler / Courtesy of BORM (tr). Garn Collection: Borsig (clb). 64 colour-rail.com: (ca). Milepost: (bc). 64-65 colour-rail.com. 65 Canada Science &Technology Museum: (tl). Dorling Kindersley: Gary Ombler / Courtesy of BORM (cra); Gary Ombler / Courtesy of RMP (crb). PROV: (tr). The Library of Congress, Washington DC: (br). 66 akg-images: ullstein bild / ullstein - Jaffø (cla). Dorling Kindersley: Gary Ombler / Courtesy of the Verkehrshaus der Schweiz, Luzern, Switzerland (tr). Mary Evans Picture Library: Sueddeutsche Zeitung Photo (bc, br). Steam Picture Library: (cb). 66-67 Dorling Kindersley: Gary Ombler / Courtesy of the Musee de Chemin de Fer, Mulhouse (c). 67 Corbis: Bettmann (bl). Dorling Kindersley: Gary Ombler / Courtesy of RMP (tr). Brian Stephenson/RAS: (br). 68 Dorling Kindersley: Deepak Aggarwal / Courtesy of NRMI (cl); Gary Ombler / Courtesy of ETS (crb); Gary Ombler / Courtesy of HSB (br). 68-69 Dorling Kindersley: Gary Ombler / Courtesy of the Verkehrshaus der Schweiz, Luzern, Switzerland. 69 Dorling Kindersley: Gary Ombler / Courtesy of RMP (tr); Gary Ombler / Courtesy of BORM (br); Gary Ombler / Courtesy of HSB (cr). Keith Fender: (bl). Brian Stephenson/RAS: T.G. Hepburn (cb). 70-71 Dorling Kindersley: Gary Ombler / Courtesy of ETS. 72 colour-rail.com: (cla). Brian Stephenson/RAS: (cl, cb). Wikipedia: Hans-Peter Scholz (bl). 72-73 Alamy Images: jozef sedmak (bc). Dorling Kindersley: Gary Ombler / Courtesy of ETS (tc). 73 colour-rail.com: (cr). Dorling Kindersley: Gary Ombler / Courtesy of BORM (tr); Deepak Aggarwal / Courtesy of RSLS (br). Getty Images: SSPL (cla). 74 Dorling Kindersley: Gary Ombler / Courtesy of VMT (tl, cl). 74-75 Dorling Kindersley: Gary Ombler / Courtesy of RMP (b). Ted Ellis: (tc). 75 Dorling Kindersley: Gary Ombler / Courtesy of BORM (tr); Gary Ombler / Courtesy of VMT (cr). 76 Dorling Kindersley: Gary Ombler / Courtesy of RMP (cl); Gary Ombler / Courtesy of VMT (bl). 76-77 Dorling Kindersley: Gary Ombler / Courtesy of BORM (t, c); Gary Ombler / Courtesy of VMT (b). 78 Dorling Kindersley: Gary Ombler / Courtesy of DRC (cl); Gary Ombler / Courtesy of RSR / Science Museum Group (bl). 78-79 Dorling Kindersley: Gary Ombler / Courtesy of DRC (t); Gary Ombler / Courtesy of RSR / Science Museum Group (c). 79 colour-rail.com: (cra). Keith Fender: (br). Brian Stephenson/RAS: (bl, cb). 80 colour-rail.com: (bc). Milepost: (clb). 80-81 Marek Ciesielski: (bc). Keith Fender: (tc). 81 colour-rail.com: (cra). Dorling Kindersley: Gary Ombler / Courtesy of the DB Museum, Nurnburg, Germany (tr); Gary Ombler / Courtesy of ETS (br). Keith Fender: (clb). 82 Dorling Kindersley: Gary Ombler / Courtesy of the Musee de Chemin de Fer, Mulhouse. Keith Fender: (cla). Brian Stephenson/RAS: (tr). 83 colour-rail.com: (tr, cr). Brian Stephenson/RAS: (br). 84 Brian Stephenson/RAS: (tr, crb, bl). Dorling Kindersley: Gary Ombler / Courtesy of RSR / Science Museum Group (cl). 85 colour-rail.com: (tc, cla). Milepost: (bc). Brian Stephenson/RAS: (cra). 86 Dorling Kindersley: Gary Ombler / Courtesy of VMT (tr, crb); Deepak Aggarwal / Courtesy of RSLS (tc). Milepost: (c). 87 Dorling Kindersley: Deepak Aggarwal / Courtesy of RSLS (tl, c). Milepost: (crb). 88 Milepost: (cra). Brian Stephenson/RAS: (cla, cb). 89 Brian Stephenson/RAS: (tr). Dorling Kindersley: Gary Ombler / Courtesy of HSB (ca); Gary Ombler / Courtesy of FWHR (c). 90 Dorling Kindersley: Gary Ombler / Courtesy of DRC (tr, clb); Gary Ombler / Courtesy of VMT (cla); Gary Ombler / Courtesy of RMP (bc). 90-91 Dorling Kindersley: Gary Ombler / Courtesy of ETS. 91 Garn Collection: (tc). Dorling Kindersley: Gary Ombler / Courtesy of VMT (cla); Gary Ombler / Courtesy of DRC (r, cr); Gary Ombler / Courtesy of BORM (br). 92-93 Dorling Kindersley: Gary Ombler / Courtesy of NRMY / Science Museum Group. 94 Dorling Kindersley: Gary Ombler / Courtesy of ETS (cl). Keith Fender: (c, cra, tc). 94-95 Dorling Kindersley: Gary Ombler / Courtesy of the Museum of Transportation, St Louis, Missouri (bc). 95 Dorling Kindersley: Gary Ombler / Courtesy of BORM (t, br). Keith Fender: (cra). Brian Stephenson/RAS: (cl). 96 Amtrak: Amtrak History and Archives (bl). colour-rail.com: (tr). Getty Images: UIG (cl). 96-97 Alamy Images: Craig Yates T (bc). 97 Keith Fender: (br). Roger Lalonde: (cr). Brian Stephenson/RAS: (cra). 98 Keith Fender: (cra). TopFoto.co.uk: RIA Novosti (cl). Dorling Kindersley: Gary Ombler / Courtesy of RSR / Science Museum Group (tr, cla); Gary Ombler / Courtesy of ETS (bl). 98 colour-rail.com: (cr). Dorling Kindersley: Gary Ombler / Courtesy of ETS(tr, b). TfL from the London Transport Museum collection : (ca). 100 Keith Fender: (tr, br). Charles P Friel: (ca). Mirko Schmidt: (bl). 100-101 Dorling Kindersley: Gary Ombler / Courtesy of RMP (c). 101 Keith Fender: (tl, tr). Don Oltmann: (bc). 102 Alamy Images: Robert Harding Picture Library (br). Dorling Kindersley: Gary Ombler / Courtesy of Transrapid, Lathen, Germany (bl). 102-103 colour-rail.com: (c). TopFoto.co.uk: RIA Novosti (tc). 103 Keith Fender: (tr, bc). Milepost: Brian Solomon (cra, cla). 104-105 colour-rail.com: Bob Sweet (c). 104 colour-rail.com: Bob Sweet (c). Keith Fender: (tr). Milepost: (cl). 105 colour-rail.com: (tl). Dorling Kindersley: Gary Ombler / Courtesy of HSB (cr).Keith Fender: (cra). 106 Alamy Images: Prisma Bildagentur AG (bl). Dorling Kindersley: Gary Ombler / Courtesy of ETS (cla). Keith Fender: (tr, cr). Milepost: Brian Solomon (cl). 106-07 Dorling Kindersley: Gary Ombler / Courtesy of DB Schenker (b). 107 colour-rail.com: (tl); Bob Sweet (cla). Keith Fender: (crb). 108 Alamy Images: Gunter Marx (tr). Keith Fender: (cl). Brian Stephenson/RAS: (cr). 108-09 Dorling Kindersley: Mike Dunning (bc). Milepost: Brian Solomon (c). 109 colour-rail.com: (tl); Bob Sweet (cr). Keith Fender: (cra). 110 Keith Fender: (cla, bc, tr). 110-111 Craig Walker. 111 Keith Fender: (br, cb). Siemens AG, Munich/Berlin: (tc). Vossloh AG: (cr, bl). 112 Keith Fender: (c, tr). Imaginechina: Gao yuwen (crb). Milepost: (bl). 113 Alamy Images: Susan Isakson (tc); Iain Masterton (cr). Japan National Tourism Organization : Awajiya (br). Ilya Semenoff: (bl). 114 Alamy Images: Avpics (bl). colour-rail.com: (c). Keith Fender: (tr). 115 Dorling Kindersley: Gary Ombler / Courtesy of Hitachi Rail Europe Ltd (b). Keith Fender: (tc). Getty Images: Gamma-Rapho (cb). Brian Stephenson/RAS. 116 Bombardier Transportation: (cla, c). Vossloh AG: (br). Chris Wallace: (tr). 117 Keith Fender: (cla, cra). Siemens AG, Munich/ Berlin: (cr, br, bl). Vossloh AG: (tc). 118 Getty Images: Car Culture (c) 120 Giles Chapman Library: (cla). 121 Louwman Museum. Corbis: The Bettmann Archive (cl). Getty Images: Ed Clark / Time Life Pictures (tl). Malcolm McKay: (cr, bl). TopFoto.co.uk: Topham Picturepoint (tr). 123 Louwman Museum. Motoring Picture Library/ National Motor Museum. 125 Louwman Museum: (crb, cr). Giles Chapman Library: (clb). 126 Louwman Museum. 127 Art Tech Picture Agency: (tr). Louwman Museum: (cr). Corbis: Car Culture (crb). 128 Louwman Museum: (tc, ca, cla, bl, br, cr, cra). TopFoto.co.uk: National Motor Museum/HIP (clb). 129 Louwman Museum. Giles Chapman Library: (bl). TopFoto.co.uk: Alinari (clb). 130 Alamy Images: pbpgalleries (tc). Art Tech Picture Agency: (cl). Louwman Museum: (cra). Motoring Picture Library / National Motor Museum: (cb). 131 Motoring Picture Library / National Motor Museum. Rex Features: Gary Hawkins (tr). 132 Louwman Museum. Getty Images: Car Culture (tl). 133 Louwman Museum. Giles Chapman Library: (cla). James Mann. TopFoto.co.uk: (cb). 134 Art Tech Picture Agency: (cl). Louwman Museum: (bc). James Mann: (cra). TopFoto.co.uk: 2006 (tr). 135 Louwman Museum: (tl). James Mann: (crb). Motoring Picture Library / National Motor Museum. TopFoto.co.uk: 2005 (cb). Ullstein Bild: (cl). 136 Motoring Picture Library/ National Motor Museum: (tl, cr). 137 Louwman Museum: (cra, c). James Mann: (tr). Motoring Picture Library/ National Motor Museum: (cl). 138 Alamy Images: Motoring Picture Library (cl). Louwman Museum: (tc, clb). Motoring Picture Library / National Motor Museum: (cr). 139 Giles Chapman Library: (cra). Motoring Picture Library / National Motor Museum: (tc, cl). 140 Alamy Images: Interfoto (ca). Louwman Museum. Magic Car Pics: (tr). Motoring Picture Library / National Motor Museum: (crb). 141 Alamy Images: Prisma Bildagentur AG (bc). Corbis: Car Culture (cla). 142 Corbis: Car Culture (c). 144 Giles Chapman Library. Motoring Picture Library / National Motor Museum: (tr). Reinhard Lintelmann Photography (Germany): (bl); (clb). 145 Art Tech Picture Agency: (bc). The Car Photo Library: (cb). Giles Chapman Library. TopFoto.co.uk: ullstein bild / Paul Mai (tl). 146 Louwman Museum: (cra). 150 Flickr.com: Ludek Mornstejn (tc). 151 Flickr.com: Stefan Koschminder (br). Motoring Picture Library / National Motor Museum: (cra). Oldtimergalerie Rosenau. : (clb). 150 Alamy Images: Autos (bc). 151 Giles Chapman Library: (clb). Reinhard Lintelmann Photography (Germany): (tr). 154 Louwman Museum: (cl). Giles Chapman Library: (cra). Malcolm McKay: (cr). Motoring Picture Library / National Motor Museum: (bl). TopFoto.co.uk: (tl). 155 Louwman Museum. Motoring Picture Library / National Motor Museum: (tr). 156 Louwman Museum: (bc). Giles Chapman Library: (cb). James Mann: (ca). Motoring Picture Library / National Motor Museum: (cl). TopFoto.co.uk: (tc). 157 Art Tech Picture Agency: (tr, br, cr, cra). Louwman Museum: (cla). Giles Chapman Library: (bl, ftr). 158 Giles Chapman Library: (cl). Malcolm McKay. 159 Alamy Images: Tom Wood (br). Magic Car Pics: (tl). Malcolm McKay: (tc). Motoring Picture Library/ National Motor Museum. 160 Louwman Museum: (cb). Image created by Simon GP Geoghegan: (cr). Giles Chapman Library: (tr). Motoring Picture Library / National Motor Museum: (ca). Reinhard Lintelmann Photography (Germany): (c). 161 Art Tech Picture Agency: (br). Giles Chapman Library: (cra). Magic Car Pics. James Mann: (tl). 162 Magic Car Pics: (tr). 164 Alamy Images: Transtock Inc. (bl). Louwman Museum: (bc). Cody Images: (ca). 165 Giles Chapman Library: (cla). James Mann: (cb). Malcolm McKay: (crb). Motoring Picture Library / National Motor Museum: (bc). 166 Art Tech Picture Agency: (tl). James Mann: (bc). 167 Louwman Museum: (tr). James Mann: (bl, br). 168 Giles Chapman Library: (clb, crb). Magic Car Pics: (tc). Motoring Picture Library / National Motor Museum. 169 Louwman Museum: (tr). Giles Chapman Library: (tl, br). Motoring Picture Library / National Motor Museum: (crb). Reinhard Lintelmann Photography (Germany): (clb). 170 The Car Photo Library: (fclb). Magic Car Pics. 171 Alamy Images: culture-images GmbH (br). Fiat Group: (cb). Giles Chapman Library. Magic Car Pics: Paul Deverill (clb); (cl). James Mann: (tl). Motoring Picture Library/ National Motor Museum: (tc). TopFoto.co.uk: Roger-Viollet (cra). 174 Art Tech Picture Agency: (clb). Giles Chapman Library: (bl). 175 Art Tech Picture Agency: (cr). Giles Chapman Library: (br). Malcolm McKay: (cl). 176 Corbis: Car Culture (c). 179 Art Tech Picture Agency: (cra). 184 Louwman Museum: (tc). Magic Car Pics: (tr). Malcolm McKay: (cla, bc). 185 Alamy Images: Coyote-Photography.co.uk (tl). Louwman Museum: (cb, fcla). Giles Chapman Library: (cra). Malcolm McKay. Reinhard Lintelmann Photography (Germany): (clb). 186 Giles Chapman Library: (clb). 187 Getty Images: Bloomberg (cb). Giles Chapman Library. 188 Archivio Storico Alfa Romeo: (cla). Art Tech Picture Agency: (cr). Giles Chapman Library: (cb). Volvo Group: (tr). 189 Art Tech Picture Agency: (cla). The Car Photo Library: (crb). 192 Giles Chapman Library. 193 Art Tech Picture Agency: (fcra). Louwman Museum: (clb, bc). The Car Photo Library: (c). Giles Chapman Library. 194 Art Tech Picture Agency: (ftl). LAT Photographic: (clb, crb). James Mann: (fbl). 195 TopFoto.co.uk: Phipps/Sutton/HIP (clb).196 Motoring Picture Library/ National Motor Museum: (fcr). 197 Alamy Images: Stanley Hare (fbr); Martin Berry (bc). Rudolf Kozdon : (clb). 200 Giles Chapman Library. 201 Art Tech Picture Agency: (fbr). Giles Chapman Library: (fcl). 208 Alamy Images: Tom Wood (clb). 210 Art Tech Picture Agency: (clb). LAT Photographic: (fbl). Giles Chapman Library. 211 Art Tech Picture Agency: (fcr, fbl). LAT Photographic: (clb, ftr). Giles Chapman Library. 212 Art Tech Picture Agency: (ca, c). Ford Motor Company Limited: (fcla). The Car Photo Library: (fbr). LAT Photographic: (cl). Giles Chapman Library: (ftr). Suzuki Motor Corporation: (clb). 213 Alamy Images: Trinity Mirror / Mirrorpix (bc). Art Tech Picture Agency: (fbl). Courtesy of Chrysler Group LLC: (tr). Giles Chapman Library. Magic Car Pics: (fbr). James Mann: (ca). Wisconsin Historical Society. : Image ID 25823 (ftl). 214 Art Tech Picture Agency: (c). 215 BMW AG: (fcla). Magic Car Pics: (ca). 217 Art Tech Picture Agency: (cla). Greig Dalgleish: (cra). Giles Chapman Library: (fcl). Reinhard Lintelmann Photography (Germany): (cb). 218 Art Tech Picture Agency: (cra, ftl, clb). 219 Art Tech Picture Agency: (ca, cb). 220 Louwman Museum: (ftr). Motoring Picture Library / National Motor Museum: (clb). 221 Motoring Picture Library / National Motor Museum: (cra). 224 Giles Chapman Library. Magic Car Pics: (fcla). 225 LAT Photographic: (cla). Giles Chapman Library. 226 Motoring Picture Library / National Motor Museum: James Mann (c). 229 James Mann (afl). 230 Art Tech Picture Agency: (c). Giles Chapman Library. 231 Giles Chapman Library. Wikipedia, The Free Encyclopedia: (tc). 232 Art Tech Picture Agency: (c). Giles Chapman Library. 233 Art Tech Picture Agency: (fbl). Giles Chapman Library. Malcolm McKay: (clb). 234 Art Tech Picture Agency. Giles Chapman Library: (fbl). James Mann: (ftr). 235 Art Tech Picture Agency. Giles Chapman Library: (fcr). 236 Art Tech Picture Agency: (fcl). (c): Aventure Peugeot: (cb). Citroën Communication: (crb, fbr). LAT Photographic. Giles Chapman Library: (clb). 237 Art Tech Picture Agency: (cra, cr). Magic Car Pics. 238 Art Tech Picture Agency: (cb). Giles Chapman Library: (cra). 239 Art Tech Picture Agency: (cla, cra). 240 Giles Chapman Library. 241 Art Tech Picture Agency. Giles Chapman Library. 242 Art Tech Picture Agency. Louwman Museum: (cla). 243 Art Tech Picture Agency: (c, bc). Giles Chapman Library. 246 Art Tech

Picture Agency: (tc). 248 Art Tech Picture Agency: (tl). 248 Art Tech Picture Agency: Giles Chapman Library. 249 Art Tech Picture Agency: (ca, ftl, fcra, fcr). Giles Chapman Library: (tc, fcl, bl, cb). 250 LAT Photographic: (fcla). Giles Chapman Library: (cra, c, fbl). 251 Alamy Images: Phil Talbot (ftl). Art Tech Picture Agency. Giles Chapman Library. 252 Art Tech Picture Agency: (cr). Giles Chapman Library: (c, fcla). Orphan Work: (fcl). Art Tech Picture Agency: (cra, fcl, ftr). Giles Chapman Library. 258 Alamy Images: Transtock Inc. (fclb); Motoring Picture Library (fcra); izmostock (c). Giles Chapman Library: (fbr). 259 Alamy Images: Robert Steinbarth (ftr). Giles Chapman Library: (fcrb). 260 Giles Chapman Library. Magic Car Pics: (fcra). courtesy Mahindra Reva: (tc). 261 Giles Chapman Library. Malcolm McKay: (fcl). 266 Art Tech Picture Agency: (ftr). 267 LAT Photographic: (fcr). Giles Chapman Library: (ftl, fclb). 269 Giles Chapman Library: (frca, bl). 272 Alamy Images: Transtock Inc. (fcrb); Drive Images (fbl). Ford Motor Company Limited: (c). Giles Chapman Library: (ca, fclb). Motoring Picture Library / National Motor Museum: (fcla). 273 Alamy Images: Drive Images (fcra). Corbis: Car Culture (ca). LAT Photographic: (ca). Giles Chapman Library. Nissan Motor Company: (tr). 274 Audi AG: c. Daimler AG: bl. Detroit Electric Holdings Ltd: br. Frazer Nash: cla. Honda Motor Co., Ltd: crb. Peugeot Motor Company PLC: cl. Renault UK Ltd: cb. Tesla Motors, Inc.: tr. Toyota Motor Europe S.A. / N.V.: tc. 275 BMW AG: cb. Nissan: cla. Peugeot Motor Company PLC: cra. Porsche Cars Great Britain Ltd: br. Vauxhall Motors Ltd: tl, tr. Volkswagen AG: ca. 278 MAS: (all images). 276-77 TSC. 279 FAAM: (cl/HMA). MAS: (all other images). 280 Getty Images: SSPL (cra). TSC. Ted Huetter: The Museum of Flight, Seattle (clb). YAM: (cla). MAS: (cl). 281 TSC: (t, cl). Getty Images: SSPL. Ted Huetter: (cr). 282 F: (tl). TSC: (cr, cla). NSAM: (b). 283 TSC: (cra). TNLTA: (tr). YAM: (bl). 282-83 BM: (t). FAAM: (c). 284 Matthew Charles Boddington/ Stephen Slater: (t). Gene DeMarco: (tl). RAFML: (c). USAM: (clb). SSA: (b). RAF F.E.2 (cra). Chris Savill: (tc). RAFML (cr). 286 aviationpictures.com: (tl). Philip Whiteman: (tr). TSC: (clb). RAFML: (bl). 287 aviationpictures.com: (cr). Michael Cook: (br). TSC: (cra, cl). F: (tl). MAS: (cra). SSA: (cl, bl). 286-87 BM: (b). 288 MAS: (ca, br). Mary Evans Picture Library: Epic / Tallandier (cla). SNASM: (crb). 289 aviationpictures.com: (crb). PRM Aviation Collection: (crb). MAS: (t, br). 290 MAS: (cl). Imperial War Museum: (bl). FAAM: (br). PRM Aviation Collection: (bc, cra). TopFoto.co.uk: RIA Novosti / Igor Mikhalev (c). U.S. Air Force: (tr). 291 aviationpictures.com: (tl). aviationpictures.com: (tl). PRM Aviation Collection: (bc, cra). TopFoto.co.uk: Roger-Viollet (crb). SNASM. 292 aviationpictures. com: (cla, bl, br). PRM Aviation Collection: (cl, tc). EBF: (cra.) SNASM: (cbr). 293 aviationpictures.com: (cl, cr). PRM Aviation Collection: (tl, tr).

294 TSC: (c, cra). Richard Seeley: (cb). PRM Aviation Collection: (cla). SNASM: (t). RAFMC: (b). 295 aviation-images.com: (cla). aviationpictures.com: (bl, tl, tr). PRM Aviation Collection: (br). TNLTA: (cra). 296 aviation-images.com: (tr, cra). aviationpictures.com: (clb, cb). Getty Images: SSPL (bc). 297 aviation-images.com: (cr). PRM Aviation Collection: (clb, tl). SNASM: (tr). MAS: (cb). 296-97 MAS: (c). 298 SNASM: (tr). aviation-images.com: (bl). Cody Images: (cra). PRM Aviation Collection: (cla). TopFoto.co.uk: Flight Collection (c). 299 TNLTA: (t). SNASM: (cla). aviationpictures.com: (cb). Roy Palmer: (b). MAS: (cra). 300 TSC: (tr). aviationpictures.com: (clb). SNASM: (cla, bl, br). 301 SSA: (tr). TSC: (cra). The Flight Collection: Quadrant Picture Library (cb). PRM Aviation Collection: (tl, cla, bl). 300-01 FAAM: (c). 302 TNLTA: (cl, cla). aviation-images.com: (cb, tr). viationpictures.com: (bl). 303 aviation-images.com: (tl, cla). PRM Aviation Collection: (tr, cb). F: (b). 302-303 F: (c). 304-05 SSA. 306 DHAHC: (tl, cla). aviation-images.com: (cra). aviationpictures.com: (cr, tr). David Allan Edwards/Anthony Maitland: (b). 307 Robert John Willies: (tr). Nigel Pickard: (crb). TSC (Peter Holloway): (c). TSC (Paul Stone/BAe Systems): (clb). TSC: (cra). SNASM: (tl). TRAC: (br). 308 TSC: (tr). SNASM: (cla). TRAC: (cb). 309 TSC (Michael Gibbs): (br). SNASM: (tl, bl). TRAC: (cb). 310 aviation-images. com: (tr).aviationpictures.com: (cla). Cody Images: (cr). MAS: (cb). SNASM: (bl). 311 aviation-images. com: (cla, cra). Cody Images: (cl). PRM Aviation Collection: (cr). SNASM: (tl). TRAC: (b). 82-83 Corbis: Bettmann (c). 84 The Advertising Archives: (bl). Alamy Images: Museum of Flight (tl). Hans Verkaik: (cl). 85 Alamy Images: Susan & Allan Parker (ftr). Rafael Cordero - AeroImágenes de México: (c). Robert John Willies: (ftl). TRAC: (tl). Philip Whiteman: (tr/PA-28 Cherokee). 312 aviationpictures. com: (cla, tl). TNLTA: (cbr, b). 313 aviation-images.com: (tr). aviationpictures.com: (c, tr). Dorling Kindersley: Mike Dunning, Courtesy of the Science Museum, London (clb). TNLTA: (cb). 314 aviationpictures.com: (cla, cra). Cody Images: (tr). 315 Alamy Images: MS Bretherton (tl). aviation-images.com: (crb). Cody Images: (cla). PRM Aviation Collection: (c). 314-15 FAAM: (b). 316 SNASM: (bl). aviation-images. com: (clb, br). DHAHC: (cb). Dorling Kindersley: Max Alexander (c) Dorling Kindersley, Courtesy of the Powerhouse Museum, Sydney, Australia (cla). PRM Aviation Collection: (tr). 317 aviation-images.com: (tl, tr, cra). Copyright Igor I Sikorsky Historical Archives: (crb). MAS: (b). 318 TSC: (tr). RAFML: (tl). Corbis: Bettmann (c). SSA: (b). YAM: (br). 319 Corbis: (tl). 320 TRAC: (tr). Corbis: (bc). SNASM: (cr). TSC: (tl). SSA: (clb). 321 TSC: (tr). SSA: (cla, cb). MAS: (bl, br). 322 B17 Preservation: (tr). aviationpictures.com: (ca). PRM Aviation Collection: (clb). Chris Savill: (bl). FAAM: (crb). F: (cla).

323 Richard Vandervord: (tl). aviationpictures.com: (cb). YAM: (cra). 324 RAFML: (cb). 325 RAFMC: (tr). Alamy Images: CS Stock (clb). FAAM: (b). RAFBBMF: (cla). 326 PRM Aviation Collection: (br). TSC (Tracy Curtis-Taylor): (b). GAO: (c). TRAC: (cb). 327 YAM: (tr). TMAF: (cla). Philip Whiteman: (b). RAFML: (clb). 328 Cody Images: (bl). PRM Aviation Collection: (cla, cl, clb). 328-329 aviation-images.com: (tc). TSC: (c). 329 Cody Images: (crb). PRM Aviation Collection: (tr, cla, cra, clb, br). TNLTA: (crb). 331 TSC (Sir John Allison): (cla). Anthony David Pearce: (br). MAM: (crb). TRAC: (clb). 330-331 Thomas Martin Jones/Margaret Lynn Jones/Paul Martin Jones: (t). 332 SNASM: (cra, cl). RAFMC: (tr). FAAM: (tl). 333 FAAM: (tr, cl). DHAHC: (tl). 332-33 FAAM: (c). 334 aviationpictures.com: (tr). DHAHC: (br). RAFML: (ca, cla, br). 335 PRM Aviation Collection: (tr). SNASM: (tl). PRM Aviation Collection: (bl, br). 336 aviation-images.com: (cra). aviationpictures.com: (cl). PRM Aviation Collection: (bc). SNASM: (cla, bl). 337 SNASM: (tr). MAS: (ca). USAM: (tlb). 336-37 RAFMC: (cb). 338 aviation-images.com: (ca). PRM Aviation Collection: (bl, bc). 339 aviation-images.com: (cl). Cody Images: (clb). PRM Aviation Collection: (tr, bc). Science Photo Library: Detlev van Ravenswaay (cra). MAS: (cr). 338-39 TSC: (tl). 340 SNASM: (tl). aviation-images.com: (cl, cra). Cody Images: (crb, bl). 341 aviation-images.com: (bc, tr). Cody Images: (cra, cla). PRM Aviation Collection: (clb). 340-41 SNASM. 342-43 FAAM. 344 GAO: (tl). F: (cl). YAM: (cra). CNAM: (bl). MAM: (br). 345 FAAM: (tr, ca). F: (tl). MAM: (c, b). RAFMC: (clb). CNAM: (crb). 346 F: (cla, cl). TNLTA: (tr, c). YAM: (cra). aviation-images. com: (bl, cb/Vickers Valiant). 347 Alamy Images: Allstar Picture Library (cla). aviationpictures. com: (tl). Dutch Historic Jet Association: (c) F: (cl). USAM: (b). 348 YAM: (cl). CNAM: (cra). MAS: (cla). TNLTA: (br). MAM: (bl). F: (clb). 349 RAFMC: (t). TMAF: (bl). F: (bl). YAM: (br). THM: (ca). 348-49 USAM: (c). 350 DHAHC: (tr). F: (b). 351 MAM: (tr). aviationpictures. com: (cra). PRM Aviation Collection: (br). F: (cla, cb). 352 RAFMC: (t). aviation-images. com: (clb, bl). PRM Aviation Collection: (br). USAM: (crb). 353 aviation-images.com: (bl, br, tr). TNLTA: (tl). CNAM: (cr). F: (cla). 354 Anthony Wakefield: (tl). Freddie Rogers: (tr). SNASM: (cr, cra). PRM Aviation Collection: (cl). TNLTA: (br). 355 TNLTA: (cra). PRM Aviation Collection: (tl, br). Gilbert Davies: (bl). TRAC: (cb). 356 RAFMC: (tl). MAM: (tr). aviation-images.com: (bc). aviationpictures.com: (cl, br). MAS: (clb). 357 aviation-images.com: (bc). PRM Aviation Collection: (clb). MAS: (cra, bl). 356-57 RAFMC: (c). 358 F: (tl, br). Corbis: George Hall (cb). 359 F: (tr). NSAM: (tl

aviationpictures.com: (cr). MAM: (cl, b). 358-59 CNAM: (ca). 360 Philip Whiteman: (br). CNAM: (cr). 361 D. Edwards/G. Harris/K. Martin/J. France/J. Bastin: (cra). Hertfordshire Gliding Club: (bl). Richard Whitwell: (cb). 362 CNAM: (cla). BM: (cr, bl). F: (br). 363 aviation-images.com: (b). USAM: (bl). 362-63 F: (t). 364 aviation-images.com: (tr, c). F: (cla). PRM Aviation Collection: (cl, bc, crb). 365 MAS: (cra). aviation-images.com: (cl, cr, br). MAS: (cb). DHAHC: (t). 366 YAM: (c, cra). MAM: (bl). 367 TRAC: (cla). Alamy Images: Matthew Harrison (b). Corbis: Bettmann (b). Global Aviation Resource: (tl). FAAM: (crb). 186 Corbis: George Hall (tl). MAM: (all other images). 368 aviationpictures.com: (ca). PRM Aviation Collection: (t, bl, br). 369 PRM Aviation Collection: (cra). aviation-images.com: (tl, bl). 368-69 RAFMC: (c). 370 Andrew Dent: (tr). TMAF: (cl). NSAM: (bl). 371 FAAM: (br). USAM: (t, cla, crb). 370-71 FAAM: (c). 372 TRAC: (tl). Philip Powell: (b). 373 PRM Aviation Collection: (cra, cl, br). Paul Stanley: (tr). 374 PRM Aviation Collection: (tr, cra, ca, cr, clb, bl, br). 375 Cody Images: (crb). PRM Aviation Collection: (tr, tl, ca, bc). 376-77 Michel Gilliand: (tc). 376 Alamy Images: ClassicStock (bl). aviation-images. com: (cb, ca). aviationpictures.com: (c). PRM Aviation Collection: (bc). 377 BM: (cra). Alamy Images: Steven May (ca). image courtesy of Bombardier Aerospace, Belfast: (c). Andre Giam: (br). PRM Aviation Collection: (cb). 378 YAM: (tl). PRM Aviation Collection: (cl, clb). F: (bl). 379 BM: (tl). Alamy Images: Kevin Maskell (tr). PRM Aviation Collection: (br, c). 378-79 USAM: (c). 380 aviation-images.com: (tr). CNAM: (cl). F: (tl, cr). TNLTA: (br). USAM: (cb). 381 CNAM: (cr). MAM: (b). 382 F: (tr). THM: (bl). USAM: (cl, cra). 383 FAAM: (cra). Alamy Images: Antony Nettle (bl). PRM Aviation Collection: (clb). 386 FAAM: (tr). NSAM: (bl). USAM: (cr). F: (cla). 387 USAM: (tr). aviation-images.com: (ca). PRM Aviation Collection: (cb, br). 388 FAAM: (tl). Cody Images: (br). 389 Dorling Kindersley: Andy Crawford, Courtesy of Oxford Airport (br). Cody Images: (c, tl). 390 aviation-images.com: (bl). PRM Aviation Collection: (cla). TRAC: (c). 391 Dorling Kindersley: James Stevenson Courtesy of Aviation Scotland Ltd. (cl). TRAC: (cr, bl). 392 aviation-images.com: (cla). PRM Aviation Collection: (cl). 393 aviationpictures.com: (cb). PRM Aviation Collection: (bc, cra, cla). 394 aviation-images.com: (tl, clb). Cody Images: (c). 395 aviation-images.com: (bl, crb, tl). Cody Images: (ca, c, cr). PRM Aviation Collection: (tr). 396 aviation-images.com: (bl, br). PRM Aviation Collection: (cb, c). 397 aviation-images.com: (br, clb). aviationpictures.com: (bl). Hamlinjet: (tr). 399 PRM Aviation Collection: (cra). TRAC: (b). 400 aviation-images.com: (clb). PRM Aviation Collection: (clb). P.L. Poole: (cla). 400-01 Phil & Diana King: (c). 401 TRAC: (t). Lasham Gliding Club: (ct). Graham Schimmin: (br). 402 aviation-images.com: (bl). Cody Images:

(cla, tc, cra, crb). PRM Aviation Collection: (t). 403 Alamy Images: Antony Nettle (cla). 402-03 TNLTA: (c). 404 PRM Aviation Collection: (bl). MAS: (clb). 405 aviation-images.com: (b). Keith Warrington: (cr). TNLTA: (cl). 406 YAM: (tl). 406-407 RAFMC: (c). YAM: (cb). 408 Nigel Tonks & Adrian Lloyd: (c). Frank Cavaciuti: (cb). Freddie Rogers: (b). 409 Lambert Aircraft Engineering: (cr). 408-09 TRAC: (c). 410 Alamy Images: Susan & Allan Parker (tr). aviation-images. com: (cla). Hamlinjet: (cr). 411 aviation-images.com: (tl). Capital Holdings 164 LLC: (ca). Philip Whiteman: (br). 412 aviation-images.com: (tr, crb, clb). 413 Alamy Images: Stephen Shephard (crb). aviation-images.com: (clb). Philip Whiteman: (tl). 414 aviation-images.com: (cl). Cody Images: (tr). PRM Aviation Collection: (cl). 415 aviation-images.com: (cr). 414-15 RAFMC: (ca). 416 Alamy Images: Susan & Allan Parker (ca). aviation-images.com: (bl). PRM Aviation Collection: (clb). Alamy Images: aviation aircraft airplanes (crb). 416-17 aviation-images.com: (cb). 417 aviation-images.com: (tl). aviationpictures.com: SJ Aircraft (cl). Fly About Aviation: Courtesy Pipistrel d.o.o. Ajdovščina (br, ca). Bernd Weber: (cra). WSM: Colman (bl). 418 aviation-images.com: (clb, bc). Corbis: Gene Blevins (tr). 419 aviation-images.com: (crb). aviationpictures.com: Helicopter Life / GHJ (bl); PC-Aero (cr). PRM Aviation Collection: (tc, cla). Sikorsky Aircraft Corporation: (br).

All other images © Dorling Kindersley
For further information see:
www.dkimages.com

Trains, cars, and aircraft featuring on chapter openers
pages 8-9 *Rocket*
pages 38-39 NER Class X1 No.66 Aerolite
pages 70-71 DR No. 52.8184-5
pages 92-93 JR West Shinkansen Series 0 22-141
pages 118-119 Napier 7-passenger Touring
pages 142-143 Wanderer W25K
pages 172-173 Ford Mustang
pages 226-227 Mini Cooper
pages 276-277 Bristol M.1C
pages 304-305 Boeing B-17
pages 342-343 Westland Wessex 5 "Jungly"
pages 384-385 Boeing C-17 Globemaster III